More Advance Praise for Hubris

"Richard Curtis has performed a service to those concerned with the recurring pattern of misconduct by presidents. By suggesting a conceptual framework within which abuse of power seems sure to occur, the author joins an impressive group of thinkers who have pondered this troubling tendency. This book is fascinating and often entertaining."

— Clyde Ingle, former Commissioner of Higher Education for Minnesota and Indiana, author of *From Village to State in Tanzania. The Politics of Rural Development*

"A spectacular volume! The research is stunning, the approach unique, and the eloquence so arresting I couldn't lay it down. For those concerned about an imperial presidency, here is an easy-read as well as a must-read."

— Andy Jacobs, former Congressman for 30 years, author of *The 1600 Killers. A Wake-Up Call for Congress.*

D1430484

About the Author

Richard K. Curtis, a native of Worcester, Massachusetts, was a P51 "Mustang" fighter pilot with the 15th Air Force in Italy in 1944-45, winning the Air Medal with four oak leaf clusters, and the Distinguished Flying Cross. He took his Th.B. from Northern  Baptist Seminary in Chicago, and his M.S. and Ph.D. from Purdue University. For 40 years he taught speech communication in a number of colleges and universities, retiring from Indiana University-Purdue University in 1993, after teaching there for 24 years. His two previous books are *They Called Him Mister Moody* (Doubleday, 1962) and *Evolution or Extinction: The Choice Before Us. A Systems Approach to the Study of the Future* (Pergamon, 1982).

HUBRIS

AND THE PRESIDENCY

The Abuse of Power by Johnson and Nixon

HUBRIS

AND THE PRESIDENCY

The Abuse of Power by Johnson and Nixon

Richard Curtis

Rutledge Books, Inc. Danbury, CT

Cover photos of Lyndon Johnson and Richard Nixon provided by
Corbis Images

ALL RIGHTS RESERVED
Rutledge Books, Inc.
107 Mill Plain Road, Danbury, CT 06811
1-800-278-8533
www.rutledgebooks.com

Manufactured in the United States of America

Cataloging in Publication Data
Curtis, Richard Kenneth, 1924-
    Hubris and the presidency : the abuse of power by Johnson
    and Nixon

    ISBN: 1-58244-086-7

    1. Johnson, Lyndon B. (Lyndon Baines), 1908-1973. . 2. Nixon,
Richard M. (Richard Milhouse), 1913-1994. . 3. United States --
Politics and government -- 1968-1974. 4. Vietnam War.

973 / .923 / 092

Library of Congress Catalog Card Number: 00-103907

To the memory of:

Albert W. Curtis,
radio operator, severely wounded in a
poison gas attack in France, World War I, 1918

Robert L. Curtis,
B17 navigator, killed in raid on Kiel, Germany, World War II, 1943

Dana A. Curtis,
mine engineer, killed in North Korea, 1951

Timothy Vicalvi,
Marine infantryman, killed in Vietnam, 1967

CONTENTS

PREFACE

All writing, fiction or non-fiction, is necessarily autobiographical, revealing the author as well as the subject. You will understand something of the incentive for addressing the subject of hubris and particularly as it applies to these two presidents when you recognize the toll that wars have taken on my family. Albert Curtis was my father, Robert my older brother, Dana my younger brother, and Timothy Vicalvi my sister's oldest child. In addition, I flew fifty-one missions in a P51 "Mustang" fighter plane in World War II, earning the Distinguished Flying Cross. Of twelve pilots assigned at the same time to the 52nd Fighter Group of the 15th Air Force, flying out of Italy, none of us with the six to nine months of the usual intermediate training after receiving our wings, I was the only one of the twelve still flying after one month and seven missions, thus the only one to complete my tour of duty.

Since that time I have been a clergyman, a college and university professor, and an author. Previous books include *They Called Him Mister Moody*, Doubleday, 1962, and *Evolution or Extinction: The Choice Before Us: A Systems Approach to the Study of the Future*, Pergamon, 1982.

To help overcome the inevitable bias of biography, I have attempted to draw opinions from many and varied sources. Examining the personality is akin to examining a sunrise. We can't appreciate the sun by looking directly at it. Rather we examine what the sun does to all it touches, to the clouds above, to the mountains, the hills, the trees, the shrubs, and finally to the mists rising from the lakes and streams below. Only then can we appreciate the sunrise. In like manner we can best examine and evaluate Johnson and Nixon only after noting the impressions they left on those lives they touched—their families, friends, colleagues, audiences, as well as other world leaders.

Since this is history as well as biography, it is necessary to study the context which these two presidents both reflected and influenced. Only then can we hope to compare them with their predecessors. Is it fair, for example, to compare these two, both of whom inherited a war neither of them started and neither of them wanted, with peace-time presidents? Is it fair to compare them with the presidents of the preceding century when life was so much more simple? Is it fair to compare these two ambitious leaders with other presidents who were largely content simply to mind the store?

A further problem intrudes, that of differentiating truth and truthfulness. Truth, or at least an approximation of truth, can only emerge as witnesses are truthful. In addition it is vital that we differentiate factual truth from typical truth. It ia a fact that Eisenhower lied to Kruschev when he denied that the U.S. was sending V2 reconnaissance flights over the Soviet Union. But a close reading of Ike's presidency indicates that, while the incident did occur, lying was not typical of Ike, and might well be justifiable on the basis of the Cold War in the late fifties.

This book is also an essay. You will find a scaffolding of some thirteen steps along the path of hubris, steps which I try to illuminate as well as corroborate in drawing from the lives of these two men. This will undoubtedly provoke questions: Why thirteen? Why these? Why this order? All I can plead is your forbearance. My hope is that you will find these steps a useful means of analyzing the effects as well as the causes of hubris in the lives of these two presidents. More importantly, my hope is you will find useful suggestions for checking, as well as preventing, the hubris of future presidents.

I am in debt to the Conference on Advanced Systems Study held in Baden-Baden, Germany in 1991 for the warm response and encouragement in the first, sketchy presentation of this subject. I am in special debt to my wife Elizabeth, an American history teacher for twenty-four years and a veritable walking encyclopedia. I am also in debt to the many biographers listed in the appendix who have done yeoman's work in ferreting out information on these presidents. The memoirs of both men have been revealing, both as to what they recalled and how they recalled it. Just as I had wrapped up the writing, there emerged three books that I have, perforce, sandwiched into the text. Two of them, edited by Beschloss and Kutler, cover recently released audio tapes of Johnson and Nixon. The third, also based on tapes, by Matthews, concerns Kennedy and Nixon.

COMPARATIVE CHRONOLOGY

Lyndon Baines Johnson		Richard Milhous Nixon
	1905	
b. August 27, 1908		
Gillespie County, Texas	1910	
		b. January 9, 1913
	1915	Yorba Linda, California
	1920	
	1925	
B.S. S.W. State Teacher's	1930	
College, San Marcos, TX,		
1930, Teacher, Sam Houston		
H.S., Houston, TX 1930-31		
Secretary to Congressman R.		
Kleberg, 1931-35. Married		
Claudia Taylor, Nov. 17,		BA Whittier College,
1934.		Whittier CA 1934
	1935	
TX State Director, NYA		L.L.B., Duke University Law
1935-37		School, 1937
		Practiced Law, Whittier, CA
		1937-41
Elected to Congress, 1937		
Re-elected to Congress		
1938-48	1940	Married Patricia Ryan,
Served in US Navy 1941-42		June 21, 1940
Lynda Bird born, 1944		Worked for O.P.A. 1942

Lyndon Baines Johnson		Richard Milhous Nixon
	1945	Served in US Navy 1942-46
		Elected to Congress, 1946
		Patricia born, 1946
Lucy born, 1947		Julie born, 1947
Elected to Senate, 1948		Re-elected to Congress, 1948
	1950	Elected to Senate, 1950
Elected Minority Leader, 1952		Elected Vice-President, 1952
Elected Majority Leader, 1954		
Re-elected to Senate, 1954	1955	Re-elected Vice President, 1956
Elected Vice-President, 1960	1960	Defeated for President, 1960
		Defeated for Governor of CA, 1962
Assumed Presidency, 1963		Practiced Law in CA, 1961-63
Elected President, 1964		Practiced Law in NY
	1965	1963-68
Dropped out of Presidential race, 1968		Elected President, 1968
Returned to Texas Ranch, 1969		
	1970	
Died, San Antonio, Texas, 1973		Re-Elected President, 1972
		Resigned as President, 1974
		Pardoned by President Ford, 1974
	1975	
		Disbarred from practicing law in NY, 1976
		Died New York City, 1994

CAST OF CHARACTERS

United States Presidents

1. George Washington	1789-1797
2. John Adams	1797-1801
3. Thomas Jefferson	1801-1809
4. James Madison	1809-1817
5. James Monroe	1817-1825
6. James Quincy Adams	1825-1829
7. Andrew Jackson	1829-1837
8. Martin Van Buren	1837-1841
9. William Henry Harrison (one month)	1841-1841
10. John Taylor	1841-1845
11. James K. Polk	1845-1849
12. Zachary Taylor (16 months)	1849-1850
13. Millard Fillmore	1850-1853
14. Franklin Pierce	1853-1857
15. James Buchanan	1857-1861
16. Abraham Lincoln	1861-1865
17. Andrew Johnson	1865-1869
18. Ulysses S. Grant	1869-1877
19. Rutherford B. Hayes	1877-1881
20. James Garfield (7 months)	1881-1881
21. Chester A. Arthur	1881-1885

22. Grover Cleveland	1885-1889
23. Benjamin Harrison	1889-1893
24. Grover Cleveland	1893-1897
25. William McKinley	1897-1901
26. Theodore Roosevelt	1901-1909
27. William Howard Taft	1909-1913
28. Woodrow Wilson	1913-1921
29. Warren Harding (29 months)	1921-1923
30. Calvin Coolidge	1923-1929
31. Herbert Hoover	1929-1933
32. Franklin D. Roosevelt	1933-1945
33. Harry S. Truman	1945-1953
34. Dwight D. Eisenhower	1953-1961
35. John F. Kennedy (34 months)	1961-1963
36. Lyndon B. Johnson	1963-1969
37. Richard M. Nixon	1969-1974
38. Gerald F. Ford	1974-1977
39. Jimmy Carter	1977-1981
40. Ronald Reagan	1981-1989
41. George Bush	1989-1993
42. William Clinton	1993-

INTRODUCTION

Today there are two great peoples who, starting from different points, seem to approach the same destiny. They are the Russians and the Anglo-Americans. The American battles the obstacles of nature; the Russian, those of man. The former combats the wilderness and savagery; the latter, civilization with all its weapons. American conquests are won with the laborer's plow; Russian triumphs, with the soldier's sword. To attain its ends, the American relies upon personal interest and allows free scope to the unguided energy and common sense of individuals. The Russian somehow concentrates the power of society in one man. The method of the former is freedom, of the latter, servitude.

Their starting point is different, their ways are diverse, yet each of them seems called by the secret design of Providence to control, some day, the destinies of half the world.

— Alexis de Tocqueville, Democracy in America

Richard Nixon was concerned. Here were his National Security Advisor, Henry Kissinger, and his Secretary of State, William Rogers, going at it again. "It's really deep-seated," the President explained to William Safire, his speech writer. "Henry thinks Bill isn't very deep, and Bill thinks Henry is power-crazy." What did the President think? "In a way they're both right. Ego is something we all have, and either you grow out of it or it takes you over." Nixon was closer to the mark in associating a towering ego with a lust for power than he was in insisting, "I've grown out of it."

Like so many leaders before him, and particularly his predecessor, Nixon was succumbing to the age-old disease of hubris. Taken from the ancient Greek "hybris," hubris was used by Aristotle, student of Plato, in the sense of deliberately humiliating others for the sheer pleasure of it. This was distinguished from the defeat or subjugation of others, whether in the Olympic Games or in the courtroom, for gaining honor for others and oneself. "Hybris" was not simply the attitude of excessive self-confidence that we link it with today. For the Greeks 2,300 years ago, it involved the malicious pleasure of committing evil with impunity, of watching others squirm or shrink in shame. Here was the abuse of power, however gained, of satisfying one's sadistic impulses by forcing someone else to suffer. Thus we have the case of Meidias, slapping Demosthenes in public for daring to speak out against him. The historian Xenophon characterized Alcibiades as "the most hubristic of those who lived under the democracy."[1]

Like all words, "hybris" evolved through the ages, broadening its meaning to stand for the wanton pride that results in the abuse of power. In the process it has been the subject of countless moral and religious maxims. The Hebrew writer of the Book of Proverbs put it, "Pride goeth before destruction and an haughty spirit before a fall." Another of the ancients wrote, "Whom the gods would destroy they first make mad." Of the seven sins, Dante called pride the first. And well he might. For he and his predecessors, of whatever religion, have warned not only of the self-destruction visited upon the perpetrator but of the far vaster destruction visited upon his victims. The fallen angel, the tragic hero, the leader mesmerized by the reflection of himself in the eyes of his followers—there are stories of hubris told again and again in religions around the world since the beginning of history. Ravana in Hindu literature had its counterpart in Samson in Hebrew literature. In Greek mythology there was Icarus, son of Daedalus, ignoring his father's warning not to fly too close to the sun. So close did he fly that the sun melted the wax on his wings and he plunged to his death in the sea below.

Among the Greek dramatists, Euripides, Sophocles, and Aristophanes, the tale of the tragic hero appears repeatedly, even as it does in the plays of Shakespeare, Sheridan, and Shaw. American playwrights Albee, O'Neill, and Williams have made much of hubris. Joseph Conrad, in his *Heart of Darkness* novella, noted that "Kurtz had no restraint." What Kurtz lacked, as so many leaders have lacked, were the very inhibitions that transform the savage infant, intent only on gratifying himself, into a civilized human being, capable of functioning in society. Hubris ensnares those who ignore Conrad's advice that "your strength comes in . . . your power of devotion, not to yourself but to an obscure, back-breaking business." (More of this in the Epilogue, where we shall consider preventives of hubris.)[2]

Emerging from the hidden mists of mankind's beginnings, hubris has managed to ensnare leaders more than followers, yet it remains no respecter of race or religion, of age or sex or party. In the wake of leaders who succumbed to its siren call have descended the Four Horsemen of the Apocalypse: famine, pestilence, war, and death. If prostitution is mankind's oldest profession then perhaps hubris is our oldest disease. Where the first affects individuals, the second affects institutions, nations, even the world. In the twentieth century alone it is estimated that at least 110 million people have died in war. If we add to this grim tally those killed in the Soviet purges of the thirties under Stalin and the Chinese purges of the sixties and seventies under Mao—as many as 30 to 40 million in each country—the total rises to 180 million. To dramatize this, imagine two of every three Americans being lined up and shot dead. By contrast, less than seven million have been killed in other disasters of this century, whether by so-called "acts of God" such as earthquakes, floods, hurricanes, typhoons, tornadoes, fires, or volcanoes, or "pseudo-acts of God" such as car, train, or airplane crashes, mine disasters, shipwrecks, or explosions. To put it differently, for every person killed in a natural or accidental disaster, there have been at least twenty-five killed in war. Is it too much to venture that hubris has played a role, perhaps a major role, in these 180 million deaths?[3] As I have emphasized in *Evolution or Extinction: The Choice Before Us*, we now exercise the power to extinguish ourselves as a species on this earth. Confronting us as we enter a new century and a new millennium is the overarching question: can we apply the same ingenuity, the same commitment, and the same sacrifice to our survival as we have to our destruction?

Religion has probably done as much harm as good in attempting to answer this question. The Christian New Testament, for example, has the Apostle Paul counseling: "Every person must submit to the supreme authorities. There is no authority but by act of God, and the existing authorities are instituted by Him; consequently anyone who rebels against authority is resisting a divine institution . . ."

From such was born the nefarious concept of the divine right of kings that plagued Western civilization for almost two millennia. From such continues to be born the mindless genuflection epitomized in Al Capp's creation of "Lil Abner" and his homage to presidents. It was just this mindset that sought to excuse the barbaric devastation of the Roman Empire by Attila the Hun in the fifth century on the basis of his serving as "the scourge of God." In our century there have been those who likewise viewed Hitler and his minions as "instruments of Divine justice, chastising those who had departed from the way of truth."[4] Such "sacred determinism" is but another name for fatalism, that breeder of resignation and cynicism which together sever the nerve of initiative and, in turn, progress.

Hubris is neither inevitable nor inexorable. Leaders do make choices, as do their followers. And once on the hubristic path, leaders can—and do—careen down that path to destruction. And, as we shall see, the further along the path, the steeper becomes its slippery slope.

Have historians, in tracing the evolution of civilization, given sufficient prominence to "the capacity of aggressive, charismatic leaders to shape the course of history?" Marcus and Flannery, in their *Zapotec Civilization*, think not.[5] Perhaps they have a point, for aggressive and charismatic leaders accumulate power, and in their power reveal their flaws—some fatal.

Let us distinguish three levels of hubris. To deprive others of discretionary choices—such as selecting which foods to eat, which clothes to wear, which car to drive, which house to inhabit—is the first level of hubris. Perhaps we can equate this with the "unalienable" right of happiness, spelled out in Thomas Jefferson's Declaration of Independence. Of more consequence is the second level of hubris, that which deprives others of the freedoms spelled out in the Bill of Rights. By far the most frightening level of hubris is that which deprives others of life itself. Perpetrated at the personal level, premeditated and executed in the name of honor, or revenge, or security, we call it murder and invoke the harshest of legal punishments. But perpetrated at the national level, and for these same reasons, we not only justify it but glorify it, going so far as to identify patriotism with religion, hallowing the names of those who have paid "the supreme sacrifice."

PROLOGUE

Congratulations, Mr. President! You have just been elected thirty-seventh President of the United States. Come January, you will take the oath of office, to be administered by the Chief Justice of the Supreme Court. But before you do, permit me, as head of your transition team, to brief you on your duties as well as your salary, expense money, and perks. Perhaps you will recall Charles DeGaulle's *The Edge of the Sword*, in which he noted, "Men fundamentally can no more get along without direction than they can without eating, drinking, or sleeping."

You have been chosen by the American voters to lead this nation for the next four years. Your job description is unlike that of any other nation's leader. When Khrushchev, at the height of his power in 1960, was asked what his job was like, he replied, "You have no idea how difficult it is. It's the most difficult thing in the world. . . . It means every minute of the day or night. Every ounce of your energy. There is no rest. No relaxation. Enjoyment? [I don't] know the meaning of the word. . . . You never know what is going to happen next."

Your job is greater still. Members of your executive branch will look to you to direct, coordinate, and implement policy. Members of Congress will look to you to establish priorities, exert influence, and provide services. The leaders of other nations will look to you to articulate your position on issues of international importance and, when necessary, to flex your nation's muscles. And the general public will look to you to safeguard them, to solve their problems, and to exercise symbolic and moral leadership.[6]

Now you may, along with this nation's first president, heartily wish this election to the nation's highest office did not fall upon you. But probably not. He described it as the greatest sacrifice of his personal feelings and wishes that he had ever been called on to make. Like George

Washington, you may be "overwhelm[ed] with despondence" at the thought of your "own deficiencies." But probably not. So fearful was Washington on entering this office that he "felt not unlike . . . a culprit who is going to the place of his execution." Surely these are not your sentiments.

Yet other presidents have had second thoughts. James Garfield, less than two weeks after his inauguration, felt "wholly unfit for this kind of work," and Abraham Lincoln confessed, "I do not think myself fit for the presidency."[7]

As you know only too well, Mr. President, modesty—and especially false modesty—has been vastly overrated. This does not imply, as some people have alleged, that anybody running for president must be possessed of a towering ego to be able to wear so many different hats. For Lincoln there were only three such hats: as the "nation's first legislator, the inventor as well as the executor of policy, and a source of the nation's political conscience."

Now, over a century after Lincoln, you will wear no less than eight hats. You will be the chief executive officer in charge of enforcing the laws of the nation; the chief administrator of the executive branch; commander in chief of the armed services; chief engineer for "fine-tuning" the economy; head of your political party; ceremonial chief of state; top diplomat; and, most importantly, keeper of world peace. As such you will inherit the mantle of your predecessor, Lyndon Johnson, in "taking giant strides over the world to catalogue [your] program and [your] duties." Not only will you be "the missionary of freedom, but the regulator of birth, the purifier of air, the healer, provider, educator." In addition you will be "the government reorganizer, the crime-stopper, the keeper of the economy." At times you will wonder at it all, as John F. Kennedy did when he mused, "I don't see how we do it." But you will do it—or at least you will try. And in the trying you will bump into the fences the Constitution has erected to restrict your power.[8]

Undoubtedly you will be able to empathize with Adlai Stevenson who, after being nominated as the 1952 Democratic presidential candidate, told his Chicago audience, "I would not seek your nomination for the presidency because the burdens of the office stagger the imagination. Its potential for good or evil, now and in the years of our lives, smothers exultation and converts vanity to prayers."[9]

With this unexpected responsibility goes unprecedented power—indeed, awesome power. Theodore White, chronicler of presidential elections, described this awesome power as befitting a king, a protector, a father figure, and virtually a god, possessed of omniscience if not omnipotence and omnipresence. The Constitution grants you certain prescribed powers, two of which must be approved by the Senate: to make treaties and to appoint officers, including ambassadors and Supreme Court justices. In addition to the power to command the armed forces, you will have the power to grant pardons; to provide Congress each year with information on the state of the union; to call it into special session; to recommend to it measures to consider, including an annual budget; and to exercise a qualified veto on the legislation it passes.

As you readily see, power and responsibility are opposite sides of the same coin. The responsible use of power was the major concern of the Founding Fathers when they drew up the Constitution. Just how difficult this will at times be for you can be seen in a more detailed look at your obligations. You will have direct supervision of more than 50 departments, as well as responsibility for personnel and decisions in an additional 197 departments, agencies, commissions, and committees. In just one department—Health, Education and Welfare—you will have ultimate responsibility for overseeing no less than 254 separate programs. You will also oversee such "trivia" as the preparation of certificates for graduates of the Capital Page School; determining the quality of food being served as rations to our armed forces; deciding where the Navy Band will play when it goes on tour; and passing judgment on some 500 bills of relief annually submitted by private citizens, most involving immigration and small claims. As though your plate were not already full, you will be weighed down with seemingly endless demands as leader, job-giver and father-confessor. Harry Truman was scarcely exaggerating when he described the concerns of the president as encompassing "Every hope and every fear of [your] fellow citizens; almost every aspect of their welfare and activity." These, he was quick to add, are not simply your concern; they are your duty.[10]

One of your most important responsibilities will be to keep the electorate informed. You will be expected to do this every week or two by means of press conferences, every month or two by means of televised speeches, and every year by means of a State of the Union address. In addition, there will be hundreds of White House press releases that eager reporters will funnel to their editors. All of this is vital to your constituency keeping tabs on you; after all, the American people have granted you unparalleled power. Still, that is not enough to satisfy those who delegate the power you wield. They will make certain the media as well as the Secret Service are tailing you wherever you go, whether to duck out for a pizza or fly to the other side of the globe for a summit meeting. The press, and through them your fellow citizens, will always be taking your measure. Partly it's curiosity, as some 1.5 million of them traipse through the White House each year, hoping against hope to see you or your family "up close and personal." When you're speaking, they will be riveted to your every word. Every inflection, every gesture, every eye contact will be scrutinized. What you wear and how you wear it, what you say and how you say it, what you do and how you do it—all will be the object of an almost surreal fascination.

Perhaps you will be forbearing with your many visitors, as was Lincoln, who explained, "they don't want much [and] they get but little." More likely, you will feel like James Polk, that "the people would not regard the presidency highly if they could look in occasionally and observe the kind of people they elected." Still, you may, before long, sympathize with Calvin Coolidge as he stood in reception lines each day for three to four hours, listening to visitors who "want something they shouldn't have." As you greet each one you will wonder if your fixed smile will wear out sooner than your legs or your handshake. Like Coolidge, you may choose to say nothing and do nothing, figuring, as did "Silent Cal," that "most will run down in three to four minutes." But, he complained, cough or provide a spontaneous smile, and they'll start all over again. Privacy, you will soon discover, is a relic of the days before entering politics. Now, as the nation's number one celebrity, you will live—as never before—in a fishbowl. Put out your best cutlery for entertaining your counterparts from other nations, as Martin Van Buren did in 1840, and you may provoke a Congressman like Charles Ogle to berate you for making the White House "a royal establishment" at great cost to the taxpayer for "knives, forks or spoons of gold that [you] may dine in the style of the monarchs of Europe." On the other hand, refuse the formality traditional with the office, as did Andrew Jackson, the quintessential populist, and invite one and all to join you for inauguration festivities in what he called a "people's collaboration." Watch the revelers prime themselves with punch from pails, plant their muddy boots on the furniture, break the dishes, and take turns jumping out the windows. Then you can understand Jackson's disgust as he headed for the nearest hotel, soon to describe his situation as "dignified slavery." Just remember that your predecessor, LBJ, made the mistake of picking up his hound dog by the ears, arousing the wrath of millions of dog lovers.

Perhaps before your inauguration you'll sympathize with Truman who, learning he was to assume Franklin Roosevelt's mantle, told the press he was going home "to get as much rest as possible and face the music." Like Harry S., you may be tempted to solicit the press, "Boys, if you ever pray, pray for me now." He'd soon be "riding a tiger," which he'd have to "keep on riding or be swallowed." Like Kennedy, you may well discover your greatest surprise is finding that "things were really just as bad" as he'd said they were during his presidential campaign. One of the "bads" may be, as Coolidge complained, that your major job seems to be running "an entertainment bureau," or, as William Howard Taft complained, to increase "gate receipts" or be a sounding board while "other people talk."

Perhaps by this time you'll conclude, with Zachary Taylor, that you "don't care a fig about the office," or with John Adams that you can't wait to return to your family and friends. Give yourself six years in the office, as did Thomas Jefferson, and pronounce it "nothing but drudgery and a daily loss of friends." You won't have to serve six years to experience, with Garfield, "a broadside of the world's wrath." Nor will you, in all probability, have to serve eight years before you long, with Washington and Jefferson, to get back to private life. On the other hand, neither of them could have imagined the great relief of your predecessor in turning over the "nuclear football" to you, a burden that dogged his every step.

But before you contemplate stepping down from this "splendid misery," as Jefferson put it in a memorable oxymoron, consider the rewards of office, beginning with your inauguration.[11] You won't enjoy the regal splendor of a gilded carriage drawn by twelve white horses, as Washington wanted until Jefferson talked him out of it. On the other hand, you won't have to "pick [your] way through the narrow winding streets of near wilderness that was the federal city," as Jefferson did on his way to a partially completed Capitol.

None of that for you, Mr. President. Once you've stopped for tea with LBJ at the White House, you will step into a luxurious black stretch limousine, and the two of you will ride in grand style to the Capitol, accompanied by a motorcade of at least twelve vehicles, and a motorcycle escort with lights flashing and sirens screaming to announce to the thousands lining the street that you are to become America's VIP extraordinaire.

As such, you are precious cargo. At least one of the cars in the motorcade will be a decoy identical to the limo you'll be riding in, down to the presidential seal emblazoned on the side. To protect you further, one car will carry a counterassault team of Secret Service agents, armed with an assortment of the latest "James Bond" weapons. Another car, devoted to intelligence, will carry a computer to track those accused of threatening you. Your own car, code-named "Stagecoach," will be armor-plated, with bulletproof glass. As your limo makes its way down Pennsylvania Avenue, you will notice that concrete barriers block the roads leading on to your route, and that the crowds are kept safely distant from your car. But you probably won't be able to see that all manhole covers will have been sealed, that all windows looking out on the route have been closed and secured, and that agents have been posted on rooftops, armed with high-powered rifles, binoculars, and two-way radios. You understand that since the assassination of John and Robert Kennedy, the Secret Service is leaving nothing to chance.

As you take your seat on the specially constructed stage outside the Capitol, you will note the hundreds of VIPs seated behind you. But that is nothing compared to the sea of faces before you, upturned to grasp what Dwight Eisenhower referred to as "the majesty of the moment" encapsulated in this "orderly transfer of power" in celebrating "the unity that keeps us free."

Having taken the oath of office and given your inauguration address, you will find the day's festivities have just begun. Unlike Jefferson, returning to his boarding house only to find no available seat for dinner, you will be the honored guest at one grand ball after another. At each you will greet many well-wishers, say a few words, and dance with the First Lady.

Here you've scarcely claimed the White House and already you may be astonished at the deference paid you by one and all. Even your Vice-President may wonder just how he should address you, as John Adams wondered if he should call Washington "Majesty," or "Elective Highness."

The great temptation here, of course. is to interpret this obsequiousness as an honor owed to you personally, rather than to your office. In fact, it is the presidency, not the president, that receives such homage.

Believe it or not, this is just the beginning of the fashioning of a new reverential attitude toward you: hero worship combined with recognition of your almost sacerdotal privilege. The "royalty trap" lies not far beyond. Every time you appear at a formal occasion, there will be a standing ovation, accompanied by trumpet fanfare and "Hail to the Chief." Abroad, there will be red carpet treatment, review of the color guard, and a twenty-one-gun salute. The First Lady will probably not want, as Martha Washington did, ladies to curtsy before her, as befitting the queens of Europe. She would be like a queen, Martha thought, high-crowned headdress and all, welcoming titles such as "The Presidentress" and "Lady President." It is probably just as well that such forms of address did not attach to Martha, so your wife will not have that to contend with.

As Congressman and Senator, you became accustomed to some deference by captains of industry. As Vice-President you were accorded even more. But being President confers on you an aura unlike anything you have ever experienced. Fortune 500 CEO's will be at your beck and call. Once in your presence they will bark out no commands, give no ultimatums. Indeed, they will scarcely speak unless spoken to, and then only in muted tones appropriate to objects of veneration. Pity the person who dares to interrupt you when deep in thought. And when those thoughts find expression in words, many if not most will hang on them as the Decalogue falling from the lips of Moses descending Sinai. When you wish to make a Presidential address, the three major networks will provide prime time at no cost. What you will come to recognize, for good and ill, is that you, Mr. President, are news.

The inaugural festivities concluded, you will enjoy settling into your new home at 1600 Pennsylvania Avenue, appropriately coded "Crown" by the Secret Service. Only a fifth as large as the American Versailles that architect Pierre L'Enfant submitted to Congress, you will, nonetheless, find it suitably impressive, with its 132 rooms magnificently situated on 18 acres of beautifully landscaped and lovingly manicured lawns and gardens.

Do recognize, Mr. President, that you've come a long way from 1857, when Congress allocated $2,500 for the first White House employee to handle secretarial duties. Before that time each president paid for any such help out of his own pocket. Herbert Hoover had fifty or so employees, and Truman some 200. But you can count on an Executive Office Staff of 1,500—including five calligraphers, who alone cost $260,000. There are an additional 1,000 employees of the White House Commission Agency—financed by the Defense Department—including those in the basement Situation Room. It is there that you'll receive reports instantaneously from the CIA, State, and Defense, providing, among other information, the latest U.S. military movements around the world. Having inherited your predecessor's war in Indochina, you'll welcome not only the privacy of the second-floor living quarters but the solicitous care of your White House staff. Do you need a leaky faucet to be fixed, a clock to be wound, a package to be wrapped, a peanut butter sandwich to be prepared? There will be a Johnny-on-the-spot servant to attend to your slightest wish. Step out of your suit with the help of your valet, and presto—it will be whisked away to be pressed, cleaned, or brushed. Take a brief afternoon nap and you can rely on having clean sheets the next time. Take a swim in your Olympic-size pool, a walk in your luxurious gardens, a workout in your own gym, or a movie in your own projection room, and you will see servants bustling about, catering to your every desire.

Let me reinforce the importance of security. You can't grab a quick pizza just a block or two away without a minimum of five of the thirty-five cars at your disposal. There is no motoring for you, Mr. President, without a motorcade. If you wish a quiet stroll around your acreage, count on Secret Service agents at your heels, and a SWAT team on the roof, following your every movement. In addition, you and each member of your family will be coded and automatically and digitally tracked on a location box, whether you move from room to room or venture out to any spot on earth. None of your thousands of staff will be permitted in the second-floor living quarters without your express permission. If you grant that permission, your visitor's every movement, every gesture, every word will be scrutinized by one or more of the thirty-five ubiquitous Secret Service agents always on duty at the White House.

As for that high fence surrounding the grounds: until FDR entertained British royalty in June 1939, the grounds were open to the public. But with World War II about to break out, the iron fence was built. Ever since its construction, visitors are required to be checked by armed guards. There are systems that will screen your drinking water for impurities as well as for noxious substances. Canine units of German shepherds will sniff for any explosives. Your windows in the White House are of three-inch-thick bulletproof glass. Infrared and electronic sensors, detected by both audio and pressure waves, supplement the many TV cameras covering every inch of the eighteen acres. And overhead, no planes are permitted to fly.

All these precautions will give you some idea of the importance you have as President of these United States. And each year they set the taxpayers back some $350 million to safeguard you, your Vice-President, and your families. [This in 1969 dollars, worth three times 1999 dollars.] If you wish to escape from this fishbowl even for a few hours, you will find some relief by hopping aboard a helicopter on the South Lawn and making for Camp David, secluded not far away in the woods of Maryland. It is, you will find, a notch above a typical Boy Scout camp. Far from roughing it, there will be virtually every comfort and convenience you have at the White House. Here, in your own cottage, "Aspen," are four bedrooms, a glassed-in living room with a table for twelve and a spectacular view, a movie projection room and an elaborate stereo system. Just outside the front door you will enjoy a luxurious swimming pool. Just inside is an elevator that will drop you into the bowels of the earth, where a bomb shelter is equipped with communications equipment and all the amenities. Surrounding this hideout are a high fence and a security gate, with one hundred Marines on duty in addition to the usual Secret Service contingent. Some one hundred Navy Seabees are stationed there to keep "Aspen," the other cottages, and the conference center in tip-top shape.

On occasion, you may want some variety, so hop aboard the presidential yacht, "Sequoia," for a cruise down the Potomac, and the amenities you will find surprising. Including its seasoned crew, the yacht will cost taxpayers one million dollars each year to maintain. But, Mr. President, we are concerned that you relax and keep well, even if it means boarding your old war buddies—as Harry Truman did—and engaging them in a game you will surely appreciate, after your war experience in the South Pacific: poker, lubricated with ample spirits.

If, however, you really wish to travel—abroad, for instance, for a summit conference—it will be, in the words of Bill Gulley, your military aide, "like moving a palace." For a week before you leave, planeloads of people and equipment will precede you to prepare the way. Personnel will include a doctor, aides, communications experts, and Secret Service agents. Equipment will include backup aircraft, cars, and communications gear. En route, no planes will fly anywhere near Air Force One, while U S. warships will be spaced every few hundred miles below in the event of an emergency

By the time you arrive—with at least two other big jets carrying staff and journalists—it will seem to the natives like an invasion force. Indeed, your predecessor used to brag to reporters that every time he took a trip he displaced no less than seven hundred people: those who preceded him, accompanied him, or stayed on for a week to mop up after him.

Know that times have changed since John Quincy Adams was unable to obtain a seat at the captain's table while aboard a ship off the Eastern seaboard. If you found Camp David to your liking, "Sequoia" suited to your demanding tastes, and the White House itself mind-boggling, you'll discover that Air Force One is the most luxurious of magic carpets. On the South Lawn you will board one of the thirteen helicopters available to you and be whisked to nearby Andrews Air Force Base, where Air Force One will be equipped and ready to go.[12] After all, Bill Gulley has 2,000 military men attached to his office and another 1,500 on call at Andrews. Nothing will escape his scrutiny regarding your safety, comfort, and convenience.

All of this, of course, doesn't come cheap. Air Force One alone, just for fuel and maintenance, will cost $40,000 per hour to fly. Taking in the cost of the crew, it adds up to a tidy $185 million per year. When the rest of the "invasion force" is considered, you begin to realize, Mr. President, that being the head of the richest and most powerful nation on earth requires first-class accommodations and strict security wherever you go. Since much of this expense is assigned to a secret defense fund, there is no need to trouble average taxpayers with figures they couldn't understand anyway. At least, that's what your predecessor thought.

On a domestic flight it will be comforting to know there will be no delay in landing, no waiting in traffic patterns. And before your pilot sets down he is assured no other plane has landed within the last twenty minutes. In addition Secret Service agents have already combed the runway for anything that might interfere with your safe arrival. Advance men will assure a respectable crowd being there to greet you.

But that will pale next to the receptions that will be the rule overseas— especially among U.S. allies. You may not draw the million or so Berliners that greeted Kennedy at the Brandenburg Gate, or the two million South Koreans that greeted LBJ. But you'll be sorely tempted to compare the tumultuous welcomes abroad with the often lackluster receptions at home, and judge, as Jesus did, that "a prophet is not without honor save in his own country." Still, abroad and even at home you will find, as Jesus also did, that there are some eager to catch a glimpse of you, others extending their hands just to be touched, and still others ecstatic at simply being able to touch "the hem of your garment." Perhaps then you can understand the feelings of LBJ who, returning to Air Force One from such an encounter with a crowd, gently nursed the cuts and bruises on his hands as though they were the stigmata of Jesus. In any event, you will be hard-pressed not to think that your position as international peace broker and benefactor is not only the role you most appreciate, but the role you fill best. Here, you will be convinced, is your forte.

Nonetheless, wherever you go and to whomever you speak, whether in person or on television, you can count on many—even millions—hanging on your every word. Here, the millions will believe, is Shakespeare's heavenly dew falling from heaven to the earth beneath. You will be sorely tempted to dismiss the caveat of Lincoln at Gettysburg that "the world will little note nor long remember" what you say. On the contrary, you may well find yourself keeping a diary, jotting down everything you can remember from the day as well as impressions, reflections, predictions, anything you can scrounge from the attic of your mind. And, to be sure that posterity will appreciate the fulsomeness of your thoughts as well as your deeds, you will want to leave a record of the memos you write, the speeches you give, and the conversations you have. To make certain history accords you your proper place for future generations, you will understandably wish to continue LBJ's taping system. Or perhaps even improve on it, making it automatically record everything you say, regardless how trivial others may think it is.

Now, Mr. President, with all of these grave responsibilities—such that no other leader on earth has shared—you will be well paid. Your $200,000 salary plus $50,000 expense money is but the tip of the iceberg. To run the White House, Congress has set aside $10 million. For your own office expenses, there's another $40 million as well as the $25 million for something called the Office of Administration. And when you need advice you don't have far to look. For the Office of Management and Budget, the

National Security Council, and similar agencies are budgeted for $94 million. Just in case you run out, there are always the deep pockets of the Defense Department, into which you can dip, knowing that precious few will be the wiser. Forget the senatorial wag, Everett Dirksen, cracking that a billion here and a billion there all add up. Simply rest assured that the American taxpayers look out for their presidents.[13]

With such weighty responsibilities, such concern for your security, such money and perks at your disposal, you will relish the attention, the acclaim, and the devotion that millions will accord you. Perhaps you may be excused for thinking yourself not simply a politician but a statesman, not simply important but great, not simply vital but indispensable—indispensable to the presidency, to the government, to the nation, to the continent, to the hemisphere, to the "free" world, and yes, to the whole world. Such is the path of hubris. Is there anyone on this planet more sorely tempted?

CHAPTER 1

DEFERENCE

A prince . . . ought to be a constant inquirer, and afterwards a patient listener concerning the things of which he inquired. . . . A prince who is not wise himself will never take good advice . . .

— Machiavelli, *The Prince*, 1513

So much is expected, so many untoward circumstances may intervene, in such a new and critical situation that I feel, in the execution of my arduous office, how much I shall stand in need of the contenance and aid of every friend to myself, of every friend to the Revolution, and of every friend of good government.

— George Washington to a friend, 1789[1]

LYNDON JOHNSON

Oh, Rayburn's so goddamned difficult—I've got to go over there to the Board of Education and kiss his ass, and I don't want to do it.

— Senator Majority Leader Lyndon Johnson
to former FDR aide, Jim Rowe, 1960

Goddammit, I have to kiss his ass all the time in Washington. I don't have to do it in Texas, too, do I?

— Senate Majority Leader Lyndon Johnson,
of Sam Rayburn, to House doorkeeper, 1960

I've been kissing asses all my life and I don't have to kiss them anymore. Tell those press bastards of yours that I'll see them when I want to and not before.

— President Lyndon Johnson to Press Secretary George Reedy, 1965[2]

WILL IT BE DEFERENCE OR FLATTERY?

"Mr. Warnke, this is Lyndon Johnson, and Bob McNamara has been telling me of all the great things you have been doing for your country, how much and how generously you have given of your time, and how helpful you have been, and I am calling to say thank you." Jack Warnecke, on the other end of the line, was an architect and social friend of the Kennedys who had provided some help to Secretary of Defense McNamara at the JFK gravesite in Arlington Cemetery. He demurred that he'd done all too little but did appreciate the President's remarks.

"No, Mr. Warnke, this is no time to be modest. We know all about you.

There is no man I hold in higher esteem than Bob McNamara and Bob is saying a lot of fine things, very fine things about you." Warnecke acknowledged that he too was an admirer of McNamara. "Mr. Warnke," continued Johnson, "it is refreshing to talk to someone like yourself, a man who could make a great deal of money in private life and yet is willing to give of himself to his country." Warnecke, modest to a fault, assured LBJ that his sacrifice was all too small.

The President would hear none of it. "Mr. Warnke, I know better. I know that you have done a truly fine job for your country, and we are not unaware of it. We know of your dedication and, Mr. Warnke, Bob McNamara needs you and I need you, and I am calling you today because I am naming you as Assistant Secretary of Defense today, and it will be in tomorrow's paper. We are proud of you."

With that Warnecke stumbled, protesting that an architect could hardly be expected to run the Defense Department. Johnson, egg on his face, admitted, ". . . it does appear that a mistake has been made," but not before assuring this total stranger, "Mr. Warnke, you too have done a fine job for your country."

We know nothing of Johnson's reprimand of the phone operator who misconnected him—a perfectly natural mistake given the similarity of surnames. But if past treatment of his aides is any indication, the hapless operator was reduced to tears. And Johnson's follow-up call to Paul Warnke took him aback with its curtness.[3]

Though Warnke did come aboard to replace John McNaughton, killed in a plane crash in 1966, Warnke was opposed to JFK's Vietnam policy and even more opposed to LBJ's escalation, becoming a vocal critic.

Several points stand out in this recruitment of Johnson's. First was his brazen attempt, through not mere deference but through outrageous flattery, to recruit an important staff member. In addition, though he apparently knew nothing of Warnecke, he persisted in flattering him as though he had the inside track on him. If, as Shakespeare suggested, we damn others with faint praise then perhaps we double-damn others with extravagant praise—the praise that fingers us as potential manipulators. Note also Johnson's choice of words in commending "Warnke" for sacrificing sizeable private income for government service—not only sycophancy but hypocrisy in view of LBJ's unprecedented enriching of himself through "public service," detailed in a subsequent chapter. Also note that Johnson made no apology to Warnecke but took it out on Warnke the next day—curt, rude, abrupt. Finally note Johnson's brazen insistence on inserting the announcement of Warnke's appointment in the press without Warnke's acceptance. It is a wonder Warnke accepted.

As for proper deference, Johnson had much to learn from our first President, who understood the importance of soliciting the advice of others, if not complying with it. Especially was this so at the start of Washington's term of office, as we have seen. To add to Washington's diffidence, his Vice-President, the cultured New Englander, John Adams, was scarcely a friend on any count as he laced into Washington as "too illiterate, unlearned, and unread for his station and reputation." All the more reason, Washington conceded, aware of his limitations, "to enlist those who (excel me) in expertise and experience." Indeed, with the exception of the acid elitism of a few, including Adams, the early Republic appears to have been a deferential society.

Flattery was one thing; honest and spontaneous deference was something else again. Like Washington, Jefferson seemed to have understood that. In 1774 he wrote, "Let those flatter who fear; it is not an American art." It was something to inquire freely of others, for that, bound to reason, offered the "only effective agents against error." It was something else again to flatter, to wheedle, to play the sycophant. Woodrow Wilson also understood that, recognizing the importance of seeking the counsel of others. "I never come out of a conference," he noted, "without seeing more of the question that was under discussion than I had seen when I went in. And that to my mind is an image of government." He went on, "The whole purpose of democracy is that we may hold counsel with one another, so as not to depend on the understanding of one man, but to depend on the counsel of all."[4]

The story of the six blind men of Hindustani, trying to describe an elephant through the sense of touch, illustrates the dilemmas we all face in depending solely on our own understanding. The first felt an ear, the second the trunk, the third a leg, the fourth the tail, and so on, so that each came up with a radically different view of the beast. Only by merging their impressions could they develop a composite nearer the truth. Assuming that all are on a somewhat equal footing, and that none is an expert, collective intelligence is superior to that of one. For if we define intelligence as the ability to come up with the greatest number of possible solutions to a problem in the shortest time—enabling us to select what appears to be the best answer or combination of answers—then Wilson's point makes eminent good sense despite his failure to practice what he preached.

It was just such a process that enabled the nation's Founders to patch together a single nation from thirteen disparate colonies, each intent on preserving its autonomy, but aware that strength lay in numbers. It was only after seemingly endless debate—and even heated wrangling—that a Constitution emerged that would become the envy of most of the world. Only through compromise, permitting each participant to feel he had a stake in the answer, was implementation possible. Here lies the beauty of democracy. And here lies the necessity of that first step in deference, soliciting the opinions of others. It is important to note that none of the Founding Fathers was an expert on democracy. Indeed, this was an experiment that would push the first systematic attempt at it—in ancient Greece—far beyond its original bounds. But even though none were experts, all were well-read and, arguably, "the best and the brightest" at the time. Today, no one other than the president has such ready access to expertise, not only on a given problem but in collective decision-making.

Lyndon Learns Limitless Flattery

It has been the failure of presidents to utilize proper deference and to substitute their own opinions, or the opinions of others who agreed with them, that has subverted this critical first step on the path to hubris. In the case of Johnson especially, it was his shameless obsequiousness on the path to the presidency that reinforced the title, "Prince of Flatterers," given him in college by fellow students.

Early on, Lyndon came to understand not simply the power of words, but particularly the power of words "fitly spoken." These were, the boy learned at his mother's knee, "like apples of gold in pictures of silver," as the writer of Proverbs put it. For Rebekah Baines Johnson was determined that her firstborn would be well-grounded in the Scriptures. What she did not foresee was Lyndon's discovery that no words were more rewarding than those of flattery. The fried chicken of a neighbor lady was not simply good, it was "better than anything in the whole wide world!" And when the neighbor beamed, Lyndon realized that when it came to flattery, there could be no excess. Not content to let it go with mere words, Johnson soon became aware of the reinforcing power of touch. Thus when the mother of a playmate was the object of his praise, Lyndon also put his arms around her and kissed her repeatedly until her own four children complained, "Mama, do you love Lyndon more than you love us?" Lyndon, remembered one of the four, "could get whatever he wanted from her." So effective did Johnson become in cajoling whatever he wanted that his friends let him do the asking—knowing, as one recalled, that "he could get them to do things that ordinarily they'd say no to." The more someone disliked him, the more hoops Lyndon would jump through to gain his friendship. He'd smile—too easily and too broadly. He'd demean himself, fawn, wheedle—even hug another boy—anything to ingratiate himself. His grades in school were nothing to bring joy to the heart of Rebekah, herself a teacher. His first grade teacher, however, remembered Lyndon crawling onto her lap, where he would "pet and pat" her. He followed her around all day, clinging to her skirt or pressing up close to her and nuzzling her with his shoulder. But one day he refused to read aloud because defective "R's" made him self-conscious, so Rebekah suggested the teacher hold Lyndon on her lap while he read. And this she did, while thirty other children looked on, whether in amazement or envy.[5]

In 1927, at the age of nineteen, Lyndon enrolled at Southwest Texas State Teachers College in San Marcos. There he soon earned a reputation as a bootlicking bully. The bootlicking part was recognized early on by Alfred "Boody" Johnson (no relation to LBJ), captain of the football team, and Ardis Hopper, student council president, who were living rent-free in two small rooms above the garage of the school's President, Cecil Evans. According to "Boody," Lyndon took him aside one day and gave him some advice. "Boody, the way you get ahead in this world, you get close to those who are the heads of things. Like President Evans, for example." When "Boody" found work as a building inspector, Lyndon claimed he had gotten him the job. Not so, "Boody" objected, he "already had it lined up." You see, "Boody" later explained, "Lyndon liked to have credit for things."

But with mediocre grades and little money, Lyndon was ready to hitchhike home before the year was over—until a friend, Ben Crider, sent him his savings of $81 and "Boody" agreed that Johnson could live free with him. Already his bootlicking was paying off. As Lyndon next focused on buttering up the Director of Admissions, a cousin, Ava Johnson, recalled that he'd come a long way from his first day on campus, when he had stood in the registration line looking like "one scared chicken."

Yet Johnson's bootlicking in college had just begun. He now set his sights on nobody less than President Evans himself. It didn't hurt that Lyndon's father, Sam—a Texas state legislator—had fought at Austin for increases in appropriations for teachers colleges. So when Sam wrote the President soliciting a job for his son, Evans complied. Soon Lyndon was busy doing maintenance work on the campus, clearing it of rocks and other debris. Still, he was never too busy to intercept Evans when the President walked by. The aloof Evans seldom talked with students, but Lyndon changed all that—disarming the President with an ear-to-ear grin, regaling him with stories of statehouse politics gleaned from Sam.

It wasn't long before the long, lanky, awkward boy with the fetching smile and the easy banter had exchanged his rake for a mop, swabbing the halls of the college administration building, Old Main. It was hardly a coincidence that whenever Evans entered his office, he would find Johnson just outside, flourishing a mop with vigor. In no time at all, Lyndon had persuaded the President to give him an even better job: office boy to Evans' assistant.

Other first-year students were aghast at the effrontery of their class-mate, who, five weeks after enrolling, was earning twice the $7.50 earned on the "Rock Squad." Years later, Johnson maintained that he'd "literally swept (his) way through teacher's college." It would be more accurate had Lyndon admitted he'd swept Evans off his feet with persistent ingratia-tion. He revealed his strategy to Cousin Ava. "The first thing you want to do is to know people . . . and don't play sandlot ball; play in the big leagues. . . get to know the first team." Astounded, like other students, at Lyndon's cheek, Ava said she'd never "dare to go to President Evans' office." "That" corrected Lyndon, "is where you want to start." Johnson had by this time a three-pronged strategy for ingratiating himself with his college President. Lyndon would flatter him to his face; he would sit at the President's feet in rapt, virtually worshipful attention in class; and, as an editorial writer for the school newspaper, he would pay fulsome tribute to Evans. One such editorial appeared in 1928: "Great as an educator and as an executive, Dr. Evans is greatest as a man . . . with depth of human sym-pathy rarely surpassed, unfailing cheerfulness, geniality, kind firmness and friendly interest in the youth of the state, Dr. Evans has exerted a great influence for good upon the students of SWTSTC. He finds great happiness in serving others." With such lavish encomiums, it is no wonder that along with such nicknames as "Bull" Johnson and "bootlicking tyrant," Lyndon was also called "Prince of Flatterers." Joe Berry, star end on the football team, sized Lyndon up: "If he thought you could help him, he would fawn all over you. If you couldn't, he wouldn't waste much time with you."[6]

So avid was young Johnson's taste for power that, in 1931, Sam again interceded for his son. Sam had rounded up a lot of votes for Congressman Richard Kleberg, and the quid pro quo was that Kleberg would hire Lyndon as his secretary. Lyndon jumped at the chance. Leaving his post as a speech teacher and debate coach in Houston, Lyndon soon found himself in Washington, D.C., aide to the heir of one-fifth of the 2,000-square-mile King Ranch back in Texas. Lyndon's days of exaggerated deference were just beginning, as he moved from sandlot ball to the big leagues.

With so much to learn, Johnson was now all ears. When the secretaries broke for lunch and headed for Childs Cafeteria, there he would be, bounding ahead of the rest, grabbing a tray and enough food to feed a horse, rushing to a large table and wolfing down his food. Then he'd start in with the questions. Who were their bosses? What did they do? How did they get done what they did? Who were the power brokers? Who were the committee heads? How could one become somebody here? Recalled one of Lyndon's coworkers, "He wanted to be sure he knew the answers."

In addition to knowing "all the answers," Johnson used gall, effrontery, and buttering up to ingratiate himself with his superiors. Tommy "the Cork" Corcoran, an aide to FDR, recalled this brash secretary introducing himself on the phone as Congressman Kleberg. Furthermore, Corcoran noticed, "He was smiling and deferential . . . no matter what someone thought, Lyndon would agree with him. . . ." He was fast becoming a political animal, with all the craven connotations the term implies.

But it was not Corcoran who became the consuming object of Johnson's wheedling, fawning, pawing attention. It was Sam Rayburn, twenty-six years Johnson's elder, the man above all others who knew the avenues of power in the House of Representatives. After all, he'd been there since Wilson was elected President in 1913. Power, as Johnson put it, has "an odor." It not only tasted good; it smelled sweet. And that sweet smell arose from the bald head of old Sam Rayburn more than any other person that Johnson found on Capitol Hill. Hubert Humphrey, later

Johnson's Vice-President, emphasized, "You must never underestimate the importance of Sam Rayburn in Johnson's career."[7]

It turned out that Lyndon had discovered in Rayburn the pot of gold at the end of the political rainbow. It was in 1934 that Rayburn interceded with FDR to make Johnson director of the National Youth Administration in Texas, even though the President had already announced another appointee to the post. At twenty-six, Lyndon was the youngest state director in the land. With Rayburn backing him, Johnson figured that when he returned to Washington he'd do so as a full-fledged Congressman himself—and told the rest of Kleberg's staff just that. Soon he had another VIP backing him: FDR's wife Eleanor, who, in her several visits to Austin, found Lyndon not only committed to eighteen-hour days but "a most ingratiating young man."

Sycophancy: The Path to Power

In 1937, when he learned that Texas Congressman James "Buck" Buchanan had died, Johnson went to work on rich, influential Texans who could stake him to a run for Buchanan's seat. Lady Bird, Lyndon's wife of three years, dipped into a trust fund left by her mother for the campaign's seed money, and his wealthy friends chipped in enough more to achieve the miracle needed to vault Lyndon from last place among seven candidates to the winner's circle. Along the way, Lyndon not only ingratiated himself with the rich and powerful in his home state but with FDR himself. Not only had the First Lady regaled her husband with the accomplishments of this young NYA director, but FDR certainly took notice when Lyndon not only defeated seasoned and favored politicians, but did so by backing Roosevelt "one hundred percent"—including his proposal to increase the Supreme Court from nine to fifteen members, a plan ridiculed by the press as FDR's "court packing scheme." Here, then, was a young man after the President's political heart, one who knew where to place his bets. As Lyndon's father had reminded him in his parting words at the train station, "Now you get up there, support FDR all the way, never shimmy and give 'em hell." A few weeks after the election Roosevelt took a fishing vacation off the Texas coast. He also found time to congratulate the freshman Congressman, Lyndon Johnson, on his spectacular, come-from-behind victory. Not to be outdone, Lyndon congratulated the

President on his fine catch of a seventy-two-pound tarpon. He, too, Johnson claimed, was fond of fishing and consumed with all things Navy—a surprise to anyone who knew him. Of course it was Roosevelt's naval background that had sparked Lyndon's sudden interest.

Not about to buffer himself against such praise, FDR took delight in the impeccable taste of this fledgling Congressman and invited Lyndon to join him on the presidential train from Galveston to Ft. Worth. Johnson soon discovered that he was a paying guest aboard the train, and it took all he had to buy his ticket. Grumbling about the cost, Lyndon was set straight by a reporter. "Let this be a profitable lesson to you. The President is very generous with everybody's money but his own, and don't you forget it." Yet the few dollars Johnson had to cough up for his ticket was a minuscule down payment on Roosevelt's subsequent investment in Lyndon. Before departing at Ft. Worth, Johnson was given Corcoran's phone number, with instructions to call the presidential aide when he got to Washington. Tommy, FDR assured Lyndon, would take care of him.[8]

By this time Lyndon had perfected ingratiation to a fine art. And there was no more important—or slick—professional pal than FDR who, after returning to Washington, issued orders to Corcoran. "I've just met the most remarkable young man. Now I like the boy, and you're going to help him with anything you can." Soon Kentucky Representative Fred Vinson, one of those in charge of congressional committee assignments, was invited to dinner at the White House. Throughout the meal, Vinson wondered what FDR "wanted from me." At last, "casually—oh, very casually—'Fred, there's a fine young man just come to the House. Fred, you know that fellow Lyndon Johnson? I think he would be a great help on Naval Affairs'." It was only a suggestion. But even a nudge from the President was all Johnson needed to become a member of Carl Vinson's Naval Affairs Committee. FDR remembered Lyndon's being enamored of "all things Navy."

So taken was the President with Johnson that he remarked to Harold Ickes, another top aide, that had he, FDR, not gone to Harvard, Lyndon was the kind of uninhibited young pro he'd like to be. Furthermore, Roosevelt sensed the balance of power was shifting south and west, "and this boy could well be the first Southern president." To Corcoran, FDR made much the same prediction: that if Johnson "can keep his friends, he could end up as President of the United States." Johnson, in embracing

FDR "one hundred percent," was to cut a swath in politics much as Roosevelt had done, with every trick, every device at his disposal. In his review of Ted Morgan's biography of Roosevelt, Max Lerner faulted Morgan for reining in his criticism of the President. Lerner himself drew a less-than-flattering picture of FDR. There were his "deceptive sleight-of-hand in dealing his political cards, his trickster skills, his duplicities, his outright unwinking lies, his incapacity to involve himself deeply with other people, his recoil from face-to-face showdowns, his flatteries and double-talk, his embittered vindictiveness when crossed, his manipulative use of people, his interests, and his discarding of loyal and faithful advisers once they fell out of favor."[9]

Stepping onto the Senate floor in January 1949, LBJ had come a long way from the brash, cocky, aggressive dynamo that had invaded the Hill less than twelve years earlier. He was now a member of the most elite club in the world, and that called for being conservative, cautious, discreet, and prudent. Still, one salient characteristic continued—an unctuous flattering of those whose power he craved.

Johnson's eleven years in the House exhibited, at best, a lackluster performance. Apart from helping to get the draft extended in 1941, his record was dismal. His name was never attached to a bill that passed muster, and much of the time he could be found dozing through long-winded speeches on the floor.

Senator Johnson: "Landslide Lyndon"

Now Johnson was a U.S. Senator, "the best that money could buy," and that perhaps meant his eventual accession to the White House, as FDR had predicted—as long as he could keep his friends.

He looked around the Senate to see who might indeed be his friends. There were, he concluded, "minnows and whales." Among the "minnows" were other newcomers: Hubert Humphrey, Estes Kefauver, Paul Douglas, Robert Kerr, and Clinton Anderson. Among the few "whales" there was but one undisputed leader, the mastermind of the Senate, the one who, as puppeteer, pulled the strings behind the scenes. And that one, fortunately enough, was another Southerner and chairman of the Armed Services Committee, Richard Russell. The Senate's answer to Sam Rayburn, Russell was old enough to be Lyndon's father. He was also a bachelor who, like Rayburn, was alone much of the time and perhaps lonely—just the kind of power broker who could succumb to Lyndon's blandishments. It was only Russell who commanded the respect of all other ninety-five senators. So Lyndon, his deference intact and his hunger for power insatiable, drew a bead. First, he later explained, he'd have to find a seat on Russell's committee to see him every day. Having had a similar seat on the House Naval Affairs Committee helped, and soon Johnson was closing in. Going if not gone was the longhorn steer in the political China closet, the brash and windy self-promoter, the know-it-all, the ostentatious dresser, the flash in the pan. In their stead Johnson assumed a new persona, more to be appreciated by the austere, aloof, and quiet Russell, the country patrician who looked for all the world like a small-town banker. The new Johnson embraced, in the words of two commentators, a "magnificent self-control" that was not to resurface until he assumed the vice-presidency under JFK. So taken was *Newsweek* with Johnson's "quiet and gentle" manner that it said of him in 1951, "Everything he does, he does with great deliberation and care."

What *Newsweek* apparently missed was Lyndon's elaborately deferential manner. He worked hard, but so did others. Yet his antennae were picking up nuances those others couldn't detect. What separated Johnson from others, and particularly from the other freshmen, was his "you-can't-praise-them-enough apple polishing." He was as overly solicitous of Russell as he'd been of Evans, of Rayburn, and of FDR. It had paid rich dividends before, and Johnson was preparing to strike a mother lode. He took careful note that Russell arrived early in the morning to breakfast at the Capitol, and stayed late at night to dine across the street. Here was his opening. As he later explained to Doris Kearns, "I made sure that there was always one companion, one senator who worked as hard and as long as he, and that was me, Lyndon Johnson." And come Sundays, "I made sure to invite Russell over for breakfast, lunch, brunch, or just to read the Sunday papers. He was my mentor and I wanted to take care of him." Before long he was a member of the family. And, as Lyndon's alter ego, Bobby Baker, recalled, Johnson didn't simply cultivate Russell, he courted him, flattering him outrageously.[10]

Whether servile or solicitous, Johnson's genuflections before the power brokers paid off. In addition to Armed Services, Johnson, with the help of "Uncle Dick," landed another plum, the Interstate and Foreign Commerce Committee.

Until 1951, recalled Majority Leader Scott Lucas, Lyndon's contributions to the Senate were "negligible." Yes, he did smile easily, probably too easily—and broadly, probably too broadly. And Lucas remembered Lyndon's "warm personality and general conduct (making) a favorable impression upon all senators irrespective of their political affiliations." Lyndon the chameleon was learning to change colors to blend with his changing environment—especially with those power brokers he was courting, like Lucas and Russell.

By 1952, Lyndon was itching to reach the next rung on his ladder to the top, but he figured his new friend, Russell, wanted the job of minority leader. So he went to the Georgian and promised his support if he chose to run. As it so happened, Russell wasn't interested, so Johnson immediately asked his mentor if he'd support him for the position. Lyndon even claimed that he didn't think he could be reelected, come 1954, without the job. Russell was convinced, promised to back him, and even to move his Senate seat directly behind Lyndon's—so as to coach him in all the maneuvering this new post would require.

On January 2, 1953, Johnson became, at forty-four, the youngest minority leader in the history of the Democratic Party. It didn't hurt that "Uncle Dick" had spent hours rounding up support for his adopted nephew. And it certainly didn't hurt when he stood to nominate his fellow Southerner. In what Lyndon fearlessly proclaimed as "a very wonderful speech," Russell praised Johnson's human values, his peerless qualities as a conciliator, his championing of party unity. And he closed by expressing "complete confidence" in Johnson's leadership. Lyndon couldn't have said it better himself. It was a shoo-in; Johnson received all but five votes. Once more, Johnson's strategic targeting of a power broker with shameless blandishments had paid off handsomely.

Come January 1955, Dame Fortune yet again smiled on the wily Texan, when Wayne Morse, the lone Independent, switched from voting with the Republicans to voting with the Democrats—giving them control of the Senate. In addition, it boosted Lyndon to the next rung on the ladder: Senate Majority Leader, and at forty-six, the youngest in history. He later recounted to Kearns, "I knew from the start that all relations of power rest on one thing, a contract between the leader and the followers such that the followers believe it is in their interest to follow the leader."[11] No longer was he bound to the advice of Russell, his erstwhile mentor. Once again he'd verified the soundness of his strategy: identify your next goal; locate the power broker able to help you meet that goal—even if that goal is to replace the power broker himself; defer to him extravagantly to ingratiate yourself; persuade him that achieving your goal is in his best interest; persuade him that his backing is absolutely essential to victory. Then distance yourself from him, or—if need be—replace him as you concentrate on your next goal and your next object of deference.

Vice-President Johnson: Deference and Servility

For all Johnson's outrageous flattery and overly solicitous care of his "sugar-daddies," and with the presidency within his reach, he stumbled and fell in large part because he'd narrowed those to whom he'd defer only to those who would agree with him. In doing so he divorced himself from reality, and when reality did set in he found it painfully disconcerting. Nevertheless, picking up the pieces, he agreed to be John F. Kennedy's running mate and was soon occupying the vice-presidency. There, for almost three years, Johnson deferred, not because JFK would help Lyndon succeed him in the White House. This was a conscious, disciplined, forced deference he owed not so much to JFK as to the office of the presidency. The Kennedys were people to both loathe and envy—the moneyed, patronizing, intellectual elite of the Northeast that Lyndon as a boy had been taught was the cause of so much trouble in Texas and elsewhere. It was Kennedy who'd come to Johnson for his Senate office and committee assignments. It was Kennedy who'd promised Lyndon his vote for Majority Leader. It was Kennedy who'd pleaded with Johnson to have a bill bearing his name come to a vote on the Senate floor. So, as Vice-President, Lyndon practiced a self-discipline that was something to behold in the longhorn steer from the Texas Hill Country.

According to Dean Rusk, Secretary of State to Kennedy and later to Johnson, the Texan, brimming with "enormous energy and drive," displayed "immense self-discipline in his deference to JFK. Without exception there was disciplined restraint and consideration." Indeed, in his eight years with both presidents, Rusk acknowledged he'd never heard either one of them say "a disparaging word about the other, even in private conversation." After all, reasoned Johnson, he couldn't attack the "pilot in the cockpit," for Kennedy was "the only pilot you've got."

Lyndon Johnson: Accidental President

It was with deep emotions—and mixed emotions—that LBJ was sworn in as thirty-sixth President on November 22, 1963. It was a time of national shock as well as national mourning, and Johnson was the epitome of moderation, good taste, and fitting deference to JFK's legacy and to his surviving family. There seemed to be no trace of the fawning sycophant paying homage to Evans, Rayburn, FDR, or Russell. The day after Kennedy's funeral, the new President received a long handwritten note from JFK's widow. Jacqueline Kennedy thanked Lyndon for "walking yesterday—behind Jack," despite the risk. She thanked him for the letters he'd written to her two children. "The touching thing is," she added, "they have always loved you so much, they were most moved to have a letter from you now." But "most of all," she thanked Lyndon "for the way you have always treated me—the way you and Lady Bird have always been to me—before, when Jack was alive, and now as President." She became more specific. "You were Jack's right arm—and I always thought the greatest act of a gentleman that I had seen on this earth—was how you—the Majority Leader [actually, Minority Leader] when he came to the Senate as just another little freshman who looked up to you and took orders from you, could then serve as Vice-President to a man who had served under you and had been taught by you." She concluded by thanking him for his kindness in letting her and the children stay until they could conveniently move out of the White House. In this, one of Johnson's first and most spontaneous acts of deference after becoming President, he struck a responsive chord in the heart of the grieving widow.

As spontaneous and sincere was this overture, LBJ's further occasions of deference were, if more calculated, restrained and fitting. In the first instance, he reasoned he would need to capitalize on the surge of national emotion rapidly projecting the assassinated President toward martyrdom. So on November 27, he addressed a joint session of Congress, urging it to pay tribute to Kennedy in the most realistic way it could: by passing the legislation JFK had put forward—and that had been bottled up in a recalcitrant Congress—and passing other legislation of the same vein. In this, Lyndon deferred to former president Dwight Eisenhower, who'd driven down from his home in Gettysburg, Pennsylvania, for the funeral, and who had given him suggestions as to what he'd do if he were in Lyndon's place. His first and most important suggestion: use Theodore Roosevelt's "bully pulpit" to address a joint session of Congress. Then Ike outlined five points that Johnson might cover in the first ten or twelve minutes, the most important being "to implement effectively the noble objectives so often and so eloquently stated by your great predecessor."[12]

Where Kennedy was usually articulate, if not eloquent, Johnson was hesitant, if not bumbling. But on November 27, he was as eloquent, as moving, as he was in any speech, before or after. So Johnson deferred. He harked back to Kennedy's own inauguration speech, "Let us begin . . ." and added, "let us continue." He called for "the earliest possible passage of the Civil Rights Bill for which he fought so long." He called for the passage of Kennedy's tax bill. And he concluded with a fitting resolve, "Let us put an end to the teaching and preaching of hate and evil and violence. Let us turn away from the fanatics of the far left and the far right, from the apostles of bitterness and bigotry, from those defiant of law and those who pour venom into our nation's blood stream. . . . So let us here highly resolve that John Fitzgerald Kennedy did not live—or die—in vain."

One could almost detect the echo of Lincoln at Gettysburg, thanks to the combined skills of his speech writers and Johnson's unusual presence of mind before microphones and TV cameras. In any event, historian Arthur Schlesinger, echoing many others, called the speech "a genuine success," with the new President "never speaking better."

This moving tribute, this protracted eulogy, was an echo, above all, of Johnson's deference to Kennedy aides—the same aides who for almost three years had heaped contumely on the Texas interloper, the man whom none of them, and least of all Bobby, had wanted as vice-president. But now Lyndon wanted them, needed them, both to maintain continuity and to help him with vexing problems, none more vexing than Vietnam. He knew, he later reflected, just how they felt. "The impact of Kennedy's death was evident everywhere—in the looks on their faces and the sounds of their voices. He was gone and with his going they must have felt that everything had changed. Suddenly they were outsiders just as I had been for almost three years, outsiders on the inside. The White House is small, but if you're not at the center it seems enormous. You get the feeling that there are all sorts of meetings going on without you, all sorts of people clustered in small groups, whispering, always whispering. I felt that way as Vice-President, and after Kennedy's death I knew that his men would feel the same thing. So I determined to keep them informed. I determined to keep them busy. I constantly requested their advice and asked for their help." Here was Johnson at his deferential best.

One of those to whom he deferred was a member of the Eastern elite, the intellectual Eric Goldman, Professor of History at Princeton. On December 4, 1963, he was ushered into the Oval Office, where he found the new President "extremely tired," yet going out of his way to accommodate—making "the extra effort to please," as the press had noted, "whatever the occasion." Johnson said nothing after the initial introductions, so Goldman noted some historical points he thought might be helpful, then stopped abruptly and apologized for giving Johnson "a history lecture." "Go on," said the grinning Johnson, "I can use a history lecture." So Goldman continued for some forty-five minutes rather than the fifteen allotted for the interview. As he did, he became aware of how little television had revealed of Johnson's "sheer physical force," his "strong-featured, weathered face, the nuances that came in looks, gestures, and intonations of the drawl." Goldman was impressed and signed on, only to leave after three years—so disillusioned he wrote of his ordeal in *The Tragedy of Lyndon Johnson*.

Lyndon spent Christmas Day at the Ranch, throwing a party for all his kinfolk. Among them was seventy-eight-year-old Aunt Jessie. And when Lyndon asked, a gleam in his eye, "How'm I doing?" Jessie answered, ". . . don't let your britches ride too high, Lyndon. Don't let those people brag on you too much and make you go forgetting you're just plain folks like the rest of us." Had Aunt Jessie elaborated, she might have warned him about buttering up others even as he should avoid being buttered up.

To Theodore White, veteran presidential campaign recorder, Johnson's first weeks on the job were something to behold. "There is no word less than superb to describe the performance of Lyndon Baines Johnson. . . . All accounts of his behavior through the week of tragedy—his calm, his command-presence, his doings, his unlimited energies—endow him with superlative grace. Yet such stories limit the tale only to his positive deeds. To measure the true quality of his take-over, one must consider not only those positive acts, but what did not happen. So much might have gone wrong—yet did not."[13]

Johnson's "superlative grace" was due in part to his fixing his eye on

1964, when he would no longer be simply an "accidental" president. And it was due in part to his determination to outdo JFK and Ike—but especially FDR—in passing a full panoply of legislation. Here was ambition to burn up all the energy he could muster. But the single greatest factor in this initial "superb" performance was his remarkable deference to the memory of the President he'd served as Vice-President.

Bathing in the warm glow of praise for his speech to Congress, Johnson was faced with an irate Richard Russell, his old friend whom he'd decided—without consulting him—should serve on the Warren Commission. After arguing at length, LBJ pulled out all the stops. Johnson: ". . . nobody ever has been more to me than you have, Dick—except my mother." At this Russell scoffed. Johnson: "No, no, that's true. I've bothered you more and made you spend more hours with me telling me what's right and wrong than anybody except my mother. . . . I just want to counsel with you and I just want your judgment and your wisdom. . . . I haven't got any daddy and you're going to be it. And just don't forget that." Here was the President who criticized McNamara for not taking "the time to personally suck up" to White House military aides, and who himself vowed that as President, "I ain't gonna kiss any more congressman's ass." Yet he was not above telling Senator Russell Long, "I saw all your Louisiana folks this morning and I told them you were the greatest man I knew." Nor was he above telling Senator Harry Byrd of Virginia, who'd helped him in the defeat of a particular amendment, "Harry, you're a gentleman and a scholar and a producer and I love you . . . God bless you. You're wonderful."

It was one thing to be deferential when the path seemed clear and the future bright. It was something else again for LBJ to be deferential when one mine after another threatened to blow up in his face. If there was one path strewn with deadly mines, it was Vietnam. And if there was one critic who persisted, day after day and week after week, in opposing Johnson's policies there, it was George Ball, Undersecretary of State. At first Johnson was deferential, even encouraging divergent points of view, much as he had insisted with aide Joseph Califano. When Lyndon labeled a particular suggestion of his aide "naive," Califano retreated. At this point Johnson snapped, "I didn't hire you to 'yes' me. If you disagree with me, you let me know it. Don't back off just because I say something." Of course, it wasn't just "something" that Johnson had said. It was the equivalent of saying Califano was simple or stupid. Califano recalled veteran aide Cliff Carter's advice when Califano was the new kid on the block: "To work for this man, you've got to remember two things: you're never as good as he says you are when he praises you, and you're never as bad as he says you are when he chews you out." And when Ball, arriving at a meeting, heard Johnson sarcastically greet him with "and now that our resident devil's advocate is here we can begin," the Undersecretary knew his days were numbered. Like John the Baptist, he had come to feel his was a voice crying in the wilderness, to which the president was giving scant attention. So Ball quit in 1966.[14]

When it came to reporters, Johnson's expansive overtures simply backfired, sending him into conniptions as he howled at the "ingrates" and "traitors." How did they have the nerve, he would ask, to put their feet under his table when, within hours, their hands were busy typing a disparaging column? One reporter, Hugh Sidey, recalled Johnson applying "the treatment" to him and other reporters. He would take a reporter "under his arm," wrote Sidey, "wine him and dine him and entertain him, treat him to a few innocuous secrets, and then suggest a story line." If the reporter "saw the light" and Johnson saw more good press, he'd invite him back for more intimate moments. But if the hapless reporter tried to do his job conscientiously, Johnson would issue orders banishing him from the inner circle of the White House press corps or even from the press corps itself.

A President in His Own Right—But Wrong

As Johnson mired his government as well as his nation in what he called that "bitch of a war" in that "pissant, third-rate country," he listened to fewer and fewer, and only those voices that would agree with his suicidal policy. Gradually he isolated himself, as a later chapter will reveal, from his staff, from the Congress, from the press, and—ultimately—from the constituency that had elected him so overwhelmingly in 1964. By the time hubris had run its fateful course, Johnson was dismayed that so few appreciated all he thought he'd done for them—if not in Vietnam, then through his Great Society. Few there were who liked him; fewer still who "loved" him—though that was the deference he felt he deserved.

After all, LBJ was fond of repeating, "I'm the only President you've got." By 1967 his patience had worn so thin that he'd become mercurial, abrasive, abrupt, and more garrulous than ever. For fifty-five years he'd been pampered and, in turn, preened himself like a prima donna who deserved the front center stage, where he could glow in the spotlight of a receptive press.

Now those who disagreed with him were dismissed with a peremptory wave of his hand and a few choice words. By 1968 his deference to others was as thin as were his chances at reelection. He'd managed to distort, subvert, and emasculate the initial deference he'd exercised when he stepped into Kennedy's shoes.

There were few who illustrated this initial deference and subsequent castigation and alienation more than William Fulbright. As chairman of the Senate Foreign Relations Committee, Fulbright had run interference for Majority Leader Johnson. By 1960 Johnson was urging Kennedy to appoint the Arkansas Senator as Secretary of State. Though Kennedy chose Rusk instead, Fulbright remained one of the Vice-President's staunchest friends and supporters. Two days after Lyndon's speech to the joint session of Congress, Fulbright joined the Club of the Effusive: "...you were absolutely marvelous at the speech the other day . . . it was absolutely first-rate."

By March 25, 1964, however, Johnson felt a growing unease toward Fulbright, who had just addressed the Senate, warning of the festering war in Vietnam and the danger of escalating it. Johnson knew that the Joint Chiefs were all for escalation, and he'd promised them their war if they would support his election in 1964. Johnson asked his National Security Advisor, McGeorge Bundy, what Rusk thought of Fulbright's remarks. Bundy didn't know. Johnson: "They all assume that Fulbright speaks for the administration . . . ." Bundy: " . . . he didn't say to you any of this was going to happen." Johnson: "Fulbright is that way though. He's a very unpredictable man. . . .As Truman said one time, he's half-bright!"

Having shepherded through the Senate the Tonkin Gulf Resolution— which granted the President broad powers to conduct combat operations in Vietnam—Fulbright was aghast to see LBJ renege on his promise to consult Congress before actually using the Resolution. Two years later, Fulbright had his Foreign Relations Committee hold televised hearings on the war, raising the prospect that the President's close ties with Brown and Root—one of the war's biggest contractors in Vietnam—would be investigated. With that, Lyndon broke all further ties to the southern Senator.[15]

Deference, Johnson's kind of elaborate deference, had figured hugely in winning him the White House. It also figured in selecting his aides, and in delegating power and responsibility: the subject of the next chapter.

RICHARD NIXON

Good God, he's going to kneel!

> — A British reporter, observing Nixon
> approaching Charles DeGaulle, 1969

I'm running the show. When I tell Dick Nixon what to do, he listens.
> — Attorney General John Mitchell, summer of 1969

Everybody, including Chou, showed (Mao Zedong) the deference that was due him.

> — Richard Nixon, meeting China's leader in 1971[1]

Discovering the Source of Power

Early on, Richard Nixon learned the art of deference. Deference to father Frank to avoid the lash of the tongue and the back of the hand. Deference to mother Hannah, to avoid the stare and the silence of a strict, no-nonsense Quaker who saw him to church three times on Sunday and again to mid-week prayer service. It was discipline that ruled the Nixon home, always under the watchful eye of Hannah. That failing, there was always the threat of temperamental Frank. Here was a discipline imposed until each of the five boys learned to discipline himself; a discipline that encouraged tough love without displays of affection. Rare was the occasion that Richard felt the embracing arms of either parent. It was work, work, work, with little time for play, and many found Richard a very dull boy. It is significant that, despite his later contention that his boyhood had been happy, not one of his early photographs shows him with even a trace of a smile.

Without the natural affection a growing child needs, Richard craved the attention he soon found in deferring to audiences. Rejected for a part in a school play, he volunteered to play the piano, something he did in church. By high school he found debating and declaiming put him in the spotlight and brought him the applause that made him feel he was, after all, somebody. When not on the platform and not busy in his parent's filling station/grocery store, he deferred to books. In college he deferred to teachers, but none more than to his football coach, "Chief" Wallace Newman. No man, save his father, did he come to admire more.

It wasn't until he graduated from Duke University Law School and took up a practice in his home town of Whittier, California, that Nixon found the affection he craved. It was no surprise, then, that he deferred, meticulously and extravagantly, to Thelma "Pat" Ryan, especially during their courtship.

After they married in 1938, he continued practicing law while she taught school. With the coming of World War II, Nixon enlisted in the Navy as a junior grade lieutenant, was put in charge of providing supplies for airmen in the South Pacific, and set up "Nick's Hamburger Stand" to cater to crewmen. Evenings were spent, more often than not, over the poker table. Yet in each of these roles it is remarkable, as a colleague later recalled, that rarely did Nixon condescend to speak with, much less to defer to, anybody below his rank. Apart from his poker games, he also seldom deferred to his peers and immediate superiors. But around the top brass, he was all ears. It was not so much what but who you knew, Nixon realized, when it came to acquiring power.[2]

Politics Is Power

Released from the Navy after four years of service, Nixon again returned to the place he'd come to cherish: front center stage, with spotlights above and audience below hanging on his every word. The surest path to power was politics. Challenging incumbent Jerry Voorhis for Congress in 1946, he discovered that the spotlight was a means of metamorphosis, transforming the dull larva into the resplendent butterfly. Preparing so thoroughly that he rarely used notes, he found directness, continuous eye contact and earnest appeal not only drew people to him, but to heed what he said. In turn, his audiences were increasingly deferring to him—so much so that, despite great odds, he was elected to Congress.

Though he came to loathe deferring to others, he came to relish others deferring to him. As Hannah later put it, "People seldom dictate to Richard." But there was one person to whom he habitually deferred in his first campaign: Murray Chotiner. Shrewd and unprincipled, Chotiner was serving as a key campaign manager to Senator William Knowland. So successful was Chotiner that he was also hired part-time to advise Nixon. One of Chotiner's axioms made a mockery of proper deference by substituting pandering: tell the people what they want to hear, tell it well, and tell it often—and you'll be elected. So Nixon pandered to his audiences, serving up what he and Chotiner figured they wanted to hear. True, he'd been raised in a home where both parents voted Democratic. True, he'd sat at the feet of his favorite professor at Whittier, Dr. Paul Smith, and imbibed liberalism. But that, he realized, would not sit well with the conservative Republican businessmen who'd persuaded him to run against Jerry Voorhis, the liberal Democrat. So he changed his tune.

He pandered to his audiences even as he deferred to Chotiner. Voorhis had to admit that Nixon "knew what they wanted to hear and how to say it." In the end, Nixon trounced Voorhis at the polls. If pandering would get it done, along with assorted dirty tricks, then so be it.

With the Congressional seat under his belt, Nixon scrounged for national attention in pursuing Alger Hiss on the charge of espionage, but had to settle for perjury. Still, he'd gotten enough favorable press not only to enable him, again with the help of Chotiner, to win a Senate seat, but to attract the attention of Dwight Eisenhower and his handlers, especially Tom Dewey. Convinced that Nixon was a comer, Dewey and other aides convinced Ike to take on his ticket the man who'd gotten Hiss "fair and square." Nixon was appropriately grateful, and at the Republican National Convention of 1952, he asked the assembled delegates, "Haven't we got a wonderful candidate for president?!" The crowd roared its approval, Ike beamed his blessing, and Nixon learned that extravagant deference had its rewards. It is ironic that Ike himself, in the eyes of the historians of the fifties, was seen as a "near failure" in the White House because he governed deferentially.

Again in 1956, after four years of deferring to Ike—knuckling under even when he disagreed stoutly with him in private, winning kudos for his prudent deference during Ike's 1955 heart attack—Nixon was at last given the nod by a reluctant Eisenhower to stay on the ticket. But Ike needed a bit more pizzazz in Nixon's deference at the 1956 convention to help counter Democratic candidate Adlai Stevenson's flak. Yes, Ike conceded, he might find heady praise a bit embarrassing. But still and all, the twinge of embarrassment was little enough price to pay for the honor of being reelected. So Nixon, determined to continue as the good soldier, deferred once again—this time laying it on even thicker when praising the man of whom he genuinely stood in awe, the man who could have become president on either party's ticket, and the man who was a shoo-in for reelection. As for Eisenhower, well, he could—in the words of Dan Rather—"glide, serene and aloof, far above the squalid tumult of partisan politics."[3]

Nixon, always a wordsmith in Ike's view, pulled out all the stops on his deferential organ. The President, he proclaimed to the assembled delegates, was a man who deserved reelection for having brought peace, prosperity, and progress to the nation. Nixon's three "sweet peas" would have warmed the heart of any Quaker preacher. Leaning over his "bully pulpit," the eager throngs of the faithful before him, Nixon climbed the ladder of deference, rung by rung. Eisenhower, he said, was a man "whom every American can proudly hold to his children as one who has faith in God, faith in America, and who's restored dignity and respect to the highest office in the land"—a backhand slap at the coarse expletives of former President Truman. Climbing higher, Nixon warmed to his subject: "the greatest leader of the atomic age . . ." Then, reaching for the top rung, Nixon genuflected before "a man who ranks among the most legendary heroes of the nation . . . the man of the century!" That was simply too much. Or was it? Nixon turned to see Ike beaming and blushing, "aw, shucks!" written on his face. The crowd ate it up, and so did the country. Ike won his second term in a breeze, Nixon with him all the way—almost.

For by 1959, his eyes on the prize, the former junior grade lieutenant had more deferring to do to the former five-star general. For seven years Nixon had disagreed with Ike on crucial issues, most having to do with the spread of Communism. There was Ike, as Nixon saw it, the chronic waffler, paying excessive homage to a balanced budget, while his Vice-President sallied forth to oppose the insidious spread of atheistic Communism, orchestrated from the Kremlin. Whether it was Ike not intervening enough at Dien Bien Phu to prevent the Vietminh from defeating America's French allies—or disowning fellow Republican Joe McCarthy, the super-patriot who was turning over rocks in the State Department to expose the Reds beneath—or halfheartedly supporting Cuba's exiles in their efforts to oust Castro—it was obvious that the President had gone soft on the Red Menace.

So when Nixon turned to hammering out a platform for the 1960 convention, he found Nelson Rockefeller parting company with him. The New York governor was unhappy with Ike's defense posture, and he felt Nixon was coddling him. Trouble was, Nixon needed them both. So he trekked to Rockefeller's plush quarters in Manhattan, there to compromise in "The Treaty of Fifth Avenue," only to return to an irate Ike. Never, the President groused, had either of them complained directly to him about "the adequacy of America's defenses." Clutching at verbal straws, desperately needing the approval of the person a Gallup poll had just revealed as "the world's most popular man," miffed that the press had scorned his "surrender" to Rockefeller—Nixon once again deferred to Ike. For the offending "Treaty" statement, he substituted one explaining that Ike's position had been just right: "To provide more would be wasteful. To provide less would be catastrophic."

But Ike was distancing himself from his Vice-President as the Republican National Convention loomed. Every poll showed Nixon the front-runner and, in all probability, the winner in a landslide. Yet there was Ike, encouraging his old favorite, Treasury Secretary Robert Anderson, to enter the race. It was bad enough that Anderson had urged Ike to spurn Nixon's advice to prime the economic pump—something Nixon felt was essential, since people tended to vote their pocketbooks. Far worse was Ike's pleading with Anderson to run: "I'll quit what I'm doing, Bob, I'll raise money, I'll make speeches. I'll do anything to help. Just tell me I'm at liberty." It wasn't only that Nixon lacked "administrative experience," as Ike had told him in trying to bump him from the ticket in 1956. It wasn't even Nixon's conspicuous lack of other qualifications, mainly his inability to deal with people one-on-one. What it came down to was that Nixon wasn't a likable person. As Tom Wicker noted: ". . . his obvious ambition and opportunism . . . his intensity, his occasional false and Heepish humility contrasted with flashes of political savagery, the sense than his public persona concealed some other man—none of this made Richard Nixon easy for anyone to like . . ." By contrast, Ike—in the opinion of fellow World War II officer, General Douglas MacArthur—". . . had a magnificent talent for getting along with people. He could get Patton and Montgomery and Bradley in the room, and before they left, they would be in agreement. Ike had a positive genius for resolving differences. Perhaps it was because you couldn't dislike him even when he disagreed with you." It seemed that people couldn't help liking Ike, even as they couldn't help disliking Nixon.

If, however, deference was what was needed to nail down the nomination, deference Nixon would provide—at least with the convention delegates. In a remarkable tour de force he shook hands with all 2,600 of them, with a photographer present to record every handshake. That calmed the waters, and Nixon won the nomination with room to spare. Then, in just as remarkable a performance, the exhausted candidate took to the podium and showed how, by deferring to his audience, they in turn would defer to him. The speech, according to *The New Republic*—hardly a Republican bastion—sent both the delegates and the millions who were watching it on network television "into raptures." It was, the magazine declared, "one of the most impressively effective fifty minutes we ever witnessed. He rang every bell."

Hardly had the reverberations ceased, however, than Ike pulled out the rug beneath his Vice-President. It seems that Nixon was making the most of his "practice at being President." Each time, however, there was Eisenhower contradicting him. He and he alone had made all those decisions. Yes, he'd given due consideration to Nixon's advice, along with the advice of others on his staff. But ultimately they were his decisions. *Time's* Charles Mohr pressed Ike for an example of an idea of Nixon's that he'd adopted. Exasperated at recent slights by Nixon, Ike answered, "If you give me a week, I might think of one. I don't remember."[4]

That was it! Nixon resolved to run his own campaign, with or without Ike's support. Undoubtedly previewing LBJ's complaints that he'd "kissed enough asses," Nixon dug in his heels. Eisenhower cautioned him about fulfilling his promise at the convention to campaign in all fifty states. This was rash, especially in view of Nixon's confinement to a hospital bed for almost two weeks the beginning of September, recuperating from an infected knee. Though this gave Kennedy a running head start in the race, Nixon ignored the President. Then Kennedy challenged Nixon to a debate, and once more Ike advised against it: Kennedy needed national exposure; Nixon didn't. Again Nixon ignored the President, losing both the debate and the election, despite heroic last minute efforts by Ike to save the White House for a Republican. Any deference Nixon showed, either toward Ike or his own campaign staff, was a case of too little, too late.

The Brass Ring Tarnishes

In 1968 the phoenix arose from the ashes of not one but two humiliating defeats to gain the presidency, this time with Ike's help. Lying on his deathbed in Walter Reed Hospital, that "senile old bastard"—Nixon's epithet for him four years earlier—gave Nixon his blessing. After all, Ike's grandson David had married Nixon's daughter Julie—so now they were family.

Eisenhower's blessing was just what Nixon needed as he sallied forth to the convention to rouse the troops with an old-fashioned, "Let's win this one for Ike!" In his previous try for the White House, Nixon had wanted Ike's support without his advice: "There was hardly a subject," wrote biographer Stephen Ambrose, "be it the pace of the campaign, or the kind of car to ride in for a motorcade, or the route to travel through a city, or the right position on civil rights or religion, or the proper makeup for a television appearance, on which Nixon went to experts [or to Ike] for advice or help." Now, in 1968, Nixon did get Ike's blessing, but not his advice; Eisenhower was too ill to give it.

But Nixon had learned his lesson. He couldn't afford to be a loner on the campaign trail. More than ever, he was determined to defer to the wants, if not the needs, of his various audiences. Long before he'd learned to pander; by 1968 he was an expert. Needing the votes of white Americans, he blasted the withholding of federal funds from school districts refusing to integrate. Needing the votes of blacks, he extolled the 1954 Brown v. Board of Education of Topeka decision, and called on the affluent to alleviate the "terrible poverty" of black ghettos. Needing the votes of the white middle class, Nixon championed law and order. Needing the votes of the working class, he charged that inflation was wiping out any gains they were getting in their wages. Needing the votes of the elderly, he assured retirees in Florida that he was for an increase in Social Security benefits, as well as an annual cost-of-living increase. Needing the small but powerful votes of the Jews, he proposed to a B'nai B'rith convention that "the balance of power in the Middle East must be tipped in Israel's favor." As President, Nixon promised, he would see to it that this island in a sea of Arabs received the weapons technology necessary to offset its numerical disadvantage.[5]

But as much as any, Nixon craved the votes of the Baby Boomers. So he dispatched David and Julie, two Boomers, to the front lines to head up Youth for Nixon. Their message: Nixon's first order of business as President would be to end the Vietnam War. When Nixon addressed the group, he muted his law and order theme as imprudent, and instead trumpeted the virtues of this new America. "Remember," he assured them, "I believe in young people. They are great. Give them a chance. That's what we want." Here was no Kennedy, challenging America's youth to join a Peace Corps. But with David and Julie, he managed to calm some of the troubled waters.

Promises, promises. Something for everybody—the more promises Nixon made, the less they counted. Here was the ultimate pragmatist, for winning was what it was all about. Stanley Long, an aide to Jerry Voorhis, had accused Nixon of lying twenty years before when he'd called Voorhis a Communist. Nixon's answer to Long: "Of course I knew Jerry Voorhis wasn't a Communist . . . But it's a good political campaign fire to use. I had to win. That's the thing you don't understand. The important thing is to win. You're just being naive." It appears that the attitude of his former football coach, "Chief" Newman—who believed that winning was more important than how you played the game—was alive and well in the twisted mind of Richard Nixon.

By 1968 Nixon had launched, with appropriate fanfare, "Operation Candor—no doubt to contrast with LBJ's fatal "Credibility Gap." The message: Nixon was one pol who could and would level with the American people, who could be counted on to keep his promises. With that in mind, he assiduously courted South Carolina Senator Strom Thurmond, the Dixiecrat and former Democrat who, four years before, had come to see the light of Republicanism. Thurmond, Nixon figured, could wrap up the vote in the Southeast like Johnson could in the Southwest. All Thurmond needed was incentive. So Nixon pulled out a sheaf of guarantees: he'd slow racial integration; he'd raise tariffs to protect South Carolina's textile mills; he'd push for a strong national defense, providing jobs for the Charleston Navy Yard, there in the backyard of this powerful member of the Armed Services Committee.

With such a slew of promises, atop his subverting of Johnson's Paris Peace Talks (to be detailed later), Nixon was elected—just barely. His inaugural address was larded with more promises, none more relevant to this chapter than his determination to "bring us together." And how would he do that? By showing himself "the new and improved" Nixon—adhering unwittingly to the advice of Machiavelli to the Prince—to be "a great asker of questions" and "a patient hearer of answers." Let's stop, sang the President in a new key, the angry rhetoric and bombast—his own trademark for twenty-two years—and "listen in new ways to the voices of quiet anguish, voices that speak without words, voices of the heart: to injured voices, anxious voices, voices that have despaired of being heard."[6] The composer? Undoubtedly Ray Price, Nixon's favorite speech writer.

If anything, Nixon found it harder to keep this promise than the others. Oh, yes, he did ask, and he did listen, to those select few he admired, or to those who obviously could be of help to him. People like California Governor Ronald Reagan, who had the good sense to play hardball with the war protesters—particularly at Berkeley, a hornet's nest of liberalism. As the nationwide crescendo of protest rose in response to Nixon's broken promise to end the war in six months, he realized he'd need every California vote come 1972. So, knowing a sound investment when he saw one, Nixon dispatched Ron and Nancy Reagan on a goodwill tour, a glorified vacation to the Far East aboard a luxurious 707, with enough room for Nancy's hairdresser. Hang the cost. It was only money. And not his at that.

While Nixon courted others for what they could do for him, he genuflected before a mythic leader like Charles DeGaulle. Hardly had the neophyte President set foot in the White House than he was off on a whirlwind tour of European capitals to take the measure of his counterparts. He would ask. He would listen. And for some he would do even more. Disembarking at Orley Airport, Nixon couldn't miss the 6'8" ramrod-straight frame of the imperious DeGaulle, there at the end of the red carpet. Approaching the towering martinet, Nixon appeared to grovel, so much so that a British reporter blurted out, "Good God, he's going to kneel!" He didn't, but he came close enough to send shudders through the ranks of Americans looking on. DeGaulle, for his part, had no trouble with this kind of deference. After all, if Louis XIV could be France, so could DeGaulle. Yet ever since Hitler made an end run around the Maginot Line, DeGaulle had suffered one humiliation after another. Spurned by FDR and

Truman in his appeal for ships to transport French troops back to Vietnam; ignored by Ike both in participating in the Normandy invasion and in his cry, ten years later, for support at Dien Bien Phu; challenged by the likes of JFK, the "poster-boy wonder;" and insulted by the coarse LBJ, who told him there was nothing he could teach the Texan—DeGaulle now had someone before him capable of appreciating his larger-than-life dimensions. For here Nixon saw a super-hero of World War II, cut in the image of Eisenhower. Here was the valiant General who, evading capture by the Germans, pulled together the French resistance movement from his headquarters in London. Here was the French President who personified the very virtues Nixon had imbibed since childhood: obedience, discipline, industry, thrift, the warp and woof of the Protestant ethic. Here obviously was a giant, worthy of due respect, and Richard Nixon would pay that respect—extravagantly. Here was the kind of deference that was second nature to LBJ on his way to the top—a fawning obsequiousness that raised the stature of its object by diminishing the stature of its perpetrator.[7]

When it came to his aides, the one to whom Nixon deferred most extravagantly was John Connally, the big Texan who'd been with Johnson since his early days in Congress. By 1972 Nixon was pointing to the tall, handsome spellbinder, exuding charisma along with machismo, as his "closest political adviser." Nixon tapped Connally as his Treasury Secretary, and gave strict orders to the military: "I want this guy to have anything he wants. He can use my plane. He can have Camp David." It was Connally who Nixon called on to whip his senior staff into shape for what both figured would be a bracing 1972 campaign. It was Connally—and only Connally—who, among aides of the President, was admitted to the second-floor living quarters of the White House.

National Security Advisor Henry Kissinger, it seems, learned of Connally's high status the hard way. Returning to the South Lawn by helicopter, Nixon greeted some of his welcoming aides. When he came to Connally, however, he put his arm on the Texan's shoulder and steered him into the White House, leaving the others trailing behind. Getting to the elevator to ascend to the living quarters, Nixon ushered Connally in and pressed the button, closing the door directly in Kissinger's face. Furious, Kissinger "turned like an enraged bull," Bill Gulley recalled, "and barreled out of there so fast he nearly knocked a woman down." Kissinger had to admit, he later wrote, "there was no American public figure Nixon held in such awe." Incredibly, Nixon wanted the Democrat Connally to be Vice-President in his second term. He was "the only man in either party," Nixon insisted, "with the potential to be a great president." This was high praise indeed from one who considered himself to be more—much more—than an average president. Fortunately for Nixon, Connally turned him down, telling Attorney General John Mitchell, "under no circumstances" did he want to be Vice-President. Nixon's jowled face fell when Mitchell bore the news. Just as well, assured Mitchell, for Vice-President Spiro Agnew maintained strong support among Republican ultra-conservatives—many of them big campaign contributors.

As for Mitchell himself, Nixon was initially deferential to his former law partner. For Mitchell, a specialist on bond issues to cities and states, rubbed shoulders with Republican fat cats. Just the man to help finance chairman Maurice Stans raise money for the 1968 campaign. So Nixon started that eventful year by announcing that Mitchell was to be his "personal chief of staff." During Nixon's first two years in the White House, there were few he deferred to more than Mitchell, the pipe-smoking sphinx. Dan Rather has described the subtle cues of the Attorney General that Nixon's antennae detected. At Cabinet meetings, Mitchell—his dour face protruding through swirls of smoke rising from his ubiquitous pipe—seemed to others both imperturbable and inscrutable. But not to Nixon. If Mitchell grunted and nodded his balding head, that was a go. Encouraged, the President would press on with renewed vigor. If, however, Mitchell let out a grunt, looked the other way, and stopped his pipe puffing, that was a stop. Nixon would back up and change the subject.[8]

As for the others on his senior staff, Nixon's treatment ranged from occasional deference to transparent contempt. Just how selective his memory had become by 1977 can be seen in his interview with David Frost, the British journalist: "I always assured all people that came in to see me, 'Look here, you tell me what you think and I'll take the blame if it should fail, and I'll give you credit and take a little of it myself if it succeeds,' and I got very good advice as a result of that tactic."

The reality was somewhat different from the rhetoric. When visitors passed Chief of Staff H.R. "Bob" Haldeman's wary eye and slipped into the Oval Office, or caught the President unaware outside its confines, Nixon was hard put to give them the time of day. His favorite device for abbreviating their stay: finishing what he considered to be their stammering or faltering with his own ready words. If that didn't do the trick, he'd throw a glance toward the ubiquitous Haldeman as if to say, "Do something: Don't just stand there!" Worse for this consummate loner were the interminable cocktail parties, receptions, and other social events that protocol insisted he attend. After an hour or two of agonizing small talk—pleasantries that went with the smile he'd pasted on his face—he was not above confiding to an aide, "I really want to kick them."

As for his Cabinet, introduced on national TV from the Shoreham Hotel with pomp, ceremony, and hype, Nixon virtually ignored them—with the exceptions of Connally and Mitchell. Part of this was the result of Nixon's wanting to centralize all foreign and domestic decision-making in the White House, where he could control it. Part of this was also Nixon's longing to impress foreign dignitaries, Kissinger noted, for Nixon figured he'd gain prestige by not only ignoring but by contradicting his aides. He was his own man.

There was one other to whom Nixon was sure to defer during his first term, and that was Lyndon Johnson. In desperate need of the votes of Texas and the rest of the South, Nixon dispatched his friend the Reverend Billy Graham—who also had Johnson's ear—to assure LBJ that if elected, Nixon would not embarrass him. Indeed, Nixon wanted nothing more than a "working relationship" with his predecessor, and promised to "seek his advice continually." After all, Nixon gushed, he had nothing but respect for "the hardest working and most dedicated President in 140 years." In addition, he promised LBJ that he'd "do everything to make you a place in history because you deserve it."

Johnson couldn't believe his ears. Here was the gadfly who'd been carping for years that LBJ was never going far enough in the war, the hawk of hawks who was constantly needling him for doing too little, too late. The "chronic campaigner," Johnson called him. So Johnson asked Graham to read it again, rolling over each word, each phrase in his mind. The word went to Nixon: I am duty-bound to back Humphrey, but if you win, count on my support.

But undoubtedly, the single most far-reaching deference by Nixon during his time in office was his surprise visit to China, followed within three months by a visit to the USSR. By the spring of 1971 he was in a position to empathize with, rather than condemn, his predecessor for closing the blinds, circling the wagons, and hunkering down behind the big black fence rimming the White House. For he, like Johnson, was under siege. Wave after wave of protests were rocking Nixon's ship of state, threatening its foundering on the reefs of Vietnam. Worse, the protests were resonating increasingly with the press and, in turn, the electorate. The polls showed Nixon trailing Senator Edmund Muskie of Maine 47 percent to 39 percent. Compounding the bad news were the imposing figures of Massachusetts Senator Ted Kennedy and Alabama Governor George Wallace, waiting in the wings.[9]

China and the Perfervid Anti-Communist

How can I appear "presidential?" he complained to his staff. "We have no monuments." Here was a nice placement of pronouns: "I" and "we." By no coincidence, this President claimed all the credit he could get, and then some, while blaming others for his shortcomings. The winter of discontent—would it never end? Then came a suggestion from Bob Haldeman, ever his faithful Chief of Staff, one to whom he came to defer. Why not pay a visit to China? There, on the other side of the shrinking planet, lumbered the xenophobic Communist dragon, breathing fire at any and all interlopers and detractors. And none posed a greater threat to its borders than its ideological counterpart, the USSR. Even then, the border clashes were heating up.

Who, better than this belligerent pol, having spent twenty-five years flaying the Communists, would be better positioned to pry open the door? The idea wasn't new. Nixon had been broaching the idea in print as early as 1967. Shortly after his inauguration, he gave orders to National Security Advisor Kissinger to explore secretly the possibilities of a rapprochement. But a year later, Kissinger had nothing to report; the Chinese had ignored each of his several overtures. It was time, Nixon then decided, to get down to the business of deferring. In his Foreign Policy Report to Congress, he urged that the U.S. "take what steps we can toward improved practical relations with Peking." A month later, in March 1970, Nixon gave orders to the State Department: relax official travel restrictions to Communist China. In April he ordered a further easing of trade controls. By October he told a *Time* reporter, "If there is anything I want to do before I die, it is to go to China. If I don't, I want my children to." Come March 1971, and Nixon ordered State to end all restrictions on the use of American passports for travel to mainland China. It was no coincidence that "Communist China" or "Red China" had become "mainland China" or the "People's Republic of China."

More concessions, the coinage of deference, were in the works. On April 14, 1971, Nixon announced the end of the twenty-year-old embargo with Mao Zedong's China, and ordered an easing of currency and shipping controls. That did it. The same day, Chinese Premier Chou En-lai personally welcomed American table tennis players to Peking. Two weeks later, Nixon let it be known that he'd like to visit China "sometime in some capacity." Soon *Life* reported that Mao would welcome Nixon to Peking.

Come June 2 and Kissinger breathlessly handed his President "the most important communication that has come to an American President since the end of World War II." That was the kind of language Nixon understood. But submerged beneath all the tall talk of the moment was the underlying issue of concern to Mao: that the U.S. end its resistance to his China replacing Chiang Kai-shek's Republic of China on Taiwan at the UN. With one concession after another by the U.S. President, Mao at last condescended to talk face-to-face as a representative of 750 million or more Chinese who, of course, were better able to represent China than a tiny island's 12 million Chinese. It was simply this that Nixon, born and bred in the shadow of Hollywood and its hype, called "a moment of historical significance."

For Nixon was envisioning previously undreamed-of possibilities. He would spring on the American voters as well as the rest of the world a "monumental" surprise. He would introduce the most populous nation on earth to the "family of nations." He would enlist them in ending the Vietnam war by playing them off against the Soviets. He would establish himself solidly in the role as the broker of international peace. He would silence his war critics, once and for all. He would be the first sitting President to visit this Asian monolith. But above all, he would command an overwhelming mandate at the polls, and be reelected to serve as the country's Bicentennial President. What more could he ask?[10] Deference—even subservience—was little enough price to pay.

Despite Nixon's hailing this a tour de force, Agnew and his right-wingers saw a disaster. Here was the putative leader of the "free" world, so desperate to be reelected that, like Faust, he would seal a compact with Lucifer. Turning his back on a stellar career of virulent anti-Communism, this President was preparing to go, hat in hand, to beseech Mao to help end the crusade against Communism in Vietnam. So did Agnew and his ilk envision Nixon's trip.

Not so, said Nixon and Kissinger, the latter pressing the point, "We would not appear in Peking as supplicants." They were also not going as adversaries, but as partners in a cooperative enterprise in which all the world had a stake. Their negotiations would not be, as Kissinger put it, "the 'salami' approach," slicing "their concessions as thinly as possible over as long a period of time as possible." They would be taking a cue from the Chinese themselves, trying to come up with a reasonable solution to a given problem, "get there in one jump, and then stick to that position."

At any rate, that was the theory. And Kissinger, true to form, put his expectations on a pedestal. The trip would be "a major defeat for Hanoi," undercutting its campaign "to exhaust us psychologically and undermine our public support." It would show Americans "their government was capable of bold moves for peace." It would send a message around the world that those depending on the United States for security could count on us. It would, in short, enable America "to dominate events rather that await them passively." Lest others judge these expectations unreasonably high, Kissinger readily admitted he had "sufficient hubris to speculate on which [goal]would be considered historically the more significant achievement": ending the war or introducing China to the family of nations. No small thinking here.

As for the President, he was not only with Kissinger in these high expectations but, ever the astute pol, was counting on the press "eating out of [his] hand." It would be a public relations coup the likes of which could beggar the coups of previous presidents! Moreover, as Kissinger noted, "It was one of Nixon's unshakable conceits that somehow he could blackmail the press into a more benign view of him by rewarding with special attention those who, as he saw it, treated him fairly."

As it was, the trip to Peking was a PR blitz. Across the world, radio and television carried the hour-by-hour image of a U.S. President in full deferential array. John Foster Dulles, Ike's imperious Secretary of State, had refused even to shake the hand of the Communist leader, Chou En-Lai, at the 1954 Geneva Conference, "deeply insulting" Chou, according to Nixon. Arriving at Peking on February 21 at 11:30 A.M.—conveniently 10:30 P.M. eastern standard time, still prime time on TV back home—

Nixon would not only shake Chou's hand but insist that cameras would catch him and Chou alone on this historic moment.

To that end Nixon made it "perfectly clear at least a dozen times"— Kissinger was counting—that he and Secretary of State Rogers were to remain aboard Air Force One until after the handshake. Then, to make sure, Nixon posted a burly sergeant at the door of the plane. Nothing, the President insisted, would detract from his momentous encounter with Chou. Not one given to understatement, Nixon later wrote, "When our hands met, one era ended and another began."[11] More importantly, polls from home showed Nixon now leading Muskie by five points. No doubt about it, Nixon was building his "monument" to history—and reelection— brick by deferential brick. Yet when it came to deference, Kissinger was giving Nixon a run for his money. If Chou was "frail" but "elegant," Mao was something else again. "Tall and powefully built for a Chinese," Mao displayed more "distilled, raw, concentrated willpower" than any man, aside from DeGaulle, that Kissinger had ever met. Indeed, Mao "dominated the room . . . by exuding in almost intangible form the over-whelming drive to prevail." Here, in short, was "the colossus into whose presence" these two worshipful Americans were peremptorily summoned five times, always on short notice. There, before the great one, "Everybody," Nixon noted, "including Chou, showed [Mao] the deference that was due him." And so did the President. After all, he'd recently told André Malraux, the French writer and philosopher who had known Mao since the 1930s, that Mao appeared to possess a mystique "present in many great men," such as Lincoln. "Five years ago," Malraux noted, "Mao had one fear: that the Americans or the Russians, with ten atom bombs, would destroy China's industrial centers and set China back fifty years at a time when Mao himself would be dead." He'd told Malraux, "When I have six atomic bombs, no one can bomb my cities. . . . The Americans will never use an atom bomb against me."[12]

Nixon was not about to take advantage of his own nation's over-whelming military power as leverage to force a deal with Mao, not when obsequiousness would do. Nixon began, "The Chairman's writings moved a nation and have changed the world." "Not so," countered the self-effac-ing Mao, he'd "only been able to change a few places in the vicinity of Peking."

So Nixon, the quintessential pragmatist, was overlooking much to placate this staunch supporter of fellow Communists in Vietnam. Gone was the Mao who'd led China's millions down the road to atheistic Communism, routing Chiang, America's ally in World War II. Gone was the Mao whose seizure of power had prompted Nixon to accuse Truman of "losing" China. Gone was the Mao who'd opened the floodgates for 180,000 Chinese "volunteers" to cross the Yalu River and throw back American troops on the verge of victory in North Korea. Gone was the Mao who'd supported Ho Chi Minh and his Vietminh for over twenty years, first against the French, then against the Americans. And gone was the Mao who, through his "Cultural Revolution," was responsible for the deaths of millions of his own countrymen at the hands of zealous young purists. This, surely, was much to overlook. But when it came to deference, Nixon could indeed be magnanimous.

On to Moscow

Of all Nixon's aides, none were more deferential to him than Connally and Kissinger's deputy, Alexander Haig. That was going some, for Nixon no praise was too much, not even from Patrick Gray, a Justice Department lawyer who would soon be named interim director of the FBI. Gray, said Nixon, was "a nice guy, loyal in his own way. But he's panting after the goddamn job [as Director] and is sucking up." Then there was Press Secretary Ron Ziegler, massaging his master's ego as Nixon was about to fire Haldeman and John Ehrlichman, the White House assistant on domestic affairs, for their roles in a scandal that would become known as the Watergate cover-up. "People trust the President, they respect the President. The presidency at this moment is not involved [in Watergate] . . . The presidency's not involved in a battle to prove whether or not they were right or wrong in doing this or that. The presidency right now is involved in the ending of an era of the greatest achievement in a generation, the achievement of peace." No wonder Nixon chose Ziegler to be his press secretary.

What remained as an uncanny loyalty—continuing to defer to Nixon despite the President's having thrown him to the wolves—was that of the White House Chief of Staff, Bob Haldeman. He'd just been "resigned" by his boss when the President phoned him. Nixon: "I hope I didn't let you down." Haldeman: "No sir, you got your points over, and now you've got to set it right and move on. You're right where you ought to be."

Nixon: ". . . God bless you, boy. God bless you. . . I love you, as you know . . . like my brother." Haldeman: "Well, we'll go on and up from here." Fully expecting to be pardoned by his President, Haldeman was dismayed when Nixon refused even to return his calls personally. After four years of investigation, persecution, indictment, and imprisonment, Haldeman, incredibly, dedicated his memoirs to—among others—"President Nixon, who made possible what was, despite its ending, the mountain-top experience of my life."[13] While Haig was concentrating on Nixon's reelection, not knowing he'd emerge as Nixon's Chief of Staff, Connally was concentrating on the upcoming Moscow summit that seemed in danger of being canceled by the Soviets. His advice must have brought back to Nixon warm memories of "Chief" Newman: The President must "show his guts and leadership on this one. Caution be damned—if they cancel . . . we'll ram it right down their throats!"

As it turned out, Nixon kept the summit but lost the war. On May 20, with his Committee to Reelect the President (CREEP) setting in place "Operation Gemstone" that would lead to Watergate, Nixon was off to Moscow. Arriving, he compared Brezhnev's "elegance and toughness" with that of Chou. Then he got down to business, determined to sign the SALT (Strategic Arms Limitation Talks) agreement even though, as State's Gerard Smith complained, "he didn't even realize what proposal we had on the table. He didn't even know what anyone reading the newspapers would know." Furthermore, as Smith warned Nixon, Kissinger had removed an important reservation from the draft paper. To this Nixon responded with a typical, "Bullshit!" In reality, the treaty was so flawed by the time Nixon signed it that journalist Seymour Hersh asserted that Kissinger and Nixon had "cheated their way to the summit, accepting less than would have been achieved in the bargaining, and then lied to the press and public about what they had accomplished."

So what had Nixon accomplished? Flushed with success, he stood before a joint session of Congress on June 1 to proclaim the summit an unqualified success. More than that, it was an unprecedented, breathtaking moment in history, sounding the end of an era that had begun in 1945 with the dropping of atom bombs on Japan. Now, exulted the President who knew not what he had signed, "We took the first step toward a new era . . . check[ing] the wasteful and dangerous spiral of nuclear arms which has dominated relations . . . for a generation."[14] Truth be told, the

President's abysmal ignorance of the pact, compiled with his obsession to be reelected, led to remarkable concessions—extraordinary deference, even for Nixon. As it was, the treaty placed no limits on multiple warheads or MIRVs, more deadly by an order of magnitude than SLBMs or ICBMs. Little wonder, then, that both sides wasted no time converting their warheads to MIRVs. In addition, Kissinger permitted the Soviets whatever size—"throw-weight"—they wanted on their ICBMs.

As a result of this deferential fiasco, Nixon, his critics charged, gave to doves the rhetoric and to hawks the reality. As Admiral Elmo Zumwalt put it, ". . . the unconscionable numbers in the SALT agreements . . . virtually froze us into five more years of high spending on U.S. strategic forces."

Nixon's stunning deference at both summits was virtually hidden from the press and the public. Thus did the summits become the "monuments" he needed to win reelection. But the foundations of those monuments would soon begin to crumble. Less than three weeks after the President returned from Moscow, the headquarters of the Democratic National Committee in Washington's Watergate complex would be broken into. At first it appeared to be nothing more than a minor burglary. In fact, it was the beginning of a scandal that would engulf the Nixon administration—and eventually Nixon himself.

It is of no small moment that, during the Watergate cover-up, Nixon the Imperial President became Nixon the Deferential President—even to his aides. Reading the Watergate transcripts, one has to agree with Irving Janis that, "Behind the closed doors of his office . . . he seems a waffling executive, a President who, instead of presiding at these critical decisions, defers continually to his subordinates." Indeed, at times he seemed to be "'a bystander, almost a yes-man, letting others take the lead. On several occasions, having made suggestions, Nixon quickly withdrew them when one or more of his top aides objected."[15]

Times had changed, and he was enough of a pragmatist to change with them. Perhaps it can be taken as a sign of his desperation, with impeachment blowing in the wind, that the Imperial President—who dressed his White House guards in the garish garb of the Swiss guards at the Vatican, who relished the pomp and ceremony "due" him, who barked out orders to aides even as he ignored his own Cabinet, who hyped his own successes even as he blamed others for his failures—should, in the end, stoop to habitual deference to his staff.

No doubt about it: Richard Milhous Nixon could be the Deferential President, the Bellicose President, the Furtive President, and as many other Presidents as changing circumstances seemed to warrant. But, as he resigned in disgrace and boarded the helicopter for California, one thing was certain. He would never be the Bicentennial President. The fault, to paraphrase Shakespeare, lay not in his stars but in himself. He, like each of us, was an underling.

CHAPTER 2

DELEGATION

The first opinion which one forms of a prince, and of his understanding, is by observing the men he has around him.

— Machiavelli, 1513

Look here, Charlie, I want you to run defense. We both can't run it. And I won't run it.

— Eisenhower to Charles Wilson, Secretary of Defense, 1953

Whenever a man has cast a longing eye on offices, a rottenness begins in his conduct.

— Thomas Jefferson, 1820

A fellow once came to me to ask for an appointment as a minister abroad. Finding he could not get that, he came down to some more modest position. Finally he asked me to be made a tide-waiter. When he saw he could not get that, he asked me for an old pair of trousers. It is sometimes well to be humble.

— Abraham Lincoln, 1865

LYNDON JOHNSON

Tell the generals [the JCS] that if they're little men like that, that believe they can pressure their commander in chief on what his strategy ought to be in war or what his decision ought to be in peace, they don't know the commander in chief."
— LBJ to Roswell Gilpatric, Deputy Secretary of Defense
December 23, 1963

For four years he was a slave to a master who destroys his slaves.
— Richard Rovere, on Hubert Humphrey as Vice-President[1]

Office Seekers Galore

Listening, learning, and—when advisable—heeding others, a president must gather around him the best people he can muster. They may not be "the best and the brightest," as Halberstam sardonically hyped Kennedy's aides, but they must be able to relieve him of some of his tremendous workload. As Coolidge emphasized in his one rule: "Do nothing that someone else can do for you."

Who, then, should a president recruit? Eisenhower had a rule that nobody looking for an office should be given it. And no wonder. Benjamin Harrison wearied of the applicants clustering around his office, hounding him for jobs. Cleveland cursed "this dreadful, damnable office-seeking [that] hangs over me and makes me want to quit." Lincoln was no less impatient, complaining that "this struggle and scramble for office, for a way to live without work, will finally test the strength of our institutions." For his part, Polk found it took all his patience "to repress [his] loathing toward the hungry crowd of unworthy office hunters" who crowded [his] office.[2]

Who then? "Select the men best qualified and most meritorious" was John Adams' rule. Washington had to be "exceedingly circumspect that no just criticism be leveled at [him] for partiality to friends or relatives." Bobby Kennedy remonstrated with Jack when he was considering his kid brother for Attorney General. "They would kick our toes off" on the charge of nepotism, he warned. But the next day the new President called him, "You hold on to your toes—I'm naming you Attorney General today."

Especially vulnerable, as Aunt Jessie had warned LBJ, is the president when surrounded by sycophants—or, as Jackson said of Polk, "by a set of parasites . . . who flatter him until he does not know himself." Coolidge cautioned that "people in high office are always surrounded by worshipers. They are constantly assured of their greatness. . . . Powerful people live in an artificial atmosphere of adulation and exaltation which sooner or later impairs their judgment. They are in grave danger of becoming careless and arrogant."

"The president," Truman noted, "hears a hundred voices telling him he's the greatest man in the world. He must listen carefully indeed to hear one voice that tells him he is not."[3]

To resist the adulation of those who would be yes-men requires rare control. FDR was determined to fill his Cabinet with strong and independent people. Truman emphasized that not only should he exercise self-control, but control of his aides, for no president will delegate responsibility—and with it power—to those he can't control. For every office the president bestows, warned John Adams, he will "make one man ungrateful and a hundred men his enemies."[4]

Presidents were apt to look to the universities. FDR turned to Columbia for his 'brain trust," whereas Kennedy turned to Harvard for many of his top aides. When Minnesota's Orville Freeman was asked why JFK had appointed him Secretary of Agriculture, he responded. "I'm not really sure, but I think it has something to do with the fact that Harvard does not have a school of agriculture."

The power vested in a president's ten or so top aides is such that FDR's Corcoran contended that they really make up the government. Poorly chosen, as they were with Grant and Truman, and the country as well as the administration suffers. So unimpressed was David Lillienthal with Truman's inner circle that, compared to FDR's, they were "bungling incompetents, old cronies from Missouri like Harry Vaughan, his Army buddy from World War I." Indeed, Lillienthal maintained, "they were as sorry a bunch of third-raters as I have seen in many a moon."[5] Yet in all fairness it should be pointed out that Truman did not assign many of them major responsibilities. They were primarily for relaxing with over poker and booze.

Retaining Kennedy Aides

Lyndon Johnson was a miser when it came to power. "Get all you can and can all you get" seemed to be his life's motto. Only reluctantly did he share that power with others. He became, in effect, a one-man band, preferring to play all the instruments himself. And when he did delegate, he made sure that every aide knew where the power came from and how easily the spigot could be closed. His lust for power coupled with his stingy sharing with others was legendary.

Nevertheless, like every other president before and since, Johnson had to delegate much of his precious power to aides. This was especially important to maintain continuity with the Kennedy administration, and a stark necessity to claim a marathon amount of legislation—much of it in Kennedy's revered name. These, LBJ felt, were essential moves if he was to be elected on his own and overcome the epithet of the "accidental" President. Furthermore, he was determined to set a record at the polls to match his record in Congress.

So "Uncle Cornpone" barged into Camelot, swallowed his pride, and hired Kennedy's aides on the spot. They may or may not have been "the best and the brightest" but of one thing Johnson was certain: he needed them. As he stressed to Florida Senator George Smathers after the assassination, "We've got to carry on. We can't abandon this fellow's program because he is a national hero and we've got to keep the Kennedy aura around us through this election." As it turned out, he was impressed with many, if not most of JFK's people, and came to envy them as well as resent them. This graduate of a mediocre college, who had finished with mediocre grades, was a San Marcos thorn among the Harvard roses. As he bent his angular frame to smell the roses, his deference was so conspicuous as to arouse resentment among his own longtime aides—those who'd stuck with him through the despondency of the vice-presidency, and some who had been around during his glory days in the Senate. Men like Walter

Jenkins, Horace Busby, Bill Moyers, and Jack Valenti. Fellow Texan Rayburn figured there was somewhat less than met the eye in these "Harvards." One day LBJ was singing their praises when Sam remonstrated, "Well, Lyndon, you may be right, and they may be every bit as intelligent as you say, but I'd feel a whole lot better about them if just one of them had run for sheriff once."

It is revealing to observe this new President in the recruiting process. When White House special assistant Arthur Schlesinger submitted his resignation the day after JFK's assassination—to return to teaching at Harvard—Johnson laid out the red carpet. No one, intoned Lyndon, possessed the profound understanding of American history, with its purposes and programs, as did Professor Schlesinger. No one could possibly understand the progressive policies that distinguished the Democratic Party as could this Harvard alumnus. There could be no question but that Schlesinger was an indispensable man, desperately needed to guide the new President. Yet, Johnson complained, there on his desk lay the resignation, something he rejected outright. Then, with tongue in cheek, he warned that, were Schlesinger to act on it, he'd have him arrested! That did it. Overwhelmed, Schlesinger stayed for four months, then went back to his beloved Harvard—because the new President, having cadged him aboard his ship of state, gave him nothing to do.

If it took intimidation, or ingratiation, or dissimulation, whatever it took, Johnson was up to it. When Walter Heller, JFK's resident economist, wanted to resign—claiming that LBJ had become a conservative—Johnson protested, "I remain a Roosevelt New Dealer." This despite his having left the fold more than twenty years earlier. Furthermore, Johnson insisted, Heller was to make sure that John Kenneth Galbraith, another of JFK's economists, understood what Johnson himself understood: there was little hope of making a smooth transition from Kennedy's New Frontier to his own Great Society without first reaffirming his credentials as a dyed-in-the-wool New Dealer.

LBJ knew that the real key to the Kennedy aides was Bobby, and when the Attorney General agreed to stay, so did the others. By the end of November 1963, Johnson was breathing a sigh of relief. He could now hitch his Great Society wagon to JFK's New Frontier horses and capitalize on Kennedy's sudden ascension to martyrdom. LBJ would pass legislation that had stalled in Congress. Here, Johnson figured, was the only way he could assure himself of winning the 1964 election.

Over all his aides, new and old, Johnson needed an experienced hand, someone he could trust. So he turned to Jim Rowe, a former aide to FDR, whom Johnson had managed to alienate during the 1960 campaign with his callous and pompous indifference. Crow was hardly a staple in his diet as he approached Rowe to apologize. No need, interrupted Rowe. "Jim," pleaded Johnson, "you're not going to deprive your President of a chance to say he's sorry to an old friend, are you?" That apology, almost without precedent for the bumptious Johnson, did the trick, and Rowe was with him but, like the others, only temporarily.[6]

Loyalty and Power Sharing

LBJ was the master chess player, moving others around with as much verve as nerve. When Adlai Stevenson quit as UN Ambassador, Johnson decided to replace him with Arthur Goldberg. But Goldberg was busy as an Associate Justice of the Supreme Court, so Johnson turned to old friend Abe Fortas to replace Goldberg. Thanks but no thanks, said Fortas, who should have known Johnson would not be deterred. "I'll go ahead anyway and make the public announcement," said the presumptuous President, "and then if you want to refuse me, go ahead!" This was the kind of pressure LBJ exerted with each of Kennedy's aides: submit your resignations if you wish, but, despite protocol and precedent, this President would not accept them!

It was one thing to shanghai the crew and to direct Rowe as coxswain to keep them in stroke. It was something else again to keep them from jumping ship with Captain Bligh either ignoring them or tyrannizing them. As one after the other chose the escape route, Johnson should have realized there was something amiss with his definition of loyalty. For this he considered to be the first prerequisite in an aide. It was not loyalty to party, as important as that was at election time. And it wasn't simply loyalty to country, although he never hesitated to sound reveille and hoist the Stars and Stripes when it suited his purposes. Nor was it even loyalty to the presidency as such. What Johnson wanted, indeed what he demanded, was loyalty to himself—absolute, unquestioning, and unhesitating. As majority leader, Stewart Alsop noted, Lyndon could whip his crew into such a frenzy of exertion that they easily slipped by the crews of previous majority leaders. Hubert Humphrey well understood the importunity of

Majority Leader Johnson. One day he astonished some of his friends after an encounter with LBJ. "Look," he said, pulling up a trouser leg to display cuts on his shins where the Majority Leader had kicked him and demanded, "Get going now!" For all his mistreatment of Hubert, LBJ thought highly of him. After covering a number of possibilities for vice-president with brother Sam Houston, the latter remarked, "Well, hell, Lyndon, that leaves only Hubert, and you're sure not picking him, are you?" Lyndon: "Now what the damn hell have you got against Hubert?" Sam: "Plenty, Lyndon. For God's sake, he's been fighting you for years. No one's bugged you more on civil rights, and look at the way he's always harping about the oil people. He's a damned maverick." Lyndon: "Dammit, Sam Houston, you've got him all wrong. Hubert's a good man. I've made a goddamned Christian out of him. He's gone along with me on a lot of things. He also happens to be a helluva good campaigner." Sam: "He talks too much." Lyndon: "Don't worry about that. I'll get Muriel [Humphrey's wife] to keep him short." And soon Hubert was number two man in the country.[7]

Repeatedly, however, Johnson had to correct Humphrey as he did on May 2, 1964: ". . . you just talked when you ought to have been listening. . . . I don't want to hurt you. I want to be helpful to you. I'm trying to build you up. I'm trying to make you the greatest man in the world. . . ." Johnson was dropping the hint that he was considering Humphrey for Vice-President. In his choice of Hubert, it was neither appreciation for past favors, nor friendship, nor Humphrey's sycophancy that determined the choice. Like Johnson himself being chosen by Kennedy, it was solely political. Who could help him the most to win in 1964? In concluding a discussion with Connally on July 23, 1964, Johnson admitted of Hubert: "He'll get a lot of smear. He votes the oil and gas companies. . . . He'll catch you unshirted hell from the Drew Pearsons [muckraking columnists]. . . . He's kind of regarded as a liberal renegade. . . . We're not going to carry any Southern states, John, and Humphrey has a lot more appeal [than Senator Eugene McCarthy] in the other states." In addition, Humphrey pledged his loyalty. "If your judgment leads you to select me, I can assure you— unqualifiedly, personally, and with all the sincerity in my heart—complete loyalty." Not only that, Humphrey assured him, but ". . . that goes for everything. All the way. The way you want it. Right to the end of the line."

In reality, the ebullient Hubert didn't realize what he was getting into, despite having known Johnson for more than a decade. As Vice-President to Kennedy, Johnson had been treated with respect, even friendship. Kennedy had gone out of his way to warn his staff that he'd fire the first one to disparage Lyndon, the oversized Texan maverick who'd helped him win the White House. But Johnson was not Kennedy. And Humphrey would suffer at the hands of his President as few vice-presidents before him—or since. Twice McNamara had refused the number-two spot. At last, turning to Humphrey, Johnson used him as his verbal punching bag for four years.

Fond of playing games with the press, determined to keep them guessing, by convention time neither the press nor Humphrey were sure who the fickle Texan was going to select. Finally Hubert turned to Lyndon and asked if he was to be the chosen one. To this Johnson replied with a sarcastic put-down: "If you didn't know you were the Vice-President [choice] thirty days ago, maybe you're too stupid to be Vice-President."[8]

Having won the post, Humphrey must have had some misgivings before settling in. Less than a month after the election, he made the mistake of departing from his prepared text on education, giving the impression he'd be in charge of education policies. Johnson—ignoring his own lunge for power under Kennedy—blistered his sidekick then regaled the press: "Boys, I've just reminded Hubert that I've got his balls in my pocket."

On December 20, 1963, Johnson excoriated Humphrey to House Speaker John McCormack: "This damn fool Humphrey put that paragraph on [an amendment requiring Johnson's report on a wheat deal to the Soviets]." Later, in the same conversation, "Hubert's got his damned amendment drafted wrong. You just tell him to quit talking first and thinking afterwards." A few months later Johnson happened on a press report quoting his Vice-President to the effect that select cities would be rehabilitated as demonstrations for others. "How in the hell," Johnson demanded of Califano, "did Humphrey know we were working on that?" Califano, chairing the committee in charge, replied he'd asked Humphrey—the former "Boy Mayor" of Minneapolis who'd become a legend in his state for so effectively governing its largest city—to join him on the task force. Johnson was furious. "You are never, never to let the Vice-President attend any meeting on the legislative program. He has Minnesota running-water disease. I've never known anyone from Minnesota that could keep their mouth shut. It's just something in the water out there." For someone who'd earned a reputation since college as being afflicted with constipation of the brain and diarrhea of the mouth, Johnson was hardly in a place to criticize. Little did Humphrey realize how much his pledge of "complete loyalty" would cost him. For it is widely accepted that Humphrey's continuing tie to Johnson's ill-fated war policy was a major factor in his forfeiting the 1968 presidential election.

How could Johnson manage to obtain yeoman's work from each and all? Partly because the captain drove himself to exhaustion, again and again, requiring hospitalization and long periods of recuperation. He showed no mercy to others because he was merciless with himself. So he laid the whip to his crew, barking out orders. They were to subordinate every other consideration to their President. They always served "at the pleasure of the President." Any aide who even hinted he was more interested in his own future than that of the President's did not last long.

In his own inimitable, earthy terms, Johnson made clear the kind of loyalty he expected. When one day he queried an aide about the loyalty of another, Johnson was told, "Well, he seems quite loyal, Mr. President." This definitely would not do. "I don't want loyalty. I want *loyalty*. I want him to kiss my ass in Macy's window at high noon and tell me it smells like roses. I want his pecker in my pocket." That was loyalty. But who would ever exhibit that degree of loyalty? His Secretary of Defense, that's who. "If you asked those boys in the Cabinet to run through a buzz saw for their President, Bob McNamara would be the first to go through it!"[9]

Exhibiting that degree of loyalty, McNamara could have just about anything his heart desired. Twice Johnson asked if he'd like to take the vice-presidency in 1964, and twice McNamara demurred. It wasn't loyalty alone that made the difference. For four years Hubert Humphrey exhibited no less. But what McNamara also laid claim to was, in Johnson's opinion, the best mind he'd ever encountered in government. On top of that, in 1960 McNamara had quit his $400,000 a year job as President of Ford Motor Company to take on Kennedy's Defense Department at $25,000 a year. Now that was sacrificial service. McNamara had done that for JFK, and stayed with LBJ, though he'd stipulated to Kennedy that he'd serve but one term. As Vice-President, Johnson not only bowed to Kennedy's wishes with scarcely a murmur, but expected others to do the same. When at breakfast with brother Sam and his wife, Johnson impatiently listened to her criticism of her boss, JFK, then interrupted, "Support him or quit." It was the same policy he carried into the White House, and was largely responsible for his plunging ever deeper into the morass of Vietnam.

Another whose loyalty Johnson never questioned was his Secretary of State. As Vice-President, he'd warmed to Dean Rusk as to few others. "He's just the kind of man," Lyndon said, "I'd want in my Cabinet if I were President." Rusk apparently displayed the kind of loyalty that Johnson found in John Connally, fellow Texan and old friend. Again LBJ spelled it out. He wanted the dutiful subservience of the servant to his master. This was the kind of loyalty he demanded above every other quality, whether intelligence, initiative, or competence. And it was this kind of loyalty he meant when he went on record as saying, "I admire loyalty above everything else." He added, "I can call John Connally at midnight, and if I told him to come over and shine my shoes, he'd come running. That's loyalty."

If there was anyone who understood that kind of loyalty, it was Presidential Assistant Jack Valenti. After announcing his Great Society in May 1964, Johnson listened to a *Newsweek* reporter commend him, "You had the crowd with you all the way, Mr. President," noting that they had interrupted his speech no less than twelve times. Not one to let well enough alone, Johnson corrected him. "There were more than that," and turned to Valenti for corroboration. "How many applauses were there?" Valenti had it right, "Fourteen." That included the cheers LBJ had gotten when he was introduced and when he sat down.[10]

Another time Valenti actually offered himself as a footstool, a hassock for the feet of his master. But it was Valenti's glowing tributes—the kind of "kissing ass," as Johnson put it, that was most satisfying. To an assembled press, Valenti once launched into a panegyric that would have passed muster with a Caesar. Johnson had told civil rights leader Roy Wilkinson on January 6, 1964, "I can't be too much of a dictator . . . they say I'm an arm-twister, but I can't make a Southerner change his spots any more than I can make a leopard change them." With Valenti he didn't have to change any spots. LBJ was, in Valenti's overblown prose, "a sensitive man, a cultivated man, a warmhearted and extraordinary man" blessed with "godly osmosis." Furthermore, he assured a hard-bitten press corps given to skepticism, we could all "thank the good Lord" that Johnson had "extra glands." Then, switching metaphors midstream, this future President of the American Motion Picture Association indulged in the kind of hyperbole for which Hollywood had become famous. Not only was LBJ a "large, gray stone mountain," but Valenti slept "each night a little better, a little more confidently, because Johnson is my President. For I know he lives and thinks and works to make sure that for all Americans and, indeed, the growing body of the free world, the morning shall always come." With that kind of hype Johnson was bound to return the compliment in kind. Valenti, he pronounced as "one of the finest humans in existence."[11]

If there was anyone who could appreciate the value of boundless praise, it was Valenti's President. For years he'd carefully swaddled one power broker after another in layers of sycophancy. And now it was his turn to be lulled into a complacency that would foster decisions as tragic as any by a twentieth-century president.

Tyranny and Sycophancy

All Johnson's hard work—and he was a workaholic—didn't help him when it came to decisions, particularly in regard to Vietnam. Driven, in his obsession for power, he anesthetized himself to the pain that ordinary mortals feel by drowning himself in Cutty Sark. "An eight-hour man," he was fond of saying, "ain't worth a damn to me." Unwittingly, he seemed to follow Aristotle in his definition of leadership as the ability to inflict pain on others. But far from advocating sadism, Aristotle was concerned with persuading others to inconvenience themselves to do what their leader asked. Johnson, however, not only asked, he persuaded—by any and all means—others to work for him. Then he'd cut them loose if they didn't measure up to his exacting standards.

In addition, LBJ was known for parceling out "no-brain" jobs. He hired Lloyd Hand, for example, to join his stable of speech writers, thinking Hand could write orations worthy of a Churchill. When Hand's speeches didn't measure up, Johnson gave him a couple of books on Churchill so he'd get the hang of it. Still his writing lacked Churchillian grace. So Johnson dumped Hand in "Menial Alley," answering the thousands of letters from Johnson's constituents back in Texas. It had been the same for Harry McPherson, a brilliant, young Texas lawyer, who spent ten years of his life largely involved in writing congratulatory letters for Congressman Johnson to all Texas high school seniors. Undoubtedly the speech writer who came closest to Churchillian standards was Richard Goodwin, author of the phrase, if not the idea of "The Great Society." Introducing his signature speech on May 22, 1964, at the University of

Michigan, LBJ began: "We have the opportunity to move not only toward the rich society and the powerful society, but upward toward the Great Society." He concluded with: "Will you join in the battle to build the Great Society, to prove that our material progress is only the foundation on which we will build a richer life of mind and spirit?" Amid the hosannas of the faithful and others in the audience, there must have been some who questioned how such polished prose could slip from the lips of a country bumpkin. But would this President give credit where credit was due? Hugh Sidey later recalled in an interview with LBJ: "As Johnson continued to talk about his staff I had the notion that he was playing a game. He certainly knew that I was aware that Goodwin wrote his speeches and indeed, had become his chief writer. Johnson wound up the interview by pulling a felt-tipped pen from his shirt and sketching the table of organization of his men. Down at the bottom under a 'Miscellaneous' category was a man named 'Goodman.' This was the ultimate put-down—misspelling Goodwin's name, as if he were a stranger in the White House."[12]

By the time Johnson strode into the White House his tyranny was legendary, demanding work from his staff as did no other President before or since. Always, day and night, seven days a week, 365 days a year, they were to be on call, ready and eager to do their master's bidding, whether to tree a possum on the Hill, to fetch a downed political bird in the swamps of Vietnam, or simply to heel. Body, soul, and spirit of his aides (and their families) belonged to this President. When he learned that his Secretary of Commerce was out on the golf course, Johnson told him to quit. He wanted no Ike-the-golfer image on his staff. When a Fortune 500 CEO suggested Johnson give his staff a month's vacation to recuperate so the other eleven months would be more productive, Johnson ignored him. LBJ's attorney, Abe Fortas, went so far as to change when his family celebrated Thanksgiving, knowing that on the scheduled holiday he could expect a phone call from LBJ that would ruin the event for him and his family.

Happening in on Assistant Press Secretary Malcolm Kilduff one day, LBJ took one look at his messy desk and remarked, "Kilduff, I hope your mind isn't as cluttered as your desk." With that reprimand, Kilduff soon straightened up his desk, only to have Johnson later enter and remark, "Kilduff, I hope your brain isn't as vacant as your desk." Trying in vain to reach Califano one Sunday morning, Johnson found that his aide had spent an hour in church. Johnson barked out that Califano should thereafter take a White House car and sit in the back of the church, where the driver could fetch him to the car phone without disturbing the service![13]

Soaring on the wings of victory in 1964, gloating over the unprecedented mandate he'd pocketed, Johnson was primed for the stratosphere. Yet the torture of witnessing his Great Society gradually being incinerated in the flames of Vietnam made him at times inconsolable. It served to lash him and his staff into a more furious frenzy of work. Shifting into double-time, they were adjusting to the "'LBJ trot." Here, in Johnson, observed journalist Theodore White, were the clear symptoms of incipient manic-depression.

Johnson had said it was one thing to tell a man to go to hell; it was something else to make him go there. Johnson could do both, and, in the process, seemed to approach divine dimensions. Yet it was hell on earth that he visited on his staff. It is not surprising that few of his staff, including Humphrey, took this President seriously when he told his soon-to-be Vice-President, on August 25, 1964, "Hubert, I'm not a sadistic person, as you well know." Not only was he an inhumane taskmaster but a cruel bully. He took delight in bullying the likes of Secretary of Health, Education, and Welfare John W. Gardner into joining him skinny-dipping in the White House pool, then gloating, "I got that intellectual, John Gardner, in my pool swimming around bare-assed naked." As aide John Roche put it, "He dropped people like that on their aristocratic asses."

As much as Johnson respected McNamara and Undersecretary of State George Ball, both came in for such a tongue-lashing at a conference that foreign policy guru Dean Acheson interposed, "Mr. President, you don't pay these men enough to talk to them that way—even with the federal pay raise." During a phone conversation, LBJ poured his profane vitriol all over Press Secretary George Reedy in the presence of an astonished visitor. But he was in for a bigger surprise after Johnson hung up and announced, "Well, let's give George his Christmas present now." When the guest expressed his astonishment, Johnson explained, "You never want to give a man a present when he's up—you want to do it when he's down." The ultimate, it would appear, was Johnson's humiliating of Mac Bundy, ordering him into the bathroom while he went about his business on the can, reading his news summaries all the while. The graduate of San Marcos would call to the former Dean of Harvard College, as Bundy kept his distance just outside the open bathroom door, "I can't hear you . . . Mac, get closer . . . Mac, get in here!"[14]

Even at the starting gate Johnson was ready to show who was boss. On his first day in the White House Johnson encountered a Navy captain and two Army generals awaiting him outside his Oval Office. Johnson: "What are you here for?" "Mr. President," said one, "we're here to make our report." Johnson: "Report of what?" "Report of our respective services" was the response. Johnson: "Look, I served for years as a member of the Naval Affairs Committee. I know more about the Defense Department than any of you, and I don't want to see you here again unless I send for you." Soon Johnson had replaced them with his Air Force One pilot, Major Jim Cross, and a Marine Sergeant, William Gulley, gloating that a major and a sergeant took a captain and two generals any day, "especially if they were Kennedy appointees."

For Gulley, meeting Johnson for the first time was a searing experience. "Mr. President, I'd like you to meet Bill Gulley," was Chief of Staff Marvin Watson's introduction as they chanced to meet in a corridor. "He's the new Marine who's going to clean up the mess in this office and replace six people on the staff." With no handshake, with no trace of a smile, Johnson shot out, "So, you're a water-walker, are you? Well, those six had better be gone by the end of the month or you'll be." And off he strode, leaving the sergeant—on the job just five days—wondering what had hit him. Could this be the same President, appearing so very caring and solicitous on television? As one friend put it, "Lyndon has a clock inside him with an alarm that tells him at least once an hour to chew somebody out. . ."

Johnson was no less the bully with his female staff, and sometimes it became both pathetic and ludicrous. As Vice-President, his secretary was Dolores Stacks. All afternoon, one day, he'd tried in vain to reach Bob Kerr. At last, suspecting a conspiracy to keep him from talking to his old and rich friend, he dialed the White House, switching on the red light of his phone and other phones in the office. Stacks picked up the phone and there, in a muffled voice, Johnson said, "This is Senator Kerr and I'd like to speak to the Vice-President." "Sir," she responded, seeing the red light, "The Vice-President's line is busy. He does want to talk to you, and I'm sure he'll return your call."

Like a shot Johnson was out of his chair, yanked the door open, and there was Stacks on the phone. She couldn't understand why Johnson was standing there glaring at her. His red light was still on. Not knowing what to do, she said to her caller, "Just a moment, Senator," then she turned to Johnson, "Senator Kerr wants you." "Goddamn you," roared the Vice-President, "that's not Senator Kerr! Goddamn you, you told him I was busy. I wasn't busy, goddamn it; I wasn't busy at all!" At that, Stacks started crying while Johnson continued to berate her for her obvious incompetence.

Johnson was accustomed to addressing his aides in the familiar idiom, "You dumb bastards!" or, in the singular, "You damn fool!" or simply, "Boy!" Even Valenti, "one of the greatest humans in existence," found himself in the less-elevated address, "You dumb son of a bitch!" The occasion was Valenti's being served by the Air Force One steward, "a beautiful slice of rare roast beef," as he put it. Leaping up and addressing Valenti in his less than sanguine tone, Johnson scolded him, "You are eating raw meat!" With that, Johnson grabbed his tray and marched to the galley where he accosted the two stewards. "You two sons of bitches, look at this! This is raw! You gotta *cook* the meat on my airplane. Don't you serve my people raw meat! Goddamn, if you two boys serve raw meat on my airplane again, you'll both end up in Vietnam!" That out of the way, Johnson dashed the tray upside down on the floor. On another occasion, over lunch, Moyers was in the midst of saying grace when Johnson shouted, "Speak up, Bill! I can't hear a damn thing." With that, Moyers looked his boss squarely in the eye and rebuked him quietly, "I wasn't addressing you, Mr. President." [15]

If Johnson deemed it necessary, he wouldn't hesitate to order an aide to perform tasks over and above the call of duty. Harry McPherson, veteran counsel to LBJ, listened one day as Johnson complained about the rhetorical lash of a certain female reporter. "What that woman needs," Johnson said to his trusted lawyer, "is you. Take her out. Give her a good dinner and a good fuck." Used to ridiculous requests, McPherson sighed and ignored the order. The disparagement from the reporter wouldn't let up and Johnson kept badgering McPherson until he did invite her to dine with him. There he devoted himself to highlighting the President's strengths. Soon the reporter's column was singing a different tune: high praise, but not for Johnson—for McPherson. Johnson saw the same column and that evening, before a few senators, he praised his legal aide as "a fine young man." Yet, Johnson added, he was "a little concerned about his family. You know, Harry's been taking out this bitch of a reporter and screwing her, and I worry about his wife and children."

Of all those Johnson enjoyed bullying, none were more put upon than his Secret Service detail. He took special pains to humble them. In a common trick at his Texas Ranch, LBJ would suddenly hop into his Lincoln convertible and hightail it down the road like a jackrabbit, his "shadows" scrambling to catch up. Eyeing them in the rear-view mirror, eating his Texas dust, Johnson would scoff, "Look at those bastards back there. They're supposed to be Secret Service, but they look like a bunch of goddamned Mexican generals! All you see is elbows and asses!"

Leaving a church service near the Ranch one day, Lyndon asked, "What kind of a car do you have, preacher?" When the man gestured at an old Chevy, Johnson turned his usual generous self—with taxpayer money. "Well, you ought to have a better car than that. I'm going to give you that new station wagon over there," pointing to the Secret Service car. With that, he ordered the dumbfounded agents out, took the keys and handed them to an equally dumbfounded clergyman. Then, in a flash, he jumped back into his own car and roared off, leaving the agents to fend for themselves.

Perhaps the most pathetic of abuses Johnson heaped on the men responsible for his safety was an incident involving agent Bob Taylor. In the spring of 1968, Taylor was trying to brief his President on the details of Martin Luther King's assassination. The two were standing by a flower bed just off the Ranch porch where several women were talking. Keeping his voice low to avoid disturbing the women, Taylor suddenly realized Johnson had unzipped his fly and was urinating on the flowers. Worse, he called out, "Goddamn it, Taylor, I can't hear you. Come over closer." When Taylor complied, the President leaned his elbow on the agent as he continued to relieve himself—directly on Taylor's shoes.

On another of his Ranch vacations, Johnson was awakened early in the morning by the screeching of his pet peacocks. It seems they'd been pecking holes in the plastic cover over his swimming pool, so Johnson had directed his aides to keep the peacocks away from the pool. Following orders, one unfortunate aide was shocked to find Johnson suddenly throw open the window and bellow, "What the hell are you doing?! You dumb son of a bitch, you're going to kill my peacocks, chasing them like that! Don't chase my peacocks or they'll lose their feathers. What do you think

I have peacocks for? For their feathers! And you, you dumb bastard, you're running all the feathers off them!"

One thing for sure, working for Johnson was a no-win proposition. Though visualizing these outrageous incidents tends to provoke a chuckle or even a guffaw, they were always at somebody else's expense. As Eugene McCarthy put it, Johnson was "playful in the cruelest way."

As astonishing were these and other abuses of his aides, it is more astonishing that they took them as long as they did. One who refused to be browbeaten was General Wallace Greene, Commandant of the Marine Corps. At his first meeting with the President, Greene was appalled by Johnson's treatment of his staff. When it came Greene's turn to speak about Vietnam, he argued that it appeared to be a case of too little, too late. Johnson, impatient with criticism of his policy, interrupted, "Speak up! Speak up! I can't hear what you're saying. Speak up!" Greene, mustering the strength to rein in his emotions, paused for a time that seemed interminable. Then, his eyes fixed on his commander in chief, his voice cold but crisp, he responded, "You can hear what I'm saying and so can everyone else in this room." With that, he calmly, deliberately, returned to his subject. Taken aback by this reprimand, Johnson ceded to Greene a grudging respect he accorded to few, in or out of uniform, and turned increasingly to him for advice.[16]

The question naturally arises: why on earth did Johnson stoop to such abysmal treatment of his aides? First and foremost was Johnson's being spoiled by his parents, and especially by his mother, who made herself a doormat for her eldest, the one in whom she placed her hopes and dreams. Another factor was Lyndon's determination to be somebody. His lust for power was insatiable as, with his boardinghouse reach, he tried to control everyone around him, especially those to whom he delegated authority. In his grasp for power, Johnson used every ounce of his strength, every minute of his time, every demeaning ingratiation. And he demanded his aides do the same, except that it was all to be done in Johnson's name. At times, especially as the war ground on, his pent-up raw energy clashed with the reality of a no-win war even as it sapped his Great Society, and he would display, alternately, signs of manic-depression or paranoia. He was no pony engine pulling a few cars down the track. He was a giant locomotive, valves thrashing, wheels grinding, whistles shrieking, as he vainly tried to pull one hundred senators, then two hundred million Americans down the track. High ambition wed to great energy meant singular frustration at being balked. Yet another factor was Lyndon's haunting demons of discontent, a deep and abiding insecurity drawing him to prove himself worthy of his mother's hopes, superior to his father's accomplishments—and the equal of anything the intellectual elite of the Eastern seaboard could produce, whether it was Wilson, FDR, or Kennedy. So sure was his goal, so enormous his energy, that he would brook neither criticism nor deviation from the path he was pursuing. Surely, as his brother repeatedly noted, up to four packs of cigarettes and two fifths of Cutty Sark each day did not help his decision-making. Constantly fingering an inhaler in one hand and a cigarette in the other, Johnson was, it seems, either sniffing or puffing between downing shots of his favorite whiskey. A psychiatrist might well have started a list of his addictions, not the least of which was sex. Faithless as a father and a husband, he was a tyrant with his staff. Ralph Waldo Emerson discovered every man to be his superior in some way, and in that way he was determined to learn from him. Lyndon Baines Johnson discovered every man to be his inferior in some way, and he would use that way to manipulate him. Some people, like wife Lady Bird, and daughters Lynda, and Luci suffered in silence—as did Walter Jenkins, his most loyal and trusted aide, whom we shall later describe in detail.

A second question begs an answer. Why did these people take it? Why did they put up with such outrageous bullying, shameless lying, and flagrant disloyalty? Johnson's wife and daughters perhaps saw a different side of him, perhaps understood him better, and in any event were his family, with bonds most difficult to dissolve. Others simply paid the price for hitching their wagons to a rising star. To live and breathe in his shadow meant that in some way, great or small, they would share in his glory. After all, as he constantly reminded them, he was the only President they had.

Groupthink in Decision-Making

Johnson's decision-making, especially in his Tuesday luncheon meetings that were devoted primarily to the war, reflected that characteristic described by Irving Janis as groupthink. According to Nietzsche, who ought to have known, madness is the exception in individuals but the rule in groups. Janis defined group madness—groupthink—as the product of discussion in which reservations are muted in the name of harmony, with each participant more concerned with a consensus in line with the leader's opinions than in hammering out the best decision on the hard anvil of open and free discussion.

Each of the eight symptoms of groupthink outlined by Janis seems to fit the decision-making of Johnson's Tuesday luncheon "Cabinet" as they escalated the war.

1) There was an illusion of invulnerability: "feeding excessive optimism" and encouraging extreme risks.

2) There were "collective efforts to rationalize in order to discount warnings which might lead the members to reconsider assumptions before they recommit themselves to their past policy decisions."

3) There was "an unquestioned belief in the group's inherent morality, inclining the members to ignore the ethical or moral consequences of their decisions."

4) There were "stereotypical views of enemy leaders as too evil to warrant genuine attempts to negotiate, or as too weak and stupid to counter whatever risky attempts were made to defeat their purposes."

5) There was "direct pressure on any member who expressed strong arguments against any of the group's stereotypes, illusions, or commitments, making clear that this type of dissent was contrary to what was expected of all loyal members."

6) There was "self-censorship of deviations from the apparent group consensus, reflecting each member's inclination to minimize to himself the importance of his doubts and counter arguments."

7) There was "a shared illusion of unanimity concerning judgments conforming to the majority view."

8) There was "the emergence of self-appointed mind-guards—members to protect the group from adverse information that might shatter their shared complacency about the effectiveness and morality of their decisions."

In the opening days of his presidency, Johnson seemed to be genuinely seeking open discussion of the war, all ears as he sought alternative views to arrive at a consensus. This had been his strategy for eight years as Senate leader, when always his consuming interest was getting something done, some bill passed, even if it represented just half a loaf. More often than not, the consensus represented compromises all around, with no one especially happy or unhappy with the result. Ever since the nation's Founders hammered out a Constitution in Philadelphia, this has been the process of discussion-based democracy. And it had worked for Johnson in piling up an unprecedented record in Congress during the 1950s. As opposed to deciding on the "right" answer—every other answer, by definition, being "wrong"—the answer that emerges in a democracy represents the "best" answer: the one that, since each member has a stake in it, each member will be committed to implementing. For, as every leader soon learns, it is one thing to legislate and something else again to implement. A half-loaf, Johnson was fond of saying, was not only better than none, but held the promise that more would be forthcoming—perhaps even the full loaf.

The most outstanding example of this was the Civil Rights Act of 1957, the first such bill since the days of Reconstruction. So opposed were the Southerners—led by Georgia's Richard Russell—that they filibustered in a marathon session, bringing about gridlock in the Senate. That is, until Johnson so compromised the bill that he alienated Senate liberals such as Hubert Humphrey and Paul Douglas of Illinois. It emerged a poor likeness of its original self, a half-loaf at best. But it was better than no bill. And seven years later, with Johnson in the White House, a new bill emerged— after another marathon filibuster led by Russell—this one a bill that could serve as the cornerstone of his Great Society.

It was just this same strategy, this "come now and let us reason together" emphasis, that was the earmark of Johnson's policies regarding the war. He would listen to the doves on one side, including Ball, Galbraith, and the CIA. Then he would listen to the hawks, including McNamara, Rusk, Rostow, and the Joint Chiefs. Then he would deliberately steer a middle course, eschewing extremes like the plague. Of course he pleased neither the hawks nor doves, but reasoned that consensus—and implementation—lay in a middle, moderate course. If, then, it has traditionally been this strategy that characterizes American democracy, what went wrong, so wrong that the tragedy of Vietnam culminates Barbara Tuchman's brilliant *March of Folly*, in which she concludes that the "prime characteristic of folly" is none other than the "rejection of reason?"

To use Janis' term, "groupthink" came to plague Johnson's Tuesday luncheon meetings. Columbia University professor Henry Graff interviewed Johnson and each of the other participants four times between

1965 and 1968. He was struck by the high degree of their cohesiveness, even the "genuine friendship and mutual support" born of loyalty to their leader and to each other, as well as the increasing adversity from an implacable foe in Vietnam and the virulent antiwar protests at home. Soon the group was listening only selectively, so as to iron out the wrinkles and present their leader with a smooth consensus in line with his thinking. Indeed, as Graff discovered, they became so familiar with his and each other's assumptions and ways of thinking—including euphemisms shrouded in Pentagonese—that congeniality became the rule. Why spoil a fine luncheon with divisive argument, or worse, acrimony?

But by 1968, Johnson was bypassing Secretary of Defense McNamara, who had "turned dovish" on him. The "war of attrition" had backfired, so that for every enemy casualty, another two or more were ready to take his place. Still, until McNamara was replaced by Clark Clifford in 1968, Graff was impressed with the "loyalty with which those around the President defended him and the decisions they had helped him reach. . . " As the stakes increased and the luncheon "Cabinet" saw their President increasingly beleaguered, they turned to one another for reassurance. As a result, Graff concluded, this informal group "exerted an extraordinarily powerful influence over its leader, perhaps more than any other presidential advisory group in American history."

After three years of meeting on Tuesdays, Johnson's advisers on the war—"the Wise Men"—suddenly reversed themselves in March 1968. But it was too late. Too late, that is, for Johnson. By the end of the month, haunted by the thought of more than 25,000 American dead in Vietnam, he fell on his political sword and declined to run for reelection. Reason, as Tuchman put it, had been overpowered by "non-rational human frailties— ambition, anxiety, status-seeking, face-saving, illusions, self-delusions, [and] fixed prejudices." As it turned out, "the structure of human thought," based as it is on logical procedure from premise to conclusion, was insufficient "proof against the frailties and the passions."

Here, then, was a President who had entered the White House surrounded by a glittering constellation of advisers, including JFK's "best and brightest:" Rusk and Ball, McNamara and Bill Bundy, Reedy and Moyers, and—towering above them all—the resplendent Mac Bundy, former Dean of Harvard College. As Halberstam put it, all were committed to the firm belief that "sheer intelligence and rationality would . . . solve anything."

Even Kissinger paid homage to Bundy in his encomium, "You can't beat brains," following that up with his concession—surely no easy thing for Kissinger himself—that Bundy possessed "one of the keenest intellects I have ever encountered."[17]

Yet with all this intellectual horsepower at his fingertips, Johnson stumbled and fell, and took the nation with him down the slippery slope of hubris. In his desperate insistence on both "guns" and "butter," on pursuing the war to "victory"—whatever that meant—and, at the same time, erecting his "Great Society," Johnson, with the help of his advisers, chopped the legs off facts to make them fit his Procrustean bed of half-baked assumptions, woeful ignorance, and monumental ego. Even as he deferred to fewer and fewer—and only to those who agreed with him— the men to whom he delegated power came to realize that to hold their jobs, they had to compromise their integrity. It is little wonder that, by the time Johnson made his fateful announcement on March 31, 1968, few were the aides who had stuck by him for five years—and fewer still were those who believed him when he said he was bowing out. As questionable as were Johnson's thinking skills, his people skills were worse. And in the end, many Americans, as well as other millions in Southeast Asia, paid a terrible price.

RICHARD NIXON

I dealt with what came before me, leaving the rest to others, and not really worrying about the whole thing. This was admittedly an unusual approach for me to take, but I had plenty of other things to worry about, and there were many other staffers such as Dean who could handle Watergate. At least that's what I believed then, to the extent that I thought about it at all.

— H.R. Haldeman[1]

A Faceless Bureaucracy?

If an electorate is known by the leaders it chooses, then perhaps a leader is known by the company he keeps, particularly the aides he chooses. Just as we cannot appreciate the rising sun by looking directly at it, so we cannot appreciate our presidents by looking directly at them. We must also know what they did to enlighten, to inspire, to energize, to transform our world, and particularly those closest to them, with whom they worked each day. Not only do presidents set the tone; they set the example. The hat industry went into a tailspin when JFK was seen, again and again, even on the coldest days, bareheaded. When it came to delegation, Nixon was critical of his predecessor: "If the President assumes too much power, his mistakes are magnified. If power is diffused, his mistakes are reduced." It appears that Nixon as an administrator was strong on theory and weak in practice. Indeed, Ambrose in 1987 concluded that "Nixon's big weakness as President was that he did not know how to administer government. He was what Lyndon Johnson said he was—a chronic campaigner; he knew how to get elected but not how to govern. His administration was replete with crossed purposes and people keeping secrets from each other."

Richard Nixon promised in his 1968 campaign to pick "a Cabinet made up of the ablest men in America, leaders in their own right and not merely by virtue of appointment." He introduced them to the public with great fanfare, then promptly ignored them, with the exceptions of Mitchell and Connally.

It is an indictment of Nixon's presidency that those who dared to speak the truth, as uncomfortable as it may have been to him—assuming they could get through Haldeman, the gatekeeper of the Oval Office— were soon fired. By 1972, Secretary of the Interior Walter Hickel, Secretary of Housing and Urban Development George Romney, and Secretary of Defense Melvin Laird had paid dearly for their effrontery in either criticizing Nixon or in giving him a steady stream of bad news.

By the time Nixon had "cleaned house" of "malcontents" and begun his second term, he had, in the words of Schlesinger, "the most anonymous Cabinet within memory, a Cabinet with one or two exceptions, of clerks, of compliant and faceless men who stood for nothing, had no national identity of their own and were certified not to defy presidential whim." Theodore White was even more scathing. Here, he declared were ". . . men of little patriotism and no principle, as self-seeking as their enemies saw them—the hustlers, the bullies and all the crawling creatures of the underground, men set in motion by nothing more than ambition, and whose authority came from the self-righteous moralist(s) at the top." These satraps "entered into government, all of them with no greater knowledge of how power works than the intrigues of the political antechambers and the folklore of advance men . . . tantalized by the temptations of power. . ." Indeed, he even tried abolishing the Cabinet, making them answerable to a "small supercabinet to which the lesser Cabinet members would report." Then, in a concession that would have "astounded all previous presidents," and unable to maintain the pretext of a traditional Cabinet, he proclaimed that henceforth he would maintain "a direct line of communication" with them. Other presidents simply assumed this to be the case.

In his 1968 campaign, Nixon plumped for a streamlined, efficient government. Just how inefficient the government could be Nixon had learned during World War II in his eight months at the Office of Price Administration before enlisting. David Cavers, one of his Duke professors, was highly placed in the OPA, and offered Nixon a job at $3,200 per year— much more than he'd been making in his California law firm. He jumped at the chance. But, answering umpteen letters to those petitioning for exceptions to the strict tire-rationing policy, Nixon was soon disillusioned. There were the long hours of tedious work, the rubbing of shoulders with law school graduates from the East—particularly Jews—and the "mediocrity" as Nixon put it, "of so many civil servants."[2]

But what really got under Nixon's skin was not only the sheer waste and inefficiency of this giant bureaucracy in which 47,000 worked in World War II, but the promotions and higher pay of fellow bureaucrats with "lesser academic records and not as much legal experience." So he protested to his superior, who advised: "Build a little staff. Request two or three people to assist you, and then we can raise you. . . ." Nixon protested, "But I don't need a staff." "Then," his superior admonished him, "you won't get a promotion." It was that simple. And that disillusioning. So much so that in the Congressional Directory he later listed his employer between January and August of 1942, not as the OPA, but as the Office of Emergency Management—tantamount to an FBI agent listing his employer as the Justice Department. When, as President, Nixon received invitations to OPA reunions from a teasing John Kenneth Galbraith—himself highly placed there during the war—Nixon did what he seemed to do best: he ignored him.

Working for the OPA, Nixon later wrote, had an "enormous effect" on his thinking. In 1968 he was determined not only to make his executive branch "lean and mean," but to keep it under his control. To that end he recruited forty-eight personal aides by 1972, compared with eleven under FDR, thirteen under Truman, and thirty-seven under LBJ. To that end he "slimmed" the White House staff payroll from 266 when he was Vice-President in 1954, to 600 in 1971. Constantly complaining about the lumbering bureaucracy, he recalled that Ike's executive office staff was 1,175, noted that Kennedy's was 1,164, and determined to "cut back" drastically to 5,395 by 1971. All this "reduction" had its effect on the budget, "lowering" it from $31 million when he took office to $71 million by the end of his first term. So much for trimming the bureaucracy.[3]

In the preceding chapter we took note of the special deference Nixon paid certain members of his staff: Mitchell, Connally, Moynihan and Haig. Here we will focus on Henry Kissinger, John Ehrlichman, and Bob Haldeman, to better understand those to whom he delegated responsibility—and power—and how he used and abused them.

Henry Kissinger

Kissinger, a Johnny-come-lately among Nixon's aides, was more responsible than any for helping Nixon formulate his disastrous Vietnam policy. Yet Kissinger emerged, to use Ike's phrase, "as clean as a hound's tooth," both from the tragedy that was Vietnam and the fiasco that was Watergate. That, of course, took some doing, but by that time Kissinger— whether as National Security Advisor or Secretary of State—had become "Mr. Teflon." No matter what was cooking or burning on the executive stove, nothing ever stuck to him.

Just how slippery Kissinger was is seen in his recruitment by Nixon in 1968. Henry, a Harvard graduate, had been teaching there when he caught the eye of Nelson Rockefeller. It wasn't hard for Kissinger to become one of the Governor's most ardent boosters when he went to work for him. At the same time Kissinger caught the eye of LBJ, who was, though a Democratic President, likewise a booster of Nelson, preferring Rockefeller as his successor over Humphrey. Soon Henry was attached to Johnson's peace team, trying to hammer out an agreement in Paris. Kissinger took note when Nixon trounced Rockefeller for the nomination, and, taking note also of Nixon's lead over Humphrey in the polls, decided it would be a good bet that Nixon would be the next president. Forgetting he'd condemned Nixon as "the most dangerous of all the men running, to have as President," Kissinger snuggled up to the Republican candidate with a blow-by-blow description of what was happening with Johnson's peace team in Paris. That, as we will detail more fully later, was the kind of information "Tricky Dick" Nixon could—and did—use to win a razor-thin victory over Humphrey in November. It was obvious to the new President that Kissinger was brilliant if unscrupulous, a man who could spot a winner a mile away and throw in with him, regardless of how he'd bad-mouthed that same man in the past. Here, in short, was a man "sensible enough to change with changing circumstances." So Nixon made this ultimate pragmatist his assistant for national security, turning to Kissinger— rather than to his Secretary of Defense, Melvin Laird, rather than to his Secretary of State, William Rogers, and rather than to his Joint Chiefs of Staff—in formulating his war policies. It is hard to imagine someone of Kissinger's background rising to the place where he wielded such enormous power in the U.S. government—particularly in preparing and participating in the two 1972 summit meetings in Peking and Moscow.

In some ways Kissinger was a reflection of Nixon; in other ways the opposite. Nixon was a product of a middle-class Quaker home in California; Kissinger emigrated to this country as a boy, a penniless German Jew who'd suffered thirteen of his kin being executed in the Holocaust. Nixon was a graduate of Whittier, a small liberal arts college on the West Coast; Kissinger graduated from the elite Ivy League Harvard, arguably the premier university on the East Coast. Nixon was the professional pol, Kissinger the cloistered prof; yet both shared a love of intrigue, of eavesdropping, secrecy, conspiracy, surprise, backbiting and, above all, power plays. Furthermore, they shared at times a cynicism so corrupting as to hold in contempt virtually all others—including each other. They were two peas in a pod, always together. Other aides took note of their three or four meetings daily, interspersed with innumerable phone calls. Like the goad that Nixon had been to Johnson, Kissinger was to Nixon, constantly egging him on to escalate the war. Always at stake was Nixon's manhood. Did he wish to go down in history as a coward? Each doubted the other's sanity more than once. Repeatedly Kissinger described Nixon as being "beside himself," while at one time Nixon urged Ehrlichman and Haig to get Kissinger to a psychiatrist.

During December 1971, Kissinger wasn't allowed to have a press conference. The problem? Nixon was furious that Kissinger was garnering all the great coverage. He'd been telling reporters how he, the reasonable statesman, managed to keep Nixon, the mad bomber, on a tight leash. Nixon's point man, Haldeman, intent on cutting Kissinger down to size, told Ehrlichman that Nixon was "nearly to the point of firing Henry, just to end the wear and tear." Apparently Kissinger was unaware of the 1937 report of FDR's Commission on White House Operations: "The President's aides should be possessed of . . . a passion for anonymity." So exasperated did Kissinger become that he later told *Time* editors, "I debated for several weeks at the time whether I should go on, and decided to." Presumably Kissinger was still seeking the rainbow, hoping to find the pot of gold in the form of the post of Secretary of State, replacing his nemesis, William Rogers.

Did Henry find what he was looking for? Yes, he did replace Rogers, climbing as high as his being a naturalized citizen permitted. But, as he confided in his biographer, John Stoessinger, he believed in "the tragic element in history." There was "the tragedy of a man who works very hard and never gets what he wants." Then there was "the even more bitter tragedy of a man who finally gets what he wants and finds out that he does not want it."[4] Presumably Kissinger included himself in the latter category. But there remains a third level of tragedy, of a man striving for what he wants, only to destroy himself in the process. It is the fourth level that is the worst, for here a man destroys not only himself, but others—including many innocents.

In a further chapter we will note the love-hate relationship between Nixon and Kissinger that lasted until the President's resignation in August, 1974.

John Ehrlichman

Kissinger's strength lay in international affairs. His counterpart for domestic affairs, John Ehrlichman, had been hired by Haldeman as an advance man in Nixon's first presidential campaign. Fellow undergraduates at UCLA after World War II, they had become fast friends. In 1959, Haldeman introduced his thirty-four-year-old compatriot to the man he'd serve, off and on, until April 30, 1973—the day Nixon fired them both. When they met, Ehrlichman recalled, "Nixon looked at me intently. 'Oh, yes. Fine. How are you?' Then he was gone, eyes down, deep in thought."

With Nixon's loss to JFK, Ehrlichman returned to his law practice—only to be recalled by Haldeman in 1967, to enlist advance men for Nixon. But John's main job was to organize the 1968 Republican National Convention in Miami. With Nixon's sweet victory, Ehrlichman was offered the position of counsel to the President. Pushing for liberal policies, he was, in Henry's words, "truly interested in substance; he sponsored or supported domestic policies that were humane and progressive." Then came the Cambodian "incursions," that embroiled one campus after another in protest, arousing the consciences of Ehrlichman's three children. Deeply moved, Ehrlichman nevertheless understood that if he wanted to keep his job, he had to go along with Nixon. So he adopted Nixon's "tough guy" approach that expressed itself repeatedly in his barbed arrow aimed at those who disagreed with him or the President: "Give him the shaft!" It wasn't, however, until acting FBI Director Patrick Gray was about to be sacrificed on the altar of Watergate that Ehrlichman stretched his imagination to recommend of malcontents, "Let them twist slowly, slowly in the wind." This kind of sadistic talk endeared Ehrlichman to few besides Nixon.

Already, by the end of the 1968 campaign, Ehrlichman and Haldeman were alienating others on Nixon's staff. Speechwriter Richard Whalen quit in disgust at the heavy-handed running of the campaign by the "two Germans." "We were under the heel of men basically unsure of themselves," Whalen complained, "second-raters playing over their heads and fiercely resentful of anyone who dared approach them at eye level."

Ehrlichman's ignorance of the issues couched in the legislation he forwarded to Congress—exacerbated by his arrogance—virtually assured the defeat of his bills and prompted him to bad-mouth Congress as "a bunch of clowns."[5] Ehrlichman, according to Nixon, was willing to "get rid of anybody with even the appearance of wrongdoing." Nixon added, of course, that he would have taken a more humane course. Humane, however, was not what Ehrlichman thought of Nixon when he decided to sacrifice both him and Haldeman for "the larger good": his own survival as President. It began with Ehrlichman's saying the word everybody—and especially Nixon—had studiously avoided mentioning even though thinking: "impeachment." "That," Ehrlichman recalled, "was like dropping a dead cat into the Kool-Ade."

Not long after that shock, Nixon dispatched Ziegler to ask Haldeman and Ehrlichman for their resignations. Nixon had been talking with Connally, Rogers, and Haig, and all three felt it would "move the problem [the Watergate cover-up] away from the President"—ensuring his "plausible deniability"—if they walked the plank. This had no special appeal for Ehrlichman, so he sat down and wrote the names of seventeen White House staffers who should precede him on the plank, men he was convinced "had committed crimes or who had been accused of serious wrongdoing in the newspapers"—including Press Secretary Ron Ziegler himself.

So desperate had Ehrlichman come to feel that on April 27,1973—aboard Air Force One with Nixon, en route to Mississippi to survey flood damage—he found himself in the cockpit behind the pilots, thinking seriously of ending everyone's troubles by throwing [himself] against the controls. "We'd all be gone in about a minute and a half." But he thought better of it and returned to his seat.

Two days later, Ehrlichman and Haldeman met with Nixon at Camp David. En route, Ehrlichman later wrote, "I was overwhelmed with self-pity. I was being disgraced, and it was unfair." He was about to be fired, he was convinced, solely on the "false accusation" of John Dean—who had been talking to journalists about Ehrlichman's role in Watergate. Furthermore, he was "being lumped with Bob Haldeman, who had some real troubles with hush money which [I] did not share: Worse, no one had the class or courtesy to deal with me directly."

That was about to end. Closeted with Nixon at Camp David, Haldeman already having been fired, Ehrlichman listened with little sympathy as Nixon told him—as he'd told Haldeman—that he'd prayed the night before that "he might die during the night." Tears flowed—Nixon had always been good at that, according to his drama coach at Whittier College—when Nixon told Ehrlichman he'd have to walk the plank. Nearly in tears himself, Ehrlichman asked only one thing: "Just explain all this to my kids, will you? Tell them why you had to do this?" But he and Haldeman, ever the good soldiers, tendered their resignations forthwith.

May and June came and went and Ehrlichman followed Haldeman before Democratic Senator Sam Ervin's Watergate Committee. Underestimating the group's North Carolina chairman, and indeed the entire panel, Ehrlichman figured they were but "a shabby collection of posturers and politicians, winding themselves in swaddles of self-righteousness." He would not testify as had Haldeman, who "smiled and deferred at every opportunity" in an effort to disabuse the American public of his image as a martinet. Instead, Ehrlichman decided to respond, "as I would have in trying a tough lawsuit, cramming the facts down their throats and not letting Ervin get away with his phony country-lawyer act." It was during Ehrichman's third appearance that national TV inadvertently picked up Hawaiian Democratic Senator Dan Inouye's whisper, "What a liar!"[6]

In his last face-to-face meeting with Nixon, on May 2, 1973, Ehrlichman departed convinced that Nixon had let him take the blame for the break-in at the Los Angeles office of Lewis J. Fielding, Daniel Ellsberg's psychiatrist, something that Nixon himself had ordered. Not so, wrote Nixon in his memoirs. Had he even known of it, he "would have automatically considered it unprecedented, unwarranted, or unthinkable." Yet, Nixon excused the break-in on the grounds that it was not as "wrong or excessive as what Daniel Ellsberg did" in releasing classified Pentagon documents to *The New York Times* for publication. So Nixon concluded that it was "a tragedy of circumstances that . . . John Ehrlichman went to jail and Daniel Ellsberg went free."

As the noose of impeachment tightened on Nixon's neck, Ehrlichman and Haldeman concluded that, in all probability, Nixon would resign rather than face the humiliation of impeachment, a trial, the loss of pension and perks, and prison time. But before he resigned, there was one thing he could do to ameliorate the rank injustice of what had happened to his two closest aides. After all, Haldeman contended, the "acts and things done" by him and Ehrlichman—for which they'd been convicted and sentenced—had been done at the President's direction, or with his knowledge and approval, or "under a general presidential authorization or direction," or finally, "for the President's personal, political, or institutional use or benefit." What they needed to right at least some of the wrongs was a presidential pardon, to include even Vietnam draft-evaders. Such an act of clemency, Haldeman explained, would give Nixon's successor "an absolutely clean slate." Furthermore, the pardon would be in the best interests of Nixon and the country. For if Nixon were to resign, "the probability is that Congress is willing to grant the President immunity rather than seek the last drop of blood."

The petition was rejected out of hand. Ehrlichman and Haldeman were not only liabilities but albatrosses, adding to the discomfort of impending impeachment. Back from the desk of Haig, Haldeman's successor as Chief of Staff, came the response, as curt as it was cold: "Pardons for everyone have been extensively considered, and the idea has been rejected as impossible; it can't be done." How fortunate is the passive voice. It appeared to absolve Nixon and Haig of the heartless act of actually ignoring the plea of two of Nixon's top aides—the same two he claimed to have prayed to die for rather than fire; the two whose firing caused him to "burst into tears;" the two who'd done everything for love of Nixon, if not for country. Instead of writing to them directly, Nixon had so little respect for his aides and so much respect for his own skin that he had Haig write the note of refusal, as if there were a larger fate governing all of them. Indeed, there is no indication that Haldeman's petition ever went beyond Haig.

The President's heartlessness in refusing pardons for any of his aides proved to be an irony made worse by its hypocrisy when, just one month after Nixon's resignation, his successor pardoned him. That successor was not Spiro Agnew, who had left office in disgrace after being hit with charges of tax evasion. The new Vice-President was Michigan Republican Gerald Ford, who assumed the presidency on August 9, 1974, and pardoned Nixon on September 9. Ehrlichman remained unsure if this was the result of a deal between Ford and Nixon. The electorate, it appeared, was more certain than Ehrlichman, and turned down Ford's presidential bid in 1976. It brought to mind the president of the steamship line of the doomed "Titanic," who was among the first to push his way into one of the lifeboats, scorning the tradition that women and children should go first. It seemed certain he would be hauled into court for brazenly saving his own neck and be judged guilty of gross negligence. Instead, he was exonerated by a judge whom he had in his pocket.

It appears that Ehrlichman was much more the man than was Nixon. For Ehrlichman later wrote that Ford did "the right thing for the nation's good." That is debatable. What is not debatable is that it was for Nixon's good. As Ehrlichman concluded, "If one cared about one's place in history, the pardon route was the best. And Richard Nixon cared deeply about his place in history."[7]

H.R. Haldeman

In considering Ehrlichman we have necessarily included Haldeman, for the two so often acted jointly. Yet there is much more to be said of Nixon's alter ego, the man who introduced Ehrlichman to Nixon in 1959. It was years earlier that Haldeman was himself introduced to Nixon by a girlfriend working in Senator Nixon's office.

Before attending UCLA, Haldeman had gone to a strict private school. Though he was later reported to have an intelligence in the genius range, the D's on his early report cards showed little promise. What he did learn at the private school was discipline. At UCLA, where he majored in public relations, Frank Mankiewicz was student editor of the campus newspaper. As such he rubbed shoulders with Haldeman, and later wrote that he never recalled seeing Haldeman laugh. Here was a man who, like Nixon, was dead serious. Indeed, working for Nixon as an advance man in 1956, as chief advance man in 1960, as a research assistant for Nixon's book, *Six*

Crises, and as Nixon's campaign manager in 1962, it soon became evident that Haldeman was Nixon's shadow.

It was something of a surprise that Nixon should have enlisted this public relations man from the staff of the J. Walter Thompson advertising agency in Los Angeles. For Nixon was as suspicious of PR as he was of the "gimmicks" he saw Johnson and others using in Congress. By 1958, Nixon was calling timid politicians "gutless wonders" or "neuter, play-it-safe" men whose counterparts in business worked in public relations. Before taking a position on a subject—at least, any subject of importance—both would first test the wind in the polls. You could thus avoid "throwing yourself on your sword," Nixon argued, by using this "neuter" type of campaign. "Though you may win," Nixon insisted, "in the long run your winning will prove a catastrophe for the country." There is no small irony in Nixon's winning the White House in 1968 through the use of a whole new set of "gimmicks" introduced by Haldeman and others, and cata- logued by Joe McGinniss in his *Selling of the President*—only to prove Nixon's point made a decade earlier that this was indeed "a catastrophe for the country."

It was at UCLA, while listening to Nixon's crusade against the Communists, that Haldeman came to see the light and made Nixon his idol. Though later accused of blind loyalty, he argued he was loyal but not blind—either to Nixon's "great virtues" or his "great faults." Haldeman's cause, he explained, was neither the presidency as an institution nor the man Richard Nixon, "but rather the unique combination of the two: President Nixon. . . . It was neither the office nor the man, but the two together that captured my loyalty, dedication, and energy." Just how com- plete this was became evident in Nixon's 1962 gubernatorial campaign. As campaign manager, Haldeman was accused of circulating hundreds of thousands of postcards to conservative Democrats, assuring them that Nixon was one of them. Then the Democrats sued the California Republican Party for $500,000. This time Haldeman was accused of replacing a picture of the March of Dimes poster girl with one of Soviet leader Khrushchev, showing Governor Pat Brown bowing and smiling and uttering, "Premier Khrushchev, we who admire you, welcome you to California." In court, Haldeman perjured himself—something that Nixon had sent suspected communist spy Alger Hiss to prison for, twelve years earlier. There, without a doubt, was loyalty of the kind that must have captured Nixon's heart. As it turned out, the suit dragged on for two years before the verdict revealed that Haldeman had lied under oath. And who was the State Republican Chairman but Nixon's future Secretary of Health, Education, and Welfare—and later Ronald Reagan's Secretary of Defense Caspar Weinberger. Thus was Nixon unknowingly setting the stage for Watergate, complete with a cast of characters that included Haldeman, Ehrlichman, and Weinberger as well as Kalmbach, Stans, Ziegler and Chapin.[8]

Come 1968, the ever-faithful Haldeman refused to join Nixon full-time until he was guaranteed the position as Chief of Staff. Promised the job, Haldeman boasted, "there will be no Sherman Adams—referring to Ike's Chief of Staff, who Nixon had forced to resign after rumors that Adams had accepted favors from a wealthy industrialist. Yet a year later, Haldeman changed his boast: "I come closer to Sherman Adams than anyone else."[']

Haldeman wasn't long on the job before he was alienating other aides with his role of doorkeeper. Kissinger considered Haldeman to be dismayingly self-important. On April 13, 1970, Kissinger, after learning of a malfunction aboard the Apollo 13 space vehicle, tried to inform Nixon, only to be blocked by Haldeman. It was 11:00 P.M. and the President was not to be awakened. But this was an emergency! Orders were orders, and Haldeman, as usual, prevailed.

During Haldeman's first days in the White House, reporter Dan Rather found him "suspicious of people, arrogant, and fiercely protective of Nixon." Presidential economic adviser Arthur Burns discovered this the hard way. In the spring of 1969 Burns met with Nixon, then left the Oval Office—only to remember something he'd left there. Turning to reenter he found the irrepressible Haldeman blocking his way. "Your appointment is over." "But," protested Burns, "it'll only take a minute." Haldeman, his steel-blue eyes piercing beneath his cropped hair, stood firm, "No, that's that." On another occasion John Connally, Treasury Secretary and Nixon's favorite, rushed to the Oval Office, only to be thwarted by the keeper of the gate, who coldly announced, "I'll convey your wishes to the President." Whereupon Connally blazoned, "*I'll* convey my wishes to the President!" With that he brushed past the astonished martinet.[9]

Besides discipline, Haldeman, the PR expert, displayed elaborate deference. Not only did Nixon exude "class," said his Chief of Staff but he was undoubtedly the best-known person in the history of the world! Such a luminary needed time alone with his great thoughts, so Haldeman was determined to ensure Nixon's privacy. No one would bother him without first convincing the gatekeeper that his issue was worthy of the President's attention. Haldeman's wife, seeing him emerge from prison after Watergate, was sure his loyalty to Nixon had been misplaced. "I thought you were blind about Nixon," she said. "You couldn't see his faults. I'd hear you on the telephone, coddling and flattering him. It just wasn't like you."

If Haldeman was out of favor with his own wife, he was persona non grata as far as Nixon's wife was concerned. Pat found Haldeman to be a petty tyrant, exerting undue and baleful influence on her husband. Neither Pat nor her good friend, presidential secretary Rose Mary Woods, could tolerate Haldeman. Woods went as far as to warn Nixon that Haldeman put his own interests first, lied to Nixon, alienated him from those he needed and, in the end, would be his ruination. But Nixon wasn't listening to Woods any more than he was to his wife. What he wanted—what he desperately wanted as the war dragged on and the protesters converged on Washington—was assurance that his course of action was "right." He needed praise, not criticism, for standing up to the Communists. Taking heavy hits from the press, Nixon turned to Haldeman and his recruits, soldiers ready and willing to do battle. Entering the White House in 1969, Haldeman saw his job, Rather reported, "as smiling, deferential . . . ever ready to usher in men of importance whose counsel the President would need. . . ."

To that end Haldeman recruited not only Ehrlichman but Larry Higby, who was to Haldeman what Haldeman was to Nixon. In addition, Haldeman brought to the White House staff a group of other true believers: Dwight Chapin, Gordon Strachan, Donald Segretti, Jeb Magruder, and John Dean. It was impressive, almost awesome, to witness this "Beaver Patrol," as some called it, heels clicking as they scurried around in pressed suits, white shirts, ties properly knotted, hair short but loyalty long—the picture of crisp efficiency. Only after they began to fall, first the tenderfoot class, then the second class, then the first class, did the members of this Scout patrol begin to ask, not how, but why? Indicted, convicted, imprisoned, they found in their jail cells, at long last, time to ask the larger question.

These, *The New York Times* reported, were "Richard Nixon's children, these sad young men who, one after the other, raised the specter of

Nuremburg, with their only excuse for Watergate and the cover-up that they were simply following orders." Theirs was not to question why; theirs was but to do and die. Or, as Haldeman made it clear to Magruder, his job was "to do, not to think." On another staffer's memo, Haldeman simply scrawled, "T.L." The miscreant at last summoned the courage to ask its meaning. Back came the cryptic reply, "Too little, too late." Learning that a Republican senator was on his deathbed and that a hospital call from the President would be appreciated, Haldeman decided Nixon himself wasn't well enough to make the visit, and responded, "Wait until he dies."[10]

Here, to coin a phrase, was the marine drill sergeant's drill sergeant. Haldeman, in his memoir, *The Ends of Power*, was unduly modest when he wrote, "I tried to submerge myself totally to the cause. . . ." And what was that cause? "I saw my mission and my opportunity as unique . . . [to] play a very special role in what I firmly believed would be a drama of enormous success and accomplishment." That it ended instead in imprisonment for Haldeman and resignation and disgrace for Nixon was in no small part due to the Chief of Staff, who had shielded his President from the very criticism he so desperately needed—and resisted. Though Haldeman claimed, "I am no worshiper of Richard Nixon," he could have fooled any number of people who saw him in day-by-day subservience to his master. Yes, he admitted, he "gained a tremendous appreciation and respect for the greatness in [Nixon]. . . ." It was apparent that Haldeman, the former PR man, saw something in Nixon that few others saw.

So sensitive was Haldeman to the call of his President that, sailing a half-mile from shore, he got word Nixon wanted him. Abruptly he reversed course, then proceeded to flog the crew verbally to hurry to shore. Finally, exasperated with the laggards, the devoted Chief of Staff dove overboard and swam the rest of the way. To make certain of the efficiency, loyalty, and morality of the various departments in the executive branch, this same martinet placed others, notably Jeb Magruder, to spy on them and report back so Haldeman could, if necessary, take prompt and drastic action.

Yet for all his devotion, Haldeman was to walk the plank, a sacrifice for his master and a sop to the persecutors out to do his master in. A month before giving him the boot, Nixon exclaimed, "I marvel [at] the strength of Haldeman. He is really a remarkable man." Later, to David Frost, Nixon must have had Haldeman in mind when he said, "Some people are competent but not loyal. Other people are loyal but not competent. And when you find one that is both competent and loyal, then you've found the rarest of gems."

Gem he might be, the rarest of them he might be, but not so precious as to avoid being fired, indicted, convicted, imprisoned and, in the process, fail to get so much as a direct reply from Nixon regarding his petition of pardon. Nixon: "I felt that I owed it to him to listen to his eleventh-hour plea. . . . I did not give him an answer." Released, Haldeman was interviewed by TV journalist Mike Wallace, to whom he confessed, "On a personal basis . . . I was not close to Richard Nixon . . . I do not love Richard Nixon . . . I have an enormous respect for Richard Nixon." Despite this, Haldeman found Nixon "weird in the sense of being inexplicable, strange, hard to understand."[11] One thing about Nixon should have been abundantly clear by this time: he prized his own skin more than the skin of Haldeman and all the other White House aides put together.

The Law of Unintended Consequences

There can be little question but that one decision after another by the Nixon administration was flawed to the point of catastrophe. The scuttling of the Paris peace talks, the expansion of the war, the prosecution of war protesters, the further dividing of the nation, the refusal to engage in serious peace talks until election time, the massive Christmas bombing of 1972, the promise of billions in reparations to Hanoi, the hyping of "peace with honor" when a cease-fire was finally declared—on terms that could have been obtained four years earlier, and the blaming of Congress for losing the war—all of these and more. There were also the dirty tricks: the break-in of the psychiatrist's office, Watergate and its cover-up. All reflected fatally flawed decision-making.

For this litany of calamities Nixon was all too willing to blame his aides. His staff, he insisted to Haig, "has got to be [blameless] like Caesar's wife." One of those who could fill the bill was William Ruckelshaus, as current FBI acting director. "Bill," said Nixon, was "not part of the old guard. . . ." Neither was Elliot Richardson, Nixon's choice for Attorney General to replace Richard Kleindienst, who had earlier replaced John Mitchell. Not only was Richardson a Harvard man but, like Ruckelshaus, was no personal friend of Nixon's. As he put it, ". . . he's sort of Mr.

Integrity, Mr. Clean. . . . He's a hell of a fellow . . . smart as hell . . . tortuous, yes, but only because he's thinking so carefully." As for Haldeman and Ehrlichman, said Nixon after firing them, they were "two of the finest public servants it has been my privilege to know."

It wasn't that his staff lacked loyalty and, specifically, loyalty to the President. It was this that Ziegler knew counted most with Nixon when the press secretary offered a spirited defense of Leonard Garment, one of many who would briefly hold the title of the President's counsel. Ziegler: "I'll tell you this. There's one guy . . . who's a fella who's really standing up [for the President.]" Nixon: "Who? Garment?" Ziegler: "Well, it's Garment." Nixon: "Well, he's a loyal [lawyer?]" Ziegler: "He's a lawyer— loyal." Nixon: "Loyal." Ziegler: "A loyal fella." There can be little question about the centrality of personal loyalty as Nixon's most important qualification in an aide. Later that loyalty of Garment came under fire when Ehrlichman claimed that Garment might be "leaking very heavily to the press." Ziegler rushed to his aid, only to be cut off by the President, wary that Garment's loyalty "is only to the institution of the presidency." If so, Nixon warned, "I'll fire him today. . . . He's working for a person, you understand, the President person." At this Ziegler protested that Garment's loyalty "very definitely goes to you the man."

Apparently Nixon had on his staff some like Gray—whose nomination as FBI director was withdrawn when it became apparent that Congress would balk at confirming a White House lackey to succeed the legendary J. Edgar Hoover. Gray was, Nixon said, "a good, straight arrow, wonderful guy, but not very smart." It really wasn't enough that they were loyal, apparently. A week after firing Haldeman and Ehrlichman, Nixon complained to Haig,"I was dragged into this [Watergate] sonofabitch because of stupid people. Well-intentioned stupid people." Two weeks later, on May 23, 1973, he took much the same line with the outgoing chairman of the Republican Party, Bob Dole, and his replacement, George Bush: "It's just one of those things where well-intentioned people made some dumb, some bad mistakes."

Yet there was another Republican leader, Howard Baker, who seemed ready to finger Nixon himself in the imbroglio. For Baker's impression, he told Ehrlichman, was that "nobody's really in charge. I kept getting information and feedback from three or four different sources, and it suddenly dawned on me no one person's calling these shots...somebody needs to be in a position to have the broad overview of every piece of this puzzle [Watergate and the cover-up]." By July of 1973 Nixon was furious with Baker for not only was he critical of the President's leadership, but he'd had the nerve to cut to the heart of the issue of the Watergate cover-up when, as a member of Ervin's committee, he asked: what did Nixon know and when did he know it? By raising this question, Baker was apparently taking John Dean's word against the word of the President! Dean's wavering loyalties were fast making him a presidential enemy—one of a growing list to which the name Howard Baker had now been added. Nixon: ". . . Baker . . . [will] never be in the White House again—never, never, never. . . . He will never be on a presidential plane again. . . . Unforgivable . . . I think it's despicable conduct. . . . He thinks he's gonna be President. He's finished. . . . Howard has no excuse; Howard's smart enough to know better. I've campaigned for the sonofabitch time and time again. He's been in here [the Oval Office]; we've done favors for him. He's not gonna get away with this now." The question, of course, is if his aides were stupid if loyal, could their leader be far behind?

One thing for sure, Nixon reminded Dean on March 16, 1973, just five days before the soon-to-be-fired counsel to the President counseled the President that he had a cancer growing in the White House, ". . . you've got always to think in terms of the presidency and the President should not appear to be hiding and not forthcoming . . . the problem is the cover-up, not the facts. . . ." In other words, it was appearances that counted, not facts; PR that counted, not truth; persona that counted, not the person himself. In that respect, it was always a balancing act between appearances, PR, and persona on the one hand, and facts, truth, and the person on the other hand. And it was easy at times to get them mixed up, even as it was to confuse the President with the presidency. It certainly didn't help, Dean countered, when, as master of the cover-up, he was "so busy putting out daily fires" that he found it hard to concentrate on his "good master plan to deal with this."

Frustrated with Dean's report about "daily fires," Nixon complained to Haldeman that Dean, in all his duties as fireman, might well be forgetting the main point of the whole exercise, namely, "there's only one thing worse than having any substantive disclosures that have not come out, and that is to have the cover-up exposed . . . you cannot have the President hurt here in a cover-up." Therefore, simplicity itself, Dean had to "try to find a way to take the offensive with regard to Watergate. . . ."

So here was the predicament for this President when it came to decision-making. With all of the problems besetting him, Nixon had to rely on aides who were good as gold—some of them; smart—some of them; and loyal—almost all of them. Yet they couldn't seem to protect the President from this enveloping miasma of troubles interfering with doing what the electorate had mandated him to do.

It was enough to make a President weep. Here were "very moral men . . . they don't drink, they don't smoke, they don't screw around, they love their families, they're very, you know, Christian Science-type of people." Beyond that, even their intentions were very moral, as Nixon stressed to Haldeman, after firing him: "It's terribly important in terms of your intentions . . . you can't be accused of illegal intent if you didn't know something was illegal . . . unless they saw your intent was—well, to shut them [the Watergate burglars] up. . . ." Of course, Haldeman assured his President, "I had no motive to shut them up. I knew nothing about the Watergate. You knew nothing about the Watergate, and I was told by Dean, on whom I was relying, that nobody else in the White House knew anything about the Watergate. . . . My interest is . . . the public relations interest. . . ." Nixon then asked if Haldeman had read *The New York Times* editorial that day. For there—"Screw it"—was NBC's John Chancellor, "lying, of course that this is so much bigger than Teapot Dome. Sonofabitch." At that, Haldeman explained Chancellor's rationale: "He runs through this litany of all the people who have had to resign as a result of this. . . " and was cut off by Nixon, eager to fix the blame: "The media has forced them out." Not only that, but the media ". . . also wanted to destroy the [presidency]." Then the President got down to the nub of the matter: "But the main thing is that all this crap about the President should resign. . . ." Haldeman cautioned Nixon, "Don't even listen." And Nixon: "Nobody should even raise such things . . . if I walk out of this office, you know, on this chicken-shit stuff, why, it would leave a mark on the American political system. It's unbelievable . . . if they ever get up to the impeachment thing, fine, fine. . . . My point is if they get to that, the President of the United States, my view is then *fight like hell*."

What comes through repeatedly here is the brazen hypocrisy of Nixon, coupled with his determination to save his own skin, regardless of what happened to his staff. Prior to that, prior to his firing Haldeman, his Chief of Staff warned, "If you fire everybody now, in effect you send them to jail. . . . And that's the danger of throwing any baby to the wolves, is you always make the wolves more hungry and prove to them that you've got some more babies."

Two weeks later, on April 13, 1973, with his own firing of Haldeman and Ehrlichman scarcely two weeks away, Nixon got his pronouns mixed up—a common problem—when he again felt for Haldeman and the rest of his aides: "...I feel for all these people. I'd like to do something to save them all, but there isn't a goddamn thing you can do, is there?"[12]

Information, while not a sufficient cause of good decision-making, is surely a necessary cause. Somewhere between information gathering and decision-making is interpretation. From these conversations recorded on Nixon's taping system, it becomes glaringly apparent that his twisted thinking would result in exactly the ill-fated decisions he made. Perhaps Janis had a point in emphasizing, "Sometimes the main trouble is that the chief executive manipulates his advisers to rubber-stamp his own ill-conceived proposals."

James B. Conant, former president of Harvard, commissioned a report in 1943 on the purposes of higher education in a free society. The report concluded, two years later, that there were four: to think clearly, to make sound judgments, to discriminate among values, and to communicate effectively. Each of the last three not only flowed from the first but became a criterion of the first. Thus, if one's decisions were flawed, it showed that thinking was not sufficiently clear. Good decisions, on the other hand, the best decisions—decisions that one could live with, that over the years proved to have been the best—resulted from clear thinking. It is here that the clarity of Nixon's thinking comes most into question. The decisions, or at least the biggest of his decisions, seemed fatally flawed. He was unwilling, if able, to engage experts in meaningful discussion of vital issues and emerge with the best answer: best not only because it drew upon varied opinions, but also because it was thus able to be implemented. Indeed, Nixon often announced his opinion at the outset of a discussion with his aides; thus he would prejudice the remaining discussion, turning it into what Janis, as we have noted, called "groupthink." Furthermore, Nixon was determined to take credit for the decision if it turned out well, and blame others if it didn't. Whatever the decision, the participants could count on Nixon not being "out-toughed" by other participants.

Nixon's decision-making was suspect even in the best of times. But under the pressure of the war turning sour, and of Watergate and his futile attempt to distance it from the White House, Nixon's decisions went from bad to worse. Increasingly, he took to barking out orders on impulse, regardless how ridiculous, or even dangerous, they might be. Some of his orders, derided by Ehrlichman as "I-am-the-President instructions," were outrageous. Once he ordered Secretary of State Rogers, for example, to fire everyone in the Laotian embassy, including the ambassador, by the end of the week. Fortunately, Rogers chose to ignore it, and Nixon later laughed at it. Another time Nixon snapped out an order to Ehrlichman to cut off all federal finding to the Massachusetts Institute of Technology (MIT). He made it clear. "Do it now. Do it today. There is no appeal. . . ." A couple of days later, Nixon checked with his domestic advisor. "What have you done about cutting off federal finding to MIT?" Ehrlichman: "Well, I haven't done anything about it." Nixon: "Well, I've been thinking about it; it's probably just as well." Increasingly, Nixon's top aides learned to sift his orders, especially those barked out on impulse, and withhold those posing a threat to him or to his administration.

Judge John Sirica, reviewing Watergate, wrote how amazed he was "to see how the White House staff cannibalized its own people to save the President." Before firing Ehrlichman, Nixon told him, "Whatever we say about Harry Truman, while it hurt him, a lot of people admired the old bastard for standing by [his] people who were guilty as hell and, damn it, I am that kind of person. I'm not one who is going to say, look, while this guy is under attack, I drop him."[13]

Within days Nixon did just what he said he'd not do, but, refusing to blame himself, he put the onus on two other aides, Kleindienst and Henry Petersen. In his diary he rationalized, "I had to fire my friends for things I myself was part of, things I could not accept as morally or legally wrong. . . . I was selfish enough about my own survival to want them to leave. . . . I had to do the right thing, no matter how painful it was."

Theodore White saw it differently, saw it in the light of a hubris that, like an infectious disease, started with Nixon and contaminated those who worked for him: ". . . stripped of power, they were what they had been in the beginning—the flotsam of politics, now left behind on the beach by the wave that had carried them so high, scavengers' trophies, their sadness gloated over by most of those who came to watch."

As it was, this thirty-seventh President of these United States managed to rack up no less than eighty-three individual counts of breaking the law in the bill of impeachment by Congress, only to wriggle through by resigning, then getting Ford to pardon him within a month.

Machiavelli, it seemed, had been born again in this American century. Yet even Machiavelli had counseled his Prince that the prudent prince was one who gave his aides full liberty to speak the truth. Furthermore, each advisor was "to see that the more freely he speaks, the more he will be acceptable."[14] Nixonism, it appears, trumped Machiavellianism.

CHAPTER 3

EXPANSION

There is no city in the civilized world which does not contain plenty of men capable of doing all that [Boss] Tweed did and more, if they got a chance. . . . He was undoubtedly an eminent man in his field, but he was not an eminently bad man. . . . He was produced by certain political conditions which grew into existence almost without the knowledge of the American public, and in which their eyes were only fairly opened by his rise and fall.

— E.L. Goodkin, "The Moral of Tweed's Career"

LYNDON JOHNSON

I was going to reach beyond my father. I would finish college; I would build great power and gain high office.

— LBJ, recounting his return home at sixteen from California.

No man ever became President who didn't want to be the best President the country ever had.

— LBJ, interview with Hugh Sidey.

Once Johnson started on one of his monologues, it was difficult to halt him. If one of the listeners interrupted, trying to pull him back to the business at hand, he would become enraged.

— Doris Kearns, on LBJ's Tuesday luncheon meetings.[1]

The Founders and Their Constitution

Once a president has sought advice for the problems and responsibilities devolving on his office, often deferring to the aides to whom he has delegated power, he typically redoubles his effort to expand his power. As Winton Blount, former postmaster general, expressed on September 21, 1974, the "history of the past thirty-five years has been one of Presidents constantly expanding their power, moving into this area and that, building bureaucracies to administer the power grabs, and then finding themselves with a bureaucratic establishment they couldn't control themselves."

Not satisfied with merely matching the accomplishments of his predecessors—and particularly his immediate predecessor—this president would outdo them. To do so he rationalized that he needed more power than granted under the Constitution and its subsequent interpretations. He stretched to the point of violating the traditional restraints on his presidential power, often by hyping, if not concocting, a national emergency. "National security" was the fig leaf Johnson used to cover his private lust for power. He was neither the first nor the last president to do so. Indeed, it was just those presidents who governed in times of war—Lincoln, Wilson, and FDR—who not only abused their power in their expansion of it—excluding Washington—but earned the highest marks as U.S. presidents. There can be great reward in expanding one's power, but not without great risk. It was Madison who, in 1788, maintained that "there are more instances of abridgment of the freedom of the people by gradual and silent encroachment of those in power, than by violent and sudden insurrection."

Arthur Hansen, president of Purdue University in the 1970s, said his greatest fear for democracy was the "nickeling" away of our freedoms, one by one, often without benefit of our knowledge, and, more frequently, our input. Speaking in Indianapolis in 1977, he cited as an example the sudden ruling by Congress stipulating that all luggage at airports must be searched for weapons before travelers could board. Here were encroachments on our mobility, our time, and our privacy—enacted without public consultation, to counter a recent wave of skyjackings The argument was not its necessity, nor the balance between sacrificing a bit more of these freedoms for safety in the air. It was, rather, that Congress rushed through a law without adequate input from the electorate. The deaths by skyjackings, hyped out of proportion when compared to travel by car, constituted a problem of "national security." And the public forfeited more of its precious freedoms.

It was just this hyping, even this concocting, of national emergencies by Johnson that enabled him to expand his power as few presidents before or since—with the singular exception of the other president in our focus: Richard Nixon. It was our first Chief Justice, John Marshall, who maintained that the Constitution was "intended to endure for ages to come, and consequently to be adapted to the various crises of human affairs." Having won independence from Britain, the Founders faced the almost insuperable task of uniting thirteen disparate colonies, each zealously protective of its sovereignty, into a single nation. Like the Greek city-states of antiquity, the colonists had great trouble forgetting they were, first and foremost,

Virginians, Rhode Islanders, and Georgians, and realizing they were a new breed, Americans. Britain took advantage of our remaining divisions to exploit us, impressing our seamen into its navy, leading to the War of 1812 and the torching of Washington.

The British could burn the nation's capital, but they couldn't destroy the Constitution, nor the spirit of independence that gave it birth. The Constitution stipulated a division of powers specifically between the legislative and the executive, those who make and those who execute the laws. As for domestic policy, the division seemed clear enough. Teddy Roosevelt discovered this in expanding his power to become a trustbuster. His niece's husband, FDR, also discovered this when he expanded his power to moderate the ravages of the Great Depression. But, as Arthur Schlesinger observed, it was in foreign policy that the Constitution appeared "cryptic, ambiguous and incomplete." As a result, presidents, notably Johnson and Nixon, relied on foreign policy to expand their powers, in sharp contrast with Washington, who cautioned against "entangling alliances."

Indeed, Washington remains "first in the hearts of his countrymen" not only because he commanded the armies that made possible our independence, but because he helped forge a union not as a king, whom he displaced—nor as a president-for-life, which he rejected—but as a citizen-president only too eager to return to his beloved Mount Vernon. In this, he refused to follow in the footsteps of other victorious generals throughout history who had become dictators. The powers of the chief executive, Washington noted, were more definite and better understood than perhaps those of any other nation. He and the other drafters of the Constitution had made certain of that. So repelled was he at the thought of leading the country in peace as he had in war that, upon learning he'd been unanimously elected President in 1789, Washington lamented that this was "the event which I have long dreaded." He greeted the news with "a heart filled with distress," foreseeing "the 10,000 embarrassments, perplexities, and troubles to which I must again be exposed." Washington well understood that, however difficult it was to rally his hungry, freezing troops at Valley Forge and press on to victory, it would be ever so much more difficult to rally his countrymen to forge out of thirteen colonies a single, united nation. There were no such qualms for either Johnson or Nixon as they aspired to—no, lusted for—office, so much so that they would say anything, do anything, to enter the White House. And once there, they would invoke "national security" to perpetrate abuses of power that, generations later, will continue to echo and re-echo in the halls of history.

By contrast, Washington, in his farewell address, cautioned that, while extending our commerce with other nations, we should "have with them as little political connection as possible." To implement that, he and the other Founding Fathers authorized Congress, not the president, "to regulate commerce with foreign nations." In addition, to further circumscribe the powers of the president, Congress was given the exclusive right to declare war and to make treaties, prerogatives that in Europe only monarchs had exercised.[2]

It was not, Schlesinger has noted, that the Founders wanted to hobble the president so he'd be unable to respond quickly to external attack. They did recognize that the occasion might arise where the president, as commander in chief, must leap to the defense of the nation without pressing his case before Congress and awaiting a formal declaration of war. As a matter of fact, the Constitution is silent on the role of the president in making war. Once Congress did declare war, it was then up to the president—with no more power, Schlesinger has insisted, than a top Army general or Navy admiral—to conduct that war. To further circumscribe the president's war-making powers, the Constitution stipulated that Congress was not to authorize appropriations for the armed forces for more than two years.

The result of this judicious balancing of legislative with executive power was, as Edward S. Corwin noted, "an invitation to struggle for the privilege of directing foreign policy." In light of the centrality of the Vietnam War in the administrations of both Johnson and Nixon, it is significant that nowhere does the Constitution define a national emergency serious enough to warrant a president circumventing the Constitution. This in itself would appear remarkable, considering that the Founders had survived a wrenching emergency in cutting our umbilical cord with the "mother country." Perhaps Schlesinger is right in maintaining that crises might occur, sufficiently serious to warrant a president sidestepping the Constitution—as did Lincoln—to save the nation.

So wary were the Founders of concentrating excessive power in one man that Alexander White, a member of the First Congress, argued that the president should have the right "to extend his power on some extraordinary occasion, even when he is not strictly justified by the Constitution, than [that] the legislature should grant him an improper power to be exercised at all times." The significance of this mistrust of power concentrated in a single individual is highlighted by its stark contrast with the utopia of Marx and Lenin, in which they anticipated that the powers vested in the state—and its leaders—would simply "wither away" and usher in a utopian Communism in which all would give according to their ability and take according to their need. Indeed, the "Founding Fathers" of Communism were so intent on uniting "workers of the world" and throwing off the oppressive yoke of the capitalists that they entertained an unbelievable naiveté when it came to vesting power in the state—albeit a temporary one—and its leaders. Not so Washington, Jefferson, Adams, Madison and others of our nation's Founders. It is perhaps no exaggeration to contend that it was just these opposing views toward power concentrated in a single leader that, more than anything else, accounts for the implosion of Communism in the Soviet Union and, by contrast, the continual thriving of Constitutional democracy in this country.

Our democracy continues to thrive despite the usurpation of power by various presidents, and particularly by Johnson's wresting of the power to engage in war, which was granted him by Congress in 1964 through the Gulf of Tonkin Resolution. Not to be rescinded for seven years, it gave license to both Johnson and Nixon to wage war "by tantrum," as some charged, and by deception, as most came to see. It was not so much to frighten the enemy as to deceive the American people. As later chapters on coercion and deception will explore, this abuse of power almost brought the country to its knees. We have come to realize, as Emmett Hughes has written, that "the opportunities for creating a 'mess' in Washington are so unlimited, the chances to make bad matters worse are so inexhaustible, that no administration should ever underestimate its capacity to surpass the folly of its predecessors."

Complexity

One biographer after another marveled at the seemingly infinite complexity of Lyndon Baines Johnson. In 1937 there was "Mr. Johnson goes to Washington," wide-eyed and starstruck, even after serving as a congressional secretary for several years. But by 1963 this President, a seasoned pol, knew the ins and outs of the nation's capital as few did. When he took the oath of office aboard Air Force One in Dallas, the world doubted that he would ever be able to fill the shoes of JFK. Before long, however, the Washington grapevine was abuzz with wonderment. How could so many different people all fit into Johnson's shoes? How could this hulking Texan walk into a room—any room—and dominate it, regardless of who and how many were there? Meeting him for the first time in 1967, Kissinger was "impressed," as he later wrote, "and oddly touched by this hulking, powerful man, so domineering and yet so insecure, so overwhelming and yet so vulnerable."

"Under Kennedy it used to be ideas," one columnist's wife explained. Under Johnson, by contrast, it was LBJ's personality that was the subject of gossip. "Indeed, Washington seemed obsessed by its President," wrote one reporter. Whether diplomats, administrators, or journalists, all appeared to have discovered in the oversized Texan a walking oxymoron. Kearns wrote that Johnson was "a mixture of primitive conduct with the exercise of imperial power, the commingling of cruelty and compassion, the suggestion of a wildness not fully tamed." Merle Miller described Johnson as "one of the most complex, fascinating, difficult, colorful personages in American history."[3] Here was a human kaleidoscope. Turn him ever so slightly. Catch him an hour—even a few minutes—later, and you see a different person. It was as though he were a victim of multiple personality disorder—thirty, fifty, one hundred different men wrapped in the same skin. Wilbur Cohen saw in Johnson a man of such manifold dimensions that it was impossible to put a verbal lasso on him. One moment, at the Ranch, Lyndon would be describing to Cohen and to John W. Gardner, Assistant and Secretary of HEW respectively, and both refined intellectuals, how he bred cattle, in the most lurid and graphic language. The next moment he'd have stopped his Lincoln convertible on a hilltop, leaned back, and described in what Cohen called "really pure poetry," the East Texas Hill Country, the setting sun, together with his hopes and dreams for the American people. Cohen concluded that Johnson consisted of the unlikely "combination of Boccaccio, Machiavelli and John Keats."

As for Press Secretary George Reedy, he saw Johnson as Pirandello, the playwright "who would leave you with the most baffled wonderment as to whether the whole thing was a figment of somebody's imagination, whether there really was a King, or whether he was just a demented lunatic. . . ."

John Connally, no simple pol himself, figured "it would take every adjective in the dictionary to describe" his fellow Texan. Johnson, he said, was, at turns, "cruel and kind, generous and greedy, sensitive and insensitive, crafty and naive, ruthless and thoughtful, simple in many ways yet extremely complex." Here was one who "could overwhelm people with kindness and turn around and be cruel and petty towards those same people." In fact, testified Richard Neustadt, special consultant to LBJ, his boss seemed to share with his mentor, FDR, "a streak of cruelty . . . of just liking to pull the wings off flies."

There were few that LBJ enjoyed tormenting more than his own Vice-President. Yet Hubert Humphrey defended him, describing him as "an all-American President." Humphrey explained: "He was really the history of this country, with all of the turmoil, the bombast, the sentiments, the passions. It was all there, all in one man. . . . Every time you saw him it was like seeing an institution. . . . Johnson thought he could pick up the globe and walk off with it." That he didn't do it was not because he didn't try.

Ambition

In Lyndon's lunge for power there were many factors playing their parts. Jealously he guarded the persona of a Texas Hill Country populist, cut from the same cloth as FDR, but bigger, brighter, and more ambitious. Ambition is the first factor we shall consider in expansion. So daunting is the president's task —and so towering the ego of a person simply to run for president—that in 1846 Zachary Taylor wrote to run "seems too visionary to require a serious answer. Such an idea never entered my head, nor is it likely to enter the head of any sane person."[4] Apparently Taylor had a change of mind, if not of sanity, for he ran and won, only to leave, at best, a lackluster record.

As far as ambition was concerned, there was no shortage in Johnson. Editorializing in his college newspaper, he asked, "What is it that makes a real man?" His answer: "Ambition." Where Sam had failed Rebekah, and left the family in poverty, Lyndon was resolute after once letting his mother down: "She would never be disappointed in me again." It was Rebekah who planted the seeds of ambition in her eldest. Much of it fell on the barren ground of an incorrigible adolescent. But a stay in California followed by a sweltering summer on a Texas highway crew, convinced Lyndon that this was not the way to get ahead in life. So he finally gave in to his mother and went to college. Her imprint was undoubtedly the single greatest influence on his life, prompting him in later years to recall her as "the most beautiful, sexy, intelligent woman, and I was determined to recapture her wonderful love." From college he wrote her several times a week, in one letter paying more than ample tribute to her influence. "There is no force that exerts the power over me that your letters do . . . I have been thinking of you all afternoon . . .I love you so much." No less effusive were her letters to her son. "My darling boy," she wrote in 1937, "Your election [to] Congress compensates for the heartache and disappointment I experienced as a child when my dear father lost the race you just won. You have always justified my expectations, my hopes, my dreams. How dear you are you cannot know, my darling boy, my strength and comfort."[5] Here, in what is surely an unusual relationship between mother and son, lies one important wellspring in Lyndon's lofty ambition. Well-born, well-educated, an oasis in this desert of scrub-brush poverty, Rebekah was convinced she'd married beneath her station, and determined that her first-born would fulfill the ambitions she'd seen unfulfilled in her husband.

Sam, too, not only stoked the fires of ambition in his son's belly, but made sure Lyndon knew everything he knew about politics. Beyond that, Sam interceded with President Evans at San Marcos to get Lyndon accepted in college. After his son's graduation, Sam interceded with newly-elected Congressman Richard Kleberg so that Lyndon could go off to Washington to serve as Kleberg's secretary. There Sam Rayburn, remembering that he and Sam Johnson had served in the Texas state legislature together, took Lyndon under his wing, becoming the boy's father away from home.

It is clear then that Sam Johnson not only stoked the fires of ambition in his son and pointed him in the direction of politics, but opened doors along the way. It is equally clear that Lyndon did not pause before entering, nor tiptoe through those open doors. He bounded through them, including those opened by his surrogate fathers: Rayburn, Russell and FDR. By the time he was Majority Leader in 1960, Johnson had his eyes on the prize—the White House itself. Defeated at the convention by Kennedy, he took second place, perhaps with the same strategy he'd used in setting new records for passing legislation: compromise if need be, for half a loaf was better than none, and eventually you might end up with the full loaf.

The "full loaf" was attained on November 22, 1963, when Lyndon was suddenly thrust into the presidency. Within hours he was laying plans for earning the top spot on his own in 1964. Using the phone on Air Force One, within a half-hour of its leaving Dallas for Washington, Lyndon offered consolation to Rose Kennedy and encouragement to Nellie, wife of Texas Governor John Connally, who had been wounded by the assassin. Returning to his old office, LBJ put in a call to Eisenhower before meeting with the leaders of Congress. Ike had already left him a message suggesting that he meet with a joint session of Congress as soon as possible—a meeting that should be televised to the distraught nation. He must calm the waters and assure the electorate that he would maintain continuity. Beyond that, Lyndon deferred to Ike: "I've needed you for a long time, but I need you more than ever now. . . . I am going to rely on your good, sound judgment and will be calling on you, but I wanted you to know how touched I was by your message." Confident that Eisenhower would support him as he—Majority Leader of the opposition Democrats during the fifties—had supported Ike, Johnson met with Congressional leaders, then was back on the phone again, placing two important calls. The first was to Supreme Court Justice Arthur Goldberg: "I want you to be thinking about what I ought to do to try to bring all these elements together and unite the country. . . ." Johnson needed help in preparing his message for the Congress. But his next call showed he was looking beyond that, indeed a year beyond that, when he could win the top spot for himself and not have to ride in on Kennedy coattails. This call was to Richard Maguire, Democratic National Committee treasurer and chief fund-raiser for JFK in 1960. Johnson: "I want to rely on you more than he did . . . I've been on your team since I got here. . . . You've got to be candid and frank and come in and tell me what we need to do and how we need to do it."

There was never any question but that Johnson, from day one, felt more than equal to the task, despite his conscientious self-deprecation to Goldberg: "I'm totally inadequate, but I'll do my best. . . ." Sympathy had given way to deference and deference to ambition. Lyndon was far more surefooted than he let on.

The next day, Saturday, Johnson was pumping the phone with FBI

Director J. Edgar Hoover, with Senate Minority Leader Everett Dirksen, with old friend Senator George Smathers, with House Speaker John McCormack, with National Security Advisor McGeorge Bundy, and finally with Senator Edward Kennedy. His closing statement to the slain President's youngest brother was significant, because LBJ was determined to get all his ducks in a row for a run that would put to rest the rumors that he was but an "accidental" President: "Know that God Almighty in His wisdom works in mysterious ways. . . ."[6] If there was anyone he wanted on his side, it was the Almighty. At least, that's what he wanted others to think. Perhaps he should have been more circumspect with the admonition, "Be careful what you pray for lest your prayers be answered."

Energy

Yet another factor in Johnson's expansion of every position he filled was his seemingly inexhaustible energy. The whirlwind that swept Lady Bird off her feet toward the altar had already been going full steam ahead for years. It was always just a question of whether his arms, his legs, or his tongue would win the race. Given a job to assist President Evans at San Marcos College, Lyndon threw himself into his work with such abandon that Evans finally exclaimed, "Lyndon, I declare you hadn't been in my office a month before I could hardly tell who was the president of the school—you or me."

Taking a year out of college to teach Mexican students in Cotulla, Texas, he was determined to impress the district superintendent. Lyndon was always the first to arrive in the morning, and the last to leave at night. And in those twelve hours he did his best to defy the laws of physics by functioning as a perpetual-motion machine. "He walked so fast," recalled the dry cleaner who patched his clothes, that "it was like seeing a blur." At Sam Houston High School in Houston, where he taught after college, colleagues and students remembered him as "a steam engine in pants," as he bolted through the corridors from class to class, defying anybody to keep up. Told the school had never won the city debating championship, "Bull" Johnson saw this as a red flag. He would not only charge it, but claim it, he assured the principal. Furthermore, he needed more money so the debate team could engage in competition with other cities. "But this has never been done," objected the principal. "But you've never had a teacher like me," countered Johnson. And who could argue with that?

Arriving in Washington in 1931 to work for Kleberg, Lyndon was prowling the corridors of the Dodge Hotel before unpacking his suitcase, "knocking on doors, shaking hands, and telling each person his life history and future plans." That night he took no less than four showers in the only bathroom on his floor in order to talk with as many of the seventy-five other congressional secretaries as possible. The next morning he invaded the bathroom five times, at ten-minute intervals, to catch those he'd missed the night before.

Enlisting two fellow secretaries to help him, Lyndon managed—with the three of them putting in eighteen-hour days, seven days a week—to get Kleberg's office up and running in less than three weeks. Within a few months, another secretary recalled, "this skinny boy . . . as green as anybody could be . . . knew how to operate in Washington better than some who had been here twenty years."[7]

By 1934, Lyndon was directing scores of men as head of the Texas National Youth Administration. At twenty-six, Johnson was the youngest director in the nation—and he was soon the most productive. Hitting on the idea of employing young people to build roadside parks, the first in Texas, Lyndon was up, up and away, working "like a crazy man," said sidekick Luther Jones. "He just worked night and day; he just worked his staff to distraction." Within two years 135 parks were under construction by 3,600 youths. Other jobs, including school walks to keep children out of the road, trimming back roadside trees and shrubs to improve visibility, filling in the gullies caused by erosion that lined Texas highways, building drainage ditches to prevent further erosion—these and other similar tasks occupied the remainder of the 12,000 jobs the NYA mandated for the state. Of the first twenty-six men he appointed to administrative posts, nineteen were, like Lyndon, in their twenties. Good thing, for they needed all the energy youth could provide to keep up with their boss. "If he wanted you to bring him a letter, he'd be edgy until you brought it." "Sometimes he'd not wait, but bound out of his desk chair," recalled one, "lunge across the room and out the door and almost run, with that awkward arms-akimbo stride" to fetch it himself. Lyndon not only walked double-time, he dictated double-time, striding about the room, "acting out the letter, gesticulating with his long arms, jabbing with his forefinger, as if making a speech."

And if a particular word or phrase eluded him, he'd wave his arms in a frenzy of frustration. Each letter of the thousands he got—from mayors, county commissioners, school board presidents, college deans, high school principals, students, state and federal officials—was not only to be answered, but answered that very day. When it wasn't, or when any one of the hundred other tasks he supervised wasn't completed on time, he'd fly into a rage. "God," recounted one aide, "he could rip a man up and down." The aide recalled Sherman Birdwell, soft-spoken, sweet-tempered, "the gentlest man who ever lived," cowering under the lash of Johnson's tongue as he battered away without mercy. With such commitment and energy, it is little wonder that, by the end of 1936, Johnson had put to work not the 12,000 quota assigned him, but 20,000.

As 1936 became 1937, Johnson might well have said, "You ain't seen nothin' yet!" For that was the year he ran, against seven others, for the congressional seat of the deceased James "Buck" Buchanan. Lyndon drove himself as he drove others, to the point of exhaustion. LBJ's biographer, Robert A. Caro, claims that the insecurity and shame of growing up in hardscrabble Hill Country was Johnson's motivation for grasping "frantically at every chance, no matter how slender, to escape that past." What others called energy Caro labeled "desperation and fear." Surely there was this, too, behind Lyndon's fantastic efforts to seize the nomination and the seat in Congress. Typical of his determination to see every voter, to miss no one in his own Hill Country, was the evening recalled forty years later by one aide. Already headed to Austin at the end of a grueling day, Lyndon suddenly remembered a particular farmer he'd overlooked. No matter how close to Austin they were, no matter how dark it had gotten, no matter how exhausted or hungry they were, Lyndon turned the car around and headed back, back, far back up a rutted, country road to a lone farmhouse—and there, by the glow of a kerosene lamp, he grasped the farmer's hand, confident he'd sealed another bargain at the voting booth.

It was inevitable that such desperate, frantic activity would take its toll on the "Chief," as his aides called Lyndon. Returning to Austin, they saw a scraggly beanpole, skinnier than ever, his shirt collar gaping around his neck, and his suit drooping over his shoulders. His pale white complexion had turned a sickly gray, his eyes looked like coals of fire in their deep-sunken sockets, his smooth cheeks had given way to harsh lines, while his ears flapped bigger than ever on either side of his gaunt, hollow face.

There were the telltale effects of nicotine on the man who'd light one cigarette from the other, and his fingers, stained yellow, were raw and red
where he'd torn at his cuticles. Some forty years later, Ed Clark, Texas
Secretary of State and chief political advisor to Governor James Allred in
1937, recalled, "I never saw anyone campaign as hard as that. I never
thought it was possible for anyone to work that hard."

By the last week or two of the campaign, Lyndon was eating little and
sleeping less, his voice alternating between shrill and hoarse, his mind giving way to paranoia. Those who attacked FDR were no longer simply "in
the dark" but "back-stabbers." Two days before the election, he awoke in
Austin in the grip of pain and nausea. Speaking to four hundred, the
largest audience so far, Johnson was holding on to the platform rail for
support when he suddenly doubled over, turned ash-white and sat, his
arms across his stomach. Told by some members of the audience that he
must have appendicitis, Johnson waved away his "instant physicians,"
stood again, apologized for the interruption, and finished. Standing as
well-wishers filed by, he was wet with perspiration. Then he turned to
Sherman Birdwell, "I'm sick. Stand here beside me." He sat again, and
couldn't get back up. Finally, Lyndon was taken to Seton Hospital, where
he learned he'd almost died from an appendix on the verge of bursting. He
was in bed there when he learned that he'd beaten his nearest opponent by
three thousand votes. Johnson had made it to Congress—just barely.

This was to be the pattern for subsequent campaigns, with nicotine
and alcohol providing the anesthetic he desperately needed to withstand the exhaustion. Trouble was, these were becoming addictions, a
lifestyle which, combined with eating and sleeping in fits and starts and
exercising even less made Johnson an accident waiting to happen. As
Rayburn put it, "Lyndon behaves as if there were no tomorrow coming
and he had to do everything today." Bounding from one appointment to
the next in a long, loping stride, Johnson soon became known for the
"LBJ Trot." When a friend was told that Lyndon would go whichever
way the wind blew, he replied, "Maybe, but if he does, he'll probably
beat the wind there."[8]

Not surprisingly, in 1955 Lyndon was stricken with a heart attack. He
came within whispering distance of the Grim Reaper as his blood pressure
dropped to zero and doctors were almost ready to give him up for dead.
So frightened was the Senate Majority Leader that he gave up smoking

and went on a strict diet—that is, until he became Vice-President. Forced to stoke the fire in his belly as he played second fiddle to Kennedy, Johnson was soon chain-smoking again, drinking more than ever, and gaining so much weight that he resorted to wearing a girdle.

By the time the 1964 campaign was in full swing, he was giving twenty speeches in a single day, and the White House resembled nothing so much as a racetrack. As George Reedy put it, "The White House [was] an indoor stadium hosting a perpetual track meet. The halls were scenes for sprint after sprint as fleet-footed messengers dashed to bring the latest bulletin or memo to their supervisors and sometimes to the chief himself." When it came to legislation, Johnson was among the superstitious, Reedy maintained, believing that "for every social ailment there is a self-enacting legislative nostrum." Thus: "Were people poor? Declare 'war on poverty!' Were people ignorant? Declare 'war on illiteracy!' Were people racist? Declare 'war on prejudice!'" As a result, there flowed from Congress—which Johnson knew better than any president before or since—a cascade of legislation in which he took great delight signing into law, with appropriate fanfare and distribution of copious signing pens.[9]

As President, further bouts of illness—kidney stones, gall bladder, bronchitis, and the removal of nodules from his vocal folds—should have reminded LBJ that he, too, was mortal. Finally, in 1973, his heart gave out at the age of sixty-five. Running full throttle from Cotulla in 1928 until he returned to his Ranch in 1969—a period of forty-one years in which he abused his body and mind as few if any presidents—the big engine from Texas finally ran out of steam. But for four decades, energy—boisterous, expansive, frenetic energy—had served to expand every position Lyndon ever occupied.

Intelligence

In addition to energy, expansion requires intelligence, and political expansion requires political intelligence. Wilson acknowledged that in public affairs, it was stupidity that was "more dangerous than knowing, because harder to fight and dislodge." Stupidity, as Paul Tabori has elaborated, is not to be confused with idiocy or mental derangement. Rather, it is the result of laziness, of one's refusal to use perfectly normal mental abilities to solve one's problems. Tabori sounded an ominous note in warning that "stupidity is man's deadliest weapon, his most devastating epidemic, his costliest luxury. . . . We have paid for our own stupidity since the beginning of the world, and we shall go on paying until we have blasted all life off the surface of the earth. . . ." It is revealing that the lion's share of Tabori's book, *The Natural Science of Stupidity*, is devoted to law and politics.

What Tabori called stupidity, Barbara Tuchman called folly. Again, it is revealing that the subtitle of her book *The March of Folly* is *From Troy to Vietnam*. Furthermore, the folly of Vietnam is the longest of its five chapters. More significantly, that chapter centers on the person of Lyndon Johnson. Yes, his predecessors—Kennedy, Eisenhower, and Truman—had laid the groundwork. But it was Johnson who, in four years, took 17,000 "advisers" in Vietnam and multiplied them to 550,000. That it was "their war"—the Vietnamese's—was iterated and reiterated by Ike, by Kennedy, and even by Johnson. But that didn't prevent LBJ from co-opting it, brushing the South Vietnamese aside and showing Hanoi—and the world—that America was a colossus, straddling the globe as the world's policeman. Unlike his father, Lyndon was, in the words of Tuchman, "forceful and domineering, a man infatuated with himself. . . ." This Narcissus-in-the-flesh was determined as he vowed, "I am not going to lose Vietnam. I am not going to be the President who saw Southeast Asia go the way China went." As leery as he was of criticism by the liberal left, LBJ was far more concerned with criticism from the conservative right. For there he saw his manhood, his Texas machismo, at stake.[10]

Central in Johnson's thinking, as Sidey has taken pains to emphasize, was the Texan's devotion to the Alamo, what Professor Joe Frantz of the University of Texas has called "the Lexington and Concord west of the Mississippi. It is tragic and enduring, and above all what Lyndon Johnson knows." Again and again it was the star by which Johnson steered his ship of state. Colonel William Travis, commander of the fort, vowed, "I shall never surrender or retreat." Johnson: "There does come a time when men must stand." It was Travis, Davy Crockett, Sam Houston, and Jim Bowie who, heroes of the Alamo, were emblazoned on the minds of every schoolchild in the Lone Star state. As Kitty Clyde Leonard, a high school sweetheart of Johnson's, recalled: "When we studied the Alamo it was the heroes who were impressed upon our minds. Heroes who were willing to fight for liberty. They stayed rather than retreated. Hard, strong, sturdy, patriotic men, willing to die for what they believed."

Johnson, dispatching troops to Vietnam in his 1965 escalation, reasoned, "It's just like the Alamo. Somebody damn well needed to go to their aid. Well, by God, I'm going to Vietnam's aid and I thank the Lord that I've got the men who will go with me." Decorating men under fire at the DMZ or learning of Marines digging in at Khe Sanh, he remarked. "It's another Alamo." He urged equal rights by pointing out a Negro who died there. Just as Travis and Bowie tried negotiating with Santa Anna before resolving to fight to the bitter end, LBJ, after sensing a rebuff from Ho Chi Minh, resolved never to surrender. Here, Sidey concluded, was Johnson's tragedy: his conviction that the only honorable course was to stand and fight—just as his great-great-grandfather had done at the Alamo, he told troops at Korea's Camp Stanley.

In this hailing of the Alamo as his lodestar, Johnson was less than honest, less than courageous, and less than intelligent. In the first place, he fibbed about his ancestor fighting and dying at the Alamo. There is no Johnson precursor listed on the roster of those in that siege. In the second place, Johnson's courage, through his youth and his six months in the Navy, was scarcely stellar. And in the third place, the battle of the Alamo was as senseless as it was hopeless—just as Vietnam proved to be for the embattled Johnson.

The vow Johnson made encapsulated the ignorance, the stupidity, the folly of the man and several of his predecessors, in their policy toward Vietnam. Was Vietnam or China even ours to lose? No, that was simply Cold War rhetoric, embracing a phenomenal presumption: that certain nations were ours to "lose" if they aligned themselves with Communism rather than capitalism. Thus, when Chiang Kai-shek or any other of a dozen dictators we supported, called their nations "free" versus the "slave" nations of Communism, we set the stage for the likes of Lyndon Johnson. In addition, his vow illustrated the camel-in-the-tent fallacy: that, as the Arabs say, if you let a camel put his nose inside your tent, soon he will be in and you will be out. Here was the essence of the domino theory. Knock over Vietnam and the other nations of Southeast Asia will topple like dominoes in a row. Here, too, was false analogy, assuming that those nations were lined up like dominoes. The fact that Vietnam did fall to the Communists, without taking the other nations in the region with it, has shown just how specious the analogy was.

What we have here, in Johnson and his predecessors who set the stage for him—notably Eisenhower and his Secretary of State John Foster Dulles—is the simplistic thinking that exacerbates rather than solves problems. For if we define a simplistic solution to a problem as one less complex than the problem itself, we realize that any adequate solution must be based on as thorough an understanding of the problem as we can muster. Barring that, we can be certain we shall make matters worse. But conceding that, it is surprising how close to an effective solution we are. As we shall explore further in the chapter on coercion, Johnson's determination to stay the course—despite its carrying the nation into the quicksands of Vietnam—was a monumental mistake, born, in part, of simplistic thinking.

From boyhood, Johnson had focused on but one subject: politics. In that hyperspecialization he had become victim of José Ortega y Gasset's "Barbarism of Specialization." He knew more of the ins and outs of politics than probably anyone in his day. But that was it. Of other subjects he knew little because he cared little. As a result, he lacked the perspective a well-rounded education could provide—a perspective absolutely vital to the task of being President. This the press came to understand. Scarcely three weeks into the presidency, Johnson, having addressed the U.N., urged George Ball ". . . to feed some of that [reactions from U.N. Ambassador Adlai Stevenson] out through your press thing because you've got to get this country-hick, tobacco-chewing Southerner [himself] off of you and get in there with you intellectuals, you know." Another three weeks and Lyndon—the echoes of "Uncle Cornpone" jibes from his vice-presidency still ringing in his ears—lowered the boom on his resident intellectuals. To Mac Bundy, National Security Advisor, he complained, "Now you-all are supposed to be a brains group and have a lot of imagination . . . I've been in government six weeks and I've just had people tell me what I couldn't do . . . go around and think and be some wise men and see if you can't come up with some proposals besides just having him [Khrushchev] run me in a corner and me dodge. . . ." In point of fact, Johnson continued "I am tired, by God, of having him be the man who wants peace and I am the guy who wants war. And I'm just a big, fat slob that they throw a dagger into and I bleed and squirm just like a Mexican bullfighter." Again Johnson pressed: "I would like to have something fresh . . . that I would at least like to massage my brain with." In agreeing with Jefferson, albeit unknowingly, that "forty years of experience in government is worth a century of book learning," Lyndon seemed blissfully ignorant of the fact that Jefferson himself was an insatiable reader. So was JFK, devouring one book after another at a 1,200 word-per-minute clip and, presumably, at a high rate of comprehension. From this steady diet of reading, from his education at Harvard, and from many and lengthy discussions with family and friends, Kennedy grasped, as Theodore White put it, his "greatest single weapon for combating a recalcitrant Congress at home and a growing Communist menace abroad." That weapon was the mighty power of reason. It also helped him with two historic problems: "how to bring thinking and intelligent men to power, and . . . how to enable power to impose a reasonable discipline on action."[11]

After four years at Southwest State Teachers College in San Marcos, meeting what standards there were, Lyndon left no record of which he or his parents could be proud. Though he bragged of earning thirty-five A's in the forty courses he took, it turned out to be but eight A's in fifty-six courses—with more C's than A's—leaving him, at best, an average student. Without his pull with Evans, one is left to wonder if he would have scored even that high. What record he did manage to leave was that of "Bull" Johnson, the motor-mouth who could hardly interrupt himself to take a breath, the obnoxious braggart who, instead of studying his lessons, studied Evans and others in power to figure out how he could ingratiate himself with them.

His moving into 1600 Pennsylvania Avenue, America's most prestigious address, counted for something, including a stable of smart speech writers. But, left on his own, he reverted to Hill Country language . "It won't do no good," was the way he put it to Russell Long, chairman of the Senate Finance Committee, who had resisted one of LBJ's suggestions. Told that the Senate was dragging its feet in approving Johnson's appointment of Abe Fortas as Chief Justice, Lyndon complained to Califano, "If they get this thing drug out for very long. . . ." To Hoover, Lyndon vowed, ". . . there ain't nobody here who's gonna take over anything from you as long as I'm living. Ain't nobody gonna take our thirty-year friendship and mess it up one bit." To Bundy he put the question, "Wouldn't it be good for he [Undersecretary of State Geoge Ball] and McNamara to sit down?"[12] It became glaringly apparent that where the Kennedy brothers, the Bundy brothers, Califano, Rusk, and Galbraith had been playing Chopin at Harvard, Johnson had been banging out "Chopsticks" at San Marcos.

Learning of rumors that he was allergic to books, LBJ instructed his aides to "correct" the grapevine. He was indeed into books. What, asked inquisitive reporters from time to time, was the President reading? Each time the response was Barbara Ward's *Rich Nations, Poor Nations*, a palliative for his second thoughts about escalating the war. In 1967 he stood before the leaders of Congress with, of all things, a book in his hand. It was Bruce Catton's *Never Call Retreat*, an account of the Civil War. Just the other night, he said, he'd run across a passage he thought would stiffen their spines on Vietnam. He proceeded to read to them, satisfied they'd realize he was no illiterate. Come to find out, Lyndon was something less than met the eye or the ear. For earlier that very day Bobby Kennedy, his nemesis, had handed him the copy, a page marked for his attention.

Johnson's alienation from those who made up the nation's intelligentsia was largely due to his being the very antithesis of what a higher education stood for. There was nothing in the report of the Conant Commission—a panel, chaired by Harvard President James Conant that had investigated American educational practices—about training for vocational skills. Nothing about preparing to be tax-paying citizens. It was the nurturing of the mind that counted, and practical results would follow. With none of the functions of higher education in a free society did Johnson appear familiar. Indeed, it was this very lack that contributed to his plunging the nation into the war in Vietnam.

It wasn't simply the swagger in Lyndon's walk and talk. And it wasn't just his repugnant sycophancy before those he needed to manipulate. Nor was it only the bullying of aides or those who opposed him on Vietnam. It was all these and more. Especially was it his desperate attempt to cut others down to size—to puncture what he regarded as their balloons of pretension. If Gordon Allport in his *Nature of Prejudice* was right in rooting prejudice in insecurity, then it may well be that Lyndon engaged in secret self-loathing.

In Johnson's overseas trips he took special pride in setting the "striped-pants set" back on their heels as he made a mockery of protocol. Arriving at one airport after another with several planes and hundreds of people accompanying him, the natives could be forgiven for thinking they were being invaded. An advance force would lay out the preparations and a follow-up force would clean up after them—the latter almost always having to apologize profusely for Lyndon's lunacy.

LBJ's disregard for protocol became legendary. He thought nothing of striding past an honor guard without a hint of recognition, much less inspection. Scheduled for a round of meetings, he was invariably late, leaving his ambassadors and aides chewing their nails, pacing the floor. When he finally did make his appearance, he dismissed any thought of small talk to break the ice, plowing in directly to the point and offending the host nation. He was a sight to behold at a formal dinner-dance-reception. Hogging the limelight, his voice sailing above the others, he'd regale his dinner companions with titillating stories, windmilling his long arms to the point that waiters could not serve him. Served at last and comparing his portions with those of his neighbors, he would pluck some tender morsel from a nearby plate. Dinner over, he would sally forth to the dance floor, there to corner the most attractive of the diplomats' wives and give them a taste of his legendary "treatment" as he danced. If a visit to a cemetery was scheduled, Lyndon could be found walking over the graves. In these and other ways, as imaginative as they were coarse, this Texas longhorn was out to tell the world nobody—but nobody—could put a lasso on him.[13]

Having done his best to bridge the chasm between the President and the intelligentsia, White House advisor Eric Goldman soon headed back to the halls of his beloved Princeton. Just how alien was Johnson from the life of the intellectual was emphasized by journalist Tom Wicker in 1967. Gathering a panel of eggheads around him, Johnson asked why he didn't get along with them and their fellow intellectuals. To his guests, the answer was obvious: the root of the alienation lay in Johnson's inability to think like an intellectual; neither could the intellectual empathize with Johnson's way of thinking. "The intellectual," Wicker explained, "may not possess superior intelligence or an endowed chair or even unusual learning; rather he is distinguished by a particular turn of mind—questing, challenging, skeptical, analytical, toughly fired. He thinks for himself. His impulse is to reason." What Johnson meant by "reasoning together" was not what intellectuals meant. More often than not, Johnson meant, if not imposing his own point of view on another, at least moving another closer to his viewpoint so as to effect a compromise.

It was this, Wicker concluded, that was the root cause of the alienation. Like other presidents, Johnson found time of the essence in his decision-making. He simply couldn't afford the luxury of sitting by the hour and analyzing the various options available. It was in life-and-death emergencies such as war produced that time became the tyrant, forcing hurried solutions. As McNamara put it, "We didn't do with tactical bombing what we did with the test ban treaty. If you're dealing with intelligent, honest people and can get them around a table, tear the arguments apart; if you take enough time . . . but it takes a hell of a lot of time." Quickly moving to the "right" answer for a given problem—all others being "wrong"—LBJ's job was to "inspire faith in what he does and chooses," as he put it. Almost invariably the intellectuals were the last to buy into the choice, if ever they did.

A question begs an answer. What concatenation of genes and circumstances conspired to elevate Lyndon Johnson from the hardscrabble Hill Country in southwest Texas to the corridors of power in Washington? Was it, as he wrote his mother from college, that Providence would "place me in a position where I can relieve you of the hardships that it has fallen your lot to suffer"? It soon became clear that it was not as much his Father in Heaven as his father on earth who was opening doors to San Marcos and to Washington. At last, ensconced in that pinnacle of power, the White House, Johnson dreamed of a Great Society while plagued with recurrent nightmares of Vietnam. As the nightmares took over and the dream receded, Johnson found himself under siege in the White House he'd struggled so hard to reach. "Do they think I'm some kind of war villain or an idiot who can't read an English sentence?"[14] His complaint fell mostly on deaf ears, as an increasing host—in the Congress, in the press, and across the land—turned to faulting him on both counts and more.

Yet one after the other of his colleagues and aides testified to his tactical brilliance which, together with his resourcefulness, his playing his cards close to his chest, and his uncanny sense of timing, succeeded in finding consensual solutions to intractable problems. Reedy, for example, couldn't get over how Johnson "would predict votes other senators didn't even know they were going to cast." He not only understood his colleagues as few if any did, but perceived how they would react to different circumstances. As a result, "he knew when to engage the opposition and when to withdraw, to mount a flank attack later and emerge victorious."

There remains, however, a singular irony in Johnson's inability to size up, much less to strike a deal with, his most formidable political opponent: North Vietnamese leader Ho Chi Minh. Lyndon knew next to nothing of the Vietnamese people or the man they called "the George Washington of Vietnam." Truth is, Johnson was an ignoramus when he waded ever deeper into the swamp that was Vietnam, a buccaneer armed with his simplistics and McNamara's statistics. In 1956, he had told reporters that he'd back Ike "when he's right and oppose him when he's wrong." It was just that simple. Too simple. Yet, paradoxically, the Majority Leader shunned extremes as he quoted Isaiah from the Old Testament: "Come now and let us reason together. . . ." During his Senate years and for most of his presidency, he was Homer's Ulysses, desperately trying to steer a course between Scylla and Charybdis, intent on arriving safely at his destination: a workable consensus based on compromise.

But as the war ground on, LBJ scrounged to rationalize what appeared to be an endless and fruitless encounter. He had difficulty at times even distinguishing two alternative courses of action. "There is always a rational answer to each national problem," he contended, "and believing this, I do not believe there are necessarily two sides to every question."

To thinking men and women, this should have aroused their suspicion, even as it would have aroused Alfred Korzybski thirty years earlier. For this Polish scientist and mathematician had founded the school of General Semantics, dedicated to removing the roadblocks that bedevil so much of our communication. Central to his thinking was our orientation to language as it relates to us and our world. To consider two alternatives, or either/or thinking, Korzybski considered almost as simplistic as considering a single solution. What he advocated, especially in regard to our most important decisions, was to take into consideration as many alternatives as possible. Ideally, that would comprise an "infinite-valued" orientation. If there were any decisions Johnson was making as President that required considering as many alternatives as possible, it was those regarding the war in Vietnam. It is here, as the chapter on coercion will delineate, that Johnson's supreme concentration on politics left him—and a nation—bereft of the responsible decision-making we expect of our presidents. The open society of which we boast was closed considerably when Congress, in 1964, effectively gave to Johnson the power to wage war as he saw fit. We will consider details of the Tonkin Gulf Resolution more fully in the chapter on deception.

If we are to assess Johnson's intelligence, and the part it played in the expansion of his power by the yardstick he applied to others—namely "smart is as smart does"—we can conclude that, though possessing the astuteness, the cleverness, the shrewdness to advance his political career, he lacked the more important aspects of intelligence that we commonly associate with wisdom. Chief among these is the ability to learn from the errors of others as well as ourselves. But Johnson, knowing precious little but politics, was hamstrung by his ignorance of others' mistakes. When it came to his own mistakes, he rarely acknowledged them, much less apologized for them. Protected by his indulgent parents from the consequences of his blunders, he grew to adulthood believing he just didn't make mistakes—or found a way to shift the blame onto others. As his world imploded around him in 1968, he said he'd made no major decision that he regretted. This, Tuchman maintained, was folly of the worst sort. The folly in Vietnam, she wrote, was not so much ignorance of the enemy as "persistence in the pursuit [of Johnson's policy] despite accumulating evidence that the goal was unattainable." Here was the "classic symptom of folly," a refusal to recognize and admit one's mistakes, thus preventing one to learn from them. Criticized by Theodore White for his intemperate attacks on American scholars in the early fifties, JFK, by contrast, acknowledged, "I was ignorant; I was wrong; I was a kid Congressman . . . I made a mistake—what else can I say?" Following the debacle at the Bay of Pigs, Kennedy sank into a deep depression and finally confessed, "I learned a lot from it. It would almost be worth it for what I learned from it—except that I can't get those 1,200 men in prison out of my mind."

Search the literature on LBJ and one is hard-pressed to find any confession even hinting at guilt or apology. Perhaps that is one of the reasons that Johnson complained to Senator Abraham Ribicoff on January 23, 1964, "I've had fifty-six days in this job, and they've been the most miserable fifty-six I've ever had." This is another example of Johnson's hype, used to manipulate Ribicoff into helping Johnson out on a Republican senator's meddling with a proposed tax cut: ". . . don't let . . . Everett Dirksen screw me this way." By March 31, 1968, Johnson would understand what Jefferson meant when he described the presidency as a "splendid misery."[15] Perhaps there is no more significant difference in intelligence between Kennedy and Johnson than this willingness to confess, and thus learn, by one's mistakes.

Speaking

One other major factor important in Johnson's expansion of his presidential powers was his speaking. Some would contend that no more important skill exists for an enterprising president than his ability to persuade voters to vote for him—and then, through their representatives in Congress, to back him in his leadership. It was here that Johnson parted company with JFK most dramatically. For LBJ brought to the White House few of the formidable rhetorical skills of his predecessor. Though Johnson retained much the same stable of speech writers that Kennedy employed—in particular Richard Goodwin—he was no JFK, much less a Churchill. Perhaps LBJ remembered Kennedy's encomium to Churchill, ". . . he mobilized the English language and sent it into battle . . . to illuminate the courage of his countrymen." Would that Johnson had known of Longinus, the rhetorician of ancient Rome, who taught "the style is the man," or that words from others—like FDR or Churchill—would ring hollow coming from the mouth of LBJ. Indeed, Roosevelt himself was eager to learn from Harry Hopkins, after his return from meeting with Churchill, who wrote the British Prime Minister's speeches. Wrote Hopkins later, "I hated like hell to tell him that Winston wrote them himself." When Johnson came off sounding more like a hick from the hills of Texas than a Prime Minister uttering the King's English, of course he blamed his speech writers.

It would be too much to expect that this comparatively unlettered pol from the Hill Country, this one who seemed to think that more talk, faster talk, and louder talk made for better talk, could fill the rhetorical shoes of his predecessors. He couldn't hold a candle to Teddy Roosevelt, astride his "bully pulpit," or Franklin, pulled up in his wheelchair by the hearth for his "Fireside Chats." Nor could he compete with Truman's modest, folksy, homespun warmheartedness that somehow came through a distinctively nasal Missouri twang. As Senate Majority Leader, Lyndon prowled the corridors and cloakrooms scrounging votes with his legendary "treatment." But he was no match for the man in the White House, Dwight Eisenhower, who, despite occasional woodenness, came across on TV screens as the confident, smiling commander, the five-star general who, in his clipped cadence, exuded decisiveness and integrity. Then, of course, there was Kennedy, the Churchill of postwar America, who could rouse a nation to cross New Frontiers, whether to land a man on the moon or commission thousands as Peace Corps emissaries to the world. How could Lyndon Johnson compete with the likes of these? He couldn't. And he didn't. But it was not for lack of trying. Raised in a home where talking was hailed as an art form, where his mother tutored others as well as Lyndon in the fine art of "elocution," where speaking was, according to Lyndon's brother Sam, "a compulsion," it was no surprise when Lyndon entered a speech contest at age thirteen. And it was no surprise—except to him—that he lost. He later recalled, "I was so disappointed I went right into the bathroom and was sick."[16]

In his first run for Congress, LBJ plied the towns with a sound truck, rousing the citizens with a rasping, "Come and hear Lyndon Johnson speak at the courthouse square." If he had a script to read, his phrasing was awkward, his gestures stilted, his inflection flat. And, lest he lose his place in the text, he looked at it more than at the audience. And he'd read on, and on, and on, until some members of the audience would start drifting away, while others prayed this young whippersnapper would quit his speechifying and get down off that flatbed truck to start shaking hands. With personal contact he was transformed. There seemed to be nobody that Lyndon didn't know personally, or at least some member of the family.

Here, one-on-one, Johnson was at his most persuasive. "No man alive," testified JFK, "ever entirely won a face-to-face argument with Lyndon Johnson." In campaigning for the presidential candidacy in 1960, the contrast between the two could scarcely have been greater. There was the "Harvard-trained, immaculately tailored, [and] superbly eloquent" Kennedy, the man whom LBJ had challenged to a debate before the Massachusetts and Texas delegations. Johnson intended to show this young neophyte a thing or two: he would prove himself the elder statesman against his young opponent.

Yet for every Johnson dig there was a Kennedy quip. Johnson boasted he'd answered all fifty quorum calls and voted for all forty-five roll calls during the Southern filibuster on civil rights, while "some senators answered no quorum calls and missed thirty-five roll calls." Kennedy: "I assume you're talking of someone else." In any event, "Congratulations to Lyndon for his wonderful record of answering quorum calls." Johnson: "I've been elected Senate Majority Leader no less than four times, and each time on a unanimous vote. Surely this qualifies me for the presidency." Kennedy: "I strongly support [you] for Majority Leader!" For forty minutes it went like this, Kennedy strewing land mines along Johnson's path to the nomination. The quips entertained delegates and press alike, even as they thoroughly discombobulated the hapless Texan.

The debate was no contest. And when it came to Lyndon's public speaking on the hustings in Texas, Theodore White was as perceptive as he was caustic. Lyndon's performance was "something like an act out of a show-boat production. He normally begins in a grave, serious tone, strictly out of Washington. Then, as his fists clench, flail and thrash the air, his voice changes. It roars like a bull's; it drops to a confidential whisper as he tells grassy jokes; it achieves a high-pitched Southern resonance; all texts are discarded, and the flavor of the slow drawl, the snapped phrases, the smirked confidences are never recaptured in the printed text. His face, which is, with the exception of Eisenhower's, the most mobile and expressive in national politics, seems a wad of India rubber—his mouth draws tight in anger, opens wide in a bellow of indignation, sucks in about the corners as he ruminates aloud, turns up in a great smile after the joke, turns down in sorrow as he wails of the nation's problems."

Goldwater recalled LBJ as Majority Leader in terms of "persuasive wrestling." "When Lyndon wanted something, he would stand face to face and put his hand on a member's shoulder. He would exploit flattery and friendship, remind you of former favors, and then if you didn't come around, he would be explicit about what your failure to cooperate might cost your state. We called the friendly approach, when he just put a hand on your shoulder, the Half-Johnson. When he put his arm clear around you and thrust his face close to yours to make his threats, we called it the Full-Johnson."

Ben Bradlee, editor of *The Washington Post*, recalled the "treatment" as "feeling as if a St. Bernard had licked your face for an hour, had pawed you all over. . . . He never just shook hands with you. One hand was shaking your hand; the other hand was always some place else, exploring you, examining you . . . he'd be trying to persuade you of something that he knew and I knew was not so, and there was just the trace of a smile on his face. It was just a miraculous performance."

Humphrey also recalled an occasion when he got the "treatment"—emerging battle-scarred after an hour or more of argument, mimicry, humor, statistics, and analogy, with Johnson pulling one supportive clipping after another from his pocket. "It was an almost hypnotic experience.

I came out of that session covered with blood, sweat, tears, spit—and sperm!"

Bad enough to be subjected to such an ordeal on land, but Califano found it almost life-threatening in the swimming pool at the Ranch. Only 5' 10" to the President's 6' 4" frame, Califano was treading water as LBJ, standing easily on the bottom, barked out one command after another. What was dismaying, however, was that Johnson would emphasize each command by jabbing his finger on Califano's shoulder, in effect dunking him with every point. At last, waterlogged and exhausted, the sputtering aide heard the boss ask, "Now, can you do that? Can you do all those things?" Califano, never one to duck an obligation, responded, between gasps, "Yes, sir, Mr. President."[17]

Rare was Johnson's ability to withstand the effrontery of formality, such as he did after JFK's assassination in addressing a special joint session of Congress on November 27, 1963. This session was to be the new President's first full-dress message to the nation—of utmost importance to a leader intent on capitalizing on what was coming to be seen as Kennedy's martyrdom, if not his beatification. Johnson turned to Ted Sorensen, JFK's wordsmith, along with John Kenneth Gaibraith, to pro-duce a rough draft. This he handed to old friend Abe Fortas, who revised it completely, recalling later, "I corned it up a little." Handing the formal draft to Lynda Bird, then a sophomore at the University of Texas, Lyndon listened as his daughter pointed out a single word she thought too restric-tive of the South, and Texas in particular. "Father," she said, "tomorrow you're going to be speaking to the world. I think we should change this word." And Lyndon did. The next day, riding to the Capitol at noon with Kennedy aides Larry O'Brien, Pierre Salinger, and Sorensen, he handed a copy of the final draft to Sorensen, giving him the credit. No, countered Sorensen, only about 50 percent of it was his. "But that's the best 50 per-cent," Johnson maintained.

So quietly did he begin the speech that those in back strained to hear him say, "All I have I would have given gladly not to be standing here today." Then, in tribute to his predecessor, who had always treated him as Vice-President with consideration, respect, and kindness, Lyndon contin-ued. "The greatest leader of our time has been struck down by the foulest deed of our time." Here Sorensen and others had capitalized on both hype and parallelism, overlooking the conservatives' jibes and brickbats, as well as the stubborn Congress that had considered Kennedy something less than a saint or a statesman. But Johnson was intent on two things: immortalizing his predecessor, and establishing his own continuity with him. "Today," continued LBJ, "John Fitzgerald Kennedy lives on in the immortal words and works that he left behind. He lives on in the hearts of his countrymen."

"No words," intoned Johnson, "are strong enough to express our determination to continue the forward thrust of America that he began." One is left to wonder how Kennedy's predecessors, and Ike in particular, regarded that tribute. But there was the first of many rounds of applause. Reassured, Johnson continued.

"The dream of conquering the vastness of space . . . of partnership across the Atlantic and across the Pacific as well—the dream of a Peace Corps in less developed nations . . . of education for all our children . . . of jobs . . . of care for our elderly . . . of equal rights for all Americans, whatever their race or color—these and other American dreams have been vitalized by his drive and by his dedication. . . . Kennedy told his countrymen . . . let us begin . . . I would say . . . let us continue."

When Johnson urged the passage of JFK's Civil Rights bill—as tribute to the New Frontiers' President, and one to be structured on LBJ's 1957 bill, the enthusiastic applause might well have obscured the stony silence of Richard Russell and other Southerners. But this Texas Southerner singled them out by indirection. "We will serve all of the nation, not one section or one sector or one group." Then LBJ began to soar airborne on the wings of rhetoric provided by Sorensen, Galbraith, et al. "These are the United States—a united people with a united purpose. Our American unity does not depend upon unanimity. We have differences; but now, as in the past, we can derive from these differences strength, not weakness, wisdom, not despair. Both as a people and as a government, we can unite upon a program, a program which is wise, just, enlightened, and constructive."

Having already drawn from George Washington, he now drew from Abraham Lincoln to fly to ever loftier heights of eloquence. "I profoundly hope that the tragedy and the torment of these terrible days will bind us together in new fellowship, making us one people in our hour of sorrow. So let us here highly resolve that John Fitzgerald Kennedy did not live— or die—in vain. And on this Thanksgiving Eve, as we gather to ask the

Lord's blessing and give him our thanks, let us unite in those familiar and cherished words:

America, America / God shed his grace on thee,
And crown thy good / With brotherhood / From sea to shining sea."

That this was a rhetorical tour de force was evident in the thunderous standing ovation, with even Russell's Southerners joining in. It was tribute to Johnson's ability, not equaled before or after, to read a script with conviction—and to his eye contact, thanks to a new teleprompter that was visible to him but not to the audience. More, it was tribute to the rhetorical skills of Johnson's speech writers, wordsmiths extraordinaire. But mostly it was tribute to the slain President, JFK himself. As huzzahs and hallelujahs rang from the rafters, editorialists, columnists, radio announcers, and TV anchormen joined in. Even the staunchly Republican *New York Herald Tribune* refused to be a spoilsport: "Fine words, fitting words, at times inspiring words. As he stood before Congress and the nation, not a fluke of history but a President." Dick Gregory, the comedian and civil rights activist, spoke for Negroes across the nation: "As soon as Lyndon Johnson finished his speech before Congress, twenty million of us unpacked."

LBJ had every reason to relish the bouquets, for this would prove to be the shortest honeymoon in presidential history. His oratorical comet would enter earth's atmosphere and burn itself out.

Apart from this notable success, Johnson's rhetoric fell flat. One factor was his intimidation by microphones and TV cameras. Another was his inability to read effectively the words others had prepared for him. Still another was the fact that he was an intellectual lightweight. Churchillian prose, even Goodwinian prose—both were a far cry from stump speaking with no notes. All that "highfalutin" language got caught somewhere between his voice box and his lips, so that by the time the words fell out in an unmistakable Texas drawl, it was at turns pathetic and hilarious.

In Johnson's case there was a fourth factor, more important than the rest, and that was his growing "credibility gap." Having won a virtual blank check to wage war in the form of the Gulf of Tonkin Resolution; having then paraded himself as the peace candidate, as opposed to Republican presidential candidate Barry Goldwater, the warmonger; and having then escalated the war dramatically, disregarding his campaign promises, as well as his promise to consult beforehand with Congress—Johnson found fewer and fewer were believing what he had to say. What confidence he'd gained by persuading Congress to pass a landslide of legislation, much of it bogged down in Congress during Kennedy's term, he quickly forfeited. By the end of 1965, the deadline by which Kennedy had planned to have all U.S. military out of Vietnam, Johnson's rhetoric summoned little more than a dull thud.

Humphrey noted that comparing Johnson to Kennedy "was like comparing a heavyweight boxer to a ballet dancer." "Of course," Johnson's Vice-President continued, "every presidency has its own personality. Kennedy's had great grace and charm and class. Johnson's presidency was more like a developer moving into an area that needs rehabilitation, renovation, rebuilding. It isn't very pretty at times." Johnson "was a builder, above all. He was a muscular, glandular, political man. Not an intellectual but bright. Not a talker, a doer. Kennedy was more a talker . . . when you look back, you will see that with Johnson—he didn't get all the little paintings on the wall, and he didn't get the gold plate on the dome and didn't shine up the doorknobs, but he got the foundations in, got the sidewalks up, got the beams put across. The structure was there."

It wasn't that Johnson couldn't talk, or that he wouldn't talk. In fact, he was as voluble a President as we've ever had. As Martin Luther King told Andrew Young: when he talked with President Kennedy, "he made you do all the talking. But when you talked to President Johnson, he did all the talking." More for Lyndon was better. More words spoken—more applause—more bills passed—more men and weapons to Vietnam—all of this was better. Had to be better. But it wasn't. In the end, Johnson fooled not only others but fooled himself. There were limits to which this human balloon could expand without bursting, and he would come to learn those limits the hard way.[18]

RICHARD NIXON

I know that you must be aware . . . that there are some . . .who would say, "I don't know what it is, but I just don't like the man; I can't put my finger on it; I just don't like him." Would you have any idea what might inspire that kind of feeling on the part of anybody?

— Walter Cronkite interviewing Nixon two weeks
before the 1960 Nixon-Kennedy debates

For years the flame of ambition burned absolutely pure in him.

— Garry Wills, of Nixon

Take anybody, no matter what his views, if he looks like a winner; desert anybody, no matter what his record, if he looks like a loser.

— Jack Bell, on "the cardinal rule of politics"

Do Not Repeat What Has Already Failed
— Sign Barbara Tuchman would have hung on Nixon's wall.[1]

Complexity

Power. What was Kissinger's aphrodisiac was Nixon's sustenance. In one college debate he took the affirmative on "Why the Powers of the President Should Be Increased." Then, as a Congressman and a Senator, he became increasingly supportive of Lord Acton's claim that power could indeed corrupt, and so made frequent, impassioned criticism of presidential expansion of power. That is, until he became President.

Having deferred to others to get power, having delegated to others some of that power, Nixon was as determined as any president to expand that power. To that expansion he brought a formidable set of strengths as well as weaknesses. Few there were who came to know Nixon well, and those few, with the possible exception of his mother, found him immensely complex. By 1968, Walter Lippman wrote he was seeing a "new Nixon, a maturer and mellower man who is no longer clawing his way to the top." Not so, protested Hannah, who, as Nixon's mother, should have known. "He has always been exactly the same; even as a boy I never knew a person to change so little."

Inside his skin, Nixon appeared to be a man of many parts, some contradicting others. He was certainly not, as he claimed while introducing Barry Goldwater at the 1964 Republican National Convention, "a simple soldier in the ranks" of the party. Goldwater thought of himself as "a simple, uncomplicated man . . . telling it like it is." But he knew Nixon was not. "Nixon," he wrote, "was a loner." As such, he kept his thoughts, like he learned to keep his cards in poker, "close to his chest." Ola-Florence Welch, Nixon's girlfriend for six years in college and law school, found him not only "unsure of himself" but "a mystery. . . . Sometimes I think I never really knew him." Once in politics, Nixon was brusque to the point of rudeness in refusing to disclose himself. In a 1983 interview he was asked by erstwhile aide Frank Gannon, "Do you consider that you've had a good life?" Nixon: "I don't get into that kind of crap."[2] Though shy and taciturn, he was fiercely ambitious. Though a frenetic workhorse in his manic phase, he could slip as easily into melancholic brooding and outright despair. Though a builder of castles in the sand of politics, he maintained most of the time a healthy respect for realities. Though no backslapper, he learned that deference, even elaborate deference, had its own rewards. Though furtive and secretive, he could, on occasion, let down his hair—especially to friends like Bebe Rebozo and Robert Abplanalp. Though given to dramatic exhibitions of gall as well as courage—all in the name of machismo—he also displayed streaks of cowardice, a refusal to hold to Truman's maxim: "The buck stops here." Though craving long periods of silent introspection, he could, given an audience, be both expansive and persuasive. Though a friendless loner, he could mix it up with the best and worst of them and emerge more often than not the victor. Though a humorless perfectionist, he could sit at a piano and bang away for hours, taking requests in a sing-along. Though too smooth for—and with—words, he was a born klutz, banging his knee twice on a car door in one campaign, almost crippling himself. Though superficial in his pandering to public simplistics, as in his "Checkers" speech, he could be both cunning and brainy. Though bored by social affairs, especially ceremonial affairs, he disciplined himself not to offend other VIPs. Though a language prude in public, he could swear like the sailor he'd been among friends and aides. Though a health nut in his eating habits, he could drive himself to the point of exhaustion. Though a political conservative, he prided himself on being a "radical" when it came to goals for the country—and for Nixon.

Of Nixon it seemed to be said, even by his closest aides and friends, what General Tecumseh Sherman said of General U.S. Grant, his closest comrade in arms: "To me he is a mystery, and I believe he is a mystery to himself." To Arthur Burns, Nixon was a split personality, incapable of being fully understood. To Henry Kissinger, Nixon was an introvert, too insecure and too "vulnerable" to "transcend his resentments and his complexes," masking them in language both ambiguous and elliptical. When Kissinger proposed a formal National Security Council system, he waited—and waited—for Nixon's response, eventually given to him by Haldeman. Nixon, after long consideration, not only approved the plan but said he'd fire anybody opposing it. Here, Kissinger wrote, was "vintage Nixon: a definite instruction, followed by maddening procrastination and ambiguity, which masked the search for an indirect means of solution, capped by a sudden decision—transmitted to the loser by two consecutive intermediaries."

What drove Burns, Kissinger, and other aides to distraction was Nixon's saying something, then immediately denying it, or saying he would not do something, then immediately doing it. Words for him were so many "billiard balls," wrote Kissinger, "what mattered was not the intellectual impact but the carom." To Bob Haldeman and Ray Price, Nixon possessed light and dark sides. But where Price found them at war with each other, Haldeman dismissed the dark side as unimportant, in view of Nixon's "great virtues." At the same time, Haldeman was convinced Nixon was "the weirdest ever to live in the White House."[3] Speech writer William Safire, on the other hand, characterized Nixon as a "three-layer cake," consisting of conservative, progressive, and liberal layers.

Reporters were every bit as baffled as his aides. To James Reston, Nixon was "a tragic tangle of contradictions." To Tom Wicker, examining Nixon's foreign policies, he was a "Jacksonian in his belief in executive power, Gaullist in his determination to exercise that power personally,

Machiavellian in his willingness to manipulate and maneuver to advance American interests, and purely Nixonian in what others might consider a grandiose ambition rather than a 'great purpose'—to achieve a lasting structure of peace."

To David Frost, interviewing Nixon at length after his resignation, he was "a walking contradiction of terms—an oxymoron," possessed of many faces: the "stern" Nixon, the "resolute" Nixon, the "pensive" Nixon, the Nixon "hounded by recollections of Watergate and other abuses." So which was the "real" Nixon? None of the above. Frost gave up the quest as an exercise in futility.

Perhaps, after all, Nixon was "all of the above" and then some. Maybe that mystery was what intrigued president-watcher Tom Wicker who, after thirty years on the beat, concluded Nixon and Johnson were the "two most interesting." In Wicker's apt title, *Richard Nixon, One of Us*, he recognized not only Nixon's reflecting the time and place in which he lived and, in turn, influencing them, but was, like each of us, a zoo in which a multitude of beasts contended with each other for dominance. Presiding over it all was the anxious and overworked zookeeper, the rational self, attempting to create order of chaos and with limited success. At night, it seems, the zookeeper slept, leaving the beasts free to roam and contend as they would, doing their dream work. Americans, Wicker noted, seldom were sure what lay beneath Nixon's facade: "From behind his appearance of pious responsibility and somewhat strained good-fellowship, someone else has looked out at us over the years, with a gaze shrewd, sharp, measuring, menacing to some, enigmatic even to those who believe in him."[4] In an attempt to unravel something of this complex Nixon, let us examine some of his outstanding characteristics in expanding his power base.

Ambition

Nixon was nothing if not ambitious. As a boy he'd sit with a brother, watch the trains pass, whistle shrieking, rails thwacking. Catching a glimpse of the waving engineer, the boy dreamed of the world out there and devoured copies of the *National Geographic* to learn more. He practiced the piano. He practiced the violin. And he dreamed of directing his own symphony orchestra or of sitting at the keyboard of a cathedral organ. Off to college, then law school, his dreams climbed higher until, meeting Pat, he told her that not only would he marry her "someday," but that he would be president. There is nothing wrong with ambition. John Adams conceived of Jefferson's ambition as equal to that of Oliver Cromwell, while Adam's son, John Quincy, took note of Jefferson's "transcendent" ambition. If the author of the Declaration of Independence and among the foremost of the nation's Founders could be that ambitious, then surely Nixon's ambition would seem well placed. Except that Nixon was utterly consumed by it, particularly as it focused on power and his means of expanding that power.

Elected to Congress in 1946, gaining national recognition in pursuing Alger Hiss, Nixon's eyes glistened as he contemplated the Senate. Then, who knows, the White House . . . entering the Oval Office that he'd been ushered into as a freshman member of the House, to meet with Truman. In six years his ambition won him the vice-presidency. But seeing Ike reluctant to expand his power, Nixon determined if he won the presidency he'd expand that power. From the time he entered politics or, as Nixon's euphemism would have it, "public service," he came to want power, to yearn for it, to crave it, to lust after it, to the point that by the time he became Vice-President he'd earned a reputation for ruthlessness—for saying anything, for doing anything, to get and expand that power. Finally ushered into the Oval Office, *his* Oval Office, having arrived at the very pinnacle of power, possessed of more raw power than any man in history, Nixon used it, then abused it—crassly, ignominiously—until it brought him, like Samson of old, down to his destruction under the awful weight of hubris.

Along the way he served as an electric prod to the GOP elephant, hibernating, as Bell put it, only to awaken "with a mighty trumpet blast at election time" before resting "calmly until the next campaign." During Nixon's heroic effort in 1954 on behalf of fellow Republicans, he found that daughter Tricia, just eight, could teach him a thing or two. Encouraging her at the piano, Nixon told her to practice, practice, practice—then she'd be perfect. Tricia wasn't convinced, and countered with, "If you'd gone on practicing like you tell me to do, you might have gone to Hollywood. Then when you died you'd be buried in an important place!"[5]

So obvious was Nixon's lust for the Oval Office that by 1960, he had enlisted Roger Ailes to change his face and talk—from the brash, tough, anti-Communist refugee from McCarthyism to a new, "warm" and "mellow" statesman. Ailes confessed he had his work cut out for him. For here, he said, was this "funny-looking guy. He looks like somebody hung in a closet overnight and he jumps out in the morning with his suit all bunched up and starts running around saying, 'I want to be President' . . . this is how he strikes some people"—including, in all probability, Ailes himself.

Losing to Kennedy, Nixon was, by 1967, preparing the ground well for his next run, including camouflaging his aims. Of March 1967, Nixon later wrote, "I didn't want the presidency in order to be someone . . . I was bored by the charade of trying to romance the media [where] the majority opposed my views and would strongly oppose my candidacy." By 1968 Nixon was determined to outdo his predecessors, especially Johnson's spectacular 1964 win. In addition, his track record would leave Ike eating his Vice-President's dust.

One night Nixon was discussing former presidents with speech writer William Safire. Nixon: "You think of Truman—a fighter. Eisenhower—a good man. Kennedy—charisma. Johnson—work. Me—what?" Safire: "Competence." Then, seeing Nixon's disappointment, he quickly added, "Sorry about that." Nixon: "Hell, if all we do is manage things ten percent better, we'll never be remembered for anything." Another time Nixon returned from a trip abroad to find the desk that Woodrow Wilson had used, and Nixon had insisted be moved into the Oval Office, had been refinished. It seems that Nixon's feet on the desk had scuffed it. Nixon: "Dammit! I didn't order that. I want to leave my mark on this place just like the other presidents!"

Taking inventory, Nixon concluded he had four of the five qualities necessary to be a good candidate: "brains, judgment, guts and experience." But did he have the ambition, the "heart," as he put it, the "fire in the belly?" He wrote he wasn't so sure. But others were convinced that he had this above all. And this despite his later writing that "the road to another presidential primary had at times been unbearably lonely."

As it turned out, Nixon had all five, and more too, including shady maneuvers, reverting to the 1950 "tricky Dick" that his opponent in the Senate race, Helen Gahagan Douglas, found so repulsive. At last in the White House, at long last at home in the Oval Office, Nixon set about expanding his power, as we have noted and will later detail. All—or most all—he did in the name of "national security." As speech writer Ray Price, reflecting Nixon's philosophy, later wrote, "the worst thing a President can do is to be so paralyzed by propriety that he shrinks from bending the rules when the nation's security requires it." After all, Abe Lincoln, the first Republican President, had done it. So why not Dick Nixon? Trouble was, Lincoln had the nation, or at least enough of the nation, behind him to warrant the stretching of his powers when "E Pluribus Unum" was in danger of Balkanization. A century or so later, Nixon had what he called but a little "bitch of a war" with a primitive, third-world country on the other side of the map, of little conceivable interest to us and of no conceivable danger. So he lacked both public and Congressional support in his grab for more power. In addition, having promised in 1968 to end the war in six months, this promise had gone the way of so many of his other promises. As a result, an increasingly skeptical electorate began to think he was deliberately timing the war's end to coincide with his campaign for reelection.[6]

Nixon's two summits, his continuing withdrawal of American troops from Vietnam, and his ability to cover up the Watergate burglary—and the part of his White House in it—was such that, coupled with his cunning device [detailed later] of removing Muskie from the field, and leaving the more vulnerable McGovern, gave Nixon the unprecedented victory at the polls he'd been lusting for. Now with this powerful mandate in his pocket, he would expand his power and who was there that would dare challenge him? In the opinion of Attorney General Elliott Richardson, Nixon was one of only a handful of people in Washington "over the last thirty years [who] really have had an overriding desire to exercise power." But, as Richardson was to discover, his President not only gloried in using his power but in flaunting it. As he saw his power evaporating in the throes of Watergate, Nixon, on May 11, 1973, less than two weeks after firing Haldeman and Ehrlichman, let go a burst: ". . . I have very little power, but, goddamn it, I can nominate people. . . . If they have any doubts about the President, let me tell you, I'll withdraw their goddamn nominations in the next five minutes, believe me. I'm not going to have any screwing around. . . ."

In his abuse of power, Nixon contrasted sharply with the President for whom the capital was named. For Washington's advisers urged him to set himself above and apart from the commoners by using the trappings of royal splendor. Washington refused. He would be no George III, even if some wanted him to be King George Washington. As Daniel Boorstin, historian and director of the Library of Congress, noted, "Washington struck a prudent balance between what he called, "too free intercourse and too much familiarity." In other words, Washington struck the proper balance between Johnson's undue familiarity and Nixon's aloofness. Yet both exerted mightily to push out the Constitutional bounds on their powers. Nixon had three professed goals in his presidency, according to Kissinger: "to win by the biggest electoral landslide in history; to be remembered as a peacemaker; and to be accepted by the 'Establishment' as an equal." Each of these, Kissinger claimed, Nixon had met by 1973. That is debatable. What is not debatable, however, was that in attempting to meet these goals he tried to make himself over into the "new" Nixon—and thereby incurred the wrath of the gods who exacted a fearful price for this presumption.[7] By 1973 hubris was alive and well in the Oval Office of Richard Nixon.

Industry

A second factor in Nixon's power expansion, without which ambition would have foundered on the rocks of indolence, was his indefatigable industry. Here was no simple search for identity, no normal hankering for recognition, no natural yearning for success. Here, rather, was a man driven, a man obsessed with power. As a boy, he'd learned about hard work from father Frank, who was willing to roll up his sleeves and build by himself his first house, a small, white clapboard affair. He'd also learned from mother Hannah who, rising before the sun, busied herself taking the too-ripe fruit from the grocery and turning it into pies—as many as fifty a day—to sell in the store. As Dick's younger brother Don recalled, Frank "worked us to death." When Dick was old enough to drive, he became the store's produce man. For six years he'd arise at four, drive the pickup to Los Angeles, make his selections from the farmer's market, wash and arrange the fruits and vegetables for sale, then go off to school by eight. Here was the quintessential grind, Horatio Alger in the flesh, or—as a law school classmate put it—"Iron Butt." Afraid he couldn't make the grade at Duke, competing with graduates of the elite Ivy League colleges, Nixon shared his doubts with Bill Adelson, who assured him, "You don't have to worry. You have what it takes to learn the law—an "iron butt." Nixon credited his earning of honors at Whittier College to simple diligence. "It wasn't because I was smarter but because I worked longer and harder than some of my gifted colleagues." Why did he do it? In his explanation, Nixon revealed much beyond merely his addiction to hard work. "What starts the process really are the laughs and slights and snubs when you are a kid. . . . But if you are reasonably intelligent and your anger is deep enough and strong enough, you learn you can change these attributes by excellence, personal gut performance, while those who have everything are sitting on their fat butts."[8]

Nixon won his first Congressional seat partly through dirty tricks. But in all fairness, he also won it because he spent long hours in preparing for his debates with Jerry Voorhis—so much so that he knew his opponent's record in Congress better than Voorhis did. It was the same dogged determination that helped him nail Hiss to the wall for perjury.

It was the same, "I'll show 'em" attitude that prompted Nixon in 1960 to run himself ragged as he campaigned for president. Late at the starting gate by two weeks, and recuperating from an infected knee, Nixon propelled himself from the hospital bed to a madcap campaign schedule, driving himself and his aides out of their energy, out of their patience, and almost out of their wits.

In Nixon's mind was the notion, firmly fixed since childhood, that the winner was invariably the one who worked the hardest, drove himself unmercifully, kowtowing to no physical or mental limits. Traveling 65,000 miles to each and every state, this marathon campaigner gave 150 major speeches in 188 cities to ten million people. At the same time some of his aides were busy writing—and Nixon signing—no less than 160,000 letters. He had outdone Truman, but, unlike Truman, it wasn't enough. Had he garnered another 4,500 voters in Illinois and 32,500 in Texas, he'd have won. Apparently Chicago Mayor Richard Daley and Texas Senator Lyndon Johnson made the difference.

With the taste of ashes of defeat on his tongue, Nixon nonetheless plunged into the writing of *Six Crises*, concluding with a quotation from Sophocles: "One must wait until evening to see how splendid the day has been." Nixon's evening would not be Sophocles' evening.

By 1962, when the book was published, Nixon was not about to content himself with reflecting on the "splendor of the day." Evening was yet far off, and there was much to do to prepare himself for 1968. Oliver Wendell Holmes had said, "Alas, gentlemen, we cannot live our dreams. We are lucky enough if we can give a sample of our best and if we can know in our hearts that it was nobly done."[9] Nixon was, by 1968, doubly determined to live his dreams, the most enchanting of which was to move, duly elected, into 1600 Pennsylvania Avenue.

In 1960 Nixon had lost in a squeaker. In 1968 he won in a squeaker. Not because he'd run another marathon, but because, listening to others like Haldeman, he substituted brains for brawn, substituted television for personal appearances, and reached, not ten million but ten times that.

Had he continued to rely on good sense, he might have avoided the imbroglio of Watergate. In fits and starts he reverted to type, phoning members of Congress for a solid seven hours one day on behalf of a certain bill. But in the end, industry was not enough. Good sense eluded him, and in the evening of his life he could only look back in bitterness and resentment at the enemies, especially the press, that had done him in.

Intelligence

Having made note of "good sense," let us turn to the third factor in Nixon's expansion of power, intelligence. Of the many characteristics of this walking conundrum, none were more important or more debatable. Though not a "many-splendored thing" like love, intelligence is many-sided, leaving Nixon positively brilliant in some aspects and moronic in others. Just as there are not enough hours in the day to be "all things to all people," so is there not enough time to develop all—or even several—of the various aspects of intelligence. Forging ahead in one area invariably necessitates not developing other areas.

Other presidents had set an example for Nixon with their exemplary minds. Madison, primary author of our Constitution—and thus no slouch when it came to intellect—paid tribute to Jefferson as a "walking library" with genius his constant companion. Just as Jefferson courted genius, so was he repulsed by ignorance. He agreed with Montaigne that "ignorance is the softest pillow on which a man can rest his head," and was determined "to estrange myself [from] everything of that character." Having served as our third President, having founded the University of Virginia, he wrote, "If a state expects to be ignorant and free, in a state of civilization, it expects what never was and will never be." If ignorance in the electorate is unfortunate, then ignorance in our leaders is intolerable.

One has only to read the three-minute Gettysburg Address to find in Lincoln a brilliance that outshone his contemporaries with rare exception.

Of our twentieth century presidents, it is probably Wilson who best epitomized intellect. Like his mother, Nixon was a staunch admirer of our twenty-seventh president. Dr. Paul Smith, Nixon's political science professor at Whittier College, recalled that Nixon quoted from Wilson, the Democrat, more than from any other man.[10]

As a student, Nixon showed unusual promise. He graduated third in his high school class and won the Harvard Club of California prize as the best all-around student. Eligible for a scholarship to Harvard, he had to forego it for lack of money. This was not an insignificant factor, because it showed in his later resentment of "Harvards," as Nixon called them. In college he graduated second, and at Duke third in his class. Yet one of his Duke professors found him neither "terribly imaginative," nor "profound." He apparently played his studies much as he played the piano and later would play his politics: mechanically, dutifully, uninspiringly.

Yet determination was there. Once in politics it was still, with little exception, unflagging industry rather than flashes of insight that impressed others. One exception was his deploring of Ike's crash program for improving science classes in American schools after the Soviets had beaten us into space with their "Sputnik" in 1957. Another was his insistence that television, not religion, was fast becoming, in Marx's words, the "opiate of the people." More often, he was the drudge rather than the innovator, relying on cunning rather than common sense, on secrecy rather than openness, on fixing blame rather than confessing fault. As a result, the mistakes he made in 1960 were but a prelude to the egregious mistakes of his presidency. If the 1960 campaign revealed glaring chinks in his intellectual armor, Watergate revealed his Achilles' heel. Just as 1960 was followed by *Six Crises*, so was his resignation followed by his *Memoirs*. Where the first earned enough in royalties to help finance his 1968 campaign, the second helped pay the fees of attorneys defending him on Watergate. Both were replete with simplistics as much as exaggeration. And both were monuments to self-serving hypocrisy, made the worse by his sanctimonious self-pity.

A trait incompatible with high intelligence would appear to be a belief in fatalism, however couched: luck, destiny, predestination, or karma. When Kennedy was assassinated in 1963, J. Edgar Hoover told Nixon that Oswald had intended to kill him as well as JFK. "Only with great difficulty," wrote Nixon, had Oswald's wife "managed to keep him in the house to prevent him from doing so." Nixon claimed that he was "fatalistic about the danger of assassination. I knew that given the number of people who, for whatever reasons, want to kill a President, it takes a combination of luck and the law of averages to keep him alive."

Sympathetic biographer Earl Mazo wrote that Nixon, "like the average successful politician [was] respectful of the mysterious power called 'luck.' " Or, as Nixon wrote, "the man who was on the scene at the right time and who pleased the voters with the words they wanted to hear would win." Here, if anything is a minced definition of fatalism, with a bow to rationalization in an ill-disguised attempt to justify his servile pandering to his audiences. Rationalization was one of Nixon's strong suits, as when, in November 1972, he appealed to the "great forces of history" to move him in the "right" direction. In this, Nixon appeared to be paraphrasing Lincoln's verdict that, "Only events and not a man's exertions in his own behalf can make a President." Maneuvering to cover up Watergate being linked to the White House, and stretching the close of the Vietnam War to coincide with his reelection, he insisted that any other than the "right" direction would be a bow to "insanity and irrationality."[11]

In 1967, Nixon declared to friend Elmer Bobst that the United States must "race to control change, rather than be controlled by it." All of his political life he strove mightily to control his White House, his administration, and the world itself—especially Vietnam. Yet he often found refuge in Churchill's verdict that, "the longer one lives, the more one realizes that everything depends on chance. If any one will look back over the course of even ten years of experience, he'll see that tiny incidents, utterly unimportant in themselves, have in fact governed the whole of his fortune and career." Theodore White interviewed Nixon in 1972 and concluded that it was fate that governed his life. Yet it was Kissinger who wrote, ". . . to hide behind historical inevitability is tantamount to moral abdication . . . ." There is abundant research showing it is a mix of genes with environment that shapes the person, notwithstanding the pivotal place of will in the process. This despite B.F. Skinner's contention that freedom of choice is an illusion. Nixon himself refused, he wrote, to bow "to the inevitable just because it is inevitable." At the same time, he registered his belief in the supernatural when, on the eve of the 1972 election, he wrote in his diary, ". . . someone must have been walking with us. The Peking trip, the Moscow trip, the May 8 decision, and then the way we've handled the campaign—must deserve some grudging respect from even our critics." That the "someone" must have been less than godly can only be assumed by looking at his campaign itself, which was far less than "clean as a hound's tooth," to use Ike's phrase. Indeed, as Taft wrote, politicians have a knack for capitalizing on luck, such that if the rain causes "the corn to grow" or makes "business good," politicians are the first to claim credit for it.[12]

Theodore White commended Nixon's mind as "tough" and "wide-ranging," while Ambrose paid tribute to Nixon's memory as "the best . . . of any modern president." Not only was he best at absorbing facts, but in keeping them in his head. Compared with Eisenhower, Ambrose found Nixon smarter in memory, in imagination, and in flexibility—the will to change, to take a chance. Yet Ambrose concluded that whereas Ike smiled, Nixon snarled; whereas Ike displayed "generosity of spirit," Nixon showed "meanness of spirit." Therefore, Ambrose concluded, ". . . it must have been a terrible thing to be Richard Nixon." Few were the questions Nixon asked, and fewer still the big questions, the "why" questions that invariably arise from a study of philosophy or history. White wrote that Nixon, all his political life, asked not so much the why as the how questions, especially how things work. But his disaster, White continued, showed he still didn't understand how the Republic worked. Nixon's philosophy was summed up in, "Shoot if you must this old gray head, but spare your country's flag." It was this, White concluded, that gave rise to Nixon's relentless search for the quixotic "peace with honor."

That Vietnam, that Watergate, that Nixon's resignation in disgrace, did not cripple the Republic was in no small part due to the wisdom of the Founders. As John Adams wrote in 1814, "Liberty . . . is an intellectual quality, an attribute that belongs not to fate or chance." Created on the bulwark of intelligent choice, seasoned in the kiln of consensual discussion, liberty found its expression in a Constitution that held power suspect, so much so that it had to be constrained by a system of checks and balances. Thus did the Constitution provide a foundation firm enough to withstand the assaults on its integrity by Richard Nixon, who expanded presidential power as none before him.

To equate cunning with intelligence and craft with intellect is to strip the mind of morality, to say that freedom can operate without responsibility, that power can operate unchecked. It was this presumption that gave

TV anchor Chet Huntley misgivings when he learned Nixon had won the White House. Huntley was overwhelmed by the "shallowness of the man . . . the fact that he is President frightens me." It turned out that Huntley had good reason to be frightened. For Nixon, like Johnson, was woefully ignorant of the enemy in Vietnam, both in the North and among the Vietcong in the South. He had little coherent picture of why he was fighting, of what victory would consist, or of what the nation was willing to pay—in terms of lives, of money, of divisiveness, of prestige. His "peace with honor" was the Holy Grail—always beyond reach because he was constantly shifting the terms of definition.

Yes, Nixon had perfected his rough-and-tumble campaign skills. Yes, he'd burnished his ceremonial skills as Vice-President. But these were not the skills he needed as President. What he needed was to find and apply the best solutions to problems, with careful, patient, probing analysis and thorough planning—just the skills, Kissinger wrote, that Nixon lacked, and that made inevitable the Watergate fiasco.[13]

Indeed, it was Watergate and its aftermath that laid bare the bankruptcy of Nixon's mind. Close friend and benefactor Donald Kendall, CEO of Pepsi-Cola, called Nixon "brilliant," while Deputy Secretary of the Treasury William Simon was "astounded," as he put it, at Nixon's powers of concentration even two weeks before his resignation. Yet a reading of the transcripts reveals no careful planning, no penetrating analyses, no deferring to others beyond his aides, also neck-deep in the cover-up. What they do reveal is a fumbling, self-contradictory, crude President, grasping at straws to prevent the inevitable, willing to sacrifice his aides to save his own skin. His claim to be an "idea" man rather than a "personnel" man was suspect.

Gone was the man who postured as statesman, who, just weeks before the burglary at the Watergate, scored what most in the press praised as a remarkable tour de force by prying open the door to Communist China—even as his aides were planning to pry open the door to Democratic National Headquarters in Washington. The burglary scarcely raised a ripple in the press at home, while China's Congress had, just previous to Nixon's visit, denounced him as a "hypocritical priest, a gangster wielding a blood-dripping butcher's knife." Gone was the private person that stood in such marked contrast to the public persona.

Reading the transcripts, the nation gasped. Was this the real Nixon?

What of the image on TV? Where was the "great intellect" that Elliott Richardson claimed to see? Where was the intent on downplaying his natural brilliance, as Ray Price put it, "in order to be one of the boys?"[14]

That there was a pronounced difference between his writing and his speaking—particularly as the latter is recorded on the tapes—is abundantly clear. At one point Ron Ziegler asked Nixon if Special Counsel Chuck Colson was involved in preparing a fake cable meant to implicate JFK in the murder of Diem. Nixon's answer was less than a sterling example of coherence: "Never, never, never, never, never, never. No. No . . . Goddamn. That Colson thing . . .Oh Christ, he's looking like a Goddamn fool . . . Please God . . . I had no Goddamn knowledge whatever. . . ." Lest this be thought to be singular, the tape transcripts are studded with examples of similar incoherence. Two other examples: "Actually, let me tell you, the thing is on this, wh, wh, we'll, we're ready to strike back but wh, we're, we've got a plan. . . ." Or: "We're gonna, they, they've started, they wanna have a gut fight, they're gonna get one . . . we're gonna, we're gonna, we're gonna force them right now. . . ." Judged by his schooling, Nixon was well-educated. If, however, by "well-educated" we mean well-rounded—men like Washington, Franklin, Jefferson, Adams, and Madison, or their successors Lincoln, Teddy Roosevelt, and Wilson—then Nixon did not meet the standard. He would, rather, be another of Ortega y Gasset's "barbarians." Nixon's specialty, to which he gave his all, was politics. Other areas needed to complete the picture were summarily and necessarily ignored. When it came to spatial intelligence, Nixon was an all-thumbs bumbler, the proverbial klutz, the man who couldn't open a car door without clobbering his knee; the man who, jabbing his pen into his hand at a bill-signing ceremony, sent aides scrambling to retrieve it when he dropped it in pain; the man who left teeth marks on a pill bottle cap he couldn't open; and the man who, trying to erase incriminating parts of the most incriminating of his tapes—that of June 20, 1972, left an eighteen and one-half minute gap. Haldeman figured that his boss finally gave up in frustration when he realized that, "at the rate he was going it would take him ten years."

Speaking

The fourth of Conant's purposes of higher education, and again flowing from clear thinking, was effective communication. Kissinger, no slouch when it came to intellect, found Nixon's use of language bewildering and bedeviling. Here, as in his *Memoirs*, was language that was serpentine as well as elliptical, vague as well as self-contradictory. Beyond these, however, there were rhetorical land mines in the form of logical fallacies endangering the path of any person trying to follow in his wake. Either-or thinking, or two-valued orientation, as Alfred Korzybski called it, is probably the most common form of simplistics. It suited itself well to the bumper stickers of Nixon's day, including "America: Love It or Leave It." Nixon's delight, as Fawn M. Brodie wrote, "was not in solutions but in a place on the platform," first in California, then in Washington, D.C.[15] To occupy that platform, to use it as a command post, to win the election, Nixon was convinced—with the help of advisor Murray Chotiner—required that he appeal to the lowest common denominator. Thus, his campaign slogan in 1946 was, "Had Enough?" Enough of what was left unanswered. Then Nixon moved on into the fallacies of loaded words and unsubstantiated assertions or lack of evidence: "A vote for Nixon is a vote against the Communist-dominated PAC [The CIO's Political Action Committee] with its gigantic slush fund." Or, let's "clean house in Washington" and rid ourselves of the "left-wing group" backing Voorhis.

On a par with his slogans, loaded words, and unsubstantiated assertions was Nixon's brazen histrionics, during a debate in the campaign. Challenged by Voorhis to show evidence of his PAC endorsement—which his opponent had charged—he simply pulled from his suit pocket a mimeographed paper and waved it in the face of the flustered Voorhis. Was it evidence? Not at all. But now Nixon had put his opponent on the defensive.

Nixon kept at it. Of 132 public bills Voorhis had introduced in the last four years in Congress, said Nixon, only one, the Rabbit Transfer Bill, ever became law. "I assume," ridiculed Nixon, "you have to be a rabbit to have representation in the Twelfth Congressional District." Amid the raucous laughter of that audience—consisting of Nixon followers who'd come early to occupy the front seats and others who positioned themselves strategically in the hall to applaud or jeer, on cue—Voorhis slumped in his chair. "From then on," wrote reporter Roy Day, Nixon "had him on the run."

Just before the election Nixon pounded the last nail in Voorhis' political coffin: circulating a rag that accused Voorhis of consistently voting "the Moscow-Henry Wallace line," and leaving Voorhis with no time to defend himself. Not surprisingly, Nixon carried the day, with almost 57 percent of the vote. This despite a 1939 consensus of Washington reporters that Voorhis was the most honest and the fifth-most intelligent Congressman on the Hill. And this despite his colleagues voting him the hardest-working among them. Even Nixon acknowledged as much when he said to a chief architect of his anti-Voorhis campaign, "All agree that he is honest, conscientious, and able."

Nixon's 1950 campaign for the Senate was largely a repeat of 1946. Like Voorhis, Helen Gahagan Douglas was in favor of retaining federal control of tidelands oil off the California coast, anathema to big business. Like Voorhis, she possessed sturdy anti-Communist credentials, and Nixon knew it. Indeed, he said it—in private—but he attacked her anyway, as "pink down to her underwear." By this time Nixon knew by heart Chotiner's first rule of politics: "Destroy your opponent." He did it, and he won, less a tribute to his intelligence than an indictment of his lack of scruples. It is worthy of note that Joe McCarthy went to Nixon's aid, breathing anti-Communist hellfire. Calling Truman the head of the "Administration Communist Party of Betrayal," McCarthy drew applause from Nixon, accompanied by an "Amen" and "God give the courage to carry on."[16] Just as McCarthy was igniting the voters on the crassest of appeals—fear—Nixon was using the same device to secure his election to the Senate and, in two years, a place next to Eisenhower on the national Republican ticket.

Perhaps the most memorable speech associated with Nixon was his "Checkers" defense in 1952, against Democratic charges that a secret slush fund, contributed by California businessmen, was financing his campaign. It was Lincoln who said, "God must have loved the common people, he made so many of them." But it was Nixon, not Lincoln, who seemed to perfect the art of pandering to them. There is a perceptible difference between the "Checkers" Speech and the Gettysburg Address. Baring his household finances may have horrified Pat, but "Joe Six-pack" and his wife ate up Nixon's firm declaration that the only gift he had received after being nominated was a dog—and he would not, under any circumstances, part with "Checkers," his cocker spaniel. Of course, the dog had nothing to do with the issue at hand, Nixon's slush fund.

Others—far fewer, but arguably a more sophisticated minority—denounced the speech as a mawkish, sanctimonious, unctuous performance that would have done credit to Uriah Heep. Many found the speech, as Ambrose put it, "one of the most sickening, disgusting, maudlin performances ever experienced."

Words were words, so one would think. But in the hands of the master manipulator, Nixon, they became more than mere words. They were alternately, carrot-and-stick-promises and warnings to polarize his audiences and secure their votes; sponges to soak up their sympathy for this pilloried underdog; barks to assure his underlings that this top dog meant business; feints to throw his enemies off guard; stilettos to thrust them through; foils to parry their retaliation; sops to appease them; strands of gossamer strung together in his solitude to hold together his house of fantasy, and—when all else failed—padding for the cell to which he could retreat to nurse his paranoia.

Nixon, it seems, was in good company when, in 1965, he defined neutrality where the Communists were concerned as: "we get out; they stay in; they take over." By 1970, Nixon, announcing his "incursion" into Cambodia, warned that anything less than "peace with honor" would make us "second-rate." Furthermore, if we failed to act in this crisis, we would be "unworthy to lead the forces of freedom in this critical period in world history." In addition, he declared himself as preferring to be a "one-term President and do what I believe is right than to be a two-term President at the cost of seeing America become a second-rate power and to see this nation accept the first defeat in its proud 190-year history." With typical inflated verbiage, he concluded, "If, when the chips are down, the world's most powerful nation . . . acts like a pitiful, helpless giant, the forces of totalitarianism and anarchy will threaten free nations and free institutions throughout the world." Here, as Nixon would have it, civilization itself hung in the balance. Unnoticed by many was the fact that, at the time, Nixon was ordering the massive withdrawal of American troops from Vietnam, leaving the South Vietnamese to fight their own battles under, of course, protective U.S. air cover. It is worthy of note that, seeing the war continue badly, Nixon within a year was laying plans to meet with the erstwhile "forces of darkness" in Peking and Moscow, to broker agreements that would help end the war and credit him with "peace with honor."

It was just this kind of twisted thinking that led to Vietnam in the first place, perpetuated our stay there in the longest war we ever fought, and ultimately spilled over in the Watergate fiasco. Overlooked in Nixon's vow not to be the first president to lose a war was the Civil War, in which the Southern half of the nation lost—as well as the Korean War, which ended, at best, in a stalemate. Certainly neither of these wars can be considered thumping victories. And with the development of nuclear weapons, it appears no nation can emerge from another world war claiming victory.

While aides and assorted friends, and of course the Pentagon—together with many citizens—praised Nixon's speech, Senate doves such as Fulbright, Mansfield, Aiken, and Kennedy denounced it, together with much of the press. *The New York Times* labeled it "military hallucination. Again . . . time and bitter experience have exhausted the credulity of the American people and Congress." *The Washington Post* perhaps said it best, deploring this "self-renewing war," supported by "suspect evidence, specious argument and excessive rhetoric."[17]

As we can see, Nixon's thoughts expressed themselves in his language, in his decisions, and in his actions. That so much of his language was mined with fallacy meant that many of his decisions would be fraught with danger. Furthermore, that so many of his actions served nothing but to subvert the intentions of the Founders in the Constitution should give us pause.

Acting

Still another factor in Nixon's expansion of power and a significant part of his speaking was his acting, his ability to project a persona manifestly at odds with the private, personal Nixon. Wrapped up in this man, suggested author David Abrahamsen, was the unlikely combination of furtiveness and exhibitionism. It was more, much more, than the natural inclination, especially among strangers we wish to impress, to put our best foot forward. Nixon would put forward a new foot, a new leg, a new body—indeed, a new Nixon, when he was trying to impress an audience or a superior. When Judge John Sirica listened to the Watergate tapes he was shocked at the glaring disparity between the private and public Nixon. So were millions of Americans who, recalling the TV images of the underdog in "Checkers," the challenger in Caracas—where, during a 1958 tour, Nixon had been accosted by an anti-American mob—and the saint in the White House, took another look as they read the transcripts, pointing to a vastly different Nixon: a desperate felon, trying every which way to escape the noose of impeachment, even to throwing overboard the aides whose loyalty he'd rarely questioned.

If it took one to know one, Nixon saw in Soviet leader Brezhnev the consummate actor. "At public functions Brezhnev's demeanor remained ebullient. He obviously enjoyed the attention he was getting and, like a skilled actor or born politician, he knew how to hold center stage." Few descriptions of Nixon himself were more apt. Kissinger, no slouch himself when it came to projecting a persona, gave Nixon "high marks for acting ability," particularly when it came to hearing a plan he'd heard before— many times. "Each time," Kissinger noted, Nixon would listen with "wide-eyed interest, as if he were hearing the plan for the first time." And each time his questions were "the same mixture of skepticism, fascination, and approval." "No wonder," wrote reporter Wicker, "that so many in the press . . . came to regard him as a cardboard man. Reporters are not so much inclined or encouraged to look past what meets the eye, and in Nixon they tended only to see the performer—to their experienced eyes, the faker."[18]

It was in high school that Nixon took to the stage, found himself front and center, and discovered there an exhilaration he'd found nowhere else. He got some hoots, whistles, and catcalls, as when he embraced his girl-friend, Ola-Florence Welch, on stage but—no matter—he was where he could transform himself from the furtive loner, the solitary bookworm, to the expansive extrovert, the one who loved everybody if not anybody, and expected their attention if not their affection in return.

In college Nixon went a step further, serving as stage manager as well as taking various parts. In 1952, Dr. Albert Upton, Nixon's college drama coach, saw on TV his star pupil, after the "Checkers" speech, sobbing on the shoulder of California Senator William Knowland. Upton was jubilant. "I taught him to cry . . . he tried conscientiously at rehearsals, and he'd get a pretty good lump in his throat and that was all. But on the evening of performance, tears just ran out of his eyes. It was beautifully done, those tears." It was through his acting that Nixon met Ola-Florence. She took note of his indulging his fantasies not only onstage but off, where, she acknowledged, he was "an excellent actor."

By the time he'd entered politics, Nixon found his acting ability cru-cial in winning votes. He could wear any one of an assortment of faces, depending on the solution. One aide described him as "a little kid in the schoolyard that all the boys were torturing. In order to escape, he put on different faces and masks."[19]

Nixon learned to play two parts with ease when he took to the political stage in 1946: watchdog and underdog. As watchdog he learned to sound the alarm. Like Paul Revere dashing through the streets of Boston crying that the Redcoats were coming, Nixon dashed across California, then across the country, sounding the alarm that the Reds were not only coming—they were here. He cast himself just as easily as underdog: the diminutive but valiant David doing battle with the giant Goliath; the piteous Job wracked by one calamity after another, left to fend for himself among his "friends" in the press; the gaunt Ehijah, whining on his mountaintop retreat that alas, he alone remained faithful to Jehovah; the righteous John the Baptist, crying alone in the wilderness, his head about to be served up on the platter through Watergate. Yet the roles were in conflict as often as not. It was hard to be the austere Puritan, pronouncing damnation on Voorhis, Hiss, Douglas and the Truman Democrats and, at the same time, crave sympathy as the perpetual underdog. So he took to alternating these roles, hoping the public, if not the press, would fail to perceive the dissonance. And he added other roles: the warm, sensitive Nixon, his hand extended to any and all in need; the valiant and gallant Sheriff Nixon, out to restore order on the American social frontier; the cunning and furtive Nixon, able to play high-stakes poker with the best of them; the pensive, reflective Nixon, the intellectual who preferred his books and his dreams; and the international Nixon, the lofty statesman who used nations as chess pieces.

Nixon, said Stevenson, was "a man of many masks," shifting effortlessly from one to the other. He was the political chameleon, changing colors with the campaign seasons. In 1952, in full orb of his anti-Communist binge, he plumped for the reelection of "my good friend, Joe McCarthy." By 1956, however, McCarthy had fallen on his sword and Nixon—his eye on the White House—changed colors to be seen as the inclusive President, the President of all the people. Seeing the anti-Communist issue had been gnawed to the bone, he left off the attacks, at least at home, and tried desperately to project the image of the statesman: cut in the image of Ike, living above the gutter fighting of partisan politics, observing protocol religiously as he rubbed shoulders with other world leaders. But it was no use. Dick Nixon still looked more like "Tricky Dick" than the open and affable Ike. He could no more take on the persona of Ike than he could the homey likableness of Truman, the jaunty camaraderie of FDR, or the robust heartiness of TR. By nature an introvert, Nixon had more than he could do to effect the persona of a gregarious, outgoing pol. And when he tried, it invariably looked calculated rather than spontaneous, convincing many voters it was an act. The one thread that appeared to connect the various parts he tried playing was simply his acting.

When JFK was asked in 1960 if he wasn't exhausted from his grueling campaign schedule, he replied: "No, but Nixon must be." Why? "Because I know who I am and I don't have to worry about adapting and changing. All I have to do at each stop is be myself. But Nixon doesn't know who he is, and so each time he makes a speech he has to decide which Nixon he is, and that will be very exhausting." Kennedy was right that Nixon kept changing faces, but wrong if he meant that Nixon couldn't help himself. It wasn't so much a matter of trying to decide who he was as contriving who he wanted to be, which role the circumstances called upon him to play. In a 1968 luncheon conversation with John Osborne, a highly respected journalist for *The New Republic*, Nixon aide Bryce Harlow asked, "Why do you hate my guy so much?" Flustered by the abruptness of the question, Osborne finally admitted, "The press corps calls [Nixon] 'the cardboard man' because we can't see past the facade of the candidate. I've never met the real Nixon."

Yet, as Wicker emphasized, Nixon tried desperately to shed the image of "an expedient ham actor," coupled with a ruthless politician who obeyed his cunning more than his conscience.[20] Here, in short, was the flimflam man, the snake-oil salesman with the rubber face and the tongue made smooth with his oil. Here was the glib pol who could make one promise after another, relying on the electorate's short memory so he wouldn't have to keep them.

For his 1960 campaign Nixon decided to trot out the "new and improved" persona in a half-hour film that cost a half-million dollars. It was not money well spent. "Richard M. Nixon: A. Self-Portrait," featured cuts of himself as a warm, affable, extrovert, the gregarious neighbor next door. It didn't even help that Billy Graham, "America's Favorite Evangelist," liked it—therefore Nixon could release it. For already the press had repeatedly pictured the quintessential loner, the introvert who squirmed in the presence of strangers, who detested small talk almost as much as he did Communists. Yet give him an audience of upturned faces, and he lit up like a Christmas tree, in Abrahamsen's description, "plugged into a temperament-charging circuit."

Wisdom, Eric Severeid pointed out, didn't seem to count in a candidate. "Rarely has the private quality of a man been the deciding factor in his election to the White House . . . the wrapping seems more important than the contents," the veteran TV reporter maintained. If a candidate "is of poor and humble origin, he must appear at ease with the rich and powerful; if he is of rich and powerful origin, he must make it clear that his heart has always been with the humble and poor. He must appear, in other words, to be the universal man." This person may be the winter's snowman, standing alone, stationary, cold as ice, his stare fixed straight ahead. But the persona had to be the man for all seasons, for spring, summer, and fall as well, the pol who would be all things to all people.

By 1960, the packaging of the persona was no longer left to chance or to amateurs. In their place was the PR professional, Bob Haldeman, convinced that the surest route to 1600 Pennsylvania Avenue was by way of Madison Avenue. Replacing Murray Chotiner, Haldeman would come into his own in 1968, after two false starts in 1960 and 1962. Nevertheless, Haldeman did his best, in 1960, to produce what Severeid noted was the appearance of "Organized Men, packaged candidates who stood for nothing but their own ambitions." Nowhere, in either Kennedy's or Nixon's speeches, could Severeid find a firm stand or a given issue vital to Main Street America. As a result, the reporter concluded, he'd be damned if he "ever thought one of them would end up running the country." Arthur Schlesinger was just as blunt. Of the two candidates, he concluded Nixon was the mid-century man, "obsessed [more] with the appearances than [with] the reality of things, obsessed above all with his own image, seeking reassurance through winning, but never knowing why he is so mad to win or what he will do with his victory.[21]

Nowhere did the contrast between Nixon's person and his persona become more striking than in his views of Ike. According to his persona, Ike was the savior of world peace, as well as civilization itself: serving as Commanding General of Allied Forces in Europe during World War II; a national hero who remained for eight years the world's most popular man; in the eyes of American voters, the true-blue statesman who camped above the partisan timberline. But according to Nixon's person, Ike was a disappointing leader . . . a perpetual waffler who was so enamored of a balanced budget that he slighted not only national security but foreign policy itself. By 1962, *Six Crises* was hot off the press, just in time to assure California voters in particular, and other voters in general, that Nixon had "no regrets" about his 1960 loss. This despite his postmortem four pages earlier in the book, where he kicked himself repeatedly for his mistakes. He'd campaigned too long, ignored major events, and emphasized substance over style. His aides concluded that he didn't lose the election as much as he simply blew it, that perhaps Nixon just "wasn't cut out to be top banana."

If Nixon wasn't to be president in 1960, it wasn't for lack of his thespian attempts. Cabill Phillips, writing in *The New York Times*, was glad to see that Nixon had jettisoned "the unctuous countenance of a superannuated 'All-American Boy' " for a "certain sedateness that better becomes his age and station." Yet beneath the mask of "disarming youthfulness," Phillips continued to discern "a ruthless ambition for whom expedience takes the place of principle. . . "[22]

When, after his defeat in the 1962 California gubernatorial race, Nixon sang his swan song to the assembled press, James Reston thought he detected in the irascible and belligerent figure "the real Nixon." Backed in a corner by Governor Pat Brown and the California Democrats—not only defeating him, but suing him and his party for a half-million dollars for the violation of campaign laws—Nixon let his hair down as he rarely did in public. Was this the person, Reston asked. Six years later, British journalist David Frost asked Nixon if he'd made any remark in his political career that he now regretted. The only one Nixon could think of was that 1962 swan song, something he vowed not to repeat "as long as I'm a public figure."

By 1968, Nixon was determined not only to avoid confrontation with the press, but to use the media to great advantage in his campaign. Some sixteen years before, Ike had retained an ad agency. Leonard Hall, Republican National Chairman, explained, "You sell your candidates and your programs the way a business sells its products." By the time of Nixon's 1968 campaign, David Boorstin wrote that advertising "has meant a reshaping of the very concept of truth."

Between the power of advertising and the power of TV, Nixon the actor thought he had it made. Was there a plague of troubles afflicting the land? Richard the Lionheart was galloping to the rescue astride his white horse, proclaiming Law and Order. Was the Vietnam War hanging like an albatross around the neck of Uncle Sam? Enter, right, Richard the Peacemaker, fingering his "secret plan" for ending the war in six months. Was there a division in the electorate, threatening to tear the nation apart as not in a century? Enter, left, Richard the Mediator, the one who promised to "bring us together." Was there too much accusatory shouting, leaving hoarseness as well as acrimony in its wake? Listen carefully, then, to Richard the Counselor who would have us lower our voices and take time to listen. Was there immorality, like termites, eating away at our nation's foundations? Time for Richard the Pure to make his appearance, to denounce sin in its every guise, and to proclaim the dawn of a new day of righteousness.

No doubt about it, Nixon could play many roles. Marrying the power of hype to the power of illusion, this consummate actor, raised in the shadow of Hollywood, relished his many roles. Late in 1967 one Nixon handler wrote, "Potential presidents are measured against an ideal that's a combination of leading man, God, father, hero, pope, king, with a touch of the avenging Furies thrown in." It was the role of hero in a morality play, Abrahamsen contended, that Nixon treasured most.

John Osborne, writing in *The New Republic*, asked the questions that millions must have had on the tip of their tongues when they saw Nixon in action. "Must he always, upon emerging from his plane onto the ramp at the door, no matter how large or small the waiting crowd, fling his arms upward and outward, his fingers wiggling in a frenetic digital dance? He always does. During his speeches, at points of maximum emphasis, must he always bend his arms at the elbows, his legs at the knees, and, rising on his toes in a curious slouching crouch, thrust his clenched fists at the audience? He always does." Osborne added, significantly, ". . . his back noticeably rounded and bowed at the neck, his whole stance [was] expressive of an overwhelming ordinariness," albeit with a remarkable talent for survival.[23]

Scrutinizing the 1968 campaign, author Joe McGinniss contended that "politics . . . has always been a con game." If P.T. Barnum was the original American flimflam man, Nixon must come in a close second. He resolved he would not make the mistake of 1960, emphasizing substance over style. He would be measured, as McGinniss noted, "not against a standard of performance established by two centuries of democracy—but against

Mike Wallace, TV host of 60 Minutes. Then "style becomes substance. The medium gets the votes."

By 1968, Nixon, in the words of Norman Mailer, "had grown from a bad actor to a surprisingly good actor." In addition to occupying front and center stage, he wrote the script, produced and directed the play, and served as stage manager and costume designer in the bargain. He selected his live audiences as meticulously as he selected his dress. Staging telethons, he handpicked his questions. Always he made certain that between his heavy jowls and heavier five o'clock shadow, there was a beaming victory grin, the mark of a confident and statesmanlike President. Nothing—no, nothing—was left to chance.

The public—or enough of the public—bought the charade and Nixon captured the White House. But behind the victory grin, behind the calm, statesmanlike facade, there raged a seething cauldron of emotions, some of them diverse, others in conflict. Only a few of his top aides, his family, and a handful of friends ever became familiar with the private Nixon. What the public saw was the image he projected, the persona that he burnished continually and changed as circumstances demanded.

Lower-echelon aides, like military aide Bill Gulley, occasionally caught a glimpse of the person. Gulley recalled Nixon welcoming a group of returning Vietnam POW's to a White House dinner, presumably in their honor. When they weren't listening, Gulley chanced to overhear Nixon's disparaging remarks about them, "even as he threw away gifts they'd brought him." Worse was Nixon's staging of a ceremony in June 1972, honoring John Paul Vann, a hero of the Vietnam War. Jesse, Vann's son, was invited to the Oval Office—a bad mistake, Nixon was soon to realize—to receive posthumously the Medal of Freedom for his father. A maverick like his father, Jesse had torn his draft card in two and placed one-half in his father's coffin saying, "Here, this is all I can give you now; this is all I can do." The other half he planned to give Nixon at the White House ceremony. Knowing it was a crime not to carry his draft card with him, and a further crime to mutilate it, Jesse was eager to see the look on Nixon's face when he handed it to him.

But Jesse made the mistake of disclosing his plan to his family, who immediately tried arguing him out of it. Brent Scowcroft, a Nixon aide, overheard the commotion and, investigating, realized this would be an awkward situation—or worse. So he told Nixon, who threatened to cancel the ceremony if Jesse persisted. So Jesse relented, making way for a photo-op with no nasty surprises.

The photo-op was vintage Nixon. He praised Vann. He extended condolences to the family. Everything was by the book. But Jesse and brother Peter couldn't help but notice that Nixon's mind was elsewhere. On Watergate? On the November election? Who knows? But it wasn't there. Nixon was going through the motions, heavy makeup for the TV cameras giving him the appearance of a Hollywood actor, smiling too much for the occasion. The boys felt ill, nauseated by the fake performance of one who knew nothing of Vann, whose script had been prepared by another, whose encomiums were too lavish: "Soldier of peace and patriot of two nations, the name of John Paul Vann will be honored as long as free men remember the struggle to preserve the independence of South Vietnam. . . .A truly noble American, a superb leader, he stands with Lafayette in that gallery of heroes who have made another brave people's cause their own." The fact was that these "brave people"—the South Vietnamese Army, holding a five-to-one ratio of soldiers over the enemy, together with the latest U.S. technical weapons and unchallenged air power—had just fled Hanoi's army. Nixon's was indeed high praise for one who'd resigned his commission in disgust over the refusal of the top brass to listen to him and others on the battlefront, even as Paul Harkins and William Westmoreland were feeding Johnson the news he wanted desperately to hear. In that respect, the generals were only giving their commander in chief what he, in turn, had been giving his audiences—just what they wanted to hear. As if all of this fakery and ignorance weren't enough, there was Nixon tying the death of the boys' father to Nixon's ill-fated war policy, to keep fighting a war as useless as it was senseless.[24]

Within months, as the Vietnam War receded, then ended in January 1973—at least for the United States—Nixon found himself in another battle: with Congress and the courts, two of the triad of checks and balances provided in the Constitution. As the tide of Watergate rose higher and higher, reaching at last the ski jump of his nose, Nixon finally, and most reluctantly, quit the stage on which he'd been performing for twenty-eight years. He left his national audience convinced that he was a better actor than he was a President, and that was saying precious little.

Insecurity

The final factor we shall consider in Nixon's expansion of his power was his patent insecurity, begun early in his life. Smaller than his brothers; the third of five boys; fearful of his father's temper tantrums; seldom touched, much less hugged, by his straitlaced Quaker mother; a "goody two shoes" Sunday-school teacher who practiced the piano so he could play in church; learning the violin as well; a "nerd" who took to books as others took to baseball—Nixon tried frantically to offset this image he thought effeminate by effecting the pose of a tough guy. To avoid being seen by other boys as he washed dishes at home, he'd draw the shade. By high school he was also effecting the pose of a girl-hater. Said one female classmate, "He'd make horrible faces at us. As a debater . . . his main theme was why he hated girls." Later, in college, he made an exception and dated Ola-Florence Welch. Yet, in six years of going with her, he never told her he liked her, much less loved her. Arguably the most attractive and personable girl in the college, Ola-Florence was simply his personal trophy, a conquest that paid tribute to his machismo. In addition, Nixon went out for football at Whittier, only to remain—for four years—a bench warmer. Just 150 pounds of klutz, he was best as a lusty cheerleader while on the bench, and as a tackling dummy during practice. Knocked down again and again, he was always back on his feet. Coach "Chief" Newman damned him with faint praise: "We used Nixon as a punching bag . . . exposing a masochistic streak to display his manliness. Anybody else would have given up after not making the first team in the first year, or certainly the second year."[25]

Nixon won more than his share of honors in college, but won few close friends other than Welch. It was the same in law school—only more so, Welch recalling his letters that revealed him as "lonely and lost." With his roommate, he left the impression he was intense, private, and humorless. Other classmates remembered him as "Gloomy Gus . . . shot through with rectitude . . . industrious, honest, reverent, all of that." And one classmate recalled how Nixon simply "bristled" when he called him "Nicky." The only time Welch found Nixon relaxed and enjoying himself was when he got word that he'd been accepted at Duke on a scholarship. "He was not only fun, he was joyous, abandoned. . . . He said that was the best thing that had ever happened to him. We rode around in his car and just celebrated."

It didn't last long, as "Gloomy Gus—alias "Iron-Butt"—dug in his heels and dug in his books, determined not to be left behind, competing with graduates of better schools in the East than Whittier could ever hope to boast. Graduating third in his class at Duke, he figured he had it made. With two other graduates he set off for New York City, there to seek his fortune with a prestigious Wall Street firm—only to be rejected while his companions, first and second in the class, got jobs. Discouraged, Nixon learned of an opening in the FBI and applied—never to hear from them. Licking his wounds, he returned to his hometown where, through family connections, he at last obtained a position with the city's oldest law firm. None of this was to help his self-image.[26]

When White House correspondent Helen Thomas commented to Julie, "Many people say your father is not warm and does not relate to people," she was out to defend him. "I don't agree. He's just a very human, warm person. . . . He is such a sensitive person."

For the very few—mostly women—who saw this side of Dick Nixon, thousands saw him as a cold fish, as insensitive as he was insecure. He not only craved the positive strokes of others but, as Theodore White put it, "Nixon was above all a friend seeker, almost pathetic in his eagerness to be liked. . . ." Yet seeking to be liked did not go as far as touching. When Elvis Presley met with Nixon in an impromptu visit to the White House to be named an honorary drug enforcement agent, he embraced the President. Observing this, aide Egil Krogh wrote, "I thought to myself, boy, this is the last meeting they let me schedule, because you don't hug Nixon."

Pat turned out to be the polar opposite of Dick when it came to making friends and touching people. For him, reaching out to others, opening up to others, made him vulnerable to rebuff, to criticism, to rejection, all too painful for his fragile ego. Pat, on the other hand, was ever ready with a smile, a handshake, an embrace. And when she summoned the courage to criticize him, she usually wrapped her words in velvet.

Virtually everybody who got to know him found in Nixon a man tormented by the demons of discontent, of self-doubt, even of self-loathing. Reporter Jimmy Breslin noted that Nixon appeared to feel guilty for having chosen his father's love of argumentative jostling rather than his mother's disciplined peacefulness and charity. "Keeping his evil internal," Breslin wrote, "ruined him, with his being judge and jury of his own sins, proclaiming a self-hatred that resulted in continual accusations against others. . . ." When, in his first term as President, Nixon found HEW Secretary Bob Finch, Communications Director Herb Klein, and Secretary of the Interior Walter Hickel summoning courage to level with him, he summarily fired Finch and Hickel, and kicked Klein "upstairs" to another slot where he'd be less offensive. Shown his daily news summaries, Nixon the tough guy, gave vent to his spleen. "Get someone to hit him," "fire him," "cut him," "freeze him," "fight him," "dump him," or "don't back off." One is left to wonder, reading the transcripts of Nixon's tapes, whether it was anger at being blocked in his pursuits of unattainable goals, or a dreadful self-loathing, or simply his awkward effort to be "one of the boys" that gave expression to his castigating others. Senator Sam Ervin was alternately, "an old fart," "a senile old shit," "a sonofabitch," and an "old incredible bastard." Not one to single out Ervin, Nixon had a few choice words for others of his adversaries. Thus Senator Howard Baker was "that simpering asshole" while John Dean became "a goddamned liar." Yet in his public appearances—or in the presence of friend Billy Graham or noted attorney Charles Alan Wright—his language was suddenly sanitized. "Goddamn" became "goodness," "how in hell" became "how in the world," "who the hell" became "who the heck," and "knowledge of the damn thing" became "knowledge of the darn thing."[27]

Frustrated by the flak he was drawing from the press, by the stalling of a lumbering bureaucracy, by the obstinacy of a cantankerous Congress, by the carping of renegade Democrats, and by the bumbling of his own perfidious staff, Nixon more and more threw aside the bonds of self-discipline his mother had drawn about him. With the pendulum of Watergate swinging closer to his neck as he struggled to free himself in the pit of despair, he found that aide Ziegler had disobeyed his orders and permitted the press to accompany them. Swinging into action, the furious Nixon gave the miscreant a shove that sent him almost sprawling, while millions watched on TV.

Nixon, it seemed, was constitutionally incapable of pinning the blame for his mistakes on himself. Refusing the advice of others in 1960—including his own campaign aides and Ike—he lost to Kennedy, only to place the blame on Ike, TV cameras, his own makeup in the debates, the press, and others. Rejecting his wife's advice, he ran for governor in 1962 and lost to Brown, only to single out the press, among others, to blame. Ignoring the advice of Senators Fulbright, Mansfield,

Aiken and other "doves," he continued the war, proclaiming a hollow "peace with honor," only to find sure defeat, and promptly blamed a recalcitrant Congress for cutting off funds. As Watergate began rattling his cage, he wrote in his diary, "Without Martha [Mitchell] I am sure that this Watergate thing would never have happened." (Fearful that her husband would take the fall for Watergate, the outspoken Mrs. Mitchell had pointed her finger at the White House—and away from the Attorney General.) And when at last this felon was drawn from office by the threat of impeachment and a criminal trial, he characteristically pinned the blame on Congress, the Supreme Court, the press, his aides, and everybody else he could summon as scapegoats. Judge John Sirica gasped in disgust at the "evidence of his role in the cover-up . . . appalled by his lying. . . . ." aghast that never once did Nixon blame himself.

Nowhere did Nixon's demons of discontent manifest themselves more conspicuously than in his prejudice and his stereotyping, thereby stigmatizing others different from himself. Such prejudice, wrote Harvard's Gordon Allport in his *Nature of Prejudice*, is invariably rooted in one's own insecurity. There is a Chinese proverb: "The taller we grow the more we must bend." But if we refuse to believe we've grown, and have cultivated the habit of branding others to pull them down to our presumed level—if, to quote the musical, we have been "carefully taught" to hate others who differ from us in color, creed, ethnic origin, build, age, or some such—we find it extremely difficult to rid ourselves of the ingrained habit. In 1972, Nixon persuaded labor leaders to desert Democratic candidate George McGovern for him because McGovern liked "labor as a mass" whereas Nixon liked them "individually;" this, he claimed, was also true of the young, blacks, Mexicans" and others.

Especially did Nixon resent the charge of being an anti-Semite, yet few presidents deserved it more. In 1956, he was plagued with the stigma, stirring up a hornet's nest in big cities like New York, where many Jews were members of National Citizens for Eisenhower. Later, recruiting Kissinger, a Jewish refugee from Nazi Germany, Nixon was hard put to show what Julie insisted was her father's extreme sensitivity. Time and again Kissinger would return from a meeting with Nixon to complain to deputy Lawrence Eagleberger, "That man is an anti-Semite!" Others of Nixon's aides heard him repeatedly complaining, "The Jewish sonofabitch is out to get me." And he had, he thought, good reason. In 1971, he summoned his

White House chief of personnel, Fred Malek, to warn him that in the Bureau of Labor was a "Jewish cabal" distorting economic figures to make his administration look bad. How many Jews, asked Nixon, were in that bureau? Malek investigated, reported back, and had to explain that the bureau's statistical methods were traditional in economics.

With Nixon's blundering "incursion" into Cambodia he found what he intended to be kept secret suddenly exposed in the press. In a rage, he ordered Hoover to tap the phones of suspects, and in particular a Kissinger aide and fellow Jewish professor at Harvard, Morton Halperin. He was, in Hoover's words, one of those "arrogant, Harvard-type Kennedy men" who just couldn't be trusted. As Ehrlichman, whose grandfather was Jewish, recalled, "Nixon would talk about Jewish traitors, and the Eastern Jewish Establishment—Jews at Harvard, then turning to Kissinger, 'Isn't that right, Henry? Don't you agree?' Thereupon Kissinger would cavil, 'Well, Mr. President, there are Jews and Jews.'" [28]

Repeatedly in Ehrlichman's notes are references to Nixon's complaining that both the Internal Revenue Service and Commerce Department were "over-topped" with Jews who were more intent on punching out early and getting a jump on the parking lots than in completing their time. Ehrlichman also made note of Safire, Garment, and economic advisor Herbert Stein experiencing "that sinking sensation in an especially personal way" when they heard Nixon on his June 23, 1973, tape complain that the arts were heavily influenced by leftist Jews, confirming the anti-Semitism "which all of us tried so hard to allay."

Visiting Israel in June 1974, Nixon encountered angry Jews parading with placards, "We're All Jew-Boys Here," a reference to Nixon's repeated slurs in the White House. With painful phlebitis in his leg and painful signs indicting him for his anti-Semitism, Nixon was suffering far worse pains as he thought of his impending impeachment. So much so that Israel's Prime Minister Golda Meir complained to Kissinger, "We still have never had a visit from an American President. Nixon was here but his thoughts were far away."

Yet two of Nixon's staunchest supporters were Jews. Walter Annenberg, a Jewish billionaire, built his own golf course at Palm Desert, California, when he discovered the local golf club barring Jews. The President's frequent slurs notwithstanding, he dismissed the charge of anti-Semitism against Nixon as "utter rubbish." "True," he insisted, "it isn't easy to get close to him no matter how cordial a relationship you may have had."

About the time Nixon visited Israel, he had in his corner—while the waters of Watergate were swirling about him—none other than a Jewish rabbi from Providence, Baruch Korff. He'd seen Nixon working to free Soviet Jews, so how could he be an anti-Semite? American Jews, Korff firmly believed, weren't sufficiently appreciative of their President. Worse, many liberal Jews were in the vanguard of Nixon detractors. In December 1973, Nixon was treated to a surprise when into the Oval Office walked Korff and a delegation pinning their faith on this beleaguered President. Some six months earlier Korff had begun a campaign to defend Nixon, so he allotted Korff five minutes for his visit—only to let him stay forty minutes, as Nixon relished this breather in his battle over Watergate. Nixon, the good rabbi suggested, had made a mistake not to destroy the incriminating tapes. This "small-town rabbi," as he called himself, "found it morally and ethically offensive that the people didn't know they were taped"—leaving "the people" unidentified. Korff's National Citizens' Committee for Fairness to the Presidency was so concerned about Nixon that they'd paid $5,000—including Korff's vacation money—to put ads in *The New York Times* and *The Washington Post* to solicit support for their organization. Before they left, Nixon, properly grateful, bestowed on them presidential souvenirs. Five months later, in May 1973, Nixon was the honored guest at a rally organized by Korff. To his intercessor Nixon explained, "Watergate is the thinnest scandal in American history. If these charges . . . were true, nobody would have to ask me to resign—I wouldn't serve for one more month. But I know they are not true."[29]

It appears that Korff and his followers believed Nixon, and stuck to him to the very end. So did Annenberg. So did Kissinger. Yet despite this support from people who happened to be Jews, Nixon, by June 1975, was criticizing President Ford for taking issue with General George Brown, chairman of the JCS, for his remark that Jews controlled the media. "Old Brown's all right," said Nixon, "but Goddamn, those guys have got to be held in check. You can't have them making off-the-cuff remarks like that. . . ." It was one thing to think it; something else again to say it.

Thus did Nixon's haunting insecurities feed his towering ambition, his driving industriousness, his penchant for acting, his obsession for front center stage, and his blatant prejudice. It also undercut his attempt to be seen as a man of letters—not only intelligent but an intellectual who could hold his own with the likes of Schlesinger. The masses were exposed to the persona of "The President of the United States," introduced with "Hail to the Chief," and other appropriate fanfare, to witness alternately the many faces of the India-rubber man. Those who knew him more intimately were exposed to the person flagrantly at odds with the persona. Here was the person Kissinger saw dreading to meet strangers. Here was the person PR expert Harry Treleavan described as weighted with a certain "grayness," while fellow expert Roger Ailes described Nixon as "funny-looking," "dull," "a bore," " a pain in the ass," and one "who was forty-two years old the day he was born." Here was the person Senator George Smathers saw sitting in a room for three hours on end, with nary a word passing between him and long-time intimate, Bebe Rebozo. Here was the person Pat Nixon described as "shy, reserved, isolated, enjoying his retreats. . . ." And, strangest of all, here was the person who confessed, "I'm an introvert in an extrovert's profession."[30] Here, then, lay the essence of the clash between persona and person. Here was a square peg in a round hole, and Nixon never—despite heroic attempts to round the corners—really fit the part of professional pol, much less the part of President. Yet despite the clash, he not only occupied the seat of the greatest power in the history of the world, but continued pushing at the constraints that were to circumscribe that power—until they were reinforced by the Supreme Court and Nixon fell, exhausted, the Godfather who'd directed every move of his political Mafia for more than five years.

CHAPTER 4

OPPORTUNISM

. . . whenever a few people, with interests of their own and little imagination, find themselves in charge of large sums of other people's money, disaster is on the way.
— John Steele Gordon

Had I been disposed to take advantage of my country a thousand opportunities had before presented themselves, in which I might have made an immense profit and escaped detection.
— James Monroe, 1825

LYNDON JOHNSON

Somewhere in Johnson is a compass that holds truest where the cash is piled highest."

— Robert Sherrill

. . . I never handled any money. Nobody brought me any money and I didn't distribute any money.

— Lyndon Johnson

. . . if the FCC was important to KTBC, Lyndon Johnson was important to the FCC. As a member of the Senate Commerce Committee, which is the overseer of the FCC, Johnson was inevitably involved in all the major decisions concerning the status and personnel of the FCC.

— Doris Kearns[1]

Integrity the Key

Johnson lusted for power, to expand every office he ever held—always with an eye on 1600 Pennsylvania Avenue—to control everything and everybody within his long grasp; to this end he seized every opportunity to do so, enriching himself in the bargain.

Opportunism, as Theodosius Dobzhansky has emphasized, is natural. Evolution is invariably opportunistic, he maintained, in that it adapts living systems to those environments existing only at the time, taking no account of future changes. As a result of such shortsighted opportunism, living systems may die and even species become extinct. Webster defines opportunism as "a policy or habit of adapting one's actions, thought, and utterances to circumstances, as in politics, in order to further one's immediate interests, without regard for basic principles or eventual conse-quences." The key to flagrant opportunism, as opposed to natural or justi-fiable opportunism, is not the lack of awareness of future consequences. Indeed, the "Law of Unintended Consequences" is but a corollary of sys-tems theory. Rather, it is a disregard of basic principles, of contradicting not only the universal values common to most, if not all, e.g. survival, but of contradicting oneself in the process. When Lady Bird wrote in her diary on June 29, 1964, that Humphrey "is as adaptable as a chameleon. . ." she could have better been speaking of her own husband. For indeed it is the chameleon that changes colors to blend with the changing background. For a chameleon the change is an inborn trait with survival value. In humans it can be deadly. Homo sapiens sapiens, by definition, means not only man thinking, and thinking for himself, but thinking of himself—or self-awareness. Given that further dimension of thought, made possible largely by the development of the prefrontal cortex in modern man, and we can plan, fix goals, and devise strategies for attaining those goals.

In that respect Lyndon Johnson was certainly a modern man, yet more. In a speech prepared largely by Goodwin, Johnson introduced the "Great Society" to an audience at the University of Michigan in 1964. This society would be born in the use of our wisdom as well as our wealth, "to advance the quality of American civilization," to move beyond a rich and powerful society to a Great Society, "where men are more concerned with the quality of their goals than the quantity of their goods."

Coming from the mouth of one who'd enriched himself as no other president, entering politics a poor man but entering the White House with a "quantity of goods" exceeding that of any president before or since, there is more than a little hypocrisy in the rhetoric. Later that year he would insist that America "open the doors of opportunity [and] . . . equip our people to walk through those doors." Johnson had not only walked through those doors, he'd pried them open—by hook or by crook—and he'd bounded through them.

We have noted that Johnson availed himself of opportunism repeat-edly. When, for example, President Evans learned at San Marcos of an opening in the school at Cotulla, he offered Lyndon the opportunity to fill the void. When Congressman Kleberg had an opening for a secretary, he turned to Sam Johnson's son to fill the void. When FDR needed an NYA administrator in Texas, he turned to Rayburn's "foster son" to fill the void.

And when the voters of Texas's Tenth District lost their congressman to a heart attack in 1937, they turned to Lyndon to fill that void. Yet it was clear that Johnson had, through contemptuous ingratiation, or through his father's pull, or both, grasped these opportunities by the neck. More inexcusable was his rank opportunism in sporting a Silver Star medal he never earned and in winning a seat in the Senate he never earned, both of which we will detail later. It would appear to many that Dame Fortune was indeed smiling on the opportunistic pol from Texas. But what most missed was the prostitution of his own integrity in the process, providing yet another step in his eventual self-destruction.

At the heart of the distinction, then, between a legitimate and illegitimate opportunism, is integrity. Taken from its root word, integer, or whole number as opposed to a fraction, integrity implies wholeness of person. It implies a person who, through the years, has constructed an inner core of values he considers inviolable, or nearly so, and open to compromise only in the most dire of circumstances. Take honesty, for example. I well remember in college meeting a couple from Copenhagen, Denmark. He had been pastor of the First Baptist Church during the Nazi invasion in World War II, and had taken in Jews to protect them from concentration camps and almost certain death. Yet when the Gestapo knocked on his door, suspecting he was hiding Jews, he remonstrated he was certainly doing no such thing. The decision he had to make was between two evils, and he chose the lesser of the two, dishonesty, to death—his own, very possibly, as well as the death of the Jews he was protecting. Here was a clear case of dire circumstances. In Johnson's case, however, as we shall note in detail in the chapter on deceit, he lied when it was simply convenient, just as he told the truth when convenient. Neither convenience nor aggrandizement can be considered dire circumstances. Thus did Lyndon illustrate what Stuart Chase explained in his classic essay, "The Luxury of Integrity." For it was Chase's contention that, to the extent integrity becomes a luxury we can ill afford, then to that extent we effectively rend the fabric of trust that binds a society together.

Lyndon Johnson, in sacrificing his own integrity on the altar of self-aggrandizement, not only violated the pledge he made to his father who came to the train to see him off for Washington, never to "shimmy," but eventuated in the "credibility gap" that became Johnson's trademark as President.

"Lyin' Down Lyndon" was the congressman who refused to take a stand on any issue lest he later have to eat those words. In that respect he was the embodiment of the story he enjoyed telling of the young man who appeared before the school board back in Texas Hill Country, applying for a job. One member asked the applicant how he would teach geography, since there was a difference of opinion in the community as to whether the world was round or flat. What did he intend to teach? The applicant had a ready answer, "I can teach it either way."[2]

Had Johnson read the classics, including Aristotle's *Rhetoric*, he would have known that this ancient Greek prized integrity as the most essential part of what he called "ethical proof" and we call credibility. Lyndon violated that integrity by scorning the values taught him by his parents, by reneging on the promises made to his parents, and by contradicting his lofty rhetoric with sordid actions. Thus was he easy prey for the rank opportunism that, like "credibility gap," became associated with him for the rest of his life.

The Pro in Quid Pro Quo

The remainder of this chapter will be devoted in large part to Johnson's enriching himself in office. In his adolescence he must have enjoyed green—the color of money—partly because he had so little of it. At fifteen he graduated from high school and fell in love with Kitty Clyde Ross, the daughter of E.P. Ross, known as the richest man in town. He would have no daughter of his marrying the son of Sam Johnson! So he paired off his daughter with the high school principal, her senior by fourteen years. Though she never married him, she never dated the Johnson boy again.

Lyndon tried anew in college. The girl was Carol Davis, daughter of the richest man in San Marcos. Lyndon made the most of it, driving her big white convertible, honking the horn long and loud at the local confectionery where she invariably picked up the tab. Passing other students trudging up College Hill, he'd again lay on the horn, broadcasting to all the world of Southwest Texas State Teachers College that he, Lyndon Johnson, had lassoed the prize of San Marcos. Recalled one student, "She was a rich man's daughter, and Lyndon was always looking for a way to help himself." And another student: "He wanted to find a girl who had a lot of money." Standing in his way, again, was the father of the girl he loved. A man of unusual physical courage, A.L. Davis refused to take part in the big Ku Klux Klan parade in town, when the Klan was at its peak of power and virtually every other prominent family was participating. A man of fierce Baptist faith, he was not only a teetotaler but loathed those who drank. A man of industry to match his entrepreneurial brains, he saw politicians, especially liberal ones, as leeches living off his taxes—and the poor on the dole as obviously immoral and lazy. In his eyes the Johnsons, and particularly legislator Sam Johnson, was the antithesis of these virtues. So Davis put his foot down. Carol would not marry one beneath her station. As devoted as she became to Lyndon, she was more devoted to her father, in whose eyes she was clearly the favorite of his four daughters. So by 1928, despite Lyndon's trying every trick in his expanding repertoire to ingratiate himself with A.L. Davis, the romance came to naught.

The proverbial big spender, Lyndon always managed to put out more than he could earn or borrow. He was always on the prowl for those with money he could either borrow or marry into. Finally, at the age of twenty-six, this congressional secretary struck gold in the person of Claudia Alta Taylor, otherwise known as Lady Bird. She may not have been the prettiest or the brightest in the northern part of Harrison County. But she was the richest. The only child of Thomas Jefferson Taylor, she found her father more interested in making money than in her welfare. By the time T.J. had married, he owned eighteen thousand acres, the general store in Karnack, and the county's most imposing residence. He was as ruthless as he was tireless, lending money to tenants and sharecroppers at a usurious ten percent interest. According to a neighbor, Taylor kept the Negroes who worked his land in peonage. He would supply them the land and the tools to work the land. Then, if they couldn't pay their bills, he'd take back the land. Here was a man after Lyndon's own heart! Davis, too, recognized in the young Johnson a kindred spirit. So when Lyndon came calling to ask T.J.'s permission to marry his daughter, Davis gave it unhesitatingly. No one to beat around the bush, Lyndon asked "Bird" to marry him on their first date. But by the time he confronted her father, he must have wondered if he would encounter the same opposition he'd met with his first two loves. Not to worry. She'd at last brought home "a real man." How much of a real man he was might have met strong arguments back in San Marcos, where Lyndon was remembered more for his silk shirts and dandy appearance than for athletic prowess or academic excellence.

By the end of 1935 Lyndon had struck gold—not only in Karnack, but in Congressman Kleberg's office: this time in the person of Alvin Wirtz. It wasn't so much that Wirtz, though looking like a small-town lawyer, was in fact a wealthy big-time lawyer whose clients included contractors Herman and George Brown. But Wirtz had also served with Sam in the Austin legislature, and learned that Lyndon was working as Kleberg's secretary. So when Wirtz came calling on behalf of the Brown and Root Construction Company, and Kleberg was out—as he usually was—Lyndon offered to introduce him to influential people in the Capital. Fortunately for Wirtz, he gained entree to Jerome Frank, chief attorney of the Federal Power Commission—through the intercession not of Kleberg, but of Kleberg's secretary. As Thomas Ferguson, a member of the Lower Colorado River Authority, put it, "Johnson called over there and got us in to see them real quick. . . . He knew Washington. He could get you into any place." In 1936, just in the nick of time for Brown and Root, the Bureau of Reclamation announced it was taking bids for a dam at the Marshall Ford—a big dam, a $10 million dam—just the kind of project Herman Brown had been yearning for since 1909. And Lyndon Johnson's intervention had been a necessary if not a sufficient step in the process. To Wirtz, Lyndon later paid tribute as "my dearest friend, my most trusted counselor. From him I gained a glimpse of what greatness there is in the human race."[3] High praise indeed, and no wonder. For Wirtz was the conduit to Herman and George Brown, and it was their money—the money they earned and would continue to earn through Lyndon's intercession—that became the mother's milk of politics for this pol.

When "Buck" Buchanan died in 1937, leaving the Tenth District with no one in the House, Lyndon went to two people to seek their opinion—and their money. The first was Lady Bird. Yes, he should make a run for it, despite the overwhelming odds against him. And yes, there was $10,000 from her trust fund to get him started, just the amount Wirtz told him it would take to put him on the starting line. The other person was Wirtz himself. Together they weighed the tradeoff in Lyndon's shedding his NYA job for a really long shot at Congress. Wirtz was no impulsive gambler. He would, however, take a calculated risk. And he knew Lyndon was counting on his pipeline to the oil and gas interests in Texas. While, in the opinion of Senator Tom Connally, Wirtz was a liberal drawn to

FDR's New Deal for the contracts it would bring his clients like the Browns, he was also a pragmatist who understood the loathing with which most big money in Texas viewed FDR. Still, Wirtz was great in the balancing act—able, in the words of Connally, "to carry buckets of bubbling acid on both shoulders without spilling a drop." And, Connally added, Wirtz pursued these conflicting interests "ruthlessly against a lot of helpless people." Still, as far as Johnson was concerned, Wirtz was not only a clever and wealthy lawyer but one who could raise lots of cash. And Wirtz was impressed with Johnson's ability, as young as he was, to spend government money for the NYA. Like manure, both figured, it did no good in a pile, but spread around carefully, it could make votes sprout and contracts bloom. So Wirtz, who was up to a calculated risk, put his money on the horse most people thought would be last at the gate. But with the right jockey, he figured, the horse from Johnson City had at least a fighting chance. Not only did Johnson need that chance, so did Wirtz. Better than a congressman's secretary was a congressman himself to wangle the federal funds to build those Colorado River dams. And, Lyndon figured, they would, in addition to controlling floods, provide the electricity that would revolutionize the Hill Country. Rebekah had always said the only reason to get power was to spend it doing good, so Lyndon figured it was nobody's business how much he spent in his campaign or where he got the money. As far as the voters were concerned, Lyndon was financing his campaign from his "own meager savings." In actuality he outspent his principal opponent, Emmett Shelton, by at least $25,000; just the amount Lady Bird's father added to the $10,000 from his daughter. This dissimulation, coupled with secrecy, would become as nothing else Lyndon's trademark for the rest of his career. In addition, there was the usual vote-buying with special interest money. After all, this was Texas politics. So here, in his first political campaign, Johnson set the pattern of rank opportunism that never blinked at sacrificing integrity on the altar of self-aggrandizement.

Lyndon, the long shot from Johnson City, succeeded in passing the other horses one by one, and in a final frenzy of working and spending, plunged through to victory. Sam's parting words to his son as he boarded the train for Washington came too late. Though he'd probably never read Machiavelli, Lyndon was a faithful disciple paying no attention to integrity: ". . . those princes who have done great things have held good faith of little account, and have known how to circumvent the intellect of men by craft, and in the end have overcome those who have relied on their word." Sam Johnson had earned a reputation as a straight shooter, a man whose word was his bond. His son, however, saw reliance on his word as a different kind of bond, a bond meant to shackle him, to tie him down in the free-for-all politics of Texas. Back in the Middle Ages, Machiavelli had counseled his Prince that it was not virtue itself, but the appearance of virtue that was important. Thus, "to appear merciful, faithful, humane, religious, upright, and to be so, with a mind so framed that should you require not to be so, you may be able and know how to change to the opposite."[4]

The trick, Lyndon soon discovered in working for Kleberg, was not to come down on any issue of importance. Even in college, one student recalled, Lyndon "never took strong positions . . . he was only interested in himself and what could help himself." Now, as Kleberg's secretary and speaker of the "Little Congress"—composed of other congressional aides— Lyndon was often pressed to commit himself on a controversial issue. Well, he'd explain, he hadn't made up his mind on that. Said one aide, "There's nothing wrong with being pragmatic. But you have to believe in something." Luther Jones, Johnson's assistant from 1933 to 1935, didn't think Lyndon was "either conservative or liberal. I think he was whatever he felt like he needed to be. . . . Winning is the name of the game." Here was the opportunist with the forked tongue, denouncing the New Deal to Roy Miller, wealthy lobbyist for Texas fat cats—and within an hour praising the New Deal to another Texan, Congressman Wright Patman.

Not only would Lyndon have been at home with Machiavelli, but with Theodore Roosevelt, who defined the most successful pol as "he who says what everybody is thinking, most often and in the loudest voice." On the one hand, a leader remains in good standing only as long as his goals remain parallel, if not identical, to those of his constituency. On the other hand, he has the obligation to be honest with his constituency, to inform them as to his departure from those goals, and the reasons for doing so, with the hope he can influence his constituents to follow him to new and different goals. It was in this latter obligation that Lyndon failed so miserably when it came to Vietnam. But it had begun many years earlier. Johnson would not only refuse to look a gift horse in the mouth, he would commandeer everything he could get his hands on. In that way he parted company most dramatically with his early mentor and long-time confidant, Sam Rayburn. For the speaker of the House died with but $15,000 in the bank, explaining he'd been unable to save much money but adding, perhaps for the benefit of his protégé, "in politics an honest man does not get rich."

William Henry Harrison may have played the cynic when, in 1840, he deplored "that all the measures of government are directed to the purpose of making the rich richer and the poor poorer."[5] But he was no more cynical than LBJ, who viewed government coffers as a gold prospector would view a proven stake—a visible means of striking it rich. If he hadn't learned this as Kleberg's secretary, or as NYA administrator for Texas, he would learn it as Congressman Johnson.

As Kleberg's secretary, he'd done his part, he figured, by introducing Wirtz and the Browns to the movers and shakers in Congress who could authorize a dam at Marshall Ford in the Hill Country. In 1937, Lyndon was, at best, a long shot. But he was the best chance the Browns held for staying in business. So they got behind Johnson 100 percent, just as Johnson was backing FDR 100 percent. Lyndon owed Brown and Root, and they would not let him forget it.

No sooner did the Browns have the dam in their pocket but they decided it wouldn't be big enough, for the $10 million, to control floods. How much more would they need, asked Lyndon. Without batting an eyelash, the Browns announced $17 million more. With the help of his sharp attorney, Abe Fortas, Johnson managed to get the additional millions.

At the same time Lyndon was courting Herman and George Brown, he found another "angel" in the person of Charles Marsh, a wealthy Texas publisher and oil tycoon. So taken was Marsh with Johnson, and his ability to steer through the jungle of Washington unscathed, that in 1939 he offered the Congressman a nineteen-acre tract of Austin real estate for a couldn't-refuse sum of $12,000. Lady Bird again turned to her father, while Lyndon turned to Brown and Root to build a road on it and landscape it. Here was but the first of what would become a princely estate, courtesy of U.S. taxpayers.

No doubt about it, with friends like these, Lyndon was prospering. So why not look the part? Soon he was sporting $195 suits, boxes of custom-made shirts, shoes, ties, hats, coats, and gloves to match: everything the successful congressman should wear. But with no bill ever passed bearing his name, and no more than a speech a year, and dozing or chewing the fat with a fellow congressman when others were speaking—it was not exactly a sterling performance, noted Horace Busby, for one with such extravagant pretensions. In those early years on Capitol Hill he may not have been looking out for the taxpayer, but he most certainly was looking out for Lyndon Johnson. There he was, doing favors for choice friends, cutting deals, learning further the ins and outs of Washington and—above all—ingratiating himself with Rayburn, Roosevelt, and lesser power-players. Not only would he not follow his father's advice never to shimmy, he would not follow his father's example of earning a pittance as a bus inspector and ending up in poverty.[6]

By 1940, Johnson, in the eyes of those he sought to impress, was "ingratiating, gay, cocksure, and on occasion, hilariously funny." At other times he was seen as restive and overbearing. Evans and Novak drew a word-picture of the fledgling congressman: "With cigarette dangling from his lower lip, just above a jutting lower jaw with a deep cleft in the middle, and just below the large, overhanging nose with wide nostrils," there was "the long, thin face, flanked by two enormous ears" serving as a "setting for two dark, intense, and often menacing eyes. His hair, combed straight back, glistened in the sun, along with his fancy gabardine suits always a cut too big for him, and trousers too long. And this 6' 4" bean pole freshman in Congress [was] racing here and there, barking orders to his staff." There was another problem with Lyndon's living "high off the hog" as a fledgling Congressman, and that was Lady Bird, the richest woman in her part of the land, the one who'd used $10,000 of her trust fund and begged another $25,000 from her father to get Lyndon elected in the first place. From their small apartment in Washington she would head for Texas during the off-session, her car packed with boxes of dishes and kitchen utensils, just a part of the scrimping and saving she did while her husband played the dandy. After all, he reasoned, how could he schmooze with the likes of the Browns and Marsh on the meager $10,000 salary paid him as Congressman?

Lyndon was indeed grateful for all kindnesses, big and small. Yet one of the biggest he refused. It seems that Marsh—not to be outdone by the Browns in his rewarding Johnson for work well done—offered him in 1940 his share in a partnership with Sid Richardson worth at least $750,000.

Lyndon didn't need so much as a down payment; he could pay the modest price back in future earnings. But Lyndon's antennae were tuned more to politics than money, and he turned Marsh down with the explanation that being an oilman could "kill me politically." Johnson needed the money from the Clint Murchisons and Sid Richardsons, just as he needed the money from Kleberg's ranch, Marsh's newspapers, and the Browns' construction. But he mustn't compromise his persona of New Dealer if he was to continue being elected every two years by the rank-and-file Texans. Yes, he could bad-mouth the New Deal and FDR with the best of the fat cats as long as he was hobnobbing with them. But he had to guard his persona with the many more voters who were counting on the New Deal for bread and butter. Until FDR died in 1945, Lyndon was the perfect chameleon, changing colors with his surroundings without a hint of misgiving. But with the death of Roosevelt, Lyndon paid a last burst of homage before cutting his ties to the New Deal founder. "He was just like a Daddy to me always; he always talked to me just that way. . . . God! God! How he could take it for us all!" Encomiums like this didn't come along often from the lips of Lyndon. By the next day he was again properly focused. To his secretary he declared, "There is going to be the damndest scramble for power in this man's town for the next two weeks that anyone ever saw in their lives." He may not have known much about history and literature, about science or math, but he knew the scent of money and the scent of power—and he knew the first was necessary to the second. He lost his first Senate race in 1941, and he was determined not to lose another in 1948. By that time, he'd voted for New Deal legislation less than half the time, and that earned an enthusiastic endorsement from the Dallas Chamber of Commerce.

By that time, too, Johnson was not above bragging that he was "worth a cool one million dollars." And where did this slick pol get this kind of money in the decade he'd been in office—on a salary of $10,000 a year? From Marsh he'd gotten some valuable Austin real estate at a bargain-basement price. From George Brown he'd gotten a few small oil leases, enough to supplement his salary without drawing attention from the press.[7] And Lady Bird, for her part, was the picture of frugality, renting out their Washington apartment while they were in Texas, and toting her dinnerware and kitchenware back and forth.

KTBC: Milking the Cash Cow

It was in another context that Lady Bird contributed the major part of their fortune. For in January 1943, she again dipped into her inheritance to come up with $17,500 so they could purchase the Austin radio station KTBC. It seems that a certain Wesley West had inherited the station on his father's death, and had given a local syndicate the option to buy. E.G. Kingsberry, a syndicate member, was about to petition the FCC to allow him to buy the station when Lyndon approached him about turning the option over to him. Why should he? Not only because Lyndon was a U.S. Congressman but because, in that capacity, he'd recently secured an appointment of Kingsberry's son to Annapolis. So Kingsberry, appropriately grateful, persuaded the rest of the syndicate to relinquish the option to Johnson. Any such purchase, of course, was subject to FCC approval. No big deal for LBJ. Whereas the Wests had been trying for three years to obtain FCC approval to boost the station power from 250 to 1,000 watts, Lyndon not only got permission to buy, but to raise the power just twenty-four days after he filed on January 23. Speaking of power, Johnson had learned long before that who you knew was every bit as important as what you knew.

Alvin Wirtz had both what and who. When Lyndon returned from his six-month tour with the Navy, he learned that his Texas constituents were reaping great benefits from the war: oil, gas, construction, air fields, cattle, cotton—all were available to the highest bidder. And no one could outbid Uncle Sam. Back from the war, this formerly poor kid from the Hill Country was determined to get a piece of the action. Where, he asked Wirtz, was the best investment, one that would do the least to offend his constituents and attract bad press? Wirtz's reply: communications. Several of Lyndon's colleagues on the Hill owned small newspapers or radio stations, so why not Lyndon, now that his wife had come into her inheritance? A journalism major in college, she favored a newspaper. But Lyndon had always preferred talking to writing. In either case, Lady Bird, after five years of childless marriage, needed an outlet for her considerable talents.

So KTBC was theirs, and it would prove to be a bonanza. While Bird was scrubbing down the station until it no longer reeked of must and cobwebs, Lyndon was off to New York to cash in on further connections as a Congressman. Outside the office of William Paley, head of CBS, Lyndon cooled his heels while Paley's secretary notified him that there was "a very tall Texan waiting . . . in a big hat and boots who [says] he is a Congressman." So Paley dispatched his assistant, Frank Stanton, to see the young Texan and before long they'd struck a deal. In exchange for network affiliation CBS would have an important Congressman in its pocket.

Just how fortunate was this influence-exchanging is seen in Paley's turning down repeatedly network affiliation for KNOW, also operating out of Austin. His reason: CBS already had an affiliate in San Antonio, capable of reaching Austin with its signal. Was it simply coincidence? Not if you consider that Paley had been leading a fight to diminish FCC control over independent stations, and that Lyndon was the protégé of Sam Rayburn, the founder of the FCC.

As it so happened, the Johnson application couldn't have been better timed. For in 1943, the FCC was in the crosshairs of two congressional committees. The first was a special House committee accusing the FCC of "Gestapo tactics" with its "bureaucratic dictatorship." The second was the rabble-rousing House Un-American Affairs Committee, the communist witch-hunt posse under the direction of "Sheriff" Martin Dies. Worse, there before the House was an amendment to the appropriations bill, cutting off further funding for the FCC. Congressman Johnson, with his wife's application pending, and knowing of the determination of both committees to abolish the agency, kept Rayburn informed, urging him to intercede. Finally, on February 17, 1943, Speaker Rayburn, in one of his rare speeches, did just that, and saved the day. No surprise then, when just three days later, Lady Bird got her approval, with FDR's right-hand man, Tommy Corcoran, helping Lyndon "all up and down the line," as the "Cork" put it.

One nosy reporter asked Corcoran: Did it make a difference that Johnson had helped intervene to save the FCC? Corcoran: "How do you think these things work? These guys [the FCC staff] have been around. You don't have to spell things out for them." Supreme Court Justice William O. Douglas, an LBJ friend, was nonetheless critical of the favoritism when he later wrote: "Among the great plums in the Washington D.C. pudding has been the granting of radio and TV licenses. The contests have been tremendous and many political allies have been marshaled in the cause. Even some members of Congress obtained licenses for themselves or their families while in office—a practice that should be forever barred as being beyond the ethical line."

Ethical lines somehow seemed to blur where Lyndon Johnson was concerned. When Lady Bird applied on June 25, 1943, for permission to operate twenty-four hours a day and on a better frequency, it took less than a month for approval—despite one of the competitors being FDR's son Elliott. It appears he'd joined forces with tycoon Sid Richardson to form a radio business in Texas. Elliott, of course, was irate that Johnson "had the skids greased with the commission," according to John Connally. It also appears that a Congressman, together with Speaker Rayburn—surrogate father of Lyndon and father of the FCC—and Tommy Corcoran, could trump FDR's son and a Texas moneybags any day. Indeed, it was just this "rich fat-cat money," as Lyndon put it, to whom he became increasingly beholden. This despite his protestation as President, twenty years later, that "I don't want to be owned by Wall Street and I don't want to be owned by the Texas oilmen."[8]

Did Johnson have to wait until 1949, when he entered the Senate chambers, to pull the necessary strings to acquire and grow KTBC? By no means. Albert Evangelista, the initial processor of FCC applications, later conceded that, yes, congressmen invariably received special treatment. He would, as he put it, "route it to the right department." And what if it so happened that a certain high-priority application lay gathering dust on some bureaucrat's desk? In that case, the FCC chairman could expect a call—an urgent call—from the concerned congressman. And he'd get it moving. "Put 'em on the air" was the order issued.

With a boost in wattage and network affiliation, the Johnsons then obtained quick approval from the FCC to incorporate as the Texas Broadcasting Corporation. Though technically Lyndon owned none of the shares, legally he owned them as much as Bird did. Furthermore, though he claimed he owned no interest in the station, under the law he was entitled to half its income. Repeatedly, he claimed he maintained a hands-off attitude toward KTBC. That it was otherwise is seen in the many letters he wrote to its sales manager, Willard Deason, revealing a detailed working knowledge of the station. Lyndon was also involved in the hiring, and several times took over in an attempt to show his wife a thing or two about running a radio station. One after the other of Lyndon's hirees left, however, when they saw how he treated Lady Bird. One station writer noted that, when alone, "Mrs. Johnson . . . came across as a very intelligent, capable person. Throw Lyndon into the management pot and she was a different person." The writer refused to go into details, explaining, "I feel disloyal to her if I tell what she took from him." Another writer elaborated, "He talked to her as though she were a serving girl . . . I saw the way he used his family . . . without conscience."

But the FCC—that was a different ball game. According to Paul Porter, head of the FCC after FDR's 1944 election, the only time Johnson actively interceded for an Austin radio station was for KVET, owned and operated by returning veterans, led by John Connally. Lyndon's reason for interceding, he said, was that if he had to have competition, better it be "responsible, able competition." Yet it must have been obvious to Porter, as well as to his predecessor at the helm of the FCC, that Lyndon was not only a Congressman but a favorite of FDR. And it was the President who appointed its members and provided oversight, if not direction. That was enough to convince any right-thinking chairman that if he wanted to continue in his job, it would be solely at the President's discretion. There was yet one big hurdle that Lyndon's connections—now that he had won a Senate seat in 1948—could help him surmount. That was to get the FCC to grant KTBC the one TV outlet warranted by Austin's 132,459 inhabitants. No coincidence again, the application lay gathering dust for four months without a single competitive application. Perhaps television talk-show host David Susskind had a point when he noted, "If the wife of a senator of the state has applied for the license, and you would kind of like the license yourself, wouldn't it look like a waste of your time to apply?"

In their first year with KTBC, the Johnsons accumulated a profit of just $18. A decade later, however, it was worth $2 million. In one more decade, they were earning $500,000 income each year from the station—and investing it in bank stocks and real estate. Like Susskind, Kearns had a point in noting that this spectacular appreciation was due less to the astute, industrious Lady Bird than to the "long string of favorable decisions handed down by the FCC." In particular, LBJ's machinations obtained approval to buy the station, to increase its power, to broadcast 24 hours a day, to incorporate, to affiliate with CBS, to branch out into TV, and—especially vital—to be assured a virtual monopoly with the exception of Lyndon's friendly competitor, KVET. It is worth noting that "among the documentaries that CBS did not make in the sixties," as Halberstam puckishly noted, ". . . was the study of how Lyndon Johnson . . . became a very rich man." Furthermore, Johnson's in with Stanton "made people in the CBS News

Division very uneasy when Johnson was President . . . they did not like it."

Members of the Commerce Committee stoutly insisted that Johnson refused to use his membership or his post as Majority Leader to influence broadcasting decisions or legislation. Yet it was vintage Johnson to conduct business not out in the open but behind closed doors, or in corridors or cloakrooms, deftly pulling strings and striking deals. "Lyndon," said Palmer Webber, an astute observer at the scene, "goes around with a basket under the trees, and he never shakes them; he just lets the fruit fall. Lyndon never shakes a tree."[9] By the time he was Senate Majority Leader it could well be that he didn't have to shake the trees.

But why stop with CBS as an affiliate? So, having Austin's only station, Lyndon soon had ABC and NBC in his pocket. And who was the mighty driving force behind the Texas Broadcasting Company, *Life* asked in 1964. Despite his protestations, it was none other than LBJ, now President. Indeed, when he descended—all 225 pounds and 6'4" of Texas longhorn with a bullhorn voice to match—he "scared the hell out of a lot of people," as one station employee put it. And these included department heads that Johnson continued to meet with regularly.

By 1956, the 250-watt pint-sized, and failing radio station, KTBC, had awakened and stretched to become the LBJ Company, including stations in other cities such as Waco. It was a monumental money machine. Rayburn may have declared that honest pols didn't enrich themselves in office, but his protégé differed from him on that critical point. After all, public service—especially as Senate Majority Leader—should have its privileges.

For twenty years, "the skids" were "greased with the Commission for the redoubtable Lyndon." By 1948, the FCC, having allocated 106 TV licenses, called a halt on further dispensations for four years until it could devise a satisfactory nationwide policy. You should get in on the ground floor in 1952, Lyndon was advised by his attorney and a local Austin businessman. But that, Johnson protested, would take heavy financing. They were just as insistent. "You, with your connections," could make "a success of a TV station in the Gobi desert."[10]

That single phrase, "with your connections," made all the difference. Who you knew always seemed to trump what you knew when it came to Washington politics. By 1952, Senate Minority Leader Johnson not only got his TV station but the assurance of no competition for the rest of the fifties. It didn't seem to matter that the Dallas-Ft. Worth area had five TV stations, and that Houston and San Antonio each had four. Even Amarillo, with but 60 percent of Austin's population, had two stations. What did matter was that in the state's capitol, Austin, the LBJ Company enjoyed the luxury of a monopoly. Just how lucrative was this? Sponsors in the comparable city of Rochester, Minnesota, could buy an hour of network programming for $325—while the Johnson's could pocket $575 for the same hour.

The White House Stakes

Louis Kohlmeier of the *Wall Street Journal* won a Pulitzer Prize in 1964 for his series, "The Johnson Wealth," exposing in particular the family radio-TV empire that had enabled LBJ to enter the White House with an unprecedented net worth, for a president, of $14 million. "Like two young oaks springing up side by side, the LBJ careers in government and business grew mightily—their trunks rising parallel and branches intertwining." LBJ, of course, scoffed at the figure and ordered an audit which, not surprisingly, showed his net worth at a fraction of that, approximately $3 million. But, persisted an inquisitive reporter, how about your land holdings? Answered the humble Texan, modest to a fault, "I own a little ranchland, something in excess of 2,000 acres." Interesting that he omitted to say how much in excess. In addition to his own LBJ Ranch was the 1,800-acre Scharnhorst Ranch outside Johnson City and the 3,900 acres in Lady Bird's name in Alabama. In April 1964, he confided in Richard Russell, "All I've got is some ranch land—six or seven thousand acres that may be worth ten to fifty dollars an acre. . . ."

This failed to take into account the thousands of acres he owned in Mexico, and many thousands more he controlled, wholly or in part, through surrogates. When two Republican congressmen—intent on defeating Johnson's anti-poverty bill—descended on the Alabama acreage, armed with cameras and hidden tape recorders to document the wretched conditions of Negroes working and living there, Lady Bird called it, "flashy, ugly information," while Lyndon called it "low-down, dirty, cheap politics."

With Johnson firmly in the White House, he was also firmly in control of the FCC. Meanwhile his beginning radio station, KTBC, was now a galaxy of radio and TV stations, even as KTBC had become the LBJ Company and this in turn the Texas Broadcasting Company. Its phenomenal growth piqued the curiosity of reporters. One asked if this didn't constitute a conflict of interest. Inconceivable, Johnson replied, "because I don't have any interest in government-regulated industries of any kind and never have had." As for the Texas Broadcasting Company, he added, "all that is owned by Mrs. Johnson," He not only played no part in its operations, but derived no income from it—which would have been news to Jesse Kellam and others in top management there with whom Lyndon was in almost daily contact.

But that wasn't all. "I have never received any funds or cast any votes in connection with it. It was her station; don't let anyone tell you to the contrary." Indeed, he wasn't even familiar with the business—which would have been news to Don Reynolds and his insurance company, from whom Lyndon had bought a $200,000 policy, with the premiums being paid by the LBJ Company. This arrangement was permitted only if Johnson was, in fact, not only an employee, but a major employee. In exchange for this policy, LBJ had pressured Reynolds into buying over $1,200 of airtime on his radio station. When Reynolds, again under pressure, revealed this quid pro quo, Johnson tried using secret government documents to impugn Reynolds and undercut his testimony.

Clark Clifford, veteran Democratic presidential counselor, warned Johnson that his broadcast holdings presented "potential conflicts of interest." Perhaps LBJ should consider divesting himself of them? Johnson: "I'm not going to do that. I don't care what anyone says." Lady Bird, however, did see a conflict of interest. Two days after her husband became President, she held a family business meeting with Abe Fortas and his wife and other financial advisers. "We obviously had to separate ourselves from KTBC," she wrote, ". . . for the good and sufficient reason that Lyndon is now in the position of appointing the members of the FCC, who have the power to license and regulate radio and TV stations. . . ."

To give at least the appearance of a blind trust, Johnson had his Texas Broadcasting Company officially hire Jesse Kellam as its business manager. It would be he who would manage the exponentially growing holdings. Yet when Kellam reported that business had taken a beating with the Kennedy assassination, there was Lyndon on the phone, giving him explicit instructions as to how he could recoup the losses.

Then, in an interesting addendum, Johnson noted that "Bird wants to give up her option" to buy a 50 percent share of Capitol Cable Company, the only potential competitor on the Austin horizon. Lyndon added, "I told her she's crazy." As it turned out, no surprise, the Johnsons did exercise the option, maintaining the monopoly that put advertisers at their mercy. Able to take his pick of programs from the three networks, Lyndon could charge whatever the traffic would bear, and that was considerably more than stations in other Texas cities of comparable size—and with competing stations. When reporter Marshall McNeill asked Johnson about the monopoly, his answer was, "Anybody that wants to advertise in the [Austin] market has to advertise on the [Johnson's] station 'cause it's the only one there."

Little wonder, then, that the touch of Lyndon seemed to be the touch of Midas. And little wonder that *The New York Times* and *The Wall Street Journal* kept digging. Little wonder, too, that Johnson's feet were soon slipping, at least with the press, as the rumbling of an earthquake of deceptions, evasions, and dissimulations began opening a credibility gap beneath him. Catapulted into office on the death of the "really rich" JFK, Lyndon persisted in the myth that he was just a poor boy from the sticks of Texas, trying, like all loyal capitalist Americans, to make an honest buck. To that end, he dispatched Reedy to notify the press, shortly after taking office, that "The President has devoted all his time and energy to the public business and he is not engaged in any private enterprise directly or indirectly."[11]

By 1958, there was little question but that Johnson was not only master of the Senate and, arguably, the second most powerful man in the country, but that he could seize an opportunity as few others could, and run with it. And he always kept before him the goal line. Trying to enlist John Hicks as station manager back in 1944, Lyndon assured him, "I want you to know that I'm going to be President of this country someday." With that goal clearly and forever in view, Johnson enlisted big, burly blockers like Rayburn, Russell, and FDR himself to run interference for him. Crossing the goal line at last, he was horrified to learn that *Life* had dispatched a team of reporters to investigate his net worth and how he'd come by it. Their figure: once again the $14 million. Johnson begged, then tried intimidating *Life* to cancel the story, or at least to change it. But Henry Luce would do nothing of the kind. After all, if he could turn on JFK, the son of his old friend Joe Kennedy, what on earth would dispose him to go easy on this Texas maverick? So the story ran.

By February 1964, Johnson the possum was fending off the news hounds that figured they'd run him up the money tree. His teeth bared, he snarled at the "smear squad . . . investigating and hiring people, and going into all your business . . . for thirty years." It seemed cold comfort when George Brown assured him, "the papers have been pretty good to you. . . ."

There was no let up. By April, *The Wall Street Journal* was inundating Johnson aides with "pages and pages . . . of pretty pointed questions," White House assistant Walter Jenkins was reporting, adding, "It's a nasty wire. It says that failure to answer these questions would also be news-worthy too." Jenkins called it a "kind of bribery." But Johnson knew black-mail when he saw it.

By this time, LBJ had armed his aides with set answers to nosy reporters. Bad enough when Kohlmeier accused him of enriching himself at the public trough to the tune of $14 million. Worse, the *Journal*, not sat-isfied with this stellar figure, cornered some of Lyndon's intimates back in Austin and revised the figure, on the basis of their estimates, to $20 mil-lion. All of this had to be stopped. How on earth could he hope to appeal to Congress on behalf of the poor, much less compete with Kennedy's gen-erosity in donating his $100,000 salary to charity? So Johnson's instructions to his aides were explicit. Lady Bird ". . . owns 50 percent of the station. It's worth two million, odd thousand, and owes about eight hundred. She owns half. So she'd be worth a million there and owe four hundred, so she'd be worth six, seven hundred thousand. So she's a millionaire and I'm worth a little under two hundred thousand." It appears LBJ's arithmetic was worse than his grammar. Michael Beschloss rightly pointed out that these were absurd figures that only the mind of LBJ could concoct, based not on their market value at the time, but on their original purchase price, some of it more than twenty years earlier.[12]

If it takes a blatant opportunist to recognize one, it is also true that one will attract others. And one of those Johnson attracted was fellow Texan John Connally. In the words of one of Johnson's secretaries, Virginia Durr, Connally was a "cold-blooded opportunist." Yet Lyndon not only attract-ed him, he liked him, indeed he "loved him," as Durr put it, establishing much "the same relationship to him that he had established with San Rayburn."

In addition to profits from his radio-TV empire, Johnson continued, as President, to reward Brown and Root with one contract after another in Vietnam, until it was the single largest contractor doing government business there. Airfields, docks, roads, buildings—you name it, and Brown and Root were at it—with LBJ always in the background, pulling strings. Of course, it would be too much to suggest that one of the reasons Johnson refused to pull out, to negotiate an end to the war, was that his good friends, the Brown brothers, were profiting immensely from it.

Before entering the White House, Johnson had forsworn any such lavish presidential perks as Camp David and the presidential yacht, "Sequoia." But sworn in, he soon settled in, confident that his stunning 1964 victory over Goldwater was both a mandate for an agenda and for enjoying one's perks. In 1966, Armand Hammer, Soviet agent, industrialist, and chairman of Occidental Petroleum, let LBJ know he had "25" presumably $25,000 he wanted to "do without," and this in a non-election year for presidents. LBJ was ever eager to accommodate tycoons who found their money a burden. He would even be ready to lift that burden and invest it in land, in bank securities, or in his radio/TV business.

Johnson's signal departure from his two most helpful mentors, Rayburn and Roosevelt, was not lost on the 1964 candidate he'd left gasping in his dust at the polls. Goldwater, following LBJ's death in January 1973, was set to wondering—then, if not before—how "a man almost penniless [came] to Washington and died . . . with over $20 million." The Texas Broadcasting Company was finally sold in 1972 for an undisclosed price. Goldwater couldn't help but figure that a story of the intertwining interests of the Senate Commerce Committee—on which LBJ sat and steered one contract after another to Brown and Root and the FCC—so benevolent to this pol—would be, as Goldwater put it, "beautiful."

If there was any president with the Midas touch, it was LBJ. Taking the more conservative estimate of his net worth in 1964 of $14 million, it must be borne in mind that this translates into 1999 dollars to be about $45 million. Just how chintzy this multimillionaire could be is seen in his haggling with a New York hairdresser he wanted to fly down to Washington to do the hair of his wife and daughters. LBJ: "I'm a poor man, and I don't make much money. . . ."

Actually Johnson's $100,000 salary was but the tip of the iceberg. The other 90 percent lay in his perks, his miscellaneous expenses, and his being able to dip into the bottomless pockets of the contingency fund provided by the Defense Department. The estimate of his annual income of $500,000 by *U.S. News and World Report* in April 1964, was undoubtedly low.

All the more reprehensible was LBJ's stinginess with his hairdresser. Johnson: ". . . how can you come down here and make them look better?" Hairdresser: "When do you want me to come?" LBJ: "That depends first on how much it'll cost me." Hairdresser "It won't cost you anything to worry about, sir." LBJ: "All right, because I just have to live off a paycheck, and I'm in debt . . . bring whoever you need, and we'll pay their transportation, but we can't pay you much else . . . I'm going to leave you a hundred dollar bill, and I'll pay your transportation. . . ."[13] Actually, Johnson had it right the first time, with "we'll pay their transportation," if he was including other U.S. taxpayers besides himself.

By the time he left the White House, as a later chapter on arrogance will detail, Johnson packed up not only his own belongings but plenty that didn't belong to him, and headed for the Ranch. No one, he was convinced, would be such a spoilsport as to attempt to deprive him of the little amenities so necessary to a comfortable retirement.

Lyndon Johnson may have left the country in 1969 neck-deep in IOU's for the war and for the "Great Society," but he made certain that this poor boy from the Hill Country of Texas would grasp each and every opportunity to enrich himself and his heirs in the process. He not only seized an opportunity; he seized it by the throat. Here was opportunism with a vengeance. Following in its wake would be the next in the steps of hubris, exploitation. The mills of hubris, like those of the gods, may at times appear to grind slowly, if at all, but they did grind, and "exceedingly sure."

RICHARD NIXON

With candidates for the highest office, as with athletes, everything depends on timing, upon an ability to seize an opportunity.

— Henry Kissinger

Don't you see what a marvelous opportunity for the committee. They can really take this and go.

— Richard Nixon, trying to revive the HUAC
to go "after all these Jews." June 2, 1971

John Dean: ". . . there's the problem of the continued blackmail. . . ."
President Nixon: "How much money do you need?"
John Dean: ". . .these people are going to cost a million dollars over the next two years."
President Nixon: "We could get that . . . in cash."

— Stanley Kutler, ed. *Abuse of Power*[1]

Taking Advantage

It was the only black-owned shopping center in the country, there in North Philadelphia in September 1968, and Richard Nixon knew an opportunity when he saw one. He needed the votes of the blacks, who were traditionally Democrats. There by his side stood the Rev. Leon Sullivan, a prominent black activist, who could also spot an opportunity at least a block away. Here was his chance to wangle federal dollars for black entrepreneurs. Lamenting the plight of poor blacks in the inner cities surrounded by affluent whites in the suburbs, Nixon emphasized, "You can't be an island in the world. You can't live in your comfortable houses and say, well, as long as I get mine, I don't have to worry about the others." Of course, with the ghetto uprisings following the assassination of Martin Luther King that April fresh in his mind, he added that America must have "law and order." These affluent whites needn't worry about blacks invading their suburbs wholesale. He, Richard Nixon, if elected president, would lift them up in their own ghettos.

Here, in a phrase, was "mutual opportunism," the quid pro quo that was the staple of political campaigns. It was as simple as trading votes for dollars, a sum-sum game in which both sides come out the winners. The losers, easily forgotten at the time, were the taxpayers—losers because it was their taxes, their money that Nixon was promising to give away, and losers also because they would be saddled with yet another president who recognized a cardinal rule of politics: raising taxes wins no more votes than cutting back on "entitlement" programs. What does win votes is cutting taxes and increasing government largesse. How can this be done? Simply by postponing the cost, leaving our children and theirs after them to pay the bills.

"Policy emerges," Kissinger maintained, "when concept encounters opportunity." In 1971, Nixon and Kissinger saw a golden opportunity for pressuring the North Vietnamese to go to the bargaining table and end the war. The plan was to exacerbate the tensions already surfacing along the boundary separating China and the USSR, play them against each other and persuade them not only to stop supporting their North Vietnamese fellow Communists, but to move them to negotiation. So Nixon, with the help of his National Security Adviser making the arrangements, decided to visit Peking, then Moscow, and eyeball Mao-Zedong and Brezhnev in two unprecedented summits that would provide the necessary "monuments" he desperately needed to ensure his reelection.

Of course, there were a few matters he would have to overlook to cozy up to the Chinese and the Soviets. He would have to overlook the tirades with which he'd tarred and feathered both nations for a quarter-century. He would have to overlook his conviction, repeated time and again, that there was a global Communist conspiracy, in which orders went out from behind the walls of the Kremlin; its intention: to enslave the world. He would have to overlook the numbing thoroughness, not to mention hype, of his headline-grabbing in going after Voorhis, Hiss, Douglas, and the Truman administration—Communists or fellow travelers all. He would have to overlook the desperate measures he used to rout and, if necessary, to assassinate the Communist Castro, who came to power in 1959—just ninety miles off our southern coast. He would have to overlook Mao's "cultural revolution," during which millions of Chinese, primarily the better educated, were slaughtered by young "true believers," intent on purifying the faith. He would have to overlook his constant dogging of Kennedy and Johnson to escalate the war in Vietnam, convinced that Moscow and Peking were using Hanoi as a surrogate to bleed Washington dry. He would have to overlook his scalding indictment of the Chinese just twenty months before, and their return rhetoric that labeled Americans as "gangsters," "hyenas," "mad-dogs," "monsters," and "paper tigers."

To many in this country, that was quite a bit to overlook. But Nixon was blinded by a heaven-sent opportunity to end the war with "peace with honor," to assure his reelection, and to see that future generations would hail him as the peacemaker extraordinaire. So it was small enough price to pay. Back in high school, a fellow debater, Morton Wray, had praised Nixon for his "uncommon ability to take advantage of a situation before and after it develops." In the fifties, Nixon told biographer Earl Mazo, "A man must be ready to take advantage of an opportunity when it is offered." And more recently he'd taken pains to distinguish the former opportunist from the current pragmatist, with enough common sense to change as circumstances changed.

Without blinking an eye, he'd grabbed hold of the anticommunist theme and played it to the hilt for twenty-five years, drawing on that basest of motives: fear. It mattered not that since his political baptism, critics had charged that he had no convictions. With no rudder on his political boat—save anticommunism—he tended to drift wherever the winds of opportunity blew him. It wasn't even faint praise that damned him when, returning to Whittier from law school to practice his profession, fellow lawyer L. Wallace Black charged him with lacking sincerity. In 1946, the *Los Angeles Times*, on the one hand, saw in Nixon a fresh face with "no ideology encumbering his old-fashioned Americanism." Others saw the crass opportunism of a veteran poker player who figured that the fear card would trump everything. It was H.L. Mencken, the cynical sage of Baltimore, who'd written that fear was self-defeating, that when the converts stopped shaking, they stopped believing—whether in religion or politics.

Nixon had a protégé, Joe McCarthy, who ran into increasing flak in the Senate and the press. Yet when Nixon turned on McCarthy, his assistant, Roy Cohn, trashed Nixon as "perfectly willing to turn on his conservative friends and cut their throats—1, 2, 3." Nixon, he concluded, was Ike's "superb hatchet man." When Adlai Stevenson charged that Nixon's "slash and burn" campaign tactics were nothing but "McCarthyism in a white collar," Nixon seized the opportunity to ingratiate himself with blue-collar Americans. Stevenson's remark, retorted Nixon, was a slander on the American working people. "What Mr. Stevenson calls me is unimportant, but I resent his typically snide and snobbish innuendo towards the millions of Americans who work for a living in our shops and factories."[2] Aside from the fact that "our shops and factories" featured white-collar workers as well, many by this time knew that Nixon's sympathies lay not with the blue-collar laborers—but with the white-collared elite that he'd met in the California Committee of 100, which had provided Nixon's first "slush fund" in his race against Jerry Voorhis.

Standing for What?

Craft, cunning, slyness—all married to towering ambition—were the marks of the inveterate cardsharp Nixon. To Stewart Alsop in 1960, Nixon insisted that "the mark of my political career [is] I'm always willing to take a chance." This was not quite the way Arthur Schlesinger saw it. Nixon, he charged, was "the consummate opportunist. He could be for or against the Taft-Hartley Act, for or against Chiang Kai-shek, and no one would be surprised." Schlesinger's conclusion: "Nixon stands for almost nothing." Dean Burch, head of the FCC and one of Nixon's staunchest supporters, was, in the end, terribly disillusioned. "He never told me the truth about the thing [Watergate]. He never even told his own family. That was why they were fighting so hard right to the last minute. . . . That was his major failure, being so cynical. The man didn't believe in anything. He didn't believe in a religion, or principle or anything. He was totally cynical."

Nelson Rockefeller, also campaigning for the nomination in 1960, called on Republicans to reject Nixon for asking them "to meet the future with a banner aloft whose only emblem is a question mark." Only after he'd been chosen as the party's nominee would Nixon reveal anything of his platform. Poker had taught him to tuck his cards close to his chest, keep his face immobile, bluff if he held deuces—and if he held four of a kind, to spring a great surprise. It was all part of the game, whether poker or politics.

The one thing that annoyed Nixon more than anything else, he complained to Mazo, was the persistent charge that he "lack[ed] convictions," that his positions "conform[ed] to the political expediency of the day." He then cited his unpopular stands on a balanced budget, on civil rights, on labor relations, and on assistance programs. Even a cursory examination reveals that Nixon stuck his neck out on none of these and that, contrariwise, as 1960 approached and he longed to be president "of all the people," he muted his two trademarks: fiery anticommunism and slashing attacks on the "Party of Betrayal"—the Democrats.

What Nixon failed to tell Mazo was that "Tricky Dick's" so-called unpopular stands on major issues were hardly stands at all. On civil rights, for example, Nixon knew Johnson was a white Southerner, and he hoped that he, not LBJ, would garner the Negro vote. Then Nixon saw Johnson pushing through a Civil Rights Act, so he decided to try to split the white vote among Southern Democrats—and pick up the larger number opposed to civil rights. And when JFK had brother Bobby put in a phone call, interceding with the Southern judge involved in Martin Luther King's case as he languished behind bars, Nixon did not similarly step in. Taking the high road, he explained that would have constituted an unthinkable breach of legal ethics. Such close adherence to high principle had never seemed to bother Nixon until then, and his explanation fell on an unreceptive press.

Especially critical was William Costello, writing in *The New Republic*: "He has shown again a taste for the transparent device, the theatrical overstatement, an aptitude for pat slogans, easy solutions, sly aspersions. His instinct all along has been to lash out against all who differ with him, and he has restrained himself, articulately, because a reversion to earlier tactics would, he knows, revive the malodorous image of the politician who climbed to power over the bodies of contemporaries in both parties. On the eve of the election, in the hot crucible of decision, Nixon's status has been shrinking. He stands revealed as a man without a spiritual home, ready to twist any circumstance to his advantage, devoid of a genuine moral commitment to either liberalism or conservatism but trying to feel at home wherever the tides of circumstance happen to lodge him."[3]

Nor did straitlaced scruples seem to hinder Nixon eight years later, when he faced another presidential election. By then, the race issue had become a powder keg. King had been assassinated, cities were burning, campuses were erupting, and Negro leaders were charging that poor blacks were carrying the burden of the Vietnam War on the front lines. In the midst of it all, there was Nixon doing what he'd criticized Eisenhower for: waffling. Yes, Nixon insisted, he certainly backed the Supreme Court's school desegregation ruling. But no, Johnson's policy to withhold federal funds from school districts failing to comply was wrong—even though this was the most effective weapon available for enforcing Brown v Topeka. Well, just how would Nixon enforce it? He refused to say, just as he refused to say how he'd end the war in six months. But enforcing deseg-regation, he insisted, was not the government's job. Indeed, "In my view that kind of activity should be very scrupulously examined"— as if the Supreme Court had neglected to do so—"and in many cases I think should be rescinded." Never did he say just what should be examined, or what should be rescinded, or how the law should be enforced. One thing, how-ever, obtruded—and that one thing was always uppermost in Richard Nixon's mind in September 1968. The greatest opportunity of his lifetime lay less than two months away. Yes, he needed the votes of Southern whites, and yes, he needed the votes of blacks. He knew it would be a close vote, and he also knew that winning wasn't simply everything; it was the only thing. To that end, Nixon had promises galore spilling from his lips, with little intention of remembering, much less keeping, them.

In addition to all the promises he made to different special interests, Nixon promised Johnson, after LBJ bowed out of the race, that he would avoid the war as an issue. Then he immediately made the war an issue; indeed, it became *the* issue by September. And by that time, he was neck-deep in the kind of skullduggery that had become vintage Nixon—and which we'll detail in the chapter on deception.

So Nixon gained the presidency. But it was one thing to gain it, and another to hold it and get reelected. As one campaign promise after anoth-er bit the dust, as the war dragged on—spilling over into Cambodia, then into Laos—as anti-war demonstrators descended on Washington in droves, as the schizophrenic nation split itself as at no time since the Civil War, Nixon saw his second term disappearing like a mirage in the desert. What saved his neck, as we have noted, was his golden opportunity to break bread with Mao Zedong and Brezhnev, despite his heroic efforts to battle Communism up to twenty months before his decision to visit China. Again, "circumstances," particularly his imminent reelection chances, had changed, and here was the ultimate pragmatist—no opportunist, mind you—ready to show his common sense and change with the circumstances. So despite his previous stands against Communism, despite his cementing of a special relationship with Chiang and Taiwan, Nixon did a 180-degree turn and went, hat in hand, to Peking and to Moscow. It was a TV extravaganza, just the kind of publicity Nixon needed to erect his "monument" for November 1972.

Dollars for Votes

It was, however, more than "monuments" that Nixon needed. Like all pols, Nixon was milking the cash cow of Republican bigwigs, particularly those with or wanting contracts with the federal government; those looking for subsidies, like the milk producers; or those looking for favorable rulings on proposed mergers, like ITT. Though Nixon in August of 1972 disclaimed any intention of participating in fund-raising, he was by October in the middle of it with Connally, who'd forsaken the ranks of the Democrats to milk the disgruntled wealthy ones on behalf of Nixon. On October 17, Nixon asked Connally: "Did you talk to John [Mulcahy, a supporter] about my idea of showing this to ten potential contributors and letting them put up 100 G's each in the budget?" Haldeman chipped in to provide specifics: ". . . you say 'Gentlemen, if we're going to get this program across like it's got to go, we need a million dollars and we need it this afternoon. There's ten of you here. You've each got to give us $100,000 yourselves or get us $100,000 immediately.' I guarantee you, all ten of them will pledge $100,000. Then you do the same thing in Chicago for another million." No small potatoes here. So when Congress, aware of embarrassing questions being raised in the press by Nixon's fund-raising, passed the Federal Elections Campaign Act in February 1972, the President hailed it as a vital step in building "public confidence in the integrity of the electoral process." At the same time, he saw his window of opportunity closing in just two months, when the law was to take effect. Get moving, he told Maurice Stans, his chief fund-raiser, and get it all by April 7, the deadline. Stans got moving. He imposed an "election tax," amounting to as much as $100,000 on those corporations doing business with the federal government. For others it was one percent of profits, and for individuals it was five percent of their net worth. For ambassadorships ". . . anybody that wants to be an ambassador, wants to pay at least $250,000." Thus did Stans put the bite on fellow Republicans, cautioning that April 7 was a deadline "which we all naturally want to avoid." Stans, it turned out, was the farmer who gathered the golden eggs of his prize geese, and by April 7 he had $20 million in "volunteer" contributions, $6 million of it coming in the last two days. By election time, CREEP had amassed—and spent— all but $4 million of a treasure chest of $60 million, no small change even in those days. One significant contributor was Armand Hammer, the same Soviet agent/tycoon who'd feathered LBJ's nest six years earlier. How fitting that his $100,000 should arrive a month or so before Nixon headed for Moscow for his Soviet summit. Nixon was grateful to Stans, as Haldeman explained to his President on June 14, 1972: "You've got to give Stans credit. It was collected over a period of three weeks . . . the sonofabitch just got on his horse and rode, and . . . he just sucked that money in as fast as he could suck it in. . . ."

Nixon was leaving nothing to chance, so intent was he on seizing the opportunity to perform "public service," as he called it, for another four years. Back from Peking, back from Moscow, flushed with his success in erecting twin monuments to his international prowess, relishing the best news from Vietnam in his first term, Nixon, by June engaged, as Ambrose aptly described it, "in the biggest poker game of his life, had put all his chips in the pot while simultaneously drawing to an inside straight and bluffing. He was about to rake in his biggest pot."[4] Such an opportunity came only once in a lifetime, and he was determined to seize it.

Dollars for Dick

When Nixon entered "public service," in 1946, his life savings, together with his wife's, totaled some $13,000, about a third of which were poker winnings in World War II. By the time he left—somewhat reluctantly— "public service," he was a multimillionaire. Just how he "seized the opportunity" to enrich himself while in office is a tale lurid enough without his sanctimonious denials. No other president, save Lyndon Johnson, could hold a candle to him.

For twenty-eight years, Nixon laid claim to the log-cabin myth that Johnson had played to the hilt. In the eight years when Nixon was not occupying office, from 1961-1969, he was running for office. And always he insisted he could have been the author of Ben Franklin's "Poor Richard's Almanac." Life was hard for the boy, raised the second of five sons—especially with the deaths of Arthur, then Harold, both from tuberculosis. When Hannah took Harold to the dry heat of Arizona in hopes of restoring his health, she cared for four other patients for three years to help pay the bills, while Dick, at 17, worked as a carnival barker.

In his *Memoirs*, Nixon recalled life in Yorba Linda, just southeast of Los Angeles, as "hard but happy. My father worked at whatever jobs he could find. Thanks to a vegetable garden and some of our own fruit trees, we had plenty to eat despite our low income. We also had a cow that provided milk from which my mother made our butter and cheese." It is of some note that Nixon wrote this in 1978, nine years after deToledano's biography told of Nixon's living in poverty. Hannah had confessed, "Many days I had nothing to serve but corn meal. I'd bring it to the table and exclaim, 'See what we have tonight—wonderful cornmeal!' "

Nevertheless, the parents scrimped and saved, the boys pitched in as best they could, and in 1922, when Dick was nine, his father borrowed $9,000, bought some land on the road between Whittier and La Habra, cleared the land, put in a tank and a pump, and opened the first gas station, in what had been a church, on that eight-mile stretch. Soon they added a general store and grocery and, Nixon later noted, would have been "modestly well off—had it not been for the illnesses" of his two brothers.

Nixon's cousin, Jessamyn West, learning that Nixon the pol was hyping his boyhood poverty, called it, "politically expedient to put on your log cabin clothes when you run for office." Raised in like circumstances in a similar house in the same neighborhood of Yorba Linda, she said she'd not felt poor. In 1960, Nixon told Stewart Alsop, "It's been said our family was poor, and maybe it was, but we never thought of ourselves as poor." Nevertheless, in his 1968 campaign film, Nixon didn't hesitate to claim, "We were poor. We worked hard. We had very little. We all used hand-me-down clothes." And in 1972, visiting with Mao, he emphasized that, like the Chinese leader, he, too, had come from a poor family.[5] It appears that Nixon was "poor" when it served his purposes. It didn't take Nixon long in politics to cultivate the habit Kissinger found so annoying: saying something, then immediately saying the opposite, without batting an eyelash. Oxymoron or not, outright contradiction or not, Nixon used words, regardless of meaning, to further his career.

For the 1968 campaign it was made to appear that Nixon had never shown any interest in making money, least of all at taxpayers' expense. Gary Wills wrote that Nixon "never had real money until 1960. . . ." In his *Memoirs*, Nixon wrote that, for his first fourteen years in politics he lived simply but comfortably. After paying moving expenses to California in 1961, he insisted "our sole asset other than personal effects was a $48,000 equity in our house in Washington." In January 1957, with a raise in pay from $30,000 to $35,000, Nixon sold his three-bedroom house on Tilden Street for $45,000, and bought a large, secluded house with eight bedrooms and five baths for $70,000, then hired a live-in maid. In addition, the *New York Times* reported, he furnished it in part with "gifts from forty nations."[6] But no matter what he liked to claim, there was no question about it: Nixon had come a long way from the little house in Yorba Linda and the gas station/grocery store in Whittier.

What Are Friends For?

Taking a page from Ike's notebook, Dick Nixon cultivated friends who could make a difference come campaign time, friends such as Bebe Rebozo, Robert Abplanalp, Elmer Bobst, and Donald Kendall. Each of them was a multimillionaire, and each saw in the rising star of Nixon the kind of "friend" each needed in government.

Take Charles "Bebe" Rebozo, introduced to Nixon by fellow Senator George Smathers in 1951. Here, it was soon evident, was "mutual opportunity," a symbiotic relationship that would enrich them both. Rebozo went out of his way to accommodate this political astronaut, long before John Glenn became the real thing. Not only did Rebozo extend his hospitality to his Key Biscayne estate, but he awarded Nixon $200,000 that he'd "earned" through his real estate trust.

After all, this was the least Rebozo could do for a friend, particularly a friend who interceded with the Small Business Administration for him to obtain loans, at a time when rival groups were getting the cold shoulder. It was too late when Representative Wright Patman of the House Banking Committee declared there was no justification for the SBA to lend money to a person posing as a small businessman, who then turned around and opened a bank. It was too late for the federal bank examiner who took one look at Rebozo's bank and declared it no bank at all, since it was so conservative with its loans—so conservative, in fact, that few, other than Nixon, could seem to meet its strict qualifications. It was not too late, however, for Rebozo to maintain a healthy cash reserve, set aside for the exclusive use of Nixon whenever he needed it, as he did in 1961. Neither was it too late to help Nixon establish his own mansion at Key Biscayne, later his "Southern White House."

Rebozo not only had ready cash; he had ready friends, eager to climb aboard the Vice-President's train of goodies. One of these was Robert Abplanalp, whom Rebozo took aboard as a bank director. Developer of the aerosol spray can, Abplanalp contributed mightily to the depletion of the protective ozone layer. He also contributed mightily to the economic well-being of the Vice-President. When, in 1963, Nixon took over as senior partner in a New York law firm, Abplanalp threw his business to him, "chiefly to keep the government out of [our] hair," he explained. "We didn't want them to know what we were doing. We were afraid they'd steal our ideas."

When Nixon tired of Key Biscayne there was always Abplanalp's palatial mansion on Grand Cay, an island he owned in the Bahamas. But that wasn't enough for "good old Dick" in 1969, when he was President. So Abplanalp threw in with seventy-five other California businessmen to build a golf course for Nixon at his San Clemente estate. The donors were limited to seventy-six in honor of the original seventy-six who had the good sense and the good dollars to make up Nixon's 1952 slush fund.[7] It seems that Bob had lent Dick $650,000 toward the $1.5 million he paid for the thirty-acre estate at San Clemente, only to later forgive him the loan. Then he and Rebozo offered to buy six acres of the thirty for the tidy sum of $625,000, an offer Nixon found he couldn't refuse. When nosy reporters asked Abplanalp what he intended to do with the six acres, the cagey entrepreneur, never at a loss for a quip, said he intended to build a "ten story whorehouse." Learning of this in the press, Nixon wrote him, 'Bob, save the piano player's job for me." Some may be forgiven the thought that, had Nixon settled for the job of piano player in a whorehouse in 1946, a lot of wear and tear on the country would have been saved.

Of the few who remained in Nixon's corner following his resignation, Abplanalp was one, claiming that Nixon's major strength was that he was "painfully honest." How so, queried astonished reporters. Why, Abplanalp explained, take a look at all the pain Nixon had suffered in resigning, simply because he'd refused Bob's suggestion to burn the incriminating tapes. Indeed, he'd offered to burn them himself, but Nixon, the "painfully honest" President refused, deploring such a criminal act as destroying evidence. "How much crap he'd have to take was not a consideration," Abplanalp continued. "It was illegal and he wouldn't do it." How could there be any doubt about Nixon's "tremendous strength of character?"

Another Republican fat cat that Nixon had the good sense to cultivate was Donald Kendall, CEO of Pepsi-Cola. A big giver to Nixon's campaigns in the fifties, Kendall found that 1959 was payback time. Learning of Nixon's intended trip to represent Ike at the official opening of the American National Exhibition in Moscow, Kendall saw an advertising bonanza. So when cameras were focused on Nixon, finger-jabbing Khrushchev in the chest during their kitchen debate in the "All-American Home," there in the background loomed a large Pepsi-Cola sign for a hundred million or more viewers to see. No, the Soviet premier wouldn't go so far as to taste it and pronounce it fit for a king, but he did hold a bottle in his hand for all the world to note, if not to long remember.

No ingrate, Kendall was duly appreciative. In 1962, when Nixon was out of a job, Kendall and another Nixon high roller, Elmer Bobst, head of Warner-Lambert pharmaceuticals, persuaded Nixon to shake the dust of California's gubernatorial defeat off his shoes and head for the friendlier clime of New York City. There the two friends had interceded with a prestigious law firm to give them their business, along with Abplanalp's, in exchange for the firm's making Nixon its senior partner. Convincing Nixon he could be the proverbial phoenix, rising from the ashes, Kendall in 1964 joined Maurice Stans and others with an up-front "gift" of $100,000 to get the ball rolling for the Issues Research Council, a front that would serve as a launching pad for Nixon's run against Johnson in 1968. For Kendall, this was not bad for a college drop-out who'd started at the company as an assembly-line worker bottling Pepsi for $400 a month. To show his further appreciation, he put his 140-acre estate in New York's exclusive Westchester County at Nixon's disposal.

Along with Nixon, it had been Kendall who'd nagged Johnson in the 1960's to settle for nothing less than "true-blue" victory in Vietnam. Kendall was outraged at the failure of other businessmen to see the growing menace of international Communism, with its tendency to stifle good old-fashioned American entrepreneurism by nationalizing U.S. businesses set up in other nations—at great cost to the Americans. If there was anybody who could empathize with this avatar of Horatio Alger, it was "luck and pluck" Dick Nixon.

By the fall of 1970, Nixon had one last good turn to perform for his close friend Kendall. Nixon was trumpeting as the keynote of his fall campaign for Republican congressional candidates "we can maintain a free society only if we recognize that in a free society no one can win all the time." But there was Augustine Edwards, a newspaper publisher and businessman who'd fled Chile to become vice-president of Kendall's Pepsi-Cola Company, warning that if Salvador Allende was installed as president of Chile, nationalization was sure to follow. Allende had won 36 percent of the vote against two other candidates in a free election, and was in a runoff with the other top man; now it was up to the Chilean Congress to decide the victor. Unfortunately, the U.S. Ambassador, Edward Korrey, was weighing in with his judgment that "Chile voted calmly to have a Marxist-Leninist state, the first state in the world to make this choice freely and knowingly."

Friends, however, were friends, and Nixon, anything but calm, ordered the CIA to intervene. Allende, this President made "crystal clear," was not to prevail. His argument: Allende had only gotten 36 percent of the vote—conveniently overlooking Nixon's 43 percent in 1968. So Nixon cut foreign aid to Chile "to make the country scream," promised another $10 million to the CIA, and ordered Agency head Richard Helms to assume their mission as "a full time job," to use the "best men we have," but above all to keep our ambassador in the dark. Allende won, only to lose, slain with the connivance of Nixon's CIA. It should be added that Kendall wasn't the only one Nixon was satisfying in ridding Chile of Allende. For, as Theodore White pointed out in his *Breach of Faith*, ITT— whose magnanimous gift of $400,000 to the 1972 campaign kitty, in exchange for favors with the Justice Department—had also offered an additional $1 million to the CIA to help overthrow Allende.[8]

Then there was Elmer Bobst who, like Time Incorporated chairman Henry Luce and Representative Walter Judd of Minnesota, was a son of missionaries to China. No longer poor and no longer in China, Bobst not only made big bucks as head of Warner-Lambert, he flaunted them. Like

Nixon's other well-heeled friends, he put his estate at Nixon's disposal, but he also journeyed to Washington's exclusive Burning Tree Country Club in his own railroad car. For his repeated "kindnesses" to Nixon during the sixties, Bobst in 1969 found time for the "quo" to match his "quid." Try as he might, Bobst just couldn't get the Justice Department to permit a merger of his company with another pharmaceutical giant, Parke-Davis. Something about a monopoly stuck in the craw of those in the antitrust division of Mitchell's Justice Department. But Mitchell, former partner in Nixon's law firm in New York, came to the fortunate conclusion that there would be no problem with the merger. So the quo had more than matched the quid, and Bobst relaxed, convinced that his investment in Richard Nixon had been a shrewd one.

Two others, wealthier by far than these four, also made it a point to latch on to Nixon's rising star. The first was billionaire Howard Hughes, with whom Rebozo became Nixon's stand-in. It seems that Hughes, sizing up Nixon's chances, after he'd been again accepted by Ike as vice-presidential candidate in 1956, saw him as presidential timber in 1960, if not before—in case of another, and possibly fatal, heart attack hitting Ike. So when Hughes learned of Nixon's younger brother, Donald, having a hard time borrowing money to open a restaurant featuring "Nixonburgers," Hughes' kindness extended to a $205,000 loan to Donald, the only collateral being Hannah's deed for a Whittier lot assessed at $13,000. That was an offer Donald found hard to refuse. Of course, Hughes lent the money through his attorney, on behalf of the Hughes Tool Company. And of course, the $205,000 was small potatoes for Hughes, who stood to gain billions in government contracts. It didn't hurt that Ike made Nixon chairman of the President's Committee on Government Contracts. Furthermore, and by 1957 a pressing matter, the Justice Department's antitrust suit against Hughes was conveniently settled out of court. In addition, just three months after Hughes's loan, the IRS just happened to reverse its previous decision, and granted the Howard Hughes Medical Institute a tax exemption as a charitable organization. This alone saved Hughes, according to Drew Pearson, "tens of millions of dollars."

Come 1960, the Democrats cast a jaundiced eye at one hand seeming to wash the other. Had the Vice-President been put in the pocket of Hughes for a measly $205,000 loan to his brother? The rumors flew and Nixon flew into a rage, protesting through his campaign manager, Robert

Finch, that this was "an obvious political smear in the last two weeks of the campaign," showing how desperate Kennedy and the Democrats had become. As it turned out, Donald was such a poor businessman that he declared bankruptcy in 1957 and defaulted on his loan. No matter. Like the other wealthy funders of Nixon, Hughes knew a sound investment when he saw one. Yet there was his attorney, warning him of the political implications of the loan, to which Hughes responded simply, "I want the Nixons to have the money." But Noah Dietrich, executive vice-president of Hughes Tool Company, warned Nixon, "If this loan becomes public information, it could mean the end of your political career. And I don't believe it can be kept quiet." To which Nixon responded, "Mr. Dietrich, I have to put my relatives ahead of my career." Whether or not he was putting Donald ahead of his career is at least debatable. For Nixon had placed Hughes deeply in his debt with all the largesse of government favors, and he figured, sooner or later, he would reap what he'd sown.

Harvest time came in 1968, when Rebozo persuaded Hughes to part with $100,000 for Nixon's presidential run. Trouble was, the money didn't get to Nixon until after he'd won the election. Therefore the "donation" was illegal, and Nixon was obliged to return it. But he was not about to look this gift horse in the mouth, much less return the money. Some of it he used to buy Pat a set of expensive earrings—diamonds set in platinum—for her sixtieth birthday in 1972. And some of the money he used to improve his Key Biscayne property. Using this campaign money for his own personal use was easy, once Rebozo had laundered it through his Florida-for-Nixon Committee. As late as August 3, 1972, Nixon was being plagued by Democrats, and especially Democratic National Chairman Lawrence O'Brien, about the Hughes loan to brother Donald. To Ehrlichman the President griped: ". . . if they bring up that goddamn Hughes loan again, we ought to break this over O'Brien's head." Furthermore, ". . . in 1961, the first year I ever made any money, when I wrote the damn book [Six Crises], those sons of bitches [the IRS] came up and they went after it. How much did you pay for your house, and all the rest. It was horrible." Learning from Ehrlichman that "six or eight guys . . . at the top [of the IRS]" were not Nixon appointees, and therefore could not be trusted to run a thorough audit on O'Brien, Nixon was adamant. "Out with them, every one of those bastards, out now . . . we'll kick their ass out of there . . . and then investigate the bastards. They're probably on the take."[9]

Hughes, a loner like Nixon, never did try snuggling up to the political astronaut. Not so the other billionaire, Walter Annenberg, son of Moses, a poor immigrant who'd earned enough money on gambling sheets to buy the *Philadelphia Inquirer*, as well as detective and movie magazines. By 1940, he was raking in $6 million a year, making him the highest paid man in the country. To show his appreciation for the nation that had welcomed him along with the other "poor, huddled masses," Annenberg balked at paying his income taxes. Uncle Sam, not given to such flagrant disobedience, clapped him in jail, leaving his only view of the world through iron bars. That taught Walter a lesson he would not forget. Furthermore, Walter was every bit the entrepreneur his father was. Before long, he'd taken his fortune and expanded it into a billion dollar media empire, including *Seventeen*, *TV Guide*, and numerous radio-TV stations. Walter not only paid his taxes, but contributed mightily to the likes of Richard Nixon, a man on the move. Nixon, properly grateful, awarded Walter the ambassadorship to the Court of St. James—the plum of ambassadorships. It was the same Annenberg who called the charge of anti-Semitism against Nixon "utter rubbish!" It was Annenberg who'd built his own golf course at Palm Desert when, as a Jew, he was barred from the local golf course. And it was Annenberg who, in 1986, described Nixon as no "conventional politician." To the contrary, he was "prepared to embrace a snake at any given opportunity." Whether Annenberg included himself among the snakes, or whether he was opportunistic enough to know another snake when he saw him, Annenberg's was scarcely the kind of recommendation Nixon needed to rehabilitate himself in the eyes of the public, which by that time was convinced that, among the sins of this thirty-seventh President, not the least of them was an opportunism so crass that it would bow to no previous promises, no previous commitments, and no such thing as integrity.

Perhaps as critical as any money Nixon ever took was the hush money he needed for the Watergate burglars, as Haldeman outlined to Nixon on March 2, 1973: ". . . one of the major problems . . . is the question of financial, continuing financial activity in order to keep those people in place. And the way [Dean is] working on this is via Mitchell to Tom Pappas." It so happened that Pappas maintained close ties with the fascist regime of Greek colonels in Athens, and was eager to retain the U.S. Ambassador—a supporter of that regime—rather than have Nixon replace him, which he'd planned to do. As Haldeman put it, "Pappas is extremely anxious that

[Ambassador Henry] Tasca stay in Greece. . . ." Here was another quid pro quo, with Pappas, as Haldeman explained, the "unknown J. Paul Getty of the world right now." Nixon: "Great. I'm just delighted." Haldeman clinched it with: "And he's able to deal in cash. . . ." Five weeks had passed, and John Dean, Nixon found, was going to blow the whistle. Ehrlichman: "He's going to say that he and Mitchell worked it out [raising hush money for the burglars]. . . ." Nixon: "This money was contributed by whom?" Ehrlichman: ". . . Kalmbach's contributors came through with most of it." Nixon: "This is money that was not reported as a contribution to the campaign? . . . of course we weren't trying to shut them out [up]. These people . . . had been employed by the committee [CREEP], and they engaged in illegal activities. We felt they were entitled to assistance until they had a trial . . . that's what he [Mitchell] has to say. . . . Hush-up money—didn't seem to work, did it?" Two months later, on June 5, 1973, Nixon was determined to show Fred Buzhardt, who had replaced Dean as master of the cover-up, that he had no part in discussing money—particularly hush money—and certainly not with turncoat John Dean. Nixon: "There was never any discussion of a million dollars, except on the 21st. Never, never, never. Good gosh, that was pure hypothetical crap, frankly . . . the whole business about dollars is to me embarrassing because we were discussing it..."

Nixon told much of himself when, trying to enlist Ehrlichman in 1968, he first offered him the job of attorney general, and Ehrlichman wasn't interested. So Nixon asked him to be White House counsel. His reasoning: "When you return to the private practice of law, you'll get rich because everybody will want to hire you because you are the President's friend." Convicted and sentenced as a felon for his part in Watergate, there is no small irony that Ehrlichman was disbarred, never to practice law again. But apart from that, Nixon's reasoning reveals much of the man, particularly his brazen influence peddling. He'd gotten rich from his connections. So could Ehrlichman.[10]

The President Reign

As Nixon prepared for the White House, LBJ told him of the decision he'd taken on the personal papers he'd donated to the National Archives. Ever the quick study, Nixon had his vice-presidential papers appraised, their value set at $2 million. So each year, starting in 1968, he took a deduction based on that evaluation. When, in 1973, he found these deductions to be illegal, he was, as he put it, "shocked and totally frustrated." On March 18, 1974, Wilbur Mills, Ways and Means Committee chairman, announced that once Nixon's tax report was released, he would be out of office. Nixon's explanation reveals either ignorance or dishonesty—or perhaps a bit of both. "Without my knowledge," he insisted, "the deed for the papers had in fact been backdated by one of the lawyers handling it for me." The Committee refused to buy this lame explanation and ruled against him, disallowing the deduction for capital gains. But that wasn't all. With Watergate roiling the waters around him, with his having to reimburse the government for these deductions, Nixon suffered abuse, he felt, when he had to reimburse the government for his family flying on Air Force One when Nixon himself was not aboard, unless it was for official business. Atop that, the IRS disallowed Nixon's use of his Key Biscayne estate as an office. Bitter at such "slings and arrows," he complained he'd perpetrated no impropriety, much less fraud.

On November 18, 1968, Nixon claimed a net worth of $47,000 plus a 1958 Olds "in need of an overhaul." For some strange reason, the $250,000 royalties Nixon cleared in his *Six Crises* never seemed to appear in his figures of net worth after 1962, nor did his $100,000 annual income from his law firm. Never, he claimed, had he "profited from public service." Nevertheless, he welcomed the chance to clear the air "because people have got to know whether their President is a crook. Well, I am not a crook. I've earned everything I've got." This cry of poverty hardly set well with the earlier release of Nixon's net worth at $515,830, over $400,000 of which he'd invested in Fisher Island, a 220-acre island off Miami Beach that Rebozo was developing.

Once the election was assured, the new President sold his New York apartment and bought two bungalows in Key Biscayne—including one owned by Smathers and another by Rebozo—and joined the three into a single compound, fenced with a high hedge of hibiscus. The two bungalows set him back $250,000. Apparently Rebozo's was a gift. A year later, Nixon sold his investment in Fisher Island and bought five acres and a house on the beach at San Clemente for $340,000. He then issued a financial statement showing a net worth of almost $600,000.

Nixon, on May 14, 1973, once again was furious that Ervin's Watergate Committee was reporting that "the President used a million dollars of unrecorded funds to buy this property [San Clemente]." "It's just a total goddamn lie. A total lie . . . I don't have a damn thing. This is why I don't own anything. I don't own stocks or bonds. All my money's in real estate. . . ." Later that day he again took off: "On this million dollar thing, we've got to attack them, assault them, and destroy them. . . that is a libel of unbelievable pretension. . . ."

On July 9, 1973, Nixon complained to Rebozo of charges being made that he'd bilked the taxpayers of millions to refurbish and renovate his properties: "With all this business [of investigations] of going into the California property and the Florida property and all the rest—they'll say how much of this has been held which is none of their damn business."[11]

By 1974 the General Accounting Office figured that Nixon had "invested" some $10 million of taxpayer money to improve his Southern and Western "White Houses." Furthermore, it ruled that Nixon had spent $1.4 million on improvements under the guise of security. Nixon, on the other hand, claimed $8.9 million, or about 90%, had been spent on "administrative and protective support." It is not too fine a point to make that virtually all the improvements went through Haldeman and thence to military aide Bill Gulley, whose Department of Defense funds were virtually unlimited for the President. In May 1974, with Haldeman fired a year before and impeachment cries ringing in the air, Haldeman presented figures sharply at odds with Nixon's: Not $10 million, but $17 million had gone to improve these two properties. Released to the press, the firestorm that erupted did nothing to ease the mind of this miscreant. It was obvious that Johnson and Nixon both had come a long way from the spartan Truman who, in the White House, kept a roll of 3-cent stamps that he'd bought with his own money, and that he licked and stuck on personal letters to the folks back in Missouri. In addition, he insisted on paying for the refreshments on the presidential yacht when he used it on the weekends.

With his lavish estates at Key Biscayne and San Clemente, renovated and upgraded with millions from the public till, Nixon resigned a multimillionaire. Yet, there he was in his swan song to his aides, complaining, "I only wish that I were a wealthy man—at the present time I have got to find a way to pay my taxes." What some in the small audience must have known, despite the hollow laughter, was that Nixon was having to reimburse the IRS for the huge deductions he'd taken on his illegally back-dated vice-presidential notes. In reality, by parting with a few more acres of bare ground at San Clemente, he could easily pay his back taxes.

As for a charitable streak, from 1969 to 1972 Nixon earned well over $1 million. Yet in those four years the total amount he gave to charity was $13,445, or about a tenth of 1 percent. And a third of it went, in 1970, to friend Billy Graham's Evangelistic Association. They may have preached tithing in Nixon's Quaker Church when he was teaching Sunday School and playing the piano there. But he had all he could do to scare up a tithe of a tithe for charity of any kind. As miserly as was Nixon with his own money, he was a spendthrift when it came to taxpayers' money. Ever aware of the importance of timing, Nixon signed a permanent 20% increase in Social Security benefits in September 1972. This was just in time for recipients to count their blessings on October 1 and to remember, come election day, who had signed the bill into law. But just in case they didn't get the point, Nixon sent recipients a helpful reminder with their checks. In addition to greasing the skids for seniors, Nixon told his Cabinet early that year to spend their budgets as soon as possible. He hounded the Federal Reserve to open the money spigots, making 1972 the year the money supply went through the roof. With it, no coincidence, went infla-tion. To curb that, Nixon imposed wage-and-price controls for two years. This gave a momentous shot to further inflation, racing ahead at a 6.6 per-cent clip. By 1980, it was double-digit, and the Fed—to stamp out the most treacherous economic condition since the Great Depression—virtually shut off the money supply, pitching the nation into the deepest recession since the thirties. The after-shocks of that inflation earthquake of the sev-enties were still being felt by the nineties: the destruction of the Bretton Woods monetary system, the savings and loan debacle, budget and trade deficits with the burgeoning entitlement payments being demanded—and, insidiously, the plunging of the dollar in value against the currencies of Japan and Germany, and the recession of the early 1990s. It is simplistic to allege that it all started with Nixon, but there can be no question that he contributed mightily to it.[12]

Politically and financially, Nixon was a career opportunist. Shorn of scruple, he was bent on "seizing the moment" whenever and wherever an opportunity opened before him. His crass opportunism paved the way for the next step in hubris, his exploiting of things, of events and, more impor-tantly, of those around him.

CHAPTER 5

EXPLOITATION

I would define liberty to be the power to do as we would be done by.
— John Adams, 1819

. . . liberty is power . . . the nation blessed with the largest portion of liberty must in proportion to its numbers be the most powerful nation on earth.
— John Quincy Adams, 1821

The natural progress of things is for liberty to yield and government to gain ground.
— Thomas Jefferson, 1788

See to the government. See that the government does not acquire too much power. Keep a check on your rulers. Do this and liberty is safe.
— William Henry Harrison, 1840

LYNDON JOHNSON

One facet of Lyndon Johnson's political genius was already obvious by 1940: his ability to look at an organization and see it in political potentialities that no one else saw, to transform that organization into a political force, and to reap from that transformation personal advantage.

— Robert A. Caro, *The Path to Power*

Now Lyndon, don't you worry. Take it easy. If you need money or anything, you just call on me.

— Sam Rayburn, 1935

John Kennedy is watching us up in heaven and we are going to wrap up all of this legislation and put it in a package and tie it up and label it JFK.

— Lyndon Johnson to Larry O'Brien, 1965[1]

Of Levers Big Enough

Having succumbed to excessive deference, especially to those whom LBJ enlisted as aides. Having then ignored them or tyrannized them as he sailed on in an unchecked expansion of every office he held, seizing every opportunity to do so even if it meant contradicting himself, Lyndon Johnson was led almost inexorably to the fifth step in hubris: exploitation. It is defined as the unethical use of others for one's own advantage or profit; the unfair or selfish turning to one's own account.

Archimedes, the ancient Greek, said, "Give me a lever long enough and I will move the earth." Lyndon presumed, on entering the White House, that he'd found that lever. His political power, translated into economic and military power, was such that it truly beggared the imagination.

No other nation, before or since, could hope to match it. He would use that power to move not only Archimedes' earth, but heaven itself. For him, many were fools but all were tools, prosthetic extensions of himself, to be used and abused as he saw fit. These people—and everything else he could lay his hands on—he exploited unsparingly, sacrificing them on the altar of self-aggrandizement.

George Reedy, who worked for LBJ for fourteen years before quitting in disgust in 1965, came to see him as "unable to understand other people except in terms of himself—which meant in terms of action." Here was a genius as a tactician, as subtle as he was clever in using others. It wasn't so much reflection on "ends and means" that he prized as much as "mental agility and verbal nimbleness." He persuaded his Senate colleagues because, Reedy added, tactically he could outthink them, phrasing issues in such a way "that they found themselves unable to vote against them." By the time he entered Congress, Johnson had developed the ability to transform a debating society, the college social club, and the Little Congress into springboards for propelling himself ahead of others.

Added to that proclivity was Johnson's knack, in politics as in poker, to bluff. What Sam Houston saw in Lyndon's ability to win "a big pot . . . with only a pair of deuces" others saw in his parlaying cleverness, shrewdness, and subtlety—all married to an insatiable yearning for power—to yield him the biggest pot of all: the White House. When do governments gain ground, as Jefferson suggested, but when our duly elected pols exploit us as citizens? With this Jefferson had trouble. "I have never been able to conceive," he wrote, "how any rational being could propose happiness to himself from the exercise of power over others."[2] One is left to wonder if Johnson was either rational or happy in his utter insistence on controlling everything and everybody within his long reach. By 1968, with the country neck-deep in the swamp of Vietnam, many were questioning his rationality. His increasing attempts to anesthetize his misery with Cutty Sark, culminating in his sulking retreat to his Ranch in 1969, left little doubt that he was, for much if not most of his presidency, not a happy man.

Of Helicopters and String Bands

Spelled out in Johnson's exploitation were helicopters and string bands. No more effectively did he use them than in his 1941 and 1948 runs for the Senate. It seems that the voters of the Tenth District had never seen the likes of Lyndon, even in Sam, his father. In place of the straight-shooter was the showman, copying not so much Sam as the state's governor, W. Lee "Pappy" O'Daniel, Lyndon's opponent for the U.S. Senate in 1941, when the two men were vying to fill the seat of Morris Sheppard, who'd died of a stroke. To warm up his audiences, Lyndon borrowed O'Daniel's idea of a string band; then the "Kate Smith of the South" would step out with a powerful "God Bless America," followed by "San Antonio Rose," "Dixie," and "The Eyes of Texas Are Upon You." Next on the platform was a narrator hitting the high points of FDR's rescue of the country from the Great Depression, gilded with more background music.

It was developing into what entertainer Ed Sullivan, twenty years later, would call a "rilly good shew." For the Texans, or 98 percent of them, had no idea that Lyndon had long since left the shadow of FDR for the bright sunlight of the Brown brothers and their friends—with taxpayers' money. So the audiences bought it when Lyndon, echoing his 1937 bid for Congress, announced he was for Roosevelt one hundred percent. "Let the conspiracy of Herbert Hoover and Calvin Coolidge take note! Furthermore, let the foreign conspiracy of the Axis—Germany, Japan, and Italy—be forewarned." To whom could the nation turn in this time of peril? Why, to FDR of course—and to his surrogate in the person of Lyndon Baines Johnson, "a man who loves his country, who loves the people. . . ." It appears the narrator knew just how to put it.

The crowd was ready, the time was ripe, and with a ruffle of drums, what should appear beneath an oversized Stetson, its brim rolled back, but a grin connecting one big ear to the other? Some said it reminded them of FDR himself. Some said it looked like Hollywood had come to Texas. But no one said it reminded them of Sam Johnson. Here was the pizzazz, the glitz, the hype, the schmaltz, all carefully orchestrated by the thirty-four-year-old from Johnson City.[3]

In appearance Johnson bore faint resemblance to his father, and little resemblance to himself four years earlier when—skinny, gawky, a nervous beanpole—he'd almost killed himself covering every last mile of his district to shake hands with every last voter. Now when he removed the coat to his two hundred dollar suit he revealed the start of a paunch, with a spreading rear end to balance it. A double chin lay beneath a big jaw jutting out in heavy jowls, giving him the look of someone ten years older.

Carefully he removed the text of his speech, written by others, and just as carefully fitted on his glasses—after all, he must look "senatorial."

As he launched into his speech, it was not so much what he said as what he left unsaid. There wasn't a word about his careful distancing of himself from FDR; not a word about betraying his friend Sam Rayburn (to be detailed); not a word about cozying up to the fat cats who made possible his elections and the fancy garb he now sported—men who positively loathed FDR and his New Deal, a fancy term for a socialist-communist state; and not a word about the affair he was having with the mistress of one of his "deep pockets."

What he did tell them was what he figured they wanted to hear. After all, there was nothing wrong with pandering if it produced the votes to get elected. Robert Caro has carefully drawn a picture of the ambitious pol, just as ready to "shimmy" as he was to exploit. His impression was one of power, of dominating power, of power that expressed itself in an authoritarian tone, a tone of arrogance. Here was a voice that was harsh, rising at times to a bellow. He sounded like a lecturer who was determined to unscrew the heads of his students and pour into them the truth, his truth, the only truth worth listening to. His tone was "dogmatic, pontifical, the tone of a leader demanding rather than soliciting support. Reinforcing the tone were the gestures, as awkward as ever . . . his big head aggressively thrust forward at his listeners," with his hand raised to "repeatedly jab a finger down at them. Sometimes he spoke with one hand on a hip, with his big head thrown back a little, shouting over their heads." His smiles were as rare as they were mechanical, like the speaking itself.

Despite seeding the audience with campaign workers, federal employees, and those from Brown and Root, it wasn't long before the audiences sensed there was less than met the eye here—a lot less. As mechanical as was his delivery, as patronizing as were his words, his greeting the crowd afterwards was every bit as bad. Justice William O. Douglas, nearby for a speech of his own, happened in on a Johnson speech and, as LBJ came to the close, Douglas shouted, "I want all you good folks . . . to line up and shake the hand of the next senator from Texas, Lyndon B. Johnson." Then Douglas made note of Lyndon giving "each of them two pumps with the arm and one slap on the back before greeting the next comer." Here was a technique guaranteed to move the crowd along—one Lyndon had carefully rehearsed, determined to shake forty-two hands per minute.

Seldom, aide Bill Deason recalled, would Lyndon let any engage him in conversation. All was efficiency, cold efficiency, but efficiency nonetheless. In case one stalled along the assembly line to say more than a word or two, there was a cordon of officious aides to hurry him or her along. Of course with "important people," like local pols, he would stop and greet them with a big smile and a bear hug to match. For these were worth hundreds, maybe thousands of votes.

Like the ones he paused to spend time with, Lyndon's words were carefully selected. "We must stop the beast of Berlin before he reaches America. Now if you want your senator to go up there to Washington to snoop and sneak and snipe at your commander in chief, don't vote for Lyndon Johnson," the man who'd "always support your commander in chief and the elected Democratic leaders of this great Republic of ours."

At this point Johnson might very well drop his voice to a whisper as he storied them. "Over yonder in that Senate chamber there's a vacant seat. It was filled by a young congressman some thirty years ago. You promoted him from the House to the Senate. He was one of Roosevelt's strong right arms, chairman of the Military Affairs Committee. He worked himself to death. He was trying to build the greatest army that any nation ever knew. You must fill that seat. When you elect Lyndon Johnson to fill that seat, your commander in chief can look at that seat and say, 'There sits the boy from Johnson City that can't be bought!' You know, folks, they don't get to be twenty-one in my country if they're not honest."

About this time the crowd would begin to thin and Johnson would hasten to remind them that at the close of his speech—sometimes more than an hour long—there would be a drawing, worth as much as $700 in defense bonds going to the lucky winner. So many would make their way back, or pause on the edge of the crowd, perhaps wondering if they could take any more, even for that kind of money. Of course, all lost the drawing but one. And that one, it turned out, was luckier than Lyndon, who lost to O'Daniel.

By 1948, however, Johnson had more money in his pockets and more tricks up his sleeves. Indeed, it was Lyndon who was probably the first pol to exploit the helicopter, in this case a Sikorski he dubbed "The Johnson City Windmill." It seems that Larry Bell, founder of the company, ordered a pilot to fly one to Texas to help this "young, forward-thinking congressman" who just happened to have his hand on the strings to pull military contracts.

FDR's Corcoran chuckled as he described Lyndon's exploiting the novel flying contraption. "There was Lyndon flying overhead in that goddamn machine, sounding the call through his PA system, 'Come to whatever the county seat was and hear Lyndon Johnson!' And they'd come to hear him. Of course, mostly they came to see the helicopter. They'd never seen one before. Christ, it was brilliant as hell!" With his mike strapped to his chest—no mike fright here—Lyndon became the aerial pied piper, luring the crowds to a nearby landing spot. In the process he'd at times put the pilot as well as himself at risk. Whether squeezing in every last stop before darkness set in, or dodging a late-afternoon thunderstorm, or flying beneath high-tension lines, even veteran pilot Joe Mashman shuddered at times.

During one such incident in Texas, Joe recalled flying twenty-five to thirty feet high along a main street, heading toward a landing site in the town park of Marshall. Suddenly the copter lost power and dropped like a rock between two parked cars, then bounced as high as their roofs before regaining power and proceeding to the park. Johnson, his head down in the speech he was about to deliver, never noticed—but later asked, "Joe, that wasn't where you wanted to land back there, was it?"[4]

Of Prayers and Polls

Whatever it was—you name it and Johnson would exploit it. Landing the whirlybird in the park, Johnson let the crowd know he was a man of surmounting faith. "My good pilot Joe tells me it'll be too dangerous if I take off with him because we wouldn't have enough power to clear those 30,000-volt high-tension lines over there. He's going to have to take off alone. And it's going to be mighty tight. I just hope and pray he'll be able to make it."

Into his speech and seeing the crowd dissipate, Johnson was no longer giving defense bonds in a final drawing. But he'd call them back with, "Now, folks, I want you to stay here and wait until Joe tries to get the 'Johnson City Windmill' off the ground. He's going to need all the help he can get—he's going to need your prayers to get through safely. We're all hoping that the good Lord sees that Joe gets over those high-tension lines over there. I know we'll all be here helping to pray for him."

As good old Joe took the dare, climbing into his cockpit amid the silent prayers, Lyndon would climax the rally with a call to prayer. "Let's pray for Joe now. Good luck, Joe. We're with you, Joe. Help him, O Lord. Help this brave man make it out of here safely." Sinclair Lewis's Elmer Gantry couldn't have said it better. This political Gantry would, as a later chapter will describe, squeak by with an eighty-seven-vote margin of victory.

Fifteen years later, Lyndon Johnson was in the White House—for better or worse. By this time he had come to regard himself but slightly inferior, if at all, to the Almighty, bringing to mind Shakespeare's definition of a politician as one who would "circumvent God." No sooner had John F. Kennedy died and Johnson been sworn in than he was on the phone to Edward "Ted" Kennedy, assuring him that "God Almighty in his wisdom works in mysterious ways and we will just bear it together."

Exploitation was the name of the game, and Lyndon was a gamesmaster. He'd make sure to lace his speeches with Scripture and allusions to his heavenly partner. He would leave little doubt that he and the Almighty were on good bargaining terms. Aware that Baptists predominated in the South, he made sure they also predominated on the Equal Employment Opportunity Commission. Sometimes he'd make use of religion in private, as when, unannounced, he'd drop in on Luci's Roman Catholic Church in the wee hours of the morning to pray—although he confessed that Catholics and Episcopalians were "hard on the knees." More often, however, he'd make sure the press would prime his persona as a religious President.

One who saw through Johnson's exploitation of religion was Francis B. Sayre, Dean of Washington Cathedral and one of the most influential people in the capital. Worse, he was the grandson of the man whose picture adorned the wall above Lyndon's desk in the Oval Office—none other than Woodrow Wilson. But worst of all, he was the man who'd called faithfully on Lyndon's brother, Sam Houston, ten years before, when he was immobilized in a body cast after a serious accident. "I owe no man"—including Lyndon—Sam said, "a greater debt."

It was the selfsame Sayre who leveled a broadside against Goldwater and Johnson in 1964. The Senator from Arizona was "a man of dangerous ignorance and devastating uncertainty." As for Johnson, he was one "whose public house is splendid in every appearance, but whose private lack of ethics must invariably introduce termites at the very foundation."

Furthermore, "we stare fascinated at the forces that have produced such a sterile choice for us: frustration and a federation of hostilities in one party, and in the other, behind a godly facade, only a cynical manipulation of power."[5]

When LBJ finished dead last in the polls among the several candidates for Congress in 1937, he was suspicious of the results and vowed to show them wrong. As polling became more sophisticated, however, Johnson came to rely on them as much as Joe Mashman relied on a windsock to determine directions for landing. By the time he'd made his home at 1600 Pennsylvania Avenue, Lyndon was a veteran and avid poll watcher. He would identify the issues, then steer clear of them until he knew which side to come down on. That was a vital matter of timing.

According to brother Sam Houston, Lyndon was never tired of reading—and rereading—the polls. He could always be counted on to have one at the ready, drawn from his suit coat pocket, when he needed to score a point during a typical "treatment." Just which took first place, prayers or polls, became evident when, kneeling at the front of a church to take communion, Lyndon nudged Califano, kneeling next to him, and showed him the latest polls.

There was no question about it, polls trumped prayers every time. It was important to know what the Almighty was thinking, but more important to know what the electorate was thinking. That is, until the polls turned nasty and showed LBJ's credibility gap threatening not only his Great Society but his run for a second term. The more negative the polls became, the more Johnson dismissed them as not only biased but under Communist influence.

Of the Media

As with prayers and polls, so with the media. Lyndon paid attention to them as long as the winds were favorable, as long as he could exploit them, manipulate them.

By the summer of 1955, Lyndon's performance as maestro of the Senate was drawing rave reviews. Once he knew the majority was in his pocket, he would plant Alan Bible of Nevada in the presiding officer's chair, and turn to directing every move on the Senate floor. Did he want to speed up the taking of the vote? He'd raise his right hand in the air, circling with his index finger like an airport mechanic signaling a pilot to rev up his motors. Did he want to delay the taking of the vote to accommodate stragglers? He trained the Senate tally clerks just how to dilly-dally. It was hard, grubby painstaking work. But it had to be done to get legislation passed. One of the thorns in Johnson's side, Paul Douglas, couldn't get over the Majority Leader's shepherding a housing bill through to a conclusion: "I didn't think you could do it, and I will never know *how* you did it, but you did it, and I'm grateful."

Soon Johnson's reputation was such that *Newsweek*, *The New Republic*, and *The Washington Post*, were not only singing his praises but touting him for the presidency in 1960, if not in 1956. Here, according to the *Post*, was the "first party leader in modern times to tame the independent Senate." Indeed, the paper added, Lyndon was riding "a presidential boom." Alas, all such speculation came to naught when first, Lyndon suffered a massive heart attack in 1955, and then, in 1960 put off entering the primaries until it was too late. Just how he could take it out on reporters was seen in 1955, when an Associated Press journalist persisted with questions about why Johnson wanted to repeal a bill he'd already voted for. "Could you explain that to us, sir? I would be very curious." With that, Johnson uttered a roar that reverberated down the corridors. It wasn't simply the reporter's embarrassing questions that were getting to him. It was also his heart acting up, for that weekend he collapsed with his heart attack.

So Johnson was not without his critics in the press. Part of the problem was the press echoing the criticisms of liberals such as Paul Douglas, William Proxmire, and Hubert Humphrey. "Under Johnson," they were heard to complain, "the Senate functions like a Greek tragedy: all the action takes place offstage, before the play begins. Nothing is left to open and spontaneous debate, nothing is left for the participants but the enactment of their prescribed roles." This process, Johnson rationalized, "requires a certain amount of deception. There's no getting around it. If the full implications of any bill were known before its enactment, it would never get passed." To rely on conscience to justify one's conduct, Lyndon took not as a sign of courage but of cowardice. To be preoccupied with principle and procedure was a sign of impotence. Get the job done, by hook or by crook, and know that it'll not get done by endless hours of debating concepts and ideas on the Senate floor. This was LBJ's strategy.

Undoubtedly the high-water mark during Lyndon's eight years of leading the Senate was the passage of the first Civil Rights Act since Reconstruction. Throughout the long debate and filibuster by his good friend Richard Russell of Georgia, Lyndon stuck to the Senate floor, determined to narrow the differences between opposing parties until both could emerge with consensus—some sort of consensus. When it finally happened on August 7, 1957, everybody in the Senate knew that it wasn't Eisenhower's bill, or the Democrats' bill, or the liberals' bill—they knew it was Lyndon's triumph. *The New York Times* called it "incomparably the most significant domestic action of any Congress in this century." Basking in the glow of this and similar praise from the media, Johnson defined the "true leader" as one "who can get people to work together on the points on which they agree and who can persuade others that when they disagree there are peaceful methods to settle their differences."[6]

It seemed to work—at least in the Senate. But by the time he'd moved into the White House in 1963, Johnson—after a brief honeymoon—found the media more often a feisty opponent rather than a reliable ally. No longer were they merely clay in this potter's hands, to be molded at his will. One reporter whom Johnson courted more assiduously than others was Marianne Means, White House correspondent for the Hearst newspaper chain. For three weekends following Christmas 1963, he invited Means to Camp David or to the Ranch: to dine, bowl, watch films, and attend church with the family. Lady Bird noted in her diary that this reporter "is somebody that Lyndon and all men, in fact, have their eye on as considered an extremely attractive woman. So I guess I'll have to look her over harder! At any rate, her articles about Lyndon have all been very favorable."

We have already noted the demands of the media for an accounting of Johnson's enriching himself in office—particularly through KTBC—demands that Johnson dismissed out of hand. By 1965, LBJ was engrossing the media with more important matters, particularly the escalation of the war. On July 28, 1965 he announced to the press, and later on TV to the nation, that he was sending 50,000 additional men—not "advisers" but "combat support troops"—to Vietnam, conceding that still more would probably follow later.

Earlier that year, in March, the media released the results of a poll showing that two-thirds of American citizens agreed we should "continue present efforts," while only 19 percent favored pulling out. A year later, with casualties mounting and body bags returning, only half supported LBJ's handling of the war, while 33 percent did not.

Perhaps Johnson's love-hate relationship with the media was epitomized best in his long relationship with Walter Lippmann, widely acknowledged as the "dean of the Washington Press Corps"—or, as Hugh Sidey termed him, one of the capital's "high priests"—or, as Evans and Novak called James Reston and Lippmann, "Brahmins of the Washington Press." It was in 1947 that Johnson prevailed on friend Bill Fulbright to introduce him to Lippmann. But the journalists felt that, as effective as was the Texan as Majority Leader of the Senate—concerned overwhelmingly with domestic affairs—he was an "ignoramus," as Lippmann put it, when it came to the world at large. Therefore, Lippmann came out for Kennedy in 1960. Three years later, Lippmann suggested to Kennedy that he follow America's example in Laos, and push for a neutral Vietnamese government. Yet by April, 1964, Lippmann was hailing the new President as "a healing man" and nothing short of a "genius" in forging a national consensus. As a result, "the country is far more united and at peace with itself except over the issue of Negro rights, than it has been for a long time." Johnson had only praise, in return, for such perception. "Did you see Walter Lippmann last night?" he asked Russell. "I thought he was wonderful." Five days later, Johnson tried to get McGeorge Bundy to "tell Lippmann to knock the tail off of him [Nixon] because he's trying to start another war with China [by urging a tougher line toward Communism in Asia]. And he doesn't know what he's doing."[7]

As 1964 ended, however, Lippmann, like other journalists, was having second thoughts about U.S. intervention in Vietnam. Then Johnson asked Lippman to preview a speech he was preparing, guaranteeing unconditional discussions in an effort to get Hanoi to the peace table. In addition, he pledged "a billion-dollar investment" for economic development in Southeast Asia, including dams on the Mekong River on a scale that would dwarf even the TVA. This seemed to satisfy Lippmann, who had begun expressing unease about America's commitment there.

But by the fall of 1966, as Tuchman put it, "Even Walter Lippmann sacrificed his carefully cultivated cordiality with presidents to the demands of truth. Denying the argument of 'extended aggression,' he stated the obvious: that there were never two Vietnams but only 'two zones of one nation.' He poured scorn on the policy of globalism that committed the

United States to 'unending wars of liberation' as a universal policeman."

"The problem," Lyndon Johnson said, was "that I was sabotaged. Look what happened whenever I went to make a speech about the war. The week before my speech, the *St. Louis Post-Dispatch* or the *Boston Globe* or CBS News would get me over and over, talking about what a terrible speaker I was and about how awful the bombing was, and pretty soon the people begin to wonder . . . that I might be wrong about the war."

So, according to Johnson, it was definitely the media that was doing him in. As for the columnists, "They turned against me on Vietnam because it was in their self-interest to do so, because they knew that no one receives a Pulitzer Prize these days by simply supporting the President and his administration. . . . The Washington press are like a wolf pack, when it comes to attacking public officials, but they're like a bunch of sheep in their own profession and they will always follow the bellwether sheep, the leaders of their profession, Lippmann and Reston. As long as those two stayed with me, I was okay. But once they left me in pursuit of their fancy prizes, everyone else left me as well."

One thing was certain. He, Lyndon Johnson, was not just going to get mad. He'd get even. When Lippmann excoriated Johnson in 1967 for breaking his promise not to escalate, that was the last straw. This President, with his inimitable ridicule and mimicry, "kept up a series of devastating and obscene little jokes," forcing Lippmann to brand him "the most disagreeable individual ever to have occupied the White House." Finally Lippman took his leave of Johnson's Washington, "laughed, as it were, out of town."[8]

Of Sam Rayburn

It was one thing to exploit things and events: helicopters and string bands, prayers and polls, the media and even collective audiences. It was exploitation of a different order to exploit individuals. As we have seen, Lyndon was not above the crass, even cruel, exploitation of his aides, not to mention "enemies." Indeed, one can't help but agree with Goldman that Johnson's underlying aim, from the time he was a boy, was "a feral pursuit of personal domination."

But undoubtedly the most shameless exploitation was that of his mentor, his friend, his benefactor, and his surrogate father, Sam Rayburn. "Few men," wrote George Washington, "have the virtue to withstand the highest bidder." Lyndon Johnson, unlike Sam Rayburn, was not one of them. Perhaps no relationship in Lyndon's long political career illumines more sharply his willingness to exploit—then to betray—than does his association with Rayburn.

By 1940, not only had the Majority Leader in the House formed a bond with Sam Johnson in Austin, but he took to Lyndon when the young man came to Washington to work for Kleberg. Since 1933 Rayburn had been FDR's point man in the House. Divorced and childless, he came to consider Sam Johnson's son as his adopted son. And Rayburn couldn't seem to do enough for the lad who'd gone out of his way to invite him to the little apartment that Lyndon shared with Lady Bird after their marriage in 1934. It was Rayburn who interceded with FDR to land Lyndon the job as NYA administrator for Texas. It was Rayburn who did all he could to get for Lyndon the congressional seat left vacant by the death of James Buchanan. And when, in 1938, Lyndon ran on his own and, uncontested, returned to Congress, it was Rayburn who awarded him "plum" committee assignments, the kind that made other congressmen's mouths water. Finally, it was Rayburn who invited the fledgling congressman from the Tenth District to join him and other seasoned veterans in Rayburn's "board of education"—held regularly in his office to share a bottle and plan strategy.

Having done so much for Lyndon, one would think he'd reciprocate with at least a show of loyalty. But loyalty for Lyndon was always a one-way street, and with the presidential race of 1940 in the offing, Lyndon had to make some hard choices. His chance for a Senate seat he tied to FDR's running for an unprecedented third term. By 1938, however, Vice-President John Nance Garner was fully expecting to take FDR's place in 1940, after Roosevelt finished serving his second term. Here was Lyndon having to choose between Garner's campaign manager—Rayburn—and Johnson's best hope for getting the coveted Senate seat—FDR. So, throwing past favors to the wind, Johnson did what any enterprising exploiter would do, and sided with the President.

At last, waiting long enough to see if FDR would back off, Garner announced he'd be running. At that, FDR, always on the lookout for a sly dig, said, "I see that the Vice-President has thrown his bottle—I mean his hat—into the ring." The enmity between them had reached its peak in 1938, when FDR took his train through Texas, encountering Johnson along the way and inviting him aboard. But Garner—a Texan—refused even to see the President in his own state, giving the excuse that he was busy "fishing." On December 18, 1938, Garner and FDR had their last private meeting. They got nowhere.

There was no question but that Roosevelt, by 1939, had overreached himself, a victim of hubris. A Gallup Poll that year showed Garner's ascendancy. If, a poll asked in March, Roosevelt is not a candidate, who would you like to see as president? Postmaster-General Jim Farley got 8 percent, Secretary of State Cordell Hull got 10 percent. But John Nance Garner got 45 percent, while 53 percent of the Democrats were opposed to a third term. Clearly, FDR was in trouble. And through all of this, Lyndon, the new kid on the congressional block, was watching, knowing he'd have to choose sides, between Rayburn or FDR, both of whom had taken Lyndon under their wings, and provided one favor after another.

Calling Garner "impossible," Roosevelt decided to attack him on his own home turf. And who would be the President's point man to lead the attack? Who would be his spy in the ranks of Texas congressmen? Why, Lyndon Johnson, the greenhorn who was not only a Texan, but fast learning the rules of the game. Before long, FDR—eager to learn more of his primary opponent for 1940—was turning to Johnson, the man Rayburn was now castigating as "a damned independent boy; independent as a hog on ice."

It was indeed a slippery business, and not without risks for Lyndon, who wrote an NYA friend, "We will be fighting for our lives the next six months and I'm expecting you to head up the ball team." Johnson had good reason to fear that if FDR lost in his bid for a third term, he would himself go down to defeat in the 1940 congressional race. In September 1939, the outbreak of World War II was an auspicious sign for FDR and his young surrogate, Johnson, as the President now made it clear that his hat was in the ring. He needed not simply a victory but a landslide, an overwhelming mandate. And to that end he appointed Johnson's friend, Alvin Wirtz, as Undersecretary of the Interior in January 1940, figuring that between Wirtz and Johnson he could throw a monkey wrench into Garner's works. Still, FDR wanted neither an open conflict nor defeat. By April, Hitler's armies were overrunning Europe, giving FDR the ammunition to parade the motto, "Don't change horses in the middle of the stream." Then FDR decided fighting for the Texas delegation was not worth the candle.

Lyndon Johnson did not see it that way. Were his efforts going for naught? Rayburn, too, was trying to steer a middle course—campaigning for old friend Garner, but not wanting to alienate himself from the man he considered a hero, FDR himself. Furthermore, Roosevelt's support was necessary if Rayburn was to achieve his dream: to be selected as Speaker of the House.

By the spring of 1940, Roosevelt was again confident, suggesting that the Texas delegation to the convention vote for him—but only after voting for Garner, their favorite son, on the first ballot. Roosevelt, said Johnson almost thirty years later, was "a goddamn clever fella! He makes all these boys around here now—well, look like kids."[9] Lyndon was learning, back in 1940, that if there are two powerful friends, side with the more powerful without alienating the other. Rayburn needed FDR even as FDR needed Rayburn. And both needed Johnson—especially Roosevelt, whose campaign was short of funds, while Garner's coffers were full of oil and gas money. Lyndon, with his hand in the pocket of George Brown, and Brown with his connections to other deep pockets, were invaluable to FDR's chances.

So when Roosevelt decided not to push for a first-ballot vote by the Texas delegates, Johnson paid several visits to the Oval Office, finally persuading the President to keep up with the fight for a first-ballot victory. Rayburn, however, was equally determined to prevent Garner's humiliation in not being able to carry his own state on the first ballot. At this point, Johnson—convinced that Garner had little chance of winning the nomination—put the pressure on his old friend Rayburn, but not in the open. Two men from Austin, under Lyndon's orders, sent a telegram to Rayburn on April 12, 1940, demanding that he take a stand either for Garner or FDR. Not only was Johnson the exploiter refusing to be open and aboveboard in this, but he was putting his friend and mentor on the spot, forcing him to make a choice that Lyndon himself refused to make—although he was getting closer. In addition to trying to force Rayburn to desert Garner, Lyndon had the telegram smearing Rayburn with allegations that his campaign had been "engaged in a very unwise, cruel and ruthless effort to politically assassinate Roosevelt." Then he warned Rayburn not to try and stop FDR. Rayburn, at this point, was in the words of columnists Drew Pearson and Robert Allen, "the unhappiest man in the bitter melee, fearing the effect it may have on his own speaker ambitions. . . ." Still, Rayburn was

Rayburn, and stuck by his old friend—though Garner, in the opinion of Pearson and Allen, was in "his last political battle . . . on the defensive in his home bailiwick." While protesting his loyalty to FDR, Rayburn spelled out carefully his continuing backing of "Cactus Jack." Here, he insisted, was "a distinguished congressman from Texas for 30 years . . . the state's only speaker and Vice-President, its most distinguished citizen since Sam Houston." Furthermore, the Texas delegation would be proud to cast its ballot at the convention for him. Lyndon had forced "Mister Sam" to make a choice but, alas, it was all done in private. So, shortly after, Johnson ordered a second telegram, and this time thought to leak it to a reporter. When still it fizzled, Johnson himself—in all probability—either directly or through subordinates—wired many Texas newspapers about the two telegrams. Soon even *The Washington Post* was blaring the headline, RAY-BURN BACKS GARNER. But that wasn't enough. So Lyndon sent yet another telegram to Rayburn, asking him for evidence that he had no intention of trying to stop Roosevelt. Now the Dallas *Morning News* had it right, as far as Lyndon was concerned, portraying Rayburn as not only trying to stop FDR, but leading the fight against him. In addition, Johnson had the Brown Brothers' money filling the coffers at the precinct and county levels to assure FDR's win on the first ballot. Still not satisfied that he'd humiliated Rayburn enough, or ingratiated himself enough with FDR, Johnson insisted that the final telegram—agreed upon by both parties to bring unity to the convention—should not be released to the press in Texas, as Rayburn wanted, but from the Oval Office itself. And who would be there to present the telegram to FDR, along with Rayburn, but the tenderfoot congressman from Rayburn's state, Lyndon Johnson himself. According to Secretary of the Interior Harold Ickes, both were escorted into the President's office on April 29: both Texans, one the wizened old Rayburn, Majority Leader in the House, and the other every bit his equal. Or so it would seem. And the press, to Johnson's delight, made the most of his sudden rise in congressional status. What gave Lyndon the additional boost in power he so desperately craved was that FDR and Rayburn were both backing him to head up the Democratic Congressional Campaign Committee. Said Joe Roberts, who went to Washington with Rayburn, this position "really gave him [LBJ] power. . . . He was brash, he was eager, he was a comer, and everybody knew it"—especially the Brown Brothers and others seeking favors.

That Johnson subsequently backed Rayburn for speaker when William Bankhead suddenly died on September 15, and that the two were subsequently reconciled, points more to the integrity and forgiveness of Rayburn than to any such virtue in Johnson. Rayburn forgave Johnson, but Roosevelt was convinced by Johnson's underhanded, deceitful allegations that Rayburn was not only out to stop his nomination but had led the charge. He had, in the words of Corcoran, "betrayed" Roosevelt. In fact, it was Johnson who'd betrayed both FDR and Rayburn, killing two birds with one small stone of crass exploitation.[10] Indeed, if there is any relationship that exposed the tawdry, sordid, slyness and double-dealing of Johnson that would characterize the rest of his political career, this was it.

Of Lady Bird

There remains one person most responsible for Lyndon's scramble to the top, the one person above all others he exploited and humiliated. That person was the one person he claimed to love, Lady Bird herself. Without her, Rayburn and others reminded Lyndon, he'd never have made it to the first rung on the political ladder. Yet nowhere else in Johnson's life was loyalty so prostituted, devotion more a one-way street. Indeed, as Jackie Kennedy put it, "Lady Bird would crawl down Pennsylvania Avenue on broken glass for Lyndon." And Lyndon gave her ample opportunity to do just that.

No sooner were they married than she began to entertain, as she put it, "a queer sort of moth-and-flame feeling." It was, she soon discovered, a remarkably accurate premonition. As the Johnsons were departing on their honeymoon, they stopped to greet friends—and in their presence, Lyndon said, "You've got to change your stockings, Bird. You've got a run." Embarrassed, she hesitated until he barked out an order. He would leave no doubt who was in command. His manners were no less odious back in Washington. All too soon she was reaffirming the axiom that familiarity breeds contempt. If he disapproved of her clothes, he didn't hesitate, in company, to tell her so, "in a voice harsh with contempt," according to one eyewitness. On one social occasion his voice rang out across a crowded room, "Lady Bird, go get me another piece of pie." Engaged in conversation, she responded, "I will in just a minute, Lyndon." That would never do. "Get me another piece of pie," came the order, loud and clear, so all would hear and wonder why on earth she put up with it.

Before long, Lady Bird was pampering her husband even as Rebekah had pampered her son. The imperious husband was barking out orders: bring his coffee and the newspaper as he lay abed in the morning; lay out his clothes and be sure to fill his pen and cigarette lighter—and make sure they were in the proper pockets, along with handkerchief and money. Oh yes, and be sure to shine his shoes and lay them out. Run and fetch, run and fetch. The solicitous swain had quickly turned into a demanding tyrant—and Lady Bird would feel that pressure the rest of their lives together. As she put it, "Lyndon was always prodding me to look better, learn more, work harder. He always expects more of you than you think you are mentally or physically capable of putting out. It is really very stimulating. It is also very tiring." To cope with his constant badgering and occasional tirades, as Robert Dallek has pointed out, she would retreat to her own psychic island, closing him out so she could retain her composure.[11]

A dutiful wife who soon learned "her place," she was nonetheless a charming hostess to any and all Lyndon invited to their apartment, whether it was Sam Rayburn or lesser fry Lyndon was determined to exploit. In addition, it was doubtful her husband would have ever won his first congressional seat had she not persuaded her father to part with $10,000 set up as her trust fund—a tidy sum in 1937. It was Lady Bird who ran her husband's office when he took a six-months leave of absence for "duty" in the Navy. Before their first child, Lynda Bird, arrived in 1946, she'd suffered three miscarriages. As painfully humiliating as these years must have been, they were scarcely improved by Lyndon's affair with Alice Glass, the mistress and future wife of Texas newspaper magnate Charles Marsh. An avid Johnson supporter, Marsh had met the beautiful Glass in 1931, left his wife and children, and moved to a lavish estate in Virginia. Welly Hopkins, a Johnson aide, called Marsh "the most arrogant man I ever met." That was saying a lot, considering that Hopkins worked for Johnson. Marsh didn't simply talk; he pontificated. He seemed like a man after Lyndon's own heart, even as Lyndon was a man after Marsh's money and his mistress. When the stakes were this high, Lyndon flattered him with both rapt attention and praise for his remarkable perception. After all, Lyndon had not only Marsh's fortune, newspapers, and estate to benefit from, but also the beautiful, refined, and talented Alice Glass to seduce. So, according to Marsh's secretary, Lyndon was not simply friendly and solicitous; he was "very, *very* deferential . . . absolutely determined to be on good terms with him." So much so that Johnson not only sought his political advice, but asked Marsh to write speeches for him—which he somehow never got around to delivering.

As deferential as he was to Marsh, Lyndon was much more so to Glass, to the point that Longlea, Marsh's Virginia estate, became, by the mid-forties, a trysting place for the young Congressman and his latest conquest. All of this, of course, was unbeknownst to Marsh who, conveniently, was often gone on lengthy trips, seeing to his expanding empire. Bad enough that Lyndon would leave Lady Bird in Washington with her newborn while he attended to "business" at Longlea. Worse, he began taking Lady Bird with him, confiding in Alice that he intended to divorce his wife and marry his new love, even if it meant the end of his political career. He could always get a job as a career lobbyist with friends in Texas. While their romance never went that far, Lyndon did learn from Alice some manners, both at the table and away from it. Twenty years later, Alice was divorced from Marsh and writing to her long lost lover—now bedding down with others in the White House. LBJ ordered an aide to write her a "ni-ice" letter for, he explained, she was "alone—and an alcoholic."[12]

As tight-lipped as Johnson was about Alice, he was perfectly garrulous as he bragged about his other extracurricular flings. During the war, he spent more time inspecting the beauties of Hollywood—including Helen Gahagan Douglas—than he did inspecting the naval facilities on the West Coast. Yet another intimate relationship he exploited in the forties was with Congresswoman Clare Booth Luce. To husband Henry, LBJ paid the compliment of being married to "the sweetest little woman I ever served with in Congress." It was never noted if the publisher pressed the Congressman for details.

By the fifties, LBJ was not only leading the Senate but, when Lady Bird was out of town, leading various ladies half his age to socials—where he'd introduce each one clinging to his arm, "Wantcha t'meet mah girl." By 1960, he was so convinced that no woman in her right mind could resist his amorous overtures that he tried climbing into bed with a female reporter at his convention hotel in Los Angeles. As Vice-President, Lyndon did little to squelch the vice in Washington, where he gained a reputation as a "regular" at the Quorum Club's call-girl service. Here he was out to set an example for other members of Congress, their staffs, and lobbyists.[13]

Later, as President, Johnson was determined that his macho Texas image should not suffer from comparison with JFK's sexploits—especially when recounted with awe by an aide. LBJ would slam down his big fist on the desk and roar, "Why, I had more women by accident than Kennedy had by design." It wasn't long after moving into the Oval Office that Johnson discovered how accessible and private was the adjoining study, where he could enjoy a well-deserved relaxation from his strenuous days. Unfortunately, it proved to be not as private as he'd hoped, because Lady Bird happened in on him copulating with one of a handful of secretaries he'd personally hired—for more than taking dictation. Frantic because the Secret Service had failed to protect him from such interlopers—especially *this* interloper—Johnson ordered a buzzer system installed in the second floor-living quarters. Now, he was satisfied, "those lazy bastards" had no excuse for not notifying him of Lady Bird's approach, whether by elevator or stairs.

Given his Texas-size dose of testosterone, it was little wonder that Lyndon, less than two months in office, issued high priority orders to John Macy, chairman of the U.S. Civil Service Commission: "I want you to get with Walter Jenkins and do one thing for me, if we have to steal the money from the diplomatic fund." It wasn't really diplomacy that intrigued our man from Johnson City. "I want the five smartest, best-educated, fastest, prettiest secretaries in Washington. And I want to put them right here in my office where I can get them and dictate." Yet it was surely more than dictation that Lyndon had in mind. "Now you just start looking . . . I don't want any old, broken-down old maids. I want them from twenty-five to forty. I want them that can work Saturday and Sunday, I want them that can work at night . . . I've got to have some people that I can trust."

But Lyndon was not about to leave the challenge of pimping solely to his Civil Service chief. Strolling through the White House, it wasn't unusual that he'd spot a particularly comely lass and soon have her working for him, but in a secondary job. If, however, she agreed to a bit of frolic in the sack, why, he was tenderhearted enough to assure her a promotion to his personal staff. Always there had to be available to him an eye-catching pool of secretaries and an instant harem, each one capable of double time, double duty, and consummate loyalty.

Bill Gulley discovered that of the President's pool, at least five of the eight measured up to all three qualifications. Yet LBJ was still not satisfied and, on a whim, would commandeer other men's secretaries. One such, technically on Gulley's staff, found servicing the President reason enough to come and go as she pleased. After all, she reasoned, sex with someone old enough to be her father had its privileges. Not one to confine his exploits to the ground, Johnson—even when accompanied aloft by Lady Bird would suddenly disappear on *Air Force One* into a secluded stateroom, there to transact business with a fetching secretary—sometimes for hours.

On his travels to press the flesh, Lyndon appeared the true believer in three useful mottoes: "If you've got it, flaunt it"; "use it or lose it"; and "the more the merrier." It wasn't unusual for him to pick a "winner" out of a crowd, then dispatch an aide to enlist her in "service" to her President.[14]

Sometimes Lyndon didn't have to take the initiative, perhaps confirming Kissinger's conviction that power is the greatest aphrodisiac. During a campaign stop in Los Angeles, LBJ was shaking hands in a reception line at the Biltmore when, lo and behold, he. suddenly found a room key being pressed into his hand by an especially attractive supporter as she passed by. Without missing a beat, he simply slipped it into his pocket, then later fell to wondering if that key really worked. So it did, and before him was his seductress lounging, ready to receive her President as he announced, "Here ah am, honey." The business at hand completed—followed by a well-earned nap—Lyndon rose, dressed, then looked down at the drowsy, young patriot and held out his hand: "Ah want to thank you for yore help in mah campaign."

Little wonder that many in on the sexual shenanigans of LBJ considered him "a notorious wolf." One chalked it up to his sexual insecurity. He simply had to prove to himself, as well as to others, that he was not as ugly as some said—and that, in fact, he was Lyndon the Lothario.

It would seem that Lady Bird's diary description of the movie *Tom Jones* would be as fitting of her husband as of Tom: ". . . Tom Jones jumps merrily from bed to bed with a peculiar and charming innocence, and always headed for the final bed that I—well, that I think is going to be permanent." Except that Tom was unattached, while Lyndon, presumably, was very much so, what with a wife and two impressionable teenage daughters. Why, from the late thirties, when he took up with Alice Glass, did Lyndon insist on risking his political career as well as his family by insisting on spreading his seed far and wide? Peter D. Kramer, Clinical Professor of Psychiatry at Brown University, offered some insight. It seems that narcissists, possessed with a "distorted or conflicted sense of self-worth"—therefore given to grandiosity—tend "to use other people to supplement aspects of the self." For Johnson the sex act was both a compulsion and a gamble, with his grandiosity at stake.

Not only did Lady Bird appear to take it all in stride, but by 1964 she'd redoubled her efforts on his behalf. In 1960 she was regarded as having been mainly responsible for his winning Texas, even as Texas largely made the difference in JFK's victory. By 1964, she was drawing rave reviews from reporters, in contrast to lackluster reviews for her husband. He was every bit as convinced about his top billing as America's premier stud as he was as America's premier President—and he resented her favorable press.[15]

No better a father than he was a husband, LBJ had little time for his daughters. LBJ's brother Sam recalled the two girls "pulling at [Lyndon] in a futile attempt to get his attention . . . then finally retreating with a pout and a hurt look in their eyes." By the time he was Vice-President, it was Lady Bird who seemed to be the sole parent, and the girls were doubly resentful when Lyndon took her on extended trips abroad. Later Luci—clearly his favorite—confessed, "I stopped thinking of him as a father and started thinking of him as a friend. Eventually I learned to love him as a person—not as a father, because he seldom had time to be a father." It would, of course, be more accurate to say he seldom took time to be a father. After all, first things first, and for fifty years he'd learned not only to look out for number one, but to engross himself in his preoccupation—so that he would not tolerate anything or anybody muddying the waters in which this Narcissus was mesmerized by his own reflection. Whether Lady Bird protested to him about ignoring his children we do not know, but she did show her concern in her diary. On March 6, 1964, she complained of her husband's priorities: ". . . I wish he would spare himself the unnecessary effort [attending an endless round of meetings and socials] and save that effort for top-notch priority things and for hopefully a longer life with me and Luci and Lynda."

He would brag that "I'm the luckiest man alive. None of my girls drinks or smokes or takes dope." And he would take credit for this, too, even though he drank and smoked to excess. He could scarcely find minutes for the girls, yet he was always busy with extracurricular as well as curricular affairs.

The Golden Rule, reworded by Jefferson in his definition of liberty, occupied little place in the value system of Johnson the exploiter. Neither did first Corinthians, chapter 13—surely memorized at his mother's knee when he was a boy, and epitomized in the paraphrased version: "If you love someone, you will be loyal to him no matter what the cost." Not that there wasn't love there, or loyalty. But it was all a one-way street. Love for Lyndon meant he needed somebody. And that somebody was his wife, described by Sam Rayburn as "the darn best lady who ever lived!"[16] Would that Lyndon had thought so, too.

By the time Johnson reached the White House, he'd used every trick in the exploiter's trade to reach that Holy Grail. He'd flattered some shamelessly, intimidated others sadistically, promised others extravagantly, bribed others outrageously, mimicked others ingeniously, and exhausted everyone with his endless demands.

Each of us, of course, partakes of some of this, from time to time. But Lyndon took them all to excess, even as he did with his indulgences—as though being a Texan were the antithesis of reasoned restraint, of prudent moderation, of civilized discipline. By the time he self-destructed in 1968, a pattern of conduct had emerged as reprehensible as it was transparent. First, he learned where the power was concentrated in an organization. Second, he determined the flow of that power. Third, he ingratiated himself with the power broker. Fourth, he wheedled favors from that broker until he had advanced to that level. Fifth, he replaced the broker, even if it meant betraying him, yet being certain to cover his flank so that the victim didn't know what or who was undercutting him. And sixth, he moved past his benefactor, ignoring him unless he continued to need him.

Like Joe McCarthy, Lyndon Johnson climbed onto the back of that tiger named hubris—and could not get off until he was devoured.

RICHARD NIXON

Well, this is what the problem is. Every sonofabitch is a self-server.
— Alexander Haig, 1973

. . . I know dear old Sam Ervin. He's been a neighbor of mine all his life, and, of course, this is his great moment of glory.
— Billy Graham to Nixon, 1973

Of Things and Groups

Like Johnson, Nixon exploited time and circumstance. On April 28, 1973, just two days before firing his chief of staff, Nixon emphasized to him the importance of timing: "The timing situation. That's what we did with the [slush] fund, you know. I kept waiting and waiting and then finally hit . . . our timing is probably about right . . . it's best to hit after they have blown a lot of their wad."

As for the "traitor," John Dean, ". . . don't assault him too soon. Let him get on a little further. But then his legs have to be cut off on national television like nobody's business; but not by me. I cannot take on the little asshole." Here was the President who bragged, "I always believe in waiting and striking at the right time."

Like Johnson, Nixon exploited the polls. By May 8, Alexander Haig had easily replaced Haldeman, and asked the President if he'd seen the latest Harris poll. From Ziegler, Nixon had learned that the public was giving him the benefit of the doubt over Dean's testimony, and that he'd be given the opportunity to finish his term. His pulse must have quickened and his resolve stiffened when be learned that a vast majority of the electorate was opposed to his resigning. The President had found not one, but two fig leaves to cover his shenanigans: "national security" and "executive privilege." Between June 17, 1971, and July 12, 1973, recordings from Nixon's automatic taping system revealed that the President appealed to the former no less than twenty-eight times and to the latter fourteen times. Typical of his appeal to national security was his telling Haldeman on March 27, 1973, that aide Egil Krogh did know of the Watergate break-in beforehand. To this, Haldeman replied, "His thing hangs totally on national security. . . ." And Nixon concluded, "But he could just say, I was on national security matters. . . ." By May 11, Nixon was maintaining to Haig, ". . . I was a babe in the woods when they told me about this thing [Watergate break-in]. I frankly thought it was a CIA thing." As for the wiretaps he'd placed on newsmen, he told Haig they were "because of leaks of national security documents" [the Pentagon Papers, already published]. As for "executive privilege," Haldeman told Nixon on May 11 that his lawyers had been studying this loophole, ". . . and your guys I'm sure will come up with the same thing—is that executive privilege is an objective and selective judgment on the part of the President." The President not only agreed but was determined that his lawyer, Fred Buzhardt, not think for a moment that Nixon was involved in the cover-up—much less having ordered Haldeman to instruct the CIA to curb the FBI investigation.

When it came to religion, and especially evangelical religion's prime representative, Billy Graham, Nixon was all too eager to use both to his advantage. Having announced the "resignations" of Haldeman and Ehrlichman on April 30, Nixon phoned Graham for support. He was rewarded when the evangelist assured him, "Well, your sincerity, your humility, your asking for prayer, all of that had a tremendous impact." And Graham felt constrained to add, ". . . I'm telling you the truth and I'm not trying to just encourage you . . . I really mean it." To which, of course, Nixon responded, "You have been a friend." Here, undoubtedly, Norman Vincent Peale would have recognized—and perhaps applauded—"the power of positive thinking." Already Nixon, for his part, had assured Graham that "nobody in the White House" was involved in Watergate, "but campaign people, they sometimes do silly things."

Just two days before, when Nixon was preparing to fire his top domestic aides, he had vowed to Ziegler, ". . . I am determined that the chips fall where they may . . . I am going to root this out. . . ." Yet he was ". . . sorry to see Billy Graham join in the chorus of saying *do something* . . . I was really surprised to see him say that. . . . Because he had indicated to the contrary. . . . He's probably jumping ship. . . ." So, on April 30, Nixon had phoned Graham to bring him back on board. When the tape transcripts were released a year later, revealing that the President was very much involved in Watergate, Graham chalked it up to "situational ethics" infecting the White House—and wondered if perhaps, Nixon had been using him.[1]

He most assuredly had been. Nixon would use the polls to find out what the electorate was approving on earth, and he'd use Graham to find out what Providence was approving from heaven. But just to make sure his enemies got the message that he was also prepared to use brass knuckles, he had the FBI, the CIA, the IRS, and the FCC at his beck and call. Beyond that, Nixon was prepared to exploit any one of a number of dirty tricks that appointment secretary Chapin and lawyer Donald Segretti had in their grab bag.

Of Jerry Voorhis

Nattily dressed in his fetching Navy whites, his chest sporting colorful ribbons, Nixon looked every bit the war hero as he stood before the Committee of 100 in the fall of 1945. Here was the ideal candidate they'd advertised for, desperate to unseat veteran Congressman Jerry Voorhis. The committee concluded that they had before them "salable merchandise." After all, as one of the members put it, they would be doing "nothing more than selling a product."

Indeed, Nixon was a product of a straitlaced Quaker home, raised in the Horatio Alger tradition of honesty, thrift, and hard work. Therefore, when he told them he'd discussed economic issues—such as free enterprise and entrepreneurship—with GI's in the foxholes of the South Pacific islands, they believed him. It impressed the small businessmen and professionals making up the committee, and later such claims would make for "salable" campaign fliers that advertised Richard Nixon as a "clean, forthright young American who fought in defense of his country in the stinking mud and jungles of the Solomons." In another six years, most of the millions watching Nixon deliver his "Checkers" speech on television would believe him when he said he'd earned "a couple of battle stars" and "a couple of letters of commendation," modestly explaining that he just happened to be "there when the bombs were falling." Perhaps by 1961, when he was writing *Six Crises*, he was having second thoughts, for the service record remarks were omitted in the text describing his "Checkers" speech—the second of his crises. Certainly he seemed to have good reason to leave them out. For while most believed him in 1952, there were some skeptics, especially reporters, in the audience. David Abrahamsen investigated Nixon's war record and concluded that Nixon's baptism of fire in the foxholes was a "fabrication." Even Henry Spalding, a sympathetic biographer, admitted that Nixon had often been criticized for trying "to pass himself off as a veteran who had seen actual combat."[2]

But in 1945, there he stood: the thirty-three-year-old veteran, returned from four years in the Navy, all spit and polish. True, he'd thrown over the traces and learned to drink, smoke, cuss, and gamble with the best of them. But the committee didn't know that. Neither did they know of his failed attempts to land a job in New York or with the FBI after law school. Nor were they aware that he'd come within a hair's breadth of being disbarred in his first appearance in court as a lawyer—when a client filed a malpractice suit after losing everything due to a Nixon blunder. They did know that Whittier's leading banker and most influential citizen, Herman Perry, had recommended him highly. That was good enough. Despite Nixon's close brush with legal death, Jeff Wingert, partner in the Whittier firm, predicted, "that boy will be President of the United States someday if he wants to."

At this point, however, all the committee wanted was someone—anyone—who could trounce the "socialist" Voorhis, the wealthy congressman who'd turned his back on his fellow moneybags and voted against California laying claim to offshore oil. Looking Nixon over, the committee was convinced that Nixon had a good shot at it. True, he avoided the eyes of the committee members when he talked to them, something one of their number would note and correct him on, as being essential to an impression of sincerity. True, he was a novice in politics, but that was nothing that Murray Chotiner, the "Californian Machiavelli," couldn't correct—for a fee of $500.

So by the time Nixon was discharged in January 1946, Chotiner was ready to take him under his wing. His cardinal rule: always attack. Don't try to defend. Remember that if you try to defend yourself, your rebuttal will never catch up to the charge, especially if delivered close enough to the election time. The rebuttal will never demolish the charge. Rule number two came via Roy Day of the committee: "Nice guys and sissies don't win any elections."

From the time Nixon learned he'd been chosen as the committee's candidate—on November 28, 1945—until he was discharged in January, he was busy boning up on Voorhis's record until, he later wrote, "I knew [it] as well as he did himself." Meeting Nixon for the first time, Voorhis got the distinct impression that Nixon "hated" him, for this, Voorhis acknowledged, was the "coldest reception I've ever had from anybody." Twenty-eight years later, Voorhis was only one of the multitude whom Nixon had learned to hate. But in 1946, the only thing Nixon may have hated more than the face of Voorhis was fungus. As he told *Life*'s Donald Jackson, describing his service as a supply officer, "I didn't get hit, or hit anyone. All I got was a case of fungus."[3] For that—and the rest of his service—he received none of the "battle stars" he claimed.

Nixon's hyping of his Navy service showed he had a way with words, a way of exploiting them, of using them to represent or misrepresent the facts. He may not have gone to the outrageous lengths that Johnson did in fabricating his Silver Star stories, as we shall detail in a later chapter. And he didn't go as far as his friend, and later Senate colleague, Joe McCarthy. "Tail Gunner" Joe claimed first to have flown fourteen bombing missions, then twenty, then thirty, and was soon sporting a Distinguished Flying Cross—a tribute to his leverage after becoming Senator rather than to his bravery.

As for Nixon, he not only took care of supplying his contingent on Bougainville in the Solomon Islands with authorized necessities—but also contrived to get additional provisions, which he used to open "Nick's Hamburger Stand." There fighter and bomber crews, on their way to battle missions would be given free hamburgers and beer. As a result, when he left the island they threw a big bash in his honor. "All of them," according to Lt. James Stewart, "were strong for him, and hated to see him go." It was just as well that Nixon enjoyed these kudos—genuine tokens of affection would become rare indeed after he entered the political fray against Jerry Voorhis.

Chosen by the committee, Nixon was exultant. "I am really hopped up over this deal," he wrote. "This deal" had ignited a fire in his belly—but

Nixon had no idea that within six years he'd be but a heartbeat away from the presidency. This catapult to the second-highest post in the nation is a tribute, in part, to his ability to exploit time and circumstance, as well as technology and people.

Kyle Palmer, political editor for the Los Angeles *Times*—unquestionably the most important newspaper in Southern California—was not impressed with the "somewhat gawky young fellow who was on a sort of giant-killer operation." This was, at best, "a forlorn effort, particularly when it is being made by a youngster who seemed to have none of the attributes of a rabble-rouser who can go out and project himself before a crowd." Before long, however, Palmer changed his tune and recommended the Republican candidate to publisher Norman Chandler—who, after listening to Nixon for twenty minutes, declared him a "comer" the newspaper would support.

Voorhis may not have been a "giant," but he was held in high esteem on Capitol Hill. A graduate of Yale Law School, Voorhis founded an orphanage, then the Voorhis School for Boys, in California. In addition, Voorhis was one of the few in the House to protest the internment of Japanese-Americans in World War II.[4]

But Voorhis was bound to clash with the likes of Nixon. For he came from Yale, one of the bulwarks of the Northeastern elite that Nixon alternately despised and envied. In addition Voorhis was wealthy. Furthermore, in the twenties he had aligned himself with the Socialists— at a time when many Americans were disenchanted with capitalism, believing that unbridled "Cowboy Capitalism" had been riding high in the saddle, helping to incite World War I. There was no doubt in Nixon's mind that Voorhis was still a Socialist when he exposed a secret contract being drawn up by Standard Oil, giving it control of the Elk Hill oil reserves. Voorhis had also cultivated the nasty habit of voting for labor unions. Finally, Voorhis continued to vote for the Office of Price Administration as an effective brake on inflation—the same OPA that had left a bad taste in Nixon's mouth from his employment there four years earlier.

So Nixon mounted his attack and put Voorhis in his sights. The OPA, Nixon charged, was "shot through with extreme left-wingers . . . boring from within, striving to force private enterprise into bankruptcy, and thus bring about the socialization of America's basic institutions and industries." Here was Nixon's shot across the bow of the "U.S.S. Voorhis." This

Don Quixote, as journalist Stewart Alsop called Voorhis, who was an idealist with his head in the clouds and no firm underpinning for his feet, had little idea what was in store for him—until Nixon lashed out, claiming his opponent was a Socialist getting support from CIO-PACs that were clearly infiltrated, if not controlled, by Communists. Nixon had struck political gold in his anti-communist stance, a stance that would reap huge rewards in the months and years ahead. Later he dissembled by claiming that the issue of Communism had played no role in the campaign. That would have been news to Voorhis, to his supporters, and to the assembled press at Nixon's rallies and especially at the four debates Voorhis had made the mistake of accepting.

Nixon was ready. So was Chotiner, with his "denigrative method," as writer Garry Wills called it. In substance, it included discrediting Voorhis even before the whistle blew to start the campaign; then organizing a separate group of Democrats to support Nixon; then branding Voorhis a Socialist with Communist support, hinting at treason; then accusing Voorhis of unfair tactics, including lying, if he objected to this defamation. It was as clever as it was unprincipled. And Nixon exploited it to the nth degree. As Wills put it, Nixon developed into a "virtuoso manipulator of discontents."[5] Aiding him in this crass exploitation was his expertise at poker. During the war he'd outbluffed, with a pair of deuces, an opponent for a $1,500 pot. Now Nixon figured he could bluff and call, fold when need be, and outmaneuver Voorhis—all with a poker face, in his biggest game yet. Keeping his cards close to his chest and a face etched in stone were naturals for this furtive pol who cherished secrecy until he could spring the grand surprise.

Also aiding Nixon was California's cross-filing system, which allowed candidates to run in both the Republican and Democratic primaries. This enabled Nixon, the rock-ribbed Republican, to collect the votes of Democrats—posing, in his pragmatic way, as one of them. Determined to appear as just a "regular guy," Nixon doffed his officer's uniform and donned civvies, his veteran's pin in his lapel. Determined to show Voorhis in the pocket of the CIO's Political Action Committee, Nixon released a statement to the press: "The choice now is: Shall it be the people, represented by Nixon, or the PAC by Voorhis?" Determined during his first debate to show that Voorhis's PAC was dominated by Communists, Nixon flashed the anonymous paper that proved nothing of the kind—but the flustered Voorhis lost his composure and never regained it. Determined to show Voorhis's voting record showed him sympathetic to the Communists—despite his authoring the Voorhis Act of 1940, requiring all Communists to register with the government—Nixon lumped Voorhis with Congressman Vito Marcantonio, an avowed Socialist from Brooklyn. Then, in a maneuver that surely warmed the heart of Chotiner, Nixon had his volunteer callers phone Democrats in the final days of the campaign with the message, delivered as soon as the phone was picked up, "This is a friend of yours, but I can't tell you who I am. Did you know that Jerry Voorhis is a Communist?" Click.

In mid-October, Nixon placed an ad in every one of the district's thirty papers proclaiming in bold type, "PAC looks after the interests of Russia" and concluding with "REMEMBER, Voorhis is a former registered Socialist and his voting record in Congress is more Socialistic and Communistic than Democratic." Before the American Legion, Nixon warned that Communists and fellow travelers were "gaining positions of importance in virtually every federal department and bureau," all part of a Moscow-directed conspiracy "calculated to gradually give the American people a Communist form of government." Did Nixon know what he was talking about? No matter. This David was in a face-off with Goliath, Voorhis. What better stone for his sling than anti-Communism? Trouble was, Voorhis was no more a Communist than Nixon, or any of the Committee of 100.

Earlier that month, Nixon had told an El Monte audience: "I do not question the motives of my opponent in voting the PAC line in Congress. I respect his right to believe in and to support that type of legislation." Having averred that, Nixon went on to do just the opposite, questioning his opponent's motives. But he, Richard Nixon, would "not be obligated to any special interest or pressure group." Indeed, he would "serve all the people impartially." When it came to foreign policy, Nixon was clearing the path for Joe McCarthy. To a Pomona audience Nixon charged, "There are those walking in high official places . . . who would lead us into a disastrous foreign policy whereby we will be guilty of . . . depriving the people of smaller nations of their freedoms."[6]

Nine years later, determined to "set the record straight," Nixon announced to an astonished reporter, "Communism was not the issue at any time in the 1946 campaign. Few people knew about Communism then, and even fewer cared." He then claimed that he'd never even implied that Voorhis was a Communist. More than that, he'd never even raised the issue of Communism in the campaign. Yet by 1955, the reporter and many others were convinced with Wills that Nixon was the master manipulator. He exploited language, the press, the electronic media, the telephone, and, of course, his audiences. Never one to leave victory to chance, Nixon had his supporters arrive early for the four debates and seat themselves in separate groups, so that Voorhis fans would be surrounded. Then, during the debate, Nixon's stalwarts would cheer him as lustily as they jeered Voorhis. Before his audiences Nixon, the man of many faces, became alternately, as Ambrose described it, "Richard the actor, the debater, the courtroom lawyer, the clean-cut Quaker kid seething with righteous indignation over Teapot Dome, [and] the poker player who had bet more than a year's salary on a bluff."

Gary Allen, in his 1971 biography, attempted to identify *The Man Behind the Mask*—the book's subtitle—convinced that his former fellow conservative had become a liberal, staffing his administration with more than one hundred members of the Council on Foreign Relations. The truth was, Nixon, the ultimate pragmatist, wore many masks, each displaying a different persona—while beneath lay the private person he rarely revealed, even to those closest to him.

Compounding Nixon's crass exploitation and dissembling was his sheer gall. His 1946 victory in place, he entered Voorhis' office to ask for his mailing lists. Voorhis, normally a mild-mannered man, had all he could do to hold his temper. Here was a man, Voorhis biographer Paul Bullock noted, who graduated from an occasional lie that he could cover up to a blizzard of lies repeated again and again. As Fawn M. Brodie wrote, "Under Chotiner's tutelage, Nixon absorbed the technique of repeated, consistent, and organized lying."[7]

In his fight with Voorhis, Nixon found, to his surprise, a sheep in sheep's clothing, willing to be led to the slaughter with scarcely a bleat. In his next major battle—with Hiss—Nixon met one who, like Voorhis, represented the cultural elite of the Northeast, but one whose main weapon against this gutter fighter was a sneer. Not until Nixon met Helen Gahagan Douglas did be find someone who, "madder'n hell," was "not going to take it any more." Douglas gave as good as she got. But it was left to Stevenson, in 1952, to combine the cultural elitism of the intelligentsia with the barb of crafted witticism to put Nixon in his place. What Nixon euphe-mized as his "public service," Stevenson lambasted as "Nixonland," the land wherein dwelt one of the "Neanderthals of American politics," given to "lies, half-truths, circuses, and demagoguery . . . the kind of politician who would cut down a redwood tree, and then mount the stump and make a speech for conservation." Furthermore, Stevenson elaborated, "Nixonland" was "a land of slander and scare, the land of sly innuendo, the poison pen, the anonymous phone call, and hustling, pushing, shov-ing; the land of smash and grab and anything to win." Finally, it was the land where Nixon, the "Little Lord Fauntleroy of the Republican Party, has no standard of truth but convenience and no standard of morality except what will serve his interest in an election."

Not to be outdone, Truman weighed in, by 1956, with questions: "Why is the Republican party offering us this over-ambitious, unscrupulous, reactionary boy orator as a possibility for the president? Why are they imposing this terrible choice on the people?"

Of Dwight Eisenhower

By the time Nixon was running for president in 1960, he was both the most feared and hated man in the country, and—save Ike himself—the most admired and desired. Nixon chalked up his loss to numerous factors. He knew that there was skullduggery going on in the Kennedy camp, par-ticularly when it came to Texas and Illinois. In all probability, however, he knew nothing of the long arm of Joe Kennedy shaking hands on a deal with Sam Giancana, Chicago mob leader. Brokered by Joe's old friend, William Touhy, Chief Judge of Cook County Circuit Court, the deal was a typical quid pro quo. Giancana's mob-controlled unions would not only get out the vote, but provide campaign contributions from the pension fund of the Teamsters Union. In exchange, Jack Kennedy would lay off the Chicago branch of the Mafia, known as "the Outfit." Just how much Kennedy's reneging on this promise—with brother Bobby as Attorney General declaring war on the Mafia—had to do with JFK's assassination is problematic. That Nixon himself contributed mightily to his own defeat is more certain.

There is no little irony in Ike, on his deathbed in the spring of 1968, being exploited by Nixon to win his party's nomination. Nixon needed

Ike's endorsement in view of the polls showing Rockefeller defeating both Humphrey and McCarthy—while Nixon would lose to either of them. Desperate, Nixon sent Bryce Harlow, a former aide to Ike, to solicit Eisenhower's endorsement. But Ike wasn't talking. So Nixon sent Admiral Lewis Strauss for an endorsement. Still no reply. Then Ike suffered his fifth and last heart attack. With one month to go before the convention, Nixon, hat in hand, sought out the dying general at Walter Reed Hospital. Yes, Ike said he wanted Nixon, and, on August 15—the day the convention would open—he'd call a press conference to say so.

Time was of the essence. Suppose, in the next four weeks, the frail, seventy-seven-year-old general, reduced to skin and bones, should die? Nixon couldn't take that chance, so back to the hospital he went, then wrote Ike a long letter. Ike read Nixon's frantic plea and the next day went public with his endorsement. After all, he acknowledged, he couldn't help but endorse Nixon in view of "his personal qualities, his intellect, acuity, decisiveness, warmth, and above all, his integrity." Nixon couldn't have hoped for a loftier encomium. Ike added, "I just want the country to know that I have admired and respected this man and liked the man ever since I met him in 1952." Fulsome praise, that. But, inquired one reporter, did the fact that Ike's grandson David was now married to Julie Nixon have anything to do with it?" "I think, " replied the general, "they [David and Julie] tried to."[8]

With Ike's endorsement, Nixon took the nomination. In his acceptance speech he announced, "My fellow Americans, the dark long night for America is about to end." It was just six years later, to the day, that he again stood before the American people to announce his resignation. By that time the electorate realized that in 1968, the "dark long night" had, in fact, just begun. By 1974, they would breathe a sigh of relief that "Nixonland"— with all its abuses and exploitation—had come to an end.

Of Pat Nixon

So intent had Nixon been on exploiting everything and everybody to win, that when Julie went to his office to tell of her plans to marry David, all Nixon could summon was a passing nod as he kept working. In tears, she fled to her mother. If there was anybody who understood Dick Nixon's compulsion to exploit people, it was Pat Nixon.

Courted assiduously for more than two years, Pat, born Thelma Catherine Ryan on March 16, 1912, in a miner's shack high in the mountains of eastern Nevada, finally gave in and joined the firm of Richard Milhous Nixon, Inc., on June 21, 1940. Life had been hard for the twenty-eight-year-old schoolteacher. Moving from his job as timekeeper and occasional prospector, Will Ryan settled on ten acres in Artesia, south of Los Angeles, to take up truck farming. There his small house was only a slight improvement over the Nevada miner's shack. With no running water or electricity, Will and wife, Kate, together with their four children, were hard put to scrape by as they hauled vegetables into the city behind the Model T.

"Pat" as Will called Thelma, found in her father a voracious reader and a stern disciplinarian. As with Dick Nixon, she was taught to hide her emotions, particularly when it came to suffering. And Pat learned to suffer stoically, especially when her father returned from a nearby tavern, spoiling to pick a fight with Kate. The temper and the violence left their mark. Later, Pat told her two daughters, "I detest temper. I detest scenes, I just can't be that way. I saw it with my father." Both Dick and Pat early learned to avoid confrontation with their mercurial fathers.

In school Thelma proved a quick study, skipping second grade. Bright, industrious, a perfectionist, she, like her father, loved to read. There in her books, "the biggest influence on my life," she learned of the world outside Artesia—and determined to be a part of it.

From her books, however, she learned little about coping with the death of her mother in 1926. "When my mother died," she told her own daughters, "I just took responsibility for my life." Not only hers, but at thirteen, the lives of her father and three siblings—as she cooked and kept house, not because she enjoyed it, but because she found she was "able to do anything" if she simply had to. With a full plate of high school activities, including debate and drama, she caught the eye of the principal who, for years afterwards, cited Thelma Ryan as an example of industriousness and self-discipline: keeping house, holding the family together, earning high grades even as she was busy in extracurricular activities. In 1930, four years after her mother's death, her father died of tuberculosis, the same disease that claimed the lives of Dick's two brothers, Harold and Arthur.

The next year, Patricia Ryan, as she now called herself, matriculated at Fullerton Junior College, using money she'd saved while working for two years after high school. It was the bottom of the Great Depression, with the farm's entire potato crop fetching less than $16. To pay for college, Pat kept books and swept floors in the local bank for $30 a month. With other odd jobs as a chauffeur and as a clerk in a TB hospital, she entered the University of Southern California on a research fellowship, graduating *cum laude* after working full-time her last two years, and picking up additional income as a movie extra.

Soon Pat was teaching commercial subjects at Whittier Union High School, and in 1938 tried out for a part in *The Dark Town* with the local community players. That night in February, the tryouts over, she told a friend, "I met this guy tonight who says he is going to marry me." Who was he kidding? The furthest thing from her mind was marriage, and she only consented to date the "guy" if he stopped broaching the subject. He then confined the subject to his letters, writing "I bet you're mad with me for pestering you. . . ." He pestered, and he pestered and at last, in March 1940, she agreed to marry him. On June 21 the knot was tied.

She was now Mrs. Richard Nixon. Alter a two-week honeymoon in Mexico, they settled down in an apartment above a garage, then moved to Washington, D.C. in January 1941, where he worked for the OPA until enlisting in the Navy that August. After a tour in the South Pacific as a supply officer, he returned stateside to work, as he put it, as "chief janitor" at the Alameda Naval Air Station outside San Francisco. Shipped to the East Coast, he'd hardly begun his new job of settling war contracts when he heard from the Committee of 100 in California. He'd been selected to run against Voorhis.[9]

On February 21, 1946, Pat delivered her first child, Patricia, or "Tricia." Six hours later, she was researching her husband's first of many political campaigns. Dick, a Republican, had voted for Willkie in 1940 and Dewey in 1944. Pat, a Democrat, had been a staunch supporter of Al Smith in 1928, but by 1937 had registered as an Independent. Now she was neck-deep in Republican politics and, though not at all sure she was cut out for the nonstop campaigning and intrusion into her private life, she gave it her best shot. Dick was irate on learning she'd given away his suits to cousins while he was on active duty, but was pleased to find she'd squirreled away $10,000 in savings bonds, plus $3,000 in savings, enough to get them campaigning. Pecking away at a typewriter, folding and addressing thousands of letters and postcards, recruiting women to volunteer, canvassing door to door, packing the rallies to cheer on the candidate, sitting in the front row, her eyes fixed on her husband though she'd heard the same pitch night after night, Pat was doing her "duty."

In a day when few women smoked, Pat did, yet would not light up in public lest she draw the stares and slights of other women. It was one thing to avoid their slights, another to avoid her husband's. One confidant recalled Pat's complaint about Nixon's incivility. "He would always hold the door open for me, but would walk through it in front of me as if I wasn't there at all." Leaving Tricia with Dick's parents, Pat would spend a rough day, much of the time feeling guilty for not being with her newborn. One afternoon, after a particularly grueling pace, she prepared to send the materials she'd been working on—only to find there were no stamps to mail them and no money to buy more. The wall she'd built up over the years to contain her emotions suddenly gave way and she sobbed uncontrollably. Despite constant financial worries and Dick's countless slights and humiliations, a friend noted that Pat talked "incessantly about what a great man her husband was." Again "duty" called.

Although Voorhis always appeared to refrain from the dirty tricks that Nixon learned to use, the same was not true of his campaign staff. One day a man walked into Dick's campaign headquarters asking for fifty of the expensive four-page brochures Pat had spent her hard-earned money to have printed. She was elated. The next day, another man entered and requested one hundred brochures. This time, at the urging of her husband, she questioned the volunteer about his plans to distribute them. Come to find out, he worked for Voorhis—so Pat held on to her brochures and ordered the man to leave. The next day, she returned to the building, only to find it broken into and the remaining thousands of brochures gone. There went the $3,000 she'd used to print the brochures, money she'd gotten from her share of the sale of the Artesia property. It was a bitter blow, long remembered. In 1972, she complained, "I wonder why it [the Watergate break-in] is played up so much. No one cared when it happened to us in '46!"

By now Pat had learned that her husband had a fuse about as short as her father's. One afternoon during the campaign, Dick was preparing a radio broadcast when Pat ventured into the studio. According to an observer, he went into a tirade and ordered her out "with as little ceremony as he would have a dog." "You *know* I never want to be interrupted when I'm working!" Tom Dixon, an aide present at the time, later said, "It gave me insight into the man. If he had been doing a brand-new speech, I could have understood it, but this speech he knew by heart."

That was just the beginning of the roller-coaster ride she'd endure with Dick Nixon. This outburst by her husband was not the first, nor was it by any means the last, in her marriage to a borderline manic-depressive bent on exploitation. One man who saw Nixon creating painful scenes with Pat was James Bassett, city editor of the Los Angeles *Mirror-News*. Bassett recalled that Nixon had "total scorn for female mentality. He would rant and rage when he had to speak before the National Federation of Republican Women, rank and file workers: 'I will not go to talk to those shitty-ass old ladies.' "[10]

Why did Pat continue at his side in one campaign after another, exploited as no other? Why did she help make up for his lack of sophistication, a failing his Whittier professor had noted in recommending him to Duke? A close friend of Pat's explained, "She gritted her teeth and did it because she felt it was her duty. . . ." Duty. It was always duty. And those watching her on TV, standing by his side—even through the dismal days of Watergate—couldn't help but see her mask of dutiful resignation under pressure. Her lack of expression earned her the unenviable reputation of "plastic Pat."

On July 5, 1948, she gave birth to Julie, the daughter who would take the time and care to write her mother's biography in 1986. Yet the next day, in a letter to his favorite college professor, Paul Smith—on what other subject but politics—Nixon made no mention of the birth of their second child. After all, first things first.

By 1950, he was busy campaigning against Helen Gahagan Douglas for the California Senate seat. With him at every one of the ten or more stops each day, as he spoke from the tailgate of their station wagon, was his dutiful wife. After winning handily, Dick found a private secretary and Pat a fast friend in Rose Mary Woods.

Busy during his four years in Congress, especially with the Hiss case, Nixon shifted into a frenetic pace as Senator. More often on the stump than in the Senate chambers, he was always on the go: flying here, driving there, crisscrossing the country as a speaker in constant demand after receiving national attention during his prosecution of Hiss. Campaigning for one senator after another, Nixon put them in his debt, even as he tried to replenish his own campaign coffers.

Between the stump and the chambers, Pat's husband had little time for family. Rarely was Nixon home for an evening meal. Receptions and other Washington social events found her with him, so much so that the girls knew their baby-sitter better than they knew their father. In April 1952, Dick took his family with him on a speaking trip to Hawaii. This, said Pat, was "the last carefree vacation I ever had."[11]

It would get worse. When Nixon was named Eisenhower's running mate at the Republican National Convention in July 1952, the news provoked "shouts of rage and disbelief" from the journalists sitting near Pat. Her mouth fell open in astonishment. Did the press have so little use for her husband? Already, as much as she hated confrontation, she'd argued with him for four hours about his undertaking a national campaign. She wanted neither the fishbowl nor the travel. But above all she cringed at the thought of being separated from her two daughters, now ages six and four. Already she'd suffered the torments of the damned when, leaving again with Dick on yet another junket, both daughters would burst into tears. Once Julie was so distraught that she threw herself on the floor, crying uncontrollably. Nixon, at a loss for an explanation, simply turned to his mother, Hannah, who was staying with them. "Mother, take her in your arms, or something." He had obligations to tend to.

It was 4 A.M., July 11, and Dick had not yet convinced his wife he should take the vice-presidential slot. Nixon needed reinforcements, so he phoned Murray Chotiner, his campaign adviser since 1946, whom Pat had come to resent. "What are you doing?" asked Nixon. "Sleeping." But no more. In minutes he'd joined the couple, who were still arguing. "What do you think?" asked Dick. "If this thing is offered to me, do you think I should take it?" Chotiner confronted Pat. "There comes a time when you have to go up or out." This was followed by, "What have you got to lose?" Plenty, Pat figured, and went on for another hour of wrangling, then, exhausted by the two men cornering her, she at last conceded, "I guess I can make it through another campaign." Yet, hoping against hope, she was sure he'd refuse the offer and not subject her and the girls to more of the same—or worse.

But Nixon was not about to lose this golden opportunity. Dragging Pat with him, he practically ran back to the convention hall, where, surrounded by reporters, he gave them the news. Pressed by the journalists for her response, Pat said she was "amazed, flabbergasted, weak, and speechless . . . ." After her husband was nominated, she was escorted to the stage, where she kissed him—then again for photographers—but only on the cheek. Through this, her husband never so much as looked at her, so busy was he shaking hands, flinging his arms around those nearest to him, a "tremendous grin" on his face. Then it was Dick standing with hands over his head, fingers in Churchill-style "V for victory," acknowledging the cheers sweeping the hall. Caught up in the pandemonium and the adulation of the crowd, Pat momentarily forgot the coming ordeal of campaigning.[12]

But not for long. Back home they found Tricia in bed asking what it meant to be vice-president. Her mother replied that Daddy's job would be to help the president. At that Tricia cried out, "Oh, you mean that you're going to campaign *again!*" And so it went. Always Pat bowed to Chotiner's advice: "Never embarrass your husband. . . . Always look at your husband when he is talking." And always she had a ready explanation as to why she put up with it all. "A wife's first duty is to help and encourage her husband in the career he has chosen." There it was again: duty. Aide Tom Dixon's theory, given during the 1950 campaign: "I think he would have made it very miserable for her if she hadn't gone along. In fact," Dixon added, "she was . . . weak with him. His ego had to be toadied to. . . . She had a little of the martyr's complex in her to take that with so little grumbling."

It wasn't just his tirades, or the slurs against her husband that she was subjected to at cocktail parties and receptions where, standing next to the Vice-President, she'd hear the barbs yet manage a smile and a handshake for the gossiper. It wasn't just the neglect of the family, as he worked far into the night, curling up on the couch, then arising for a hurried breakfast and a shave before heading again to the Senate chambers. Even when his parents underwent surgery and stayed with Pat and Dick to recuperate, Nixon saw little of any of them. But what really got to her was his total obsession with politics. He had no hobbies, played no games apart from an occasional stab at golf. As Pat put it, "He can keep right on thinking and working at politics from the time he wakes up until he goes to sleep."

As little time as he had for Pat, he had none for other women. Politics was his sustenance as well as his consort. He had no lack of critics, and was accused of virtually everything under the sun—except womanizing. Indeed, at a Republican fund-raiser in Hollywood, he was surrounded by a galaxy of female stars, prompting reporter Adela Rogers St. Johns to exclaim, "You never saw such beautiful flesh." Yet there was Nixon, seemingly oblivious to it all, acting "like a man utterly unsexed. It was as if he didn't know they were there." The only relief from the daily grind that Nixon seemed to enjoy was when, after whipping his aides all day and into the night to work harder and faster, he'd invite them over to his big, new house—and there, seated at the piano, take requests in a sing-along for a couple of hours.

Rose Mary Woods gave some idea of the exploitation, the hectic pace to which he subjected one and all within his grasp. To a reporter, "Rosy," as Nixon called her, explained her daily workout. "I fly with a typewriter strapped on a table across my lap, so I can type without interruption during landings, takeoffs, thunderstorms, and rough air. I've typed on chairs, couches, card tables, and boxes. . . . I'll run alongside him taking dictation. In a few minutes he can give me a list of twenty phone calls to make, twice as many notes to write, have me change luncheon dates, assign people to dig up facts on a handful of subjects. . . ." At times it seemed that the only person more dedicated to Nixon than his wife was Woods. And that's saying a lot—because, as Nixon faithfully recorded in his *Memoirs*, "Pat and I traveled 46,000 grueling miles during the 1952 campaign. I made 92 speeches, 143 whistle stop appearances, visited 214 cities, and held several press conferences.[13]

It certainly couldn't be said that Pat lacked loyalty. Weathering the jibes of cynical reporters aimed at her husband; ignored by him while he gave his all to his political career; accompanying him on one campaign after another as she left tearful daughters with baby-sitters; taking Julie, Tricia, and a picnic lunch to his Senate office so her daughters wouldn't forget what their father looked like—she worked like a trouper whether on or off the campaign trail, forever deferring to her increasingly imperious husband.

After being elected with Ike, Nixon seldom paused to look back, intent on running for president in 1960. But Pat was fed up. Bad enough that for four years Ike had used her husband as a hatchet man, who in turn became a lightning rod for all the bolts hurled at the administrtion by Democrats and even some Republicans. Apparently Ike had been reading Machiavelli: ". . . princes ought to leave affairs of reproach to the management of others, and keep those of grace in their own hands." Worse, Pat saw Ike's aides trying to convince him to dump Dick from the ticket in 1956. But worst of all was the press, particularly Herblock's cartoons in *The Washington Post*, portraying her husband in brutal caricatures. She broke down—something she rarely did, even in private. She'd come to hate politics, she told Dick, then insisted he quit at the close of his first term. He said he would. Not good enough; he'd said that before. So Pat insisted that he put it in writing. He did, then placed it in his wallet to remind himself. And a lot of good that did.

For Dick Nixon had tasted power—real power—power so close to the pinnacle that he was hooked. He could no sooner shake the political habit than a heroin addict could quit cold turkey. Gradually Pat was coming to realize this insatiable thirst in her husband, and it was, to say the least, disconcerting. So he stuck with Ike through a second term, ran for president, and was defeated. Why had he reneged on his promise again? It was, he rationalized, "circumstances." Yes, he acknowledged, "Pat felt very, very strongly about it. . . . Ever since the fund thing [the slush-fund allegations that had led to the "Checkers" speech] she hasn't been keen on this business." But what could he do? What other choice did he have? As he put it, "Once you get into this great stream of history you can't get out. You can drown. Or you can be pulled under by the tide. But it is awfully hard to get out when you're in the middle of the stream—if it is intended that you stay there."

So that was it. "Circumstances" equaled destiny equaled fate. It was all in the cards this poker player had been dealt. Pat didn't believe it. She'd gone along with his growing imperiousness, his manic phases that alternated with periods of deep depression, his furtiveness, his neglect of her and the girls, and his rampant exploitation. She'd gone abroad with him on one "goodwill" tour after another, braving anti-American taunts, spittle, rotten vegetables and stones hurled their way—then she would brush protocol aside to visit the sick, the poor, the schools and hospitals, rather than indulge in mindless cocktail parties at various embassies. As Attorney General Herbert Brownell described her, "Plastic Pat" could also be "Gracious Pat," and "Spontaneous Pat," given her own "circumstances." She could also be "Humble Pat." One day in Washington Dick was using the car so Pat decided to walk to an appointment. Afterwards, snow was falling, so, carrying her shoes, she trudged home even as the long white limos of VIPs passed her by. On a ten-week tour of the Far East with the Vice-President in 1953, she visited over 200 schools and hospitals, including a leper colony, to assess social and educational conditions. This prompted Ike—who'd given Nixon a "pretty good" for the trip—to say that Pat had been "wonderful!". When she returned home from Africa in 1956, a reporter was "amazed at Pat's stamina." After a trip to Ireland, she was greeted by friend Jessamyn West, who asked if Pat wasn't tired after this strenuous journey. "No," she replied, "I am never tired, never sick, and never afraid." She thought nothing of intervening in a fight in New York City when she saw two boys bullying a younger child. *The Washington Post*, typically hard on Dick, wrote of Pat in 1956 that she "seems to be a woman [unlike her husband] without enemies." At the Republican National Convention that year, the Associated Press reported "she received a roaring ovation." Even Ike's wife, Mamie, had a good word for her, saying that Pat was "always gracious and never one to put on airs."

Place Pat Nixon beside her husband in front of an audience, and she was "Plastic Pat," the actress who could play the part of dutiful wife. But place her out among the people, as in her trips abroad, and she was transformed. Spontaneous, gracious, with a bright smile and a warm handshake, she always seemed ready to extend a helping hand.[14]

Ever the dutiful wife, ever the inexhaustible trouper, ever the paragon of graciousness, what goodwill did emerge from the Nixons's 1958 Latin American trip was largely due to her unfailing generosity, even under fire. Yet on the evening of their return—instead of being home with daughters she'd missed for more than two weeks—duty prevailed and, with her husband's insistence, she stood next to him at the Women's National Press Club. Washington columnist Betty Beale sketched a pathetic picture. "You probably have never seen a more exhausted woman. . . . Usually responsive and keen, Pat stood beside her husband as he spoke, with arms hanging limp beside her, her face so numb with fatigue it couldn't smile. . . . She seemed to move like an automaton. . . ."

Nixon's loss to Kennedy in 1960 showed he had yet to learn perhaps the most important lesson Pat could teach him: that honey attracts, vitriol repels. The defeat was a double blow for Pat. Her husband had promised not to run again in 1956, only to renege, and then subjected her to another campaign that again separated both of them from their adolescent daughters. And for what? To lose to Kennedy. As for JFK, he could forgive Nixon his slurs against the Democrats. What he couldn't forgive was Nixon's call for Pat to be by his side, on national TV, the night of the election, appearing close to a nervous breakdown. Exploitation knew no bounds for Nixon.

During the 1960 campaign the contrast was striking between the way the two candidates treated their wives. Ever solicitous of Jackie, holding her hand, dancing with her, putting his arm around her, kissing her, JFK convinced the public—at least most of them—that he truly cared for his wife. Nixon, by contrast, was so indifferent to Pat in public as to suggest contempt. Rarely did he dance with her, and when he did it was awkward, as though he were a stranger. Rarely did he hold her hand, and then only when, emerging from a plane, he knew photographers were at the ready. Rarely were they seen embracing, and when she kissed him it was always a peck on the cheek. Ever since a boy, raised by a strict Quaker mother, he had, as Brodie put it, "a problem with touching." Indeed, when the public did get a glimpse of them together, she was usually trotting along behind him.

The election over, one would have thought Nixon would have packed it in, found another job less strenuous, and spent more time with Pat and the girls. But he didn't. Already he seemed to be running for something, as well as plumping for himself, in *Six Crises*. With Haldeman at his elbow doing research, Woods at the typewriter banging it out, an election somewhere in the offing, and Pat at home with their daughters, Nixon did what Nixon did best—he bragged on himself. He thought so little of his indispensable helpmeet that he paid her about as much attention in the book as he did to her in public. In the first 204 pages—comprising almost half the book—he referred to her in just 16 of over 8,000 lines. More often it was, "Everywhere I went that afternoon, I was hailed as a hero in Peru." Or, quoting Ike's wire to him, "Dear Dick, Your courage, patience, and calmness in the demonstration directed against you by radical agitators have brought you a new respect and admiration in the country." Concluding his crisis in Caracas, Nixon wrote, "It wouldn't be complete without describing at least briefly the impact those events had on the nation, as well as on me personally." In the next 230 lines he went so far as to include "Mrs. Nixon" as they were "applauded by spectators in hotel lobbies, railroad stations, and other public places. . . ." It wasn't as though Pat were lacking in those qualities that made for an extraordinary spouse, even for a President. Stewart Alsop called her Nixon's "major political asset." Paul

Smith, Nixon's favorite at Whittier College, called Pat "a far stronger man [sic] than Dick . . . I don't know of anyone who has so disciplined herself to endure a life she does not like. . . . She's the hero in the whole lot, highly disciplined, instinctively moral." During the difficult 1960 presidential campaign, Pat acknowledged, "If I have a problem I keep it to myself."[15] Yes, her husband, she repeated again and again, was "a man of destiny." But no, she'd not comment on their marriage except to profess her husband was "easy to live with." But was he?

From all indications, it wasn't his persistent lack of attention that caused Pat to reach her breaking point. It was, rather, his ignoring of the children that was getting to her after his defeat by Kennedy. Adela Rogers St. Johns, interviewing Nixon about *Six Crises*, overheard Pat threatening Dick, "If you ever run for office again, I'll kill myself." It sounded serious but, incredulously, it was not enough to keep Nixon from running again, this time for governor of California. At home, in the precious little time he spent there, Pat and the girls found him, as he later admitted, "short-tempered." Nixon just had to get back in the "arena" where he could be center stage, basking in the spotlights. And of course, there was Ike, urging him to run. He "dreaded bringing up the subject with Pat," Nixon later confessed, so I left it until the last possible moment," September 27, 1961. Pat, pale and trembling, refused to "be out campaigning" with him as she'd done in the past. Nixon took to his study, ostensibly to compose an announcement that he wouldn't run, when Pat appeared. "I am more convinced than ever that if you run it will be a terrible mistake." But, she added, if he was determined to do so, she'd help him once again.

That was all the "chronic campaigner," as LBJ labeled him four years later, needed to be off and running. "My heart," he later wrote, "is in public service"—even if Pat's wasn't. So Nixon ran again, and lost again. After the gubernatorial loss, Pat confided to a physician that she wanted a divorce.

Apparently she thought better of it, what with the trauma it would impose on her daughters—and with Nixon moving the family to New York where he joined a law firm. Supposedly taking up a law practice, he was, in fact, building for a 1964 presidential campaign—as a dark horse in the event of a standoff between Rockefeller and Goldwater. That misfired, so Nixon promptly set his sights on 1968. When Julie asked why her father was running again, Pat was ready with, "He's a great man, a man of destiny." This despite her intense misgivings in 1966, when she'd confessed to her daughters that she just couldn't face another presidential race because the "humiliation" was too much. All she wanted, she confided to close friend Helene Drown the next year, was the "peace of mind [of] a normal life." By campaign time, however, she was convinced—or so she told her daughters—that her husband was not only a man of destiny, but that his destiny was her fate. Years later, when attempting to explain her father's 1970 appearance at the Lincoln Memorial to confront war protesters, Julie remembered her mother's words, though less succinctly. "I think he's sort of the idealistic type, and the whole idea of a man of destiny."[16]

Jt was somewhat less than convincing that Nixon was "destined" to become president when he had to resort to the biggest "trick" in his grab bag to win the election (which will be detailed in a later chapter). Once again Pat was by his side in the campaign. Asked what her greatest contribution was, she replied, "I don't nag him. The best that I can [do] is cheer him up." With the war dragging on and Watergate ahead of him, she had her work cut out for her. And she did her best, even though there was a lapse or two. At a dinner for the White House Press Corps in California Nixon was obviously uncomfortable with those at his table, including his wife. He detested small talk and refused to discuss major issues with any of them. At last, in a determined effort to break the embarrassing silence, he remarked how great were the decorations in this Mexican restaurant. "But Dick," Pat interrupted, "they're plastic." Nixon's face darkened as he retreated once again into the safety of his own thoughts.

Not only were the decorations plastic—so was Pat's appearance when events later closed in on her husband. Her face was a mask of utter resignation, and White House physicians worried as Pat, smoking and drinking more than ever, continued to lose weight. Even the few chores her husband had once given her—like choosing guest lists and menus, and making seating arrangements for state dinners—he'd now usurped. At Julie's wedding, Nixon danced with her but not with Pat. The only time Chris Palmer, chief steward on *Air Force One*, ever saw even a hint of affection between the Nixons occurred when, alighting from the plane—for the benefit of TV cameras and the public—he'd grasp her hand and descend the stairs, looking for all the world like inseparable lovers. At the second inaugural she would not embarrass her husband with a public kiss, to her husband's relief. "Mrs. Agnew kissed Agnew," he later wrote. "Pat doesn't kiss me. I am rather glad she didn't. . . . These displays of affection . . . [don't] quite fit."[17]

As early as 1948, aide Tom Dixon wrote: "I never saw him touch Pat's hand . . . she was farther away from him than I was . . . I have never seen quite as cold an arrangement." Twenty-five years later, Pat was celebrating her sixty-first birthday at the 1973 opening of the Grand Old Opry in Nashville, Tennessee. They wheeled out an upright piano on the stage, whereupon Nixon thumped out "Happy Birthday" while all joined in. Then, as Pat's press secretary Helen McCain Smith recounted, "At the last chord, her face glowing, Pat rose from her chair and moved toward her husband." He had things other than a public embrace in mind and, eager to move on with the program, he turned his back on her and "stepped brusquely to the center stage"—something he'd gravitated to ever since a child—"and ignored Pat's outstretched arms. I shall never forget the expression on her face."

Shortly after this snub, Nixon told a group of women journalists that Pat could go along with him on his trips if she cared to, but that frankly she would be "excess baggage." A year later, on the eve of his resignation, he managed to damn Pat, as Shakespeare put it, "with faint praise." "I have a wonderful family," he acknowledged to a group of congressmen, "and a pretty good wife." The next morning, in a tearful farewell speech to his staff, he mentioned his Cabinet, his parents, his dead brothers—everybody, it seemed, except his wife.[18]

By this time there was scarcely a relic of the "beautiful new teacher" Nixon had courted at the Whittier Playhouse. Gone, it seemed, was the "warm and fun-loving, unselfish and tender" Pat. Gone was the "beautiful and vivacious young woman with titian hair" with whom he'd become infatuated, "a case of love at first sight," as he recounted in his *Memoirs*. Gone was the one hundred thirty pound "smiling woman with flashing eyes, a mass of red-gold hair, and cheeks . . . like apricots." Thirty-five years of living with Richard Nixon had taken their toll. Now all that remained was a hundred pound skeleton, frail, fragile, bitter—duty written on her forehead, all emotions hidden behind a mask that gave no hint of the fury beneath the surface. Pat Nixon was now only a caricature of Pat Nixon—one that left millions wondering if perhaps, she was no longer even human.

But she *was* human. Try as she might to hold it all in—as she'd learned to do with her violent father, try as she might to drown herself in alcohol—retreating to three or four martinis a day to anesthetize herself to the Watergate scandal crashing down upon them, she finally gave vent to it all as she raged at him, "You have ruined my life!"[19]

Nixon's preening hubris led to his exploitation of many people, but none was more unconscionable than the ruination of his life partner. Here was the one he'd courted assiduously for two years until she could no longer resist his importunities. Here was the one who bore him two girls, yet who found him ignoring them just as he ignored her, who was reduced to bringing a picnic basket to his office so his daughters could catch an occasional glimpse of this father for whom politics was the be-all and end-all. Here was the one he'd promised—again and again—that he'd quit politics to enjoy his family, only to renege—again and again—in favor of front center stage. Here was the one who, trying to hold him to his promises, found herself—again and again—badgered and hounded, until at last, wounded and exhausted from hours of argument, she gave in. And here was the same Pat who, determined to maintain her persona, admitted to an incredulous press that her first duty to her husband was not "to nag him" but "to try and cheer him up." If there was anybody who needed "cheering up," especially after the children left home, it was Pat. Indeed, one can't help but think she would have been content with even a few crumbs of solicitous attention that might fall from the master's table.

As the next chapter will detail, exploitation, thy name is arrogance.

CHAPTER 6

ARROGANCE

Insolence breeds the tyrant; Insolence…when it hath scaled the topmost ramparts, is hurled to a dire doom. . . .

— Sophocles, *Oedipus the King* c. 425 B.C.

. . . rulers of states, if they are true rulers, never think of their subjects as sheep. . . .

— Plato, *The Republic* c. 360

. . . a question arises: whether it is better to be loved than feared or feared than loved?. . . a prince ought to inspire fear in such a way that, if he does not win love, he avoids hatred. . . .

— Machiavelli, *The Prince*

I have ventured, like wanton boys
    that swim on bladders,
This many summers, in a sea of glory,
But far beyond my depth, my high blown pride
At length broke under me, and now has left me,
Weary and old with service, to the mercy
Of a rude stream, that must forever hide me.
Vain pomp and glory of the world. I hate ye.

— Shakespeare, *Henry the VIII*[1]

LYNDON JOHNSON

. . . the written word of the intellectual, of the contemplative mind he connected with stillness, paralysis, and . . . death.

— Doris Kearns

In later years as Lyndon rose politically, MacArthur, no mean politician himself, said that had he but known he would have given him an even higher award, what was then called the Congressional Medal of Honor. . . .

— Merle Miller

Issues, to Johnson, had never been anything more than campaign fodder; caring about none himself he had, in every campaign he had run, simply tested, and discarded, one issue after another until he found one which, in his word, "touched"—influenced—voters.

— Robert A. Caro, *Means of Ascent*[2]

America the Arrogant

Insinuated in each of the foregoing steps in hubris, one cannot help but detect arrogance. Yet this deserves a full chapter for no other reason than it is most often associated with hubris. Indeed, the two terms are often interchanged. Taken broadly, arrogance is defined as "the act or quality of having unwarranted pride and self-importance." Taken more narrowly, however, as we shall do here, arrogance is rooted in "arrogate," meaning "to claim or demand unduly or presumptuously." As such, it is often associated with haughtiness or a contemptuous manner. What leaders like Lyndon Johnson have been most apt to covet, to arrogate to themselves, is power—the authority to influence and ultimately to control others. Emerging from World War I relatively unscathed seemed to be continuing proof that Providence was on the side of this nation. If the nineteenth was Britain's century, then, proclaimed Henry Luce in *Life* in 1940, the twentieth was America's. Unwilling and perhaps unable to return to the China where his parents had been missionaries, Luce would undertake the challenge of exporting "Christian capitalism." Many were convinced, but theologian Reinhold Niebuhr was not among them. He excoriated Luce's "egoistic corruption of other nations under the banner of free enterprise." Most, however, weary of the Great Depression, eagerly grasped the coming war—and the abundance of jobs it would bring—as welcome respite from the economic catastrophe of the 1930s. Once again we would stand in the breach and prevent Germany, now allied with Italy and Japan, from taking over Europe, the Far East, and perhaps the world.

There was no stronger proponent of capitalism in 1940 than the fledgling Congressman from the Tenth District of Texas. He was making the most of what many were calling socialism, incarnated in FDR's New Deal. Lyndon would bring Washington's largesse to the Hill Country. He'd clean the water, pave the roads, build the libraries and schools, and, above all, dam the lower Colorado to provide electricity. Here was an unlikely Santa Claus—bringing $70 million of federal money to his one district.

By 1940, Lyndon was also taking all the money he could from the Browns and their friends to get elected and reelected. And they'd begun thinking of Johnson more as Robin Hood—robbing the rich to feed the poor—than as Santa Claus. While dipping into FDR's pocket as a hundred percent New Dealer with one hand, Lyndon was dipping with the other hand into the pockets of Texas fat-cats in order to lubricate his campaign machinery. Just how he could pull off this shrewd balancing act is testimony to his political astuteness, as well as his moral obtuseness. It wasn't lost on Lyndon when Senator Kenneth Wherry stood in the Senate in 1940 and—manifest destiny burning in his bosom—proclaimed, "With God's help, we will lift Shanghai up, ever up, until it is just like Kansas City!" The only surprise was that Wherry, a Nebraskan, didn't picture Shanghai as a Chinese Omaha.

Five years later, the second global war was over, the Marshall Plan was in place, and the Cold War was beginning. We would be not only the world's banker but its policeman. So right was our cause, so pure our motives, so sacred our mission, that Eisenhower hit just the right note in proclaiming, "Here are forces of good and evil, amassed and armed and opposed as rarely before in history. Freedom is pitted against slavery, lightness against dark." This was to be an epic struggle, a holy war, with the Judeo-Christian tradition arrayed against atheistic Communism. On such simplistics enthusiasm, extremism, and terrorism all feed. It was all black and white, with no room for pallid grays.

Again we had emerged from global conflict relatively unscathed, proof once again of our exceptionalism. It was this banner that Kennedy raised high when he laid down the gauntlet at his inauguration. Absolutes, interspersed with either/or simplistics, were the order of the day. The torch had been passed to a new generation—the generation of GIs emerging from World War II—willing to "pay any price, bear any burden, meet any hardship, support any friend, oppose any foe to assure the survival and the success of liberty."

The rest of the world was either free or enslaved, good or evil, right or wrong, allies or adversaries. But all must know that this new generation was not to ask "what America will do for you, but what together we can do for the freedom of man." Finally, this new generation could bank on the help of the Almighty, assured that "here on earth God's work must truly be our own."

Ted Sorensen, the man most responsible for Kennedy's speech, looked into the faces of the crowd and thought, "They had forgotten the cold, forgotten party lines and forgotten all the old divisions of race, religion and nation."[3] Hardly. As the new decade unfolded, it brought with it the most malevolent divisiveness in eighty years. Sorensen, it appears, was seeing what he wanted to see.

By 1966, we had become, as Fulbright's *Arrogance of Power* put it, not only the most powerful nation on earth but the most arrogant. "America," he wrote, "is now at that historical point at which a great nation is in danger of losing its perspective on what exactly is within the realm of its power and what is beyond it. Other great nations, reaching this critical juncture, have aspired to too much, and by overextension have declined and then fallen." Arnold Toynbee had sounded the same alarm almost twenty years earlier in his massive *Study of History,* and Paul Kennedy took up the alarm some twenty years later in his *Rise and Fall of the Great Powers.*

Why, Fulbright asked, should we invite hubristic destruction? Its causes, he wrote, "while not entirely clear," were rooted in what had become "one of the uniformities of history: power tends to confuse itself with virtue and a great nation is peculiarly susceptible to the idea that its power is a sign of God's favor, conferring upon it a special responsibility for other nations—to make them richer and happier and wiser, to remake them. That is, in its own shining image."

LBJ the Arrogant

Lyndon Johnson both reflected and reinforced this arrogance. And inasmuch as arrogance arises from ignorance, Johnson's distancing himself from history, literature, philosophy, and the arts prepared him to both reflect and reinforce this country's image as America the Arrogant. He may have flattered Princeton history professor Eric Goldman by listening intently to his lecture on American history—but Johnson was more interested in recruiting Goldman as a resident intellectual, who could forge links with academics across the country, than in learning about Goldman's subject. Though considered brilliant by Kearns, though convinced he was "a true leader" in his ability to create alliances among opposing forces, though eschewing the simplistics of "classifying, labeling, and filing [of] Americans under headings," Johnson was in important respects an ignoramus, Merle Miller contended, when it came to comprehending "the culture of almost any country outside his own." And even of his own, as Goldman came to realize, he had precious little understanding.

What Lyndon did come to understand, early in life, was the importance of attention. In all probability he emerged from the womb in 1908 vocalizing and, with few interruptions, continued vocalizing until the Grim Reaper stopped his mouth as well as his heart in 1973. Supremely confident that his tongue could rescue him from any situation, indulged shamelessly by his mother if not by his father, Lyndon entered college a preening peacock, strutting where others walked, shouting where others talked, grabbing where others asked. And never—but never—apologizing. By the time he was in Kleberg's office, coworker Estelle Harbin recalled, Lyndon "couldn't stand not being somebody, just could not *stand* it." He would brag, "I'm not the assistant type. I'm the executive type." Yet after

Even his speakership of the Little Congress, made up of aides like himself, was wrenched from his grasp when they, like the students at San Marcos, came to resent this chest-thumping braggart who stuffed ballot boxes to win elections. When, in 1939, a later speaker of the Little Congress inquired why they went to such lengths to count the ballots and check them against the membership, he was aghast to learn the story. "My God," he cried, "who would cheat to win the presidency of something like the Little Congress?"[4] Lyndon Johnson, that was who. By 1939, he'd become a practitioner of the art of arrogating to himself—whether by ingratiating himself with his betters who would, like the Browns and Rayburn, go out of their way to reward him, or by stuffing ballot boxes and buying votes.

What better topic of conversation was there than Lyndon Johnson? And what better way to show him larger than life than to brag? And, in the process, to exaggerate? Having ingratiated himself with Rayburn to land the job as NYA administrator for Texas, Lyndon was not only its youngest director, but became its most productive. With the help of the Brown brothers, he outspent the rest of the candidates to win a seat in Congress. Through his rapport with Roosevelt, he became the moneybags for Democrats in 1940, earning one IOU after another.

The Navy "Hero"

On August 12, 1941, in his first major speech in Congress, Lyndon reminded his colleagues that "Texas boys come from a race of men who fought for their freedom at the Alamo. Texas boys prefer service now to slavery later." Fitting words, he thought, for the times—because, he emphasized, the war "may wash over our shores any time." Johnson had never earned a reputation either for courage or for athleticism. One boyhood classmate recounted that Lyndon "threw a baseball like a girl." When he started to lose, he'd "run home crying, a tall, skinny, awkward, teenaged boy . . . running through the streets of that quiet little town sobbing loudly." Indeed, Emmette Redford recalled, "All anyone had to do was touch Lyndon, and he let out a wail you could hear all over town." As soon as Sam laid a hand on him for one of his many shenanigans, Lyndon would scream so loudly and hysterically that the screams would echo and re-echo down the lonely streets. Other families, hearing the cries, could count on "Ol' Miz" Spaulding, the telephone operator, dialing them up to report, "Sam's killing that boy again."

In college, the nickname "Bull" was not given him for his courage. The only muscle that seemed to work overtime was his tongue. Sucking up to the President and other faculty members, ingratiating himself with Evans through his flattering editorials in the student paper, lording it over other students when Evans put him in charge of assigning student jobs, strutting around in his fancy white silk shirts, he managed to antagonize almost all the other students.

One day, another student figured he'd had all he was going to take and challenged Lyndon to a fight. At this, the stalwart Texan, whose bloodline he'd traced to the Alamo, fell back on his bed, legs flailing. "If you hit me, I'll kick you!" he yelled. The students watching couldn't believe their eyes or their ears. One later recalled, "Every kid in the State of Texas had fights then, but he wouldn't fight. He was an absolute physical coward."

After enlisting, here was one Texas boy who, despite his promises back home in the Tenth District, shunned the foxholes of the South Pacific for the finest hotels on the West Coast. In between his many parties—arranged by Edwin Weisl, Paramount Pictures counsel, and where Lyndon took opportunities to inspect movie stars such as Veronica Lake, Bonita Granville, and Deanna Durbin—he and companion John Connally would inspect naval facilities along the coast.

Always a step ahead of his superior, who was desperately trying to keep tabs on him, Johnson—with Connally in tow—was having, as Connally put it, "a lot of fun." Apart from the parties, Weisl also arranged for lengthy sessions with a top-notch Hollywood photographer, providing Lyndon with his "best face," shots of him giving a "speech" so he could develop his "best gestures," and a voice coach to help him produce his "best voice."

Obsessed as he was with projecting his best persona, Lyndon was hardly at his best in service to his country. On what must have been a well-deserved vacation, Lyndon was on his way to Sun Valley, Idaho, by train when, in the middle of the night—lubricated with one drink after another—he engaged in a violent wrestling match with Jesse Kellam, his successor at the Texas NYA. The brawl could not be broken up until Connally threw cold water over them. Alighting from the train next morning at Sun Valley, Lyndon greeted fellow travelers with a hearty "good morning!"

only to be grumped at, "It may be good for you, but you kept us up all night."

With Hollywood beauties at his beck and call, one would think Johnson's testosterone would have leveled off. But no, he was lonely for none other than Alice Glass, by this time Charles Marsh's wife. Nevertheless, she came running. Always a step ahead of Marsh, as well as his military superior, Lyndon found this life more to his liking than slogging along in "the mud and the blood," as he put it, of the trenches. Just as heroism was for the heroic, indulgence was for the indulgent. But somewhere along the line Lyndon confused the two when he later regaled audiences about his South Pacific exploits. Lyndon's West Coast heroics stood in sharp contrast with those of two fellow congressional members of the Naval Affairs Committee, who had enlisted about the same time. Warren Magnuson was serving on an aircraft carrier in the battle off the Solomon Islands, while Melvin Maas, serving with the Marines in the South Pacific, earned both the Purple Heart and the Silver Star.

But Lyndon's lavish lifestyle was about to come to an abrupt end. After all, his were hardly the kind of exploits that would win for him the medals Maas was winning, something every self-respecting congressman coveted if he were to go for a Senate seat. And that's exactly what Lyndon intended to do, even though the incumbent—Pappy O'Daniel—was well-entrenched. So on March 7, 1942, Johnson wrote his commander in chief: "Things are very dull here with me." Which would have been news to Connally and Kellam, as well as Weisl. "How I yearn for activity and an assignment where I can be reasonably productive." His "yearning" was apparently encouraged by digs, even from his friends, that his service record was something less than stellar and that he was jeopardizing his political career. "Get your ass out of this country at once," advised Marsh, not so much to keep Lyndon from Alice—of which he remained blissfully unaware—but to get "to where there is danger, and then get back as soon as you can to real work. If you can't sell the Navy on ordering you out, you are not as good as I think you are . . . for God's sake, get going and quit talking." Wirtz was saying amen to that. And there was the friendly *Houston Post*, warning that if he were "merely getting himself a safe, warm naval berth . . . the voters would be certain to react accordingly."5 Johnson's secretaries, meanwhile, were doing handstands to distract nosy reporters. Yes, according to the last reports, Congressman Johnson was on the West Coast, undoubtedly en route to the Pacific war zone. In fact, he may be already there. But, you know, secrecy and all: "Loose lips sink ships." This was the watchword.

Then, out of the blue, Lyndon learned that one of O'Daniel's supporters had been spying on him, knew where he was and what he was doing. Worse, the man went public with it, suggesting that if Johnson were going to spend the rest of the war on the West Coast, he might as well return to Congress—where he could at least be representing his district. This was a low blow, coming from the man who'd trounced Lyndon for the Senate just the year before. By March 16, FDR was seriously thinking of recalling all members of Congress from active duty. If that happened, Lyndon would be home from the war—without ever having set foot in a war zone. O.J. Weber, a Johnson aide. cautioned his boss, ". . . it is doubly important that you get on a boat and get to Pearl Harbor or some other place like that now and as quick as you can. . . ." The voters were asking, Weber added, and "any way you take it, the situation will be embarrassing." Other congressmen, like Magnuson and Maas, were winning plaudits and garnering headlines—while Lyndon's record, like his congressional record, was something less than lackluster. Finally Johnson realized, as Marsh had kept telling him, that he had to put up or shut up. An LBJ aide wrote at the time that Johnson "wants for the sake of his political future to get into the danger zone though he realizes his talents are best suited for handling speakers and public relations." After FDR turned down his audacious request to become an admiral in charge of all naval production, Lyndon had to make do with a lieutenant commander's rank.

At last the President had an overseas job for him. It seemed there was an officer who, after being driven from Corregidor by the Japanese, had fled to Australia—vowing to return to the Philippines. His name was General Douglas MacArthur, Commander of all Allied Forces in the Southwest Pacific—and he was concerned about his persona. In fact, he'd gone to the trouble of hiring the best PR man and photographer he could find on the West Coast to look to the care and feeding of that persona. Nothing of any moment was ever done without first examining the public-relations impact. Then photographers would be well-placed to provide the best possible shots. One can never be too careful with one's persona.

Knowing this, FDR was not sure that the general's reports actually pictured the grimness of the situation in MacArthur's command. Indeed, the commander in chief was quite sure they didn't. He was also anxious to find the truth behind a rumor that MacArthur was giving short shrift to the Army Air Corps. So FDR dispatched his favorite Congressman to assess the situation in the Pacific. And Lyndon departed, all dolled up in his officer's uniform, carrying an ample supply of his formal Hollywood portrait that showed only his "best face," so all would see and remember him. In going to Australia, was Johnson putting himself in harm's way? Not really. Yes, the Philippines had fallen to the Japanese, along with a number of other islands. This, as FDR noted, put Australia, New Zealand, and India at some risk—for Japan was now, the President concluded, in "a dominating position from which it would prove most difficult to eject her."

Yet to be "at risk" is not quite the same as being in a battle zone, and Lyndon realized that. He also realized that this commanding general— who a decade later would be fired as Allied Commander in Korea for insubordination to Truman—was unhappy under FDR. Eager to return to the Philippines, if for no other reason than to fulfill his promise, he chafed that Roosevelt put Europe ahead of the South Pacific.

So Lyndon was off to do the bidding of his commander in chief, and some were unhappy. White House aide Jonathan Daniels took a look at the "slim and curly-haired [Congressman] joking and laughing," and thought he bore as little resemblance to a fighting sailor as he did to a congressman; what he did look like was a movie actor in a seagoing costume. A Capitol Hill observer sized up Lyndon—who was being sent with "a special escort through a combat area" so that he could pose before the voters as a combat veteran—and concluded "it was really, of course, a political charade." Actually, the charade was just the beginning. MacArthur met Johnson, knowing full well that he was "inspecting" if not "spying" for their commander in chief, eyed this congressman dressed in the garb of a Navy lieutenant commander, and said acidly, "God only knows what you're doing here." But MacArthur was aware that this was no ordinary Navy officer, and certainly no ordinary congressman, so he dispatched a team—headed by nothing less than a brigadier general—to escort Johnson and two Army observers, Lieutenant Colonels Samuel Anderson and Francis Stevens.

When the three men arrived at Garbutt Field in Northern Queensland, Lyndon must have thought that the rumor of MacArthur and the Air Corps was indeed true. For instead of flying there in a B-17 Flying Fortress as he'd planned, Lyndon was told that the plane had been grounded for a lack of parts to repair it, so he and his companions had to fly in an obsolete Australian airliner. At the field, Johnson found twelve battle-scarred B-26 twin-engine bombers, their mechanics scurrying about trying to scrounge parts to make them airworthy for a bombing run over Lae, in New Guinea.

Crew members seemed to be on a par with their planes, dressed in Aussie shorts, bush hats, and cowboy boots, their own uniforms worn out and no new ones available. Some, their red eyes sunken from exhaustion, wore fresh bandages stained with blood. Lyndon tried empathizing. After all, back home he had driven himself to exhaustion—until the skin hung loose on his frame, his eyes were like coals of fire in his head, his body trembled with fatigue, and his hands were red and raw. Of course, the difference was that Lyndon had been fighting for votes; these men were fighting a war.

There is some irony in the lesson that as President, Johnson professed to have learned from his World War II experience: ". . . that war comes about by two things—by a lust for power on the part of a few evil leaders and by a weakness on the part of the people whose love for peace too often displays a lack of courage that serves as an open invitation to all the aggressors of the world." Truth be told, there were few in Johnson's day that exceeded him in that "lust for power," though he would be the last to admit it—or to acknowledge that he, too, might qualify as an "evil leader." There is further irony in Majority Leader Johnson taking on, as chairman of the Senate Subcommittee on Preparedness, one of the most decorated generals of World War II, Lieutenant General James Gavin, head of the 82nd Airborne Division. Learning that Gavin was planning to retire, Johnson excoriated him. "If men like you . . . tuck your tail and put up a white flag and say, 'I can't take it any more,' and run from this crowd [the sub-committee, the press, the audience], we are going to have a second-rate Army. . . ."[6]

This from the costumed lieutenant commander who, in 1942, spent six months in the "service," and who was, by 1958, flaunting his Silver Star in his lapel. Just how Johnson "earned" this coveted award for valor in combat is a glaring example of arrogance—of arrogating to himself an honor he neither earned nor deserved. Garbutt Field was still a long way from harm's way, so Lyndon—mindful that his political career would suffer if he didn't see action—insisted on accompanying a flight over enemy territory. The Army officers in Johnson's inspection team, Anderson and Stevens, had already received permission to observe the bombing of Lae from two of the twelve B-26s. But no arrangement had been made for Lyndon, because the Army was reluctant to put at risk a Navy officer, who had no connection to the mission. Johnson put his foot down, and was finally begrudged approval for the flight to New Guinea.

The next morning, June 9, 1942, Johnson arrived late at his assigned B-26, the *Wabash Cannonball*—to find that his fellow observer, Lt. Col. Stevens, had taken the only available spare seat. Go find another plane, said the colonel, so Johnson ambled over to another B-26, the *Heckling Hare*. Of course, he immediately had to press the flesh as a good politician must do, shaking hands with the seven-man crew. Did they mind if he went with them as a spectator? The tail-gunner, an enlisted man, was blunt. "You're out of your goddamned mind. This ain't no milk run, believe me! You don't need to come along and get shot up to find out about conditions here, or the things we need. We'll *tell* you that. . . ."

What they really needed, another crew member interrupted, was fighter planes. "Get us some fighters out here. It would be a pleasure for those Zeros to have something to worry about, instead of our worrying about them. Fighters—that's what we need. Fighters that can go all the way over the target, and let us really get those bombs in where they belong."

The same crew member later let go on MacArthur, as "probably the most unpopular man we know of . . . a lot of our people [were] being killed without any real reason. All we ever [knew] about MacArthur [were] his fancy press pictures and his statements about the war. We'd read official communiqués that went back to the States about smashing air attacks and how many Zeros were shot down. . . . Well, if we ever shot down as many planes as his headquarters used to say, we'd have wiped out the Jap air force in two months." It was obvious that Lyndon would have plenty to tell FDR about conditions in the South Pacific. But first things first. Johnson had a mission to fly; he just had to see it for himself. And, as it turned out, he saw plenty. Donning a chute, he climbed aboard and took his seat in a small cubicle just behind the cockpit. Above him was a plastic bubble for the navigator, and across the cramped passageway was a small window. By standing on a stool he could look across the top of the fuse-lage.[7]

Within an hour they were approaching their target at Lae when suddenly the twelve B-26's were set upon by Zeros. As luck would have it, the *Heckling Hare*'s right-engine generator began to fail, and with it engine power. Within minutes they were sitting ducks, trailing the rest of the mission. It looked bad, so the pilot jettisoned his bombs, turned one hundred and eighty degrees, and started for home—as seven Zeros put the *Heckling Hare* in their sights, their bullets shredding the plane. There, taking it all in from his little side window, grinning from ear to ear, was the Navy observer. Finally, he moved up to the navigator's bubble for a better view. "Boy, it's rough up here, isn't it?" Lyndon asked, to which a crew member answered, "Yeah, I'm always scared up here." At that Johnson "burst out laughing at me," the scared one recalled. "I'm sure he felt exactly the way I did, but he just didn't show it." This, apparently, was the same Lyndon who, fifteen years before, had hitchhiked to college by standing not to the side of the road with his thumb out, but in the middle of the road—forcing cars to stop to avoid hitting him.

By the time the pilot found refuge in some clouds, the *Heckling Hare* had become the "Limping Hare," as it coughed, sputtered, and faltered, barely making it back to base. There they found the plane perforated with bullets and shell holes, but miraculously, no one was hurt. To the crew, Lyndon observed with a smile, "It's been very interesting." Then they waited as nine other B-26s made their way home. At last a tenth appeared—so badly shot up that it couldn't lower its landing gear and had to take the runway on its belly, grinding to a stop in a cloud of dust. They continued to wait for the eleventh, but in vain. Hit by shellfire from a Zero, the *Wabash Cannonball* had crashed into the sea, killing all aboard—including Stevens, the lieutenant colonel who had taken the lieutenant commander's place.

Lyndon Johnson returned to Australia and met with an incredulous MacArthur, who was obviously irritated that Johnson, a Navy man, had so put himself in danger. Had he been killed, MacArthur would have the devil to pay when he answered to the commander in chief about the fate of his favorite congressman. Why, MacArthur asked Lyndon, did he insist on putting his life on the line? Why, simple enough, replied the intrepid observer. Many of the airmen knew he was a Congressman from Texas, and some were his constituents. After all, he'd promised to hunker down with them in their foxholes when war came, and this was a flying foxhole.

Johnson, concluded MacArthur, had rushed in where even angels feared to fly. The more the general thought about FDR's affection for this politician, the more it made sense to confer upon Lyndon a medal.

Suddenly MacArthur announced he was awarding the Distinguished Service Medal, second only to the Congressional Medal of Honor, posthumously to Stevens—though none of the *Wabash Cannonball* crew were so recognized. Then, seemingly as an afterthought, MacArthur said he was awarding Silver Stars to the two surviving members of the inspection team, an honor that ranked next to Steven's medal for valor in combat. Unfortunately, MacArthur had no such medals on hand, the citation had not been written up, and there would be no awards ceremony. Johnson and Anderson should just pick up the ribbons at the outer office. No matter, here was proof positive that Lyndon Baines Johnson, direct descendent of an Alamo hero, had not only gone to war but had emerged a genuine hero! Of course, none of the three observers had ever fired a shot, none were in danger more than an hour or so, and none of the seven-man crews on any of the three planes were so decorated. But business was business— and to MacArthur, with an eye toward challenging FDR for the presidency in 1944, that business was politics.

Johnson had begun his assignment to the South Pacific suffering nightmares, and concluded with the loss of twenty-five pounds from pneumonia. In between, heading from Queensland to Garbutt Field on the ancient Aussie airliner, Johnson complained in a letter to Lady Bird— whom he addressed as "Miss Jesus," that he "Almost froze for three hours. Stood up, beat my legs, stomped my feet, put on windbreak sweater, fur coat, etc.—to no avail."[8] But, he later recounted to Kearns, it was all worth it, for receiving the Silver Star was one of the high points of his life.

Lyndon returned to Washington enveloped in second thoughts about the award. After all, he'd only been an observer, and on the one mission. Perhaps MacArthur's last-minute, backhanded compliment of awarding a medal without a ceremony—lest other observers might chalk it all up to cynical politics—was a ploy meant to blunt the harsh edges of any report Johnson might give the commander in chief. So Lyndon drafted a letter to the Adjutant General of the War Department. He could not, he confessed, "in good conscience, receive this decoration and wear the coveted medal . . . for the inconsequential part I played. . . ." Here was Johnson out of character, honest as he seldom was, especially with himself. It was obvious he was being victimized by what others called conscience. So he struggled with the monster courageously and emerged the victor. He would not only keep the medal but wear it conspicuously on the lapel of his suits, so that all the world may know this was a true descendant of the Alamo!

It is worthy of note that, before leaving for the Pacific, Johnson told FDR aide Jonathan Daniels that he wanted to go only "for the sake of [his] political future." And on July 10, 1942, Daniels noted that Johnson was "back from his politically essential plunge into the Pacific," the day after FDR ordered all congressmen in the armed forces to return to Congress. This recall was prompted by none other than Lyndon Johnson, who convinced FDR that these politicians could better serve their nation in the halls of Congress than in the "halls of Montezuma," as the Marine Corps song put it. The wording of the order was, in fact, a Johnson master touch. All members of Congress serving in the armed forces would be placed on inactive duty, "except those who wish to remain on active duty for the duration of the war." Here was the perfect out for Congressman Johnson, late of heroic action in the Pacific, highly decorated for valor in combat, now to return to "public service" in the Congress. But just to cover all the bases, Lyndon got Navy Secretary Frank Knox to write him a letter, stating "the President has determined that your services to the nation in this critical period are more urgently required in the performance of your duties in the House . . . than as an officer on active duty with the Navy." Lyndon could not have worded it better himself.

That Roosevelt had sent fellow pol Johnson to the Pacific as a political ploy, rather than a sincere desire for information, is evident in FDR's studied lack of attention to Johnson in an hour-long interview on July 15. Instead of listening to Johnson recount MacArthur's problems, FDR—according to Secretary of the Interior Ickes—"drowned out Lyndon's report with talk of his own." "You know," Johnson later confided to Ickes, "how it is when you are trying to tell something to the President."[9]

Of the eight congressmen on active military duty, four resigned their congressional seats to remain in uniform. One of them, Vincent Harrington of Iowa, was later killed in action. Of the four who returned, Johnson had the most polished explanation: "I had been ordered out of uniform and back to Washington by my commander in chief." After all, duty called. Within a week he was on Capitol Hill, his uniform replaced by a top-of-the-line tailored suit—emblazoned, of course, with a Silver Star.

In an increasingly rare moment of candor, Johnson confessed to reporter Marshall McNeill that he didn't deserve the medal. He'd gotten it "for a flight, not for a fight," and he'd "never wear the thing." In one of his Texas speeches, he admitted "the small part I played in the trips [sic] did not entitle me to the same honor that went to the men who risked their lives in daily combat." These mea culpas and resolutions disposed of—and the fact that the "same honor" went to none of the crewmen of the *Heckling Hare*—it is noteworthy that Johnson's fantasy was already beginning to outrun his memory. For, in a Freudian slip, he recalled not the one "trip" or mission, but "trips."

Johnson's recounting of his heroics in earning an award for valor in combat took on a life of its own, which grew with the telling. Upon returning to Washington, he purchased a Silver Star from an Army-Navy store, then arranged to have it pinned on him in a proper ceremony, something MacArthur had overlooked. Not once but several times, Johnson went through the charade, having the Silver Star pinned on him in his home state, so that all could see and hear this brave man from the Hill Country. And each time, he acted as though it were the first. At Fort Worth he requested the commander of the local American Legion post pin it on him. While Legionnaires cheered, Johnson stood, according to Caro, "head bowed, face somber, hardly able to blink back the tears." It was all so moving.

This was just the beginning. In the years to follow, he made a habit—when referring to his combat service during a speech—of pulling his lapel forward and backward, brandishing the precious silver bar with the bright star in the middle, so that everyone in the audience could pay proper homage. Ever eager to chronicle his six months of "military service"—four of which he'd actually spent living high off the hog on the West Coast—Johnson's fantasy was soon leaving reality in the dust. The twenty-five pounds he'd lost from pneumonia were soon forty pounds from dengue fever. The twenty thousand miles he'd flown became sixty thousand; the minutes he'd been in combat were now months; the single bombing run grew into multiple missions. On one flight, he'd been too tall to fit into the lone chute provided for the crew and, with characteristic altruism, had handed it to a crew member. The engine that had lost power from a failed generator had, in reality, been knocked out by Japanese Zeros. He'd personally glimpsed fourteen Zeros going down in flames and, of course, several of his crew members were wounded. "Raider" Johnson was the name these crew members gave him.

As he told and retold the story, there were bound to be some who'd "heard that song before," but with different words to the music. One, Harold Young—counsel to Vice-President Henry Wallace—caught the spirit of Lyndon's college classmates when he noted, "Sometimes you could hardly restrain yourself from shouting, 'Oh, bullshit, Lyndon!'"

After another twenty years of polishing this tale, it was clear that Lyndon had won the war single-handedly. In 1966, he unwittingly demonstrated why a "credibility gap" was opening beneath him like a chasm— by recounting, once again, his illustrious contributions to World War II. "During the months we [three observers] were there, we must have talked to ten thousand men, flown to hundreds of bases." On one particular mission, he recalled, the squadron had lost not one but many planes. "We came back," as he put it, "with a lot fewer planes than we left with." By December 13, 1967, the war in Vietnam was going so badly that he was hard put to cheer himself up. So Lyndon fell back once again on his precious wartime memories in an interview with journalist Ronnie Dugger. Wrote Dugger, "He not only let falsehood pass for truth, he faked his record himself. Telling me about the mission over Lae, he said that when 20 Zeros attacked them 'it was like shooting fish out of a barrel . . . 14 of the planes got the hell shot out of them.' He said that everybody who survived that mission got a Silver Star; everybody who died got the Distinguished Service Cross." Of all those who took umbrage at Johnson's arrogating to himself the Silver Star—then plumping the story for all it was worth as he flaunted the unearned medal—fellow Texan Joe M. Kilgore most resented it. Kilgore had captained a B-17 Flying Fortress over Europe on twenty-five missions. Then, his tour of duty completed, he re-enlisted and went back for ten more missions. On one of these, he was heading for home when he saw German fighters laying waste to another B-17 that was trying to limp back to base. Kilgore turned his plane around and returned to fly cover for the crippled aircraft. For his heroism he was awarded the Silver Star.

Later, as a young Texas attorney, Kilgore was enlisted to help Johnson on the campaign trail. Lyndon constantly reminded Kilgore that he, too, had been awarded the prestigious medal. Yet, Johnson didn't stop there, always making it clear that the Silver Star was little enough for all he'd gone through. Unfortunately, Kilgore had learned the truth about

Johnson's mission: "a routine raid in which he got shot at." So it irked Kilgore no end to hear Johnson "complaining that he had gotten only the Silver Star for an experience that thousands of people had had. . . ." The man appeared "almost irrational [as he] "bitched and bitched because he only got the Silver Star."[10]

General U.S. Grant wrote in 1886 that "wars produce many stories of fiction, some of which are told until they are believed to be true." With this, Joe Kilgore and others would heartily agree. For they had come to understand, as Kilgore later put it, that Lyndon could "convince himself of anything, even something that wasn't true."

Johnson succeeded in arrogating to himself an aura of heroism in combat, not only undeserved but wholly out of character. He not only wore the Silver Star but flaunted it, while increasingly embellishing the details of his valor under fire, until those around him understood he was never satisfied to let well enough alone. Here was a strutting arrogance that became the mark of the man who would do anything, say anything, to further his own goals.

The utter gall in Johnson's claiming the Silver Star as rightfully his, and fabricating his accounts in earning it, stand in naked contrast to the suicide of Admiral Jeremy Boorda, Chief of Naval Operations, on May 16, 1996. For on that day, wracked with guilt over having worn two simple battle stars for the Vietnam war to which he was not entitled, Boorda killed himself. Ironically, retired Army Colonel David Hackworth, who had publicly accused Boorda of falsifying his colors, had not only bragged that he himself was "America's most decorated living soldier," but later confessed that two of his own ribbons had been unearned. It appears that Hackworth was a kindred spirit with LBJ—although he couldn't hold a candle to Johnson's sweeping fabrications.

By 1942, the one goal that Johnson shared with MacArthur was the White House. Although he'd finally decided to pass on the Senate race that year—later saying he had been "in the jungles of New Guinea"—Lyndon would not long be deterred from taking the next logical step toward the presidency. "The road to hell," Lyndon had written Rayburn while "inspecting" on the West Coast, "is paved with indecision and inaction."[11] The road to the special hell that lay at the end of hubris, Johnson would come to find out, was paved not so much with indecision and inaction as with arrogance and perfidy.

Arrogating a Senatorship

Lyndon Baines Johnson expropriated fame he neither deserved nor was content with. But far worse was his expropriation of power. He did it as a spineless sycophant, fawning over those who wielded power. And he did it by outright theft.

Nowhere was this more evident than in Lyndon's theft of the 1948 Senate election, when he ran against Texas Governor Coke Stevenson. Unfortunately Lyndon was carrying the baggage of a less-than-sterling record in his eleven years as congressman. He would soon exchange the epithet, "Lyin' Down Lyndon—earned for his conspicuous ability to avoid taking a stand on any issue of importance—for "Landslide Lyndon," earned for a razor-thin margin of eighty-seven votes in the 1948 race. Helen Gahagan Douglas—recounting the ten speeches Lyndon made on the floor of the House, as well as her personal conversations with him—observed that the Texan would say nothing that "might be repeated or remembered, even years later." At dinner parties, she noted, Johnson monopolized the conversation, yet managed "never to say anything substantive." No such care seemed to attach to his telling and retelling of his Silver Star heroism.

By 1948, he was determined to arrogate to himself by theft what he was not able to buy outright. He had long since departed FDR's New Deal, anathema to big oil and gas tycoons. As he made plans for his campaign, Lyndon realized that he had much riding on it, not the least of which were—since he could run for only one office—his eleven years of seniority in the House. In February 1948, Lyndon learned that Coke Stevenson was favored in the polls over all his likely opponents combined; obviously, it would be a long, long shot to beat the Governor come primary day, July 24. So, despondent, LBJ delayed entering the race, later telling Kearns, "At first I just couldn't bear the thought of losing everything." Not until May 12, did he finally toss his hat in the ring, after friends urged him to back John Connally for the Senate. The idea that his old friend might go after the seat *he* wanted galvanized Lyndon—who immediately launched, according to Dallek, "the most energetic, all-consuming drive for office he had ever made."[12] It would come down to a face-off between Stevenson and Johnson, a contrast in character so striking that it was hard to believe they had a common heritage in the Hill Country.

Johnson at sixteen was begging money from his mother for college. Stevenson at sixteen was herding steers across the rugged Continental Divide, saving enough from his meager earnings to buy a wagon and six horses and start his own freight business. Logging upwards of 20 miles a day, sometimes marooned in mud for 11 days at a stretch, Coke invariably found time by the evening campfire to read and teach himself bookkeeping. Lyndon at eighteen was earning a well-deserved reputation as "Bull" Johnson, the student suffering from constipation of the brain and diarrhea of the mouth. Coke at eighteen was janitoring in a bank at half his former wage, because he saw the chance to move up. By twenty, he'd been promoted to cashier and was teaching himself law at night, even as he was building a new house for his bride. At twenty-five, Coke passed the bar, took his first legal fee, and with his savings bought a 520-acre ranch for $8 an acre. At twenty-five, Lyndon was stealing the election to head the Little Congress.

Before long, Coke was earning a reputation as an outstanding advocate in the courtroom, earning the tribute of a fellow attorney: "Coke would never say a word that he didn't believe . . . [so] when he spoke to a jury, the jury believed him." He didn't talk much, but when he talked, people listened. Not so with "Bull" Johnson, the man who craved center stage, talked incessantly, yet could never seem to tell the truth—unless it happened to be convenient.

At twenty-six, while Lyndon was marrying Claudia Taylor, Coke became county attorney and brought to justice rustlers stealing his and neighbors' cattle. He did such a thorough job that at thirty he was county judge, bringing order where there'd been none. Lyndon at thirty had bought two elections for Congress and was FDR's favorite sycophant. He loved public life, his high being applauded by crowds on the campaign trail, winning with special-interest money that had been carefully—and craftily—cultivated. Stevenson, on the other hand, wanted nothing so much as to be left alone, and refused even to campaign for county judge, so his supporters pitched in and campaigned for him.

When friends urged him to run for Congress, Coke begged off. He'd had enough. "My public life," he recalled, "came about by accident. I did not deliberately set about entering public life. On the contrary, each time I held an office, it was for the purpose of getting a particular job completed."

Contrast this most reluctant of officeholders with that other man from the Hill Country—who *craved* office, regardless of what it took.

In 1920, at age thirty-two, Coke returned to his law practice, where he was conscientious in observing two cardinal rules: never defend a person you don't believe is innocent, and never defend a person accused of cattle rustling. Before long, attorneys and judges from the cities such as San Antonio, Dallas, and Houston were returning from the Hill Country with the word that Coke was "one of the greatest trial lawyers in the history of Texas." Judge A.B. Martin of the Texas Court of Criminal Appeals went so far as to call him "the best all-around lawyer" he'd ever seen. Coke Stevenson even wrote a number of "landmark" cases for law books that were studied at major universities.

By 1928, at age forty, Coke had founded several small businesses, including a bank—and owned a 6,000 acre ranch, the envy of his county. He built his own house; it burned to the ground, so he built another. Yet in what was an exceedingly productive and busy life, Coke always found time to read, especially at night and before sunrise. His favorites were government, history, and biography—books that helped him to learn more about the world beyond the borders of Texas. Lyndon prided himself on keeping his distance from books.

Some eight years out of office, but continually prodded by his wife and fellow ranchers, Coke finally ran for the state legislature. By 1933, he was Speaker of the House. Come 1938, and Coke was persuaded to run on Pappy O'Daniel's ticket as lieutenant governor. When O'Daniel took to the hustings, singing with his hillbilly band, Coke's friends urged him to follow suit. Coke's answer: "I've got a record, and if that ain't good enough—well, that's all I've got." Stevenson wasn't a backslapper, he was even loathe to ask people to vote for him. No platform. No campaign promises he couldn't keep. No loudspeakers. No signs on his car—not even a bumper sticker. His explanation: "I don't want to go into a town looking like a circus wagon." "Quiet dignity" was the way one reporter described his style.

Yet that unadorned style won Stevenson admirers—and votes. He'd pull into the courthouse square, step from his dust-covered Plymouth with no fanfare, make his way over to a small crowd, shake a hand here and another there, as he conversed with them. And what he said, he meant, noted one political observer. "He was sincere. You just looked at him and you said, 'I can trust him.' "

O'Daniel knew next to nothing of politics, apart from high-octane campaigns. If it weren't for Coke, the state under Pappy may well have gone belly-up. As it was, Coke spent his three years in quiet, private conferences with the legislature to eliminate an unheard-of deficit of $34 million. It was so bad that the state's employees were being paid in warrants, or IOU's, which were accepted only at a discount in the stores. So fed up with O'Daniel's malfeasance were Texas businessmen that when the U.S. Senate seat became vacant in 1941, they figured O'Daniel could do less harm in Washington than in Austin. So O'Daniel went off to Capitol Hill, and Stevenson moved to the governor's mansion. "To me the plan of government of our forefathers is a divine inspiration," he said at his inaugural. "It is a government of laws and not of men."

Governor Stevenson's record was as illustrious as Congressman Johnson's was lackluster. With Coke in Austin, the Texas economy would thrive, because this straight-shooter—unlike Lyndon—was the bane of special interests. "No one," recounted one lobbyist, "would have *dared* to offer Coke Stevenson a dime." One Austin pol noted that, far from being the air Johnson breathed, politics was something Stevenson "really hated." He "truly *hated* it—the deals, the maneuvering"—all those aspects that sent Johnson's blood racing. "If," the pol continued, "you started talking about wheeling and dealing—trading votes, whatever—what you got from Coke was that stone stare.... But if you were talking about what government should do and why we should do it, then you had his interest."

Coke learned that state agencies were not auditing their books, so he got the legislature to pass a bill authorizing a state auditor. Having been responsible, as House Speaker, for the only paved road in Texas—a 165-mile stretch between San Antonio and El Paso—he discovered that the state's highway construction was riddled with corruption. He not only cleaned it up, but proposed a bill authorizing a gasoline tax to build more paved highways; it lost its two-third required majority by a single vote. Learning that the state's prison system was also a scandal, he donned the garb of an inmate and slept with convicts in their cell—and used that experience to introduce long-needed reform. In his two terms as Governor, Coke was most certain of one thing: "What has kept this country is that it's a country of laws. Otherwise it's all influence." Yet it was influence and influence-peddling that had sent Lyndon to Congress and gotten him reelected six times. There were few things that money—special-interest money—couldn't buy.

By the time Stevenson left office he'd added to his luster by reforming the abysmal social welfare program that put his state at or near the bottom. He improved education spending, moving Texas from 38th to 24th place. He tripled pensions for the elderly. And while accomplishing all this, he replaced the $34 million deficit with a $35 million surplus. Coke's impressive record made him lionized in the press as the "Abraham Lincoln of Texas," the "Horatio Alger of Llano [a river in the Hill Country]," the "Log Cabin Statesman," and the "Cowboy Governor." The *State Observer* noted that this staunch fiscal conservative "makes fewer public statements than any other man in Texas political life today, yet is credited with greater wisdom."

Some idea of the immense appeal of "Mr. Texas," as Coke was known in 1944, was his reelection that year with 85 percent of the vote, carrying every one of the state's 254 counties, despite—or perhaps because—he refused to attack any of his eight opponents for governor. There was no state law prohibiting a third term, yet it was traditional to quit after two. So in 1946, he refused to run again and returned, instead, to his ranch. A nephew recalled this "former governor of Texas milking cows, standing buck-naked washing himself in the river, eating the same beans every day—you could hardly believe it. But there was no pretense about Coke Stevenson, none at all."

There on his beloved ranch Coke was undisturbed by phone calls, for he'd never installed a phone. And the mail came only weekly. Yet each week the bundle got heavier as, across the state, more and more believers in this legend urged him to run for the U.S. Senate in 1948.

On New Year's Day, 1948, Johnson learned that his fellow Texan from the Hill Country, this man of few words and many deeds, would be one of his opponents if he declared for the Texas senatorial seat. It was as if "high noon" had arrived at the "O.K. Corral." Separated by ten paces, the two principals were about to face off in a duel to the political death. One candidate had but a single cartridge in his six-shooter, and that was his record; the other had all six cartridges, and a backup gun with six more. If one didn't do the job he had plenty more to choose from. Indeed, observers might wonder if Lyndon would start firing before he quit pacing, while Coke's back was still turned. After all he'd done to Rayburn eight years before— to his staunch friend and supporter, the man who'd virtually adopted him in his home away from home—betrayal of a comparative stranger would not seem so farfetched.

By May 12, when Johnson finally entered the race, the incumbent, Pappy O'Daniel, had withdrawn—leaving virtually just the two, Coke and Lyndon, in a countdown to the primary on July 24. Lyndon had his work cut out for him. With a jaunty air that belied his trepidation, he announced that with O'Daniel out, "Now we stand one down and one to go."

With scarcely two months to campaign, with his political career in both House and Senate riding on the outcome, with his determination to reach this next rung on the ladder toward the White House—Lyndon was nevertheless off to a less than auspicious start in Austin on May 22. He had his speech writer incorporate the three P's—preparedness, peace, and progress—into his political sermon and, in the process, stole important parts of Stevenson's thunder by railing against government, unions, and civil rights. Lyndon had his fiddle bands warming up the crowd. He had his two "sweethearts," Rebekah on one side and Lady Bird on the other, when, at the right moment, he stepped out on the platform, doffed his Stetson, and sent it sailing into the crowd, announcing, "I throw my hat into the ring." Ramsey Clark, who would one day be Johnson's attorney general, was only a boy at the time. He watched it all in wonder, later calling it "the corniest thing I'd ever seen."

High noon was arriving with the forty-year-old Johnson—described by Senator Paul Douglas as "an intensely ambitious man anxious to get power and hold on to it"—lined up against the fifty-nine-year-old Stevenson, the cowboy who'd taught himself law and who only reluctantly had turned to politics. Here was the man whose word was his bond, whose sterling record was known throughout Texas, pitted against the great equivocator, the man who Rayburn had called "slippery as a hog on ice." Over eleven years in the House, he'd learned to hold his cards close to his chest, to bluff, to call, to fold, and—when necessary and no one was looking—to deal from the bottom of the deck. The bland three P's were his style as he alighted from his helicopter, sometimes as many as twenty times daily, feeding the crowd his fourth P: pablum.

He would not "sling mud," Lyndon promised at the outset, yet as the weeks passed and the enormity of Coke's popularity pressed in on him, he began to renege on his promise and play loose with the truth. "One of my [ten] opponents is *sixty-one*," he would emphasize, though Coke was fifty-nine at the time. But sixty-one sounded like he just wasn't up to the rigors of office in the U.S. Senate. Furthermore, Johnson proclaimed, ". . . I am *not* for the $15,000 *pension* you'd give him if you elected him," that, of course, being a senator's salary. Yes, and Lyndon would sling no mud, but when it came to mimicking Coke, Lyndon was more like Coke than Coke himself. Johnson would borrow a pipe, stick it in his mouth, and regale his audience, "With one eye on the labor bosses in Ft. Worth and one on the millionaires in Houston, he sits and smokes." Then, with hands on hips and pipe clenched between his teeth, he'd swing back and forth as he sputtered, "I'm for state's rights; I'm for state's rights."[13]

But, doubled over in pain from a kidney stone on May 26, two things became evident to Lyndon; Coke, though twenty years his senior, was in far better shape than he was; and there would be no leaking of his condition to the press, this despite campaign manager Connally's insistence they had to let the cat out of the bag. When Lyndon threatened to quit the race altogether if Connally persisted, the campaign manager replied, "Well, you re going to have to withdraw because we're going to release it." With that, Johnson agreed to a trip to the Mayo Clinic—where he spent a week recuperating from surgery, sharing his pain with all and sundry attending him, insisting on hourly news releases assuring his public he was campaigning with no less energy, and working three phones at a time, making as many as sixty-four calls in twenty-four hours. Lyndon was suffering from a pain in his gut, but he'd soon made himself a genuine "pain in the ass," as Connally recounted it.

Back in February, the polls showed Coke leading Lyndon four to one, and in March three to one. Adviser Alvin Wirtz tried consoling him: even if he lost, he'd have gained enough publicity to give him a running start in 1954. "1954!" wailed Johnson, "by 1954 I'll be fifty-five years old!" In reality he'd be forty-six—but then, why should he be a stickler for accuracy when there was more to gain by fudging. And if there was one dish Lyndon could cook, it was fudge. Finally back on the campaign trail, he started dishing it out. Civil rights he castigated as "a farce and a sham," requiring "a police state in the guise of liberty." He, for one, had voted *against* repealing the poll tax, *against* the so-called "lynching bill," *against* the Fair Employment Practices Commission. He would have Texas in his pocket as he sang "Dixie." And yes, he was *against* "socialized medicine," and *against* Truman's deploring the anti-union Taft-Hartley Act. Johnson had not only voted *for* the act, but "with the utmost enthusiasm."

At last, Lyndon was actually saying something. Mounting his white horse, he railed against Stevenson, the "fence-straddler," asking at each stop, "Do you want to vote for a man who wouldn't tell you where he stands?" This from the Congressman who, over eleven years, had carefully cultivated the epithet "Lyin Down Lyndon," the man who avoided like poison committing himself on any issue of importance. Now he found that his resolve against all matters pertaining to big government—especially in its becoming a "police state" to enforce civil rights—was helping him. So was his stand *for* Taft-Hartley, which convinced Texas business interests he was a dyed-in-the-wool conservative

It wasn't these positions alone that won Lyndon the election. Nor was it solely his continued bragging and flaunting of his Silver Star, nor his inimitable mimicking of Stevenson, nor his micromanaging of every aspect of his campaign—even to having aide Warren Woodward walk among the audience and start the applause at a preset time to rouse the crowd, nor the taking of names and addresses of politicians pressing Johnson to do something for them. It was also because Lyndon was flush with special-interest money, thanks to George and Herman Brown and other assorted deep pockets—especially those of oil man Sid Richardson. At the time Johnson was griping about the bargain-basement prices of war surplus plants that could be essential to continuing national defense, he was also arranging for Richardson to buy one of the largest munitions facilities built during the war. It was a huge complex of 447 buildings on 426 acres with 50 miles of pipelines and the capability of producing 45 million pounds of carbon black each year. The price for Richardson: a paltry $4.3 million. But that wasn't all that Johnson did for Richardson. He also proposed that the government designate carbon black a critical defense material and store it at Richardson's new plant. And when the government threatened an antitrust suit for alleged collusion between Richardson's company and the United Carbon Company, who but Johnson stepped in to ward off the suit.[14]

Lyndon was covering all the bases, and John Gunther described one such base when he wrote, "The way to play politics in San Antonio is to buy, or try to buy, the Mexican vote, which is decisive." With at least 10,000 votes for sale in this third-largest city in the state—and more than enough cash to buy them—Lyndon was ready. He'd not stoop to peeling off a $5 bill from a big roll; instead, he would simply buy off the opposition poll watcher for $10 or $20, or the election judge for $50. For that kind of cash they would find it inconvenient to stay after the polling places were closed, at which time the doors would be locked, the ballot boxes opened, and those who'd paid their poll taxes but hadn't voted were added to the count. It is instructive that south of San Antonio, the towns in the Rio Grande valley were populated by illiterate Mexican-Americans with, as historian V.O. Key Jr. has put it, "only the most remote conception of Anglo-American governmental institutions."

Come July 24, the day of the all-important primary in a virtual one-party state, and the scene in such towns was hardly the fulfillment of Jefferson's dream of an educated, responsible electorate. As Key described it, typically a half-breed deputy sheriff armed with a couple of six-shooters, a Winchester rifle and a bandoleer of ammunition slung over his shoulder, would march the voter to the polling place where he'd be handed a folded ballot to drop in the ballot box. Rewarded with a shot of Tequila, he would then be escorted out, where he would touch the hand of "one of the local political bosses or some of his sainted representatives." It was hardly the kind of performance meant to quicken the pulse of the Founding Fathers. But it did win votes, and votes won elections—and Lyndon would win, whatever it took.

Scarcely more noteworthy, but surely more efficient, was the handling of the votes on the big ranches, the prima donna of which was Congressman Kleberg's King Ranch. There the Klebergs could count on the unquestioning loyalty of at least 700 *vaqueros*. The procedure: pay the poll taxes for them and then simply cast their votes for them. Then there were other loopholes, like voting in the names of those who lay, unaware, in cemeteries—or emptying the saloons on the other side of the border and trucking the customers across the Rio Grande.

Where there was a will, there was bound to be a way. And Lyndon Johnson had both the requisite determination and the imagination, shorn of legal niceties, to devise any number of ways of accumulating, say, 25,000 votes from Duval County, ruled by the Parr machine. Big-city bosses across the country wielded no more rigid control over their voters than did George Parr. As one reporter described it: "It is not easy for the average person to imagine what it was like . . . to oppose Boss Parr in his own county. A word from him was sufficient to get a man fired from his job or denied welfare payments or surplus commodities distributed to the needy. Merchants who opposed him faced the sudden loss of most of their trade.

Little farmers and ranchers were intimidated by the *pistoleros*.

It was obvious to Lyndon Johnson that it was important to have Parr on his side if not in his pocket, for he could easily produce 80 percent of the local vote. In his 1940 gubernatorial race, O'Daniel had paid the price and gotten 95 percent of the vote. But come 1944, and Governor Coke Stevenson queered himself with Parr by refusing to appoint Parr's man as district attorney in Laredo. The commanding general of the Air Force base there, with fully half of his men laid up with venereal disease contracted from Parr's prostitutes, had pleaded with Stevenson to deny the position to any man connected with Parr. Even with no war, it made sense; but with the war on, it was his patriotic duty. So Stevenson alienated Parr, leaving Johnson to play this field uncontested.

Lyndon and George were—in the words of Luther Jones, Johnson's former aide and Parr's favorite attorney—"good friends." After all, it was Lyndon who'd won a pardon for George for a tax evasion conviction. So by 1948, Johnson had 25,000 or more Parr votes rung up in his political cash register—votes that would prove crucial come July 24.[15]

On that day, when the votes were counted, Lyndon was losing to Coke 34 percent to 40 percent—with a third candidate, George Peddy, trailing at 20 percent. So Peddy withdrew, leaving the two leaders facing a runoff election on Saturday, August 28. For this do-or-die second primary, Coke campaigned as he always did: refusing to ask people for their votes, relying on his performance as governor to convince the voters that he would make a good U.S. Senator. Driving into a town in an old Ford, he'd give a short, matter-of-fact speech, pointing to his record, then invite questions. Smoking his pipe, he would reflect carefully before giving his best answer, straight from the shoulder with none of the "shimmying" that Sam Johnson begged his son to avoid—and which he had become famous for. No more questions, so Coke would turn to the weather, or crops, or cattle, or simply reminisce. This was the laid-back, you-see-what-you've got, style of Coke Stevenson.

It was in stark contrast to the frenetic, frantic style of the Congressman from the Tenth District who, trailing in the polls, was resorting to long auto caravans, hovering helicopters, bleating PA systems, fiddle band music and—of course—pressing the flesh till his hands turned raw and bled.

Come the day of the runoff August 28, and the Texas Election Bureau was all set to monitor the voting. Trouble was, one Johnson supporter noted, it consisted of a newspaper organization in which reporters obtained their figures from each candidate himself, who would hold back votes to see how many votes his opponent had. By that night, Stevenson was confident he'd won, fair and square. But he hadn't anticipated a challenge from the land of the Parr machine, where votes suddenly seemed to be materializing from everywhere as the tallies were checked.[16] The counting and recounting would drag on for another week.

Sunday, September 5, was not only the Lord's Day, but Lyndon's day, as he went over the top by 162 votes. The next night he declared himself the winner. Yet neither man could truly claim victory until the state convention met and announced the official results. So there was time for Lyndon and the Parr machine to firm up and expand his lead. Suddenly a bloc of about 200 votes materialized from Jim Wells County in southern Texas. Coke immediately smelled a rat and dispatched three young attorneys to the town of Alice in George Parr's fiefdom. Don't wear coats so they can see you're not carrying guns, was Coke's order. Given just five minutes to check the voting list for Precinct 13, the trio discovered that the last 202 names were all in the same handwriting and the same color ink. Furthermore, they discovered that the eleven names they had time to write down were those of people who had never voted. More suspicious yet, one lady who arrived to vote at 6:59—a minute before closing time—testified there was no one else there when she voted, and no one entering when she left. Yet those 202 names appeared after hers on the list.

The three investigators notified the chairman of the county Democratic Executive Committee—an honest man who had somehow slipped into his position when George Parr wasn't paying attention. He was about to omit the 202 names when ruffians burst in, grabbed him "by the scruff of his neck, and marched him right out of there," according to one of the young lawyers.

Coke was furious. With a Texas Ranger in tow, he headed for the town of Alice. The ranger, Frank Hamer, had been responsible for the deaths of Bonnie and Clyde, the two notorious bank robbers who had terrorized the area years earlier. Clearly, Hamer was not a man to be trifled with. When he walked down the main street of Alice and headed for the bank vault where the votes were stored, onlookers parted to let him pass. The bank was surrounded by Parr's henchmen, heavily armed and ordered to block

Coke and Hamer from entering. "Git!" said Frank, and they too fell back. There at the door were other fierce-looking *pistoleros*, who cowed before the fabled lawman and the former Governor. "Fall back!" was Frank's command, and they did just that. The two quickly examined the evidence and left, convinced they had proof that Parr and Johnson, Inc. had tried to steal an election.

Still, the shenanigans weren't over yet. Coke and Hamer had to convince the 58 members of the state Democratic Executive Committee—most appointed by Coke himself—that there was outright fraud, and that Coke's name, not Lyndon's, should appear on the ballot for the general election in November. That should not have been difficult, for here was a former Governor, with a reputation for honesty that Johnson could only dream of, together with a Texas ranger who'd become a legend throughout the Southwest.

But Coke hadn't gauged the power of his opponent, a man who was as unscrupulous as he was loaded—with special-interest money to buy off as many committee members as he needed. As it was, Coke got just half of them to vote for him, so it looked as if it was going to be a tie. Then suddenly a committee member, seized with a heart attack, dropped like a stone. He'd hardly hit the floor when a quick-thinking Johnson aide rushed to his side, scribbled a proxy on the back of an envelope, and had the unfortunate victim sign it. That turned the tide by one vote, 29 to 28, in Johnson's favor. It was a fluke worthy of the man who had ridden the *Heckling Hare* back to safety six years before, while the officer who'd taken his place on the *Wabash Cannonball* flew to his death.

At the state Democratic convention the next day, the recommendation of the Executive Committee was accepted—but not without protest. Supporters of Stevenson converged on the stage and made off with the furniture and equipment that Johnson's men had borrowed—adding machines and typewriters as well as desks, tables, and chairs. Rayburn, sitting there at a table, stood to protest, only to have his chair taken from beneath him. Then someone rolled a barrel out onto the stage and started singing "Roll Out the Barrel," while Johnson's crowd took up the song. After all, it was all good clean fun. Except it wasn't. And Coke Stevenson was not about to let the charade rob him of victory. Immediately he petitioned Federal District Court Judge Whitfield Davidson to issue a temporary restraining order to prevent Johnson's name from appearing on the

November ballot. Convinced that there was a "prima-facie showing of fraud," Davidson granted the injunction and dispatched two investigators to Jim Wells county.[17]

In a further hearing Stevenson's lawyers called for the crucial ballot box from Precinct 13, now securely locked where, a week before, it had not been. Worse, no one could find a key. When a locksmith came and cut the lock, every eye was fixed on that ballot box. The cover was opened and inside they found absolutely nothing. The drama was heightened by the arrival of a telegram bearing an order from Senior Circuit Court Associate Justice Hugo Black to stop the investigation. It appeared this was strictly a state matter and outside the jurisdiction of the federal courts.

Abe Fortas, Johnson's brilliant legal pal, had not only done his homework, but had sprung into action. Davidson had made his ruling on September 21 at Ft. Worth. There was scarcely a month to go before the ballots had to be prepared for November. Fortas figured there'd be no chance to go directly to the Supreme Court from a district court, so he presented a brief summary of events—that was to Johnson's taste—to the Court of Appeals. Then Fortas went to Hugo Black, who just happened to get a call from the White House at the same time. Black subsequently ordered the Secretary of State, as Fortas's associate Paul Porter recalled, "to certify Lyndon Johnson's name as the Democratic nominee." Fortunately for his friend Lyndon, Fortas had the law on his side and, he announced, "It made no difference who Lyndon Johnson was. The law is the law."

If there was anyone in Texas who believed—and preached—that this country must be a country of laws and not of men, of equal justice and not of special privilege and influence-peddling, that man was Coke Stevenson. When, before Davidson's ruling, Lyndon had challenged Coke to a statewide referendum to determine the winner, Coke had refused. Now he was down, but not yet out. In October, two U.S. Senate investigators arrived in Texas with no fewer than fourteen subpoenas. They were bound and determined to get to the bottom of the shenanigans that, by now, had become an open secret across the country. But the gremlins had already done a thorough job, and not only all the ballots but all the records in Boss Parr's territory had suddenly and mysteriously vanished into thin air. The rumor persisted that they'd been burned, and the perpetrators were all in Mexico—on vacation. According to Johnson supporter George Reedy, Coke's fatal mistake was in not going to the highest court in the state, which would have immediately impounded the ballots and records. As it was, "Parr was able to burn the ballots. Nobody could stop him." Did the truth ever come out?

In the fall of 1959, Lyndon was determined that a mail fraud conviction against Parr not jeopardize his chance either for reelection in Texas or his run for the presidency. Suppose Parr were to blow the whistle on Lyndon's 1948 theft of his senatorial seat? So Lyndon sought out the one man who, in the final analysis, had saved his neck in 1948: Abe Fortas. Together with Paul Porter, they appealed Parr's conviction all the way to the U.S. Supreme Court. As the hearing continued, Fortas and Porter described the deliberations, blow by blow, for the nervous Johnson, but always and only through his assistant, Walter Jenkins. Even with that precaution, Johnson was taking no chances; he ordered Jenkins to "burn your memos up on phone calls." This was one of the few orders from "the boss" that Jenkins disobeyed. Again Fortas was successful, Parr and Johnson were both off the hook, and it was all kept quiet.

In 1975, Parr, facing five years in prison and a $14,000 fine for perjury and income tax evasion, put one of the many bullets available to him through his head. But two years later, one of his henchmen, Luis Salas—seventy-six at the time and eager to clear the slate before the Grim Reaper came calling—released the story to the Associated Press. It seems that three days after the 1948 primary runoff, Lyndon had met with Parr, his lawyer, the city commissioner of Alice, and Salas, one of the local election judges. Johnson told the group that he had to have 200 more votes to win, so Parr ordered Salas to come up with them. About three weeks later, on September 29, Lyndon and this same cast of characters boarded Harry Truman's whistle-stop campaign train in Corsicana. There Truman was informed that Lyndon was about to lose the primary election in a court battle. That same afternoon, according to Salas, "Black's telegram ordering a halt to the probe came..." Salas concluded, "That was all it took to give the election to Johnson. A telephone call from Truman to Hugo Black. That's the way it works in party politics."[18]

As tantalizing a story as it was, Salas and the AP reporter, James W. Morgan, couldn't sell it to a book publisher, for it wasn't quite true. Truman's train was not in Texas on September 29, but in Oklahoma. Johnson had boarded the train in Texas on September 26 in San Antonia, not Corsicana. These and further holes were poked in the "deathbed confession" of Salas by an enterprising *New York Times* reporter. Yet for all the holes, one salient fact emerged: Salas actually stole the votes, because the 202 votes were in his handwriting.

Come November and it was Lyndon's name, not Coke's, on the ballot, with just an eighty-seven-vote margin of victory out of almost a million votes cast. Johnson owed much to George Parr And he also owed much to Abe Fortas. Twenty years later, Lyndon returned the kindness by nominating Fortas to the U.S. Supreme Court. The political poker game that Johnson had quickly mastered after coming to Congress in 1937 was called quid pro quo. Its rules were reduced to two: I do you a favor. You reciprocate. How better, then, to continue this symbiotic relationship?

On February 15, 1964, LBJ said to reporter Marshall McNeill, ". . . I don't want to be arrogant. . . ." Yet long before, he'd learned the ropes that would eventually hog-tie his presidency. As late as June 1964, the ghost of George Parr, like the Ghost of Christmas Past, was haunting this modern-day Scrooge. On June 26, Jenkins reported to LBJ that Carl Phinney—Commanding General of the Texas National Guard until 1961 and a close lawyer friend of Johnson's—had learned that the Republican campaign committee was investigating the deal Johnson had made with Parr, while the Republicans themselves had made a deal with Coke to "ship him around the country explaining how he lost the election. . . ." Johnson: "Well, none of it's true."

Lyndon the Arrogant had mastered the art of quid pro quo and arrogated himself riches in office unequaled before or since—with the possible exception of his immediate successor, Richard Nixon. Johnson had arrogated to himself a Silver Star and the honor that medal connoted, never having earned it. Finally, and fatally, he had arrogated to himself such power that, ten years after stealing the election to the Senate, he was widely recognized as second in power only to President Eisenhower himself But justice would not be forever denied, and ten years later, Lyndon would fall on his own political sword, a victim of hubris. Too bad that Lyndon the Arrogant was almost Lyndon the Illiterate. For, had he read and heeded the words of preceding presidents, he might have spared the nation as well as himself untold grief. John Adams had written Thomas Jefferson in 1787 that he was terrified by "elections . . . to offices which are a great object of ambition." Again, in 1796: "Corruption in Elections has heretofore destroyed all Elective Governments." In 1912, Teddy Roosevelt maintained that, "No people is wholly civilized where the distinction is drawn between stealing an office and stealing a purse."[19] Lyndon the Arrogant, it seems, was adept at both—stealing offices as well as purses, and stealing honor as well.

RICHARD NIXON

Politics would be a hell of a business if it weren't for the goddamned people.
— Richard Nixon

The only problem, the major problem [is] our image . . . the language in the first draft [of the Huston Plan] . . . said that I . . . ordered that they [the Plumbers] use any means necessary, including illegal means, to accomplish this goal [of stopping the leaks]. The President of the United States can never admit that.
— Richard Nixon

Cultivating Arrogance

William Fulbright, in his timely and insightful *Arrogance of Power*, emphasized the arrogance of this nation, and particularly Johnson as its President, at the pinnacle of power. It was arrogance that stemmed from unchecked power. What this chapter attempts to do is to show how arrogance is compounded when it is used to attain that power. That is, when Nixon, following Johnson, arrogated to himself power that was not rightfully his—power that by craft, deception, and betrayal he took for himself.

It was one thing for Nixon to arrogate to himself riches while in "public service," as we have seen. It was arrogance of a far more ominous dimension to arrogate to himself the power of a congressman, a senator, a vice-pesident, and finally the ultimate power of the president. This last usurping of power we consider later.

Here we shall concentrate on Nixon's further arrogating of power to himself in seeking and gaining a second term, despite his reneging on his promise to end the war in six months, despite his enlarging the war into Cambodia and Laos, despite his ordering his aides to break into the Brookings Institute to retrieve the Pentagon Papers, despite his ordering—by extension—their break-in of a psychiatrist's office, despite his ordering—again by extension—the break-in at the Watergate, despite his tight-fisted hold on the money he'd raised for his campaign, and despite his ham-handed efforts at covering up the connection of the Watergate burglary to his White House.

It wasn't that Nixon lacked for examples of arrogated power run amok. His idol, Woodrow Wilson, had fired Secretary of State Robert Lansing for presuming to arrogate Wilson's power. Walt Whitman expressed amazement at "the never-ending audacity of elected persons."[1] There were few more audacious with the start of the Cold War than Nixon's "fellow traveler" Joe McCarthy. Presiding over the Senate, Nixon helped Johnson ring down the curtain, in 1954, on the Senator in whom lawyer Joseph N. Welch saw "no sense of decency." Nixon was sufficiently aware of McCarthy's meteoric rise and summary eclipse to take heed, when Ike suffered his near-fatal heart attack in 1955, not to presume to arrogate to himself any of Ike's powers. Whether leading the meetings of the National Security Council or the Cabinet, Nixon was careful not to take Ike's seat. So grateful were Secretary of State John Foster Dulles and other Cabinet members that they gave him a round of applause, probably the only one the Vice-President ever received for deference.

Schlesinger observed there was "no more earnest critic of presidential presumption" than Nixon. That was, *until* he became President. The trouble with Nixon was that by 1968, he'd been long embracing arrogance and had found it—well—bracing. As far back as 1937 he'd found arrogating power to himself akin to the independence he prized. It was just ten days after being admitted to California's bar that he took his first case as a trial lawyer and learned something of the harsh penalty for undue presumption. Standing before the presiding judge, Nixon heard the words, "Mr. Nixon, I have serious doubts whether you have the ethical qualifications to practice law in this state of California. I am seriously thinking of turning this matter over to the Bar Association to have you disbarred." It wasn't simply that this green lawyer was inept. Rather, he had presumed to enter a record showing his client had been satisfied with the judgment of the court when, in fact, she had not. More, he had presumed to order a Los

Angeles marshall to attach the property of the defendant without notifying his own client. Atop that, he'd presumed to put the property up for sale and, without other bidders, went on to buy it. Succumbing to one presumption after another, Nixon put his client in the unenviable position of finding that there were already two mortgages on the property, and that when it was foreclosed and the mortgages paid off, there was nothing left for her.

Nixon was in a peck of trouble. So he filed an affidavit on behalf of his client to try to justify his course of action. The judge was not impressed, and neither was Nixon's law firm, forced to ante up $4,000 to settle the claim of Nixon's client. This was anything but an auspicious beginning for this presumptuous greenhorn in his chosen field of law. Had the judge sought disbarment, had Nixon's law firm fired him—which they probably would have, if the senior partner had not been an old friend of Hannah's—Nixon's career would have been aborted.

By 1946, Nixon was a tenderfoot in the House of Representatives and in need of intervention for committee assignments. Again he was fortunate to have Herman Perry from Whittier in his corner, writing to Speaker Joe Martin. Martin was convinced Nixon must be a clever lawyer, if not an entirely honorable one. In addition, he was a flaming "Red-baiter." So Martin appointed him to the House Un-American Affairs Committee where, chairing a subcommittee, his job was to root out communist subversives in New York.

Ignoring his family and everything of less consequence, Nixon threw himself into the challenge, working feverishly day and night. This bloodhound soon caught the scent of infiltration by Reds— particularly Alger Hiss—into Truman's State Department,. One would hardly have guessed this to be, as Nixon later claimed, "probably the most unpleasant and thankless assignment in Congress" by the gusto with which he pursued Hiss. Or by the way he stood before his congressional colleagues for one and one half hours, claiming he'd worked virtually alone, regaling them with his heroics in "getting" Hiss on the charge of perjury. To be certain others also appreciated his "thankless" work, he sent copies of his speech to newspapers across the country. Others could be forgiven if they saw no hero plodding on in a most "unpleasant" assignment, but a grandstanding politician, lusting for name recognition in preparation for a run for the Senate in 1950. The press tended to the latter view and Nixon complained,

"No one can consistently take strong positions in public life on the issue of Communism, and particularly subversion at home, without expecting to pay the penalty for the rest of his life." As if the press were in cahoots with the Kremlin!

Driven by his lust for power, Nixon alternated roles as super patriot, grand inquisitor, punctilious lawyer, relentless hawk, boastful hero, and whining victim. The common thread among them was an arrogance befitting Machiavelli's Prince, an arrogance that prided itself on an unprincipled pragmatism that refused to embrace any precept but that of galvanizing people with fear—in this case the fear of Communism.

By the time Nixon had disposed of Douglas much as he'd disposed of Voorhis, and taken his seat in the Senate, he was hitting his stride as a Red-baiter, the slightly more civilized brother of Joe McCarthy. Here Eisenhower found the perfect hatchet man, somebody who could relieve the general of the messy battles on the front lines while he directed strategy from the safety of the rear. It wasn't that Ike was especially happy with the choice. He couldn't forget the 1952 embarrassment of his running mate drawing fire for a slush fund. And he couldn't forget Nixon having arrogated his power to choose—and retain—this running mate by appealing over Ike's head to the voters. Neither could he forget Nixon's call for all major candidates to release the financial information he was releasing in his "Checkers" speech. And then, of course, there was the "shit-or-get-off-the-pot" criticism from the lieutenant commander to the five-star general—the last straw.

Eisenhower, the Commanding General of all Allied Forces in Europe in their stunning victory over Hitler's Germany, may have been a neophyte in politics, but he was a veteran when it came to judging people and choosing aides. So he stuck with Nixon, only because abandoning him may have cost him the election. Pressed to the wall, Ike had little choice in 1952. But 1956 was different, and Ike was eager for Nixon to take another job—any job but that of Vice-President. Nixon, he found, had a nasty way of alienating himself from others with his furtiveness, his grimness, his ferocious slashing attacks, his relentless bragging, his maudlin self-pity. He was hardly the man Ike wanted to replace him, whatever his public remarks. So Ike put Nixon off—keeping him at a distance until, hat in hand, Nixon virtually begged to be taken aboard again. Ike told Nixon to announce the decision to the press himself. One slight after another, and

Nixon was counting. But the worst came in 1960, when Ike professed he would need a week to recall some advice from Nixon that he'd taken in promulgating administration policy.

Nixon's arrogance seemed to reach a new height in 1960 when he studiously ignored the advice of Ike as well as campaign aides. Colonel Earl Black, former West Point football coach and a legend in his time, wrote at length to Nixon, warning him that visiting all fifty states, as he promised in his convention acceptance speech, would exhaust him and his staff—leaving him unfit to debate Kennedy on the now-vital medium of television. Nixon took the time to read the caution, to note "Right" in the margin, then to promptly ignore it.[2] With a small army of advisers, aides, secretaries, advance men, speech writers, PR experts and others at his elbow, Nixon proceeded to ignore them all. If familiarity bred contempt, so did arrogance. Then there were friends and supporters, well-wishers and a gaggle of reporters. Amid this crowd, Nixon was, in the words of Stephen Ambrose, "one of the loneliest men in the United States." There was no doubt about it: as deference wore thin, it was replaced by a surly arrogance that could scarcely compete with the confident, jocular, urbane, and deferential Kennedy.

Robert Oppenheimer, head of the Manhattan Project that had developed the A bomb, met with Nixon in the early fifties to try and retrieve the security clearance McCarthy had stripped from him. In the course of the conversation they discussed nuclear weapons, something that Nixon had joined Admiral Radford in recommending be used to relieve the French at Dienbienphu. It was not McCarthy but Nixon who Oppenheimer concluded was "the most dangerous man I have ever met."

Within weeks of his loss to JFK, Nixon was feverishly working on a book to pave the way for his candidacy for governor of California, if not for another presidential run. His life, as Nixon maintained, had been a series of crises, yet nowhere did he pin the blame on his arrogance or any of the other unpleasant traits so many found in him. Always the fault lay in his enemies. *Six Crises* became as patent a self-serving book as any president or vice-president had ever written. Here was this "luck and pluck" Horatio Alger mounting his soap box: *the* lesson of these six crises was to remember that "the period of greatest danger is in neither the preparation, nor the battle itself, but in the immediate aftermath, when the body, mind, and spirit are totally exhausted and there are still problems to deal with."

At the close of his sorrowful 1960 campaign, lost by the thinnest of margins to Kennedy and his enterprising father, Nixon was, in the words of Murray Kempton, "wandering limply and wetly about the American heartland begging votes on the excuse that he had been too poor to have a pony when he was a boy." It seemed to be a repetition of his 1952 "Checkers" speech, reminiscent of Uriah Heep's "Umble as I am, umble as my mother is, and lowly as our poor but honest roof has ever been. . . ." Deprived of a pony as a boy, Nixon would be deprived of the White House in 1960 and again in 1964. Worse, even his home state deprived him of the governorship. But Nixon laid it all out in *Six Crises*: he had learned, as Harry Truman had learned, to stand "the heat in the kitchen." "It might seem," Wills noted, "that the publication of a story of moral growth is not the mark of a 'umble' person but of a boaster. For a man of self-esteem does not spell out the moral justification for each of his acts. He presumes that people will credit him with good intentions." But Nixon, ever the actor, knew—he thought—what played well to his public audience. As Wills put it, Nixon "has gone through most of his career knowing that he is better, brighter, more profound than he lets himself appear."

Many in that public audience may have sensed a vague unease at Nixon's pose, his deprecating himself over and over again, his portraying of the "log-cabin syndrome" of his upbringing, his moral mandate to unearth Communist infiltrators of our government, and his sanctimonious appeals to that public to defend himself against his immoral enemies. Some believed him. The press, for the most part, did not. They had "heard that song before," and it still sounded off-key. Never, however, was it so jangling as when Nixon descended the stairs of his hotel in Los Angeles, having lost the governorship to Pat Brown, the incumbent, there to read the riot act to the press assembled in the lobby. He was leaving politics for good—something he'd promised his wife he'd do for ten years, in vain—and would thereby deprive the press of their favorite target. Alas, he was no more truthful to his word with the reporters than he had been with Pat.[3]

The reason he always gave for reneging on his promises to quit politics was that he was not a quitter. If only others, and especially Pat, would understand that the victory goes to the one who wants it the most, strives the hardest, and prevails the longest. If there was one asset Nixon prided himself on, it was his resilience, his staying power, his ability to pick himself up off the ground—as he had done as the team's football dummy back at Whittier College for four years—and get set for the next punishing blow. Here was a masochist who was proud of it! When reporters queried him in the spring of 1968 about his reaction to LBJ's bowing out of the race, Nixon recalled that Rockefeller and Romney had both thrown in the sponge and quipped, "This is the year of the dropouts."

Kept at a respectful distance by Eisenhower; knocked down by Kennedy, then by Brown, then by Republicans who refused to see him as the dark horse in 1964; pummeled by the Democrats as well as by the press—Nixon would keep coming back for more. If there was, as the Good Book had taught him as a boy, such a thing as an unpardonable sin, that would be quitting. His mantra: "You're never defeated until you quit." "Chief" Newman's words were emblazoned on his forehead.

By June 1968, it was apparent this phoenix was again rising from the ashes of defeat, determined to arrogate to himself the brass ring that had eluded his grasp for eight years. His new address, he would make certain, would not be in Rockefeller's building on Fifth Avenue in New York, there to be ignored for five years by the Governor. He would reside at 1600 Pennsylvania Avenue in Washington, there at the pinnacle of international power. Yet to Cabinet member Arthur Burns he confided that he'd probably be a one-term President. Why? Because he would have done so many "unpopular things." In addition, he would simply be too exhausted to run for a second term.

Why on earth, one is tempted to ask, did the Republicans, who wanted nothing to do with Nixon in 1964, settle for this three-time loser? Few put it as graphically as did Wills: "The Party had not undergone any great internal convulsion. It had simply caved, sifted and crumbled in upon its center, and the name in the resulting sand pile was Nixon."[4]

The Arrogance of Presidential Presumption

No sooner did Nixon hear the vote count assuring his victory in November than he began preparing for his reelection. The first order of business had to be the war, specifically the timing of the war's end to coincide with his reelection. There would be nothing he could do to guarantee that reelection as surely as bringing the disastrous war to a successful conclusion of "peace with honor." Timing was of the essence. Forget the six-month deadline he'd imposed upon himself in the heat of the campaign. Voters had a notoriously short memory anyway. Jonathan Schell was generous in writing that Nixon would not "subordinate the cause of human survival to the cause of personal political survival. Rather, he appeared to have decided that the two causes were one."

That may be. It is certain, however, that Nixon was out of character in making the promise in the first place. Theodore White found that Nixon had become so adept at ad-libbing that it was futile to try "to pin him down to a major policy statement." Moving into the presidency, he was determined to control everybody and everything within his reach. What he couldn't control directly he controlled through aides, whose only redeeming characteristic appeared to be their unquestioning loyalty. His wish was their command. His preening, narcissistic arrogance manifested itself in countless ways, yet seldom if ever aroused his White House aides to protest.

Once he'd made himself comfortable at 1600 Pennsylvania Avenue, Nixon proceeded, as he'd done in his 1960 campaign, to ignore his Cabinet, the Congress, the Court, and the press, all those checks on his power that had been safeguarded by the Constitution. It didn't seem to matter that he'd made it by the skin of his teeth. Or that, as Joe McGinniss went to lengths to point out, that he'd been prepackaged to appeal to the voters just like Madison Avenue prepackaged cigarettes to appeal to consumer tastes. It didn't seem to matter that Nixon had tailored one promise after another to various groups, with little intention, if any, of following through with them. Nor did it matter that, with the help of Kissinger in Paris feeding him supposedly secret information on the progress of Johnson's peace talks, he was able to appeal to South Vietnam's President Thieu to toss a monkey-wrench into them by refusing to participate, reneging on his earlier promise to Johnson.

The point was, he'd been riding the political carousel for sixteen years, eight of which he'd been within inches of the brass ring, and now he'd finally grasped it. He at last had arrogated to himself power undreamed of by previous presidents or world rulers. It was a moment to savor. Assurance gave way to confidence, and confidence to cockiness, next door to the wanton pride usually associated with arrogance.

Nixon had concluded his morality play, *Six Crises*, six years earlier by noting that he didn't know what the future held for him. At the same time,

"... whatever happens, I shall have no regrets about the past." To suffer regrets would seem to imply he'd made mistakes, something his burnished persona would not tolerate. Would he also shake the Washington dust off his feet, six years later, as he boarded the helicopter on the South Lawn, a deposed ruler headed for San Clemente to lick his wounds? Wouldn't he then admit to mistakes? Did he ever? Well, yes and no. In the spring of 1972, escalating the war by bombing Hanoi and mining the harbor at Haiphong, he concluded he'd made mistakes. Yet, truth be told, they weren't really *his* mistakes for "the only real mistakes I've made were times when I didn't follow my own instincts." In other words, when he heeded the advice of others. Was it Shakespeare who wrote, "The abuse of greatness is when it disjoins remorse from power"?

The moot question, of course, is where did Nixon get his own instincts? Perhaps some emerged in the battle between the memory of his gentle but austere mother and the memory of his mercurial but boisterous father. Or was it the clash of genes he'd inherited from both? Were his instincts, on the other hand, drawn from role models as diverse as his football coach, "Chief" Newman, and Woodrow Wilson, the predestined Presbyterian? It did seem that many of his decisions, if not his "instincts" were drawn from his intimate circle of friends: Kendall, Abplanalp, Rebozo—especially Rebozo. Discussing the invasion of Cambodia in April 1970, Nixon found Rogers, his Secretary of State, in sharp disagreement with Laird, his Secretary of Defense, leaving Nixon up in the air. So to Bebe he went. Over drinks he learned that this former Cuban cigar manufacturer who'd made it big through the same luck and pluck that Nixon had relied on, was for the invasion. Still, Nixon wasn't fully convinced, so he took to his pool where—doing laps with Kissinger walking alongside—he declared he wanted a "big play." He would go "for all the marbles" since whatever he did, he expected "a hell of an uproar at home."[5]

For all the tough talk—the badge of machismo for this renegade Quaker—he still wasn't certain, and neither was his goad to manhood, Kissinger. So Nixon decided a change of scenery was in order, hustled Rebozo and Kissinger aboard his presidential yacht, *Sequoia*, and added old friend Mitchell. There, over a sumptuous roast beef meal, they imbibed freely, lest pesky inhibitions subvert their stiffening resolve. Returning to the White House, Nixon served up yet another course: *Patton*, starring George C. Scott, by this time a staple in Nixon's motivational diet. That did the trick. Within hours, Nixon, Mitchell in tow, met with Rogers and Laird. Having hearkened to his "instincts," his mind made up, he would hear no more discussion of it. Cambodia was a go.

The next day the wire services carried the news. The United States had invaded Cambodia, touching off a firestorm of protest, especially among college students dismayed at Nixon's widening rather than ending the war. Would their numbers soon be coming up in the draft lottery? Did they wish to offer themselves as a supreme sacrifice for a war in which they had no say, no confidence?

Demonstrations broke out on campuses across the country, but none with the repercussions experienced at Kent State in Ohio. In a hail of fire, four students—two of them innocent bystanders—were shot dead by National Guardsmen summoned by Governor James Rhodes to "eradicate the problem" of campus unrest. These dissidents, who'd earlier burned the ROTC building to the ground, were "worse than Brown Shirts," Rhodes declared, referring to Hitler's youth organization. Eleven other students were wounded in what had been a peaceful demonstration. Nixon, never at a loss for words, called a spade a spade that evening on network TV, warning, "This should remind us all once again that when dissent turns to violence, it invites tragedy."

The next day Nixon really said what he had in mind, this time to a sympathetic audience—where?—at the Pentagon itself. These demonstrators were nothing but "bums . . . blowing up the campuses . . . burning up the books, storming around the issue" in stark contrast to the forsaken GI's slogging through the rice paddies and jungle swamps of Vietnam, "kids who are just doing their duty . . . stand[ing] tall and proud. . . ." That was language the military could understand and appreciate—especially if they were safely ensconced in the world's largest building, devoted solely to the military—and far from the increasingly disillusioned, fragging, and drug-addicted GI's in Vietnam—and now Cambodia.

Though virtually all of the demonstrations on the one hundred college and university campuses were peaceful, Nixon saw the protesters as perpetrators of violence, as hoodlums who refused to see that they were "the luckiest people in the world, going to the greatest universities. . . ." Trouble was, they wanted to stay on the campuses and not be shipped off to some God-forsaken sinkhole on the other side of the earth.

In the aftermath of the massacre, some thirty-seven college and university presidents signed a letter to the President, warning that he was alienating himself and his administration from America's youth, and requesting an urgent meeting with him. So Nixon trotted out advisers John Ehrlichman and Daniel Patrick Moynihan to a news conference, there to brand the request presumptuous and arrogant. Agnew, the hatchet man that Nixon had been for Eisenhower, had choice words to say about this "predictable and avoidable" tragedy. It emphasized "the grave dangers which accompany the new politics of violence and confrontation." Reduced to their essentials, these lame explanations were simply saying, "These bums got just what they deserved." In his *Memoirs*, written years later, Nixon papered over these crass, in-your-face, warnings. He'd been "haunted" by the photos of the dead students and the reactions of their classmates. He'd written "personal letters" to the grieving parents, "even though I knew that words"—especially Nixon's words—"could not help." And he "felt utterly dejected when I read that the father of one of the dead girls had told a reporter, 'my child was not a bum.' " What Nixon did not tell those parents, or the press, or the nation, was his less-than-illustrious method of arriving at that decision to invade Cambodia, bowing inevitably to his "instincts." Kissinger, one of the principals, shortly received a letter from his Harvard colleagues demanding that he resign. Told of this, Nixon's answer was short, pointed, and scriptural: "Henry, remember Lot's wife. Never turn back. Don't waste time rehashing things we can't do anything about."

It boggles the mind to wonder at the decision-making of this most powerful of presidents. One such decision, more ludicrous than most, was Nixon's decision to clothe his White House police in garb befitting his imperial presence. Away went the drab blue; in its place was glistening white, with ample gold braid and topped off with pillbox hats. Even Washington himself had scoffed at the idea proposed by colleagues that he be addressed "Your Majesty," thereby to compete with England's king. "Mr. President" would do, thank you. But this was a new President for a new day, this thirty-seventh, and he would be paid the honor due him!

The press enjoyed a field day. The *Buffalo Evening News* ventured that "even ushers at old-time movie palaces were garbed with greater restraint and better taste." Nixon—of course—was furious and ordered Haldeman to inform the staff that they were to bow to "RN's position on this *regardless* of their own views. . . ." Before long, however, public pressure forced

Nixon to back down, to store the costumes in mothballs and restore the police to their navy blues. Like Hollywood funny man Rodney Dangerfield, Nixon just couldn't seem to get "the respect" he felt he deserved. Back in his first inaugural address, Nixon had let drop something like "greatness comes in simple trappings," very possibly Ray Price's words and therefore easily forgotten.[6] The film shown at the 1968 convention had been carefully scripted to show Nixon as one of Norman Rockwell's homey stock, an ordinary American just like all the other Americans he wanted to vote for him. Would Joe and Molly Six-Pack, Main Street rather than Wall Street Americans, buy the package? They seemed to, at least enough of them to edge out Humphrey. But four years later, they may have been forgiven some regrets. By 1972, many were convinced that here was no "Poor Richard," care of Ben Franklin; and no "Richard the Lion-Hearted," after England's twelfth century Richard I; but rather the same old "Tricky Dick" from the barbed tongue of Helen Gahagan Douglas; or just plain "Dick the Arrogant." Here was the one who, when push came to shove, could shove as hard or harder than any of his predecessors—and keep on shoving.

The one enemy who could and would shove right back was the press. In Nixon's choice words, Marvin Kalb, Dan Rather, Joseph Kraft, and other journalists were simply "press pricks" who deserved to be ignored. So rather than hold press conferences with the give-and-take so necessary to an informed public, Nixon ran an end-run around them and took to television with a script prepared by others, which he simply had to read with some semblance of conviction, and with no embarrassing questions. When the indignant press weighed in with less-than-rave notices of the President's behavior, he raged at them and ordered them put on his official enemies list—to be hounded by the FCC, the IRS, and the FBI.

Determined to make it on his own in the 1972 election, Nixon needed neither the Republican National Committee nor its chairman, Senator Bob Dole. Though Dole respected Nixon, the feeling was scarcely reciprocated. When Dole called repeatedly for an appointment with Nixon, he was shunted off to some second-string assistant. "Hey, Bob," the assistant put it, "do you still want to see the President?" Dole: "When?" Answer: "Tune in on channel 9; he's coming on the tube in ten minutes."

When, at last, Nixon was able to replace Dole as chairman, he found a successor in George Bush, whom he had met in 1952 when Bush organized a reception for the vice-presidential candidate in Midland, Texas. Twenty years later—despite the disapproval of America's deepening involvement in Vietnam by his father, former Senator Prescott Bush—George Bush sided with Nixon. Needing another voice in the Senate to help parry the thrusts of Senate Democrats, Nixon urged Bush to run for the Senate seat from Texas, promising him "every form of help" if he lost—which he did. But instead of a major Cabinet position or even the vice-presidency in 1972—possibilities Nixon dangled before Bush—he offered him the UN Ambassadorship, and that only after several others, including Moynihan, turned him down. Safely reelected, Nixon then offered Bush the thankless job of chairman of the RNC, just in time to go to bat for Nixon during the spreading scandal of Watergate that had become, as John Dean put it to Nixon on March 21, 1973, "a cancer within—close to the Presidency." Reluctantly, Bush accepted the post, and even more reluctantly asserted Nixon's innocence in the face of mounting evidence that Nixon had perpetrated "crimes and misdemeanors" that were leading to his certain impeachment. At last, on August 7, 1974, Bush wrote Nixon, urging him to resign for the good of the country. This Nixon labeled not simply as treachery, but "candy ass" treachery, coming as it did from a "weakling and a wimp."

This brings us to the most execrable and most unforgivable aspect of Nixon's arrogance: his extending and enlarging the war for another four years after his inauguration in 1969, then desperately trying to time its conclusion with his reelection so that he could properly be labeled as the great peacemaker. Not only did more than 25,000 GI's die for this highhanded prolongation of a conflict he'd resolved in his 1968 campaign to end in a matter of months, or resign. It also cost more than a million lives of Vietnamese, North and South, and of Cambodians and Laotians as well. In addition, the four years took a frightful toll—several times the number of those killed—on the wounded, most of whom were civilians, and the majority of whom were women and children. Repeatedly Nixon, like Johnson, vowed he'd not be the first American President to lose a war. That he did lose is proof enough of the futility of gaining "peace with honor," the spin he put on the war's ending in January 1973.[7]

One of the many reasons for Nixon's vainglorious handling of the war was his insistence on making foreign-policy decisions out of his vest pocket, usually with nobody but Kissinger privy to them. Having embraced the war as his own, Nixon found Fulbright warning him that his policy of "messianic globalism," as Schlesinger called it, was fraught with danger. America was courting disaster, Fulbright maintained, by insisting it could and would do what Wilson, then FDR, had instead planned to do through a world organization. The United States was usurping the power it had helped delegate to the UN. American global hegemony, Fulbright warned, "could only lead to endless foreign exertions, chronic warfare, burgeoning expense, and the militarization of America." This was just the specter that haunted Eisenhower in his farewell address in 1961, when he inveighed against the entrenched power of the "military-industrial complex."

By 1969 and Nixon in the White House, Fulbright was clearly worried. "Whatever lip service might be paid to traditional forms," he warned the Senate, "our government [will] soon become what it is already a long way toward becoming, an elective dictatorship," dedicated at home and abroad to the military-industrial establishment. "If, in short," he concluded, "America is to become an empire, there is very little chance that it can avoid becoming a virtual dictatorship as well."

Fulbright had ample cause for alarm. Kevin Phillips, a Mitchell aide, mounted the barricades at the White House to lob verbal grenades at the Hill. In *Newsweek*, he wrote that the current system of checks and balances was "obsolete." What the country needed, he proposed, was a "fusion of powers" to replace the constitutional separation of powers, because "the separation of powers [may be] doing more harm than good by distorting the logical evolution of technology in government." In the *New Republic*, he lobbed another grenade: "President Nixon treats Congress with contempt which . . . is richly deserved." Indeed, he continued, "our biggest problem is whether Congress can be salvaged, because if it can't, our particular 18th century form of government, with its separation of powers, can't be salvaged." Worse, where there should be something, there is nothing, and "a vacuum has to be filled. The authority of Congress has decayed till it is overripe and rotten. Mr. Nixon has merely proclaimed it."[8]

Unfortunately, it was a domestic affair that was to ring down the curtain on Nixon's presidential presumption. And neither Ehrlichman in domestic affairs, nor Kissinger in foreign affairs, nor Haldeman standing guard at the entrance to the inner sanctum, nor any of the rest of Nixon's aides or hired lawyers, could keep the roiling waters of Watergate from inundating the White House.

The Arrogance of Watergate

Nixon was, in the eyes of his aides, what LBJ called a "water walker." By the summer of 1972, there were the White House aides, rushing to and fro, jabbing their fingers in the holes of the leaking dike Nixon was desperately trying to build around Watergate. Wrote Haldeman, ". . . I believed Nixon could accomplish anything . . . nothing could hurt him now [after his Peking and Moscow summits]." Dean was just as certain: "I had faith that the President would overcome the Watergate scandal by his infinite power and wisdom." For good reason, then, did Theodore White note with alarm, "It was as if, intoxicated by the power of the White House, they truly believed that they could circumvent what had taken 200 years of American civilization to build. They could not imagine that to use the powers of office to erase the crime would wipe out all that Nixon had really accomplished."

Just as Johnson had belittled "the little yellow men in black pajamas" opposing the unprecedented firepower of the world's greatest military force, Nixon viewed the Watergate break-in with the disdain that he'd carefully nurtured through twenty-six years of political arrogance. He dismissed the burglary as "a joke," "a caper," or "a little trick and treat," performed by "a few pipsqueaks," or "some jackasses." Before long it became successively "a stupid thing," a jackass operation," " a silly-ass damn thing," "a goddamn thing," "a goddamn escapade," or "a son-of-a-bitch of a thing." However others may look at it, especially those Democrats who were suing the Republican Party for a cool $1 million, Nixon clung to the certainty that it was "no crime!" The most he would concede was that it was "a third-rate burglary attempt," and "a can of worms."

By the time Dean was assuring him the containment of Watergate was working so well that he had nothing to fear in the election five weeks later, Nixon was feeling his oats and declaring it part of a "war" between Democrats and Republicans. But having announced the dismissal of his two top aides on April 30, 1973, Nixon's mood was turning foul as he struggled with a torn conscience. Now the break-in and the cover-up were "chicken shit," "a crappy business," and "a horse's ass crap." But there was the press, "comparing it with the Teapot Dome, for Christ's sake, which was thievery on a massive basis!" For his part Nixon had sense enough to realize it was all just a "PR game." It may be a "PR problem," but still it was all just "PR."

If there was anything in the life of this refugee from Whittier that illustrated dramatically the danger of unchecked arrogance, it was his blundering into Watergate, then exerting frenetic efforts to conceal its connection to his administration.

Dean was right when, on September 15, 1972, he assured the President he'd done his job of covering up so well "that 54 days from now that not a thing will come crashing down to our, our surprise." Indeed, so vital was this that on March 21, 1973, Dean reminded Nixon that there had been "no price too high to pay to let this thing blow up in front of the election."[9] There was scarcely a Watergate ripple in the press when Election Day dawned in November. By November 1, Nixon was so confident of a landslide victory that he told Ehrlichman that *The Washington Post*, with its continual nosing into the Watergate mess, was "finished." Furthermore, "There ain't going to be no forgetting, and there'll be goddamned little forgiving. . . ."

Back in 1968, Nixon had done his best to reorganize the executive branch by placing power precisely where he thought it should be centered—in the Oval Office. Now, in 1972, he again tried to enlarge his power by ridding himself of those whose loyalty to him was less than wholehearted. To that end, his landslide victory assured, he demanded that the top 2,000 of those in the executive branch submit their resignations. Forty of those he interviewed, one-on-one, at Camp David. He would tolerate no slackers, no aides with less than one hundred percent loyalty to *the President*. Only later did Nixon realize the "chilling effect," as he put it, "this action would have on the morale of the people who had worked so hard during the election and who were naturally expecting a chance to savor the tremendous victory instead of suddenly having to worry about keeping their jobs." As it was, instead of savoring his resounding victory on election night, Nixon confessed he was "at a loss to explain the melancholy that settled over me." "Was it Watergate? Was it his "failure to win Congress?" Was it his failure "to end the war in Vietnam?" Was it that "this would be my last campaign?" Always, everywhere, it was Nixon the introvert, Nixon the arrogant, Nixon the egomaniac. Chances are he was so wrapped up in trying to end the war, cover up Watergate, and assure his honorable place in the history books, that he scarcely gave a thought to the 2,000 who Haldeman ordered to submit their resignations.

When—four days after the Watergate burglary—on June 21, 1972, Nixon first started his cover-up, he suggested that one of the Watergate plotters, G. Gordon Liddy, confess. Then the President would appeal for compassion on the grounds that Liddy was "a poor misguided kid who read too many spy novels." After all, reasoned Nixon, "if he and the Cubans entered guilty pleas [three Cuban-Americans had been part of the burglary team] they'd get only fines and suspended sentences [as] first offenders." In addition, Nixon was confident that the reaction to Watergate "is going to be primarily Washington and not the country because I think the country doesn't give much of a shit about it. . . ."

But less than a week later, Haldeman had his eye on Mitchell as the next one to walk the plank. Nixon protested, "I won't do that to him. I'd rather, shit, lose the election." By June 29, Mitchell appeared ready to fall on his sword, surely the good soldier. For not only did he tender his resignation as head of CREEP, but added, ". . . nothing is more important to the future of our country than your reelection as President." There, that should stiffen Nixon's spine just in case he started to weaken in sacrificing the crew to save the captain. Come July 8, Nixon told Ehrlichman that they should throw in E. Howard Hunt, head of the White House "heavy operations team," and CREEP's deputy director, Jeb Magruder, to sweeten the pot of Liddy and the five burglars; then Nixon could grant clemency to all eight. On July 19, Ehrlichman agreed that Magruder should be offered up as a sacrifice, "to take a slide. . . ."

By this time, Nixon was getting so worried that he slammed Democratic presidential candidate George McGovern for his obvious "lack of character" in dumping Senator Tom Eagleton from the national ticket for having visited a psychiatrist to treat a "nervous breakdown." At the same time Mr. Hypocrisy himself was considering who should be next to walk the plank. Would it be the President's special counsel, Chuck Colson, the "lightning rod for criticism"—or Dwight Chapin, Nixon's appointments secretary who'd let "political espionage" coordinator Donald Segretti's "pranksterism [get] out of hand?" By the following spring, it was obvious that Haldeman and Ehrlichman themselves were not indispensable. Yes, they were "great men, fine men trying to do what was right." In fact, they were "two of the finest public servants it has been my privilege to know." Furthermore, Nixon would have speech writer Ray Price know that this President always suffered from a peculiar "weakness," namely, "I'm one of the few men in Washington that never blames the secretary when the poor damned secretary misspelled a word . . . I'm responsible." With that, Nixon announced on network television the "resignation" of the two men who'd made life miserable for others on the White House staff. Few could sympathize with Nixon's lament, ". . . from that day on the presidency lost all joy for me."[10]

There was Rogers, in response to Nixon's call, telling him, "Gee, that was terrific, really superb." This was surely appropriate, coming from the Secretary of State who, just the day before, was castigating them for their reluctance to "resign": "They can't perform their duties now, for Christ's sakes. The whole government is at a standstill because these guys are reluctant." Continuing his fishing expedition for surcease from what remained of a conscience, Nixon called friend Hobart Lewis, who called it ". . . a tremendous job. . . . The best job you've ever done." Next the president checked in with Colson, just before midnight, to make sure he understood his marching orders. No, Colson wasn't about to rock the boat by testifying before Ervin's committee: "I don't intend to talk about it . . . I don't think they can make me because . . . it's a national security operation. . . ." Nixon breathed a sigh of relief and reminded him, "You just say . . . we were protecting the security of this country," then pronounced the benediction, ". . . God bless you and keep your faith, boy." The Almighty may have forgiven Himself if He refused to bless either Colson or Nixon, for if there was a heaven, the stench of all that was going on in Nixon's White House must have reached that lofty abode and made even the angels weep.

Back on February 3, Nixon had been in a tirade. It seems that the presiding judge at the trial of the Watergate burglars, John Sirica, was not only a Republican, but had been in the trenches in 1952, supporting the Eisenhower-Nixon ticket. If there was anybody on God's green earth who ought to be making the "right" decisions, it was this son of Italian immigrants who, like Nixon himself, had managed to pull himself up by his own bootstraps. There was the jury convicting Liddy and burglar James McCord. There was Hunt, pleading guilty to six counts and insisting it all stop with him; no higher-ups had been involved, and certainly not the White House. There were the Cuban burglars, also pleading guilty. Yet despite his credentials, there was Sirica, pretending he smelled a rat in the woodpile, holding all seven until a bond hearing, determined to get at "the truth." Nixon was predictably furious as he castigated this turncoat Republican before favorite stormtrooper Colson. Sirica's "Goddamn conduct" was truly "shocking." Finally, thoroughly exasperated that his aides weren't doing enough to keep the tawdry business of Watergate from the White House and its President, Nixon exploded with something less than a benediction: "For God's Christ, why doesn't somebody get into this thing?!"

It seems that somebody was about to "get into this thing," because the Senate had appointed Sam Ervin to head a Select Committee on Presidential Campaign Activities, focusing primarily on Watergate. Astoundingly, this was done by a unanimous vote, 77 to 0, showing Nixon's chickens were coming home to roost—for, among so many other slights, he had been positively niggardly in doling out to fellow Republicans running for Congress even a fraction of the $60 million that CREEP had succeeded in shaking loose from the Republican money tree. Immediately Nixon swung into action, calling a summit meeting of his top aides at his "Western White House" in San Clemente, California. He would hew to his cardinal rule in a crisis: the best defense is always an offense. So they went into a huddle and emerged with a strategy for "hampering, discrediting, and ultimately blocking this investigation."

Nixon figured he had a lot going for him. Here he'd emerged with a landslide victory over McGovern; he'd concluded the war with "peace with honor," bringing home the POW's; he'd held two unprecedented summits in China and the Soviet Union; and he was buoyed by a 68 percent approval rating by the electorate. So when McGovern on January 21 warned that the country was "closer to one-man rule than at any time in its history," Nixon scoffed at this spoilsport who couldn't admit defeat. Then he lambasted Congress and the courts as being "timid and depleted" in contrast to a President who was "active and strong." Nothing, nobody could touch him now.

Recalling Truman's invoking "executive privilege" to forestall Nixon's investigation of Hiss, Nixon decided it was time to use the same pretext to block Congress. Not only would Nixon himself refuse to honor the requests of Congress for evidence—so, ruled Attorney General Richard Kleindienst, would all three million employees of the executive branch!

Nixon would defy any subpoena, and if the senators persisted, then, challenged Nixon, let them impeach him! This clear defiance sent shock waves through Congress, the press, and the nation. Was there no end to Nixon's arrogance?

Like his predecessor, Nixon was determined to project a persona larger than life, a persona that would elicit hosannas from future readers of history books. In his resignation he made certain that Americans would realize how far he'd come from the little four-room, white clapboard house of his youth to the 132-room mansion on Pennsylvania Avenue—a very different white house. They would appreciate, too, the time he'd put in as their President so that he, and only he, could handle foreign affairs on a first-name basis with his international counterparts. Finally, they would be forewarned that our democracy was in grave peril of deteriorating to the British parliamentary system—in which the Prime Minister could be summarily removed when he lost a vote of confidence among the electorate. In a word, the constitutional system of checks and balances was both fragile and obsolete. Thus spoke Nixon.

What was fragile and should have been obsolete was Nixon's inflated ego, a monumental sense of self-importance that expressed itself in a braggadocio matching that of Johnson, and a chronic raging at those who would dare puncture the inflated balloon. Any attempt, especially by the press, to take note of his foibles, to cast him in human dimensions, he met with studied indifference, then with annoyance, and finally with a rage that signaled revenge was in order.

Yet Nixon's arrogance, his consuming fury at those attempting to check his grab for more and more power, had to await his ascendancy to the White House in 1968 and his reelection in 1972—in both cases by theft and deception, however euphemized. One has only to peruse one of a score or more biographies of the man to have his senses assaulted by the repeated, virtually continuous references to Nixon's fury. His chronic distemper plagued him from the time he entered politics in 1946 and put Voorhis in his crosshairs, until he flung his V-for victory arms skyward on boarding the helicopter following his resignation. In all probability, a middle finger would have been more representative of the feelings of the man who, in his consuming arrogance, invariably considered himself better than others—than *all* others.

Despite his pretensions of humility, despite his recurrent emphasis on the presidency being simply "public service," despite his sanctimonious moralizing, and despite his wallowing in self-pity, Nixon in the end was seen at war with himself. The persona he'd tried hard to project was finally stripped from him, revealing an imperious pretender to the throne, one with no honor, no nobility, no scruples—truly a naked man. In one important respect, as Wicker would remind us, Nixon was, in the final analysis, "One of Us." His role, as Walter Lippman emphasized, "has been that of a man who had to liquidate, defuse, deflate the exaggerations of the romantic period of American imperialism and American inflation. Inflation of promises, inflation of hopes, the Great Society, American supremacy—all that had to be deflated because it was all beyond our power."[11]

Arrogance, after all, whether in Nixon or the nation he was both leading and reflecting, did have its limits. As surely as exploitation leads to, as well as partakes of arrogance, so does identification represent a further step on the slippery slope of hubris.

CHAPTER 7

IDENTIFICATION

The powers of the Executive of the U. States are more definite, and better under-stood perhaps than those of almost any other country; and my aim has been, and will continue to be neither to stretch, nor relax from them in any instance what-ever, unless imperious circumstances shd. render the measure indispensable.

— George Washington, July 2, 1794

The danger is that the indulgence and attachments of the people will keep a man in the chair after he becomes a dotard, that reelection through life shall become habitual, and election for life follow that.

— Thomas Jefferson

If you can't keep the two separate, yourself and the presidency, you're in all kinds of trouble.

— Harry S. Truman

LYNDON JOHNSON

For Johnson, the United States is more than a Senate: it is faith, calling, habit, relaxation, devotion, hobby, and love. For him the Senate, with its hallowed traditions, is the most glorious instrument of government known to man. And each facet of its life—its majestic decisions, its sordid little deals, its prickly personalities, its open clashes and back-room intrigue—fascinates him. Over twelve years the Senate has become almost a monomania with him, his private domain, and he confuses the United States Senate with life itself. By the time that the politics of 1960 were coming to a crisis, Lyndon B. Johnson all but believed that the Senate was America and that he was the Senate.

— Theodore White[1]

Symbols and the Self

"That's your helicopter over there, sir," said the junior officer to his commander in chief, watching him head for the wrong plane. "Son," corrected Johnson, "they are *all* my helicopters!"

Here is identification at work. As commander in chief, Johnson presumed not only military equipment but military personnel were his. All of it—all of them—belonged to him personally. Whether introducing Ellsworth Bunker as *his* new ambassador to Saigon, or introducing the new senior commanders as *his* generals, LBJ made sure the South Vietnamese leaders understood that *he*, Lyndon Johnson, was not only in charge but taking it all very personally. For Lyndon laid claim to the war. It was *his* war and only he could manage it, indeed, micromanage it. Brother Sam recounted how, "Almost every morning at three o'clock he [LBJ] would crawl out of bed, often without ever having gone to sleep, wearily slip on his robe and slippers, then go down to the Situation Room . . . to get the latest reports coming from Saigon. . . . Even the loss of one American soldier [*his* soldier] could bring on a mood of sadness and frustrated anger that would keep him awake the rest of the night."

No matter how often he touted his "Pacific tour," or flashed his Silver Star, it was clear that war was a stranger to him. Kennedy, Eisenhower, Truman—all had been personally acquainted with the risks and rigors of battle, while Johnson had attempted to inflate an hour or so of watching others in combat into a crusade in which he was indispensable; a crusade, this time, against Communism.

Johnson was not only "the only president you've got," as he never tired of telling others, but successively saw himself as the presidency, the government, the nation—even the world itself. Occasionally he actually identified himself with these larger entities. More often he implied or declared himself to be indispensable to them, the degree of which was the degree of identification.

All of us engage in a lifelong process of attempting to identify just who we are. We are not simply *Homo sapiens* or thinking man. We are, more than that, *Homo sapiens sapiens*, or man capable of thinking about himself. Or to resort to Descartes, it is not simply, "I think; therefore I am." It is, rather, "I think, and I think about myself; therefore I am." This process of self-awareness, of self-reflection, is most importantly illustrated in self-definition, a symbolic and ongoing process.

There are many ways in which we attempt to identify ourselves at a given time. The most common way is by lineage. We simply give our names, thus connect ourselves with our forebears. Or, we may identify ourselves by place. Thus, to differentiate ourselves from others of the same name in the big-city phone directory, we give our address. Or, we may identify ourselves by vocation. We are computer programmers, or bank clerks, or whatever. Then, too, we may identify ourselves by avocation, as skiers, or stamp collectors, etc. We may go further and identify ourselves not simply by what we do, but by what we possess—whether homes, car, clothes, and so forth. We may define ourselves by structure—by age, sex, race, height, weight. As we have seen, we can identify ourselves by contrast, by differentiating us from others who may or may not resemble us.

And this brings us to comparison by emphasizing similarities with others. Here is one important reason, as Tocqueville emphasized, that we Americans tend to be joiners.

From birth to death we are continually defining and redefining ourselves. In the process, as the word "definition" implies, we draw fences about ourselves, separating what we are—or think we are—from what we are not—or think we are not. In all of this we are engaged in a symbolic exercise, substituting marks on a paper or sounds in the air for what we think we experience.

The word for "symbol" derives from "symbolon," the ancient Greek practice of hospitality. In that case a ring or coin was divided in two, one half retained by the host, the other half given to the guest, but each to recall the experience of hospitality. Recall itself gives way to higher orders of thinking such as imagination, goal-setting, choice, freedom, responsibility, morality, conscience, or remorse. These higher orders all rest on the foundation of symbolization, that process by which we think, that process by which we most importantly differ from other species.[2]

Vanity of Vanities

From the time the growing child learns to speak, he is using his symbols to tell himself and others who he is. Much of this he learns from the verbal—and nonverbal—cues of others. In Lyndon's case, his mother, if not his father, made him understand that he was apart from others, including his siblings. Lyndon would be the fulfillment of Rebekah's hopes and dreams, dashed on the altar of matrimony when she took Sam Johnson as her husband. As Lyndon grew to manhood, she increasingly identified herself with her firstborn. By the time he was a teenager, Lyndon was treating her like a maid, ordering her about, defying her, interrupting her and others with a bossiness accompanied by a vanity that would lead to his identification.

In college Lyndon was self-conscious about his nicknames, "Bull," "Slat," and "Old rattle-and-bones," the latter referring to his having to almost unwind to stand in class. Was he poor? He took extra measures to deny it, dressing carefully in a suit, silk shirt, and bow tie to match. Preparing for a date, a friend recalled, he stood before a mirror, primping like a girl, "patting his hair to make sure the waves were right . . . or scrunching his neck down into his collar to make his face seem fuller." His stint in the Navy only served to heighten his vanity as well as his fantasy. One reporter who knew Johnson before his "milk run" of six-months Navy duty, remarked to Rayburn that after the war, Lyndon seemed changed. Rayburn replied that Lyndon hadn't been the same "since he started buying two hundred dollar suits." By the time he left his uniform to return to Congress—Silver Star shining from his lapel, having distributed photos of himself from Hollywood highlighting his "best side"—vanity had taken over. His persona would reign supreme.

Were it not for his exuberant energy, it might well be said of Johnson as it was of Lafayette, that he was a statue forever in search of a pedestal. For Lafayette's contemporary, Washington, there appeared to be a pedestal even before he died, and a corps of faithful to clean and polish both statue and pedestal for years to come. Indeed, an 1844 biography intended for America's youth, already spoon-fed on the axioms and truisms of *McGuffy's Reader*, went so far as to say, "the first word of infancy should be mother, the second father, and the third [the father of our country] Washington." Washington, of course, had done his best as commander in chief to project a persona no less majestic, no less resolute, no less heroic than what he thought necessary to win the Revolution. That was no small order, given his sparse education, his ramshackle army, his divided country, and his immediate enemy. With victory, he was equally concerned that the presidency of this new nation, with all the wrangling attendant upon democracy as opposed to the relative efficiency of army command, would not tarnish his persona. Indeed, he seemed obsessed "to maintain the dignity of office, without subjecting himself to the imputation of superciliousness or unnecessary reserve." It appears that, 175 years later, Lyndon Johnson had no such worry.

Elected Majority Leader, Johnson was determined to let one and all know just who was in charge. He began by commandeering offices for his Preparedness and Space Committees, then took over the Majority Conference Room on the second floor. This was just the start for the "Maharajah of Texas," as the *Chicago Tribune* dubbed him. For his "Taj Mahal" he needed no less than a seven-room suite across from the Senate floor, renovated by a New York interior decorator who furnished it with royal green and gold. The order of the day was the plushest of carpeting, chandeliers of crystal, and the finest furniture that taxpayer money could buy. Then to remind this dirt-poor boy from the Texas Hill Country just how far he'd come, he made sure that, upon opening the door to his inner sanctum, he (and others) would first see a well-lit, full-length portrait of himself standing next to a Texas-size desk. To further enhance the royal ambiance, he made sure that three elevator operators appeared at the deserted Capitol on Sundays, just in case he took a fancy to appear. In addition, he required operators of the underground railway between the Capitol and the Senate Office Building, who usually quit at 6 P.M., to remain on duty as long as he was there. Peter Hurd—a portrait artist who LBJ summoned to project his best side—disappointed him, and he denounced the picture as "the ugliest thing I ever saw." One is left to speculate how Johnson greeted the face he saw in the mirror each morning.

To be certain that history would not be impoverished in trying to document the record he was determined to make, LBJ not only installed a taping system to record his words, but hired a full-time presidential photographer. Within two months, Yoichi Okamoto had shot virtually every waking moment of the vainglorious President, yielding no less than 11,000 stills. This was not to go unnoticed by his critics, who ridiculed both the vanity and extravagance. So, with his election coming up, Johnson had press secretary Pierre Salinger announce on February 4, 1964, that Okamoto had simply been "on loan" and that his "mission" was now finished. With the election in his pocket, however, Okamoto was back "on loan" to the White House.[3]

Whatever others thought, whether an "accidental" or legitimate President, Johnson had, at long last, arrived at the office for which he'd spent his political life lusting. And he would not be denied—not by the bumptious Bobby Kennedy—not by the sour grapes of defeated Republican presidential candidate Barry Goldwater—not by the holier-than-thou Francis Sayre, Dean of the Episcopal Washington Cathedral, who had denounced LBJ's "private lack of ethic"—and certainly not by the skeptical press. So he ostentatiously emblazoned the presidential seal on everything he could get his hands on: cowboy boots and rancher's jacket, cufflinks and cigarette lighters, even on disposable drinking cups. Had he been able, LBJ would undoubtedly have emblazoned his seal on the foreheads of his aides. Not that he needed to, for the aides were there, above all, because they'd passed the ultimate test: absolute, unquestioning loyalty to the President.

Not content with simple two-dimensional photographs, Johnson posed for a bronze bust, then had scores of copies made, to be dispensed only to those he felt worthy, those convinced this was indeed a prize worth savoring. According to the White House chief of protocol, James Symington, Lyndon had no less than two hundred of the busts made, "a mass-production gesture [that] really boggles the mind." Arriving in Manila in October 1965 for a conference with the leaders of South Vietnam, Australia, and New Zealand, he ordered Symington to get busy and distribute them to all the heads of state and their aides that evening. So up and down the hotel corridors the chief of protocol pushed his big cart, bestowing on one and all the likeness of America's leader. Years later Symington acknowledged, "Today there are heads of state all over Asia who are trying to decide what to do with the President's bust." In Seoul, South Korea, a year later, the commander in chief presented to the GIs a grand token of his appreciation for their valiant efforts in holding the line between North and South: yet another bust of himself. Surely they would treasure this monument of their illustrious commander in chief. Or would they? There is some evidence that they were underwhelmed. This trip to the Southwest Pacific was memorable if for no other reason than that it reminded LBJ of the salad days of his World War II service, for which MacArthur had justly awarded him the Silver Star. In addition, the trip offered sanctuary from the increasingly hostile chorus of voices back home, led by Richard Nixon, William Fulbright, and Robert Kennedy.

What Johnson increasingly craved—because he was getting less and less of it by 1966—was favorable publicity. He took all he could get, and then some. But when it turned sour, he always found a whipping boy on his staff. When Califano made the mistake of releasing information about welfare—in a speech that LBJ had approved—Johnson was merciless. There he saw not *his* picture splashed in newspapers and on TV across the nation, but an aide's. So furious was the President that he refused to release photos of himself with Califano, and ordered his underling to release none of the photos he'd already given him.

There, in the Southwest Pacific, Johnson not only bequeathed his bronze bust to GI's stationed in Korea, but showered upon his hosts in New Zealand and Australia a veritable cornucopia of personalized mementos. That was the least he could do for the turnouts, as crowds pressed forward to catch a glimpse, and perhaps a handshake from the mighty one, the first U.S. President to make such a visit. As the crowd at the New Zealand airport surged forward, Johnson, instead of calling for increased Secret Service protection, called for a CBS camera to record this auspicious and well-deserved moment for Americans' consumption. Having drunk deep of the witches' brew concocted by his detractors at home, here in New Zealand he relished the moment. Waving jauntily to the throng before him, beaming from ear to ear, LBJ put it to a photographer, "Ever see crowds like this before?" He hadn't. So Johnson made an all-too-accurate prediction, at least as far as U.S. crowds were concerned: "You never will again." One lady, feeling herself luckier than the rest, greeted the President with, "You're doing a helluva job!" Apparently referring to his escalation in Vietnam, this was no indication of the increasing disillusionment gripping his homeland. A man in the crowd sized up Johnson as though he were a Texas longhorn on the beef market, "The best hunk of flesh that's ever been to New Zealand!"

The visit was capped with a formal reception in which the governor-general raised his glass in a toast: "The President is not tired. He is supernatural!" To which the assembled guests responded, "Hear! Hear!" This was sweet music indeed to the big ears of a Texas maverick who'd felt the lash of the bullwhip of criticism at home. Of course, there would be spoilsports in the cynical press—there, as in the United States. One reporter groused, "He walks in a happy, loose-shouldered way, winks and grins at starched dignitaries, lunges and chews, and drawls as he says, 'Good to see ya! Glad to be among ya! All that's missing is the horse." As the encomiums washed over this weary traveler like a soothing balm, LBJ must have wondered why so many Americans were blind to what was so obvious to these New Zealanders.

On to Australia and bigger crowds, where, like a college cheerleader, Johnson launched into "Hurray for Australia! A is for America. A is for Australia. Long live AA!" The crowds roared their approval. Lyndon was in seventh heaven. Here was a heaven he'd come to miss in America, of crowds hanging on his every word, drawl or no drawl, and in no obvious need of a horse. When his comments reverted to almost a quarter-century earlier, standing shoulder to shoulder with the Aussies against the encroaching Japanese, he didn't let any penchant for accuracy stand in his way. The prime minister boasted, "He's the biggest fish I ever speared!" Johnson beamed.

That he himself was invariably the focus of his thoughts became increasingly evident to Hugh Sidey, a reporter accompanying him. In Manila, LBJ held a news conference during which he mentioned his favorite person eleven times in the first few minutes. This prompted Sidey to note, "One of those minor tragedies in the makeup of LBJ. . . . He just does not become engaged with the people he meets. He does not respond to their overtures, does not pick up opportunities to endear himself . . . his mind is on Johnson . . . his interest is personal, not in the culture. Johnson is too determined that he is going to prove that he is loved. Because of this intensity, he sometimes misses the very best chances for the things he wants most."

Part of Johnson's vanity manifested itself in his identifying power with love. In Malaysia, a mother cautioned her child as they stood to welcome Johnson, "You watch. You are about to see the most powerful man in the world. You will never forget this moment." Here was power acknowledged, but no hint of affection. Each vote cast for him in 1964's overwhelming mandate he interpreted as a valentine, not—surely—as the choice of the lesser of two evils. Whether power brought love depended on whether Lyndon hewed to Rebekah's admonition to the adolescent: that the only reason to accumulate power was to do good for people. By 1966, however, Johnson was so obsessed with his persona, with his place in history, that he had little time or inclination to care about others. He may not have agreed with the writer of Ecclesiastes that "All is vanity." And he certainly would remonstrate with those like Sidey who were seeing in him an obsessive vanity. But by now, Johnson's personal plate was so full that he was no longer thinking clearly.[4]

In Seoul, Johnson basked in what he considered the unfettered admiration of no less than two million people whom President Chung Hee Park had managed to shoehorn out of their homes and into the public square, myriad tokens of appreciation for American largesse and "Keeping the Commies at bay in Vietnam." To show there was simply no limit to Johnson's pretensions, Sidey noted that LBJ had gotten to the point where he simply would not—could not—change. One definition of divinity is "one who changes not." If, after all, you have arrived at perfection, how can change possibly represent improvement? To be on the safe side, if not on the side of divinity, Lyndon was proving to himself that he was omniscient. Robert Young's TV series, *Father Knows Best*, was but prelude to the real father: Lyndon Baines Johnson, who knew best for Americans as well as the rest of the world. LBJ was omnipresent, flying everywhere and anywhere with a mighty entourage, while those back home could observe every move on their TV screens even as it was happening. And, of course, LBJ was omnipotent. What was there he could not do? To those who pointed to the war in Vietnam, he simply pointed out that his nuclear arsenal could spare a few missiles and wipe Vietnam off the face of the earth. What greater proof of omnipotence was there? Even God Almighty had to go to all the trouble of flooding the earth with forty days of non-stop rain to rid it of all but Noah and Company. But Lyndon, with a touch of the nuclear trigger, could waste not only Vietnam but touch off World War III and its global devastation. Omniscience, omnipresence, omnipotence—here surely was a rival for the God that Rebekah had drilled into the growing boy, never dreaming that he would himself offer competition! One is left to wonder just how the Pope rated Johnson when, on his return home from Southwest Asia, he stopped to visit him in the Vatican. There the uninhibited Texan gave His Holiness one of his bronze busts. Later, Johnson told his brother that the Pope had called him "One of the great leaders of our time." High praise indeed. But not quite God himself. If, as Moyers asserted, "hyperbole was to Lyndon Johnson what oxygen is to life," then there was nobody he enjoyed hyping more than Lyndon. Undoubtedly this was one of the many reasons why 1965 polls, while showing remarkably high approval of the job he was doing, nonetheless showed he was not *liked* by the public. Other politicians, in private, agreed with them.

Lest there was anyone on his staff entertaining doubts about LBJ's hallowed status, expressed in leaks to the press, he would dispatch at home what he casually ordered in South East Asia: "a search and destroy" mission to root out the offending culprit. In this way, Sidey pointed out, Johnson sowed terror "in the back offices of the White House and related agencies." Loyalty meant exactly that. He would tolerate no chinks through which his enemies might inflict grievous wounds. After all, he reflected more than once, had he not graduated high school the youngest in his class? Had he not been the youngest NYA state director, the youngest Texas Congressman, the youngest Party Whip, Minority Leader, and Majority Leader in the Senate? He was not only precocious, Lyndon was convinced, but precious in the eyes of right-thinking constituents. By 1968, *Time* described Johnson as "egotistical enough to turn a sizable chunk of

Texas into a memorial to himself." This included "a special plaque at the Hye Post Office immortalizing it as the spot where four-year-old Lyndon Johnson mailed his first letter."[5]

Identification with Individuals

With such preening, consuming vanity, it was but a hop, skip, and jump to identifying himself with others. As a boy, Lyndon identified with his own parents, as well as with the parents of other children more than with the children themselves, and more than with his own siblings. In college, he identified with the leaders of the student body and football team, then with President Evans and the rest of the administration and faculty, more than with fellow students. As aide to Kleberg, he not only identified himself with this Texas playboy, heir to the King Ranch, but posed as Kleberg in his phone calls. He discovered Rayburn and identified with him. Elected to the House, then to the Senate, he chose to identify with FDR, Eisenhower, Richard Russell, Robert Kerr, and other power brokers. At last, sitting behind his desk in his Oval Office in his White House, he identified with the illustrious leaders of other nations, notably Churchill and DeGaulle. When it came to FDR, Johnson took the extra step and, according to aide Busby, would carry on an imaginary conversation with his political godfather. During the late thirties he'd be "talking to the President, and thirty years later he believed the fiction." Yet the fiction was not hard to come by. After all, had not Roosevelt, as Corcoran recalled, been Johnson's mentor, "laying his hand on him and saying, 'This is my boy!' "

Thus did Johnson come to define himself by associating, as much as possible, with those whom he admired, envied, and emulated—men of power. For, whether by wealth, birth, force, appointment, or election, such men wielded influence. They were the ones who threw the switches to make the machinery of government operate. All hail to the movers and shakers! Lyndon's job was to make himself as indispensable as possible to them.

Identification with Institutions

In addition to identifying with others, Johnson found it natural to identify with the institutions about him. Though Woodrow Wilson cautioned

---

that there was no indispensable man, Lyndon set about to prove him wrong. Elected Speaker of the Little Congress—by stealth—he convinced himself that he was the indispensable man. Appointed NYA director for Texas, he soon *was* the Texas NYA, without which it would not—could not—operate. That is, until he shucked it and ran for "Buck" Buchanan's seat in Congress. By dint of "luck and pluck," this modern-day Horatio Alger, bankrolled by the Browns and their friends, as well as by his wife and her father, soon occupied a seat in the House. In the midst of a less-than-valorous six-month Navy stint in 1942, he was suddenly recalled by "Big Daddy" FDR on the pretext that he, like the other members of Congress in the service, were more needed on the Hill than "over hill and dale," marching with the caissons. Another six years would pass, with a career in the House no more stellar than his goldbricking in the Navy.

It was in the Senate that for the first time, Lyndon gave full vent to institutional identification. By 1954, he was not only Majority Leader of the Democrats; the Democratic Party, he claimed, was *my* Party. Soon the "Taj Mahal" was *my* office, and the bills that worked their way through committee to a House vote were *my* bills. The Senate was, by 1957, *my* Senate. With the Civil Rights Bill before him, he complained, "*I* want to run the Senate. *I* want to pass the bills that need to be passed. *I* want my party to do right. But all I ever hear from the Senate is 'Nigra, nigra, nigra.'" By the time the Civil Rights Bill, emasculated as it was in the name of consensus, passed to the Senate, Johnson made clear to one and all that not only was this *his* bill, but it put him in line to be President of *all* the people. "If only the good Lord," he said, "would just give me enough time to do a few more things in the Senate." According to aide Harry McPherson, "Johnson thought the presidency of the United States was the one great office of the system. He thought to attack the president inevitably was to attack the presidency." This was undoubtedly one reason that Johnson was easy on Eisenhower and, as Vice-President, not only refused to criticize Kennedy in private as well as public, but took to task those who did so.

On the other hand, it didn't seem much of a stretch to identity himself with the Senate. By 1958, he was not only Majority Leader and the second most powerful man in the country, but he had seen a record number of bills passed by his Democratically-controlled Senate.[6] Furthermore, he was chairman of the Democratic Policy Committee; chairman of the Democratic Conference; chairman of the Democratic Steering Committee; chairman of the Defense Preparedness Sub-Committee; chairman of the Appropriations Sub-Committee on State, Justice, and Commerce Departments; and, finally, chairman of the new Space Committee. With so many different hats to wear, Johnson assembled a sizable staff with each one, and before long his total staff was unprecedented for a single senator in the history of that august institution. It wasn't, then, such a stretch to consider himself so indispensable to the Senate as to identity himself with it.

As one senator after another fell under his spell, victims of his special "treatment," he assembled a claque of Republicans as well as Democrats to do his bidding. Who could resist anywhere from ten minutes to four hours of what Evans and Novak described as "supplication, accusation, cajolery, exuberance, scorn, tears, [and] the hint of a threat"? This was invariably nonstop, with interjections, much less protests, rare indeed. Already he'd anticipated them. "He moved in close, his face a scant millimeter from his target, his eyes widening and narrowing, his eyebrows rising and falling. From his pockets poured clippings, memos, statistics. Mimicry, humor, and genius for analogy made 'The Treatment' an almost hypnotic experience and rendered the target stunned and helpless."

It wasn't enough, as George Smathers recounted, that Johnson's presence in the Senate was as "a great, overpowering thunderstorm that consumed you as it closed in around you." He *was* the Senate, and Johnson's top brass, including Senators Kerr and Russell, would attest to that. They understood loyalty. They knew who was responsible for their committee assignments, their office assignments, their staff, their budgets—and, for Democratic senators, their campaign money. Surely they would not look a gift horse in the mouth. Regardless of how they felt about a given bill, Lyndon could count on not only their votes, but their scurrying about lining up other senators for Johnson. Among his lieutenants was Mississippi's John Stennis, of whom Lyndon could boast to Lady Bird, "He's one of my finest senators!" Even Oregon's Wayne Morse, prickly pear that he was—and in 1964, only one of two to vote against Johnson's Tonkin Gulf Resolution—recalled Majority Leader Johnson as "not only a great statesman, but a good man."

With such loyalty, such encomiums, it isn't hard to understand how Lyndon came to see himself as indispensable, as the embodiment of the Senate. It was, as he became accustomed to saying, *his* Senate. And since the Senate was more prestigious than the House, he easily came to fancy himself as the embodiment of Congress. Furthermore, since it was the Congress who laid down the laws governing the country, it was a small step to conceive that Congress was, in fact, the country. After all, it was LBJ who ran the Senate as if it were his fiefdom. And it was staunch friend Sam Rayburn who ran the House. And it was another friend, Texas-born Eisenhower, who ran the executive branch.

The three of them, meeting regularly and in private, schmoozed over Cutty Sark and assorted beverages as they planned what was best for the country. As Ike put it a decade later: "Our friendship came of a birth state in common, and a long personal acquaintance. We had our differences, especially in domestic and economic policy. . . . Yet when put in perspective, he [LBJ]was far more helpful than obstructive. . . . For this I was grateful and frequently told him so." Chairman of the Democratic Party Paul Butler, who was unhappy with Johnson's refusal to face down Ike on important issues, would have been more unhappy had he known that the highballs enjoyed by the three Texans—meeting in the second-floor study of the White House at the cocktail hour—were often mixed with high jinx.

By 1958, Johnson was fully convinced he was the Senate, the truly indispensable man. But soon he was to discover he was, indeed, dispensable and, overplaying his hand, he found even his friends were backing off. Still, he simply wouldn't believe the Senate could run without him, and refused to toss his hat in the presidential ring. He had business to attend to on the Hill, even as Kennedy was out on the hustings—and had been since 1956—drumming up his candidacy, establishing flourishing political campaign offices in each state, and, of course, absenting himself from his job in the Senate. Johnson was confident that since his fellow senators owed him for all the goodies he'd bestowed, he could count on their loyalty, and the loyalty of their individual states, come campaign time. But he was wrong. The voters in each state were under the thumb of big-city mayors and local town supervisors much more than U.S. senators. And Kennedy knew that.

By 1960, when LBJ finally, in the eleventh hour, entered the race, he was embarrassed to be running behind the junior Senator from Massachusetts. Texas was a long way from the Bay State, and Johnson was a long way from catching up to Kennedy. It didn't help, either, when Republican Hugh Scott needled LBJ by referring to JFK as "the Majority Leader's leader." As Scott and other Republicans were gathered around

Everett Dirksen one day, Johnson eavesdropped on the perimeter until he could take it no more. Listen, he interrupted, as he launched a tirade against JFK. If he, Johnson, were not around "tending shop" on the Hill, Kennedy "would fall flat on his face"—as, presumably, would the Senate itself.

However, neither the Senate nor Kennedy fell flat on their faces when Johnson left to become Kennedy's Vice-President in 1961. Less than three years later, JFK was assassinated and LBJ became President. By 1964, with a landslide under his belt, the "accidental" President was a full-fledged President, beloved of the people—he believed—because so many had embraced him in the voting booths across the country. By this time, he truly felt himself indispensable to the presidency. *His* legislative record was unsurpassed, even by his mentor, FDR. *His* Great Society was a "city set on a hill," a beacon for all other nations to try and emulate. And *his* war in Indochina he was micromanaging from *his* White House, confident that *his* decisions as commander in chief were not only being carried out implicitly by loyal aides at Defense and in the military, but were the *right* decisions.

If only Lyndon had listened to the advice of Harry Truman: "When you get to be President, there are all those things, honors, 21-gun salutes, all those things. You have to remember it isn't for you. It's for the presidency." This is none other than the respect paid a commissioned officer in the armed forces when he is saluted. It is not the person, but the office he represents in the armed forces of his country, that is being paid tribute.

Coolidge was undoubtedly right when he wrote, "It is difficult for men in high office to avoid the malady of self-delusion." For some time LBJ had been building sand castles between his ears; but as President his fantasies would affect millions, at home and abroad. Years before, Dean Acheson had warned Johnson that the one thing a president should never do is let his ego get between him and his office. As usual, Johnson was undoubtedly talking when he should have been listening. And when he was talking, according to one aide, he was fond of saying "*my* government," "*my* Army," "*my* taxes," and "*my* Supreme Court." Once he went so far as to refer to the "State of *My* Union Address."[7]

By February 1965, the war had been escalated hugely, and Johnson could rightly claim it as *his* war. Learning of the Communist attack on the giant American air base at Pleiku in the Central Highlands, he announced to the National Security Council and congressional leaders he'd convened to deal with the emergency, "*I've* gone far enough! *I've* had enough of this!" Soon Operation Rolling Thunder was his own personal answer. The pilots were *his* boys, flying *his* bombers. And they were not to bomb so much as a North Vietnamese outhouse without *his* explicit direction. The Vietcong Christmas-Eve bombing of the Brink's Hotel in Saigon was the last straw. From then on, there was no doubt: this was very personal, pitting Johnson against Ho Chi Minh. As LBJ complained to the press, he was like a man standing on a newspaper in the middle of the ocean. Move one way or another and he'd topple over. But if he stood still, "the paper will be soaked up and I'll sink slowly to the bottom of the sea." By this time, the nation was referring to it as Johnson's war, even as the War of 1812 became known as "Madison's War"—although both presidents had inherited the wars from their predecessors.

When the Vietcong made an attack, as they did at Pleiku, Johnson invariably took it personally. These attacks, adviser Clark Clifford noted, Johnson interpreted "as somehow personally aimed at him. He reacted by thinking: 'they can't do this to Lyndon Johnson! They can't push *me* around this way!'" When South Vietnam's leaders fell short, as they always seemed to do, Johnson's complaint was, "Thieu and Ky let *me* down." Opposition to the war at home he invariably took personally. They were "pushing *me* around."

By 1967, Johnson was identifying himself with the presidency, insistent that no one else—and certainly not professional soldiers—should be micromanaging the war. And no one else could hope to launch that noble effort, the Great Society. He was indispensable to the presidency. Had LBJ read Shakespeare's *Henry IV*, he'd undoubtedly have agreed, "Uneasy lies the head that wears the crown," even in a democracy. By 1967, LBJ was lucky to catch four hours of sleep, from two to six in the morning. How could this "king" be expected to sleep with the raucous rattle of what he saw as "intellectual crazies, nervous nellies, belly-achers, domestic Communists, and assorted longhairs yelling from across the street in Lafayette Square: "Hey, hey, LBJ, how many kids did you kill today?!" Here was outright treason. As Johnson put it to Moyers—before Moyers quit and joined the opposition—"Don't they know they're Americans? They're making a terrible mistake. You know, they're attacking the country. . . . For them to attack this country is to attack the immortality of most of the bastards who make up this country." Here was, indeed, a mouthful of illogic. To attack Johnson was to attack the country. To attack the country was to put the immortality of all its "bastards" at risk. For immortality, as LBJ took pains to instruct his fellow Texan, a former theological student, stemmed not so much from one's religion as from one's nation. "If you say I am an American," Johnson explained, "you're saying I'm as immortal as this Republic." It was obvious that Moyers was at risk, not having imbibed this creed in seminary. Washington journalist Roulhac Hamilton noted that what bothered White House aides was "Johnson's equating of constructive, informed dissent with personal disloyalty and, beyond this, with disloyalty to the nation itself."[8]

This increasing chorus of dissenters, Johnson was convinced, was simply giving aid and comfort to the enemy—as though Johnson had never heard of Britain's party out of power referring to themselves as "her majesty's loyal opposition," which would oppose the party in power but remain loyal to the Queen. When Everett Dirksen took LBJ to task for not consulting the Senate enough in the conduct of the war, Johnson asked, "Now why do you say that, Everett?" "Well, Mr. President," responded the Minority Leader of the Republicans, "you must remember that I am the leader of your loyal opposition."

With Johnson's gift for equivocation, circumlocution, rhetorical pyrotechnics, and twisted logic, who could offer reasonable argument? When he appealed repeatedly to the ancient Isaiah, "Come now and let us reason together," those who knew him understood that his was a most unusual form of reasoning. In 1968, Wilbur Cohen, Secretary of HEW, put a question to his President that his fourteen-year-old son had put to him earlier: "Why are we in Vietnam?" For half an hour Johnson spelled it out, then spelled it backwards—so that by the time his tongue took a rest, Cohen later recalled, "The answer didn't make any sense whatsoever. I can't remember the words now, but it was very shocking to me. If he had given that answer publicly, he would just have been laughed out of court." When Lyndon's brother, Sam, returned from speaking at Williams College in Massachusetts, he told Lyndon that he'd been "publicly insulted by a grandstanding member of the faculty, whose hatred of [LBJ] seemed pathological." Lyndon's response: "Stay away from those meetings. You can't tell what kind of nuts are floating around these days . . . you're my brother, and that alone ought to be enough to make some crazy bastard go off his rocker."

By the close of 1967, it appeared that it was Johnson himself who was going "off his rocker." He would have been right at home in the Wonderland of Lewis Carroll's *Alice*. Bumper stickers were sprouting, bearing the motto, "America. Love it or leave it!" The reasoning: To disagree with Johnson's war policy was to attack him as President, in turn to attack the presidency and the nation itself—the ultimate treason. Into this category of chronic malcontents bugging LBJ were those who quit him, like Ball, Moyers, and most of his other top aides. As far as Johnson was concerned, orchestrating the opposition was none other than former friend William Fulbright, now reduced to "Senator Half-Bright." With him in front-row center section of Johnson's hell was former friend Mike Mansfield, his successor as Majority Leader. For it was Mansfield who'd dared to announce to the press, "We are in the wrong place, fighting the wrong war."

But it was the lesser lights, like Townsend Hoopes, McNamara's Undersecretary of Defense, who bore the brunt of Johnson's fury. Learning that Hoopes had been the source of a March 10, 1968, *New York Times* story about Westmoreland's request for an additional 206,000 troops, Johnson hit the ceiling. "Hoopies! Hoopies! Who the hell is Hoopies? Here I take four million people out of poverty and all I ever hear about is Hoopies!" Not only had Johnson himself rescued four million Americans from poverty—but, as he had told reporter Gould Lincoln four years earlier, when he'd called back Congress over Christmas 1963, to complete its work on a foreign aid bill— ". . . the whole Communist world was watching to see any sign of weakness or temporizing or compromising or running on the part of the President. . . ." He, Lyndon Johnson, had his finger in the dike, preventing the flood of Communism from washing over the free world. No question about it, LBJ was indispensable to maintaining freedom across the globe.[9]

By 1968 and the Tet offensive, Eugene McCarthy and Bobby Kennedy were taking turns breathing down LBJ's neck. His intimates, including old friend James Rowe, were forecasting doom for Johnson and the Democrats come November. Said Rowe, "Hardly anyone is interested in winning the war. Everyone wants to get out, and the only question is how." At last Johnson was catching glimpses, through the morning mists of self-delusion, of the rising sun of reality. To Clifford he at last confided, "I've got to get me a peace proposal."

It is, of course, inevitable that each of us sees the world through the unique prism of our own eyes, reflecting our own experiences as well as expectations. What is not inevitable, however, is that each of us should interpret all events as happening to us personally. In infancy and the first few years of childhood, we have come to expect such egotistic orientation. By the age of eight or ten, surely most of us come to realize that there are others in the world affecting and being affected. But Johnson never seemed to have set foot out of the megalomania that insisted everything that happened was concerned with him personally, so he, in turn, had to dominate others. It was he who must order events, control circumstances, and buttonhole every last leader, even if it meant sitting down—one on one—and accosting Ho Chi Minh at the negotiating table.

Whether it was Ho and his Communist minions, or aluminum manufacturers threatening to push prices through the clouds, or railroad strikers threatening to paralyze the nation's transportation, it was all done to tie Lyndon's hands personally. In the case of the 1965 railroad strike, LBJ closeted representatives of labor and management and threatened to keep them there until they emerged with a settlement. If nothing else, he, the President—who knew nothing of running a railroad—would take it over. One executive protested that, after all, he was "just an old country boy" and Johnson interrupted him with, "When I hear that, I put my hand on my billfold." The executive persisted, "By God, all I wanted to say was that I'm ready to sign up!" That was more like it! In a flash Johnson saw victory in his grasp and immediately headed for the nearest CBS station with a motorcycle escort, just in time to make the announcement on the evening news.

Here was vintage Johnson, putting a railroad strike on a very personal level. It was, obviously, a strike meant to cripple him—by tying up *his* railroads and preventing *his* materiél and *his* troops from moving out to the coasts and overseas to Vietnam. If they didn't settle, *he* would take over and run them *himself*.

It was the same way with the aluminum profiteers, making a bundle on the war while thousands of body bags were making their grim journey home. Here again was treason, aimed at the President, the presidency, the government, and the nation. The manufacturers turned a deaf ear to Johnson's plea to roll back the prices, so he pulled out the ace up his sleeve. "Well, *I'm* the commander in chief and I can go out and get [their giant stockpiles] smelted." That was that, and the prices were rolled back. One is left to speculate how the Supreme Court, "*my* court," as Johnson called it, would have ruled on the constitutionality of Johnson's intimidation.

A further extension of Johnson's identification occurred in his tying his own credibility to that of the nation. How would the world look at us if we reneged on our SEATO commitments? We must, at all costs, let the world know—Communist and non-Communist, "slave and free"—that *I*, Lyndon Johnson [that is, we, the nation] would stand by my [our] word. He not only identified himself with the nation, but with the "free world," something he never seemed to tire of reminding others. Australia's prime minister, he declared, was *his* prime minister, just as the troops he reviewed in Vietnam were *his* troops.

From there it was just a jump up the ladder of unreasoning to imagine himself as leader of the entire world, as the world's essence if not its embodiment. To his aides he wondered aloud just how he would run the world if he could somehow be given the chance. There were simply no limits to his egomaniacal identification. As Walter Lippman charged, "The root of his troubles has been pride, a stubborn refusal to recognize the country's limits or his own."[10]

So, as we have seen, Johnson turned to confrontation, the next step in hubris, following hard on the heels of identification, even as identification followed hard on the heels of arrogance.

RICHARD NIXON

. . . Other people than the President [don't matter] . . . those around you cannot in any way look at their self-interest. There's only one thing involved here [the presidency].

— Richard Nixon

. . . there's never been such a massive attack on the presidency. . . .

— Richard Nixon

. . . they say that half of them is worth two of anybody else, that nobody else can do it . . . they think they're sort of indispensable...

— Richard Nixon, speaking of Haldeman and Ehrlichman

Identification as Diversion

Kissinger was irate. It was "unconscionable," he stormed, "that America would ever conduct its foreign policy with a view to domestic political considerations!" Though Nixon and Kissinger had been doing this for almost five years, timing the ending of the war to Nixon's 1972 reelection, it was the press that in the fall of 1973 was at it again. It seems that Nixon had issued a worldwide alert of the armed forces following his "Saturday Night Massacre" of October 20—when the firing of Special Prosecutor Archibald Cox and the subsequent resignation of Attorney General Elliott Richardson and his deputy was provoking a firestorm of protest in the press. Journalists suspected that this alert was simply a diversionary tactic to draw attention from Nixon's deepening Watergate morass. Kissinger, of course, was not referring to America but to Nixon, aided by the likes of his National Security Adviser. But by this time Kissinger, following the President's lead, was identifying Nixon and his administration with the nation itself.

Identification With Others

Like Johnson, Nixon began by identifying himself with others he admired. There was Eisenhower, whom Nixon saw for the first time after the hero's triumphant return and ticker-tape parade in Manhattan following V-E Day in 1945. There he was, in the open car, his arms held high over his head, Nixon noticed, in Churchill's gesture that soon became his and Nixon's trademark. In 1950, Nixon listened to Ike speak at the annual retreat of San Francisco's Bohemian Club. Nixon was "deeply impressed" with "Eisenhower's personality and personal mystique." The following year Nixon was introduced to Ike, now president of Columbia University, at NATO headquarters in Paris. There, in a brief conversation, Nixon noted the five-star general was "erect and vital and impeccably tailored" in his uniform. In his *Memoirs* Nixon recalled, "I felt that I was in the presence of a genuine statesman, and I came away convinced that he should be the next president." So convinced, in fact, that Nixon would renege on his promise to support Earl Warren and persuade the California delegation to the Republican Convention to vote for Ike rather than their favorite son. Nominated, along with Ike, Nixon realized "the hero needed a point-man," or, as "Beetle" Smith, Ike's aide in World War II, called it—based on his own experience—a "prat-boy."

For eight years Nixon tried his hardest to identify himself with the one man most popular not only in the nation but across the world, the one man who could have won with either party and who was stronger than either party. That Ike would counsel him to seek another job in 1956, and only lamely accepted him for his second term was bad enough. But what stunned Nixon was that his hero turned his back on him, refusing to endorse him with any enthusiasm, and listing a half-dozen others as better choices for president in 1960. Added to this was Ike's "give me a week" remark to reporters when asked what policy matters Nixon had been instrumental in deciding. To hold Ike in such high esteem, to try desperately to identify with him and ride on his coattails to the presidency, only to find him rejecting his Vice-President, was too much to bear. The depth of Nixon's bitterness was the measure of the height to which he had elevated his President over eight years.

Another general with whom this World War II supply officer tried to identify was the egotistical, mercurial, and unpredictable George "Blood and Guts" Patton. Again and again Nixon viewed George C. Scott in the title role of the movie *Patton*, and urged his friends and aides to do the same. Nixon took to swearing like Patton to show, as Parmet put it, that his aides could hear, "the old amateur thespian assuming the language of one displaying the balls of command: General George Patton." So enamored was Nixon of Patton that he kept at his bedside the biography on which the movie was based. Though this maverick managed to kill himself in a jeep accident in 1945, he would live in the mind if not under the skin of Richard Nixon. William Safire, a Nixon speech writer, saw the President identifying himself with Patton, another "patriot misunderstood by carping critics." Ike himself had compared the two. Both had blundered, and he'd forgiven both.[1]

By the fall of 1971, Kissinger was neck-deep in preparations for Nixon's visit to Peking. Apparently Nixon's idolizing Patton had reached the ears of Chou En-Lai, who took the time to view *Patton* himself. Perhaps this would give him a further window into the mind of the man he'd be negotiating with, come spring.

Reelected in a landslide, Nixon, instead of rejoicing, spluttered that the North Vietnamese would not renegotiate the terms of the peace agreement that they had already agreed to in early October—terms which even Thieu found objectionable. Well, Nixon—like Patton—would show those Communists a thing or two. Perhaps Nixon called to mind Patton's imploring Ike to let him go after the Soviets, once the Nazis had surrendered. In any case, Nixon gave the order to start bombing the North, only to have foul weather hold him up.

Exasperated, he took the posture of Patton, as Kissinger noted, "his romantic streak" fancying himself the beleaguered military commander who, against the superior forces of "the Desert Fox" Rommel in North Africa, had won the day. To his aides Nixon barked out the command: "Try and get the weather; damn it, if any of you know any prayers, say them. Let's get the weather cleared up. The bastards have never been bombed like they're going to be bombed this time." Patton couldn't have said it better! Yet Nixon apparently saw no problem in implicating the Almighty in the unprecedented devastation he was about to unleash on the North— killing and maiming women, children, and the elderly, nine of them for every enemy soldier. He was but God's avenging angel to those Communist atheists!

It was no coincidence that the third man Nixon idolized and did his best to identify with was also a general, in this case Charles DeGaulle, the commander of the French Resistance after the fall of his country to the Nazis in 1940. Ironically, it was Nixon himself who quoted a DeGaulle critic as saying that "DeGaulle in political matters thinks that he has a direct telephone line with God and that in making decisions all that he has to do is get on the wire and get the word straight from God." As imperious as he was mercurial, DeGaulle—as we noted in chapter one—was only too eager to receive Nixon's elaborate deference at the Paris airport in 1969. Later, at a state dinner in his honor, Nixon toasted DeGaulle's life as "an epic of courage, an epic of leadership seldom equaled in the history of the world." There was more. DeGaulle was "a leader who has become a giant among men because he had courage, because he had vision, and because he had the wisdom that the world now seeks to solve the world's problems." High praise indeed for the one stiff-armed by Eisenhower during World War II, ignored by Roosevelt and then by Truman in seeking to regain Indochina, ignored again by Ike in 1954 in his desperate attempt to get relief at Dienbienphu, and ignored by Johnson and even Nixon himself in his attempts to intervene to secure peace in Vietnam. But though Nixon disregarded the general's advice in 1969 on ending the war, Nixon continued to look up to the 6' 8" giant, and not only because of his height. Indeed, as Wicker noted, Nixon's main objective, upon assuming the presidency in 1969 and planning a European trip that spring, was to cement relations with the general who had come to realize the inevitable: that the United States and its President would play a continuing major role in the European Market and the formation of a European Union.

Perhaps Kennedy was right when, in 1960, he remarked that whereas he was not tired, Nixon must be exhausted for having to assume so many different roles and wondering which one would best suit the occasion. And perhaps Abrahamsen was right in psychoanalyzing Nixon in 1960 as a man "fighting with himself on all fronts. His inner impulses pushed him in different directions and created a multiplicity of contradictions in his behavior."[2]

Yet in the turmoil that raged within him he constantly sought direction—from Hannah and Frank; from "Chief' Newman; from Woodrow Wilson and Abe Lincoln; but as much as any from those with whom he desperately tried to identify, primarily three generals: Eisenhower, Patton and DeGaulle.

Identification With Institutions

In 1958, Nixon asserted to Mazo that there was no such thing as an indispensable man. But in another ten years, with the White House won, he'd changed his mind. In stringing along one special interest bloc after another with an exhibition of campaign promises that seemed to dazzle and seduce the voters, Nixon gave the impression that he could do almost anything—if he were President. The longer he was in the White House, the more indispensable he saw himself to the office. Always he was careful to give himself the credit when there was some to be taken, particularly when he thought Kissinger was usurping what Nixon saw as *his* peace.

It was the first week of November 1972, and Nixon's Watergate cover-up—something he wanted no credit for—was so successful that, as Ambrose put it, it was "dead in the water as an issue." Furthermore, in Buchanan's pugnacious prose, Democratic candidate George McGovern was in desperate condition, "on the verge of a breakdown . . . a state of bitchiness and exhaustion," a state of "increasing bitterness toward the President personally." Underlining this last point, Nixon sent it on to Colson and Haldeman with his cryptic, "I agree."

He was less willing, however, to agree with McGovern's claim that, far from peace being "at hand," as Kissinger had declared on October 10, the war was intensifying. Nixon, McGovern warned, was deliberately misleading the nation, claiming that a peace agreement was virtually in his pocket, while dropping no less than four million pounds of bombs on Vietnam in a single day. In addition, Nixon was rushing additional matériel to South Vietnam, including enough aircraft to equip the South with the third-largest air force in the world. Atop that, Nixon's Pentagon was claiming the North was already withdrawing some of its units from the South, something McGovern claimed was "completely false." Nixon took to national TV to "set the record straight." Yes, there were "some details" that he was still working on, but only because of his insistence that "this will not be a temporary peace but a peace that will last." Indeed, he was "completely confident" that a final agreement would be reached "soon." But above all, Nixon made sure that the electorate understood that this was *his* agreement. It was *he* who was entitled to be proud of it.

Insistent on taking whatever credit there was, Nixon was just as apt to identify himself with the office of the President, the presidency, if "circumstances" convinced this pragmatist that course was the right one. Unfortunately, as Schlesinger pointed out, Nixon failed to see a vital connection between the President and the presidency. Repeatedly in his public discourse Nixon hit on the need for maintaining due respect for the office. "The possibility that such respect might be achieved simply by being a good President evidently did not reassure him. He was preoccupied with 'respect for the office' as an entity in itself." Schlesinger then asked if Nixon's predecessors, Washington, Lincoln, Roosevelt, Truman, or Kennedy had insisted on going public, again and again, about maintaining "respect for the office." What in effect Nixon seemed to be saying was "respect me!" Identifying himself with the office, showing that he was indispensable to that office, he demanded of others due respect for him *as* the office. Confronting the Watergate burglary, Nixon was intent on maintaining "plausible deniability" in dissociating the White House from the obvious tomfoolery that had gone on at the Watergate complex. In his diary of June 1972, Nixon wrote, "We have to live with this one and hope to bring it to a conclusion without too much rubbing off on the presidency before the election." Treasury Secretary William Simon later made a similar claim that Nixon was more concerned about protecting the presidency than himself. But Simon added the important point that it was Nixon who initiated the cover-up.[3]

By the beginning of 1973, it was evident that Watergate was down but not out. With Democratic control of Congress assured by Nixon's stingy parceling out of funds to congressional candidates of his party, Nixon could only fear the worst as he stood before the Congress to deliver his inaugural address. If worse came to worst, would he resign? Never. For "to resign would inevitably weaken the office of the president . . . impair[ing] the ability of presidents of the future. . . ."

But the Senate Democratic Caucus was not listening. Or if it was, it was not heeding. For the following month it called for an investigation of 1972 campaign practices. This, Nixon sneered, was simply "a Democratic ploy to put the presidency on the defensive." By March 16, 1973, Nixon was drawing on the example of Eisenhower, ridding himself of Sherman Adams to protect "the presidency." Nixon: "And I feel the same way. I mean, I cannot—you cannot figure the President is covering up the god-damn thing. . . ." Come March 21, and all hell broke loose. For there was the counsel to the President, John Dean, reporting, "We have a cancer with-in—close to the presidency—that's growing." So Nixon understood that it was the presidency, rather than merely this President that was at stake, Dean emphasized that "the real problem" was to "keep the Watergate cover-up away from the presidency." Dean understood priorities, and his first job, drummed into him "since my first day in the White House," was "plausible deniability." The deniability was becoming less and less plausi-ble, Dean warned. Nixon was grateful for Dean's emphasis on the office rather than him personally, and wrote in his diary that Dean "was earnest-ly concerned about the presidency—he'd earnestly hoped to save the pres-idency from encroaching cancer."

But it seemed no use. The cancer was metastasizing, and radiation and chemotherapy in the form of continuing cover-up seemed to be unavailing. By April 17, Kissinger was emphasizing that "the major thing now . . . is to protect the presidency. . . ."[4] By April 22, Nixon, having forced one aide after another to walk the plank, approached Haldeman and Ehrlichman. They would have to "step out," said this President, not so much to save his neck but "for the sake of the presidency."

On April 25, Nixon made no bones about asking Assistant Attorney General Henry Petersen, who stood in awe of the office of the presidency, to break the law by feeding him information on the proceedings of the grand jury investigation. By this time, Nixon suspected that Dean was try-ing to blackmail him, and wanted to catch him in a lie so as to disprove his contention that Nixon had been plotting the cover-up since day one. So Nixon ordered Petersen to have his office bugged. "You get it done . . . the presidency has got to go ahead here. . . ." Like Kissinger, Ziegler was doing his best to convince Nixon that he and the presidency were one and the same. On April 28, Ziegler assured Nixon that threats by Hunt and Dean could backfire, for "the presidency of the United States doesn't have to put up with that." When Ziegler learned that Nixon had secured the promise of both Haldeman and Ehrlichman to take "a leave of absence" but not—surely not—to resign, Ziegler congratulated the President on this "masterstroke."

Again, on May 1, Nixon was on the phone with old friend Robert Finch, telling him that Senator Charles Percy had "cooked his goose with me when he came out and said, 'Well, we've got to have a special prosecutor to work with Elliott [Richardson].' Well, my God, that son-of-a-bitch . . . I always just say, we must have confidence in the integrity of the presidency." Then, identifying the office with himself, he described himself as "One of those rare presidents who has the guts to conduct an investigation of his own people. Yeah. It's true. Then they're going to realize that this whole Watergate thing was about a crappy little thing—that everybody shouldn't have gotten excited about. It will pass. It will pass. . . ."

A week later Ziegler joined Nixon in savaging Dean, telling Nixon he'd better lay it all out in a press conference, telling reporters, "I had a man on my staff who was my counsel and who was a trusted aide, and in the course of that, I talked freely with him, not about illegality, not about wrongdoing. That man has taken much of what I said in the sanctity, the privileged sanctity of the Oval Office, and attempted to use that for his own self-service—in order to discredit the presidency of the United States." Always, it seemed, the young Ziegler was trying to pinch himself to believe he was actually serving the President of the United States, just as Nixon kept emphasizing his role as President by using the third person for the first—"the President . . . " for" "I . . . ."

Destroy him, Nixon warned repeatedly, and they will destroy "the presidency." Then he explained to another sycophant, his new Chief of Staff, Alexander Haig: "I mean, the country rallies around the president." And he, Richard Nixon, had "done some quite considerable things for this country. . . ." Haig, of course, picked up this bone that had fallen from his master's table and proceeded to chew on it. He was incensed, he declared in no uncertain terms, that the Watergate Committee was believing Dean over the President. After all, "the institution [the presidency] has got to be protected. . . ." What Nixon had concluded was only "a hopeless mess" he now saw as Dean's mad scramble "trying to save his own skin." In any event, Haig rejoined, ". . . we have to stand firm because the *goddamn presidency* can't run in the future with this kind of challenge. . . ." With that,

Nixon could only agree: "... .. for Christ's sakes, here it is, this goddamn Dean out here attacking the presidency. . . ." Again, to Ziegler, ". . . the attack is on the presidency. . . ." Then to Kissinger, ". . . we cannot allow the crappy business about Watergate and campaign crap . . . to destroy the presidency of the United States." And one more time to Ziegler, before Nixon disconnected the taping system: ". . . we can't lose sight of the major goal here and that is protection and preservation of the presidency."[5]

As more and more supporters deserted Nixon in the face of increasing evidence of his complicity, if not direction, of the cover-up, his critics multiplied. And each criticism he took personally, yet contended that each was eroding the presidency. By the end of 1973, Simon noted Nixon living increasingly in a daze, making gestures mechanically, with apparently no thought to their meaning.

Christmas 1973, was not a day to celebrate. The courts, Nixon complained, in ruling against his claim of "executive privilege" in refusing to turn over additional incriminating tapes to Congress, were in fact stripping away not so much his power as the powers of the presidency. On the last day of that eventful year, Nixon was in no more mood to celebrate New Year's Eve than he had been to celebrate Christmas. Before him stood James St. Clair. Nixon was determined that his new attorney understand what be was defending. It was not the President, he made clear, but "the office of the presidency exclusively."

This was in contrast to Nixon's instructions to Elliott Richardson earlier that year. For, on April 29, the President gave instructions to his new Attorney General, who'd replaced Richard Kleindienst to add badly needed credibility to the administration. Said Nixon, "You must pursue this investigation even if it leads to the President." Then he insisted he was innocent. "You've got to believe I'm innocent. If you don't, don't take the job. The important thing is the presidency. If need be, save the presidency from the President." Richardson understood his orders as, "If the monster is me, save the country."

That was a tall order, but St. Clair seemed nonplussed when he wrote the Judiciary Committee that he was representing nothing less than the presidency itself. To make sure that all understood the enormity of his task, he also wrote to prosecutor Leon Jaworski. He, St. Clair, could not submit more of the President's tapes, for that would "erode the presidency."[6]

Alas, there were some, such as Herb Block of *The Washington Post*, who weren't convinced the presidency itself was on the line. As Herblock, the cartoonist who, with his caricatures, had savaged Nixon in the fifties, Block could write as well as draw. "Americans have come to think of the president as an institution rather than a person," he wrote, "shielding the president from accountability. It is often said that whatever we think of any current occupant of 1600 Pennsylvania Avenue we should 'respect the office.' I feel that respect for the office should begin with the person who occupies it. I am boggled by the concern for 'failed presidencies'—as if the person temporarily occupying the White House is some kind of holy icon more important than the Constitution or the nation. What I think the nation cannot stand is failed justice and the failure to demand that officials uphold their oaths of office."

Nixon's oath of office, taken the previous January 30, scarcely appeared on the horizon as 1974 hove into view. If 1973 was a bad year, 1974 was to be a disaster. Still this football tackling dummy kept bouncing back, kept fighting with every device at his disposal, including continuing identification with the office of the presidency. On April 13, he wrote, "Any more tapes will destroy the office. It is better to fight and lose defending the office than surrender to win a personal victory at a disastrous long-range cost to the office of the presidency." Just what "personal victory" he could gain by surrendering the tapes he never made clear. In fact, as the weeks passed, his thinking became less and less clear. On April 29, he stood in the Oval Office before national television, not with the incriminating tapes before him, but with sanitized versions in the form of transcripts, impressively wrapped in blue folders, in which much that was incriminating had been expunged. Then, in a redux of his "Checkers" speech twenty-two years earlier, he stressed that laying bare his private life for public scrutiny was both unprecedented for a president and a painful sacrifice. Reverting to the rhetoric that had proven so effective in 1952, he wallowed in self-pity, pleading for fair play. "I know in my own heart that, through the long, painful, and difficult process revealed in these transcripts, I was trying in that period to discover what was right and to do what was right. I hope, and I trust, that when you have seen the evidence in its entirety, you will see the truth of that statement." Here, by no means, was "the evidence in its entirety," as succeeding weeks would reveal. But what they did reveal showed that Nixon was not the Lincoln he then drew

upon to clinch his point. Identifying himself with the sixteenth president—
and one of the greatest in our history—Nixon said he understood how
Lincoln must have felt as he was "subjected to an unmerciful attack." Then
this second "Honest Abe" quoted from his predecessor: "I do the very best
I know how, the very best I can, and I mean to keep doing so until the end.
If the end brings me out all right, what is said against me won't amount to
anything. If the end brings me out wrong, ten angels, swearing I was right,
would make no difference." By identifying himself with Lincoln, Nixon
did nothing less than slander that honorable man. Indeed, it would be
hard to find a speech by any president so obviously distorted, cynical, and
manipulative. By identifying himself, the President, with the office of the
presidency, Nixon wanted nothing so much as to show himself—the current occupant—as thoroughly indispensable to the office. Impeach him,
destroy him, and the Congress would destroy the very office responsible
for leading the nation. Thus it was but a short jump to identifying himself
with the government itself.

Early on, Haldeman and Ehrlichman had come to see Nixon as the
government. Ehrlichman won few plaudits in Congress when he insisted
"the President is the government." Steve Bull, another Nixon aide, was
perceptive enough to note, "The White House is full of arrogance. The
nicest people can come . . . and after a few weeks they start [becoming arro-
gant]. I think it is an infirmity endemic to almost any administration that
they start confusing their personal importance with institutional importance."[7]

Like an infectious disease, this arrogance that led to such identification started with the man on top, who set the tone if not the pace for others in the administration. For Nixon was not above seeing himself as
utterly indispensable to the government. To impeach him would undercut our foreign initiatives, raise havoc at home, and throw the government into such chaos as to threaten collapse. On May 8, 1973, Haig
assured the President that whatever they had to do, whether "through
innuendo and what have you," they had to "manage" Watergate. For
"there's enough goddamn at stake in terms of the country and the interest of the country. . . ." At which point Nixon butted in to carry it to its
"logical" conclusion: "It has to be managed. The hopes and dreams of a
hell of a lot of people in this country and the world are going right down
the tube, and we're not this kind of a son-of-a-bitch [Dean]. That's what's

really involved here." By July 22, Nixon was complaining that Watergate had so consumed the nation that both foreign affairs and the economy were being neglected. So indispensable had he become to the government that to abdicate his position of leadership could only worsen an unstable world situation. Watergate was making it hard for the nation to compete in world markets.

Joseph Alsop, political columnist and a confidant of Kissinger and Haig, grew increasingly contemptuous of Nixon, whom he came to describe as "99% nutty as a fruitcake," or as "the armpit of humanity." Still, Alsop reeled at the specter of impeachment, believing that the government simply couldn't operate effectively without Nixon. And to picture Ford in the White House, a Republican from a single Michigan district, with no experience in foreign affairs, with no idea—much less experience—with executive authority, was a prospect too absurd to contemplate. Still, by March 20, Alsop concluded "it is a reasonable bet that a bill of impeachment will be voted and sent to the Senate."[8]

Alsop was right, and to avoid impeachment Nixon chose to resign, even though convinced that he was indispensable, not only to the presidency and to the government, but to the nation itself. After all, if the presidency were crippled with his resignation, so would the government be crippled. And if the government, then what of the nation? Thus by one stretch after another Nixon came to identify himself with the nation. Nixon was in the habit of calling on Kissinger to recount for him, at the end of a day, the President's conspicuous role in the events of that day. It seemed to the National Security Adviser that this "poor, somewhat resentful young man from a little town in California," simply couldn't get over the privileges and perks of the highest office in the land. "To land with *Air Force One* on foreign soil [in this case, Britain], to be greeted by a king and then a prime minister. . . . He was exuberant; he adored the vestigial ceremonies and was new enough to it to be thrilled at the succession of events." This was spring 1969, and Nixon's first European tour after taking office. By 1974, it is understandable how he, as the official representative of the people of the United States, as its ambassador plenipotentiary to the world, would come to see himself as indispensable to the nation, indeed *as* the nation. After all, DeGaulle, following Louis XIV, conceived of himself as the embodiment of France. Why not Nixon of this nation?

When antiwar protesters spilled out of the cities and campuses and headed for Washington, they were, in Nixon's eyes, disloyal not simply to Nixon but to the nation. When Nixon, on December 8, 1971, found the State Department leaking information about Nixon's upcoming trip to China, he was irate. If members of that department couldn't be loyal to the President, he maintained, they should at least be loyal to the nation. According to Kissinger, this "was one of the emotional comments Nixon later regretted and that cost him so much support. The Department was being loyal to the United States by its lights; it happened to disagree with the President's policy."

Nixon liked to think that what was at stake was nothing less than the security of the nation, when in reality what was at stake was the securing of his reelection. This he had planned cautiously, methodically, completely from the day he entered the White House in 1969. As Kissinger noted, Nixon saw himself "the target of a liberal conspiracy to destroy him." Indeed, ". . . he could never bring himself to regard the upheaval caused by the Vietnam war as anything other than the continuation of the long-lived assault on his political existence."

Not only was the war his own, so was the peace plan his own. By the time of his second inaugural address in 1973, he was positively lavish in self-praise: "Because of America's bold initiatives, 1972 will long be remembered as the year of greatest progress since the end of World War II toward lasting peace in the world." These were, of course, Nixon's own initiatives, taken in secret, with no consulting whatever with his own State Department or Defense Department, much less Congress or the nation. And they were undertaken to provide the "monument" he so desperately craved to assure his reelection. In summary, Nixon had come to identify the nation's security and its credibility with his own.

By 1974, Nixon was a President under siege. His back to the wall, he decided to pull out all the stops on his rhetorical organ. It was not, he would make "perfectly clear," his prosperity that was at stake; it was the nation's prosperity. Indeed, it was not his survival that was in jeopardy; it was the nation's survival. By extension, since the nation was the world's leader, the world, too, was at stake in Nixon's impeachment. When on April 27, 1973, Nixon was fulminating against Dean for trying to "save his own ass," there was King Timahoe—the Irish setter Haldeman had gotten for his President to calm his spirit—presumably jumping up on him.

"Goddamn, get off of me!" He could rid himself of the dog sooner than the Watergate hounds. What they really wanted, Nixon put it, was "frankly to see Agnew [as] president." Warming to that absurd proposition, Nixon determined to open the eyes of Ziegler: ". . . they've got to want this country to succeed. The whole hopes of the whole goddamn world of peace . . . rest right here in this damn chair. . . ."

It had been eighteen months since Nixon stood before a crowd in Ontario in his home state and exulted, "Wherever you go across America, this nation is getting together." In a written statement released to the crowd he elaborated, "When it comes down to the important things, Americans shall stand together—we are one America in conscience, in purpose, and in inspiration." Unfortunately, Ray Price's rhetoric was lagging behind Nixon's reality: the consuming cover-up of the Watergate burglary, as he desperately tried to prevent it from becoming an issue in the election. As Nixon concluded his televised address to the nation, he sounded like Bertha the Bench Warmer, Red Skelton's character, leading the cheers for his team at Whittier: "Let's make the next four years the best four years in America's history."[9]

That they were not, that they were anything but the best four years, that they concluded in less than two years, was the measure of the distance Nixon's "conscience," his "purpose," and his "inspiration" were from those of the American people, the people with whom he had presumed to identify. In another year, Nixon's cover-up would be uncovered, like a stone overturned, revealing the scattering of insects in all directions to escape the glare of the sun's rays. One especially bright ray was the publication, in 1973, of Leonard Lurie's *The Impeachment of Richard Nixon: A Call to Action Now!* There were many Americans who'd succumbed to the pomp and ceremony of an imperial President, who dreaded even the thought of impeachment, who equated the President with the presidency, indeed with the government itself, without whom the nation would collapse. Among those were William F. Buckley: "In deference to the office of the presidency, he must not be removed. Censured, yes; humiliated, yes. But to remove a president is to remove the sovereign." It appears that Buckley, well-read as he was, was unfamiliar with the constitutional system of checks and balances, and particularly with the provision for impeachment, as we shall elaborate in our last chapter.

Nixon's arrogance led him to believe he could identify with the presidency, with the government, and with the nation itself. That presumption led to the crimes and misdemeanors that made impeachment certain. That he escaped impeachment had less to do with "conscience, purpose, and inspiration" than with craft, cunning, and duplicity.

Just as arrogance led to identification, so would identification "follow, as the night the day," with confrontation.

CHAPTER 8

CONFRONTATION

This is an office in which a man must put on his war paint.

— Woodrow Wilson

The way to get ahead is to fish in troubled waters.

— Tommy "The Cork" Corcoran

Screwed again!

— LBJ, upon learning that Bobby Kennedy had foiled the President's attempt to record their confrontation in the Oval Office by using a scrambling device, July 29, 1964

The world is an arena with everyone a warrior doing battle with others. The key question is, who is doing the fucking and who is getting fucked.

— Lyndon Johnson[1]

LYNDON JOHNSON

Wilson and Roosevelt were presidents who, in their long reach for yet more power, abused that which they had. Yet they were forgiven by many because they were war presidents. Emergency powers given to the president at such times can only be gotten by risking confrontation with the legislative or judicial branches. For executive power can only be gained by the one or both the other branches of government forfeiting some of theirs. Strong presidents, those who have amassed unusual power, have invariably been confrontational presidents. Indeed, any social change is bound to incur the discontent, if not the wrath, of those content with and benefiting from the status quo. The more frequent and disruptive the changes, the greater the confrontation.

Few presidents have tried as hard as Lyndon Johnson to change the face of America. It was a solid record of legislation that he, as Majority Leader, shepherded through the Senate. Seeking radical change in his 1957 Civil Rights Bill, he was forced to compromise it again and again, until it became virtually a toothless law. Not until he was President was he able to initiate the radical change he wanted in the Civil Rights Act of 1965. This, the cornerstone of his Great Society, produced some of the most dramatic confrontation of his political career.

Let's Talk

It was not that Lyndon courted confrontation. He much preferred cooperation, especially if the odds were long against him. In this respect Lyndon was scarcely the image of his father, facing down night riders of the Ku Klux Klan on the porch of his house—or facing down super-patriots in the Austin legislature who never saw a German-American they liked, much preferring them behind bars during World War I. Here, rather, was a teenager, flattered by another whose girl Lyndon bragged he could steal. Here was the college student who, challenged to a fight, fell back on his bed, windmilling the air with his long legs, screaming he'd kick his opponent if he got any closer. Here was the Congressman who promised his constituents that when the war came, they could count on him fighting at the battlefront in the mud and the blood; and who then pestered FDR until the President gave him a cushy job "inspecting" Naval installations—and night clubs—on the West Coast. Here was the Vice-President who wasn't about to confront the Soviets in West Berlin, even when ordered there by JFK. After all, who knew when war would break out with the Soviets? Then where would he be? Not until Jack sent Bobby to tell this wearer of the Silver Star that an order was an order did he relent and reluctantly go to West Berlin. Here was no son of the flint-and-steel Sam Johnson. What Lyndon did prefer, especially when the odds seemed about even, was cooperation.

By 1965, President Johnson was going out on a limb with his counterpart in North Vietnam, Ho Chi Minh, offering a cool $1 billion in aid to rebuild the country—if only Ho would sit down with him so they could settle this "bitch of a war." Here, Johnson figured, was an offer "old Ho" couldn't refuse. But he did. If only, Lyndon complained repeatedly, if only Ho would sit down with him, man to man, Lyndon knew he could make him see "reason"—that being meeting Johnson's terms—so he could claim "victory" and not be the first American president to lose a war. But Ho was a man after Eisenhower's heart, not Johnson's. And Ike would not let Johnson come near him with his "treatment," insisting on interposing an aide lest Johnson manhandle him. Ike tended to keep others at a distance, and made doubly sure that in any confrontation with Johnson, the distance would be maintained.

As for Lyndon, he shunned confrontation with Ike, for it was clear the sides were uneven. Liberal Democrats, however, were forever egging on their Majority Leader to have a showdown with their President. Johnson's response: "Any jackass can kick down a barn but only a man can build and keep one."

As Minority Leader, Lyndon had long suffered the jibe of "Landslide Lyndon," and his eighty-seven-vote margin of victory—stolen votes at that—in the 1948 Senate race. These were a constant sore, festering on his memory. He would do nothing to jeopardize a healthy margin of victory in 1954. So he accommodated Ike, not only meeting regularly with him and Rayburn to cooperate in a grand "Texas strategy" for the land, but going out of his way at a Jefferson-Jackson Democratic fund-raiser to hail the "good soldier." He, Lyndon Johnson, was heading an unusual form of bipartisanship, consisting of Democrats and liberal Republicans, to prevent Ike's program from being sabotaged by Old Guard conservatives led by Robert Taft.

When it came to handling the swashbuckling Joe McCarthy, Ike backed off and Johnson kept his distance, until he saw he had a clear advantage. Then, with Ike's blessing, he narrowed in on his target. By the end of 1954, "Tail Gunner Joe" was finished in the Senate. As for Lyndon, he won his reelection handily back in Texas. All the while, of course, he was shaking the Brown and Root money tree whenever the spirit moved him—especially at campaign time.

It was not until 1958, when the Democrats surged to a striking victory in Congress, that Lyndon felt the odds begin to favor him in a confrontation with Eisenhower. Liberal Democratic hounds like Hubert Humphrey and Paul Butler, head of the Democratic Advisory Council, had long been nipping at Ike's heels. Not only was he a lame-duck President, but he lacked the strength in the Senate to sustain a veto. So when the Senate reconvened in January 1958, Lyndon declared to his assembled Democrats in their caucus that it was time to draw a line in the sand. It was time, he declared grandly, for "the start of a new era." Furthermore, "we have an obligation to lead and we shall honor that mandate." Thus did "obligation" and "honor" lie at stake in Johnson's coming confrontation with his President.

Lyndon's handling of Ike with tenterhooks had infuriated his own party liberals. They smelled a sellout as, time and time again, they proposed social programs, only to have their less-than-illustrious leader lop off big chunks of money in deference to Ike and the Texas fat cats. By this time, Lyndon had so alienated himself from his fellow Democrats that he couldn't summon the two-thirds majority necessary to override Ike's "veto pistol." There was Butler condemning Johnson's "time-consuming efforts to water down the proposed legislation to limits the President might accept." There, too, was William Proxmire, McCarthy's replacement from

Wisconsin, maintaining a steady drumbeat of attacks on the Majority Leader who refused to lead. At last, exasperated to the point of desperation, Lyndon confronted him on the floor of the Senate. Proxmire, he ridiculed, needed either "a fairy godmother" or a "wet nurse" to pass his legislation. Then, juxtaposing himself as the courageous politician, willing to confront all odds, Johnson went after Proxmire's hide, ready to hang it on the wall: "It doesn't take much courage . . . to make leadership a punching bag." To the contrary, Proxmire and Butler, along with fellow liberals, knew Johnson dealt out the goodies, and that it took more courage to face him down than Lyndon had ever displayed. Lyndon's leadership was fraying badly, and by his last two years as Majority Leader he found the rug being pulled out from beneath him repeatedly, Ike on one corner and liberal Democrats on the other.[2]

The Kennedy Brothers

By the end of the fifties a pattern was evident. When it was clear that Johnson enjoyed the upper hand, he could be merciless. If it seemed like a draw, he'd opt for cooperation. And if he was confronting more than his match, he'd back down or procrastinate, sulking in a corner. Each of these lines in the pattern became evident in his dealing with the Kennedys. Of all his confrontations, none penetrated so deeply, or left him so paranoid, as his face-off with the Kennedys. Actually, the story began with Jack's election to the Senate in 1952, after serving six years in the House. When Lyndon got Russell to back him for Minority Leader, the freshman Kennedy stopped by. "I want you to know," he assured Lyndon, "you can count on my support." Recalled brother Sam Houston, Lyndon said Jack "looked like a nice kid and probably had some future in politics." At the same time, Johnson typed Kennedy as "weak and pallid," a scrawny man with a bad back, a weak and indecisive politician, a nice man, a gentle man, but not a man's man."

Here was a reflection of the tendency of Johnson to denigrate others he thought might be superior to himself. For JFK, entering the House in 1946 was, like Richard Nixon, a "comer" in politics. Rich, cultured, Harvard-educated, Kennedy was the epitome of the Northeast elite that Johnson both feared and envied. Worse, Kennedy's father, Joe, was as influential as he was ambitious for his son. By 1956, Jack was vying with

Tennessee Senator Estes Kefauver for the vice-presidential slot on the Democratic ticket. The previous fall, recuperating from his heart attack at the Ranch, Johnson had gotten a call from Joe, saying he and his son would work for Johnson's nomination at the convention if he chose to run. No, Johnson had no interest in this, he said, only to find himself a favorite-son candidate from Texas. For although he did have an interest, it wasn't enough. He couldn't seem to get sufficient backing even in his home state.

With his own delegates, Johnson had them cast their vote for Kennedy's nomination as vice-president, but not until there had been considerable hedging. To Jack, Lyndon appeared noncommittal. Both vice-presidential hopefuls Hubert Humphrey and Missouri Senator Stuart Symington thought Lyndon was in their respective corners. Perhaps, Kennedy figured, Tennessee Senator Albert Gore thought the same. "Maybe," Jack added, "Lyndon wanted them all to think that. We never knew how that one [LBJ] would turn out." As usual, "that one" was playing his hand close to his chest. On the first ballot he delivered his delegation to Gore, even though Johnson and Gore were notorious antagonists on the Senate floor. When the roll call on the second ballot reached Texas, Lyndon grabbed the mike and shouted, "Texas proudly casts its fifty-six votes for the fighting sailor who wears the scars of battle. . . ." Johnson, that quickly, had switched to Kennedy. All the while, though, Lyndon was playing out his own strategy, nursing the hope that, deadlocked, the convention would turn to the Senate Majority Leader. Instead of circulating among the various state legislators, however, Lyndon stayed in his hotel room, a phone stuck to his ear as he talked with other leaders of the Senate. Surely the convention was aware, as the press would pick up in a year or so, that Lyndon was the second-most powerful man in the nation, next to Ike himself. Yet, as Evans and Novak maintained, at that convention "the power was scarcely aware of Lyndon Johnson," described by Theodore White as "the traditional hopeless Southern candidate."

Neither was the convention much aware of Jack Kennedy, and it was Estes Kefauver whom Stevenson chose for his running mate. Writing to Joe, Lyndon explained that he simply couldn't back the Kennedy choice of Stevenson. Yet Lyndon made sure the elder Kennedy understood his warm regard for his son. "How proud I am," he wrote, "of the Democratic senator from Massachusetts. . . ." Supporting him "lighted the brightest lamp of hope for a truly great Democratic Party."

It wasn't long, however, before Lyndon was singing a different tune about Jack. Told by Rayburn that Kennedy was out on the hustings, beating the bushes in preparation for a presidential run in 1960, Lyndon dismissed it. "Oh, I don't know about that. He might want to be vice-president—but that's about all." Johnson was in for a rude awakening, as he saw, day by day, Kennedy absenting himself from the Senate to get a leg up on other candidates—including Lyndon—in 1960. As Theodore White pointed out, "Between 1956 and 1960 no Democrat, not even Adlai Stevenson, spoke in more states, addressed more Jefferson-Jackson Day dinners, participated in more local and mayoralty campaigns of deserving Democrats than did John F. Kennedy. By the spring of 1960 Kennedy had not only visited every state in the union, but his intelligence files bulged with what was possibly the most complete index ever made of the power structure of any national party."[3]

Jack, however, was unhappy with the lack of press coverage, so he nudged journalist Arthur Krock, "Why do you give all that space to Lyndon Johnson's achievements? Why don't you think of some of us younger men?" Soon Kennedy was getting his share of favorable coverage. And Theodore White, among others, was impressed, partly because of the striking contrast between the speaking styles of the two men. On the one hand was the "Harvard-trained, immaculately tailored [and] superbly eloquent" Kennedy. On the other hand was the provincial Southerner, the first to be seriously considered for the presidency since the War Between the States. Priding himself on the "touch of gray in his hair," Lyndon's campaigning on his own home stamping grounds was a "show-boat production," something to behold.

As in 1955, Jack had been anxious to know if Lyndon was a serious candidate. So he dispatched Bobby to the ranch to discover Lyndon's intentions. While Bobby was there, Lyndon insisted they go hunting, and armed him with a powerful shotgun. Bobby targeted the game, fired, and was knocked to the ground, bleeding above one eye. "Son," said the fifty-one-year-old elder statesman to the thirty-four-year-old as he helped him up, "you've got to learn how to handle a gun like a man."

More than a gun, Bobby discovered, he had to learn how to handle Lyndon. Off to his brother Bobby carried the news: No, Lyndon had no intention of running, but he'd remain as Majority Leader, above the fray as other senators dirtied their hands in the rough-and-tumble of campaign politics. He would stay, Lyndon promised, strictly neutral. Here he was adopting the same tactics that had failed him in 1956: hoping, planning for a convention deadlock, after which the delegates would come to their senses and choose the man most capable of leading the country. Having promised to be neutral, Lyndon immediately reneged on his promise and poured money—big money—into the West Virginia primary, a contest essentially between Humphrey and Kennedy. As a largely Protestant state, it was a must-win for the Catholic Jack. Despite Johnson's interference, he took the state handily, and Hubert bowed out of the race for lack of money. This was not what Johnson wanted. To achieve a deadlock at the convention required a close race right down to the finish. There, however, was Jack Kennedy, gaining ground rapidly, too rapidly. Kennedy's staff was irate that Johnson had not only reneged on his promise but had tried to defeat their man. Back off, Lyndon threatened these carping critics, or he'd take steps to counteract.

There was Johnson's interference in West Virginia, his double-dealing with Kennedy, his criticizing Kennedy for failing to vote to censure Joe McCarthy, his digs about Kennedy's health, and his disparaging of Joe as a Hitler sympathizer while ambassador to the Court of St. James in the thirties. Yet JFK not only continued to win, but to praise Lyndon to the press for treating him so well in the Senate. Jack had no intention of clashing openly with the Majority Leader. When, later, Jack chose Lyndon as his vice-presidential candidate, Bobby let it be known that the choice was based on his brother's not wanting LBJ as Majority Leader during his Presidency.

When at last, in the middle of May, Johnson gave an unofficial announcement of his candidacy, he would become, in the words of Kearns, "the perpetual tourist in the alien land of national politics." Said Kennedy, after learning that Johnson had tossed his Stetson in the ring, "Johnson had to prove that a Southerner could win in the North, just as I had to prove a Catholic could win in heavily Protestant states."[4] Still, Johnson was optimistic, envisioning himself as president, with JFK his vice-president. In addition, he boasted, he'd harvest the necessary 530 votes on the first ballot at the convention.

Here was the first of many blunders that managed to sink Johnson's ship, even before it made port at the convention. He not only vastly overestimated his own qualifications but underestimated the potential of his opponent—something he would continue to do as a President bogged down in the quagmire of Vietnam.

Kennedy, he said, not only needed "a little gray in his hair," but was a "lightweight." Yes, he seemed "smart enough," but more given to play than the kind of hard work and tough decisions he'd encounter as president. Furthermore he, Lyndon Johnson, knew ten times more about running the country! One moment Lyndon was the righteous, hardworking Puritan, his nose to the grindstone of the Senate. The next moment he was the grandiose showboater, bragging that just as Texas was oversized, so was he larger than life. In another moment he was the sharp wheeler-dealer, dressed to the nines, who never saw a deal he didn't think he could exploit. Then again he was the crude cowpoke, unabashed at wiping the cow dung from his boots at a formal reception. And always, it seemed—and especially in the late afternoon and into the evening—there would be his mainstay Cutty Sark, to anesthetize him from the reality that ever seemed to be closing in on him. So who was Lyndon Johnson, the *real* Lyndon Johnson? More to the point, who was the persona he was projecting? Whether observing him up close and personal, as few did, or observing him from a distance, or on TV, the man simply did not ring true with many Americans.

As it was, Johnson presumed much. He hadn't learned from his 1956 failure to get the nomination by hoping for a deadlock. He waited until the last minute to declare himself a candidate. He figured that by having Democratic senators in his pocket, he could not only count on their support, but the votes of their respective state delegations. Kennedy knew better, and had been courting the support of mayors and state party chairmen across the country. An example of this mistake was Connecticut's Senator Thomas Dodd, who had promised Lyndon his support and that of the state's delegation. But already Kennedy had lined up John Bailey, the Connecticut party chairman.

Lyndon had other problems. His staff was a patchwork consisting of Texas Governor Price Daniel, John Connally, George Reedy, and Irvin Hoff, who had been lent to Johnson from the staff of Washington Senator Warren Magnuson. Kennedy, in contrast, had a top-notch staff, even by his exacting standards: veterans of almost four years experience, savvy in the ways of national politics. Lyndon also made the mistake of joining Jack in co-sponsoring a labor bill. When Texas conservatives rose up in arms, LBJ assured them he'd opposed labor in every preceding bill for the past twen-ty years. This, of course, set alarm bells ringing in union halls across the country. In addition, Johnson alienated himself from both liberals and the elderly by branding the steer of Medicare "the socialization of the medical profession."

A Harris poll in Indiana put it all in a nutshell. Johnson was not a "people's politician" but a "politician's politician." As such, he'd gained a reputation as a slick, cool calculator, rather than a warmhearted empathiz-er with the rank and file from which presidential majorities emerge. He'd earned his reputation as Majority Leader, as White put it, being "liberal, sound, wise, masterful," using his constant presence in the capital to shep-herd conventional legislation "through the hidden ambuscades and open hostility of the Washington jungle." However, White added, "cunning, clever, adroit, even masterful have never been a match for empathic, warm, and friendly, especially to one's competitors."

Before the convention opened, there was Sidey again interviewing LBJ, and there was LBJ venting "all of the enmity and hostility" that he felt for the Kennedys in what Sidey recalled as "the most vicious evaluation of Senator Kennedy," getting "quite violent at times." Johnson's trouble was that he'd met more than his match, and in the form of a Senator nine years his junior—who'd come to him as Majority Leader, like all the rest, for favors.

Not about to reveal his strategy as a dark horse at the convention, Johnson was asked by reporters why he'd dithered so long before announcing his candidacy. "I don't want to get a bug in my mouth I can't swallow," he explained, with unusual insight. So, from his commanding view in the elaborate "Taj Mahal" of his office suite, he watched—as he would watch eight years hence from the White House—the unfolding of events "like a man trapped," as White put it.[5]

Lyndon would take the initiative, and therein lay more mistakes. On June 24, a full-page ad ran in major newspapers across the country, urging Johnson to run—and paid for, without a doubt, from Lyndon's campaign treasure chest. Two days later, at the Governor's Conference, Johnson reverted to type in using "the treatment" on governors as he'd done on senators. Vote for Kennedy, he warned fellow senators, but don't count on me for campaign money for your reelections. Vote for me and get your state delegates to follow your lead, and you'll get money as well as choice committee assignments. Nothing subtle about this quid pro quo, the same tactic he used with the governors. Governors and senators alike fled to the Kennedy camp.

But Johnson wasn't ready to throw in the towel. In his most egregious blunder yet, he refused to adjourn the Senate before the start of the convention. Instead, beginning the first week in July, he recessed it for five weeks—to reconvene after the convention had voted its nominations. Here was yet another power play, and it only served to alienate Johnson even further from fellow senators. Drawing his last ace from his sleeve, Johnson prevailed on Rayburn, as convention moderator, to violate the cardinal rule of moderating by siding openly with Johnson. Kennedy was dismayed but hardly surprised.

Not until July 5 did Johnson formally announce his candidacy, and that from the theater off the new Senate Office Building, surrounded by hundreds of friends and a cynical press corps. Never short on boasting, he predicted he'd win the nomination—this time—on the third ballot. Unfortunately, this dark horse was so silhouetted against the bright Kennedy that few delegates took him seriously. Neither would he let the occasion pass without taking a few swipes at "the bug" he'd caught in his throat. Kennedy, he said, had forsaken his obligations as a Senator to elbow his way among 179 million Americans, shouting. "Look at me and nobody else!" On the other hand, here was LBJ, Majority Leader of the U.S. Senate, fulfilling his sacred obligation as he tended the store he'd been elected to manage. The contrast was that simple, and bound to be as insidious as it was stark.

The press was unmoved. One reporter asked, would Johnson settle for the vice-presidency if he didn't get the presidential bid? Johnson ignored him, only to find the reporter persisting. So Johnson used words that left no doubt as to who was the elder statesman: the mature, responsible master of the Senate. And this, he presumed, was enough to qualify him—and him alone among the slate of candidates—to succeed Eisenhower. On the other hand, there was the brash, immature, and impulsive Kennedy, throwing his first responsibility as a Senator to the winds as he made for the hustings, there to scrounge for just a few more votes. Just how demeaning Kennedy's behavior was must surely be evident, even to a cynical press.

Few in the press agreed—and few at the convention. It didn't help when Lyndon ridiculed Jack as the "little scrawny fellow with rickets." To one reporter he asked, "Have you ever seen his ankles?" With that he traced a small circle with his fingers, adding, "they're about so round." Then Johnson pulled from his pocket an electrocardiogram showing, ostensibly, that his own heart had healed perfectly from his attack five years earlier. Kennedy, Johnson insisted, was not only scrawny and sickly but a "Daddy's boy," whom Johnson assigned to the Foreign Relations Committee only after his "Daddy" had intervened to plead for "his little boy." This over Cutty Sark as LBJ schmoozed with reporters.

There were few criticisms of Kennedy that his staff resented more than Johnson's ham-handed attempts to discredit their chief on the basis of poor health. In July, Lyndon's campaign manager, John Connally, went public with a demand that Kennedy air the fact of his potentially fatal Addison's disease, a malfunctioning of the adrenal glands. Though Jack had been keeping it under control with doses of cortisone since the early fifties, the last thing he wanted to do was to broadcast it. Bobby, Jack's campaign manager, answered that his brother suffered no such thing as "an ailment classically described as Addison's Disease." The devil was apparently in the details of the definition of "classically." Then Jack himself went public with a medical report testifying his "health is excellent." To Minnesota's Walter Judd, in a chance elevator meeting, Lyndon jested, "Jack's pediatricians have just given him a clean bill of health!"[6]

It was nomination time at the convention and Johnson was on pins and needles. Here was Kennedy, who'd captained a PT boat in the Pacific during World War II—at great personal cost. And there was Johnson, who'd spent four months goldbricking on the West Coast before his star-spangled trip to Australia to pick up his political favor from MacArthur—his Silver Star. At the wheel of the convention ship was Rayburn, ready to guide it through rough waters. No need to worry, he assured Johnson. But at the end of the first ballot JFK had racked up an impressive 806 electoral votes, almost twice Johnson's 409, and 45 votes more than he needed for the nomination. It was a thunderclap of humiliation. Only once in his twenty-three years in politics had Johnson been defeated, and that paled next to the humiliation of falling at the hands of the "kid with the rickets." Just prior to the first-ballot vote, Johnson had again put his big foot in his bigger mouth and again attacked Joe Kennedy as a Nazi sympathizer. Here was overkill, the Johnson strategy when he figured he clearly had the upper hand. He didn't, and it backfired, not only costing him votes on the first ballot, but further alienating him from Kennedy's staff—and particularly from Bobby.

This did nothing to aid Johnson's chances as Kennedy's pick for vice-president on the ticket. Indeed, so dismal were Lyndon's chances for the number-two berth that the press was ranking him below both Symington and Washington Senator "Scoop" Jackson. Having listened to Johnson say he'd never exchange his post as Majority Leader for the vice-presidency, and having been spurned by Humphrey for the job, Jack turned to Symington. By July 11, however, reporter Joe Alsop and publisher Phil Graham were urging Kennedy to go with Johnson, confident that, in the last analysis, he'd accept.

In retrospect, many have wondered why on earth, especially in view of Johnson's continued fulminating against Kennedy, Jack chose him as his running mate. If ever there was a case of oil and water not mixing, it would appear to be the urbane, sophisticated Bay Stater and the devil-may-care, swashbuckling Texan. There was no doubt that the distance separating the two was considerably more than the 2,000 miles between their homes. Furthermore, Kennedy's staff could not have been more dead-set against Johnson, even as Rayburn was dead-set against the Kennedys. On Wednesday night, with Jack's nomination, Tommy Corcoran asked Johnson if he'd take the number-two spot if offered. Lyndon: "He won't give it to me." Corcoran: "Will you allow me to develop an option?" Lyndon: "It's all right with me, if Sam goes along with it. He hates the Kennedys." So "the Cork" went to Sam. Would he agree? Rayburn: "Never! I won't go along with it. I wouldn't trust Joe Kennedy across the street. He'll double-cross us sure as hell." If there was anyone who could spot a double-cross, it was Rayburn. Twenty years before he'd gotten that same treatment from his protégé and adopted son, Lyndon Johnson.

But how things change, and in a matter of hours. At two in the morning on July 14, Rayburn phoned Johnson to tell him it would be "idiotic to accept." Then, nine hours later, he urged Johnson to accept. Asked why he'd changed his mind, Sam admitted, "I am a damn sight smarter than I was last night." Who'd "smartened" him up were two of Kennedy's men from Massachusetts, John McCormack and "Tip" O'Neill, one a past, the other a future, speaker of the House. Kennedy, they assured Rayburn, had no chance of winning without the Southern vote. Of the 806 electoral votes he'd gotten, only nine were from the South. Should Kennedy lose, Richard Nixon, the front-runner among the Republicans, would in all probability be the next president. If there was one person Rayburn despised more that Kennedy, it was Nixon. So, going with the lesser of two evils, Rayburn resigned himself to a Kennedy-Johnson ticket.

Sam Houston saw the situation: "As a Catholic attempting to overcome an historical bias against people of his faith, [Kennedy] particularly needed someone to boost him in the Bible Belt of the South and Southwest." The subsequent results clearly showed Kennedy was right in his prognostication. For without the electoral vote of Texas and two or three other Southern states, Kennedy would never have squeaked by Nixon.

Johnson repeatedly vowed that "never, *never*" would he trade his berth as Majority Leader of the "World's Most Exclusive Club" for what former Vice-President John Nance Garner had claimed wasn't worth a "pitcher of warm spit." Just the night before leaving for the convention in Los Angeles, Lyndon had broken bread with Henry and Clare Boothe Luce in New York City. Told that Kennedy had the nomination wrapped up, and that Johnson's best shot would be the vice-presidency, Lyndon was furious. Why, as Senate Majority Leader "[I] exercise more power over the country than any man other than the president." Furthermore," he said in his own Texas manner, "all vice-presidents are political eunuchs, and I am not, by God, about to let Kennedy cut my balls off."

Now, only days later, Kennedy had gotten "the warmest and most cordial telegram of congratulations" from Johnson. Here was a hint that maybe, after all, Lyndon was open to an invitation, despite his dismissal of a vice-president as "generally like a Texas steer. He has lost his social standing in the society in which he resides."[7]

Kennedy, with more than a measure of foresight, had gone so far as to tell Rayburn that Lyndon would be "the most qualified man for the presidency if anything should happen to me." His immediate foresight was the need—the desperate need, despite the stubborn resistance of his staff—for Johnson on the ticket. So the next morning, Thursday, July 14, Kennedy was in Johnson's hotel suite, telling him that he was JFK's choice. Lyndon, sensing the upper hand, reverted to type and decided to play hard-to-get. He wasn't so sure about this offer. He needed time to think it over, even though that evening the number-two slot on the ticket was scheduled to be chosen.

Kennedy, for his part, was mystified why Johnson would sacrifice his leadership in the Senate, where he was not only busy but calling the shots, for what most previous vice-presidents considered a thankless job. John Adams had called it "the most insignificant office that ever the invention of man contrived or his imagination conceived." And he was Vice-President to none other than Washington! Told that her husband had been nominated for that lowly office, Mrs. Coolidge asked Calvin incredulously, "You're not going to take it, are you?" To which he responded, "I suppose I'll have to." And on Warren G. Harding's death in office, Coolidge suddenly found himself President—just as Lyndon would be catapulted into that office on the death of Kennedy. "Power is as power goes," was Johnson's explanation for accepting, as he tried to explain to his befuddled staff. Always super-sensitive to the smell of power, Lyndon was now sensing that the greatest power on earth was settling around the head of Jack Kennedy. Perhaps, with Texas and more of the South, he could win against the impossible Nixon. After all, it was the same John Adams who, taking the vice-presidency 175 years earlier, had said, "Today I am nothing, but tomorrow I may be everything." Furthermore, Johnson was counting on continuing to pull strings in the Senate. Montanan Mike Mansfield, Johnson's successor, had long before realized that few were more determined than Lyndon to find a way.

So Johnson decided, reluctantly at best, to cast his lot with JFK, called by Rayburn, "The Pope's President." Even Lady Bird came around, relieved that her husband's sixteen-hour days, catch-as-catch-can meals, and a grinding pace that had almost left her two daughters fatherless five years before, might at last be over.

All, however, was not well in the Kennedy camp. Howls of protest erupted from his staff and reverberated throughout the convention hall as delegates learned of Kennedy's choice. Soon Kennedy was having second thoughts, so he dispatched Bobby to sound out Lyndon in his suite. Jack's message: Did Johnson really want that spot on the ticket? If he'd changed his mind, Jack would understand. In fact, Jack would give him the post of Democratic National Chairman "or anything else" his heart desired. After all, Lyndon, no more than Jack, would want to risk the barroom brawl that would ensue on the convention floor if he persisted in deciding to stay on the ticket.[8]

Soon Bobby was at Johnson's door, but on the advice of Lady Bird, Lyndon refused to see him. Instead, Bobby gave the news to an unbelieving Rayburn. What was going on here? For, unbeknownst to Bobby, Jack had checked out the protests in the hall and found them confined largely to Governor "Soapy" Williams' strong labor state of Michigan, and to Washington, D.C. So he'd experienced another change of heart, picked up the phone, and while Bobby was en route to Lyndon's suite, assured Johnson that he was still his vice-presidential choice.

Now, with Bobby communicating—eagerly communicating—Jack's message, Rayburn's pudgy face got redder and redder. On the bed in an adjoining room of the suite sat Lyndon, Lady Bird, and Graham, the latter reminding Lyndon of his earlier vow. "You don't want it, you won't negotiate for it, you'll only take it if Jack drafts you, and you won't discuss it with anyone else"—least of all with Bobby. As far as Bobby was concerned, he was simply a messenger for brother Jack. Lyndon didn't see him that way. Here, he was convinced, was the young whippersnapper who could no more handle Lyndon than he could a shotgun, yet heading a conspiracy to deprive him, first, of the nomination for president, and now the nomination for vice-president. Jim Rowe, a long-time friend and adviser, agreed with him.

Johnson was as flabbergasted as Rayburn was livid at this turn of events. By this time, Graham recalled, "LBJ seemed about to jump out of his skin." Finally, to resolve all the hubbub, Rayburn told Graham to call Jack. "Bobby's down here," Graham recalled his telling Jack, "saying such and such," to which Kennedy responded, "Well, Bobby's not up to date. I've already announced that Johnson is the candidate." Then Jack asked to have Bobby put on the phone. Hanging up after Jack's explanation, Bobby seemed depressed, but resigned to his older brother's resolution. "Jim," he said to Rowe, "I guess we were all too tired." Still he persisted. "Don't you think Symington or Jackson would be better?" As far as Bobby was concerned, it appeared anybody would be better than the hulking Texan who'd gone out of his way to humiliate him at the Ranch; who'd gone back on his word and poured money into West Virginia to defeat Jack; who'd savaged Jack on many scores, the least tolerable of which was his health; and who'd gone after his father, tooth and nail, as the American Neville Chamberlain. It was enough to choke on, and Bobby would not soon forget it.

Still uneasy as he watched Bobby leave to meet with Jack again, Lyndon decided to clear up the matter once and for all, face-to-face. Yes, Jack reassured him, he was definitely on the ticket. So Johnson shook hands on it and promised to support him. Kennedy would call the plays from now on, and Johnson would be a team player.

With that, Johnson held a news conference, standing on a chair in the hotel corridor. "If my country thinks I can serve better as a private," announced the humble Lyndon loftily, "I want to serve. If they want me to serve as a general . . . whatever my country wants. Jack Kennedy has asked me to serve. I accept."

So ended round one of the Johnson-Kennedy confrontation. Lyndon, with one blunder after another, recognized he'd met superior forces and had decided if he couldn't lick them, he'd join them. That Thursday evening, it was a mere formality, with Johnson being nominated by acclamation amid a few jeers and cat-calls from disgruntled Michiganders. Learning the news, Arizona Senator Barry Goldwater, whom Lyndon would confront in the presidential election four years later, declared, "I'm nauseated!" The next day Goldwater wrote to Johnson: ". . . I still have a numb feeling of despair over your actions of yesterday in accepting the candidacy for vice-president. . . . You were intended for great things, but I don't think you are going to achieve them now." Learning the same news, Joe Kennedy confided to a friend that Jack had made "the smartest political move he'd ever made."[9]

Round two opened anything but auspiciously. There was Kennedy making appointments, without so much as consulting his running mate. "I think I'll go back to Texas," complained the maverick steer, "and make a couple speeches and to hell with it." But that wasn't all of it. "Tell me," he asked a friend, "what is it that people like so much in Jack Kennedy?" Here was this rich, spoiled, stripling of a "Daddy's boy," depending on Lyndon running interference for him, if not actually calling the signals. The contrast must be evident to all. And here, on the other hand, was the maestro of the Senate symphony for eight years, exchanging harmony for the cacophony and listlessness of the Senate he'd inherited. What more could the American people expect from the Majority Leader? What more, in particular, could Texas want? Truth be told, and Johnson often found that unwelcome, he'd be about as welcome back in Dallas, Houston, and San Antonio as a Yankee carpetbagger during Reconstruction. For now he'd disgraced the Lone Star State by joining the ticket of this "socialist," as the Texas business community called Kennedy, this Catholic boy still wet behind the ears. Furthermore, he was hardly out of the cocoon of Boston, the epitome of the Northeast, hated if envied, home of the nose-in-the-air blue-bloods who got their kicks out of disparaging the ignorant poor, especially those from Texas. At least, so thought Johnson. And the more Lyndon thought about it, the more agitated he became. Here was "junior," the fresh-faced kid who would be president, the boy who'd come to him since 1952 for favors: for committee and office assignments, for staff, for support on bills he wished to introduce, for campaign money—for everything his Senate career depended on. In addition, had not Lyndon gone the extra mile and backed him for vice-president in 1956? It was simply too much.

Well, Lyndon Johnson remained a power to be reckoned with. It wasn't long before he was tossing one monkey wrench after another into Kennedy's well-oiled campaign machinery. He canceled or rearranged abruptly the carefully planned itineraries, leaving aides, welcoming committees, and audiences in an uproar. He threw out meticulously scripted speeches and substituted those from Reedy and others of his own speech writers.

Theodore White had written, "Whoever runs for the presidency of the United States can . . . never shape his own problems. America and America's problems at home and in the world shape it for him. . . ." Yet White placed too much emphasis on happenstance. For history shows that not only is a president's career shaped by which of the many problems confronting him he chooses to deal with, but just how he deals with them. Arnold Toynbee has argued that civilizations have risen and fallen on the basis of problems they chose to confront and how they chose to cope with them. Thus, civilizations, like nations, reflect in large part the choices of their leaders.

From his formal acceptance speech on Friday morning of the convention, Jack Kennedy, Lyndon's beneficiary—turned competitor—turned nemesis—turned ally—was, despite his wan and haggard appearance, primed to go against Nixon. Gathered about Kennedy on the platform that morning were the vanquished: Hubert Humphrey and Stuart Symington, Adlai Stevenson and Lyndon Johnson. It is safe to say that none felt the humiliation of defeat at the hands of the junior senator from Massachusetts more acutely than did the Majority Leader who'd taken Kennedy under his wing in the Senate. Still, he was JFK's vice-presidential choice, whatever that was worth.

With the campaign off and running, Kennedy was soon aware that Nixon wasn't his only problem. Johnson seemed intent on strewing JFK's path to the presidency with land mines, interspersed here and there with an occasional flower. One such flower emerged in the form of Brown and Root. Early on, Lyndon realized how desperate was Jack for money when a man approached them in the Senate cloakroom with a "gift"—an investment on which he was anticipating a hefty return: "I want to give you this, Senator." Johnson intervened, "Not here! Let's get out of this building." Kennedy, however, with no such qualms, grabbed the money and stuffed it into his pocket. Steve Smith, treasurer for the campaign, thereafter made a weekly trip to Kennedy's house to search his wardrobe—ransacking every pocket of every suit, emerging, more often than not, with thousands of dollars. Surely Jack had a lot to learn from Lyndon in the way of efficient fund-raising. For Johnson had only to drop a hint to George Brown, and money would come tumbling from the Brown and Root jackpot, along with more money from choice friends in Texas.

In addition, Johnson went to bat for Kennedy on the problem of his religion. Here was the most important issue of the campaign, according to the Rev. Norman Vincent Peale and 150 other Protestant clergymen. Meeting in Washington on September 9, they warned of the pernicious influence of the Vatican's foreign policy on a Catholic President. Three days later, pickets at the Alamo in San Antonio confronted Kennedy and Johnson with placards: "We want the Bible and the Constitution" and "We don't want the Kremlin or the Vatican." But the protesters were silenced when Lyndon introduced Jack as a "little old war hero," followed by Kennedy's brilliant comment that on this site, alongside "Bowie and Crockett, died McCafferty and Bailey and Carey, but no one knows whether they were Catholics or not, for there was no religious test at the Alamo." The audience erupted with thunderous applause and most of the pickets abandoned their signs.

Throughout Johnson's whistle-stop tour of the South, he repeatedly scored the point that Jack's brother, Joe Jr., had been killed in World War II together with his copilot, a Texan. "I'm sure," Lyndon would say, "that they didn't ask each other what church they went to; they both died for their country."[10]

With JFK's victory, Lyndon was, at long last, within a heartbeat of the White House. Garner wasn't the only one who had little use for the vice-presidency. Wilson disparaged the post as so bereft of influence and power that its "chief embarrassment in discussing it is in explaining how little there is to say about it. . . ." And Wilson's Vice-President, Thomas Marshall, described his situation in even more dire terms: He was, he confessed, like "a man in a cataleptic state. He cannot go up. He cannot move. He suffers no pain. And yet he is conscious of all that goes on around him."

Still, Marshall was better off—far better off—than was this ego-driven whirlwind, who had once swept up everything and everybody in his wake, but who now had to cool his heels and await orders. Suddenly Johnson's main function, to borrow a line from John Adams, was "to remind the President of his mortality—a ghastly function at best."

Lyndon agreed with the assesment of America's first vice-president. "Every time," he recalled, "I came into John Kennedy's presence, I felt like a goddamn raven hovering over his shoulder." Away from the Oval Office it was even worse. "The vice-presidency is filled with trips around the world, chauffeurs, men saluting, people clapping, chairmanships of councils, but in the end it is nothing. I detested every minute of it." Once LBJ had taken over the reins of government, he told the slain president's brother-in-law, Sargent Shriver, "a man [who] runs for vice-president is a very foolish man. [A] man [who] runs away from it's very wise. I wish I had run further away from it than I did."

Especially painful was his being made the butt of jokes and sneers—not by JFK, but by his aides, with the Attorney General, Bobby, leading the jeers. As for Jack, he bent over backward to accommodate the man who had sent him over the top—just barely—and into the White House. JFK warned his staff he'd tolerate no ill treatment of Johnson. If they disobeyed, he'd fire them. "After all," he put it to them, "I spent years of my life when I could not get consideration for a bill until I went around and begged Lyndon Johnson."

Perhaps it was that order, circulated back to Johnson, that helped prompt him—shortly after taking office—to lay on Kennedy's desk, awaiting his signature, a memo authorizing Johnson to exercise unprecedented power over large areas of the executive branch. Here, in any case, was vintage Johnson, a man already wilting in the political desert, thirsting for the water of power. Shown a copy, one of Johnson's senator friends was astonished at what he called the most presumptuous document ever sent by any vice-president to his president. Prudently, Kennedy chose to ignore it, lest his aides find yet another rich lode to mine for their jibes about "Uncle Cornpone."

For eight years Lyndon had sat under FDR. For seven years he'd sat under Truman. Then for eight more years he'd sat under Eisenhower. All without complaint. As Vice-President himself, he was not about to level broadsides against this President who did his best to reciprocate Lyndon's respect. But Kennedy would learn what it was like to have, as Evans and Novak worded it, this "great grizzly bear" who'd hugged people "until they gave in to his demands . . . now in hibernation.. . ."[11]

Kennedy ignored Lyndon's power-grab memo, but the President did assign him to chair two important committees: the National Space Council and the Equal Employment Opportunity Commission. His job on the EEOC was to monitor business contracts with the federal government to make sure that no racial discrimination prevailed. But always Lyndon, in the eyes of Bobby, seemed to be dragging his feet. Again and again Bobby was the hound dog, yapping at Lyndon, urging him to get moving. As for the Space Council, Bobby seemed to have little awareness of Lyndon's significant contribution there. Early in 1961, Kennedy had asked Johnson for recommendations as to America's role in space. Lyndon appointed a task force to address the issue, consisting of RCA's David Sarnoff, CBS's William Stanton, and old friend Donald C. Cook. Their report recommended an exponential increasing of expenditures for space development. It was this that led Kennedy, later that year, to challenge the nation to put a man on the moon "in this decade."

It seems that Bobby was ever out of sorts with Lyndon, and it was reciprocated. Johnson resented Jack's turning inevitably to his Attorney General rather than to his Vice-President for advice. "Every time they have a conference," Lyndon complained. "don't kid anybody who is the top adviser. . . . Bobby is first in, last out. And Bobby is the boy he listens to."

Fed up with one slight after another, Lyndon at last faced down Bobby and told him he knew why the younger Kennedy didn't like him: It was his slighting of Bobby's father, and his likening Joe to Neville Chamberlain, the woeful appeaser of Hitler in the late thirties. As for this,

Johnson lamely explained, "I was misquoted." Bobby, feigning ignorance, said, "I don't know what you're talking about." Lyndon: "Yes, you do, you know what I'm talking about and that's the reason you don't like me." Bobby, not to be done in by Lyndon's excuse, had an aide check four different newspaper accounts of Johnson's disparaging his father. His conclusion: there had been no misquotation. Johnson was not only a liar, he concluded, but an interloper arrogating to himself the vice-presidency.

Johnson the grizzly occasionally rubbed his eyes and, mistaking his own ethereal ambition for the sun, sauntered forth from his hibernation to confound Jack as well as Bobby. Seeing Jack pick up on his space report, the emboldened Vice-President asked JFK if he could fly to the spot in the Bahamas where the first astronaut, John Glenn, was scheduled to touch down. Kennedy: absolutely not! Then Johnson asked if he could accompany Glenn on his ticker-tape parade in New York City. Kennedy: that is out of the question. This is to be Glenn's day, not yours. Let him bask in his own glory. But Johnson kept at it, as he'd learned to do with Rayburn, Russell, and FDR. Like the judge in the Scriptures who gave in to the importunate widow, JFK acceded just to get Lyndon off his back.[12]

Bobby Alone

With JFK's death and Lyndon in the driver's seat, he was aware there was a consensus forming in favor of Bobby as his vice-president come 1964. By this time, however, Johnson had threatened, "If they try to push Bobby Kennedy down my throat for vice-president, I'll tell them to nominate him for the *presidency* and leave me out of it." LBJ could make such a rash statement because he'd read the polls and, confident they were right, saw that he could easily win without Bobby. Johnson was exultant. "I don't need that little runt to win. I can take anybody I damn well please." With that, he began laying plans to remove this albatross from his neck.

The red-letter day came on July 29, 1964. As his Attorney General was ushered into the Oval Office, Lyndon flipped on the tape recorder. He would make certain that Bobby's version of the showdown coincided with his own. So—reminiscent of his judgment more than a decade earlier that the new Senator, JFK, might have some sort of political future—Lyndon laid it on the line for forty minutes. His feigned sadness could scarcely hide his determination as he broke the bad news. "You have a bright future in politics, but not this year." Bobby just couldn't serve his party, his country, or his President as well in the position of vice-president as he could in some other position—any other position. And, of course, he was free to stay on as Attorney General—*his* attorney general. It almost sounded like a replay of Bobby's offer to Lyndon four years earlier in trying to get him off Jack's ticket. Bobby's face fell, then darkened. As Attorney General, he knew *his* FBI had forfeited its evidence to the Warren Commission. Would he ever know the truth of his brother's assassination?

After escorting Bobby to the door, Lyndon couldn't wait to read the transcript of their conversation, being prepared by his secretary. Except she wasn't typing. Earphones on, all she got was static. It was at this point that the big Texan's fist hit the desk, and he exploded, "Screwed again!" The expletive reverberated down the corridors of the White House as it dawned on Lyndon that, once more, he'd been outfoxed by his nemesis. For Bobby had come well-prepared, a scrambling device in his pocket.

No matter, Lyndon still held the upper hand. He could scarcely wait to announce that evening that no Cabinet member would be running on his ticket. Nothing personal about Bobby, of course. Then he regaled the press, mimicking Bobby's face when he'd heard the news, hyping his pervervid description of the showdown as he painted himself the hero and Bobby the villain.

For four more years Lyndon continued to lock horns with Bobby. When LBJ resumed the bombing of North Vietnam at the end of January 1968, Bobby warned, "This may become the first of a series of steps on a road from which there is no turning back—a road that leads to catastrophe for all mankind."

But Johnson wasn't thinking about all mankind. Neither was he thinking of the tens of thousands of women and children "his" bombers were maiming and killing. He wasn't thinking of the tens of thousands of soldiers on both sides falling on the battlefield, or of the thousands upon thousands of body bags making their way back to families crushed by the war. What Lyndon Johnson, commander in chief, was thinking about was his increasingly precarious political fixture.

Kennedy's dire warning only served to exacerbate Johnson's confrontation with him. Were he to lose Vietnam, Lyndon predicted, "There would be Bobby out front, leading the fight against me, telling everyone that I had betrayed JFK's commitment to South Vietnam. That I had let a democracy fall into the hands of the Communists. That I was a coward. An unmanly man. A man without a spine. Oh, I could see it coming, all right. Every night when I fell asleep I could see myself tied to the ground in the middle of a long open space. In the distance I could hear the voices of thousands of people. They were all shouting at me and running toward me: 'Coward! Traitor! Weakling!' " Lyndon was having waking nightmares as well. "Night after night," wrote Merle Miller, "He'd shake his head and say, 'That little runt will get in. The runt's going to run. I don't care what he says now.' "

It was on March 14, 1968, just two days before announcing his candidacy, that Bobby made an offer to Lyndon he couldn't refuse—so Bobby thought. He would stay out of the race if Johnson would admit publicly that his Vietnam policy had been wrong, and appoint a commission, including Kennedy, to recommend a new course of action. The offer was DOA, dead on arrival. Far from accepting it—and perhaps accepting Lincoln's refusal to be tarred and feathered and run out of town on a rail, but for the *honor* of it—Johnson couldn't conceive honor in this course of action and, instead, branded Kennedy as both devious and arrogant.[13]

On March 31 LBJ withdrew, ostensibly, from any further consideration for reelection. And on April 3, Lyndon had his last encounter with Bobby Kennedy. The personal animus seemed to have evaporated with the President's resolve not to seek or accept the nomination. To all the candidates Johnson had extended the invitation to meet, so that they could be briefed on presidential matters—particularly Vietnam. Bobby was the first to take him up on it. During their meeting, Bobby praised LBJ's March 31 speech as "unselfish" and "courageous." At that, Lyndon said, "People try to divide us, and we both suffer from it . . . I feel no bitterness or vindictiveness." Again, Lyndon pressed the point—he held no enmity against Bobby. Jack had always treated him well as Vice-President, and in turn he'd tried to support JFK.

Having come this far from his true feelings, LBJ waxed expansive. Never, he said, had he wanted to be president. Indeed, he'd been "counting the days to the end of his term ever since the beginning." Furthermore, his administration, in reality, was the "Kennedy-Johnson administration," and he'd simply been carrying on what was essentially a family matter. Could Bobby believe his ears? Was Lyndon just another member of the family? It seemed too good to be true. But Lyndon wasn't finished. He had the benediction to pronounce. He had done his best to perpetuate JFK's policies and programs—and "he liked to think," as Miller put it, "that every day Bobby's brother looked down at him and approved and agreed that yes, he had kept the faith." Then, in his last sentence to the man he had, over eight years, come to detest, Bobby responded in kind. "You are a brave and dedicated man."

Minnesota Senator Gene McCarthy, who was also seeking the Democratic nomination—and whom Johnson considered merely a stalking-horse for Kennedy—repeatedly challenged Kennedy to debate. But Kennedy was miffed over McCarthy's statement that Bobby's backers were "among the less intelligent and less educated people in America." So he had initially refused the challenge until, under pressure, Kennedy relented and agreed to one debate on June 1, three days before the California primary.

In Los Angeles on June 4, Bobby issued a victory statement at the Ambassador Hotel. "We are a great country," he concluded, "an unselfish country, and a compassionate country. I intend to make that my basis for running." But he had not far to run. After the speech, he made for a short-cut through the hotel kitchen; then shots rang out, and Kennedy fell to the kitchen floor, dying. At 3:30 the next morning, Lyndon was awakened by a phone call from National Security Adviser Walt Rostow. Bobby had been shot. Johnson's initial reaction: "Oh my God! Not again. Don't tell me it's happened all over again . . . too horrible for words." Soon this gave way to a strange elation. Could it be that he was about to be released from that "damned albatross," as he called Bobby, which had been clinging to his neck for almost a decade? But Bobby wouldn't release his hold on life. As he lingered on—and on—Lyndon kept calling the Secret Service. "Is he dead? Is he dead yet?" And Califano, listening, couldn't tell whether Johnson wished the answer to be yes or no.

At lunch that day, Lyndon's mind was not much on food. Bobby was still holding on. "God help the mother of those boys," said Johnson. "Thank God He's given her such faith that she can withstand the tragedies the good Lord has seen fit to subject her to." That night, June 5, Johnson put on his best sanctimonious manner and urged the nation to pray "to God that He will spare Robert Kennedy and will restore him to full health and vigor." Actually, Johnson initially had no such intention to pray and less to address the nation, deciding that someone else could speak in his name. But his advisers told him he had to do this himself. So, reluctantly, LBJ did as he was told—for a change—and went on the air with his mournful proclamation. As Califano put it, "Now, in the last months of his presidency, a murdered Robert Kennedy would likely leave a legacy of what-might-have-been that would rival his brother's. In life Robert Kennedy had been a political hammer; in death he would be a haunting nightmare." As it turned out, LBJ had not long to wait for the nightmare to begin; at 5:00 A.M., June 6, he received word that Bobby had died. Again he was most reluctant to address the American people. But, his aides argued, he'd taken to the airwaves after the death of Martin Luther King. Could he do less for Kennedy? That would appear to be "small-minded," Clark Clifford wrote. So, once more, LBJ went before the nation on TV, a nation that knew little of the bitter animosity that had plagued his relationship with Bobby for a decade. Despite those confrontations, Johnson proclaimed Sunday, June 9, a national day of mourning.

Bobby was dead, but not yet buried. Would the family insist on a full state funeral? Would the body lie in the Capitol Rotunda? That LBJ should even contemplate such questions constituted, Clifford wrote, "one of the saddest experiences of my long friendship . . . with him...dumbfounded" that he should ask such questions. Lyndon was relieved to learn that the family was contemplating no such formal arrangements. There would be no military presence, no honor guard, no gun salute at the gravesite. In death Bobby would continue to repudiate the violence that, along with a "credibility gap," had become the earmarks of Bobby's archenemy, Lyndon Johnson.[14]

Though Lyndon had at first refused to proclaim publicly a day of mourning, no such qualms beset him as he determined to attend Bobby's funeral at St. Patrick's Cathedral in New York City. He did, however, insist that his "Mexican generals"—his Secret Service contingent—be kept out of sight. As he entered the church he may well have sensed something of the smoldering resentment of the audience. For many were convinced that Lyndon had, in fact, contributed to the death of their hero, at the least by convulsing American society in a violent schizophrenia unequaled since the Civil War. In so doing, Johnson had deprived them of the chance that this second Kennedy could have taken the place of Jack in the White House.

After the funeral, Bobby was interred next to his brother at Arlington

Cemetery. But there remained the question of a permanent gravesite there. This would require a special $500,000 appropriation of federal funds. Johnson wouldn't even discuss it. Not until January 12, 1969, during his last weekend at Camp David as President, did Johnson finally order the Bureau of the Budget to request $431,000 from the presidential contingency fund..

There was no other personal confrontation in his life that dramatized more pointedly the "full press" that LBJ brought to bear on those he opposed. There were many such encounters, and Johnson remembered each one. Indeed, as William S. White has noted, "Johnson's memory for outright and implacable enemies is long, though rarely vindictive." Not quite. For even during Lyndon's rule as Majority Leader, when White was writing, Johnson could be vengeful, especially when it came to the Kennedy dynasty. Kearns saw it differently from White: ". . . Lyndon's resentment would not remain unburied; self-esteem wounded by humiliation became vindictive."

In Johnson's confrontation with Bobby, he displayed a singular lack of ability to build bridges. This would be, in the end, also his failure with most of his aides and with the American people. As Grant McConnell has written, "The essence of presidential leadership is the ability to appeal publicly to large and widely different constituencies at the same time." Any such appeal implies bridge-building. Perhaps Senator Strom Thurmond expressed it best when, in 1995, at the age of ninety-three and with more that sixty years of public service behind him, he called Johnson the most intimidating person he'd ever met.[15] Confrontation it was, but only when it was clear that Lyndon had the leverage to win. Here was a zero-sum game of competition, with the odds stacked in Lyndon's favor. The abiding temptation was to bend the rules, or make them up as he went along, giving rise to coercion and deceit, the next two steps on the slippery slope of hubris.

RICHARD NIXON

. . . if I walk out of this office . . . on this chickenshit stuff, why it would leave a mark on the American political system . . . if they ever want to get up to the impeachment thing, fine, fine . . . the President of the United States [will] fight like hell.

— Richard Nixon, May 10, 1973

I'm not going to allow this slick Southern asshole [Ervin] to pull that old crap on me. He pretends he's gentle and he's trying to work things out—bullshit. . . . . . . in the fall we'll attack the Committee . . . if I thought the President ought to . . . sit here like a little chimp and take this carload of shit—I'm not gonna do it.

— Richard Nixon, July 12, 1973

Roots of Conflict

If there was one word that characterized Nixon's stance over twenty-eight years of politics—according to Haldeman, who'd been with him through five campaigns—it was "fight!" Furthermore, Haldeman averred, Nixon never missed a chance to counterattack when in trouble. In this, he was like Truman, who was ready to fight even before the hat hit the ground. When the Soviet ambassador rejected an invitation to the annual presidential diplomatic dinner, the White House Chief of Protocol was fit to be tied. Wringing his hands, he asked Truman "What shall we do?" To which Truman responded, "Tell that son of a bitch Pincushion (Panyushkin) we don't give a damn whether he comes or not!" At that, the Protocol Chief turned to Secretary of State Acheson: "My God, how am I going to translate that into diplomatic language?!"

Nixon, too, enjoyed a good fight. When he refused to turn over the Watergate tapes to Judge John Sirica in 1974, Sirica predicted that Nixon would fight it down to the wire, because "he had spent a lifetime fighting."[1]

Avoiding Confrontation

Nixon learned as a boy to avoid confrontation with his father, dreading the fiery showdowns that left their indelible mark on the family. In his *Six Crises,* Nixon noted seven instances of outright fraud in his loss to Kennedy by a mere 113,000 votes of 68,000,000 cast. Three of these were in Johnson's Texas and four in Democratic Mayor Richard Daley's Chicago. Yet Nixon, despite Eisenhower's urging, refused to confront JFK in a recount. Though the loser cited numerous reasons for not doing so, conspicuous in its absence was probably the paramount reason: that Kennedy could cite similar cases of fraud by the Republicans.

This was much the same problem when, in 1964, Nixon told fellow Republican governors George Romney of Michigan, William Scranton of Pennsylvania, and Nelson Rockefeller of New York that he had the goods on the Johnson-Baker connection, at a time when it could be embarrassing to the Democratic contender. Baker, an LBJ friend and protégé, was thought to be involved in all sorts of financial misdeeds, including fraud, theft, and income tax evasion. Rockefeller, however, had done his homework—and knew that if the Baker stone were overturned, there'd be Republicans as well as Democrats scurrying out from beneath it to face the glare of public scrutiny So, in front of three of the biggest names in the Republican party, Nixon was forced to back down, tail between his legs.

Rising from the ashes in 1968 to capture the White House, the "painfully shy" president-elect, according to Kissinger, found it all he could do to be direct in even offering a job to the German immigrant. Perhaps overawed by the brilliant though mercurial Kissinger, Nixon resorted to one of what Kissinger came to see as "such elliptical ways that it was often difficult to tell what he was driving at, whether in fact he was suggesting anything specific at all." Later, after this awkward meeting, Kissinger came to realize that Nixon "would resort to any subterfuge to avoid a personal confrontation," and wondered how such a thoroughgoing introvert could become President—for Nixon's "meeting new people filled him with vague dread, especially if they were in a position to rebuff or contradict him." His "show of jauntiness" was just that, for it "failed to hide an extraordinary nervousness. . . . His manner was almost diffident; his movements were slightly vague and unrelated to what he was saying, as if two different impulses were behind speech and gesture." It seems that Nixon was offering Kissinger the post of national security adviser, in so many words—and those words so elliptical that Kissinger was baffled as to the meeting's purpose. It was two days later that Kissinger realized what Nixon had proposed, when John Mitchell asked him, "What have you decided about the national security job?" Kissinger answered, "I did not know I had been offered it." "Oh, Jesus Christ," sputtered Nixon's old business partner, "he has screwed it up again." With that, Mitchell walked out, found the president-elect, explained the confusion, and ushered Kissinger back into Nixon's presence. At last Nixon came out with it, and Kissinger, relieved, accepted the job. If it wasn't ellipticism, or subterfuge, then it was delay by which Nixon avoided personal encounters. Thus, according to Kissinger, "When Nixon told a Cabinet member he would 'think about' something, it almost invariably meant that he wished to avoid a face-to-face confrontation and that he would confirm his original decision either through Haldeman or by memorandum."

Of all his aides, Haldeman and Ehrlichman were the ones Nixon most dreaded confronting directly. Still, by the spring of 1973, confrontation was inevitable, because a lot of underhanded activities were being traced back to "the two Germans." In 1971, government employee Daniel Ellsberg had released to the press the top-secret Pentagon papers—a massive review of America's role in Vietnam. Under the always-convenient umbrella of national security, the administrtion decided to prosecute Ellsberg. But it went further. In an effort to discredit him, the Plumbers unit—a secret White House team set up to investigate news leaks—burglarized the office of Ellsberg's psychiatrist. On April 27, assistant attorney general Henry Petersen warned the President that Matthew Byrne, the presiding judge in the Ellsberg trial, would expose the role of the Plumbers. Therefore, Petersen told Nixon, "everybody should go," including not only Dean, but Haldeman and Ehrlichman as well. It wasn't Dean alone who posed a problem, although he was threatening to turn over, in Nixon's choice words, "some goddamn memos from that fucking Colson," and thus lay the groundwork for impeachment.

By April 29, Secretary of State William Rogers was insistent that Nixon fire his two Germans. Haldeman's brusque manner appeared to have set Rogers' teeth on edge. Nixon told him he was planning—at long last—to confront Haldeman and Ehrlichman that afternoon, "Would it be too much," Nixon put it to Rogers, "if I really need some backing, for you to come up and help me talk to them about this thing [firing them] a little?" Rogers: "I'll be glad to do it." But an hour later he called Nixon back: "I think you ought to give a little thought to whether you have somebody else, anybody else . . . I have no idea what they'll say if they get desperate . . . I don't want them to feel . . . that this was my decision." At this, Nixon cited Ziegler's opinion that the idea of a leave of absence for the pair was only "going to attract more flies. . . ." Therefore, should Nixon simply say, "Fellows, you've just got to go?" With that, Rogers fully agreed: ". . . they should resign now." But, Nixon countered, "If you would come up [to Camp David], and then if we get into a donnybrook then could I ask you to come over and help?" Rogers: "I really don't think it should be a donnybrook . . . you should just say, 'I've thought it over, I know how tough it is, and you told me that you'd do whatever I decided on, and this is my judgment,' period." Rogers said he dreaded getting "in a pissing match with them." Likewise Nixon.

By May, Haldeman had resigned, under orders from Nixon—who was thinking of replacing him with Alexander Haig. But because Haig had been an aide to Kissinger, Nixon was fearful of Kissinger's reaction. Rather than confront him head on, Nixon had Rose Mary Woods phone him in a ploy that Kissinger called "Vintage Nixon: the fear of confrontation; the indirect approach; the acute insight into my probable reaction; and the attempt to soften it through a preposterous charade that would get him over the first hurdle." It was only later that Nixon phoned Kissinger directly, still "not yet ready to face a direct confrontation," but with "an irresistible argument for Haig's appointment: it was designed to enhance my influence; it was aimed at, of all people, Agnew, 'to keep him,' said Nixon, 'from trying to step into things.' " Kissinger found it "mind-boggling to think that a Chief Executive needed a high-powered Chief of Staff to control a Vice-President who had been given little to do, had a skeleton staff and was in no position to 'step into things.' " To such ridiculous measures would Nixon go, Kissinger concluded, to avoid confrontation at the personal level. When it came to confronting foreign leaders, Nixon again showed that "the give-and-take of negotiations made him nervous." According to Kissinger, Nixon "hated any personal encounter that was not a set piece; he found it painful to insist on his point of view directly." While he thoroughly enjoyed surprising others, he dreaded surprises when sprung on him. Control was his great concern, and when he lost control over others he lost control of himself. A dramatic example of this occurred on December 11, 1972, when Ehrlichman informed the President that, with Liddy's case collapsing and Hunt pressing for money, "they don't get to the point you raise of how do you separate this from the White House and the President." Nixon was exasperated and defiant as he sputtered, "Just say, the President approved the goddamn bugging of the National Committee, which I approved—I didn't disapprove of."[2]

The lengths to which Nixon would go to avoid confrontation were remarkable. When Britain's Prime Minister, Harold Wilson, bet on a Democratic victory in 1968, he named John Freeman—an old friend of Humphrey's—as Ambassador to the United States. But back in 1962, Freeman, as editor of the *New Statesman*, had relished Nixon's defeat in California and written a congratulatory piece to Americans for removing "a man of no principle whatsoever except a willingness to sacrifice everything in the cause of Dick Nixon." It was a blow to his integrity that Nixon would not forget, and eleven months after Freeman's appointment to Washington, Nixon was in the driver's seat. Freeman, he was convinced, should himself be removed. But that was not to be so. Wilson stuck to his guns, and Nixon was outraged. He had sworn from day one of his election that he'd have nothing to do with Freeman. Nixon had his aides ask Wilson to drop Freeman from the guest list for the President's dinner at 10 Downing Street. Wilson would not. So, at the close of dinner, Nixon rose to speak and many in the audience dreaded what he would say, as he looked directly at the Ambassador across the table. "Some say there's a new Nixon. And they wonder if there's a new Freeman. I would like to think that's all behind us. After all, he's the new diplomat and I'm the new statesman, trying to do our best for peace in the world."

"The impact," Kissinger wrote, "was electric." Wilson jotted down a note for Nixon, "You can't guarantee being born a Lord. It is possible—you've shown it—to be born a gentleman." And Freeman, close to tears, turned out to be "one of the most effective ambassadors" Kissinger came to know, and "the only ambassador invited to the White House for a social occasion during Nixon's first term." Thus did Nixon, to avoid a major international flap—and with our principal ally—break down, offering the hand of peace and cooperation to one who'd savaged him.

As President, Nixon found it prudent more than once to back off from a confrontation. One such incident occurred on April 15, 1969, with Nixon barely three months in office. The North Koreans, Kissinger told Nixon, had shot down an unarmed Navy plane on a routine mission off the North Korean coast, killing the plane's thirty-one men. To his National Security Council Nixon vowed, "We're going to show them." Cautioned Rogers, "That's what Lyndon Johnson said about Vietnam, and we're still there." Defense Secretary Laird asked what the United States would do if, in retaliation, the North Koreans again invaded the South. A second ground war would require nothing less than full mobilization. On the other hand, cabled the U.S. ambassador to South Korea, William Porter, any strong reaction by the United States might well trigger an invasion of North Korea by the South. Mitchell, Agnew, and Kissinger were all for a tough response. Even though the Soviets were helping in a search for survivors, Kissinger warned Nixon not to be soft, "for the Soviets, along with the North Vietnamese and the Chinese, would all be watching." Had Rogers, on the other hand, taken a hard line, chances are that Kissinger would have called for moderation—because at that time, the two were in a struggle to capture the heart and mind of Richard Nixon. But since Rogers had advised caution, Kissinger was bellicose. "If we strike back, even though it's risky, they will say, 'This guy [Nixon] is becoming irrational—we'd better settle with him.' But if we back down, they'll say, 'This guy is the same as his predecessor, and if we wait he'll come to the same end.' " Kissinger urged an air strike against an airfield in the North, destroying every last plane there. He even suggested that, if necessary, Nixon should use nuclear weapons. But Nixon hesitated, wanting no second ground war—then decided on a milder response, much to Kissinger's consternation. Kissinger blamed Nixon's hesitant, halting reaction on the President's personality. And though Nixon chose the only safe and sane course given the circumstances, he vowed to Kissinger, "They got away with it this time, but they'll never get away with it again." Years later, the old bellicose Nixon revived and he remarked that his failure to respond quickly and strongly to North Korea "was the most serious misjudgment of my presidency, including Watergate." Hard as it may seem to believe, the kick-'em, sock-'em verbal pugilist not only dreaded personal, private confrontation, but went out of his way on several occasions to mediate disputes between others.

Brokering Confrontation

One of the first of these contenders with whom Nixon had to develop negotiating skills was his Senate colleague, Joe McCarthy, the same Senator who had learned much from Nixon's garnering headlines across the nation as a result of his facing down Alger Hiss. Never one to impugn McCarthy's motives, Nixon fell in line with the old guard of the GOP that "Joe might well have something" in his "take no prisoners" battle rhetoric. Nixon, in time, discovered how ignorant McCarthy was of American Communism—when he found that Joe had never so much as heard of their leader, Earl Browder. But, like Nixon, McCarthy found anti-communism to be a great tool for stirring the masses. Reluctantly, and at great personal sacrifice, claimed Nixon, he served to broker a peace between Ike and McCarthy. "I soon learned," Nixon said, "That the go-between is seldom popular with either side."

But serving as mediator between McCarthy and Eisenhower was less fraught with physical danger than the time Nixon had to step in between the fiery senator from Wisconsin and the Quaker pacifist, Drew Pearson. In his "Washington Merry-Go-Round" column, Pearson had been hounding McCarthy about his suspect income tax returns. It was December 1950, and they were at a dinner dance, when McCarthy began heckling Pearson. "You know, I'm going to put you out of business with a speech in the Senate tomorrow. There isn't going to be anything left of you professionally or personally by the time I get finished with you." At which Pearson, in a deadpan, asked, "Joe, have you paid your income taxes yet?" That was it. The gauntlet had been thrown down. McCarthy challenged Pearson to step outside and settle the matter man-to-man. Pearson declined. But as the party broke up and both men were in the cloakroom, McCarthy suddenly grabbed Pearson by the neck and again issued the challenge. Then he kneed him twice in the groin, leaving Pearson struggling for air. Seeing Nixon walking in, McCarthy gave Pearson the back of his hand, hard enough to snap his head back. "That one was for you, Dick," the hubristic Senator bragged. At that Nixon stepped between them and pushed them apart with, "Let a good Quaker stop this fight." It had not been so much a fight as a mauling by the thirty-four-year-old bully against the fifty-three-year-old columnist, who grabbed his coat and fled. "You shouldn't have stopped me, Dick," complained McCarthy.

By March 1954, McCarthy was riding high in the polls, with more than half of Americans declaring him to be good for the country, and only 29 percent opposed to him and his brass-knuckles tactics. But that 29 percent included enough who felt strongly against him that he was admitting visitors to his apartment only at gunpoint. When McCarthy accused the U.S. Army of harboring communists, the two sides confronted one another in nationally televised hearings. Nixon refused to watch the hearings on TV, explaining, "I just prefer professional actors to amateurs." On March 8, with not only Ike's Army but his administration taking broadsides from McCarthy, Ike told Republican leaders it was time to do something about the Wisconsin senator. All well and good for Joe McCarthy to smear Democrats as the party of treason, but now he was getting personal. Ike, as usual, was not to do it himself. "The difficulty with the McCarthy problem," he said, "is that anybody who takes it on runs the risk of being called a pink." So he decided to put forward Nixon. "Dick . . . would not be subject to [that] criticism." Being in the middle, Nixon found himself in a pickle. It was one thing to attack Adlia Stevenson and the Democrats; Nixon thoroughly enjoyed bashing them every chance he got, and with only slightly less ferocity than McCarthy. But, per Ike's orders, he had also to admonish Joe McCarthy for refusing to back off his assault on the Army. Nixon was at wit's end when he declared, "Frankly, we tried to mediate with McCarthy until we were blue in the face." Finally Nixon concluded, "It's probably time we dumped him."[3] So, in a televised speech, Nixon rebuked McCarthy—but not by name.

In the same speech, Nixon had also been told to defend Ike's record at home and abroad—although the Vice-President's attitude ranged from ambivalence to hostility. For Ike had stopped short of victory in Korea, had refused to commit to Vietnam, had continued with Truman's Europe-first policy and his foreign aid program, and, to top it off, had neither balanced the budget nor cut taxes. To make matters worse, Ike had called Nixon to the Oval Office the day before, claimed that the Vice-President didn't need any advice on preparing a political speech—then promptly gave him some. Nixon was to remain positive, not negative, concentrating on the pluses of Ike's programs, not the minuses of the Democrats. And, above all, Nixon was to smile.

So on Saturday night, March 13, 1954, Nixon became the great mediator, upholding Ike's administration without bashing the Democrats. After all, Eisenhower was "the greatest military leader in the world today." He knew what he was doing, and Americans should place their confidence in him. As for John Foster Dulles, "isn't it wonderful that finally we have a Secretary of State who isn't taken in by the Communists, who stands up to them? We can be sure now that the victories that our men win on the battlefields will not be lost in the future by our diplomats at the council table." In the year that the Republicans had been in charge, "in not one area of the world have the Communists made a significant gain"—obviously overlooking the predicament of the French in Vietnam who were about ready to fall to the Viet Minh. Then, in a rebut of Stevenson's charge that Ike had refused to speak out against McCarthy, Nixon cleverly compared the statesman-like Ike to the rash Truman. "It is true," said Nixon, "that President Eisenhower does not engage in personal vituperation and vulgar name-calling and promiscuous letter writing in asserting his leadership, and I say 'thank God he doesn't.' "

Then, without mentioning McCarthy's name, Nixon, avoiding a frontal assault, came at him obliquely, from the side. "Men who have in the past done effective work exposing Communists in this country have, by reckless talk and questionable methods, made themselves the issue rather than the cause they believe in so deeply." The Democrats, ready to pounce on Nixon's overlooking Communist gains in Vietnam, found further prey in Nixon's next gaffe. "I have heard people say, 'Well, why all this hullabaloo about being fair when you're dealing with a gang of traitors?. . . After all, they're a bunch of rats. What we ought to do is go out and shoot 'em. Well, I'll agree they're a bunch of rats, but just remember this. When you go out to shoot rats, you have to shoot straight, because when you shoot wildly, it not only means that the rat may get away more easily, you make it easier on the rat."

Then, copying his 1946 style with Voorhis, and McCarthy's style since 1950, Nixon ticked off the numbers—rats all. He had in hand the files of no less than 2,400 who'd been dismissed from their government jobs since Ike had taken over. He was more specific: 422 for subversive activities or associations, 198 for sexual perversion, 611 for their criminal records, and 1,424 for "untrustworthiness, drunkenness, mental instability, or possible exposure to blackmail." All had been hired by Truman and all had been fired by Eisenhower.

The speech, given without notes, was a tour de force. Ike phoned his congratulations: "magnificent . . . the very best that could have been done under the circumstances." And, believe it or not, Nixon had even managed a smile or two. But the speech, ostensibly given to build a bridge between Ike and McCarthy, proved to be nothing of the kind. McCarthy was furious, "sick and tired" of the "constant yack-yacking from that prick, Nixon." Had McCarthy backed off and recognized he was in a losing fight with Ike, Nixon's speech would have served its purpose. As it was, McCarthy became more strident, more bellicose than ever, and by December fell victim to hubris: the only senator in history to be condemned by his colleagues. The question Winston Churchill asked when he visited the country that June was, why did it take so long? To which Nixon responded that the Senate was reluctant to establish a precedent of investigating a colleague "for fear it might someday react in a case against themselves."[4]

Relishing Confrontation

By 1946, Nixon found himself in the "arena," as he called it, relishing the give-and-take of political confrontation to the point that, despite his promises to Pat, he could no sooner quit it than stop breathing. It began with his wiping the floor with Jerry Voorhis and running off with an election nobody thought he could win. He followed this up with bearding the lion, Alger Hiss, in his own den; this, the brightest star in the firmament of the State Department. The House Un-American Activities Committee, on which Voorhis had sat, was in tatters when Speaker Joe Martin got a letter from Herman Perry, Nixon's guiding spirit on his Committee of 100, urging Martin to "take an interest" in the fledgling congressman who had clearly shown "a promising future and considerable drive and ability." So Martin approached Nixon about replacing Voorhis on the committee. As its only lawyer, maybe he could "smarten it up." That it was in need of this appears in its less-than-rousing endorsements. William Rogers called it a "hare-brained" outfit if there ever was one. And Nixon acknowledged that the committee was notorious for its "gaggle of primitives" that were "habitually unfair." Neither its original chairman, Martin Dies, nor his successor, J. Parnell Thomas—later jailed for accepting kickbacks from his staff—ever produced any legislation, convicted no one they ever investigated, and succeeded only in devastating the lives of people they smeared. When Nixon, twenty years younger than the average member, joined the committee, he pronounced it "a den of ignorance, provincialism, and bigotry," the latter epitomized by Mississippi's John E. Rankin, a virulent anti-Semite, anti-Negro, and anti-Catholic.

Despite this disparagement, Nixon did little more, in his dogged pursuit of Hiss, than garner national publicity for himself—and prepare the way for the likes of Joe McCarthy and almost five years of "McCarthyism," a name reminiscent of the witch hunts and barbarism of seventeenth century Salem, Massachusetts. Virtually the only accomplishment of Nixon during his two terms in Congress was his persecution of Hiss.

Just as Nixon jumped on Voorhis for his Communist sympathies, despite showing no interest in Communism until that time—now he jumped on Hiss, although he knew virtually nothing of the man who'd prepared the draft for the U.S. position at Yalta; who'd accompanied FDR to that conference; who'd organized the World Monetary Conference at Dumbarton Oaks; and who'd helped found the United Nations at San Francisco.

So Nixon had a lot of catching up to do. From Whittaker Chambers, a senior editor of *Time*, Nixon learned that not only Chambers but his friend Hiss had been members of the American Communist Party, whose purpose was to infiltrate the government. Hearing about Chambers' charge, Hiss asked for an opportunity to refute him—and, when given that chance, denied even knowing Chambers. In what Nixon called a "virtuoso performance," Hiss brought down the house, gaining the sympathy of many in the press, some of whom cornered Nixon afterwards. One of those whom Nixon respected was Ed Lahey of the *Chicago Daily News*, yet there was Lahey, shaking with anger as he confronted Nixon. "The HUAC," he charged, "stands convicted, guilty of calumny in putting Chambers on the stand without first checking the truth of his testimony." Then there was President Truman, fingering the event as a "red herring," meant to divert attention from a Republican-controlled, "do-nothing" Congress.[5]

Ed Hebert, a committee member, urged them to turn the matter over to the Justice Department. Not on your life, Nixon as much as said as he protested taking such a PR bonanza out of his hands. To run for the Senate in 1950, he desperately needed the national attention he could wring from this case. Furthermore, Nixon the bloodhound had caught the scent of duplicity in Hiss's vehement protest of innocence. So Nixon the veteran poker player, convinced that Hiss was bluffing, decided to call. The Justice Department, Nixon discovered, had been sitting on these charges that had emanated from the FBI months before. In addition, the department was being investigated for this alleged cover-up. Now Nixon widened the scope of his hunt. He would bag Hiss, and along with him the big game: Truman's Justice Department. This, he was convinced, would assure Republican Thomas Dewey's election as president in 1948. Truman, hiding behind "executive privilege," issued an order forbidding federal employees—particularly the FBI—from releasing information about government employees to congressional committees. Nixon smelled a cover-up and persuaded the HUAC that turning the matter over to Justice would not only fail to salvage the committee's reputation, but would destroy it for good—for it would imply that the committee was reckless in bringing the charges, and incompetent in not following through. At this point South Dakota Republican Karl Mundt, acting chair, asked Nixon to head a subcommittee to question Chambers again, this time in closed session. Nixon realized something of the stakes in this political poker game. Here he was, a thirty-five-year-old neophyte Congressman, taking on the darling of the State Department, the Truman Administration, and the Democratic Party, as well as many in the press— the very press that Nixon had alienated by his rough-and-tumble tactics with Voorhis. But he also realized that if he could prove Hiss was lying, he would emerge in heroic proportions before the nation. There is irony that this flim-flam artist, this huckster cut in the image of P.T. Barnum, this flailing, irresponsible politician who fired his blanks across the bow of Voorhis in 1946 and Douglas in 1950, should warn fellow Republicans investigating the Hiss case to beware of "indiscriminate name-calling and professional Red-baiting [that] can hurt our cause more than it can help it." Yes, we must fight, and fight we will, but "we must fight with proper methods for those things in which we believe."

So Nixon took on Hiss, determined to call his bluff. First he and his subcommittee met with Chambers. Nixon found him credible, this fellow Quaker—short, pudgy, awkward, rumpled, and speaking, as Nixon noted, in a rather bored monotone. Here was the antithesis of Hiss, the cultured, debonair intellectual of the Eastern establishment.

So Nixon, the inveterate gambler, shoved his whole stack to the middle of the table. He was betting it all on Chambers. It was a long shot. Arrayed behind Hiss were Truman and his State Department, Supreme Court Justices Felix Frankfurter and Stanley Reed, journalists Alistair Cooke and Walter Lippmann. And there was Leslie Fuller, literary critic, calling Hiss's background "the prototypical history of the New Dealer at its best: the distinguished years at Harvard Law School, the secretaryship to the almost mythical justice Holmes, the brilliant career that began in the Nye Committee and culminated at Teheran."

Long shot it was, but Nixon had taken on Voorhis in an equally long shot and pulled it off. Now, however, he'd have to set the example of prudence, fairness, and objectivity in this epic battle. At the final HUAC session—on August 25, 1948, with the election little more than two months away—Hiss challenged Chambers to repeat his charges in public, without congressional immunity. Undaunted, Chambers appeared on *Meet the Press* and repeated, "Alger Hiss was a Communist and may still be one."

With Truman reelected in a stunning upset, Chambers—fearful of a lawsuit and a Justice Department investigation—hid his evidence on microfilm in a hollowed-out pumpkin at his Maryland farm. On December 1, Nixon was told that, two weeks earlier, Chambers had produced sixty-five pages of State Department documents from the thirties, insisting these had been given to him as a Communist courier—by none other than Hiss. Still, Nixon had booked passage for a Caribbean cruise with Pat, and was not about to interrupt it. Robert Stripling, HUAC's chief prosecutor, pleaded with Nixon not to abandon the case. Nixon was adamant. "I'm so goddamned sick and tired of this case, I don't want to hear any more about it. . . . And the hell with it, and you, and the whole damned business!" Stripling could scarcely believe his ears. Nixon had been putting in eighteen-hour days trying to solve the case, and now he was turning tail and running. He wouldn't even drive to Chambers' Maryland farm to capitalize on the latest cache of information. Stripling was ready to drive to the farm by himself when, in a peevish funk, Nixon gave in. "Goddammit. If it'll shut your mouth, I'll go!" Stripling, as of 1991, made no secret of his dislike for Nixon, theorizing that Nixon had been "brownnosing" Chambers to obtain information for a book he intended to write. When Chambers refused to give Nixon the vital documents and instead passed them on to the FBI, Nixon was angry and "terribly disillusioned."

To Chambers' farm Stripling and Nixon drove, there to hear Chambers say he'd turned over a "bombshell" of documents to the Justice Department. But, he added, he had "another bombshell in case they try to suppress this one." Be sure, Nixon warned, to give the second bombshell to the committee. Yet after they left, Nixon told Stripling he doubted there would be any such further revelations—and said he still planned to take his Caribbean vacation. The next day, however, true to his word, Chambers withdrew five rolls of microfilm from his pumpkin and gave them to the committee. Stripling wired this news to Nixon on his cruise ship, urging him to return immediately to Washington. Nixon, sensing the opportunity of a lifetime, took a Coast Guard seaplane to Miami, then a flight to the Capitol—where, with Stripling, he held aloft the microfilm for news photographers to record. From that time, until Hiss was indicted for perjury, Wicker noted, "rarely did [Nixon's] name leave the headlines or his picture from the front pages."

But another bombshell hit—striking Nixon this time—when a routine check by Eastman Kodak revealed that the pumpkin film had not even been manufactured until 1945, years after Chambers claimed that Hiss had turned over to him the stolen State Department documents photographed on the film. Apparently Chambers was lying. Nixon hit the ceiling, "Oh, my God, this is the end of my political career!" Then he lit into Nicholas Vazzana, the attorney who'd originally put him on to Chambers. "You got us into this. . . . What are you going to do about it?!" Despite Vazzana's protests, Nixon continued to rage. "You'd better get hold of Chambers!" At that, Stripling warned Nixon not to call off the scheduled news conference, insisting "No, damn it, we won't. We'll go down and face the music . . . tell them we were sold a bill of goods . . . that we were all wet."

As it turned out, Nixon was saved by the bell, in this case the ring of a phone from Kodak correcting their earlier information. It seemed that they had, in fact, manufactured the film prior to 1938, then discontinued it, only to resume production in 1945. The relief of Chambers, Vazzana, and Stripling was nothing compared to the huge sigh of relief from Nixon, whose political career was still intact.

What is of particular interest here are the self-serving accounts in Nixon's *Six Crises* that describe events leading up to and following Hiss's conviction—not for espionage [a hung jury] but for two counts of perjury, for which he was indicted by a grand jury on December 15, 1948, then convicted and imprisoned in 1950. Stripling's judgment of Nixon's accounts, years later, was succinct and to the point: "pure bullshit!"[6] Little wonder, then, that the majority of the press, the Democratic Party, and many others held Nixon in contempt for years to come.

The reasons are many. Because, after all the hullabaloo, Hiss was not found guilty of espionage, the major reason the HUAC had pursued him. When Hiss's first trial, on espionage charges, resulted in a hung jury, Nixon went after the presiding judge, Samuel Kaufman—denouncing him and threatening a House inquiry into the judge's "fitness." Kaufman, however, refused to be intimidated, refused to budge an inch, and was never investigated.

Because the perjury of which Hiss was convicted and sentenced for five years—with forty-four months actually served—was of a piece with Nixon's confession to reporters in the fall of 1948: that though he'd called Voorhis a Communist, he knew, of course, that Voorhis wasn't. The only difference the press saw was that Nixon's lie, and further lies he told about Helen Gahagan Douglas two years later, were not told under oath.

Because Nixon, in his *Six Crises*, glossed over his own mistakes or omitted them altogether, and self-righteously attributed to himself the highest possible motives while attributing to Hiss the lowest. Hiss, after all, was shown to have been a member of the Communist Party in the twenties and thirties—times when many Americans were critical of both fascism and the "cowboy capitalism" that was running roughshod over millions, and that led, in its frenzy of speculation, to the crash of October 1929 and the subsequent Great Depression.

Because many, including Stripling, felt that Nixon, the Horatio Alger of a small town in California and a graduate of Whittier College, went after Hiss as the apotheosis of the Eastern Establishment. In 1978 Stripling told historian Allen Weinstein, author of the definitive book, *Perjury*, that "Nixon had his hat set for Hiss . . . it was a personal thing. He was no more concerned about whether or not Hiss was [a Communist] than a billy goat." Hiss, a Harvard alumnus, was, by his words as well as his attitude, contemptuous of Nixon, who'd graduated from Whittier. On his first day before the committee, Hiss impressed Nixon as being "coldly courteous and at times almost condescending."

Because Nixon's attack on Hiss undermined public confidence in the Democratic Party, in the liberalism of the New Deal, and in FDR and his dealings with Stalin.

Because the case flew in the face of public sentiment, a public that had just pulled out the rug from beneath Dewey and the Republicans. Yet here was Nixon, branding Truman with being "soft" on Communism, and blaming him for the "loss" of China—when, in fact, the Truman Doctrine and the Marshall Plan were both virtual declarations of war on international Communism.

Because Hiss had enjoyed an illustrious career of public service and was, at the time, president of the Carnegie Endowment for International Peace, having been recommended to its board by none other than the fire-breathing anti-Communist—and subsequent Republican Secretary of State—John Foster Dulles. The day following Chamber's initial testimony, Nixon was delighted to read headlines across the country carrying a variant of "*Time* Editor Charges Carnegie Endowment Head Was Soviet Agent."

Because Nixon—contrary to his statement in *Six Crises* fourteen years later that he'd never even heard of Hiss before August 3, 1948—had undertaken an intensive study of him long before. Yet Nixon refused to divulge this to the HUAC because, Wicker has suggested, Nixon "was plotting to manage personally an investigation of Hiss, and to take the political credit for disclosing what he knew was already in the government's files."

Because Nixon, in Hebert's words, was a victim of "hysteria for headlines." He had next to nothing to do with the infamous pumpkin papers, he threatened to abandon the case and pursue his vacation, and he reluctantly returned only after Stripling's importunate pleadings. Yet when he met again with Stripling, there he was, holding aloft for all to see, the booty from the pumpkin. Once the picture appeared on the front page of *The New York Times*, other papers across the country followed suit. Clearly Nixon was the David who'd slain Goliath with his one stone, selected from the shell of a pumpkin.

Because Nixon was relentless in reminding the press, the public, and his congressional colleagues of his heroic deeds. On January 23, 1950—

with his eye on a Senate seat—Nixon gave a blow-by-blow account to the Congress, taking all of ninety minutes to portray himself the national hero in a speech entitled, "A Lesson for the American People."

Because later that year, when Nixon and Pat ran into Stripling, Pat put it to him: "Strip, we know you broke the Hiss case." But since her husband was now pledged to run for the Senate, "Do you mind if Dick claims credit for it?"[7]

Because Nixon's clash with Hiss and the accompanying headlines paved the way for McCarthy—who, taking the cue, figured he could garner for himself the national spotlight Nixon had gotten. After all, his reelection was coming up in 1952, and he needed that spotlight. Just two weeks after Nixon's recounting of his ordeal before the House, McCarthy spoke to a women's club meeting in Wheeling, West Virginia. There he made his notorious and unfounded charge that no less that 205 Communists were working for the State Department.

Because Nixon was named to Ike's ticket largely because Eisenhower was convinced that Nixon had gotten Hiss "fairly"—whereas most Americans were convinced he'd merely gotten Hiss.

Because Nixon, ten years after the grand jury indicted Hiss for perjury, was part of a Republican plot to oust Joseph Martin as speaker of the House. Here was the man who'd given Nixon his seat on the HUAC—that would serve as his springboard to the vice-presidency—and who'd also given the freshman congressman two plum assignments: one to the Labor Committee, and another to the Herter Commission, which was responsible for the Marshall Plan and which would make way for Nixon's lifelong interest in international affairs. But Nixon, determined to "modernize" the party in preparation for his 1960 run for president, must have thought Martin was one of those timid politicians he called "gutless wonders"— those who, making a fetish of avoiding controversy, were "neuter, play-it-safe politicians." Martin, disillusioned, complained, "I expected Nixon would come out in my favor. After all, I gave him his first break in Congress."

Aside from the Hiss case, Nixon did little more in Congress than he alleged that Voorhis had done in getting the "Rabbit Bill" passed. The only one of Nixon's proposals that came close to passing was the Mundt-Nixon bill, which required all Communists in the country to register with the government. It foundered in the Senate, yet prepared the way for the

McCarran Act of 1950; an act so badly conceived and executed that it was forever tied up in the courts—never exposing any Communists, much less destroying the American Communist Party. Dewey, defeated by Truman, and a subsequent backer of Nixon, nevertheless derided the act as embracing "nothing but the method of Hitler and Stalin . . . an attempt to beat down ideas with a club."[8]

It is just at this crucial point that Nixon repeatedly revealed his astonishing ignorance—in practice, if not in theory—of the nature of democracy as an open society. For democracy has traditionally rested upon the foundation of free and civil discourse. It implies that the antidote for bad ideas is better ones, that they must vie with one another not in the "tooth and claw" of the jungle arena, but in the civilized atmosphere of the marketplace. From Milton's *Aeropagetica,* through the Federalists and the anti-Federalists, to John Stuart Mill's *On Liberty,* one message has come through consistently: that though we can never know absolute truth, we can approximate what we idealize as truth—by considering as many points of view as possible on a given subject, and discussing them freely, civilly, and thoughtfully.

Nixon never seemed to grasp this critical point. Contriving his audiences to achieve a programmed response, including shouting down speakers, heckling them so others couldn't hear, demonizing them, condemning them, refusing to listen to contrary ideas, pandering to his audience's tastes regardless of his own convictions, resorting to half-truth and innuendo, and a dozen other fallacies well known to students of logic: these are the tactics that eroded not only Nixon's credibility, but our democracy as well—impoverishing each of us. For society is held together by a thin fabric of verbal trust. Rend that fabric through any of these tactics and society erodes, tending either to the extreme of anarchy or the extreme of authoritarianism.

That the price of liberty is eternal vigilance is axiomatic. That a further price of liberty has been paid in the blood of our young men in one war after another we accept as fearful yet necessary. That liberty has more to do with positive fulfillment of our potential than simply with the removal of oppression is sometimes forgotten. That we should do battle with those who would chain our ideas as much as those who would chain our persons is easily overlooked. Furthermore, it isn't just chaining our ideas that threatens our liberty. It is also prostituting our ideas, twisting them, distorting them, stretching them, whether by positive grading as in euphemism, or in negative grading as in denunciation. To deprecate the enemy in Vietnam as "gooks" was as bad as invoking "national security" to justify that ill-begotten war. Since all of our ideas are expressed in symbols, and most of those symbols are words, we prostitute our ideas when we prostitute the words that stand for them, that express them, that communicate them.

It was the corrosive force of Nixon's extreme rhetoric that served to diminish each of us, as well as the ideas that serve to guide our lives. In turn, it made suspect the political process by which we govern ourselves. For it is by means of the political process—making, executing, and interpreting our laws—that we impose the responsibility on each of us that makes our liberty meaningful. Divorced from responsibility, liberty becomes license, and that, unchecked, becomes anarchy. Invariably, the answer to anarchy has been the imposing of authoritarianism in one form or another. For when we refuse to govern ourselves, others will step in to govern us. That is why the nation's Founders were so intent on an educated electorate. Just as surely as fear and hatred are opposite sides of the same coin, so just as surely did Nixon's fearmongering become hatemongering. And just as surely did these base appeals lead, step by step, to Watergate and his political destruction.

It is no surprise that in his *Six Crises*, Nixon made much of the "national fame," as he put it, resulting from his battling Hiss in the courts. "It was two years later," he boasted, that "I was elected to the U.S. Senate and two years after that when General Eisenhower introduced me as his running mate to the Republican National Convention as 'a man who has a special talent and an ability to ferret out any kind of subversive influence wherever it may be found, and the strength and persistence to get rid of it.'" Nixon acknowledged that "the Hiss case brought me national fame." But that fame came at a price, in this case the price of "hatred and hostility toward me, not only among the Communists, but also among substantial segments of the press and the intellectual community"—a hostility which, in 1962, he acknowledged still persisted, despite the passing of ten years since Hiss's conviction was upheld by the U.S. Supreme Court.

For his trouble, Nixon was charged with a whole gamut of misconduct in public office, ranging from unethical to downright criminal activities. We have already made note of Nixon's facing down Khrushchev in their infamous 1959 "kitchen debate," when Nixon presided at the opening of the American exhibit at the Soviet exposition in Moscow. In Khrushchev, Nixon may well have seen his father, Frank, the hothead who never found an argument he didn't like, who was abrasive, loud, "boorish and obtuse," as Nixon described him. And what did Khrushchev see in Nixon? As Nixon put it, "He kept looking at me up and down from head to toe, as a tailor might estimate a customer's size for a suit of clothes, or perhaps more as an undertaker might view a prospective corpse with a coffin in mind." Krushchev discovered a troublemaker pushing—along with Congress and the President—the Captive Nations Resolution [for "Captive Nations," read *Communist* Nations]; a man fearful of, yet woefully ignorant of Communism; a forty-six-year-old pitted against his own sixty-five years; "a slick, dishonest manipulator of words." Later, when Khrushchev visited the United States, he made much of the Captive Nations resolution, declaring in Los Angeles: "There are still some people in your country who keep harping that people in the Soviet Union are little short of slaves . . . the reason why Roman civilization, as well as Greek civilization declined . . . was that it was a civilization built on slave labor, which shackled men's energy, will, and freedom."

Nixon was not about to let Khrushchev have the last word, especially in view of the 1960 presidential run. So, on September 27, 1959—the last day of Khrushchev's visit—Camp David reverberated, and Eisenhower cringed—before Nixon's onslaught against their guest from the Soviet Union. It was a Sunday luncheon to which Ike had invited Cabinet members and other top government officials, a ready-made soapbox for Nixon's grandstanding. While the guests took their seats at the table, Nixon presumed to continue his Moscow kitchen debate with Khrushchev, firing verbal torpedoes at the honored guest. As Evans and Novak noted, Nixon was oblivious to the boorishness and obtuseness that he had detected in both his father and Khrushchev. The Vice-President continued the barrage of rude, offensive questions "long enough to make the back of Eisenhower's neck redden with embarrassment for himself and anger at Nixon." As one of the luncheon guests described it later, "Ike wanted to pick Dick up by the nape of the neck and drop him out in the woods." As it was, Ike was powerless to intervene lest it appear he was chastening his own Vice-President, a breach of diplomacy—as well as etiquette—more drastic than Nixon's. When Nixon finally stuffed his mouth with food to stop his tongue from badgering, he showed not the slightest sign that his conduct had offended either Khrushchev or Ike. It would be almost another year before Ike took Dick to the woodshed in the form of his "give me a week" disparagement, a disparagement that may well have cost Nixon the election. All of this was but prelude to Nixon's face-off with Kennedy in the 1960 debates when Nixon learned that confrontation came at a fearful price. Yet he seemed to have forgotten it when he stepped into the White House, there to confront later the charges of "crimes and misdemeanors" that Congress prepared in its Articles of Impeachment. Nixon always enjoyed a fight, knowing that people loved to watch one, knowing that a fight, whether verbal or otherwise, drew the media. Though he shrank from confrontation on the personal, private level, in the ring and under the spotlight he gloried in confrontation. By means of it, especially in the Hiss case, he suffered, as he put it, not simply agony but "exquisite agony," for it provided publicity "on a scale most Congressmen only dream of achieving." The same spotlight that made possible his accession to the Senate, thence to the vice-presidency, and finally to the Oval Office itself could be, as he put it, "merciless." Try as he might to hide his cover-up of the Watergate-White House connection, Woodward and Bernstein kept the light on him. If Nixon had once understood the Fundamentals of Democracy 101, it is certain that by the time he was under siege from Watergate, he wasn't practicing them. Here, rather, was the alternately sputtering, snarling, and self-pitying President, tied on his back in Poe's pit, with the pendulum of impeachment swinging ever closer to his neck.

It seems that Fred Buzhardt, White House counsel for Watergate, was talking more about—rather than to—Nixon, when he criticized Ervin. The Senator, Buzhardt said, was conducting "terrible hearings, Mr. President. . . . He stutters, he stammers—you can't understand his questions. He garbles them up. . . ." By June 1, 1973, Nixon's language showed him to be beside himself. Of the Ervin Committee he vowed to Kissinger, "We're gonna, they, they've started, they wanna have a gut fight, they're gonna get one, Henry. . . . So let your assholes know that they're going to get this, Henry. Right in the can . . . they think they know how to fight, but never they've never fought anybody before . . . we're gonna, we're gonna. We're gonna force them right now—if they're gonna play this game." By June 13, Nixon was promising Haig, ". . . one day I'm gonna attack that [Ervin] Committee, and when I do, it's gonna be a blockbuster. I'm gonna take it apart like it's never been taken apart . . . they'll be destroyed like the McCarthy Committee was destroyed. Absolutely destroyed. . . ." On this fire, Haig poured verbal gasoline, "They don't realize what they're up against, this stupid Ervin. Drinking too much and pointing his finger. Hah! That's right. That's right. . . ."

On July 12, 1973, Nixon realized the jig was up, what with Haldeman's former assistant, Alexander Butterfield, exposing the existence of the White House taping system. Too late, the President had it removed. It is significant that the last three words recorded were to Kissinger: "Keep, keep fighting." Just before pronouncing this benediction, Nixon promised Kissinger: "As far as I'm concerned, so we'll have a constitutional crisis [over his not releasing incriminating papers to the Ervin Committee]. If we do, it'll be a goddamn ding-dong battle and we might, if we lose. I'll burn the papers. 'Cause I got them. That's the point, 'cause I would never turn these papers over to a court. Never give them over to the Committee, you know that. . . . I said [to Ervin] oh, no, your counsel isn't gonna *paw* through my papers. I just used that word. He got the message."[9]

Here was vintage Nixon, Frank's spitting image, the born fighter who, when he got his Irish up, would revert to the "rock-'em-sock-'em" verbal pugilist and who was not particular about where his blows fell once he was in the political ring. One of the great difficulties with competition, whether economic or political, is that it easily turns to coercion. In a subsequent chapter we will examine the paranoid Nixon, wallowing in self-pity, raging at the manifold enemies out to do him in.

CHAPTER 9

COERCION

. . . there are two ways of contesting, the one by the law, the other by force; the first method is proper to men, the second to beasts; but because the first is frequently not sufficient, it is necessary to have recourse to the second.

— Machiavelli

A corrosive careerism had infected the Army, and I was part of it . . . the troops became numb to what appeared to be endless and mindless slaughter. . . . Just as I came to reexamine my feelings about the war, the Army, as an institution, would do the same thing. We accepted that we had been sent to pursue a policy that had become bankrupt.

— Colin Powell

LYNDON JOHNSON

Mansfield is . . . for pulling out. Humphrey said, 'Well, we're not doing any good.' The Frank Churches said we don't want any part of it. The Dick Russells and the twenty-odd in that group say we ought not to have ever been in there. . . . What the hell are we doing in there anyway? And Dulles and Eisenhower got us in there and we oughtn't have stayed. Yet when you go to reason with 'em and say, 'How in the world you gonna get out?' they say, 'God, if some government would ask [us] to get out, it'd be wonderful' . . . it's the hottest thing we got on our hands and the most potentially dangerous.

— LBJ to Robert Kennedy, May 28, 1964

I thought you guys had people everywhere, that you knew everything, and now you don't even know anything about a raggedy-ass little fourth-rate country.

— LBJ to John McCone, CIA Director

You know, they could hang people for what's in there!

— Robert McNamara, Secretary of Defense,
on initial reading of the Pentagon Papers

In 1969 I was the same age as many of the girls raped and murdered in that village [My Lai] . . . I have never forgiven my country for what it did to the Vietnamese and to young men like my brother. I wish I could.

— Elizabeth Weber, 1968. Sister of Bill Weber, radio operator
for Lt. William Calley, killed near My Lai, 1968[1]

The Art of the Bully

Lyndon Johnson was as sure of himself as any nineteen-year-old could be when he bragged to friends at a dance, "I'm just going to take that little Dutch girl away from that old boy tonight, just as sure as the world." The bumptious braggart proceeded with one obnoxious attempt after another to steal the girl until, at last, "that old boy," Eddie, challenged Lyndon to step outside. There, as Lyndon's cousin Ava described it, "Lyndon never got in a lick. It was pitiful. Every time he got up, that old boy knocked him down—he had fists like a pile-driver. Lyndon's whole face was bloody, and he looked pretty bad." Finally, sprawled on the ground, Lyndon called uncle, "that's enough." This was not the first time, but it was about the last time Johnson ever resorted, personally, to physical force. From then on, he would, as he did in World War II, prefer others do the job.

As we have seen, confronted with superior power, he not only sought an accommodation, but relied on shameless flattery or maudlin sycophancy to ingratiate himself. Faced with equivalent power, he backed off, procrastinated, or—as he did as Majority Leader—searched high and low for a compromise to effect a consensus. But faced with inferior power, the tyrant emerged.

Incredibly, Johnson bragged that he never did anything because someone else told him he had to. "I don't push worth a damn," as he put it. Yet he not only pushed, but bulldozed others—with no thought for their feelings, their reputations, or their careers. Many, including Lady Bird, caved in simply to "humor" this loathsome bully.

Intimidation, outright threat, ridicule, "the Treatment," all of these paled next to the form of coercion most deadly: the taking of a human life. But, like all methods of coercion, it, too, is counterproductive. An extension of the law of physics, it says for every action there is an equal and opposite reaction. This, however, doesn't limit the counterproductive force to one of equivalence, as Johnson found out with "that old boy," Eddie.

To move from physics to game theory, if all human relationships could be reduced to three—cooperation, competition, and coercion—these would correspond to a sum-sum game, a zero-sum game, and a zero-zero game. In the first, both sides win. Here is the ideal relationship, illustrated in an ideal marriage. The two need each other, bring out the best in each other, and complement each other, no more dramatically than in sexual union, by which they reproduce.

Yet no marriage is ideal. Invariably there develops competition, perhaps as breadwinners, perhaps as objects of affection by their children, perhaps as performers of household chores. One of the surest signs of a marriage deteriorating into competition is the practice of keeping score. "You owe me one" is a give-away that the two are competing. One of the difficulties of competition is that it puts husband and wife at risk for coercion, usually in the form of spousal abuse, in which both sides stand to lose. When the deterioration gets bad enough, divorce ensues, and seldom if ever can one, in retrospect, say he or she "won."

Coercion may range from social pressure to a threat to life itself. Johnson's infamous "treatment" was a subtle form of individual pressure, an invasion of one's body space by someone bigger and bolder. Yet Johnson could also exert a more subtle pressure, as he did in his "stare-down" with Soviet Premier Alexei Kosygin at Glassboro, New Jersey, in 1967. Aware that Khrushchev had become reckless when he thought the "boy" President, Kennedy, was a pushover, Johnson was determined that Khrushchev's successor would see nothing but a big, raw-boned Texan— so sure of himself that he would triumph in the bargaining. Meeting Kosygin, Johnson gripped his hand as though he meant to crush every bone, then hovered over him, a head taller. Seated at the table, Johnson needed to sip his coffee, but felt for the cup rather than break eye contact with Kosygin, who finally blinked and looked away. This, LBJ figured, was a singular human triumph.

To coerce is to deprive another of one or more rights or privileges. At its extreme, it is a form of violence, the deliberate violation of the rights of another, whether "purse or reputation," as Shakespeare reminded us, or of life or liberty, as Jefferson put it. Just as the most egregious form of murder, war, under whatever guise—whether to defend ourselves against unjust taxation, or to prevent us as a nation from splitting in two, or to "Christianize" the "pagan" nations of the world, or to make the world "safe for democracy" or "diversity," or to rid the world of the "scourge" of atheistic Communism, whether ordained by the state or sanctioned by the church—remains mass murder: the deliberate taking of many lives. The recent war in Bosnia only underscores the futility of war in attempting to "even the score," or to "restore our honor," whether real or imagined.

There have been those who not only believe war is inevitable but that it serves a noble purpose. Since the dawn of history, there have been, as the apostle Matthew wrote in his Gospel, "wars and rumors of wars." "War is the obsession of the prince," wrote Machiavelli, for "it is better to be feared than loved." In his *Germany and the Next War*, Bernhardi wrote, "The inevitableness, the idealism, and the blessing of war, as an indispensable and stimulating law of development, must be repeatedly emphasized."[2] As we were to discover in Vietnam, war was, in fact, not inevitable, nor ideal, nor "an indispensable and stimulating law of development."

Johnson's War, 1963–1969

As Senate Majority Leader, our thirty-sixth President—though he'd not earned his reputation for the bravery in action that his Silver Star signified—had fully earned his reputation as a bully. Now he would earn his reputation as commander in chief in a war not to be declared, not to be financed through taxes or cuts in other spending, not to interfere with his quixotic dream of a Great Society, and not to be negotiated to a peaceful settlement through compromise. Indeed, Johnson's conduct of the war would live on, as FDR declared of the Japanese attack on Pearl Harbor, "in infamy." Coercion: thy name is Johnson. By the spring of 1964, there could be no question but that we'd installed a bully in the White House, a bully with little interest and less understanding of history, a bully who would not benefit from its lessons, and, as Santayana put it, would be doomed—along with the nation he led—to repeat them.

Until he became Vice-President, Johnson's knowledge of other nations was abysmal. Apart from his overnight inspection trip to the Southwest Pacific in World War II, a brief European trip in 1945, and a NATO conference in the fall of 1960, he had, with the exception of Mexico, scarcely been out of the country. He spoke no foreign language apart from a feeble understanding of Hill Country German and Mexican Spanish.

As Vice-President he did considerable traveling, but he also took greater pains to offend foreign dignitaries and embarrass the State Department than he did to learn the history, the culture, or the language of his destinations. Every country, every people, he tended to see as merely an extension of his own Hill Country. With the war in Vietnam, the enormity of his ignorance at last came home to roost. In his grandiose offer of

$1 billion to build dams and other projects there, to bring electricity there—as he'd brought it to the people along the Pedernales—in exchange for Ho's coming to Johnson's terms at the peace table, LBJ betrayed an ignorance truly remarkable for a man leading the most powerful nation on earth. Just as he saw others as an extension of himself—prostheses to be manipulated to aggrandize himself—so he saw other lands as simply extensions of the Texas Hill Country.

Overnight, Johnson, like Elisha of old, assumed the mantle of Elijah, in this case, Kennedy. Except that it was an albatross. It was not simply "a bitch of a war," or "that war thing," or "that damned thing," as Lyndon put it, but a way of thinking that betrayed "the best and the brightest—as Halberstam described them in his book of the same title—for almost three years. Supremely confident, they, like the Marines they were thrusting into battle, would do the difficult immediately, while the impossible would take a little longer. Armed with state-of-the-art computers, relying on the synergy of ideas from the smartest people Kennedy had been able to find, Vietnam would be a breeze—so they thought. In addition, they would have the proving ground they needed to test weapons and personnel in their new strategy of counterespionage and counterterrorism. Driven by crises, obsessed with the near-term, unable to see the war in perspective, ignorant of the ways of the Vietnamese, determined to keep their escalation of the number and the involvement of "advisers" from the American public, they neglected to go beyond the procedural "how" questions to ask the critical "why" questions.

In addition to qualifying as barbarians, the "best and the brightest" were arguably simpletons. They refused to deal with the "why" questions that historical perspective required. They satisfied themselves with number-crunching, hailing McNamara as the quintessential computer-brain, the man who would brag that at no time in history had so many men and so much materiél been transferred so far and so efficiently to fight a war. This from the man dressed, most would assume, in an accountant's "green eyeshades and sleeve protectors," who could make numbers, if not men, jump through hoops. Unfortunately, as McNamara confessed almost thirty years later, winning a war took more than logistical efficiency.

Not only did the Kennedy aides Johnson inherited neglect the silent question of "why," but provided simplistic answers to the questions they did ask. If we define as simplistic any answer to a problem less complex than the problem itself, then these men majored in simplistics, for all their formal training. On the other hand, as Edwin Land, developer of the Polaroid-Land camera has asserted, to define a problem adequately puts one in a position to find the best solution. Whatever else a simplistic answer does, it tends to exacerbate the problem. No more poignant demonstration of this can be found than in the repeated bumblings of Kennedy and Johnson and their staffs as they stumbled into the longest and most unsatisfactory war in American history.

The most pressing question for the new President was Vietnam. Uttering the mantra that became his hallmark for his first year in the White House, "Let us continue," Johnson assembled his top aides. Which way should he go? According to Reedy, "The Kennedy people knew the realities of power and they were looking to him for a cue to their future conduct. He, on the other hand, was looking to them for a cue as to what Kennedy would have done." For twenty-five years, LBJ had learned that in politics you get ahead by capitalizing on every situation in which you find yourself. Now he had a nation mourning the loss of the King of Camelot, cruelly slain by one of our own. Johnson would wring from that grief, that guilt, that remorse, every ounce of advantage he could.

It was only fitting that they should honor the memory of the murdered president, just as later he would use the same "honor" to justify escalating the war. As Reedy explained it, a president sends a hundred men into battle and loses them all, then finds he made a mistake in sending them. Of course he's not about to admit his stupidity, implying that those men died in vain. So he sends in a thousand to "keep faith" with those who've died. To abandon the battlefield was unthinkable. We would not turn our backs on the sacrifice of brave American soldiers fighting to defend our freedom. It was a question of honor. Thus did "peace with honor" become an elusive will-of-the-wisp goal for our involvement in Vietnam. Reduced to the bare facts, Johnson was perfectly willing to escalate the war and sacrifice 30,000 American lives to assure his re-election in 1968. For to acknowledge—as McNamara later acknowledged—that it all had been "a terrible mistake" would have foredoomed his reelection chances. As he repeated again and again, he was not about to be the first president to lose a war. Nor was he about to lose his election.

By December 1963, Johnson was meeting with the Joint Chiefs of Staff, gung-ho on escalation. This despite the report of Generals Ridgeway and

Gavin nine years earlier that any such involvement was prohibitively expensive in terms of men and money. This despite Kennedy's repeated resolve to withdraw by the end of 1965. This despite the reasoned caution of men like George Ball, John Kenneth Galbraith, and Averell Harriman. And this despite the conclusion of the JCS themselves, after playing war games at the Pentagon earlier that year, that it would take "at least a half-million U.S. combat troops" to do the job. Ball had earlier protested to Kennedy that it might take 300,000 and the President responded, "Well, George, you're supposed to be one of the smartest guys in town, but you're crazier than hell. That will never happen." But the more JFK thought about it, the more he thought that Ball might be right. Maybe, as Kennedy put it, it would be like Berlin—where the troops "will march in; the bands will play; the crowds will cheer; and in four days everyone will have forgotten. Then we will be told we have to send in more troops. It's like taking a drink. The effect wears off, and you have to take another." With that, our thirty-fifth President came to the conclusion that, in the final analysis, this war belonged to the Vietnamese.

There is some significance in the fact that two of the most persistent "doves" on Vietnam were two of the three coauthors of *U.S. Strategic Bombing Survey*, a landmark analysis of U.S. air power in World War II. Their finding: that bombing German cities, far from breaking the spirit of the inhabitants, in reality fortified their will to resist, just as German bombing of British cities like Coventry and London had done.[3]

Despite all this caution, despite its own finding as a result of its war games, the JCS were of a different mood when they joined Johnson in December 1963. "We're swallowing flies," complained Curtis Le May, Commanding General of the Air Force, "when we should be going after the manure pile." Amen, echoed the others. Unleash Le May's bombers and team them up with commando raids, and this "war of attrition" will soon have the Commies crying "uncle." Here was the same bombastic, bellicose Le May who, before retiring as Air Force Chief of Staff, gave his prescription for ending the war to a top State Department official: "We ought to nuke the Chinks." By that time, LBJ was convinced that any preemptive nuclear strike—such as advocated by author Herman Kahn in 1962—would result in the ultimate horror of World War III. There were the Joint Chiefs calling for massive escalation. But Johnson had a priority ahead of that, and at last conceded, "Just let me get elected, and then you can have your war."

Years later, Kissinger wrote of the costs of the war. "Vietnam is still with us. It has created doubts about American judgment, about American credibility, about American power—not only at home, but throughout the world. It has poisoned our domestic debate." Thus far, Nixon's National Security Adviser was on target. But his conclusion rings hollow: "So we paid an exorbitant price for the decisions that were made in good faith and for good purpose."

But the "good faith" and "good purpose" were as ambiguous and as shifting as they were elusive. Here was Kennedy, prepared to bring the troops home—after he'd been reelected. Here was Johnson, prepared to accede to the war's escalation proposed by the JCS—after he'd been elected. And when Nixon stepped into the role of commander in chief, he would wind down the war—after expanding it into Cambodia and Laos—just in time for his reelection. If this constitutes "good faith," it is reasonable to ask "faith in whom?" Here, rather, was crass self-aggrandizement, the willingness to sacrifice others—millions if need be—to assure their own political futures. Having promised the JCS that they could have their war once he was elected the following November, LBJ pumped out an "action memo" to the Pentagon: "Help the ARVN [Army of the Republic of Vietnam]." There, at his disposal as commander in chief of the most powerful nation in the history of the world, was, as Reedy emphasized, "one of the most important revelations of my tour in the White House, the entire apparatus of the Defense Department, the State Department, the CIA, and the USIA . . . dedicated to making his commitment work."[4]

Not a month had passed since LBJ had taken the oath of office, and he was committed: "We must go on bending every effort to win"—whatever that meant. This despite the fact that in South Vietnam, there was one coup after another as 1963 became 1964, testimony to the venality, the corruption, and the brutal suppression of Communist sympathizers and Buddhists by successive Saigon regimes. This despite the monumental siphoning off of both U.S. aid and the cream of the ARVN to enrich and protect the particular regime in power at the time. This despite the fact that ten years earlier the French, with 400,000 men under their command, couldn't prevent the fall of Dienbienphu to the Vietminh. This despite the Pentagon's conclusion it would take 500,000 U.S. combat troops, in addition to the 200,000 ARVN, to do the job—and even then it was doubtful. This despite obviously doctored reports from the ARVN brass as well as our own Commanding General. This despite our forced stalemate in Korea as the result of Chinese intervention. This despite the waning influence of Communism in Europe. This despite the growing differences between China and the USSR, putting the lie to the allegation of a worldwide conspiracy directed from the Kremlin. Above all, this despite the repeated attempts of Hanoi to negotiate, brokered by other nations—as well as a UN that was increasingly distraught by the tragic and colossal blunder of the most powerful of nations coercing a tiny, poverty-ridden nation, inflicting untold devastation, misery, and death on a people interested only in pursuing the livelihood they'd practiced for centuries. So LBJ plunged ahead, determined, as he put it, that "no crackpot assassin would alter American policy."

With 1964 and his election coming in less than a year, LBJ announced "the first reality: North Vietnam has attacked the independent nation of South Vietnam. Its object is total conquest. . . . Let no one think for a moment that retreat from Vietnam would bring an end to the conflict. The battle would be renewed in one country after another. The central lesson of our time is that the appetite of aggression is never satisfied." The two lodestars seeming to guide Johnson were Chamberlain at Munich and Crockett at the Alamo. He, Lyndon Johnson, would be wary of the first and faithful to the second. By March 2, 1964, LBJ reinforced his earlier warning to Hanoi that "it is dangerous when anybody starts aggression." McNamara wasn't so sure about it all: ". . . we don't know what's going on out there. The signs I see coming through the cables are disturbing signs— poor morale in Vietnamese forces, poor morale in [our] armed forces, disunity, a tremendous amount of coup planning against Khanh [the current leader of South Vietnam]." McNamara saw a grim situation, yet cautioned LBJ in letting the American people know just *how* grim. Disinformation always seemed to be in the works.

Yet there was Ho Chi Minh in North Vietnam: "It is crystal clear that the U.S. is the aggressor who is trampling under foot Vietnamese soil." And there was Chou En-Lai in China: "America is rapidly escalating the war in an attempt to subdue the Vietnamese people by armed force." And there was Brezhnev, Khrushchev's replacement in the Kremlin: "The normalization of our relations [with the U.S.] is incompatible with the armed aggression of American imperialism against a fraternal Socialist country— Vietnam." As for forming a neutralist government, such as JFK had approved for Laos in 1962, LBJ would have none of it, that is, unless Hanoi would also embrace one. His National Security Adviser Mac Bundy, on February 6, 1964, encouraged Johnson "to show them [the doves] you're a man of peace without letting them call the tune. . . ." And Lyndon was "damned good at that." Furthermore, Bundy added, the doves, like political writers Walter Lippmann and Joseph Kraft, were "intelligent men . . . [but] they're tempted by neutralization in Vietnam, which doesn't make any sense at this stage. . . ." After all, Bundy persisted, Vietnam was not Laos, where we had "strength on the scene." In South Vietnam ". . . there's no balance of forces like that. . . . If the U.S. forces were withdrawn, that thing [the Saigon regime] would collapse like a pack of cards."[5]

In 1967, American authors John Farrell and Asa Smith weighed in with eight types of evidence to back the Communist charge of American aggression:

1. The 1954 Geneva Accords had only temporarily divided Vietnam in two, until nationwide elections could be held in 1956—something the United States refused to support, despite its agreement to abide by the Accords.

2. Between 1950 and 1954, the United States, far from remaining neutral, provided arms and money on a huge scale to the French, the colonial oppressors—when they were fighting against a clear majority of the Vietnamese people, interested primarily if not solely in their own independence.

3. The Communist-led majority of Vietnamese actually won their war for independence in 1954.

4. Vietnamese nationalization was mobilized for twenty years, and much more behind Ho Chi Minh than French-backed or American-backed governments in Saigon.

5. The peasants of South Vietnam wanted nothing more than the return of their land confiscated by the Saigon government.

6. Diem and his U.S. allies imposed far greater suffering on the South Vietnamese peasants than did the Vietcong.

7. Diem's government [and its successors] were shot through with inefficiency and corruption.

8. The remarkable military success of the Vietcong, against overwhelming odds, was testimony to its widespread popular support.

To these can be added others, including Johnson's continued spurning of peace overtures by the North Vietnamese. The overall strategy of General William Westmoreland was to fight a "war of attrition": we would wear down the Communists until they caved in to our demands. Trouble was, it backfired, and for each Communist killed there were others eager to take his place.

Johnson's war of attrition proved to be as bankrupt as his early misgivings about the war were ephemeral. By May 1964, Johnson was a frustrated President who called the war "the biggest damn mess I ever saw." So bad was it, he lamented, that "I don't think it's worth fighting for, and I don't think we can get out." Try as he might to withdraw, he worried that Congress would have his hide. "They'd impeach a president . . . that would run out, wouldn't they," he asked Richard Russell. The last thing he wanted to do was put our GI's at risk there. Then he told Russell of his "little old sergeant that works for me over at the house, and he's got six children, and I just put him up . . . every time I think about [escalation]." Indeed, "thinking about sending that father of those six kids in there. And what the hell we're going to get out of his doing it? And it just makes the chills run up my back." Russell, chairman of the Senate Armed Services Committee, agreed. "We're just in the quicksands up to our very neck, and I just don't know what the hell is the best way to do [sic] about it."

Soon Johnson was on the phone to his National Security Adviser Bundy: "The more that I stayed awake last night thinking of this . . . it just worries the hell out of me. . . . It's damned easy to get in a war but it's gonna be awfully hard to ever extricate yourself if you get in. . . . What the hell is Vietnam worth to me? What is Laos worth to me? What is it worth to this country?"

Johnson had good reason to worry about escalating the war. From the time JFK entered the White House, to May 16, 1964, the U.S. had lost 229 soldiers. Now not only was McNamara feeding him grim reports from the Saigon regime, but there was Russell telling him, "It's the damn worst mess I ever saw. . . . I knew that we were going to get into this sort of mess when we went in there. And I don't see how we're going to get out of it without fighting a major war with the Chinese. . . ." LBJ: "That's the way I've been feeling for six months." Then there was UN Ambassador Adlai Stevenson: "I've been shuddering on this thing for three years and I'm afraid that we're in a position now where you *don't* have any alternatives. And it's a *hell* of an alternative [escalation]. And it really gives me the shakes."

When, in November 1964, LBJ expressed doubts about his win over Goldwater—doubts which by that time had no basis in fact or in the polls, which were predicting a grand sweep for the Democrats—William Fulbright, chairman of the Senate Foreign Relations Committee, assured him that "great presidents weren't necessarily greatly *loved* presidents." So appreciative was Johnson that he had a picture taken of himself with Fulbright, which he inscribed, "To J. William Fulbright, than whom there is no better." But less than a year after that—bitter at being deceived by Johnson regarding Vietnam, Fulbright and George Ball lashed out, protesting that Johnson was dragging the United States into a "bloody and protracted jungle war." We must, Fulbright insisted, get serious about negotiating an end to the war. Johnson was furious at this "betrayal," and ridiculed "Mr. Half-Bright, the stud duck of the opposition . . . a lazy and vain man." With that, the two never spoke to each other again.

Fulbright also called for hearings on Vietnam and published *The Arrogance of Power*, the result of the Christian Herter Lectures at the Johns Hopkins School of Advanced International Studies. His thesis, put by Dean Francis Wilcox, was that great empires collapsed because their leaders had lacked "the wisdom and good judgment to use their power wisely and well." Where "the U.S. has made good use of its many blessings usually, we are now at that historical point at which a great nation is in danger of losing its perspective on what exactly is within the realm of its power and what is beyond it. In the past other powerful nations have aspired to too much and by overextension of effort have declined, then fallen. It is this tragic fate, this fall from the pinnacle of power, that the writer hopes we can avoid." Both Wilcox and Fulbright were writing of hubris, the hubris that caught up both Lyndon Johnson and the nation. Though he should have, Fulbright had no quarrel with Johnson's aims as far as he understood them: "To defeat what is regarded as North Vietnamese aggression; to demonstrate the futility of what the Communists call 'wars of national liberation'; and to create conditions under which the South Vietnamese people will be able freely to determine their own future." What Fulbright did question was if the United States could achieve its aims "by the means being used": our ability "to go into a small, alien, underdeveloped Asian nation and create stability where there is chaos, the will to fight where there is defeatism, democracy where there is no tradition of it, and honest government where corruption is almost a way of life."[6] What provided the ideal glue to bind our nation together, as Fulbright quoted Lincoln, was the idea of decency and humanity, not of war's devastation.

Here was a prudent, reasonable warning to both America and its President to back up and take a hard look down the fateful road we were traveling. There is no evidence that LBJ ever read the book. There is evidence, however, that Fulbright convened his committee in February 1966 for six days of testimony regarding our Vietnam policy.

Additionally, and ominously, several members of Fulbright's committee were anxious to probe the construction scandal in Vietnam, and particularly the involvement of Brown and Root. It seems that in 1962 McNamara's Defense Department was determined to build the infrastructure necessary for modern warfare—the very plan that Ridgeway and Gavin, seven years earlier, had warned would be prohibitive. McNamara told Congress it would cost $1.2 billion, partly because time didn't allow the military to do the work. So Congress permitted the private sector to get involved and—no surprise—in stepped Brown and Root, now renamed RMK-BRJ, a conglomerate of four companies. Immediately, problems arose. The local Vietnamese were paid but a fraction of what American workers were paid. The Americans, after a day's work, took to booze, to abusing the locals, and to driving their cars up the steps of Buddhist temples. Worse, the losses due to waste, mismanagement, and outright theft amounted to hundreds of millions of dollars. It was clear that old friends George and Herman Brown were reaping what they'd sown.

To distract the press—and particularly the White House press corps—from these hearings, Johnson quickly arranged an ad hoc conference on Vietnam in Honolulu. So while Fulbright was hearing testimony, much of it questioning and condemning the President's policy in Vietnam, Johnson was listening to South Vietnamese prime minister Nguyen Cao Ky promise to undertake the reforms necessary to quiet the Buddhists. He went so far as to tell Johnson there could be nothing better for his country than the Great Society that Johnson was bringing to America. It was music to Johnson's ears. And it should have been—for the remarks had been composed by American advisers in Saigon, employed to write just the speech that would further ingratiate Ky with LBJ. Indeed, at the end of Ky's address, Johnson turned to him: "Boy, you speak just like an American!" Then he called for, in typical Hill Country lingo, "coonskins on the wall!"

Unfortunately, Ky couldn't promise coonskins. Indeed, though LBJ issued a "Declaration of Honolulu" with a pledge by Ky to eradicate "social injustice," to embrace "true social revolution," and to usher in "a modern society in which every man . . . has respect and dignity," it was simply highfalutin rhetoric which, like the clouds overhead, soon disappeared beyond the horizon.

Ky actually had no intention of grounding his promises in action. Returning to Saigon, he resolved *not* to hold the elections he had promised, and *not* to goad his ARVN to bring him "coonskins." His was a different agenda. Quickly he disposed of his chief rival, a favorite of the rebelling Buddhists, which provoked renewed demonstrations against the United States as well as Ky. Large signs appeared before television cameras, "Down with the CIA," and "End Foreign Domination of Our Country." Johnson was bewildered as he watched it all on his TV screen. What had happened to Ky's promises? All Johnson had to do was look in the mirror at the master of dissembling. For Ky was a quick study. Soon he'd convinced Bundy that the Buddhists were in league with the Communists. Nevertheless, Ky vowed that he would honor his word to Johnson and resign in five months to permit elections. Instead, he reneged on that, and the nation was plunged deeper into chaos. So what did Ky do but dispatch 2,000 troops to slaughter demonstrators in Danang. Indeed, he'd have reduced the city to rubble had U.S. Marines not intervened. Reading of these "tragic and unnecessary" demonstrations, Johnson asked why on earth these Buddhists couldn't get behind their government instead of rebelling against it. Soon Ky dispatched Nguyen Ngoc Loan to Hue—the self-same colonel who horrified Americans with his later picture on television as he shot a suspected Vietcong in the head on the streets of Saigon. In Hue, Ky got down to work, jailing hundreds of students and other demonstrators for years without even a hint of a trial.

When Fulbright resumed his hearings on February 11, the press realized they'd been bushwhacked by the White House. They were attentive as Bobby Kennedy stood before the Senate Foreign Relations Committee: "If we regard bombing as the answer, we are headed straight for disaster." Furthermore, he added, it was ridiculous to protest that we couldn't simply withdraw from Vietnam. We must, in fact, grant the Vietcong "a show of power and responsibility in a new coalition government in Saigon." Coming from Kennedy, Johnson's nemesis, it meant the gauntlet had been flung down. In response, the President branded Kennedy, Fulbright, and the lot of them as "nervous Nellies," "bellyachers," or just plain "traitors."

Finally, on March 10, 1968, just three weeks before Johnson fell on his political sword, he attributed Fulbright's "betrayal" to the fact that LBJ had not made him secretary of state. When Johnson learned Fulbright was complaining that he hadn't understood "the meaning of it all"—referring to the Tonkin Gulf Resolution—LBJ was scathing: "For a Rhodes Scholar to say that he didn't know what was in that resolution is more than this hillbilly will ever believe." There was no doubt about it as far as this President was concerned. His chairman of the Senate Foreign Relations Committee was not only a son of a bitch but a "revolving" son of a bitch, or "someone who's a son of a bitch any way you look at him."[7]

Johnson could swear off booze as of January 1, 1967, lest it interfere with his decision-making on Vietnam. But he could rid himself of Fulbright no more than he could the protesters across the street in Lafayette Square, yelling their infernal chant, "Hey, hey, LBJ, how many kids did you kill today?" By the fall of 1967, Johnson should have seen the handwriting on the wall. There were the protesters, growing in number as well as intensity, virtually besieging this stubborn Texan as he hunkered down behind the big iron fence ringing the White House. There was McNamara "turning dovish on me"—because the secretary of defense had a son leading the protesters on his college campus, and developing, along with his mother, ulcers. And there were LBJ's "Wise Men," having second thoughts about it all as they began veering from the path they'd so confidently outlined for their President three years earlier.

So on November 2, 1967, Johnson put five questions to them.

What could we do that we are not doing in South Vietnam?

Concerning the North, should we continue what we are doing should we mine the ports and take out the dikes, or should we eliminate our bombing of the North altogether?

Should we adopt a passive policy of willingness to negotiate, should we passively seek negotiations, or should we bow out?

Should we get out of Vietnam?

What positive steps should the administration take to unite and better communicate with the nation?

The last question was undoubtedly prompted by McNamara's memo, given him the day before. Not surprisingly, his Secretary of Defense warned that continuing Johnson's present policy would "not bring us by the end of 1968 enough closer to success . . . to prevent the continued erosion of popular support for our involvement in Vietnam." For Johnson's policy would require increasing the draft, mobilizing the reserves, and doubling U.S. casualties in 1968—adding perhaps 13,000 dead and three times that many wounded.

So McNamara suggested three steps to get us out of the mess.

Announce a policy of stabilization.

Halt the bombing of North Vietnam before year's end in order to bring about negotiations.

Review ground operations in the South in order to reduce U.S. casualties, transfer greater responsibility to the South Vietnamese for their own security, and lessen the war's destructiveness to South Vietnam.

When dealing with his "Wise Men," Johnson deliberately omitted mention of McNamara's dire predictions and three recommendations—but he also never gave so much as a reply to the Defense Secretary. LBJ was dead set against negotiations until and unless he could bargain from strength, meaning when he could dictate terms to Ho Chi Minh. With this position, one of the "Wise Men," Dean Acheson, was in full agreement. Negotiations would be, Acheson told LBJ in December, a "pain in the neck," adding, "Apparently Hanoi doesn't want to negotiate. Good. I just hope they stay that way." Why so? Because, he concluded, any such negotiations were likely to be long and inconclusive.

Learning of the former Secretary of State's distaste for negotiations, *Saturday Review* editor Norman Cousins took issue: ". . . painful though they may be to the necks of diplomats, they are clearly to be preferred to the pain caused by a bullet in the human gut, or deep burns in human flesh by exotic fire devices, or the destruction of huts." Just how the North could take this kind of punishment and come back for more is clearly seen in the heroic efforts of a sixteen-year-old girl on the Ho Chi Minh Trail. By November 1967, the North Vietnamese troop infiltration rate along the Trail had soared to 20,000 a month—up from 35,000 for all of 1965. Most of those who died along the way fell from disease, so this teenager was headed south to serve as a nurse. The rifle, shovel, and 60-pound pack on her back would have taxed a burly Marine. Furthermore, this was the rainy season, with the monsoons turning the Trail to mud as "flash floods," she wrote in her diary, "forced us to cling to trees and shrubs to keep from being washed away." Then there were the leeches, snakes, and vermin of the jungle, and the steep mountains she had to scale with ladders and bare feet. And always, when the weather brightened, she could count on U.S. planes overhead, constantly harassing her, laying bare the trees with defoliants, leaving no place to hide. At night the planes would drop their flares, lighting up the Trail so the Americans could better pinpoint their bombs. "One night," she wrote, "the bombs were dropping everywhere" so, using her shovel, she dug a foxhole. As "the bombs fell close, I shook with fear. My heart would throb, and my whole body trembled inside as the bombs exploded. Even after the bombing had stopped, I couldn't focus my eyes, and my head ached for hours."

Arriving in Laos, she set up a primitive underground hospital in the jungle, with logs for a roof. Then she promptly vomited at the sight and "smell of blood and pus as the wounded were brought in, their arms and legs missing, their "bellies ripped open by bomb fragments, and their intestines spilling out. Others were horribly burned with napalm." Still others, lying for days in the jungle, "were brought in with maggots crawling out of their infected wounds." Malaria, too, was taking its toll, its victims "delirious with fever," rampaging "like madmen." At last the young nurse came down with malaria and was sent home. She was one of the lucky ones.

Certainly Vietnam was no extension of Texas. Whereas Americans paid scant attention to their ancestors, the Vietnamese virtually worshipped them. Whereas Americans tolerated occasional wars as long as they were successfully and quickly ended, the Vietnamese had lived for 1,000 years as a subject people: first under the Chinese, then the French and Japanese and now the Americans. Whereas Americans had to gear up for each new war, the Vietnamese bequeathed to successive generations a gun along with a plow. Whereas Americans concentrated on the future, confident that it would bring progress, the Vietnamese concentrated on tradition, confident that the past was the only sure guide to the present. Whereas Americans spelled freedom in terms of independence, the Vietnamese conceived of freedom as interdependence, with the value of the individual determined by his value to his society. The American idea of individualism—idealized in the *McGuffey Reader* and its successors, nourished by Horatio Alger, Ralph Waldo Emerson, and the cowboys of the ever-expanding frontier of the nineteenth century—was anathema to the Vietnamese to whom individuality was immoral because it was selfish. Indeed, there was no word in Vietnamese that could be translated into our first person pronoun, "I."[8]

But how were Johnson and his staff to know Vietnam? None of them spoke Vietnamese. None had a working knowledge of their history or their culture. JFK had been fortunate to have the likes of Soviet experts Llewellyn Thompson, Charles Bohlen, and George Kennan assisting him in his dealings with the USSR. With the Far East, it was a very different story. For the three top Asian experts—John Paton Davies, Jr., John Stewart Service, and John Carter Vincent—had been forced to resign their desks at State in the wake of McCarthyism. In retrospect, McNamara bemoaned the resultant ignorance, reminiscent of the bumper sticker: "If you think education is expensive, try ignorance." The Defense Secretary later noted that "Without men like these to provide sophisticated, nuanced insights, we—certainly I—badly misread China's objectives and mistook its bellicose rhetoric to imply a drive for regional hegemony." Worse, "We also totally underestimated the nationalist aspect of Ho Chi Minh's movement."

By January 1968, *Time*, the flagship of Henry Luce's publishing fleet, was outright pessimistic as it quoted the equally pessimistic National Committee for an Effective Congress: "America has experienced two great internal crises in her history: the Civil War and the economic Depression of the 1930s. The country may now be on the brink of a third trauma, a depression of the national spirit." And who was the nation, yes, even the world, focusing upon as "the chief repository of the nation's aspirations and the supreme scapegoat for its frustrations"? Why, none other than *Time*'s Man of the Year, Lyndon Johnson. From a high of an 80 percent approval rating by the American public, he had plummeted to 38 percent in October 1967. Why? Partly because of his personality: ". . . immense, complex, contradictory, and downright unpleasant," but more because of his policies. Though historical generalizations are dangerous, according to author John L. Steele, "one is tempted to suggest that not even Lincoln was faced with such internal questioning, such intense and wide-ranging dissent as did Lyndon Johnson in 1967." It was his war policies, said Michigan's former Democratic state chairman Zoltan Furency, who quit Johnson to form a Dump-LBJ movement behind Gene McCarthy. Here, Furency emphasized, were "the youth, the academicians, the women, the intellectuals—they are dropping out of politics, they are turned off."

Turned off perhaps, but they could hardly tune out their thirty-sixth President and his endless justifications for waging an immoral war.

America's first president, Washington, was called a crook and the "stepfather of his country." His successor, Adams, displayed "in plain sight . . . the cloven foot." And his successor, Jefferson, was berated as a "mean-spirited hypocrite." Then there was Jackson, called a murderer and adulterer. Lincoln fared no better as a "baboon," and Wilson was—in TR's choice epithet—"a Byzantine logothete [an emperor's bookkeeper] backed by flubdubs and mollycoddles." During the Depression, Hoover took it on the chin, with newspapers dubbed "Hoover blankets," and an empty pocket turned inside out designated a "Hoover flag."

If these, then—some of our most illustrious presidents—faced such ire, how could Johnson expect to fare better? Black Power apostle Stokely Carmichael labeled him a "buffoon," and a "liar." H. Rap Brown, Carmichael's successor, suggested that both Lyndon and Lady Bird should be shot. Journalist Robert Sherrill called Johnson "treacherous, dishonest, manic-aggressive, petty, [and] spoiled." And the play "MacBird" referred to him as:

". . . this canker . . .

this tyrant whose name alone

blisters our tongues . . .

Villain, traitor, cur."

One cartoon at the time pictured an aide trying to comfort an obviously disconsolate LBJ: "Maybe if you're abused enough you'll get popular again!"

By the end of January 1968, the war was going anything but smoothly. The Tet offensive, carefully planned by the North Vietnamese and launched on a broad front, entered the living rooms of millions of Americans via TV, awakening them to the lie that LBJ had been perpetrating for three years: that victory was just over the horizon. There were the pictures of Communists overrunning, of all places, our own embassy in Saigon! Other reports reached home, like that of the Marine ordered to take the Citadel—the fortress in the center of Hue—that had been captured by the Communists. There the Marine found himself "face to face," and "eyeball to eyeball," as he described it, with an enemy also striving to survive. Sitting there in the darkness he could see little. But his ears were assaulted by the constant firing of guns, even as the sweet acrid smell of the dead wafted over him, permeating even his clothes. And then there was the taste: "You tasted it as you ate your rations, as if you were tasting death." It was the Grim Reaper that was the constant companion of our troops there. Before the Tet battles finally subsided, nearly 9,000 U.S. and ARVN had been killed. But there was Westmoreland, dismissing these as a small price compared to the "58,000 enemy dead." If the traditional Johnson-era counting of enemy dead was continuing, those figures were highly suspect. Nonetheless, this was a glorious victory, Westmoreland bragged, even as he raged at the press for calling it a "psychological victory" for the Communists. Such reporting he denounced as "lurid and distorted," because it "transformed a devastating Communist military defeat." Here, Westmoreland insisted, was a last-ditch stand by the Communists, similar to Hitler's Battle of the Bulge in 1944. Moreover, Westmoreland bragged, he'd smoked out the enemy from their labyrinthine tunnels and jungle hideouts to do battle in the open, where our tanks, artillery, and planes could take their toll.

And where was Johnson, our illustrious commander in chief who fancied himself—even as Hitler did—a modern-day Napoleon? There in the Ready Room in the bowels of the White House, he could be found at all hours of the night, dressed in his bathrobe, poring over a sand model of Khe Sanh—a city on which he ordered dropped no less than 100,000 tons of bombs, the deadliest deluge of firepower ever unloaded on a tactical target in the history of warfare. Moving from the model to the clacking teletype machine, he'd follow the latest blow-by-blow accounts from the field. Thence to the latest aerial photos. Then he'd bark out his orders. One of them went to the JCS, whom he instructed to sign a formal declaration of faith in Westmoreland's ability to hold Khe Sanh. Declared the commander in chief in no uncertain terms, "I don't want any damn Din-bin phoo!"

It wasn't long, however, before Johnson learned that Khe Sanh had been abandoned by the Marines. This he would not divulge to the press, for already he'd gone on record as saying that the Marines were dying there to secure a "crucial anchor" in the defense chain of that section. Nevertheless, Walter Cronkite—widely respected as America's most trusted journalist—returned from Saigon, and on February 27 predicted that "the bloody experience of Vietnam" would, like Korea, "end in a stalemate." If, Johnson complained, he'd lost Cronkite, he'd lost middle

America. To make matters worse, back from Saigon came State's Richard Holbrooke with a description of Westmoreland not as the spirited, defiant, and perennially optimistic Commanding General, but as a "dispirited, deeply shaken, almost broken man . . . stunned that the Communists had been able to coordinate so many attacks [in Tet] in such secrecy. "

Johnson was not about to take this lying down. After all, his own reelection in less than nine months was at stake. So he ordered JCS Chairman Earle Wheeler to tell Westmoreland that he, LBJ, was "not prepared to accept defeat." If you want more troops, said this commander of commanders, "just ask for them." So Westmoreland asked for them, cabling Wheeler, "A setback is fully possible if I am not reinforced. . . . Time is of the essence."

What was LBJ to do? There was Westmoreland calling for another 205,000 troops, with 108,000 to be on the field by May 1. And there was Wheeler telling him he'd have to mobilize the reserves. But this meant political suicide. So LBJ ordered another 30,000 to Vietnam, promising to "study" the issue of the reserves. Johnson had cried "wolf!" in the name of "national security" or "national defense" so often that the electorate was increasingly turning a deaf ear to him. As Wisconsin Democrat Gaylord Nelson had warned on the Senate floor, "We all know that the two biggest words in the English language are 'national defense.' If you just shout them loud enough, you are in the clear. It is just plain unpatriotic to question any appropriation for national defense. Defense against what? It does not matter. Just utter the magic words." But that was no longer true; the electorate was taking seriously—at long last—Eisenhower's warning in his farewell address to beware of uninformed professionals, their civilian colleagues and superiors at the Pentagon, their supporters in Congress, and their suppliers among big business and big labor.[9]

Even some of the professional military, by this time, were casting a jaundiced eye at their own ranks. General David Shoup, retired Marine Corps Commandant and holder of the Medal of Honor, was accusing the armed forces of relishing war for the sake of self-aggrandizement, of making the United States "a militaristic and aggressive nation." At the same time, civilian physicist Herbert York, former chief of research at the Pentagon, warned that Americans were facing a "Frankenstein monster that could destroy us." Yet invariably, it seemed, the JCS were beating their war drums. When Johnson in 1965 decided to escalate the war in a major way, it was with the complicity—indeed the *urging*—of the JCS. As the scholar and war critic Hans Morganthau put it, "No general was going to admit that the U.S. couldn't win this lousy little war against a couple of hundred thousand peasants in pajamas."

The record of the JCS in America's post-World War II policy is scarcely encouraging. MacArthur based his strategy in Korea on the conviction of the JCS that the Chinese would never intervene. Most of the JCS were heartily in favor of resorting to nuclear arms to aid the French in Vietnam. JFK went along with the Bay of Pigs invasion partly because the JCS were pushing for it. Had Kennedy heeded the JCS during the Cuban Missile Crisis, he'd have bombed and invaded Cuba before Khrushchev had an opportunity to comply with the President's demands. When LBJ inherited the White House, the JCS lost no time in urging him to escalate and win the war in Vietnam—and the JCS, in turn, were told they could have their war if they'd help him win the 1964 election. When a revolution in the Dominican Republic erupted, the JCS urged LBJ to dispatch 20,000 U.S. troops, when a far smaller force would have done the job. Indeed, at the time Clark Clifford replaced McNamara, he learned, to his horror, that the JCS had no concrete plan for ending the war, aside from using nukes—thus threatening the intervention of China and the Soviet Union, and the outbreak of World War III. If there was anyone familiar with the military-industrial complex, it was Eisenhower. In 1965, he warned in *Waging Peace* that "every addition to defense expenditures does not automatically increase military security. Because security is based upon moral and economic, as well as purely military strength, a point can be reached at which additional funds for arms, far from bolstering security, weaken it."

On February 27, 1968, an emotional McNamara reminded his replacement Clifford and other senior officials that Westmoreland was demanding an additional 205,000 men—bringing the total to over 700,000 U.S. troops—and requiring at least another $10 billion allocation: a tenth of the total federal budget. There was no way, McNamara insisted, to do this without calling up the reserves and imposing a big tax increase. Johnson aide Harry McPherson, aghast, called America's commitment in Vietnam "unbelievable and futile." But there were Rusk, Rostow, and Wheeler, all beating the war drums. Then Rusk called for an escalation in the bombing. At that, McNamara could take it no longer. "The goddamned Air Force, they're dropping more on Vietnam than were dropped on Germany the last year of World War II, and it's not doing anything!" Then, between suppressed sobs, he pleaded with Clifford, "We simply have to end this thing. I just hope you can get hold of it. It is out of control."

That, Clifford already suspected. The previous July, LBJ had sent retired General Maxwell Taylor and Clifford on a scouting tour to find out if the other members of SEATO, to whom we had pledged our defense, were concerned enough about the Communist takeover of Vietnam to pledge their troops to support us there. When they left Saigon, they got a rousing send-off. Westmoreland and Ellsworth Bunker, the U.S. ambassador to Vietnam, were in high spirits. The tide had definitely changed. We were winning, but we needed help from other SEATO countries to finish the job in short order. Yet one after another of the member nations had begged off: Australia, New Zealand, Thailand, Singapore—even South Korea.

These SEATO allies were more interested in celebrating what they had done than in anticipating what more they *might* do, Taylor and Clifford told a disgruntled Johnson. Indeed, reported Clifford, "I found no concern anywhere in Asia that the Chinese . . . or the Soviets . . . might enter the war." The Communist bogeyman seemed to be sitting only on the U.S. doorstep, far removed from Southeast Asia. The nations of that region—including South Vietnam—were all perfectly willing to form a cheering section for us as we sent more and more men and matériel to do the job. It was not until 1968, in fact, that Johnson finally put pressure on Ky to draft eighteen-year-olds, something the United States had been doing for some time.

By March 1968, Johnson was furious that the three major reasons for our involvement in Vietnam— to bolster the Saigon regime even when it didn't care enough to draft its own young people; to remain faithful in our commitment to SEATO; and to keep all Southeast Asia from falling under the dominion of China/Soviet Communism—had disappeared in one fell swoop. Johnson was at his wit's end. Murphy's law was at work wherever he turned: whatever could go wrong *did* go wrong. Worst of all, his own reelection was disappearing in the smoke of continuing battle. Since Gene McCarthy and Bobby Kennedy were both calling for a bombing halt, Johnson on March 4 decided to show them that another halt would do no more good than the previous eight had done. So to Rusk he gave the order, "Get on your horse on that one."

Four years earlier, in June 1964, Lyndon was complaining to Russell that if he lost the war the people would say, "*I've* lost. . . . At the same time, I don't want to commit us to war. And I'm in a hell of a shape." To which Russell responded, "We're just like the damn cow over a fence out there in Vietnam." Then Johnson quoted another friend, fellow Texan A.W. Moursunel: "Goddamn, there's not anything that'll destroy you as quick as pulling out, pulling up stakes and running. America wants, by God, prestige and power." Russell then predicted, "It'll take a half-million men. They'd be bogged down in there for ten years." By 1968, Johnson realized how right on target Russell had been.

LBJ was crestfallen. Soon Wheeler was cabling Westmoreland: Don't press for the 205,000 lest you "raise unshirted hell in many influential quarters." In fact, don't even count on the 30,000. Worse, there was UN Ambassador Arthur Goldberg putting it on the line to the JCS. How many of the enemy were killed in Tet? JCS—revising Westmoreland's figures: 45,000. What was the kill-to-wounded ratio? JCS: 7 to 1. And what was the strength of the enemy at the start of Tet? JCS: 100,000 to 175,000. And their ratio? JCS: 3.5 to 1. So, Goldberg concluded, "they have no more effective forces left to fight!"[10]

Back in Washington, Johnson remained as bellicose as ever. "Today we are the number one nation," he bragged to the National Foreign Policy Conference at the State Department, "and we are going to stay the number one nation." In reality, what obsessed him was not only his reelection but his place in history. What would future books say if he were the first president to lose a war?

On March 19 Clifford suggested at a Tuesday Luncheon Meeting that LBJ reconvene his circle of advisers, the so-called "Wise Men." Johnson was skeptical, figuring any de-escalation would prompt people to "think we were complying with Kennedy's proposal." Nevertheless LBJ met with them, only to find that ten of the fourteen men were dead set against the war. One of them, deputy assistant secretary of defense Morton Halperin, later recounted, "We were going to write what we thought even if that meant we all got fired." They questioned even the very presence of U.S. forces in Vietnam, as well as the "fundamental motives" of our policy there. Wheeler and Westmoreland were aghast at this "betrayal." So Clifford put it to them: How long to victory? They didn't know. How many more troops to assure that? They weren't sure. Do you need more? By all means. Can the enemy match them? Probably. So how will you assure that victory? Keep wearing them down till they throw in the sponge. Any indication that our policy of attrition has done that? None.

All good questions. But another, even more fundamental question, that Clifford *didn't* ask was, what do we mean by victory? When we've gotten Hanoi to promise not to harass the South Vietnamese—or its government in Saigon? Or when we've driven the Vietcong to the North where they belong? Or when the North Vietnamese surrender so we can occupy the entire country? Given a positive answer to any one of those definitions of victory, what then?

Those are also the questions McNamara should have been asking in the fall of 1966, when LBJ called him "The best secretary of defense in the history of the nation."[11] Others took a more jaundiced view of McNamara at the time, including the JCS, who considered his undercutting of their demands outright betrayal. So strongly did the JCS feel about this that in 1967, when McNamara told Johnson that the best he could hope for in Vietnam was a stalemate—such as had occurred in Korea—they threatened to resign as a body. And this despite the CIA's finding that no amount of bombing would deter the North Vietnamese from supplying the South with troops and supplies over the Ho Chi Minh Trail.

Then there were student protesters wherever McNamara went, walking out when he rose to speak or to receive an honorary degree, or even threatening him—as they did at Harvard. There were others, like Jackie Kennedy, whom he confessed he "admired enormously." Years later, McNamara would describe how, at the conclusion of a dinner party, Jackie began "to beat on my chest," and—"in fury and tears"—demand "that I 'do something to stop the slaughter!' " Then there was the stranger at the Seattle airport, spitting on him and shouting, "Murderer!" McNamara couldn't even take a breather to ski at Aspen without a woman interrupting his Christmas dinner by screaming, "Baby burner! You have blood on your hands!"

Of one thing McNamara was certain. It wasn't only his war. So the next summer he ordered his assistant, John McNaughton, to initiate a study of America's relationship to Vietnam since World War II. Soon McNaughton had a task force of thirty-six researchers delving into our murky business 10,000 miles from U.S. shores. Receiving initial reports, McNamara was dumbstruck: "You know, they could hang people for what's in there!" Leslie Gelb, the leader of the research team, noted in 1971—after the Pentagon Papers had been leaked to the press—that McNamara left clear instructions to the task force "to let the chips fall where they may." The group was composed of eighteen military officers, nine civilians from different parts of the government, and nine professional scholars from think tanks and universities. Perhaps a quarter of them supported Johnson's policies, a few others were highly critical, and the rest fell in between. Yet none was ever questioned about his views before signing on. The result was forty-seven volumes and 2.5 million words, with the crucial question of governmental credibility the salient feature. It wasn't that presidents and their underlings engaged, Gelb noted, in "flat lies." Rather, secrecy and half-truths were the rule, a pattern based on what Gelb called "rank paternalism." "It is the courtly conviction that the American people cannot appreciate the problems and have to be brought along. . . . Issues of diplomacy, war and peace . . . are too subtle and sophisticated for the common man. . . . Besides, telling the full story to their own people makes for 'complications' with other nations." Thus, Geib concluded, "In their desire to do the best for the nation, our leaders felt they had to protect themselves against public pressures, and in the process shielded us from the information we needed to make up our own minds."[12]

Beset at home and abroad by what Lady Bird described as "this miasma of trouble," Johnson took the country by surprise when, on March 31, 1968, he announced on national television that he'd not run again. (The details of this decision we will cover in our last chapter.) By the time he left the White House in January 1969, LBJ had left 30,000 Americans dead in the jungles and rice paddies of Vietnam, and three times that many severely wounded. In addition there were at least a million Vietnamese dead, over 90 percent of them civilians, and most of these women and children. The 17,000 "advisers" he'd inherited from Kennedy had been multiplied thirty-two times, making a total of over 550,000 Americans in the backwater nation of Vietnam. He'd managed to undercut many of the programs he'd gotten Congress to pass as part of his Great Society. In all, he'd managed to spend over $100 billion—much of it borrowed money—on a war as fruitless as it was reckless, as immoral as it was vainglorious. If anything taught Lyndon Johnson just how counterproductive coercion could be, it was the war in Vietnam.

RICHARD NIXON

. . . Brookings [Institute] has no right to have classified documents [the Pentagon Papers]. . . . Goddammit, get in and get those files. Blow the safe and get it.
— Richard Nixon to Haldeman, June 17, 1971

God, Pearl Harbor and the Democratic Party . . . will have gone without a trace if we do this correctly . . . the first things I want to go back to [are] . . . the Cuban Missile Crisis and . . . the Bay of Pigs."
— Nixon to Haldeman, June 24, 1971

. . . I want Brookings, I want them [the Plumbers] just to break in and take it out. . . . Don't discuss it here. You talk to Hunt. I want the break-in. You're to break into the place, rifle the files, and bring them in. . . . Just go in and take it . . . go in [ostensibly] to inspect the safe. I mean, clean it up.
— Nixon to Haldeman, June 30, 1971

I really need a son-of-a-bitch like [Tom] Huston [a White House aide] who will work his butt off and do it dishonorably . . . I'll direct him myself. I know how to play this game and we're going to start playing it . . . I want somebody just as tough as I am for a change. . . .
— Nixon to Haldeman, July 1, 1971[1]

Arms and the Nation

Jefferson's Declaration of Independence was intended to indict Britain for depriving the colonies of their right of liberty. There, in a bill of particulars, he made note of the "repeated injuries and usurpations" intended to establish "absolute tyranny over these states." Given this "long train of abuses and usurpations," it was not only our right but our duty "to throw off such government and to provide new guards for their future security." It was not that "our British brethren" had not been warned, reminded, appealed to and conjured repeatedly. But they, like their king, "have been deaf to the voice of justice and consanguinity." With that, Jefferson, speaking for "the general Congress assembled," and "in the name, and by the authority of the good people of these colonies," declared "these united colonies . . . free and independent states."

Thus did Britain, by its intransigence in repeatedly coercing its colonies, lose its single greatest prize, one of only many it would continue to lose until today, when the sun no longer always sets, as it did a century ago, on some part of the Empire. Britain has paid dearly for its coercion.

The United States, having gained its freedom, in turn coerced the Native Americans to enslave them and, that failing, to annihilate them and replace them with Negro slaves, imported from Africa. Indeed, our history of coercing others is no brighter than that of Britain's. Before a century had passed from Jefferson's Declaration in 1776, we had succeeded in virtually tearing ourselves apart over the issue of slavery and secession. We would do to the Native Americans, then to the Negroes, what we would not tolerate from the British. And in both cases we have been bedeviled by our resort to coercion.

With the coming of two world wars, fought—we assumed—to prevent others from conquering and enslaving us, we found ourselves in the postwar years facing yet another tyrant, bent—we were told—on world dominion. Communism was rooted in Marx's horror of a capitalism that he saw exploiting women and children in the manufacturing maw of Victorian England. In the hands of Stalin, Communism became a means to power he could never have dreamed of as a young man training for the priesthood. But in 1922, at the age of forty-three, he became secretary general of the party's Central Committee. With that, Marx's rallying cry, "Workers of the World, Unite," became, in effect, "Workers of the World, Unite *Behind Me*."

Perhaps Marx's central failure was to be overly optimistic about power in the hands of leaders, something Jefferson and the other Founding Fathers distrusted. Marx, therefore, failed to cumber delegated power with a system of checks and balances. It is without doubt that system for protecting people from its elected leaders that has figured largely in this nation's surviving and prospering for more than two centuries. Furthermore, it has made our Constitution such an ideal for emerging nations that many have copied it.

In a continuing effort to "contain" Communism's spread—following Stalin's refusal to honor his word and hold free elections in Eastern Europe after the war—we became embroiled in a Cold War that from time to time blew hot, as in Korea and Indochina. What prevented these conflicts from becoming world wars was, above everything else, the introduction of nuclear weapons that vanquished our enemy, Japan. In countering the long arm of international Communism we have paid dearly. We remained on a semi-wartime footing that poured at least five trillion dollars into our military over the past fifty years. We became the premier arms merchant of the world. We consolidated our various intelligence-gathering organizations into a Central Intelligence Agency that, by its very nature of surveillance and secrecy, has—along with the Federal Bureau of Investigation—eroded the open society that is the foundation of our democracy.

Richard Nixon played an important part in this postwar legacy, much of it through his coercive leadership. Because our involvement in Vietnam played such an historic role in his administration, this chapter on coercion is largely confined to America's relations with Indochina. Furthermore, had it not been for the Vietnam War—as Haldeman and others have maintained—there would have been no Watergate.

Vietnam, 1968–1974

How could Nixon have botched the war so badly, capping Johnson's fiasco with his own? It began in 1968, with his reversing himself one hundred and eighty degrees from the stance he'd assumed for over twenty years. By the spring of 1969, he was emphasizing two conditions for peace talks: the return of all American POWs—including an accounting of the MIAs—and an agreement not to attempt an overthrow of South Vietnamese President Nguyen Van Thieu. On the other side of the scale from these two conditions were two ways with which the United States could win the war: by bombing the elaborate system of dikes irrigating the North, or by resorting to tactical nuclear weapons. It wasn't so much the monstrous cruelty of either one that bothered Nixon. It was, rather, the resulting outcry that might very well ruin his chances for a second term.

We recoil, and rightly so, at the thought of a man deliberately killing another to gain high office, even the presidency. While this may be commonplace in authoritarian regimes, it has no place, we believe, in a society that calls itself either civilized or democratic. But what of a man who, having assured a war-weary nation in his Inaugural Address that his legacy would be that of a peacemaker, envisioned but two ways to win the war—both of which would result in megadeaths tantamount to genocide? What of a man who, promising to end the war in six months, prolonged it for another four years, to coincide with his reelection? What of a man who authorized the equivalent spending of $402 for armaments against only $2.50 to feed the hungry at home? What of a man who, to stay in power another four years, sacrificed 25,000 of our own men as well as a million or more Indochinese? What of a man who, in the face of these mind-boggling casualties, prompted Wicker to write, "It wasn't so much the casualties that deterred [Nixon]; it was the *reaction* to the casualties that bothered him." For that reaction, he knew, could spell disaster at the polls in 1972. In the face of such a monstrous ego, it is almost irresistibly tempting to demonize Nixon—even as we were tempted to demonize the Indochinese as "gooks," as something less than human. But we are brought up short by Wicker's insistence, spelled out in the title of his biography of Nixon: *One of Us*. What had happened was, it seems, that the pious Quaker boy, soaked in religious respectability, had been transmogrified, step by seductive step, by the siren songs of the nymphs of hubris.

Convinced that Nixon and his administration were becoming the twentieth-century counterpart of ancient Rome, the Center for the Study of Democratic Institutions released in June 1970 a report of an earlier paper by Stringfellow Barr: "Second Edition/Consulting the Romans." The Romans taught that their eternal city had been founded by none other than the son or grandson of Aeneas, son of the goddess Aphrodite. The Americans taught that the *Mayflower*, like the ship that brought Aeneas from the East, came to the new land, New England, bearing a saving remnant from the Sodom that was Europe—"God-fearing, honest, energetic men" who would leave their mark in the "Puritan Ethic." But they also brought death, through disease and war, with weapons the natives could not hope to match. Like the Romans, hungry for land to broaden their empire, the Americans moved to expand ever westward. Unlike the Romans, however, the Americans confronted an enemy unlike themselves, an enemy primitive and tribal, holding no ground individually, but living in common. But above all, they worshipped not Jehovah and His Son, but an assortment of gods embracing animism, totemism, and magic. So the Elect, as Barr put it, "took [the land] partly by purchase but mainly by force, by pitched battle, by ambush, by massacre, and by broken treaty."

Unable to enslave the aborigines, as the Spanish had done in the South, they imported slaves from Africa, "many of them prisoners of war like the slaves the Romans captured or bought." The "chosen" not only bought the slaves, separating families, but drove them hard, not hesitating to flog them just as the Romans did their prisoners. Even while the Europeans looked on, aghast at the incredible energy, greed, and cruelty of the new nation, the Americans did not hesitate to proclaim themselves as the "saving remnant, guided by God to found a new City," stretching from shore to shore—and, by 1970, eager to prove its sacred place in the light of Providence by battling atheistic Communism. Rome stretched itself across its world, proclaiming its specialness, insisting on enlightening others even as it incorporated the new peoples into the Empire. The United States stretched itself across the world, insistent that we would not only make that world "safe for democracy," but export that democracy—American style—to the distant and benighted peoples of Vietnam.

"Society becomes barbarism," Barr concluded, "when men are huddled together under the rule of force or fear." It was we, the Center's John C. Murray insisted, who were the barbarians—not the native Americans we'd virtually annihilated in genocide, not the black Africans we'd enslaved to do our bidding. As Barr added, "The barbarian need not appear in bearskins with a club in hand. He may wear a Brooks Brothers suit and carry a ballpoint pen." For the barbarian, Aristotle wrote, is one who refuses reasonable conversation according to reasonable laws: living together, talking together, and resolving differences through civil discourse.

Despite Nixon's clever gambling in 1972 to pit the two Communist giants, China and the Soviet Union, against each other to extract concessions from both—including forcing Hanoi to the bargaining table—the year proved to be a land mine. In the midst of Nixon's maneuvering with Peking and Moscow that spring, Hanoi was doing its own maneuvering.

While Kissinger was laying plans for the Moscow summit, the North Vietnamese Army (NVA) launched a broad offensive, reminiscent of Tet four years before, pushing into the Central Highlands from Laos and Cambodia. Nixon, scorning the proposals of Senate doves to stop the bombing in order to bring Hanoi back to the peace table, took to national TV to blast this invasion as "a clear case of naked and unprovoked aggression across an international border." Then, mounting his rhetorical white horse, he compounded hypocrisy with hyperbole: "If the United States betrays the millions of people who have relied on us in Vietnam . . . it would amount to a renunciation of our morality, an abdication of our leadership among nations, and an invitation for the mighty to prey upon the weak all across the world." There is classic irony in this, for other nations, including our World War II allies, were viewing us as the irrepressible bully laying waste to a small, primitive nation—in order, we claimed, "to save it."

With that balloon of bellicosity Nixon added a zinger, ordering Kissinger back to Paris to lay down the law—again—to Hanoi: "Settle or else!" With an enormous arsenal of nuclear weapons at his disposal, the trigger finger of this madman was becoming itchier by the day. Here, Nixon figured, was a message even the obdurate North Vietnamese would understand.

By the end of April 1972, with the Moscow summit just weeks away, Nixon was in for more bad news. From Saigon, he learned that the ARVN had collapsed before the NVA, losing all will to fight. From Paris, he learned that—far from moving Hanoi to the bargaining table to settle on our terms—there was North Vietnam's principal negotiator, Le Duc Tho, just as "icy and snide," Kissinger reported, as he'd ever been. And from New York, Nixon learned in the *Times* that it had garnered the Pulitzer Prize for its publication of the Pentagon Papers.

More bad news was in store for Nixon, the reaper who was harvesting what he'd sown, prompting Max Frankel of the *Times* to describe Nixon's "propensity for psychic rage and for diplomacy by thunderclap." Indeed, Frankel added, Nixon seemed to have taken leave of his senses. He had no use for TR's admonition to "speak softly and carry a big stick." With a nuclear arsenal as his "big stick," Nixon figured he had no need to "speak softly," regardless of his 1968 campaign promise. Frankel ended his column, "no one really does know what he might do." Of course, this was just the persona Nixon was trying to project to Hanoi, to Peking, and to Moscow: that of the unpredictable mad bomber.

To Nixon's relief, there was Kissinger on one side, urging him to throw caution to the winds as he protected his manhood. On the other side was Connally with his fighting words: Don't lose the war, don't cancel the summit, show guts and leadership on this one. "Caution be damned—if they cancel . . . we'll ram it right down their throats!"[2] That was the kind of encouragement Nixon needed.

With the NVA invading the South en masse—with his Moscow summit in jeopardy—with Hanoi thumbing its nose at him—Nixon, the first week in May, gathered with his aides to "discuss" his plans, playing the role of MacArthur as, with pipe in mouth, then in hand, he strode the room, emphasizing a point now and then with a wave of his pipe. In what Kissinger called "one of the finest hours of Nixon's presidency," the President emphasized that to pull out meant "the United States would cease to be a military and diplomatic power. . . ." Rather, it "would look inward towards itself and would remove itself from the world." Each resort to hype demanded an escalation the next time, until one is left to wonder how his aides figured Nixon was living in the real world. Then, with an air of bravura, Nixon solemnly announced he'd made up his mind. He would ratchet up the bombing again, and this time, mine the harbor at Haiphong. No consultation, as usual, with State, Defense, or even the National Security Council, much less congressional leaders. Again bypassing any news conference where reporters could well put him on the spot, he took to network TV on May 8, 1972, to announce to the nation that "there is only one way to stop the killing. [That is] to keep the weapons of war out of the hands of the international outlaws of North Vietnam."

But there was his Moscow summit just two weeks away, and he knew the mad-bomber image hardly did him credit as the international states-man who would bring peace to Vietnam. So he conceded that, if Hanoi would release all POWs and a cease-fire would prevail, he would remove the mines and withdraw completely from Vietnam within four months. Here was a significant concession in his definition of "peace with honor." No more would he demand an accounting of MIAs, no more that the NVA withdraw from the South, no more that Thieu's government remain in power. Still Hanoi refused to budge. Why should it? There remained but a skeleton force of U.S. troops, while the ARVN had crumbled, leaving virtually no resistance to the victorious NVA. Here, then, was Nixon, on the ropes, pretending he could call the shots. The picture was ludicrous, and Le Duc Tho knew time was running out for the United States.

Nixon, exasperated that he'd made no impression on Hanoi, again assumed a go-for-broke posture. "I intend to stop at nothing," Nixon told Kissinger, "to bring the enemy to his knees. . . . I want the military to get off its backside. . . . We have the power to destroy [the enemy's] war-making capacity. The only question is whether we have the *will* to use that power. What distinguishes me from Johnson is that I have the *will* in spades. . . ."

What America was in fact learning was that this President had not only the will to use his power, but to abuse it. And with the Watergate break-in scarcely more than a month away, the public would soon learn much more of Nixon's will to abuse his power.

As it was, Nixon was supporting no less than 85 percent of Thieu's ARVN budget, and a third of the South's economy. Vietnamization, far from being "astonishingly successful," as Laird puffed it, was proving a dismal failure. With the NVA pushing south, Thieu ordered the ARVN—after it had suffered 3,000 fatalities in this latest offensive—to quit fighting; he knew he couldn't prevent a coup were fatalities to multiply. Meanwhile, his Roman Catholic officers, most of them taught in American schools at taxpayer expense, gloried not so much in the honor of defending the South as in helping themselves to the bountiful largesse of American money and goods—including weapons and ammunition that they readily sold to the enemy. This "damned war," as Nixon called it in his politest language, was the longest in U.S. history, and had consumed more than 15,000 dead since he took office. And this despite the wholesale withdrawal of U.S. troops.

Still there was no light at the end of the tunnel. If anything, for the United States the war seemed to be run by one law: Murphy's. Nixon was desperate as he put it to Kissinger, "Whatever else happens, we can't lose this war!" He would abandon the Moscow summit, he would do anything to win the war—except jeopardize his reelection chances. One major regret, he told his aides, was in quitting the bombing he'd started in 1970. If only he'd continued it, he was convinced, "the damned war would be over now."

Needling him from the sidelines was Democratic presidential hopeful

George McGovern. The bombing escalation, the mining, all this was "reckless, unnecessary and unworkable, a flirtation with World War III . . . to keep General Thieu in power a little longer, and perhaps to save Mr. Nixon's face a little longer."

It was not only to save his face but his reelection that inspired Nixon to have the Republican National Committee organize a letter-writing campaign that sent out no less than 22,000 phony letters to the media—ostensibly from the "silent majority" plumping for Nixon's Vietnam policy. In addition, he had his aides take out $8,000 worth of phony ads in newspapers across the country, certainly a sound investment, what with his reelection just six months away. Surprise! Soon the polls were showing 60 percent of Americans favoring Nixon's decisions regarding Vietnam. There was no question; advertising paid off.

As though his reelection were the last thing on his mind—and after being told that the JCS were opposing the SALT agreement he'd secured in Moscow—Nixon said, "The hell with the political consequences. We are going to make an agreement on *our* terms regardless of the political consequences if the Pentagon won't go along."[3] That the political consequences of his decisions were always in his mind, indeed uppermost in his mind, is shown by subsequent events in Vietnam.

So upbeat was Nixon on returning from Moscow with a SALT agreement—and then regaling Congress with his "historic negotiation"—that he held one of his rare news conferences. A few weeks before, reporters had heard Admiral Elmo Zumwalt, Chief of Naval Operations, point out, ". . . the unconscionable numbers" in the SALT agreements "virtually froze us into five more years of high spending on U.S. strategic forces." So why, Nixon was asked, have an arms agreement that would escalate the arms race? Answered Nixon, you'll see new negotiations achieving a permanent agreement of "far greater significance." But, the reporters persisted, why put all this money into new weapons? Because, explained the President, he could only negotiate with the Soviets—like the North Vietnamese—from a position of strength. Nixon patronized the press as he explained to the dunderheads that he was building these new weapons so his successors wouldn't have to. Didn't that make sense? The reporters weren't so sure as they left the meeting, shaking their heads at this presidential logic.

Learning the ARVN was putting up lukewarm resistance at best, Nixon sent Haig and Army Chief of Staff Creighton Abrams to tell Thieu to "get off his tail and punch this outfit [the NVA]. . . . " Even though he ordered another 10,000 American ground troops home in June—leaving but 39,000 in Vietnam by September 1—Nixon was satisfied he was doing his share. For Mao was now pressing Hanoi to let up on its demand to remove Thieu. "Do as I did," said Mao, "I once made an accord with [his archenemy] Chiang Kai-shek when it was necessary."

Nixon's propaganda seemed to be paying off. A September poll found 55 percent favoring heavy bombing, 64 percent favoring the mining of Haiphong harbor, and 74 percent favoring the prevention of the South falling to the Communists.

By the first week in October, Nixon was on pins and needles, what with the election scarcely a month away and the war still dragging on. What to do? He decided that a neutralist coalition government might not be such a bad idea. Except he would not call it a coalition government— since he'd been criticizing that notion for years—but a "Committee of National Reconciliation," consisting of the South Vietnamese, the Communists, and neutralists, each entitled to one-third representation. The plan was to have them "review" the South's constitution and to oversee elections. Inevitably, it would see put in place the very neutralist, coalition government that Thieu was dreading. It would mean the end of his regime, so he did what any dictator would do. He refused to cooperate, just as Nixon had urged him to do in 1968 to prevent a Humphrey victory. Nixon's chickens were coming home to roost.

Nixon was predictably furious and again sent Haig to Saigon to bribe, cajole, or threaten Thieu—whatever it took. Go along, said Haig, or Nixon will refuse to continue support. Thieu broke down in tears at the prospect of losing his firm grip on this "freedom-loving democracy" and the hundreds of millions, even billions, he was skimming off U.S. aid to maintain himself in power and to enrich his friends and relatives. It was a prospect too grim to contemplate. Haig hastened to assure Thieu that there'd be no settlement without discussing it with him beforehand, implying, Thieu believed, that he wouldn't necessarily have to cooperate. Oh, yes he would, Haig told him, because Nixon simply could not tolerate any continuing failure to join in the agreement. The President followed up with his own veiled threat. Resistance to the White House plan—and here Nixon was ready to use his "big stick"—might develop "an atmosphere which could lead to events similar to those which we abhorred in 1963." Here was a typical Nixonism. For what he was getting at was: go along or end up like Diem, the South Vietnamese leader who had been overthrown—and assassinated—on November 1, 1963.

Thieu, it turned out, was also adept at poker, and decided to call Nixon's bluff. As time passed and election day neared, Nixon's blood pressure rose. He called on his ambassador to Saigon, Ellsworth Bunker, to lay it out "cold turkey" to Thieu. If he continued his willfulness, insisting on the tail wagging the dog, Nixon would "break it off with him after the election." After all, if Nixon could sell his Committee of National Reconciliation to the North's Le Duc Tho, he certainly could sell it to the South's Nguyen Van Thieu. Nixon ordered Kissinger to get Thieu's agreement to the plan—even, if necessary, to "cram it down his throat." Here was the old Nixon, the master of coercion.

Yet Nixon was having second thoughts about the timing of an armistice just prior to his reelection. Maybe American voters would suspect that he'd meant to synchronize the two all along. Furthermore, Nixon was becoming suspicious of Kissinger: "That son-of-a-bitch," the President told Chuck Colson, "want[s] me to be in his debt for winning this election." Nixon was having enough trouble with Thieu to have to also worry about Kissinger seizing the credit. So he sent Colson to tell Kissinger to slow down. "Please tell him it will hurt—not help us—to get the settlement before the election."

Having settled the matter with Thieu, and now with Kissinger, Nixon went public at a news conference. He would come up with a settlement "just as soon as . . . it is *right.*" Of course, the timing of the election had absolutely nothing to do with it. He would not be like Johnson, who, in 1968, had been "motivated by political considerations . . . [making] a very, very great mistake in stopping the bombing without adequate agreements from the other side."[4]

As luck would have it, Hanoi was willing to go along—provided that the United States withdraw the last of its armed forces and ante up to rebuild the North. For its part, Hanoi would release American POWs and accept the Committee of National Reconciliation. Kissinger called it "essentially . . . a mixed electoral commission, while Hanoi called it a "Provisional Government of National Concord," with emphasis on "Provisional." In fact, it was essentially a pretext for a coalition government.

Kissinger, eager to put his own spin on the agreement in order to complete it before election day, reported to Nixon that Hanoi's Provisional Government was "not inconsistent with their eventually turning their coalition government into an irrelevant committee in order to give a face-saving cover to a standstill cease-fire and de facto territorial control by both sides." Furthermore, Kissinger trumpeted, Hanoi made "an even more stunning concession" to withdraw its troops from both Laos and Cambodia after the settlement had been finalized. This further concession Kissinger hyped as "a remarkable breakthrough."

But Kissinger's excess didn't end there. "I have participated in many spectacular events," he later wrote. "I have lived with power; I have seen pomp and ceremony. But the moment that moved me most deeply was when the agreement was reached, surely my most thrilling moment in public service."

Just as euphoric, according to his National Security Adviser, was Nixon, now to take his turn in spinning the agreement. It was nothing less than "the complete capitulation by the enemy; they were accepting a settlement on our terms." And his promise of reparations to help rebuild the North meant that taking "money from the United States represented a collapse of Communist principle."

Kissinger was scornful of those who dared imply that Nixon could have settled four years earlier for essentially the same terms, including the eventual establishment of a coalition government—something Nixon had bad-mouthed for a decade. "Not even the slightest acquaintance with the record," Kissinger maintained, "sustains that argument. Never before October 8, 1972, had Hanoi agreed to abandon its unacceptable demand for a coalition government."

Indeed, a "slight acquaintance" with the agreement might lead the unwary to conclude that this was an historic first, worthy of Kissinger's self-praise. But a closer reading cannot help but reveal Kissinger's sugar-coating of the settlement. And this but confirms Thieu's continuing intransigence, based upon his sure knowledge that he would, in short order, be the odd man out.

Here was but a continuation of the hype, the spin, the twist, the stretch, the distortion that Nixon and his sidekick had used since January 1969. Now, with Nixon's snowjob transformed into a snowballing of public opinion, he was determined not simply to win in November, but to win in a landslide of historic proportions. To that end, Kissinger prepared a timetable that would call for a signing of the armistice on October 31, just days before the election.

Among the skeptics was McGovern, a bomber pilot in World War II, pointing up "the reality of this war" in terms of "the news photo of the little South Vietnamese girl . . . fleeing in terror from her bombed-out school," her flaming clothes torn off as she ran in stark terror into the eye of the camera. "That picture," said McGovern, "ought to break the heart of every American. How can we rest with the grim knowledge that the burning napalm that splashed over [her] and countless thousands of other children was dropped in the name of America?" He added, "General Thieu is not worth one more American prisoner, one more drop of American blood. Our problem is that we have asked our armed forces to do the impossible—to save a political regime that doesn't even have the respect of its own people."

Back from Paris on October 12 came Kissinger, his face wreathed in a broad smile. "Well, Mr. President, it looks like we've got three out of three!" First China, then the USSR, and now Vietnam. Caught up in the exhilaration of the moment, Nixon ordered steaks and a rare wine to celebrate. Alas, the toast they offered each other was premature. For the next day, Nixon poured not wine, but cold water on the agreement by upping the ante. In addition to "technical issues," there was the cardinal issue of the status of the Vietcong in the National Council of Reconciliation. Furthermore, what exactly were its duties? Kissinger's prolix agreement begged clarification.[5]

Hanoi was upset. Here was Nixon demanding changes in an agreement already accepted by both sides. At this point, it became evident that the President and his National Security Adviser were at odds. Nixon wanted to delay any signing until after the election, lest the public think he'd been playing politics with the war all along. Kissinger, however, was certain a completed agreement would not only redound to Nixon's place in history, but serve as a powerful mandate for his second term. In addition, Kissinger wasn't averse to either taking credit for the agreement—or replacing Rogers as Secretary of State in Nixon's new administration. So Kissinger urged Nixon to call a complete bombing halt as a token of good faith. Nixon balked, "absolutely opposed" until the ink was dry on the agreement. Furthermore, Nixon was determined he'd not be seen as another

LBJ, calling for a bombing halt on the eve of the 1968 election. On October 16, Nixon wrote Kissinger, "Do what is right with regard to the election. At all costs we must avoid the fact or the impression that we have imposed or agreed to a coalition government."

On that same day, the Rev. Nixon preached to the choir as he addressed a thousand members of the National League of Families of American Prisoners and Missing in Southeast Asia. He lambasted McGovern for his pusillanimous approach to the war. He pledged not to leave the fate of the POWs "to the goodwill of the enemy." He promised to make draft evaders and deserters "pay a price for their choice." And he brought down the house when he vowed, "We shall not stain the honor of the United States."

It seems, however, that honor, like patriotism, in the words of the good Doctor Johnson, has often become "the last refuge of scoundrels." Just how close "honor" brought this country to World War III was graphically demonstrated in the Cuban Missile Crisis. Norman Cousins, editor of the *Saturday Review*, recounted an interview he had with Khrushchev several months after Kennedy's ultimatum. According to Khrushchev, "When I asked the military advisers if they could assure me that holding fast [to the continuing supplying of nuclear missiles to Cuba] would not result in the death of 500 million human beings, they looked at me as though I was out of my mind or, what was worse, a traitor. The biggest tragedy, as they saw it, was not that our country might be devastated and everything lost, but that the Chinese or Albanians would accuse us of appeasement or weakness. So I said to myself; 'To hell with these maniacs. If I can get the United States to assure me that it will not attempt to overthrow the Cuban government, I will remove the missiles.' That is what happened. And so now I am being reviled by the Chinese and the Albanians. They say I was afraid to stand up to a paper tiger. It is all such nonsense. What good would it have done me in the last hour of my life to know that our great nation and the United States were in complete ruins, while the national honor of the Soviet Union was intact?"

On October 18, Nixon wrote to Thieu, "I believe we have no reasonable alternative but to accept this agreement." Trouble was, he and Kissinger had decided not to give Thieu the complete text because, Kissinger wrote, "of our growing distrust of [Thieu's] entourage; because we thought . . . further improvements were possible; and above all because

I supposed he would be pleased by the outcome and therefore there was no need to engage him in detail before we were clear on our own game plan."

Presumably, the "Devil" in any such "game plan" would be in the details. Not being shown the complete text did nothing to set Thieu's mind at ease. So it must have come as no surprise to Nixon when Thieu, in response to Nixon's communication, responded in words as much as to say, "Over my dead body." Now it was Kissinger's turn to get on his high horse as he complained to Nixon that Hanoi "had in effect lost the war [yet] was acting as if it had won; while [Saigon], which had effectively won the war, was acting as if it had lost." But that was not the way Thieu saw the agreement—or as much of it as Kissinger gave him: The NVA would keep 150,000 of its troops in the South, the Vietcong would influence the South's political discussions, the National Council would inevitably result in a coalition government, and Thieu would be removed, politically if not physically, from the land of the living. It was not a happy prospect. To add to his consternation, there was Haig, warning that the Communists, as they had done in Hue during Tet, would kill their enemies once a cease-fire had been announced. Is it any wonder that Thieu objected long and loud?[6]

Nixon, to prove to Thieu he was nothing if not reasonable, launched "Operation Enhance Plus" on October 20. It involved a massive airlift of military equipment, supplies, and planes to Saigon—making its air force the third largest in the world. Neither Saigon nor the Pentagon were pleased, Admiral Zumwalt going as far as to say, "There are at least two words no one can use to characterize the outcome of that two-faced policy. One is 'peace,' the other is 'honor.'" Kissinger defined honor as a U.S. withdrawal conditional on Thieu's government remaining in power pending "truly free" elections. Never mind that Eisenhower, following Dulles, encouraged Diem in 1956 to renege on nationwide elections as stipulated in the Geneva Accords, because the victory of Ho Chi Minh was a foregone conclusion. Never mind that when Thieu finally held elections in 1971, his name was the only one on the ballot and he was elected with almost 100 percent of the vote. Kissinger and Nixon, like Johnson before them, were hoisting a specious argument that, in addition, made too much of honor— scarcely a substitute, as Khruschhev emphasized, for survival. Kissinger protested that to withdraw without retaining Thieu in office, regardless of his record of nepotism and corruption, was tantamount to dishonor, to "an outright, humiliating American defeat," and which "poll after poll showed the overwhelming majority of the American public unprepared to accept. . . ." It is little wonder that the poll results were so favorable, considering Nixon's continued cranking up of his propaganda machine: blizzards of fake letters to the media, distortions of all kinds in his news releases, and the rarity of his press conferences in which reporters would have a chance to put him on the spot.

To burden honor with such a lopsided definition was to sink it beneath the conscious acceptance of most Americans. "Honor," given its best definition in time of war, is invariably suspect. How many wars in this century alone have been fought to avenge the "dishonor," real or imagined, wrought upon the avengers by past enemies, often removed by centuries? This is not to say that there is no substance to honor as a value. It is rather to say that, especially in time of war, it is subject to crass manipulation by politicians seeking to arouse a credulous public. Like "national security," it has often been used to cloak all manner of mischief.

No matter. Nixon, his political antennae sensitive to the winds, took to his diary to exult in what would be "an enormous mandate," leaving him clearly in the driver's seat, with both Tho and Thieu having "to settle or face the consequences." But on October 22, Thieu showed he was still the same fly in the ointment. There was no way he'd settle without the 150,000 NVA troops evacuating the South, and without an abandoning of the idea of a National Council. This, Nixon complained, "verged on insanity." Yet he had more to complain about when Hanoi threatened to go public with Nixon's reneging on the October 8 agreement. But, Nixon complained to Tho, Thieu wouldn't go along. Couldn't they agree to another meeting to iron out the differences? Never, insisted Hanoi. A deal was a deal. So Nixon, like Johnson, called for a preelection bombing halt once the details of the text had been agreed upon.

Tho had only threatened to go public. Now Thieu *did* go public with his allegation that if the NVA stayed in the South, "the war will have proved to be only a U.S. war of aggression and the GI and ARVN sacrifices will have proven unnecessary. . . ." This time, it was McGovern's turn to go public, with his branding the Nixon administration as "the most corrupt . . . in history." With his Ph.D. in American history from Northwestern University, McGovern presumably was in a place to judge. And that wasn't the worst of it. McGovern tarred Nixon as a modern-day Hitler and feathered him as resorting to KKK tactics. As the *New York Post* put it, McGovern had less than undying admiration for his President, calling him "a liar, barbarian, immoral, cruel, and murderous."

Then, to Nixon's further consternation, there was Kissinger bragging to the press in frequent news briefings about his "historic" accomplishments. On October 25, he told Nixon that he'd just briefed Max Frankel of *The New York Times* "on the general agreement." Nixon was apoplectic. His teeth clenched, he seethed as he told Colson, "I suppose now everybody's going to say that Kissinger won the election." Furthermore, Nixon had told reporters on October 5, "The elections, I repeat, will not in any way influence what we do at the negotiating table." The day after his meeting with Frankel, Kissinger, in his first live TV appearance, uttered the words that made millions of Americans rejoice even as they set Thieu's teeth on edge: The war was over. "We believe," Kissinger announced, "that peace is at hand. We believe that an agreement is within sight." "Just how close at hand," *Newsweek* sniped, "was a most beguiling question." Yes, Kissinger conceded, there were still "occasional difficulties in reaching a final solution but . . . the longest part of the road has been traversed" with only "relatively less important" issues remaining. But, he served notice to both Saigon and Hanoi, "We will not be stampeded into an agreement until its provisions are *right*. We will not be deflected from an agreement when its provisions are *right*." One is reminded of the legendary journalist and satirist, H.L. Mencken, who observed, "For every problem there is a solution which is simple, neat—and wrong." This was not the only reason that Kissinger, post-Watergate, thought he might be considered foolish. He observed to Haldeman, "You know, we are going to look like perfect fools when all of the tapes are released. Nixon will be heard delivering one of his tirades, saying all sorts of outrageous things and we will be sitting there quietly, not protesting or disagreeing. You and I know that's the way we had to do business with him, but I think we will be judged harshly all the same." This kind of "right" thinking, implying two-valued orientation, the most common type of simplistics, scarcely did credit to Kissinger's alma mater and the university in which he taught: Harvard. In addition, to state "peace is at hand" just days before the election—knowing of the intransigence of Thieu, and the insistence of Tho that Hanoi had already settled on an agreement and would certainly not entertain modifications imposing more hardship on the North—would appear to counsel caution. Kissinger later wrote that, though this was an unfortunate turn of phrase, it wasn't accidental; and despite his plea that only semanticists would argue that it was a stretch—a big stretch—to say "at hand," the phrase could in no way apply when almost three more months were to pass before the agreement was finally signed. These were months in which Nixon was to appear to many, including our allies, as a commander in chief bereft of his senses—a "mad bomber" determined to bludgeon not only Hanoi but Saigon into submission, as historian George Herring put it.[7]

Kissinger's "at hand" message served at least three distinct purposes. It put the spotlight on Kissinger, not Nixon, as the international peace broker, preparing the way for his Nobel Peace Prize. It credited the Republicans with bringing the war to a close, something two Democratic presidents had been unable to do in eight years. And it created such excitement that the public and the press all but forgot the burglary of the DNC at the Watergate the previous June.

Nixon, of course, was happy for the last two benefits, yet there was Gene McCarthy asking the question on the lips of many: "Why was this not done four years ago?" The same question hit Kissinger at his first press conference after his stunning announcement. His answer: it had been impossible, because Hanoi was demanding the ouster of Thieu—as if the National Council were not going to see, in time, to his ouster. Among those taking issue with Kissinger's claim was the strongest naysayer, Thieu himself. There was no difference, he insisted, between this agreement and the one given Nixon by Hanoi in May 1969. In keeping with this insistence, on October 27 Thieu vowed again he had no intention of signing such an agreement. So to Tho Kissinger went, hat in hand. Could they have another meeting to iron out "minor details?" Tho again gave him the cold shoulder, emphasizing, "Peace is at the end of a pen." As for Thieu, he charged that the United States was negotiating nothing less than surrender. By October 29, Nixon was boxed in. There was Kissinger claiming credit for the peace, if not for the election itself, yet Nixon couldn't fire him—or if he could, he certainly wouldn't. There was the settlement agreed upon by Hanoi three weeks earlier, an agreement Nixon called "complete," and due to be signed—according to Kissinger's schedule—on October 31. There was Kissinger's "peace is at hand" announcement, something Nixon knew nothing about until after the fact—and he couldn't undo that. But the hardest nut to crack was Thieu, who continued to refuse to preside over his own demise.

Then there was McGovern, castigating Kissinger's "peace is at hand" business when everything—the four million pounds of bombs dropped on Vietnam, as well as the rushing of many more planes to bolster Thieu— militated against it. Furthermore, McGovern alleged, the claim of the Pentagon that some NVA units were turning tail and leaving the South was "completely false." Nixon, meanwhile, went public to announce that he was "completely confident" that an agreement to end the war was imminent. But, he took pains to explain, this was *his* agreement, one that *he* had negotiated, one that *he* took pride in, and one that *he* would stand by—as soon as "minor details" were ironed out. The root of Nixon's problem, contended journalist James Reston, was that "there is mistrust in the President because he trusts no one, even many of the men in his official family." Including—and especially including—Henry Kissinger.

It was just three days before the election, November 4, when Kissinger, feeling his oats, was interviewed by Ariana Fallaci, an Italian journalist. Did the journalist wish to know the secret of Kissinger's remarkable popularity? Why, it was because, like the Western cowboy, Kissinger always insisted on acting alone. He prided himself in his independence. As hubris surged he announced, "I've by no means decided to give up this job yet. You know, I enjoy it very much. . . . When one wields power . . . for a long time, one ends up thinking one has a right to it." Luckily for Kissinger, the interview wasn't published until after the election, or he may have found he'd suddenly been terminated from that job he so enjoyed.

As it was, Nixon's reelection was an overwhelming win, yet he was in a funk the next day, fretting that he'd not set a record landslide. There was no joy in Nixon's White House. How long before the two snoopers on *The Washington Post* uncovered the connection between Watergate and his administration? How long before Thieu would finally cooperate so he could finalize the peace treaty? How long would he have to put up with the likes of McGovern's carping liberals, particularly in the press? And finally, how long before both houses of Congress would enjoy a Republican majority, leaving him in the meantime at the mercy of the Democrats? His "melancholy" that Nixon described overtaking him once the returns were in masked, as Ambrose put it, "an anger that knew no bounds." So, the next morning, he abruptly called for the resignations of more than two thousand of the top employees in the executive branch, many of whom had worked tirelessly for his reelection. And many of whom, along with Republican supporters across the country, had—at Nixon's request—sent in such a blizzard of congratulatory telegrams that they inundated Nixon's desk for days, before he finally relinquished them so he could use the desk again.[8] Nixon had long before recognized he could leave nothing to chance, nothing to sheer spontaneity, nothing to genuine outpouring of appreciation. Everything had to be scripted; everybody had to be under his thumb.

The one person who continued to balk at Nixon's thumbprint on his forehead was Thieu. So Nixon, ever fast and loose with his promises, vowed, "if Hanoi fails to abide by the terms of this agreement, it is my intention to take swift and severe retaliatory action." Five years later, the British TV journalist David Frost questioned Nixon on the basis for this promise—since the war would be over and he'd need congressional approval and funding to take such action. Nixon answered that he'd not have returned ground troops there, but would have bombed "on a new scale," and that he was confident Congress would have backed him. But, interposed Frost, wouldn't that result in the loss of more American lives, in addition to the massive costs? And just to keep the peace he'd claimed he'd already won? With that, Nixon shifted into gear, "I would have broke [sic] the case strongly. It would have been swift. It would have been massive. And it would have been effective."

It was evident that the ghost of General George "Blood and Guts" Patton had been alive and well in the heart of Richard M. Nixon. Furthermore, this modern-day Patton was, by November 1972, fed up to his eyeballs with the shifty headline-grabber named Kissinger. Just two weeks after the election, Nixon revealed to Colson at Camp David that Kissinger was "to go back to Harvard. . . . It's the best thing for him. He needs to do it." And he *would* do it, Nixon vowed, as soon as the peace talks were concluded. It appears, however, that Kissinger, during his Christmas vacation at Palm Springs, was of a different frame of mind. Asked by a Harvard research scholar whether he planned to return to the University, Kissinger responded with, ". . . impossible." Why? Because, "No job could be as important as this. There is nowhere to go."

On November 14, Nixon sent Kissinger to Paris with no less than sixty-nine amendments to the treaty—courtesy of Thieu—amendments that Kissinger called "preposterous." These resulted in both sides hardening their positions, and on December 13 Tho left for Hanoi, leaving Kissinger sputtering. These Communists, he raged, were just "a bunch of shits! Tawdry, filthy shits!" This was a fine preparation for Kissinger's candidacy for the Nobel Peace Prize, or for Nixon's inauguration, coming up in a month.

Here was obviously a time to "seize the moment." So Nixon, fond of issuing ultimatums, leveled with Hanoi: start talking "seriously" within seventy-two hours, or else! No talk of the fact that Hanoi had already subscribed, two months earlier, to the treaty Nixon and Kissinger had agreed to—and which had prompted Kissinger's premature but timely, "peace is at hand!" The obstacle in this course, Nixon and Kissinger well knew, was not Tho, but Thieu. Nixon had to convince the former to return to the talks, and the latter that the President meant business when he promised swift, retaliatory action if Hanoi reneged on the treaty. So the middle of December, Nixon ordered a Christmas present to be delivered to Hanoi— in the form of a bombing campaign so massive as to be unprecedented in the history of aerial warfare. He would have "peace with honor" to announce at his inauguration if he had to kill every last North Vietnamese! Or so it seemed.

To Admiral Thomas Moorer, Chairman of the JCS, Nixon laid it on the line—just as Patton would have done: "I don't want any more of this crap about the fact that we couldn't hit this target or that one. This is your chance to use military power to win this war, and if you don't, I'll consider you responsible." It was vintage Nixon—not exactly cut from the same mold as old Harry S. with the sign on his desk, "The buck stops here."

Moorer did his best to oblige his impulsive commander in chief, just at the same time Kissinger went public with the disingenuous announcement that the peace treaty was "99 percent completed." But the remaining one percent was of such moment that "we will not be blackmailed . . . nor stampeded . . . nor charmed into an agreement until its conditions are *right*." [Italics added.] Kissinger was simplistic as well as disingenuous; Hanoi was intransigent as well as suspicious; and Nixon was exasperated as well as determined to nail down that treaty—even if he had to nail Tho's hide to the wall.

So Nixon, again without notifying—much less consulting—Congress, and without notifying the press or the public, ordered Moorer to put every last plane in the air on December 23 and lay waste to the heavily populated corridor connecting Hanoi and Haiphong. With that, the huge B-52 bombers took to the air in 3,000 sorties over twelve days, dropping 40,000 tons of bombs, stopping only for thirty-six hours to "celebrate" the birth of the Prince of Peace. There is no small irony in Nixon's diary notations of December 24: "On this day before Christmas it is God's great gift to me to have the opportunity to exert leadership, not only for America but on the world scene, because of the size of the mandate. . . ."

On learning that more tons of bombs had rained down than in the previous three years, inflicting heavy civilian casualties, Vermont's Republican Senator George Aiken called it "a sorry Christmas present for both the Vietnamese and the American people." Much of Hanoi and Haiphong, aside from military targets, was reduced to rubble. Despite both cities having evacuated most of its civilian population, over 1,300 were killed in Hanoi and over 300 in Haiphong. In addition, thousands were grievously wounded. After the war, one young woman broke down in tears as she recounted the deaths in these raids of her mother, two brothers, a sister, and a brother-in-law, killed when a bomb blew apart their house. A doctor later described how he'd had to amputate the limbs of patients to remove them from the rubble after a bomb demolished a hospital, killing eighteen patients and staff.[9] Hanoi reported that the Bach Mai Hospital, the city's largest, had been reduced to rubble by no less than a hundred bombs. Workers' housing areas were laid waste. While Kissinger downplayed civilian casualties to 400–500, historian Guenter Lewy estimated up to 1,600. In addition, *U.S. News and World Report* noted, "between 5,000 and 10,000 North Vietnamese soldiers may also have died in the raids..."

American losses were heavy, although the Pentagon claimed only 15 planes were lost, as opposed to Hanoi's claim of 34. At least 93 crew members lost their lives. At this, Nixon chewed out the JCS for ordering the bombers to fly "over the same target at the same time." Finally, this glorified Navy quartermaster was able to convince the generals "to change their minds" about the scheduling and routes of the strikes, as he later wrote in his *Memoirs*. Until now the press had been largely kept in the dark about the progress of the negotiations. As journalist Seymour Hersh put it, "The press was hopelessly outgunned. Kissinger had negotiated in secret, and relentlessly controlled information about those negotiations. He had fought with Nixon and his aides in secret. He had spoken sternly with the hawks and softly with the doves. It was impossible for the press to trip him up."

At home and abroad, Nixon himself became the target of vilification. *The New York Times* accused him of reverting to "Stone Age Barbarism" with the bombing attacks, while *The Washington Post* blasted him for the "savage and senseless" assaults, resulting in millions of Americans having to "cringe in shame and to wonder at their President's very sanity." Several distinguished journalists agreed. Joseph Kraft called it an action of "senseless terror which stains the good name of America." James Reston labeled it "war by tantrum," and Anthony Lewis charged Nixon with acting "like a maddened tyrant." No doubt about it, Nixon's persona, if not his person, was invested with "the mad bomber," as unpredictable as he was bloodthirsty.

Congress was just as appalled. Ohio Republican Senator William Saxbe asked if Nixon had "left his senses on this issue," while Mike Mansfield scorned it as a "stone-age tactic." At the Vatican, meanwhile, the Pope condemned the bombing of those "blessed Vietnamese people" that brought him "daily grief." Again, Nixon took to his diary—rather than to the press—to defend himself. "The record of the liberal left media on Vietnam is perhaps one of the most disgraceful in the whole history of communications in this country!" As for the President, his conscience was untroubled. He had made a stop in Ohio during his 1972 campaign to "set the record straight" for a dead GI's father, who'd written Nixon "to be sure that [his son] didn't die for nothing." Those draft dodgers, Nixon assured him, "will never get amnesty from me!" Just how much comfort the distraught father took from that is left for one to speculate. In reality, Nixon had few tears for this dead GI, nor for the almost 30,000 others shipped back in body bags. And he had no tears whatever for the hundreds of thousands of Vietnamese, North and South, or for the Laotians and Cambodians killed and maimed by U.S. forces. What truly bothered Nixon with the approach of the holidays was the lack of Christmas cards he was receiving, especially from Republicans on the Hill and in his own Cabinet! One is hard put to shed a tear for this President who later complained to Frost, "It was the loneliest and saddest Christmas I can ever remember." Even the usual solace he found in his "Christmas cheer" failed to take the edge off the dreary holiday. Nixon's incredible callousness more than matched that of Grant at the Battle of the Wilderness. At the end of the day, with hundreds on both sides burning to death in a forest inundated with gunfire, Grant took to bed and slept like a baby.[10]

Nixon had other reasons to be sad and lonely. On December 19, he had pressed Thieu with his "final offer," and said he would settle, with or without the South Vietnamese leader. Whereupon Thieu complained to the press that Nixon was out to coerce him with an ultimatum. Then there were those on Nixon's own staff who, troubled by the relentless, unprecedented bombing, pleaded with him to extend the Christmas truce through December 26. Never! Time was of the essence. Congress would soon be reconvening and Nixon feared a cutoff in funding for the war. Three days after Christmas, Hanoi signaled that it was willing to resume the Paris peace talks, and Nixon exulted "This is a very stunning capitulation by the enemy to our terms." Yet privately, again in his diary, he hoped that "1973 will be a better year." Alas, he was in for a bitter disappointment.

On January 2, the House Democratic caucus voted, 154 to 75, to call for an immediate cease-fire, and indeed to cut off all funds for the war, once the withdrawal of U.S. troops was complete and the POWs were returned. Two days later, Senate Democrats followed suit by a vote of 36 to 12. To Nixon, their strategy was obvious: If we get an agreement, they'll take the credit for having stopped the bombing. If we don't, they'll insist on the withdrawal they've favored all along. By January 6, Nixon's funk was deepening; the war was consuming so much of his time and energy that it was having "a detrimental effect on our international relations, not only with the Soviets and Chinese, but even with our allies."

Kissinger soon adopted a new ploy. Tugging at the heartstrings of Tho, he proposed to resolve the remaining differences as a sixtieth birthday present to Nixon on January 9. To Thieu, meanwhile, went the expected ultimatum from Nixon: Cooperate or I'll cut off all aid to you. The next day, Kissinger rejoiced with Nixon at a "major breakthrough," resolving "all outstanding questions." This, Kissinger was quick to assure his President, was due to Nixon's "firmness," leaving Hanoi to believe that Nixon would "not be affected by either Congress or public pressures." Therefore, cautioned Kissinger, "it is essential that we keep our fierce posture . . . the slightest hint of eagerness would prove suicidal."

Kissinger was as ebullient. It was done! Tho had agreed to settle! In a rare moment, Nixon walked Kissinger to his car and told him, "The country is indebted to [you] for what [you've] done." Though he could never get enough credit himself, Nixon was positively miserly in bestowing it on others—especially on an aide so patently and completely ambitious.

Finally, on January 15, 1973, Nixon ordered a stop to the horrendous bombing campaign. It had "done its job." Setting January 27 as the date for the signing of the peace agreement, he again served up an ultimatum to Thieu: "I will sign on the 27th, if necessary, alone." Furthermore, if forced to do so, "I will announce publicly that your government obstructs peace." Within hours of Nixon's inauguration on January 20, Thieu at last promised to go along. At that, Nixon conceded, "I had to admire his spirit."[11]

No sooner was the ink dry on the agreement than Nixon took to the airwaves to announce to the electorate that had given him such a powerful mandate, "We have finally achieved peace with honor." Among the ancient Romans no battle could be hailed a victory without a body count of enemy dead exceeding five thousand. On that score, Richard Nixon could declare a superlative victory!

Come January 31, he again repeated his peace-with-honor claim in a press conference. Seeing the skepticism on the reporters' faces, Nixon added, "I know it gags some of you to write that phrase, but it is true, and most Americans realize it is true." In his diary he penned. "It is really curious how people have come to run down the country the way they do." Again, disagreement with Nixon was tantamount to disloyalty to country.

There was no question that Nixon had his finger on the pulse of the nation, for his popularity soared to an incredible 70 percent.[12] Apparently many, if not most, overlooked the fact that he could have settled on essentially the same terms four years earlier. Nor were they privy to all the dirty tricks he'd pulled—including the cover-up of Watergate and the thousands of fake letters—or the extent of the disastrous bombing campaign just concluded.

There is consummate irony in the actual wording of the treaty, in that conditions that had served to prolong the war had suddenly disappeared. No longer would Thieu have to remain in place, no longer would the NVA have to withdraw from the South, no longer would the Vietcong be barred from participating in the government, and no longer would the 17th parallel be seen as dividing two separate nations. It had been a civil war all along and we, like the French before us, were the invaders. No coincidence, however, that neither Nixon nor Kissinger were eager to have the actual terms of the treaty made public.

As an additional sop to the North, Nixon secretly promised Hanoi that America would pay $3 billion in reparations to help rebuild the country to which it had laid waste, something he'd also promised in the 1968 campaign. Yet this pledge, like the pledge to Thieu to take swift, massive retaliation if Hanoi reneged on the treaty, was worth no more than the paper it was written on.

Though Nixon hyped the superficial changes—some twenty of them—in his *Memoirs*, the treaty remained essentially the same as Tho and Kissinger had agreed to on October 12. Even Kissinger conceded, "We thought the agreement of October 12 adequate or we would not have proceeded with it." Kissinger then asked a question he didn't answer: "Were the changes significant enough to justify the anguish and the bitterness of those last months of the war?" An even more vital question, which also begs an answer: what had the United States accomplished since taking the place of the hated French oppressors twenty years earlier?

By the summer of 1974, 90 percent of the ARVN were not getting enough pay to support their families. Quartermasters, their warehouses bulging with equipment and supplies—courtesy of U.S. taxpayers—were demanding bribes to release their supplies to their own army units! With little money, officers forced poor peasants to ante up. Meanwhile, a roaring inflation devalued the pittance that most were earning—an inflation fed in part by widespread corruption, and airily dismissed by the American ambassador as necessary "to oil the machinery." King of the corruption mountain was none other than Thieu himself, his relatives and top brass clustered about him, reaping fortunes in real estate and other sweetheart deals.

By August 9, 1974, with Nixon's resignation, Thieu was counting the days he'd remain in office. One of the President's last acts had been to sign a bill limiting American aid to Vietnam to $1 billion, subsequently whittled down to $700 million. Even at that, only 40 percent ever reached Vietnam. Come December, and the Communists—with oil, highways, and communication in their hands—started the long-awaited, and long-dreaded drive on Saigon, culminating in the widely televised rout of April, 1975. Fixed in the minds of viewers around the world were U.S. helicopters plucking hapless allies and native workers from the roof of the U.S. embassy.

Who was to blame for this final catastrophe? Nixon blamed Congress, which on June 25, 1974, cut off further funding for the Cambodian war and stipulated that any further funding for fighting in Indochina would require congressional approval. It thereby deprived Nixon of "the means to enforce the Vietnam peace agreement." Nixon vetoed it, then compromised with a cut-off date of August 15. "This cut-off," Nixon later wrote in his *Memoirs*, "led to the fall of South Vietnam on April 30, 1975." Nixon elaborated: "The war and peace in Indochina that America had won at such a cost over twelve years of sacrifice and fighting were lost in a matter of months once Congress refused to fulfill our obligations. And it's Congress that must bear the responsibility for the tragic results."[13]

Just how bankrupt is Nixon's argument, how specious is his fingering Congress for the blame, can be seen on several counts. In the first place, Congress was, as is often the case, lagging behind the American public— which had years before tired of the war, and which would settle for anything to bring it to a close. In addition, Nixon, despite his promise to end the war six months after entering the White House in January 1969, not only widened it to Laos and Cambodia, but continued it so as to time its conclusion to his reelection. Finally, the way decisions were made—when and if others besides Kissinger were consulted—was but a continuation of the scandalous decision-making of the Johnson era, as outlined by Leslie Gelb, the leader of the research group that produced the Pentagon Papers. That decision making, he concluded, could be faulted on four counts. "First, the choices were loaded by false options." Of the three usually given, the first and third were invariably so extreme as to warrant instant dismissal, leaving the second the odds-on favorite. "Second, tactical arguments, not fundamental ones, were the order of the day. . . . Third, fundamental assumptions were rarely, if ever, questioned. . . . Fourth, policy was 'fine-tuned' to the point of being grotesque. The neat plans and careful calculations in the memos of our leaders belie their own sense of uncertainty. . . . The language of the memos portrays a sense of puppeteers and puppets, with little grasp that unpredictable human beings and lives were at the end of the strings." Gelb then quoted Alexander Butterfield, the Nixon aide who let the cat out of the bag with his admission of the existence of the White House taping system. "The hardest strokes of heaven fall in history upon those who imagine they can control things in a sovereign manner, playing Providence not only for themselves but for the far future . . .

and gambling on a lot of risky calculations in which there must never be a single mistake."

On August 9, 1975, just one year to the day of his resignation—and with a $2 million advance from Warner Books for the publication of his *Memoirs*—Nixon signed a contract for a series of interviews with David Frost. One of Frost's first questions had to do with the horrendous cost of the war during Nixon's tenure.

As it so happened, we had managed to outdo the 1,000 years of Chinese invaders, the 100 years of French invaders, and the 5 years of Japanese invaders in laying waste to a small, primitive nation of no conceivable threat to us. In our destructive wake, under Nixon's tenure alone, we left 28,000 of our own troops dead, together with 138,000 South Vietnamese, 500,000 North Vietnamese, and 500,000 Cambodians. Add to this grisly toll three times these numbers of severely wounded, many impaired for life. In the air alone, we lost 9,000 planes and 2,000 of their crew members. There were also 1,000 MIAs and 600 POWs. Nixon spent at least $100 billion of taxpayer money, much of it in weaponry and equipment that we left behind at the conclusion of the war. In view of this dreadful toll, Frost asked, was it all worth it? Nixon: It was a "close call, a very difficult call, but it was definitely worth it." Frost: Why? Nixon: Because we settled in January 1973, for "peace with honor. That meant that all POWs would be returned, and the North Vietnamese would not violate the agreement in the South." Frost: But what of your speech at the time of the Cambodian "incursion" of 1971, in which you vowed that America would never settle for becoming a "pitiful, helpless giant?" Nixon: "Whatever we did, mutual withdrawal, unilateral withdrawal— nothing that we offered would they consider unless we agreed . . . to over-throw the government of South Vietnam and allow them to take over." Of course, neither Nixon nor anyone in his administration ever offered unilateral withdrawal.

Then, as if blaming Congress were not enough, Nixon took to blaming Kennedy and Johnson for getting us there in the first place, conveniently overlooking his own hawkish egging them on to escalate. Frost: Do you still hold to the domino theory, in view of the renewed stability of the other Southeast Asian nations? Nixon: It's too soon to judge. Frost: Do you consider yourself the last casualty of Vietnam? Nixon, his face contorted in affected pain: Yes, indeed. I've made enemies who were "paranoiac" [sic] because I've chosen to do what's "right"— to win "an honorable peace abroad" and "to keep the peace at home."

In this manner did the uncanny twists and turns of Nixon's serpentine mind guide him through $200,000 worth of interviews. The gutter fighter had become an international outlaw, inflicting grievous harm on millions, yet his overriding concern was that in doing what was "right," he'd alienated himself from many, enough so they were his "enemies." One who took a dim view of the whole affair was Bui Diem, Saigon's ambassador to the U.S. "Small nations must be wary of Americans," he cautioned, "since U.S. policies shift quickly as domestic politics and public opinion change. The struggle for us was a matter of life and death. But for Americans it was merely an unhappy chapter in their history, and they can turn the page." George Ball, the resident iconoclast during Johnson's administration, later called the war "probably the greatest single error made by America in its history."

Ball was even more perceptive than Diem, since, for hundreds of thousands of Americans, it was impossible to "turn the page." In addition to the 58,000 killed and 300,000 wounded, 700,000 GIs returned to the United States suffering from various forms of "post-traumatic stress disorder"— what was called "battle fatigue" in World War II and "shell shock" in World War I. Many were physical and/or mental cripples, relying on drugs to anesthetize them against the frustration of not knowing why they'd had to see buddies killed or wounded, or why they'd had to kill not only Communist military personnel, but civilians as well. And they sought surcease from the ingratitude and occasionally outright hostility they encountered at home. A quarter-century after America bowed out of Vietnam in what can be described, at best, as a stalemate, a third of all homeless men in the United States were veterans—and 42 percent of those were Vietnam vets, struggling with identity as much as guilt. In addition, one might well ask, how many of America's 600,000 hard-core drug addicts were Vietnam vets—and how many of those would be strung out had it not been for Vietnam?

Since World War II, authors Warren Hinckle and William Turner maintain, the CIA and its predecessor, and the intelligence arms of the Army and Navy, have been engaged in a quid pro quo with the Corsican network and the Sicilian Mafia, with other drug networks—including Southeast Asia's "Golden Triangle"—and with Cuban exiles. These two authors state that by the fifties, "the CIA was knee-deep in the operations level of the heroin, marijuana, and LSD trade—cocaine would come later." Indeed, during that decade the CIA, "fearful that the Soviets were getting a leg up on mind control drugs . . . unloaded hundreds of millions of tabs of LSD on unaware Americans, many of them university kids." In the sixties, the CIA was busy "buying" information on the Communists from the drug network in the Golden Triangle—with its own fleet of planes, "Air America," flying the dope to market. Disillusioned by Kennedy's lack of promised air support leading to the fateful Bay of Pigs fiasco in 1961, "the CIA's paramilitary anti-Castro Cubans drifted from their Miami base into major narcotics smuggling and by the seventies had developed alliances with far-right, dope-financed terrorist organizations."

In addition, thousands of vets returned from Vietnam having been exposed to the defoliant, Agent Orange—which led to skin disease, cancer, and a host of other disorders, including the fathering of deformed children.[14]

When all the casualties—and only the worst of these—of our ill-fated venture into Indochina are added to our own losses, the figures are staggering: for combatants only, 223,748 South Vietnamese and 5,200 allied dead, as well as 1.1 million Communist Vietnamese. All told, it is estimated that no less than three million Vietnamese, or about a tenth of the population, North and South, died as a result of the efforts of Vietnam to win independence from both the French and the Americans. These numbers do not include civilian dead and wounded, or casualties in Laos and Cambodia. These figures also do not include the two million Vietnamese refugees left homeless, crowded into squalid refugee camps, living from hand to mouth. Nor do they include the millions of acres of land denuded of its forests, pitted with bomb craters, and sowed with over a million land mines that have continued to take their grisly toll on civilians—especially children—ever since. On April 16, 1998, ABC News took note of the death of Cambodia's Pol Pot by implicating the United States in his murderous regime. As a result of Nixon's dropping 25 million pounds of bombs on Cambodia in a fruitless attempt to interdict personnel and supplies on the Ho Chi Minh Trail, Cambodians by the thousands joined Pol Pot's Khmer Rouge—"Red Cambodians"—eventually making it a force capable of genocide. Thus, these figures do not account for its murderous campaign between 1975 and 1979, during which between one and a half and two million Cambodian civilians were slaughtered—due, in part, to U.S. meddling in what was, in fact, a civil war.[15]

As if all this were not bad enough, the United States not only refused to establish diplomatic relations, but effectively prevented other nations—as well as the World Bank and the International Monetary Fund—from helping the ravaged Vietnam to its feet. Its economy was in tatters, its social structure fractured, its people exhausted from two decades of virtually uninterrupted warfare. We had knocked them down, and then we set about kicking them to keep them there.

This, the most powerful nation on earth, this Philistine Goliath, refused to lend a hand to the David who had beaten him in combat—yet who now lay prostrate. Goliath, meanwhile, sobered, sorrowful, yet still vengeful, lumbered on in his own hubristic way. Richard Nixon, history will record, did much to exacerbate that war, little to bring peace, and achieved nothing that even faintly resembled honor. National hubris afflicted Nixon, just as Nixon contributed to national hubris. The tragedy lay not in Nixon's political immolation but—through his incessant determination to resort to coercion—in the millions who, through a vale of tears, suffered at the hands of Nixon and Johnson.

Just as surely as coercion violates the rights of others, and especially the right to life, so is coercion counterproductive. Nixon had sown the wind. And, in the remaining chapters, we will see that he reaped the whirlwind.

CHAPTER 10

DECEPTION

. . . be a great pretender and dissembler; [for] men are so simple, and so subject to present necessities, that he who seeks to deceive will always find someone who will allow himself to be deceived.

— Machiavelli

This above all; to thine own self be true
And it must follow, as the night the day
Thou canst not be false to any man.

— Shakespeare, *Hamlet*

To be honest as the world goes
Is to be one man picked out of 10,000.

— Shakespeare, *Hamlet*

LYNDON JOHNSON

Integrity means that the exhortation to see people and politics as they are need not be an invitation to lose sight of what they ought to be. To be sure, it is no small achievement to keep your feet firmly on the ground without taking your eyes off the heights. Such harmony of head and heart is too seldom contemplated and still more seldom seen. It proposes a distinction between a pragmatic accommodation in the service of principle and an accommodation of principle to pleasure and prof-it. It depends on accustoming one's eyes to the shifting shadows and hazy lights of politics where circumstances are ambiguous, motives are mixed, consequences are unclear, and decisions of grave consequences must be taken. It requires seasoned and refined judgment to determine when to endure hypocrisy and when to crush it, when to withhold the truth for a greater good and when to proclaim what is right and let the chips fall where they may.

— Peter Berkowitz, *The Political Moralist*

The strength of our society does not rest in the silos of our missiles nor in the vaults of our wealth—for neither arms nor silver are gods before which we kneel. The might of America lies in the morality of our purposes and their support by the will of the people of the United States.

— President Lyndon Johnson, at Howard University commencement, Washington, D.C., June 4, 1965[1]

An Abomination to the Lord

There is no little irony in these preceding words issuing from the mouth of Lyndon Johnson, words that came from one of his stable of speech writers, very possibly Richard Goodwin. The irony is seen on several fronts. It is in the conclusion of many close observers of Johnson that—apart from Richard Nixon—no American president was less principled. Beyond that, it was *this* American president who sought—by evasion, by duplicity, by doubletalk, by outright lies—to circumvent the will of the people in what many Americans now regard as the most immoral war in history. LBJ was very much aware of Roosevelt's deception in 1940 when he made the campaign promise, "Your boys are not going to be sent into any foreign wars." All the while, in cahoots with Churchill, FDR was trying to figure out how to arouse the electorate sufficiently to justify entering the war—justification that finally came through the Japanese attack on Pearl Harbor. Johnson had no Pearl Harbor, and neither did he have a declared war. All he had was a "piss-ant" little country that we were intent on using as a staging ground for our new counterterrorism policy and our new weapons. Always Johnson was prepared to stretch an analogy out of shape to justify his reckless decisions.

The irony is also seen in the timing. Less than a year before, during the first week of August 1964, LBJ sank to a new low, fraught with dire consequences, in obtaining by deception the Gulf of Tonkin Resolution. Within a month from the time of his Howard University commencement speech, he would—again by stealth, and without consulting Congress in advance—start a series of escalations in the war that would leave little doubt in the opinion of other nations, including our allies, that we were the most powerful bully on the international block.

Another irony lies in the fact that Johnson was speaking at a black university, yet he was about to send black soldiers—in far greater proportion than the black percentage of America's population—to do the dirty work in Vietnam. Yet what is amazing in all of this is Reedy's conclusion, after working closely with Johnson for years, that "the man never told a deliberate lie. But he had a fantastic capacity to persuade himself that the 'truth' which was convenient for the present was *the truth* and anything that conflicted with it was the prevarication of enemies." Reedy also attested that LBJ "could not fairly be accused of going back on his word, once he had given it. The difficulty was his inability to see a public speech as anything other than a crowd pleaser." As for language itself, Johnson "subscribed to . . . a primitive form of word magic," since he thought it was "unfair for anyone to cite past addresses as contrary to present intentions." Reedy then quoted Sidey: "He has no respect for the integrity of the language."

Some sixteem months after his speech at Howard—on October 3, 1966, during the swearing in of Nicholas Katzenbach as undersecretary of state—Johnson compounded his hypocrisy by declaring, "We Americans do not believe in moral double-bookkeeping." Again, there is no little irony in the timing. For George Ball, whom Katzenbach was replacing, had resigned in bitter frustration at Johnson's escalations without so much as a nod toward Congress, toward the press, or toward the public. He would convince the electorate that his policy in Vietnam was simply one of continuity, that we were winning the war, that all we needed was a little more time and patience. This was about a year after Ball had submitted a sixty-two-page memo that emphasized in detail his opposition to the President's course of military action. Johnson, however, did not lay eyes on the memo until February 1966, thanks to the collusion of Rusk and McNamara. And when LBJ did see it, he completely ignored it. By this time the President's patience with his "resident devil's advocate," as he called Ball, was wearing thin.

There was staggering hypocrisy in Lyndon's doing just what he claimed Americans were *not* doing, that is, keeping two sets of morality books. The persona he projected to the public on television was one of earnest concern for the casualties we were suffering in the war. The person he projected to those closest to him, by contrast, was one of stealth, of guile, of intimidation, and of obsession with his reelection and his own place in history, regardless of the cost. If Lyndon Johnson was a study in guile, it was in no small part due to his spending eight years as a congressman sitting at the feet of that guile-master, FDR.

By the time the President was condemning moral double-bookkeeping, he was raising hackles among reporters and members of Congress that led to their conviction, and in turn the public's conviction, that Johnson had a credibility problem. Increasingly, people were simply refusing to believe what be said. Had he not been as wary of history as he was of truthfulness, he might have learned as a teacher of public speaking in Houston what Aristotle, 2300 years before, had taught about credibility and integrity.

Taken from the root word, integer—or whole number, as opposed to a fraction—integrity implied wholeness. And that, in turn, implied a set of core values at the heart of the speaker that would issue in a critical consistency—both in what he said, whatever the circumstances, as well as between what he said and what he did. Without that essential consistency, as Emerson noted, "What you *do* speaks so loudly I cannot hear a *word* you say." One's word, Aristotle and Emerson agreed, was one's bond. Most of us, and surely Lyndon Johnson, have learned the bitter truth in Scott's "O! what a tangled web we weave, when at first we practice to deceive."[2]

The "tangled web," the stark chaos that ruled in the White House from 1965 to 1968, is testimony to the far reaches of deception to which Johnson would go. Long forgotten, if ever learned, were the words of our first president. In his farewell address, taking leave of the highest pinnacle of power in government to return to private life in his beloved Mount Vernon, Washington stressed morality as the "necessary spring of popular government." And this from the man to whom Lincoln paid tribute: ". . . as the mightiest name of earth—long since mightiest in the cause of civil liberty, still mightiest in moral reformation. . . ." And the one to whom Eisenhower paid tribute as "the greatest human the English-speaking race has produced." John Adams, Washington's successor, was even more specific in insisting that "the first of qualities for a great statesman [is] to be honest." Well had the Founding Fathers taken note of Montesquieu, who'd emphasized that "the deterioration of every government begins with the decay of the principles on which it was founded." Why, then, do a government and its leaders take leave of their senses as well as the country's founding principles? Anatol Rapaport has pointed to the gap that opens up between a leader and his followers. The larger the gap, the less the backing of popular support, and thus the less a leader's legitimacy. The more illegitimate a government becomes, Rapaport continued, the more it resorts to coercion and deceit to survive.[3]

What Rapaport did not develop, however, was the necessary link between coercion and deceit. Indeed, deceit can be seen as a vital part of coercion in that it deprives a leader's followers of the information necessary to make an intelligent choice. Whatever else freedom implies, as Erich Fromm has emphasized, it implies freedom to choose. The best choices, the best decisions, Benjamin D'Israeli made a point of noting, arise from the best information. Deprive the electorate of adequate and accurate information, and you deprive it of the ability to make intelligent and free choice. Thus did Jefferson reason that democracy can only be as robust as its people are intelligent.

Jefferson well understood that society is held together by a fabric of verbal trust, rooted in truthfulness rather than that will-of-the-wisp, truth itself. For truth is an ideal neither attained nor attainable, varying from person to person and from age to age. Truth is no more absolute than the bastion of physics, the second law of thermodynamics, commonly known as entropy. Given new worlds, perhaps new universes, and all bets are off. Even those laws of physics, those vested with the highest degree of probability, no longer appear to hold. Likewise, there is no absolute truth, if by that we mean unchanging truth. The best we can hope for, by far, as we consider this further stage in hubris, is truthfulness: the divulging of information as we understand it, at the time we divulge it. This is not to say that any of us can always be, or ought to be, completely candid. The Gentiles who hid the Jews from Nazi concentration camps and certain death during World War II were opting for the lesser of two evils—whether to lie or become complicit in the murder of those they were hiding. Physicians who refuse to divulge to their patients the onset of cancer, fearing the stress of knowing will exacerbate the disease, likewise believe that they are choosing the lesser of two evils. Less critical—but surely a vital part of the oil of discourse that lubricates the wheels of social interaction—are the many evasions or "white lies" that we tell in the name of tact, reasoning that it is better to be less than perfectly candid than to hurt others.

In each of the foregoing we can rationalize, in the name of conscience, something less than truthfulness. But what becomes intolerable is the deceit that issues from the desire to avoid responsibility, or, as Johnson would put it, "to save our own asses." And this, the electorate became increasingly convinced, was LBJ's "credibility gap." Broadened to a chasm, it became Johnson's curse. For telling the truth or lying really made no difference, since it was all in the name of convenience or ambition, of assuring his reelection, or confirming his stellar place in history. This the electorate could neither forget nor forgive.

It wasn't always that way. One of the key verses of Scripture that Lyndon learned as a boy at his mother's feet was, "A lie is an abomination to the Lord." When Rebekah's sister-in-law caught Lyndon in a lie and told Rebekah, she stoutly defended her firstborn, "My boy never tells a lie!"

Barbara Tuchman has suggested three elements in Johnson's character that led to his mishandling of the Vietnam war: "an ego that was unstable and never secure; a bottomless capacity to use and impose the powers of office without inhibition; a profound aversion, once fixed upon a course of action, to any contra-indications."

To these we can add a fourth: his apparent inability to distinguish fact from fiction which can be seen in his determination to use words in any way he saw fit to aggrandize himself. Lyndon was a moth, drawn by *A Bright and Shining Lie*, Neil Sheehan's title of his account of the Vietnam war.

Here was the President who, addressing U.S. troops in Korea in 1966, recounted how his great-great-grandfather had died fighting at the Alamo. Curious, Hugh Sidey discovered the truth and took LBJ to task for the fib. When Doris Kearns related the incident later to LBJ, he exploded; "Goddamn it, why must all these journalists be such sticklers for detail!" Dismissing it as an inadvertent slip of the tongue, Lyndon explained he had meant the Battle of San Jacento, then proceeded for fifteen minutes to prove that this battle actually superseded the one at the Alamo. Furthermore, he made it clear, his forbear was not simply *a* hero, he was *the* hero. Kearns decided, like Sidey before her, to check it out. Come to find out, Lyndon's ancestor had paid the "supreme sacrifice" of dying in his own bed, after a long career as a real estate broker.

It was deception of a vastly different order, however, to deceive the press, the Congress, and the people concerning life-and-death issues such as the war.

After scarcely three months on the job, LBJ told a news conference there was nothing "more important than being accountable to the people." Words, words, words. Like money, their worth was no more than the authority to back it up. In Lyndon's case, the "government" was virtually bankrupt.

Reedy put a sympathetic gloss on it when he maintained that Johnson was not guilty of duplicity; he simply disconnected words from actions. Words were meant to entertain rather than to inform, to garner spontaneous applause rather than measured appreciation for enlightenment. Rarely was LBJ candid, Reedy acknowledged, "and when he spoke of personal matters his words were such a mixture of fantasy, euphemism, and half-truth that it was impossible to separate out the nuggets of revelation."

Never, Reedy conceded, did this former teacher of speech communi-

cation learn "the role of the communication process in a democratic society." Never did he understand that open and free discussion had been, since
the nation's founding, the rock upon which our democratic structure
stood. Never did he understand that the verbal fabric of trust was what
bound a society together in interdependence, that to rend that fabric at any
point was to invite anarchy, and, in turn, authoritarianism. Never did he
understand that a speaker's credibility was based on his integrity—on his
word being, in fact, his bond. So in the end, Reedy concluded, Johnson
became "a prisoner of his own words."

There was a fatal disconnect between Johnson's words and reality. In
truth, the reality lay in a doting mother who was willing to be a servant to
her firstborn, convinced that he must fulfill the dreams she saw unfulfilled
in her husband. Lyndon would be, if Rebekah had anything to do with it,
larger than life. Cast in this heroic image, as Tuchman emphasized, he was
determined to loom larger on the pages of history than his predecessors,
Kennedy, Eisenhower, and Truman; even larger than his mentor, FDR. To
polish this image, he would tolerate few distractions and fewer criticisms.
So rare were his confessions of wrongdoing—and never in public—that he
could take Santanya to task: he, LBJ, made no mistakes of personal history
from which to learn. But when it came to praise, that which he'd perfected
as a "back friend, a shoulder-slapper," as Shakespeare put it, Lyndon
expected no end of it from his subordinates. As a result, according to his
aide Jim Jones, there developed "an unreality to the White House . . . that
made you think you [were] above the law."[4]

By May 1964, Lyndon was bent on outdoing all his predecessors. His
"Great Society" would be "city on a hill," a beacon light to the benighted
nations of the world. It would be a city where poverty would disappear
along with racism, where every child would get a decent education to
equip him to get a good job, and where children and the elderly alike would
be properly cared for. It was a vision that would do Lyndon right proud in
the eyes of his mother. And it could all be gotten without raising taxes. Even
while taking care of that little "bitch of a war" in Southeast Asia.

The Tonkin Gulf Resolution

Before dealing with LBJ's most egregious deception, his finagling the
Tonkin Gulf Resolution, it is well to note the wisdom of the Founders in

the Federalist Papers: ". . . a well-constructed Senate . . . [in its] cool and deliberate sense of the community ought . . . in all free governments, ultimately [to] prevail over the views of the rulers." Especially was this so where ". . . the people, stimulated by some irregular passion, or some elicit advantage, or misled by the artful misrepresentations of interested men [particularly presidents], may call for measures which they themselves will afterwards be the most ready to lament and condemn."

But his war—like a little cloud on the distant horizon "no bigger than a man's fist," as Elijah of old described it—was growing, was beginning to pose a distinct threat to his Great Society. What LBJ needed, once and for all, was the kind of leverage FDR found in Pearl Harbor: a crisis to set America back on its heels, then to dig in with a united determination to remove the threat to "national security." No, he didn't want a congressional declaration of war. Far too drastic, upsetting his Great Society and, who knows, leading to World War III. What he *did* want was an incident like the German attack on the destroyer USS *Greer* in September 1941. A similar incident would convince Congress that he needed the power of a commander in chief in time of war, without the declaration. As Ball put it, "many in the administration were looking for any excuse to initiate bombing North Vietnam."

Acheson, returning in June 1964, from Saigon, broke the news to a dispirited President: the situation in Vietnam was far worse than he'd imagined. Indeed, it might well jeopardize Johnson's chances in November. Still, polls were showing the public paying scant attention to the war on the other side of the planet, in a country few could find on a map, a war that Connecticut Democratic Senator Thomas Dodd was contending involved "a few thousand primitive guerrillas."

Before June slipped into July, Johnson convened a meeting of his top aides, including those from Saigon, to consider a "policy of attrition": developing a bombing campaign that, with a minimum of casualties and no ground troops, would force Ho to the bargaining table, there to meet LBJ's terms. What he needed was a pretext sufficient to convince Congress, the press, and the public that what we confronted was a national emergency.

There was Wayne Morse, however, stirring up trouble in the Senate, accusing Johnson of planning "an American war in Asia." What he and his staff were doing was planning to extract from Congress the kind of resolution that Ike had tried to obtain ten years earlier—and which Johnson, as

Minority Leader—had opposed. Clearly, Johnson was on the horns of a dilemma. Choose the one on the right, escalate the war, and he'd not be able to run as the peace candidate, in contradistinction to the trigger-happy Goldwater. Choose the one on the left, and he might find himself backing out of Vietnam, his tail tucked between his legs, the first president to lose a war. In either case, he felt he'd jeopardize his chances in November. So Johnson was resolute in determining to stick to the middle ground.

As early as January, Johnson had learned that the United States was training and escorting ARVN commandos, in American PT boats, in a campaign of sabotage and terrorism along the coast of North Vietnam. Hanoi could easily be forgiven for regarding this as an act of war by the United States, since we were penetrating with our warships the twelve-mile territorial limit they and many other nations observed, and not the three-mile limit we ourselves observed. Furthermore, these raids were proving virtually useless. Atop that, LBJ just happened to forget to notify UN Ambassador Adlai Stevenson about the raids—so in Stevenson's protestations of charges by the North Vietnamese, he simply didn't know what he was talking about. Johnson ordered the raids to continue, despite all this. Who could guess? Maybe some incident like the *Greer* would repeat itself. This President would be ready with a resolution—just in case—so he ordered his aides to come up with a rough draft, written primarily by the assistant secretary of state for Far Eastern affairs, William Bundy, and purposely vague.[5]

Johnson was rarin' to go. All he needed was an incident—and he didn't have long to wait. For, on July 30, two ARVN patrol boats attacked shore bases in North Vietnam. Providing cover, the USS *Maddox* destroyer moved ever closer to shore, provoking the North's gun batteries into revealing their positions. On August 2, a local North Vietnamese commander, convinced that the *Maddox* was not only an integral part of the mission but had invaded the North's territorial waters, dispatched three PT boats to attack the destroyer. The *Maddox*—with the help of planes from the nearby aircraft carrier *Ticonderoga*—returned fire, sank two of the three, left the third dead in the water, and emerged unscathed. McNamara later testified that Hanoi knew the *Maddox* was not part of the operation, yet radio intercepts contradicted this. The Defense Secretary also claimed that the *Maddox* was attacked thirty miles off the coast when, in fact, it *started* its mission just thirteen miles from the coast, and earlier that day had clearly been within the twelve-mile limit. Thus the North's attacking the *Maddox* was, in the eyes of the North and of other nations observing the twelve-mile limit, fully justified.

As it was, Johnson was leery of any large-scale response because he figured the attack had perhaps been the result of a local commander's orders—and also because he figured that this was a legitimate response to the *Maddox* having provided cover for ARVN sabotage along North Vietnam's shore. So Rusk downplayed the incident: "The other side got a sting out of this. If they do it again, they'll get another sting."

Truth be told, Johnson needed more than this minor skirmish to shake a resolution from Congress. So he ordered the destroyer *Turner Joy* to accompany the *Maddox*, and for the two to assert America's freedom of the seas. Furthermore, there was Maxwell Taylor, former chairman of the JCS and now ambassador to Saigon, complaining that failure to respond to an unprovoked attack on a U.S. destroyer in international waters would be taken as a sign "that the U.S. flinches from direct confrontation with the North Vietnamese." It seemed Taylor had not really shed his gold braid as a general for the civvies of an ambassador.

Weighing in with Taylor was Robert Anderson, Ike's treasury secretary. Lyndon explained to him—and through him to Ike—that "we've been playing around up there and they came out, gave us a warning, and we knocked hell out of 'em."

Already Goldwater, in his acceptance speech as the Republican presidential candidate, had blasted Johnson for the "failures [that] infest the jungles of Vietnam. . . . Don't try to sweep this under the rug. We are at war in Vietnam. And yet the President . . . refuses to say . . . whether or not the objective over there is victory, and his secretary of defense continues to mislead and misinform the American people. . . . I needn't remind you, but I will, [that] it has been during Democratic years that a billion persons were cast into Communist captivity and their fates cynically sealed."

These were fighting words. LBJ realized he had to do better—had to provoke, if not another Pearl Harbor, at least something comparable to the attack on the *Greer* in order to jump-start Congress on the road to a resolution. So the commander in chief ordered that his administration "reassess our situation [and] do something about it." To reporters he added, "We must lay all of the cards on the table so that the American people will be fully informed, and then take action to correct the situation." Just go up on Captiol Hill, LBJ instructed McNamara and ". . . tell 'em awfully quiet though so they won't go in and be making a bunch of speeches." Johnson was not about to "lay all of the cards on the table." The fewer that knew the details, the better.

To Johnson's right was Admiral U.S. Grant Sharp, American commander for the Pacific. Ignore the twelve-mile limit, was his advice. Show the enemy that we don't observe that by moving our destroyers within eight miles of shore. Beyond that, don't be satisfied with simply destroying the attackers. Go after the base from which they're dispatched.[6] Always Johnson could depend on advisers to the left and to the right—but he feared those on the right more.

On August 4, there was, ostensibly, a repeat of the August 2 attack. McNamara had just been briefing the President on possible North Vietnam targets for retaliation, including three petroleum supply dumps holding 70 percent of the North's supply, and a key bridge on the rail line heading south from Hanoi. Within minutes, he was back with the news from Admiral Sharp "that the destroyer is under attack." LBJ immediately ordered Rusk, Bundy, and McNamara to join him to plan the U.S. response.

Captain John Herrick, commander of the Tonkin Gulf Patrol, had objected to the orders beefing up his patrol as an "unacceptable risk." Not surprisingly, LBJ ignored this objection and turned to his trusty JCS instead. Their advice was predictable: continue provoking the North with other attacks. While this was occurring, Johnson was drafting a new resolution for Congress, to replace the sketchy one prepared by Bill Bundy. It appeared that Johnson was, as usual, leaving nothing to chance.

It was Herrick who, on August 4, had notified Sharp of the second attack. Though his report and subsequent ones were fragmentary and vague, Johnson was not about to wait for "finicky details." Within the hour the decisive President had issued an order: bomb the bases in the North harboring the PT boats. Even the JCS, however, were uneasy, demanding confirmation from Herrick before unleashing LeMay's mighty air force.

They had good reason to be skeptical. For Navy Captain James Stockdale, a forty-year-old veteran pilot, was leading a patrol over the Gulf at the time the attack was reported. Yet neither he nor his fellow pilots saw a PT boat in the area, and concluded none were there. Obviously, there was a mix-up of some kind. Just how confusing was the so-called attack that the initial report claimed the U.S. had repulsed it and, in the process, had sunk two gunboats. In 1969, further investigation revealed that the August 4 attack must have been "imagined or invented"—despite Herrick's further confirmation at the time that there had been an ambush. In his memoirs, McNamara conceded that "Visibility . . . was very limited." In addition, ". . . sonar soundings—which are often unreliable—accounted for most reports of the second attack; [therefore] uncertainty remained about whether it had occurred." In November 1995, General Vo Nguyen Giap— vice-premier for defense in North Vietnam in 1964—convinced McNamara that no second attack did in fact take place.[7]

On the afternoon of August 4, Johnson was furious at Humphrey for "his big mouth"—to the point where he was reconsidering him as the vice-presidential candidate. It appears that the day before, "he went on TV," LBJ complained, "and just blabbed everything that he had heard in a briefing." The reporters had asked Humphrey, "How would you account for these PT boat attacks on our destroyers when we are innocently out there in the gulf, sixty miles from shore?" Humphrey: "Well, we have been going in and knocking out roads and petroleum things." Johnson was irate, for he remarked to Rowe, "And that is exactly what we *have* been doing!. . . The damned fool . . . just ought to keep his goddamned big mouth shut on foreign affairs, at least until the election is over. . . . "

Interestingly, the North Vietnamese, as well as the South Vietnamese, knew exactly what we were doing. So did the Soviets and the Chinese. But Johnson was determined the American people would *not* know, and neither would Congress nor the press—that is, "until the election is over."

That same afternoon, McNamara and his deputy, Cyrus Vance, were meeting with the JCS to convince them that a second attack had actually occurred. During this discussion, however, the Secretary of Defense learned that someone had leaked word of Johnson's call for a meeting that evening with congressional leaders. That put LBJ in the awkward position of trying to show a second attack had occurred when the evidence was so vague. But he couldn't withhold his plans for retaliating without inviting criticism—just three months before the election—that he was a coward involved in a cover-up.

During the meeting that evening, Johnson, in a high dudgeon, put it to congressional leaders. Not once but *twice* had our ships been attacked by Communists in international waters! Could we, would we—the most powerful nation on God's green earth—sit idly by and permit such aggression to continue?! As far as *this* President was concerned, *Never!* With that, he laid out his plans to retaliate. But there was a slight hitch. He didn't have the power; only Congress did. No, he didn't need any declaration of war. All he needed was a simple resolution.

Indeed, it was all so simple. "I'm not going in unless Congress goes with me." There, standing before them, was the resolute commander in chief—proud wearer of the Silver Star for "exceptional valor" in combat, a decorated veteran of World War II—daring to "go in." All he needed was a Congress willing to protect his flank. Already congressional plates were full, what with November elections just three months away. Traditionally, they'd been preoccupying themselves with domestic issues, leaving foreign affairs to the President. Furthermore, when it came to the insidious spread of international Communism, fomented and directed from the Kremlin itself, they well understood the mood of their constituents. With few exceptions, the voters would expect them to stand alongside their brave commander in chief.

Even as Johnson was laying it on the line to congressional leaders, Mac Bundy was notifying the White House staff of the President's decision to go for a congressional resolution. "But isn't this a little precipitous?" asked one aide. "Do we have all the information?" Crisp and to the point, as befit the National Security Adviser, Bundy answered, "The President has decided, and that's what we're doing." The aide, obviously a "nervous Nellie"—to use what would become one of Lyndon's favorite terms for those less valorous and resolute than he during the war—persisted with the complaint, "Gee, Mac, I really haven't thought it through." Bundy: "Don't."

While these briefings were going on, the Pentagon was busy trying to get confirmation and more details from Herrick. At the same time, it was learning that U.S. planes had done their job: damaging four PT-boat bases and twenty-five of thirty boats, and sending an oil depot up in flames as well. Learning of this good news, Lyndon crowed to a reporter, "I didn't just screw Ho Chi Minh; I cut his pecker off!"

Just as he was about to meet with his National Security Council on the evening of August 4, LBJ got a call from friend Olin Johnston, saying that he was going to vote for the President because he was committed to "keeping us out of war." To that, Johnson replied, "I'm going to do my best." Then the good Senator from South Carolina told the President, ". . . you are going to find in my state and in the South these mothers and people are *afraid of war*."

At the NSC briefing, McNamara made it clear that the North's PT boats had "continued their attacks" on the two destroyers—to which the Secretary of State, no dove like Olin Johnston, responded, "The unprovoked attack on the high seas is an act of war. . . ."

It is of no small moment, considering Johnson's stance as a peace candidate, that he phoned Goldwater just before making his public announcement of the attack, to tell his rival, ". . . we're going to take all the boats out that we can and all the bases [from] which they come." To this, the super-hawk answered, ". . . you've taken the right steps and I'm sure you'll find that everybody will be behind you."[8]

But he needed that resolution. So he took to the airwaves that evening, and on TV laid it out to the public. As millions watched, the grave but resolute President described the Communist attacks, and there in international waters! What was a President to do? So he'd ordered planes to retaliate, striking boat pens along the North Vietnamese coast, one near the Chinese border. Then he intoned, so all the advanced industrial nations of the world could hear and heed their putative leader, "Aggression by terror against the peaceful villages of South Vietnam has now been joined by open aggression on the high seas, against the United States of America. . . . Yet our response, for the present, will be limited and fitting. We Americans know, though others appear to forget, the risks of spreading conflict. We still seek no wider war." He concluded, "Repeated acts of violence must be met not only with an alert defense but with a positive reply. . . . That reply is being given as I speak to you tonight." "Positive reply" was not the first—nor would it be the last—glaring euphemism to be used by this President, as he escalated a war as barbaric as any fought in the long course of history. The impression LBJ left was carefully crafted, in keeping with the words he used: he was no umbrella-toting Neville Chamberlain, cozying up to Hitler in a cowardly attempt to appease him.

In 1995, McNamara wrote that, had we been certain there had been no second Tonkin Gulf incident, "we would not have carried out that military attack on North Vietnam." McNamara's thirty-year-old reflections were as specious as LBJ's language had been euphemistic. For a Defense Secretary to expand the war so dramatically, without confirming that a second attack had actually occurred, must stand as an act both irresponsible and unconscionable.

That Johnson's conduct was no better is seen in his taking the time, next day, to pose in the Oval Office with each Democratic congressman running for reelection that November. Always it was politics, and the focus of those photo ops was not so much their *reelection* as Lyndon's *election*. Everything else paled by comparison.

There were certainly no doubts in Johnson's mind, it seemed, when he took again to national TV on the August 5. Not only had there been a first attack, but a second—"repeated in those same waters against two United States destroyers. The attacks were deliberate. The attacks were unprovoked. . . .The government of North Vietnam is today flouting the will of the world for peace." Meanwhile, Khrushchev, among others, was finding Johnson's rhetoric hard to swallow. In a stern letter to the American President, Khrushchev wrote that putting our warships in the Gulf of Tonkin constituted a "military demonstration" to strengthen the "corrupt and rotten South Vietnamese." Worse, it might risk a "serious military conflict."

The next day Rusk let the Senate Foreign Relations Committee know in no uncertain terms that these attacks on our naval vessels were "no isolated event." Rather, they were "part and parcel of a continuing Communist drive to conquer South Vietnam . . . and eventually dominate and conquer other free nations of Southeast Asia." There was no doubt that the domino theory remained alive and well in our Secretary of State. Wayne Morse was not about to take this rhetoric at face value. "I think we are kidding the world," he said, "if you try to give the impression that when the South Vietnamese naval boats bombarded two islands a short distance off the coast of North Vietnam, we were not implicated." To this, McNamara replied that the *Maddox*, "so far as I know today had no knowledge of any possible South Vietnamese actions in connection with the two islands. . . ." a statement that beggars belief. For if the Defense Secretary was unaware of actions that had been occurring for seven months, actions in which our destroyers were running interference for South Vietnamese PT boats—known as OPLAN 34A—then he was certainly something less than LBJ's "best defense secretary in the nation's history." In his 1995 memoirs McNamara was at long last forthcoming. This reply to Morse, "[he] later learned, was totally incorrect."[9]

Lyndon Johnson was nothing if not resolute. No philosophical theorizing for him. No namby-pamby doubts, hesitations, or caveats for this tall Texas cowboy-turned-gunslinger. The order of business now was to get that resolution through Congress. In the House he had his old friend Rayburn as Speaker. In the Senate, he had another old friend and fellow Southerner, Fulbright. As head of the Foreign Relations Committee, Fulbright was in even a better place than Majority Leader Mansfield to shepherd that resolution through to a successful vote. Trouble was, Fulbright was having second thoughts about our commitment in Vietnam; nothing, however, like the misgivings he'd face in the months and years ahead. But a rumor was circulating that he had his eye on Rusk's job. "Fulbright's problem," as Johnson later said snidely, "is that he's never found any president who would appoint him secretary of state . . . he wants the nation to stand up and take notice of Bill Fulbright, and he knows the best way to get that attention is to put himself in the role of critic. He would have taken that role whichever way I moved on Vietnam." Thus did Johnson later rationalize his falling out with Fulbright.

Whether or not Fulbright was actually seeking that job, he formed a fast friendship with LBJ during Johnson's tenure as Majority Leader. Furthermore, for the chairman of the Senate Foreign Relations Committee to stand opposed to the President on a matter of national security would hardly do. So he threw in with his commander in chief and promised to run interference in the Senate.

There, in the chambers on August 7, several questions and criticisms were raised. Sam Ervin asked, "Is there any reasonable or honorable way we can extricate ourselves without losing our face and probably our pants?" Satisfied by Fulbright there was not, Ervin went along with his Democratic President and fellow Southerner—something he would not do a decade later with the Republican from California, Richard Nixon.

As it was, of the 516 on the Hill, there were only two holdouts, Democratic Senators Wayne Morse of Oregon and Ernest Gruening of Alaska. Morse, a member of Fulbright's committee, denounced the proposed resolution as simply a "pre-dated Declaration of War." Having listened to "briefing after briefing," he insisted, "There isn't a scintilla of evidence . . . that North Vietnam engaged in any military aggression against

South Vietnam, either with its ground troops or its navy." Morse's trouble was that he knew both international law and Lyndon Johnson. Furthermore, on the night of August 4, Morse had gotten a phone call from an unidentified person at the Pentagon, urging him to put two questions to McNamara: Where is the *Maddox* log? That would place the ship closer to shore than LBJ alleged. And what was the destroyer's real mission? The bombs were already dropping from U.S. planes, committing America to a massive escalation, when Morse hung up the phone.

In view of all the evidence, Morse declared himself "unalterably opposed to this new aggressive course of action on the part of the United States." There was but one other senator with him in this opposition, and that was Gruening, who'd gone on record in October 1963 as being opposed to JFK's sending so-called "advisers" to Vietnam. This was, Gruening contended, an outright deception—used to elude the stipulation of the Geneva Accords that no U.S. troops should be sent to intervene.

Later, on March 10, 1964, he'd given a speech, "The U.S. Should Get Out of Vietnam," the first such statement by anybody in public life. An old newspaperman, Gruening expected front-page coverage in *The New York Times* and *The Washington Post*. "Not a line," he recalled. But the wire services did pick up on it, sending it out to smaller papers, and he was deluged with over four hundred letters, all but four backing him. Significantly, he found overwhelming approval among the intelligentsia, who were already weary and disillusioned with the war. Now, with this "accidental" President grasping for the power that the Constitution had restricted to Congress, the Senator smelled a rat.

"All Vietnam," Gruening contended, "is not worth the life of a single American boy." For his trouble, he earned no praise from Johnson when the President talked with House Speaker McCormack. Gruening, groused Johnson, was just "no good . . . worse than Morse . . . I've spent millions on him up in Alaska. . . ." What LBJ had done was provide federal assistance in the wake of the March 1964 Alaska earthquake. As for Morse, he "is just undependable and erratic as can be."[10]

Just what did the Tonkin Gulf Resolution stipulate? That North Vietnam, "in violation of international law . . . deliberately and repeatedly attacked U.S. naval vessels lawfully present in international waters . . . [as] part of a deliberate and systematic campaign of aggression . . . against its neighbors. . . . the United States, therefore, is prepared, as the President determines, to take all necessary steps, including the use of armed force, to assist any member or protocol state of the Southeast Asia Collective Defense Treaty requesting assistance in defense of its freedom."

Obscured in all the fog of noble rhetoric were several facts. North Vietnam was simply repelling attacks by the South—attacks made in consort with the United States and in defiance of the Geneva Accords, to which America had pledged its cooperation. As for assisting SEATO nations under attack, South Vietnam was neither a nation nor a member of the Southeast Asia treaty organization. In addition, as Johnson would discover three years later, other SEATO nations had no fear of the Communists in North Vietnam, China, or the USSR. Therefore, they would not assist the United States in its continuing war against North Vietnam. Furthermore, despite the noble sentiment that America would assist South Vietnam "in defense of its freedom," it was in fact no more free than North Vietnam. Indeed, if anything, South Vietnam was more repressive, particularly toward the Buddhists, who comprised over 80 percent of its population. Finally, the North had not been stigmatized by either corruption or the deployment of its best troops to protect the Hanoi administration. By contrast, the Saigon government—whether under Diem or his successors—was riddled with corruption, and made self-serving use of the cream of the ARVN to protect each regime. In brief, the resolution was as devoid of truth as Johnson, the "emperor," was devoid of clothes. A few days after it occurred, this naked emperor airily dismissed the second Tonkin Gulf incident with, "Hell, those dumb stupid sailors were just shooting at flying fish." Furthermore, he later quipped, the resolution was "like Grandma's nightshirt—it covered everything."

But the Tonkin Gulf Resolution flew by Congress with but two opposed, almost as great an indictment of its members as it was of the deceptive wording of the resolution itself, of the baiting of the North to retaliate, and of the hyping of the first incident together with the invention of the second.

In the brief debate over the resolution, Morse pleaded with Fulbright to enlarge the scope of the hearings to cover America's commitment to Vietnam—something his antagonist, McNamara, would undertake three years hence. Fulbright would have none of it. This was an emergency; there was just no time for extended hearings. Morse protested that now was the time to take a hard look at our stance on Vietnam. But Fulbright stuck by his guns and by his President. In a joint meeting of his committee and the Armed Services Committee, lasting but a single day, the resolution was presented by Rusk and McNamara in words that stretched the truth out of shape.

There was one senator, Wisconsin Democrat Gaylord Nelson, who did offer an amendment that would have limited LBJ to Kennedy's assumed role of providing advice, training, and support, with no "extension of the present conflict"—surely, in view of the stakes, a reasonable and prudent caveat. Fulbright took the proposed amendment to Johnson, who would have none of it. Others, he protested, would hang on additional amendments and before long the whole resolution would come apart at the seams. And how would *that* look to Hanoi? As if Johnson's own Congress was refusing to back their commander in chief! So Johnson assured Fulbright he wanted no land war; the resolution was already restrictive enough. That was it. Fulbright went to Nelson, assuring his fellow Senator that LBJ had no intention of widening the war.

In his strenuous objection Morse prophesied: ". . . history will record that we have made a great mistake in subverting and circumventing the Constitution of the United States . . . by means of this resolution . . . we are in effect giving the President . . . war-making powers in the absence of a declaration of war. I believe that to be a historic mistake."[11]

In none of his other myriad deceptions were there the awful consequences of this classic hoax. Incredibly, McNamara later wrote that Johnson never misled Congress: "Critics have long asserted that a cloak of deception surrounded the entire Tonkin Gulf affair . . . that the administration coveted congressional support for war in Indochina, drafted a resolution authorizing it, provoked an incident to justify support for it, and presented fake statements to enlist such support. The charges are unfounded." Had there been other McNamaras, Johnson's image in history would be more heroic than deceptive. Unfortunately, the evidence—some of it provided by McNamara himself—belies the Defense Secretary's confidence in the President's integrity. Ever the astute if deceptive pol, LBJ had long before learned, as Kearns put it, that words spoken in public had little relation to the practical conduct of daily life. Furthermore, she noted, his ability to ride "two horses in different directions at the same time" was more a tribute to his deceptiveness than to the riding skills he'd learned in Texas as a boy. Nevertheless, Kearns concluded, this feat initially drew unstinting praise from most Americans.

So complete was Johnson's snow job on the Congress, the press, and the people that 85 percent of the electorate endorsed his actions in the Gulf of Tonkin. There was no doubt about it. With his resolution in one pocket, and the latest polls reflecting his big and widening lead over Goldwater in another pocket, Johnson was on a roll. Emerging the epitome of the eagle on our national seal, arrows in one claw, olive branches in the other, Lyndon figured he had the best of both worlds. "I never had it so good," he gloated to reporters.

By the fall, the world his oyster, Johnson was in seventh heaven. The press was with him, the Congress was with him, and the polls showed clearly that the vast majority of Americans were with him. In fact, everone *loved* him—or so he interpreted the overwhelming victory that voters gave him in the presidential election that November. Eight months later—his electoral mandate in one pocket, his Tonkin Gulf Resolution in another, and the Silver Star shining from his lapel—Johnson was preparing to escalate the war dramatically, without so much as a nod toward Congress.

Once again truth—or truthfulness—had fallen, the first victim of war. At no time did Lyndon display as much as a hint of misgiving for deceiving Congress, journalists, or American citizens. The people would have done well, that election day, to have heeded the words of Norman Thomas: "The only way to throw your vote away is to cast it for somebody you don't really want, and then get him."

Ever intruding in Johnson's charade of reasons for his mounting escalations of the war was the personal concern of a President with Texas-size ego: willing to be called a liar rather than a coward, a bully rather than a weakling, a man whose word was not his bond rather than the first American President to "lose" a war. How sure was LBJ of all this, asked reporters. Johnson: ". . . as nearly as anyone can be certain of anything." It was G.W.N. Sullivan, science editor for *The New York Times*, who emphasized in his *Limitations of Science* that dogmatism, coupled with zeal, flourishes in ignorance. Or as Barbara Tuchman put it, "No one is so sure of his premises as the man who knows too little."[12]

Of one thing we can be reasonable certain after more than thirty years: that Lyndon Johnson's series of deceptions in obtaining the Gulf of Tonkin Resolution was compounded by his abuse of it. His own political destruction remains but a ripple in the history of the nation compared to the tidal wave of destruction he unleashed at home and abroad. Like an enormous earthquake beneath the ocean, unseen at the time, it would register high on the Richter scale of deceit, leaving an unprecedented swath of death and destruction in its wake.

Coercion and deceit, as we have noted, are invariably counter-productive. In this case they were followed, "as night the day," by paranoia—the next fateful step in hubris.

RICHARD NIXON

If only Nixon would confess what he'd done in Watergate, just lay it all out, then we're a forgiving people, and I can go back to fishing.

— Sam Ervin, Chairman, Senate Watergate Committee, to journalist Hugh Sidey

. . . the whole thing [Watergate] is a can of worms . . . the way . . . you've handled it . . . has been very skillful . . . putting your fingers in the dikes every time that leaks have sprung there. . . .

— Richard Nixon to John Dean September 15, 1972

. . . in national security investigations they burglarize all the time. . . .

— Richard Nixon to Ron Ziegler, May 3, 1973

The difficulty with [presidential] papers, if you ever break into them . . . you could hang any president.

— Richard Nixon to Charles Alan Wright, June 6, 1973

Civility and Honesty

"Mr. President," said Richard Nixon to John Kennedy as they walked together at Key Biscayne following JFK's victory, "your new rank entitles you to walk on my right." So did the defeated Nixon remind the new President, both former naval officers, of Navy protocol.

Had Nixon been as attentive to civilized protocol he might have been spared this further step in hubris. For civilized behavior, as we have noted, is built on a fabric of verbal trust. Rend the fabric at any point through deception, and barbarism looms. Put another way, mutual trust is the thin layer of ice separating the laws of civilized society from the depths of barbarism. When deception places too great a weight on that thin layer of ice, the ice gives way, and society is plunged into the frigid waters of anarchy. Thus, anarchy is to barbarism what law is to civilization. There has never been a law written that cannot be penetrated or circumvented by lawyers more clever than scrupulous. For that reason, all law must rest on a firm foundation of mutual trust.

The very word civilization comes from the basic root "civil," referring originally to the city. The development of the city made necessary the keeping of records and the development of literacy, just as literacy made possible the development of history. Man was no longer dependent on the foibles of oral tradition; he could learn far more from the past than from his own contemporaries. And one of the most important lessons that history could teach him was the importance of truthfulness. With the advent of modern science, truthfulness could be easily determined by replicating the experiments that led to certain conclusions. Were truthfulness as easily determined in the arts and humanities, they would have a better chance of influencing the modern mind.

George Wilson was one of many who winced at the chronic deception of the Vietnam War. For he was the mayor of Bardstown, Kentucky, a town of just 7,000 people of whom 16 had given their lives in Vietnam. Nobody, maintained Wilson, could fault Bardstown for a lack of patriotic fervor. Yet with the war over, Wilson voiced a lament that resonated the length and breadth of the land when he said, "We realized . . . that the government was pulling a bit of flim-flam. We weren't getting the truth. The Vietnam War was being misrepresented to the people . . . though I'm still a patriot, I ended up very disillusioned."[1]

Here, in the almost universal disillusionment of American citizens, lay a more subtle but equally devastating cost of the war. Over the more than a quarter-century that has elapsed since the signing of the peace treaty in 1973, there has developed a chronic skepticism—worse, a pervasive cynicism—on the part of the electorate toward their government. Few occupations rank lower on the scale of prestige than politicians. The very word tends to summon in the minds of most people the lament of George Wilson: that "flim-flam" lies at the heart of government, even as it lies in the hearts of the politicians who run the government. There is much wrong with cynicism, but arguably its most sinister aspect is that it cuts the nerve of initiative, leaving a deadening anomie in its place, a feeling of frustrated helplessness expressed by the axiom, "You can't fight city hall." Cynicism tends to lead either to fatalism or to revolt. It was Jefferson who, in the Declaration of Independence, wrote: ". . . whenever any form of Government becomes destructive of those ends [unalienable rights], it is the Right of the People to alter or abolish it, and to institute a new Government. . . ." Our country had its share of revolts, the most horrendous being the Civil War. Why is it, asked Alfred North Whitehead, that "the major advances in civilization are processes that all but wreck the societies in which they occur?"

What the good mayor of Bardstown and so many other Americans came to recognize, as the Vietnam War ended and Watergate began, was that deception in government started at the very top: in the White House itself. As Shakespeare has written, "O! That deceit should dwell in such a gorgeous palace."

Richard Nixon, the consummate pragmatist, was all too willing to exploit the public's fear of Communism to further his own ends. Winning—in this case not just football games, but elections—was what it was all about, and if to win he had to lie, to dissemble, to equivocate, or to resort to any number of verbal high jinks in his grab bag of tricks, then that was the price he had to pay. Shortly after Nixon's win over Douglas in 1950, Stuart Chase published his classic essay, "The Luxury of Integrity," deploring the increasing tendency of Americans to consider integrity a luxury too dear to pay. Integrity, as Shakespeare observed, began with self—with intellectual integrity: "To thine own self be true, and it must follow, as the night the day, that thou canst not be false to any man." One is left to conjecture if perhaps the obverse is true. If a man cannot be honest with himself, can he be honest with other men? Perhaps in either case it would be closer to the mark to place truthfulness, integrity, and honesty on a continuum. Thus, will the extent we are true to ourselves be the extent to which we will be true to another? Or will the extent we are false to ourselves be the extent to which we will be false to another? This, as we shall see, is most relevant in dealing with the thirty-seventh President of the United States.

What mystifies the student of Nixon is that he was aware of all this, yet his practice appeared to be far removed from his understanding. In

June 1974, with impeachment rearing its menacing head, Nixon recalled the words of Aijub Khan, Pakistan's leader: "Trust is like a thin thread. Once you break it, it's almost impossible to put it together again." Despite this, Nixon took LBJ's "credibility chasm" that he'd inherited along with Vietnam, and widened it into a gulf. McGovern was but one of many who disparaged Nixon's deceptions. Truman once had this to say, in his own salty but forthright language: "Nixon is a shifty-eyed, goddamn liar, and people know it . . . he not only doesn't give a damn about people; he doesn't know how to tell the truth. I don't think the son-of-a-bitch knows the difference between telling the truth and lying." On another occasion, Truman laid into Nixon as "a no-good lying bastard. He can lie out of both sides of his mouth at the same time, and if he ever caught himself telling the truth, he'd just lie to keep his hand in!" Or as Bill Gulley, head of Nixon's military office, put it: "This guy is a consummate liar. I don't think he knows he is lying."[2]

Avatar of the Protestant Ethic?

By 1952, with the corpses of Voorhis, Hiss, and Douglas in his wake, Nixon was just warming up. Thomas Dewey, who had been the 1948 presidential candidate against Truman, now persuaded Ike to run on the Republican ticket—and suggested as a running mate the "new kid on the block," the thirty-nine-year-old who'd managed to garner national publicity in prosecuting Hiss. Then Dewey told Nixon that Ike would certainly show his "generosity" if Nixon would switch from supporting Earl Warren as California's favorite son candidate and persuade his delegation—a key delegation—to follow suit. Nixon had already pledged his support to Warren, but circumstances had changed and he had enough common sense to be pragmatic. Already he'd been sufficiently shrewd to mail 23,000 questionnaires to the state's voters asking for their first choice as president. Their overwhelming response: Eisenhower. So Nixon released the results to the public. Then, in a cagey maneuver to ensure "plausible deniability," he boarded the California delegates' train in Denver and alighted in a suburb outside Chicago, site of the 1952 Republican convention. On board he had spread the word that Ike was a shoo-in, so at the convention—no surprise—the delegation cast its first ballot not for their Governor, Earl Warren, but for Dwight Eisenhower. Ike was indeed generous and put Nixon on the ballot. The Warrenites would get even, however—they were the first to sic reporters on Nixon about his $18,000 "slush fund." A decade later, Warren's son, Earl, Jr., switched to the Democratic slate—then publicly denounced gubernatorial candidate Nixon for having "wronged my father and the whole state [by] back-door tactics [undertaken] for political gain for himself."

During that 1962 race, Tom Wicker heard from a staffer that Nixon, in his presidential campaign two years earlier, had refused to listen to suggestions—and "now there's no one who dares say no." Wicker surmised that Nixon was no cinch, even for governor of his own home state. Here, rather, was a man "if anything more reserved and inward, as difficult as ever to know, still driven by deep inner compulsions toward power and personal vindication, painfully conscious of slights and failure—a man who has imposed upon himself a self-control so rigid as to be all but visible." For former Lieutenant Governor Harold Powers, a Republican, Nixon was "a discard from the rubble heap of national politics."

Though the presidency was the capstone of his political career, it would crumble beneath the weight of hubris, and in particular the multitude of his deceptions. He managed to win seats in the House and Senate through deception. He won his place at Ike's side through deception. But in 1960—spurning the advice of friends, supporters, and aides, and with the brand "Tricky Dick" still burned into his hide by Douglas—he lost to Kennedy. In 1962, he again fell under the spell of that master of deception, Murray Chotiner, and ended up not only losing to Pat Brown but facing a half-million dollar lawsuit for election fraud. In 1964, despite his vow that he was not running, Nixon held out hope that Goldwater and Rockefeller would create gridlock at the national convention—and that, in desperation, delegates would turn to the veteran who'd proved himself fit for the presidency through eight years of dedicated service by Ike's side. Again, Nixon's hopes were dashed. But alas, he would succeed four years later.

Scuttling the Paris Peace Talks

How did Nixon go from being a dyed-in-the-wool anticommunist, a hawk of hawks, to being a dove of peace, eager to leave a legacy as the international broker of peace? For twenty-two years, Nixon had done nothing so much as divide the nation. As Walter Lippmann maintained in

February 1960, ". . . Eisenhower unites the country and heals its divisions. This is precisely what Nixon does not do. He is a politician who divides and embitters the people."

As late as September 1967, Nixon was boasting that no nation had ever "sought to use its power to a nobler purpose" than what the United States was doing in Vietnam. Yet, he complained, ". . . seldom has a nation been so mistrusted in its purposes or so frustrated in its efforts. . . ." A month later, he was warning that America's painful experience in Vietnam would encourage isolationism and with it a refusal to counter communist expansionism elsewhere.

But the Tet offensive early in the new year traumatized Americans watching and listening to the sounds of their countrymen under siege at the U.S. embassy in Saigon—giving the lie to the hyped statistics that Johnson had been pulling from a cocked hat. By March, Bobby Kennedy was becoming synonymous with peace in Vietnam, and his popularity was on the rise. Nixon quickly realized that most Americans were sick and tired of the war and eager to settle, at almost any price. So, overnight, he did a complete about-face, telling the baby boomers that he had a secret plan to end the war—but one he couldn't divulge, naturally, for reasons of "national security." After all, he'd seen Ike use the same ploy regarding Korea, and figured that fifteen years later, it could still pack a punch. In the 1968 New Hampshire primary that March, Nixon was asked just how he planned to end the war. His answer: "I'm not telling yet." Later, a reporter asked if indeed he had "a secret plan to end the war." "Yes," assured Nixon, "I have *a plan* to end the war." Yet he dropped the "secret" without wishing to divulge just what it was—thus making it truly secret.[3] At other times, queried about his plan, Nixon would feign reaching for an inside pocket, giving the impression that he had the plan safely tucked away there.

Of all Nixon's many deceptions throughout his career, none was more contentious, more egregious, or more ominous than his scuttling of Johnson's Paris peace talks in the fall of 1968. Henry Kissinger—with his ties in both the Democratic and Republican camps—was able to provide Nixon with inside information on the talks. Learning of Johnson's strategies during the last few weeks of the campaign would prove of inestimable value to Nixon. This was particularly true after presidential candidate Hubert Humphrey's sudden rise in the polls when, at the end of

September, he parted company with Johnson by calling for a complete bombing halt. Seeing Humphrey closing the lead, fearing that the Democrat would overtake, then pass him, by election day in five weeks, Nixon was all too eager to use this information from Kissinger. Obsessed with winning, there seemed to be no scruple that would forbid Nixon's resort to the greatest deception of all: the sacrificing of countless lives in order to win that greatest of political prizes, the presidency. It wasn't simply that Nixon loved the arena that Pat hated, the arena where gladiators fought to their political death before an entranced multitude; where the emperor, in the form of the electorate, would on November 5 turn its thumb up or down. Having tasted the heroin of politics, Nixon was hooked. By 1968, it had been twelve long years since he'd experienced a "fix," and that by clinging desperately to the coattails of the ever-popular Eisenhower. Now he would do it on his own. There was no question that Nixon was addicted. The only question seemed to be how far he would go to get the biggest fix of all: the White House, where power was concentrated as in no other place on earth.

It soon became evident that Nixon would stop at nothing—including the deaths of another 28,000 Americans and 50 times that many Vietnamese, Cambodians, and Laotians—to gain the prize. On September 24, Nixon learned, via Kissinger's grapevine, that LBJ intended to reduce American forces in Vietnam by 90,000 before June 30, 1969. Nixon immediately jumped on the Johnson administration for being "so intent on ending the war that it [will] impair the negotiating position of the United States. . . ." Yet already Nixon had promised to "end the war on an honorable basis," drawing such applause from the Young Republicans that by the end of September, it had become his campaign platform's major plank.

Nixon was first attracted to Kissinger by the latter's writings in which he embraced the concept of maintaining a balance of power among nations. But as author Donald Kagan has emphasized, this is but one school of thought in international affairs. It "relies on one set of great powers, with an interest in the status quo, checking the other powers with radical, hegemonic ambitions; as great powers rise and fall, there must be constant attention to the balance." Yet there is another philosophy, Kagan maintained: the United Nations school of thought. It relies on international institutions, "fortified by a sense of interdependence generated by economic and sound linkages, which encourage a recognition that armed conflict is foolish and counterproductive." Once the institutions were firmly based and consolidated, they would be able to cope with changing circumstances. The first school displays little confidence in human nature, while the second is more optimistic. "A balance of power depends on strong states; strong international institutions cut states down to size." It is no surprise that Nixon, as well as Johnson, favored the balance of power theory, continually bypassing the UN—whether in mounting their war in Vietnam, or expanding it into Laos and Cambodia, or by rejecting the efforts of the UN to mediate an end to the war.

At the same time, Humphrey—labeled "squishy . . . soft on Communism" by Nixon's running mate, Spiro Agnew—was promising a systematic reduction of American forces. At this, Nixon took the high road and vowed, "I don't want to pull the rug out from under our negotiations in Paris"; therefore, our military presence "should remain at the present level." On September 24—the same day that Nixon learned of Johnson's plan to cut back the number of U.S. troops in Vietnam—Clark Clifford pressed LBJ also to halt the bombing in order to promote the Paris talks. After all, Clifford insisted, Johnson should have the "honor" of settling the war, not Nixon. In the same conversation, LBJ questioned Humphrey's ability to be president. If only, he maintained, Humphrey would show "he had some balls." The best way to prove that, of course, was for Humphrey to free himself from Johnson's apron strings, but LBJ would never admit that.

Just five days later—certain that Humphrey was indeed going to part company with Johnson and call for a halt to the bombing—Nixon went public to declare that he was "pleased" with the administration's "Vietnamization" program that would turn the fighting over to the ARVN. Nixon also insisted that he'd long before advocated this as "the best route of hope for reduction of military units." However, after his election he would "advance this program far more vigorously than [has] the present administration." Here, in a nutshell, was Nixon's "secret plan" for ending the war.

As the campaign was reaching its climax, it was obvious Kissinger was performing yeoman's service in providing Nixon with a blow-by-blow description of the Johnson-Humphrey strategy—a service that Nixon wouldn't forget—and that Kissinger would make sure he didn't forget. Not that Kissinger was sold on Nixon; he was simply hedging his bets. To

David Davidson—an aide of America's chief negotiator in Paris, Averell Harriman—Kissinger confided, "Six days a week I'm for Hubert, but on the seventh day, I think they're both awful." Whether he became an assistant secretary of state or of defense in either administration, Kissinger promised that Davidson would become his principal deputy. By September 27, Nixon was leaning toward appointing the "tough-minded" Kissinger as his National Security Adviser—if he won the election. Three days later, Kissinger was warning Nixon that LBJ would probably call for a bombing halt in mid-October—this despite Johnson's freezing out Humphrey after his "betrayal" in calling for a similar halt and his insistence that it was the Vice-President, not Nixon, who was undermining the negotiations. Ahead in the polls by twenty points in mid-September, Nixon shuddered as he saw the lead close to five points by October 7. So that same day he publicly announced his willingness to accept the peace terms that appeared to stick in Johnson's craw. Indeed, as president, Nixon would offer Hanoi a "generous" peace, including helping to rebuild the North. After all, he had no interest in conquering North Vietnam, much less in destroying it.[4]

Just how secretive Kissinger was in his double-dealing with Johnson and Nixon is seen in his contact with journalist Joseph Kraft. Having been told by Nixon that Kissinger was a top contender for the job of National Security Adviser, Kraft took note of Kissinger's presence among the Johnson administration negotiators at Paris, and wondered what was going on. When Kraft asked Kissinger what he was doing there, the journalist recalled that Kissinger "became a totally scared rabbit, pleading, 'Please don't mention this to anybody else.' " Though Kraft may have had a hunch, he had no hard facts that Kissinger was playing both sides of the political fence. Nevertheless, Kraft was surprised to receive several phone calls later that day—from airports in Washington, New York, and Boston, as well as from Kissinger's house—all with the same plea, "Please don't mention it; keep it a secret."

By late September, Kissinger had fed Nixon his second report from Paris. "Our source," as Haldeman put it, warned "there is a better than even chance that Johnson will order a bombing halt at approximately mid-October." Therefore, Haldeman continued, "Our source does not believe that it is practical to oppose a bombing halt but does feel thought should be given to the fact that it may happen. . . ." Kissinger was "extremely concerned," Haldeman added, "about the moves Johnson may take. . . ." The wild card in the game was Johnson. There was no doubt that LBJ, however upset by Humphrey's "double cross," might step in and upset the Republican applecart. So, reneging on his promises not to indulge in "personal charges" against his opponent, Nixon accused Humphrey of being permissive toward lawlessness and of building his public career by "buying the people's votes with the people's money." Then, with truly breathtaking cynicism, Nixon described his own worst qualities—and attributed them to Humphrey: "You know politicians are in trouble when they start to name-call, when they start to panic, to hit below the belt."

Haunted by the thought of another lost election, Nixon panicked. One of his first resorts was to call on Humphrey to agree to a popular vote rather than an electoral vote to determine the winner. Fortunately, Humphrey knew the Constitution—even if lawyer Nixon did not—and refused. So Nixon, incredibly, needled Humphrey for turning "away from the moment of truth for democracy . . . proof of the depth of [his] desperation."

But by October 16, it was Nixon, not Humphrey, who felt desperate. For on that day, Johnson placed a conference call to the three presidential contenders—including third-party candidate George Wallace—to tell them of a major breakthrough. Hanoi was ready to allow Thieu's government to participate in the talks if Johnson would stop the bombing. Furthermore, Thieu would go along if Hanoi would respect the five-mile Demilitarized Zone between North and South Vietnam and stop attacking cities in the South. There was no doubt about it. Nixon was challenging Johnson in a game of high-stakes poker, and it looked as if the President held the winning hand for his proxy, Humphrey. What was Nixon to do? Publicly, he declared that far be it from him to "play politics with peace." Privately, however, Nixon resolved to scuttle the peace plan, despite his vow, made during Johnson's phone call, that he would do nothing to interfere. Nixon decided to use Anna Chennault as his emissary to Thieu, hoping she would convince the South Vietnamese president to back out of the talks. The Chinese widow of General Claire Chennault—heroic leader of the famed Flying Tigers during World War II—Anna had co-chaired with Mamie Eisenhower the Republican Women for Nixon. In addition, she enjoyed close ties with Thieu. Vice-President Nixon had first met her at a banquet in Formosa [later Taiwan], given in his honor by Chiang Kai-Shek.

Over the years they'd developed such a fast friendship that in 1967 she had consented to serve as his adviser on Southeast Asia affairs. Now Nixon decided to take advantage of that friendship—just as he did every other friendship, whenever "circumstances" warranted. So to "Little Flower" Chennault went the instruction to promise Thieu that South Vietnam would get a better deal from Nixon than from Humphrey.

That Chennault's involvement had immediately done the trick became evident on October 17, when Thieu called Ambassador Ellsworth Bunker to his office and raised a series of objections to the agreement the United States had reached with Hanoi. These, Bunker assured him, were but "minor problems" that would be cleared up quickly. But four days later, Thieu was more emotional as he faced Bunker, insisting that the Vietcong should participate in the negotiations only as part of the North Vietnamese delegation—not separately, which would give the Communists a numerical advantage. This was a proposal Thieu had never made in the previous five months of negotiations—and one he knew Hanoi would not approve.

Further evidence of Chennault's role in sabotaging the peace talks can be seen in a message she received from John Mitchell later that month. "Anna, I'm speaking on behalf of Mr. Nixon. It's very important that our Vietnamese friends understand our Republican position and I hope you have made that clear to them." Having done her job and done it well, Chennault was invited to a White House reception early in 1969—during which the new President took her aside to voice his appreciation: "Anna, you're a good soldier and we are grateful."

By the second half of October, with the election just three weeks away, Kissinger had Nixon on pins and needles with his insistence that LBJ would order a last-minute bombing halt. Nixon swung into action. Through Mitchell, he implored Chennault to persuade Thieu to refuse to go to the peace table. This, Nixon figured, would make Johnson's bombing halt look unwise if not cynical and, in the end, would be sure to backfire on the Democrats. So Nixon established a relay of information from Thieu to Bui Diem, South Vietnam's ambassador to the United States—to Chennault—to Mitchell—and finally to himself: all in the interests of "plausible deniability." Nixon also cautioned that messages be relayed in crypto-language to befuddle Hoover's FBI, listening in on Chennault's tapped phone, who were sure to notify the President. Why had Johnson ordered Hoover to tap Chennault's line? Because the National Security Agency had intercepted cables to Saigon from Ambassador Diem, revealing that the Nixon entourage, working through Chennault, was both pressuring Thieu to boycott the peace talks, and promising that he would be better off under the Republicans than the Democrats. In response, LBJ had told Hoover to install taps on the phone lines of Diem and Chennault, and to provide surveillance of the Nixon campaign itself. It is of some moment that, on January 8, 1973, Nixon was turning somersaults to justify his own widespread bugging, and insisting that any congressional investigation of 1972 campaign practices should also include those of 1968. Then Haldeman asked if there was "any hard evidence that the plane [in the 1968 campaign] was bugged." Nixon was betwixt and between. He craved the precedent, but dreaded the revelation that he'd scuttled the peace talks. Yet finally he urged Haldeman to "play that fight up to the hilt." Why? Because, he emphasized, *They should not have bugged the candidate's plane.* But he also cautioned Haldeman that, without hard evidence, he should not try "to take this to court." Nonetheless, this shouldn't stop him from "just put[ting] it out as authority, and the press will write the goddamn story, and the [*Washington*] *Star* will run it now."[5]

On October 26, 1968, Nixon broke his seven-month moratorium on criticizing LBJ's conduct of the war by announcing that he'd been informed of a flurry of White House activity, aimed at achieving a bombing halt and a cease-fire. He went on to say there were reports that this activity was "a cynical, last-minute attempt by President Johnson to salvage the candidacy of Mr. Humphrey," something, Nixon added, tongue-in-cheek, "I do not believe." That was enough to release the gate; out came the Texas maverick, bellowing that Nixon was not only the shallow and deceitful man the Democrats had always said he was, but that these were "ugly and unfair charges," made by "a man who distorts the history of his time." That same day Hanoi's emissary in Paris told Harriman that if the United States stopped the bombing immediately, the first serious negotiations could start on November 2. LBJ was skeptical: "I still think this is a political move to affect this election." But with Dean Rusk, Maxwell Taylor, and Clark Clifford pushing for a bombing halt, Johnson was weakening even as he protested, "I would rather be stubborn and adamant than be seen as a tricky, slick politician. Everyone will think we're working toward electing Humphrey by doing this." Uppermost in Johnson's mind was the question: was it to be Nixon or Humphrey? At times, LBJ even seemed to favor the Republican over the man who'd betrayed him. Nine days before the election, Clifford mused, "In his heart of hearts, does Lyndon Johnson really want Humphrey to win?"

With the race going down to the wire, Kissinger was determined to play both sides against the middle. He was covering all bets. So about this time he wrote a letter to Humphrey, criticizing Nixon and volunteering his services to the Democratic candidate. Already Kissinger had offered his secret Nixon files to Humphrey, only to renege when he saw the Republican with a commanding lead in the polls. Ted Van Dyke, a top Humphrey aide, couldn't believe his eyes as he read Kissinger's latest ploy. "It was so grotesque"—just the Kissinger that Van Dyke later recalled as "being a both-sides-of-the-mouth kind of guy." In his *Memoirs*, Nixon admitted it was Kissinger who'd kept him informed about the peace process, since "he continued to have entree into the administration's foreign policy inner circles." Yet incredibly, Nixon went on to write that "Kissinger was completely circumspect in the advice he gave us during the campaign. If he was privy to the details of negotiations, he did not reveal them to us."

Chennault, in a 1982 interview, was a bit more forthcoming; she admitted Mitchell had confided to her that Kissinger was supplying inside information about LBJ's last-minute negotiations to end the war.

Believing one good turn deserves another bad one, Nixon on October 27 pledged again to "do nothing that might interfere" with the peace talks. Then he warned that any coalition government in the South—something that neither Johnson nor Humphrey had even hinted at publicly—would constitute a "neutralist" force that would lead inevitably to a "thinly disguised surrender"—what he had for years castigated as "surrender on the installment plan."

Things were heating up, and Nixon was determined to keep the upper hand. The same day, Hanoi agreed to all conditions; the negotiations for ending the war were at last in place. Johnson, worried that Nixon was making headway with Thieu, called a top-level meeting to discuss the Republican's use of Chennault to subvert the negotiations. Defense Secretary Clark Clifford agreed it was "reprehensible," but warned against going public with it, lest it reveal that Chennault's phone was tapped illegally. So Johnson did nothing.[6]

For Nixon's part, he figured he had Johnson and Humphrey boxed in. On *Face the Nation*, his first televised confrontation with reporters in two years, he insisted *he* was backing the President and only wished that *Humphrey* would do the same. Just twelve hours before Johnson ordered a bombing halt, Kissinger placed his last call to the Republican camp before the election. "I've got important information." It appeared that a halt had been negotiated and would soon be announced. All the upbeat rumors about Johnson's intentions had already given Humphrey a boost, closing Nixon's lead in the polls to just two points. This information from Kissinger was therefore explosive. "Absolutely hot stuff," said Richard Allen, a member of Nixon's staff: "My heart went into my mouth." Later, Allen paid tribute to the Republicans' favorite source: "Kissinger had proven his mettle by tipping us. It took some balls to give us those tips . . . it was a pretty dangerous thing for him to be screwing around with national security." On October 31, Johnson told a national TV audience that in view of Hanoi's willingness to agree to expanded peace talks, he was ending the bombing north of the DMZ. North Vietnamese and U.S. negotiators would meet again after the election, on November 6. Both Thieu's government and the Vietcong, Johnson added, were free to participate.

With that momentous announcement, the nation breathed a collective sign of relief. The next day polls showed the public favoring a bombing halt by 55 to 28 percent. However, while Thieu was "free" to join in, Nixon by this time knew that he would not, and that Johnson's peace plans would soon go up in smoke. But, of course, Nixon would not—could not—reveal his hand. Instead, the Republican candidate declared unequivocally that he would "say nothing to undercut" the President. After all, "Peace is too important for politics, and that's the way we're going to play it."

On November 2, Humphrey passed Nixon in the polls, 43 to 40. Still, Nixon figured Johnson was bluffing, because Thieu was not in his corner. Sure enough, that same day Thieu announced that his government would not join in the talks as long as the Vietcong were permitted. Nixon could not have been more relieved. He announced that "prospects for peace are not as bright as we would have hoped a few days ago," and that he, of all people, was "surprised" by Thieu's refusal to go to Paris. Then Nixon had aide Bob Finch tell reporters that Johnson had obviously acted too hastily, just to help Humphrey at the last minute. On *Meet the Press*, Nixon was asked if he agreed with Finch. Of course he didn't, Nixon said. "President Johnson has been very candid with me throughout these discussions, and I do not make such a charge." But, he was asked, would his aides contradict him in public? Why of course, Nixon assured them, "Finch . . . completely disagrees with my appraisal of this." The true poker player that he was, Nixon all the while maintained the face of a sphinx. In addition, with his inside track to Thieu, Nixon figured LBJ was bluffing—and he would call his bluff. To compound his deceptions, Nixon offered, if he won on Tuesday, to be Johnson's emissary to Saigon: "to get the negotiations off dead center..."

Johnson was predictably furious. He grabbed the phone and dialed Nixon. "Who's this guy Fink?" The picture of calmness, Nixon assured the exasperated Johnson, "Mr. President, that's Finch, not Fink." Well, Johnson demanded, what about Mrs. Chennault? He knew what she, Mitchell, and Nixon had been cooking up with Thieu. Again, Nixon the Cool assured the President that Mrs. Chennault was acting solely on her own and that he, Richard Nixon, was only interested in helping Johnson secure that elusive peace. Johnson, himself the consummate liar, knew another when he saw one, yet pretended to go along. After complaining more about "Fink," he abruptly hung up.

If Johnson was furious at Nixon's duplicity, Humphrey was panic-stricken. He took to his diary to vent his fears, his hesitations, his questions. Should he "have blown the whistle on Anna Chennault and Nixon?" After all, "He must have known about her call to Thieu. I wish I could have been sure. Damn Thieu. Dragging his feet this past weekend hurts us. I wonder if that call did it. If Nixon knew. Maybe. I should have blasted them anyway."[7]

As it was, Nixon conceded in his *Memoirs* that had he not held a four-hour telethon on election eve, "Humphrey would have squeaked through with a close win." That may well be debatable. What was not debatable was the importance of Kissinger's double-dealing and Nixon's use of this information, which had made him realize that without some dramatic move, he would lose. Persuading Thieu to back out of the peace talks and to place all his chips on a Republican victory was the deciding factor in the election—even though the South Vietnamese leader needed little persuasion to try and avoid his inevitable eclipse. Unfortunately, the Democrats had been between a rock and a hard place. Humphrey didn't have the hard evidence he needed to accuse Nixon of sabotaging the peace process—while any presidential accusations would have revealed that LBJ had broken the law.

Johnson was less than honest when he later wrote that he "had no reason to think . . . Nixon was himself involved in this maneuvering." After all, Johnson couldn't let on that he was tapping supposedly secret calls between Saigon and their embassy in Washington. He'd also overheard "Little Flower" Chennault tell the South Vietnamese ambassador that it would be best not to accept any peace terms before the election. Asked if Nixon knew what she was up to, Chennault revealed her hand: "No, but our friend in New Mexico does." And who was campaigning in New Mexico at the time? None other than Spiro Agnew. So the Republican's vice-presidential candidate became the next target of LBJ's continuing surveillance. In a later interview, Chennault told historian Herbert Parmet that the full story was "far from known, that more confidential messages went from Washington to Saigon through couriers [than] through Ambassador Diem."

After his inauguration Nixon turned to his trusted chief of staff, Bob Haldeman, to make sure no damning details about the sordid affair would be discovered. As might be expected, Haldeman found nothing in the FBI flies or in the intercepted messages that personally implicated the new President; Nixon had long before learned how to cover his tracks. The worst Haldeman could come up with was that Nixon may have been "indiscreet" in his contacts with Chennault and Diem.

As it was, Nixon's win was a matter of deception and timing. Had the election been held the previous weekend rather than on Tuesday, or had LBJ waited two or three days before making his dramatic announcement, Nixon believed Humphrey would have won. Maybe. But that his deception continued through to the eve of election day was a certainty. That night on national TV Nixon announced he'd heard a "very disturbing report" that for the previous two days "the North Vietnamese [had been] moving thousands of tons of supplies down the Ho Chi Minh Trail," despite U.S. bombing attacks. He said this without one scintilla of evidence that the "disturbing report" was true. Instead, Nixon had simply done what habit had taught him to do when his back was against the wall: he plucked the tale out of thin air, completely fabricating his charges. At the close of the telethon, Nixon executed a Churchillian "V" for victory that had become his trademark, performed a quick Jackie Gleason shuffle and joked, "And away we go," then strode from the studio.[8]

That election eve lie was Nixon's final campaign deception. Though Humphrey immediately denied it, having checked with the Pentagon, Nixon had made his point. He'd pulled his last ace from his sleeve, put his whole stake in the pot, and emerged the winner. Despite a clear-cut victory in the electoral college, Nixon emerged the winner with no more mandate than Kennedy had received in 1960. Furthermore, Nixon was the first candidate since Zachary Taylor—in 1848—to win the White house despite his party's failure to carry either the House or the Senate. Clark Clifford was on target when he later wrote that "Humphrey had lost to a man of shrewd cunning and inherent dishonesty. I felt immensely sorry," Clifford added, "as I watched Lyndon Johnson's thirty-two-year public career coming to an end in such disarray." But as Nixon slipped in, Clifford would not have long to wait before, in greater disarray, the thirty-seventh President fell victim to hubris.

After squeaking out his win by the slightest of margins, Nixon was appropriately grateful to Kissinger. In his *Memoirs* the former president noted that, although "Kissinger had privately made a number of disparaging comments about my competence in the field," he, Nixon, was the forgiving type—especially toward a man of such "knowledge and . . . influence." More to the point, "Kissinger was providing us with information about the bombing halt." Furthermore, in their first meeting, Nixon soon became aware that "neither of us was interested in small talk . . . we shared a belief in the importance of isolating and influencing the factors affecting worldwide balances of power." Finally, Nixon urged Kissinger to read his recent *Foreign Affairs* article broaching the "need to re-evaluate our policy toward Communist China."

Kissinger's reaction was predictable, "delighted that Nixon was thinking in such terms." Indeed, they were made for each other. Both were secretive, ambitious beyond words, willing to sacrifice any and all to achieve their aims, and eager to conduct "vest-pocket" foreign policy. They were entirely willing to use each other, as long as the National Security Adviser understood his place, giving total credit to Nixon for foreign policy successes—whether deserved or not. It is little wonder that Kissinger emerged from Watergate not only unscathed, but with more power than ever.

Having achieved the presidency largely by deception, it would also, less than six years later, cost Nixon the presidency. And when he left the White House in a resignation as sordid as it was inevitable, it was clear that deception—like power itself—had become a fateful addiction for Richard Milhous Nixon.

Nixon's monstrous deceptions only served to reinforce how little he'd learned from his predecessor. In 1964, Johnson campaigned against escalating the war, then promptly escalated it after he'd won by a landslide. "Credibility-Gap" Johnson was run out of the White House, in effect, because by March 1968, very few believed anything he said. That same year, Nixon was campaigning on the theme, "We will end this [war] and win the peace." Then—like Johnson—he promptly expanded the war after being elected, while simultaneously dickering for "peace with honor."

By August 1974, Halloween had come early, and the witches' brew was simmering. Little did Nixon realize that the full bag of tricks he'd dipped into, the incredible lies he'd told, would all come back to haunt him until, driven to distraction, he would immolate himself. But one is left to speculate just how Nixon now regarded the advice he'd given a close associate years before: "You don't know how to lie. If you can't lie, you'll never go anywhere." His associate said Nixon sounded like a lawyer for the Mafia.[9] As surely as coercion was leading to, if not including, deception, so would both lead to paranoia.

CHAPTER 11

PARANOIA

A few hair shirts [are) part of the mental wardrobe of every man. The President differs only from other men in that he has a more extensive wardrobe.

— Herbert Hoover

About all I receive are the bricks. It's a good thing I've got a pretty hard head, or it would have been broken a long time ago.

— Harry S. Truman

LYNDON JOHNSON

I have a desire to unite people. And the South is against me and the North is against me. And the Negroes are against me. And the press doesn't really have an affection for me or an understanding . . . just look in that Philadelphia Inquirer this morning . . . 'a textbook caricature of a fast-dealing politician. . . . He has not aroused any excitement as a person or any emotion or enthusiasm as a human being.'

— Lyndon Johnson to Press Secretary George Reedy, August 25, 1964[1]

An Accident Waiting to Happen

From the day he entered politics in 1937, Lyndon Johnson was buffeted by more than his share of ills, mental as well as physical. If it wasn't his appendix, it was kidney stones. If it wasn't his gallbladder, it was his heart. If it wasn't the eczema-like rash on his hands, it was the nodules on his vocal folds. Yet this twentieth-century Job refused to believe his curse was the result of flagrantly abusing his body. Smoking three packs a day, and continually repairing to his Cutty Sark for surcease from suffering, only compounded his ills.

In addition to his physical ailments, LBJ showed all the earmarks of an egomaniac and a narcissist, driven to meet his mother's lofty expectations, to excel where she had not, to become the leader her father and her husband were not. In so doing, her firstborn came to exhibit the symptoms of an incipient manic-depressive. One moment he was a whirlwind, sweeping up everything and everybody within reach of his vortex; the next moment he was a semi-catatonic, a bundle of misery drowning in self-loathing and self-pity, driven to the anesthetic of alcohol. It should have come as no surprise to those closest to him—his wife, his aides, his Senate colleagues, the White House press corps—that they in turn would bear the brunt of his reckless and merciless abuse. It was during the inevitable downside, when all his efforts appeared increasingly hopeless, that a pervasive paranoia set in. Refusing to admit he was at least partly responsible for his miasma of troubles, he rushed to judgment those closest to him, lashing out in ways that eventually drove most of them away.

Webster defines paranoia as "a psychosis characterized by systematized delusions as of persecution or grandeur." Men rarely surrender delusions, even when they are scraped away by the sharp edges of reality. One of Johnson's persistent delusions—to which he clung even after being driven from the presidential race and back to his Ranch in Texas—was the rock-firm conviction that all those voters who'd cast their ballots for him in his spectacular 1964 win over Goldwater truly loved him. Author Robert Sherrill helped let the air out of this myth: "In presidential years, faced with the alternatives of a psychotic Wallace or some dull Republican troglodyte, millions of us—effectively disenfranchised for lack of a candidate—drag ourselves sullenly to the polls and vote for what those South Korean banners proclaimed as the 'Great Texas Giant.' "

Injustice, Plato wrote 2,400 years ago, invariably leads to unhappiness for the perpetrator. More recently, David Hume wrote that, while we cannot know reality, we must try to approximate it by systematically eliminating those images that prove to be false. To fail to do so means persisting in the illusion that is symptomatic of mental illness.

No sooner was Lyndon in the White House than he began to complain that Vietnam would foreclose his presidency. "With a few drinks under his belt," Reedy noted, Johnson "was ready to tell anyone within hearing range that the war would be his downfall." It was a catch-22. "He felt," Reedy added, "he had an obligation to continue the war but he also felt he was not going to win it." Indeed, Johnson complained "he could go down in history as the first president ever to lose a war."

It would seem that Lyndon was feigning paranoia when, in 1964, he dispatched spies to infiltrate the Goldwater camp. Back they came with information he could use as ammunition for what would prove to be a massive blowout at the polls. Yet he talked of running scared, Eric Goldman recalled, summoning "hobgoblins galore which could defeat him."

Yet about that same time Johnson was breathing a huge sign of relief after disabusing Robert Kennedy of any notion Bobby entertained of being Lyndon's sidekick on the Democratic ticket. "Now that damn albatross is off my neck!" declared this political Moby Dick.[2]

Lyndon would have done well to have immersed himself in the travails of some of his predecessors. Jefferson, for example, had no easy sailing with his ship of state. So badgered was he that he resolved "to take no notice of the thousand calumnies issued against me, but to trust my own conduct, and the good sense and candor of my fellow citizens." He apparently had learned a valuable lesson from Washington, who, scarcely ten months after his inauguration, declared, "I suffered every attack that was made upon my Executive conduct . . . to pass unnoticed while I remained in public office, well knowing that if the general tenor of it would not stand the test of investigation, a newspaper investigation would be of little avail."

In 1867, Ulysses Grant described Chester Arthur as "more afraid of his enemies . . . than guided either by his judgment, personal feelings, or friendly influences." Teddy Roosevelt liked being President, but he confessed, "The attacks on me worry me." Especially relevant for Johnson was Coolidge's attributing the little abuse he got to his habit of trying "to refrain from abusing other people."

However, none of Johnson's predecessors suffered "the slings and arrows of outrageous fortune" from critics more than did Abraham Lincoln. In 1863, just a century before LBJ took the oath of office, Lincoln wrote, "I have endured a great deal of ridicule without much malice, and have received a great deal of kindness not quite free from ridicule." Having been tarred and feathered in the press by 1865, he declared in his last public address, "As a general rule, I abstain from reading the reports of attacks upon myself, wishing not to be provoked by that to which I cannot properly offer an answer."

Lincoln, it seems, was able to put it in perspective, no doubt partly due to his extensive reading as well as to his genuine kindness and ready wit. Johnson, however, was no Lincoln. Not only did he pride himself in not reading books, in not getting lost in "philosophical theorizing"—but, paradoxically, he was as sensitive to the slights, the digs, the ridicule of others as he was insensitive to his own boorish attacks on those around him.

Books had figured prominently in one of Lyndon's recurring nightmares at the age of fifteen. There he was, sitting alone in a small cage, bare except for a stone bench and a pile of dark, heavy books. As he bent down to pick up a book, he saw an old lady, mirror in hand, walking in front of the cage. Then, catching a glimpse of himself in that mirror, he saw himself not as a teenager, but as "a twisted old man with tangled hair and speckled, brown skin." He pleaded with the woman to release him from the cage, but she simply turned her head and walked away. By this time he was awake, dripping with sweat as he vowed, "I must get away—I must get away."[3] What Lyndon did get away from was not so much the cage or the old woman, but from those "dark, heavy books."

By 1965, LBJ was doing battle with an increasing army of critics. Once the exuberation of replacing JFK—then finagling a blank check to wage war—then trouncing Goldwater—had worn off, Lyndon's manic phase began sinking into Pilgrim's "Slough of Despond." Of no help was the press. For his first eighteen months as President he'd pretty much had them tamed. But by the fall of 1965, having begun the first of a series of massive escalations in Vietnam, LBJ was coming under increasing attack from the media. Not that the honeymoon had been without its spats. On January 27, 1964, he complained to Abe Fortas that he'd just held a press conference where "We were going to be candid. We were going to be open. We answered them all and then what did they do? They misinterpreted, misconstrued. . . ." leaving Johnson "just getting burnt with this press corps over here." He should have listened, LBJ maintained, to Ted Sorensen, because, "He just told me tonight he just thought I was just a big, fat, cigar-puffing, pot-bellied numskull by following the advice to get out here in front of the press." There can be little doubt that this was Johnson's increasingly disparaging self-description, rather than one issuing from Sorensen.

That March, Lyndon had Paul Miller, chairman of the board of the Associated Press, on the phone, complaining he'd been on TV fourteen times in one hundred days—whereas in the same span of time, JFK had been on just six times and Ike only three. Yet ". . . I had about a dozen columns giving me hell for not being on television enough!" If it wasn't *The Wall Street Journal* snooping "all over Texas . . . into every business transaction we ever had," then it was the United Press reporters, "little chickenshits," hounding him back at the Ranch. "I saw where they said I was in the area," he complained to Reedy, "and that meant I was probably with my big trustee of my fortune." Told by Reedy that the reporters wanted to be there if something happened to him as had happened to JFK in Dallas, Lyndon exploded, "That's the goddamnedest chickenshit thing I ever saw of grown men. . . . They're a pretty bunch of chickenshits. . . ." Johnson, on the other hand, was paranoid that journalists were digging into his relationship with Judge A.W. Moursund, who had been made the trustee of LBJ's business affairs in an effort to circumvent his blind trust. Lyndon couldn't bare his scar for appendicitis surgery, he couldn't lift up his hound dog by the ears, without the media broadcasting these crudities to the public. The trouble was, his person kept intruding on the persona he was trying to project.[4]

If the press he'd been getting had its share of thunderstorms, it was placid compared to the tornadoes that lay ahead in the next four years.

The Slough of Despond

By the fall of 1965, hints of a siege at the White House began to appear in print. One after another of his escalations-on-the-sly were chickens coming home to roost. Despite the heroic efforts of both General Westmoreland and presidential aides, the truth about the setbacks America was suffering in Vietnam continued to make its way into the newspapers, thanks to skeptical reporters like David Halberstam of *The New York Times*. So paranoid did Lyndon become that he took to the phone, challenging not only the reporters but their editors and publishers. But that was counterproductive, since there was a new round of stories about his ridiculous phone calls. So he turned to his staff to make the calls, rationalizing "at least those bastards know what I think of them." In addition, Johnson ordered Reedy to script his press conferences, with all the questions and answers explicitly noted. Reedy, as press secretary, was dumbfounded. LBJ stubbornly maintained that was the way Kennedy had done it, so what was wrong with Reedy? Try as he might, Reedy couldn't persuade the President that Kennedy only occasionally had press secretary Pierre Salinger "plant" a question—and that Reedy's job, as Salinger's before him, was simply "to assure public access to the President's thoughts and actions."

To add to LBJ's woes, there was no more progress in Saigon's promised reforms than on the field of battle. Yet another coup thrust a pair of generals, Thieu and Ky, into the limelight. Of the two, Ky commanded center stage, with his brash, unpredictable, swashbuckling role as a fighter pilot. He dressed as though for a Hollywood movie, drank, gambled, and caroused as though his reputation, if not his life, depended on it. Asked by a reporter who it was he admired most, his answer was "Hitler." Then, to underscore his point, he added, "We need four or five Hitlers in Vietnam!"

Meanwhile, back on Capitol Hill, Johnson's Great Society was crumbling—while the press, those increasingly suspicious hound dogs, kept nipping at his heels. Dissent, hardly more than a murmur in 1964, was by 1966 developing into a full-throated cry. His attempt to placate the hawks on one side and the doves on the other succeeded only in alienating both. An aide attempted to explain to Johnson his predicament: "The American people feel we are withholding information." In June, even Secretary of Defense McNamara was admitting, "We're in a hell of a mess!" There was more bad news from the Joint Chiefs. It seemed, McNamara said, that the JCS "won't stop at 175,000 men" in Vietnam. By June 21, spring may have given way to the brightness of summer, but Johnson's mood had only darkened. "We can't continue to fight this war so far from home," he complained to his Secretary of Defense, "with all the men there and more on the way." Then he acknowledged, "I'm very depressed." He explained he was "just praying and grasping to hold on during monsoon [season] and hope they [the enemy] will quit. And I don't believe they're ever goin' to quit. And I don't see . . . that we have any . . . plans for victory. . . . " Then Johnson turned to old friend Richard Russell, head of the Armed Services Committee, who told the President that America should "get out of there." Alas, Johnson moaned in despair, that was impossible, what with "our treaty [SEATO] like it is and all we've said. . . ." Worse, ". . . it would just lose us face in the world and I shudder to think what all of 'em would say." Some six hundred years before, Machiavelli had counseled the Prince to fear everybody when the populace is hostile. More recently, Thomas Hobbes had noted that dejection subjects a man to ceaseless fears. Johnson's depression was both being fed by and feeding his paranoia.

As early as the fall of 1965, LBJ's teeth were on edge. It was less than a year after his monumental win over Goldwater. To one and all he'd shown he was no longer the "accidental President"—and, if not "first in the hearts of his countrymen," at least in their hearts. And now this "bitch of a war" was getting to him. He complained he had a "terrible feeling that something [had] grabbed [him] around the ankles and won't let go." Worse, it was sucking him down, down, ever deeper into the quagmire that was Vietnam. What, he asked his Defense Secretary, could he do? McNamara's advice: "Keep careful watch, run scared, and hope for the best."

LBJ's "ceaseless fears" were taking their toll, as the White House increasingly became the haunted house. Scarcely able to sleep, even from two to six A.M., the President found his increasingly aggressive war on the other side of the globe to be mirrored in increasingly aggressive protesters at home. Goldman recalled an event that revealed not simply a depressed President, but one who was "downright frightening." Lunching on potato chips and a Dr. Pepper with a small group of aides, Johnson "rambled on pleasantly with political anecdotes." But one of those stories introduced the name of a liberal Senator who opposed the Vietnam War. Suddenly, the President stopped munching and his face darkened. "These men," he sneered—"knee-jerk liberals," crackpots"—were such "troublemakers that they force politicians to the right." Then he cited old friend John Connally, Governor of Texas, as an example. Connally had started as a "progressive," but liberals had "hacked away" at him until he "had to move to the right to get some support."[5]

Johnson was just winding up. Waxing vehement, he pounded his knees as he berated these "liberal critics," who had been "stirred up" by the Russians—or so the FBI and CIA assured him—to urge a halt in the bombing. Yes, this was all simply a ploy by the Russians! He knew better than to do it but he had suspended the bombing "to show the nation how foolish such a move was." Those Russians were also in "constant touch with anti-war senators"—and the President named names. These senators, LBJ said craftily, "ate lunch and went to parties at the Soviet embassy." They were even so gullible that the Russians told them what to say. "I often know before they do what their speeches are going to say."

Worse, Johnson knew of a member of the Soviet embassy who actually delivered instructions to a member of a committee during hearings on Vietnam—undoubtedly Fulbright's Foreign Relations Committee—in February, 1966. At last Goldman could take no more of it. "Mr. President, you *know* that what you are saying simply is not accurate." LBJ stared at Goldman with an unfathomable look.

Johnson's paranoia deepened as the cries of critics turned more shrill. So consuming was his hatred for the protesters that he showed it in some absurd decisions. Goldman recalled that the parents of a "brilliant, seventeen-year-old girl" were not invited to the annual White House ceremony honoring Presidential Scholars—a program honoring intellectual achievement that had begun under the auspices of this "Education President." Their crime? They were considered "radical" opponents of the war. Worse yet, the House Un-American Activities Committee had even cited the father as a security risk. Goldman, appalled at LBJ's pigheaded ruling, warned him that if word of this reached the public, Johnson would be caught "in an embarrassing position." The threat of more unfavorable publicity made the President begrudgingly cave in. But in the future, before a Presidential Scholar was named, both the student and the student's parents had to be checked out by the FBI!

That year, 1966, was also the year that Bill Gulley entered the military office of Johnson's White House. And what was the atmosphere? A "tangled web of money, secrecy, and suspicion, largely spun out of Johnson's . . . distrust [and] a paranoia of legendary proportions." Indeed, that paranoia was spreading "like a contagion through the White House." Part of it was based on Johnson's stark fear of being assassinated, as his predecessor had been. But part of it was also the fact that the President of the United States was increasingly showing signs of mental instability.

It seemed clear to Johnson that reporters would not stop gnawing on the bone of Vietnam because they were after his hide. He was on such tenterhooks that, spotting a particularly nasty dig in the press, he'd grab a phone—any phone, even when a secretary was using it. Dialing the miscreant, he'd bellow, "What the hell are you doing to us here?! What does this mean?!"[6]

Reflecting on his fortunes as 1966 drew to a close, LBJ realized it had not been a good year. "Nervous Nellies," he complained, were running loose in the land, "ready to turn on their own leaders, and on the country, and on our fighting men." Worse, they were infecting some of his own aides; both Reedy and Ball had already thrown in the towel. Even worse, they were being led by the likes of Fulbright. "Is he helping the cause of his country," complained Johnson, "or is he advancing the cause of himself?" Never one to tolerate the impugning of his own motives, Lyndon found it easy to impugn the motives of his multiplying "enemies."

By 1967, it was fast becoming apparent that Lyndon Johnson was about to get his just desserts. For so long had he resorted to coercion and deceit, dodging those he couldn't bulldoze, that the howling war protest-ers, keeping up their everlasting din day and night, drove him to circle the wagons around 1600 Pennsylvania Avenue. He had become its virtual inmate.

Civilized society, based as it is on free and responsible choice, holds us to account for our decisions. However, convinced that we had no other choice, society tends to exonerate us from the consequences of our actions. Convinced, on the other hand, that we are deluded into thinking there *is* no other choice, society commits us to a mental institution, as it did John Hinckley in his assassination attempt on Ronald Reagan. Johnson simply could not, by this time, bear to look in the mirror and find there a Hitler, a Stalin, or a Mao looking back at him. So he did what he'd always done—ignored it. He resolved that history would record the persona he later described for Kearns: a persona who was saving the world from the rav-ages of nuclear war.

Paranoia had a firm foothold in the Johnson White House long before he made for the sanctuary of his beloved Ranch. What Goldman found frightening in 1966 festered until, a year later , Johnson was fearful of almost everybody around him. And that fear infected those closest to him. His once-incipient paranoia finally metastasized into occasional full-blown psychosis.

Avoid travel and hunker down in the White House seemed to be what the Secret Service was saying. And Johnson, incredibly, was blaming not the war, but his own humble origins: outright prejudice was exhibiting its ugly face against this poor hillbilly from the rough-and-tumble Hill Country of Texas. No, he'd enjoyed neither the leisure of Eastern privilege, nor the education of an Ivy League school. Always, in their patrician eyes, he'd be remembered as "Uncle Cornpone," the boorish ignoramus who mistook scatological language for machismo, whose boarding house reach he used to grasp power just as he'd grasped food in his college days, who fancied himself larger than life itself.

All of this, Johnson was convinced, was further corroborated when Ted Kennedy was acquitted of causing the death of a young woman at Chappaquiddick Island off Martha's Vineyard. Johnson's initial gloating at the fall of yet another Kennedy gave way to outrage when he learned that Kennedy had been exonerated. Had that been Lyndon Johnson, he com-plained, and that girl had suffered a mere bee sting, he'd be cooling his heels in Sing Sing! Then there was the press, the infernal, pestiferous reporters who were always second-guessing their President. "If something works out," Johnson claimed, "Joe Alsop will write that it was Bundy, the brilliant Harvard dean, who did it. And if it falls flat, he'll say it was the fault of that dumb, ignorant, crude baboon of a President."

By 1967, all it took was a single glance, a slight change in voice into-nation, or a hint of a gesture—and Johnson's paranoia would interpret each as a dig, a slight, an attempt to lord it over the unwashed Texan. Johnson was so clearly exhibiting the symptoms of psychosis that Walter Lippmann, like others of the "Eastern liberal press," was centering him in their cross-hairs. Here, wrote Lippmann, was a "first-class boor," priding himself on his "swashbuckling bravado." Uncouth, unmannered, unwashed, and unnerving, LBJ was as tempting a target as the media, and especially the cartoonists, could find.

Taking their cues from the press, protesters converged on Lafayette Square opposite the White House, and held high their placards, bearing the scowling, implacable face of this war criminal, with the single caption, "MURDERER!" Accompanying this was the taunting refrain, repeated endlessly: the question of how many kids he'd killed that day. Yet LBJ never showed any sign of understanding that, by lifting the draft exemp-tion of the white middle class who could afford college, he was now, in effect, putting them not only in harm's way, but—many were convinced—on death row.[7]

It was a classic siege. The wagons were circling, the troops were ready, the protesters converging, chanting and singing arm-in-arm as they marched. Lyndon Johnson, hunkering down behind the black bars of the big iron fence, occasionally staring out through his bulletproof window, was fast developing cabin fever in the White House. He was not about to take this! Exasperated at this monumental showing of disloyalty across the street, Lyndon put it to his aides, "How can I hit them in the nuts?! How can I hit them in the nuts?!" His solution: out went the CIA, the Army, and the FBI to infiltrate the ranks of the protesters.

In the turmoil that was the White House, Mary Rather, one of LBJ's secretaries and a loyal, staunch supporter, found the going getting rougher by the day. The contrast between working for Johnson as Senate Majority Leader—"the bliss, the joy, the fun, the good humor, the pleas-antry,"as she put it—was now replaced with "absolute horror." Virginia

Durr, a colleague, "just hated every minute of it. She just couldn't wait to get out of the White House." And each departure was, in Johnson's murky mind, a betrayal.[8]

By this time, speech writer Richard Goodwin, convinced that LBJ was paranoid, had consulted a psychiatrist—then considered going public about Johnson's deteriorating mental state. Robert Coles, the psychiatrist, came to see him as increasingly "mean and sour . . . a restless, extravagantly self-centered, brutishly expansive, manipulative, teasing and sly man." George Reedy recalled "a wild drinking bout in El Paso in which [LBJ] spent the night cursing and raving at a good friend," with continuous torrents of abuse directed at presidential aides; it was LBJ as the very image of "an insufferable bastard." In 1982 Reedy wrote, ". . . I can still blush with rage over the petty sadism with which he bullied his staff." Paranoia was tightening its grip on him, and he alternately became terrifying, brutish, and ugly, or whimpering, self-pitying, and pathetic.

In 1967 LBJ sent Humphrey to lay down the law to Thieu. The United States had assumed control of the economy, the fighting, and virtually Americanized the whole of South Vietnam, bringing jobs and prosperity. "Even Thieu's inaugural address had been largely written by our embassy," noted Hubert. Now it was time for Thieu to prove his mettle and take back the war, the Vice-President insisted. How could he expect the United States to continue its support when he, his regime, and his ARVN were not pulling their weight? Casually, Thieu flicked the ash from his cigarette, and arrogantly contradicted Humphrey: "No, you'll be here for a long time."

The picture was grim, and so was Johnson. It was evident the public was getting a different picture of the war than that released officially from his White House. When Reedy dared to suggest in a memo that the statistics of enemy casualties appeared to be inflated, Johnson tore up the memo "ostentatiously," Reedy recounted, and "gave me the kind of look that meant I should never do anything like that again." LBJ railed at "gutless" bureaucrats leaking "defeatist" information to "simpleton" reporters. "Why," he expostulated, "you can't have intercourse with your wife without it being spread about by traitors."

As bad as were the leakers, the press was worse. Columnists, he was convinced, had turned against him "because they knew that no one received a Pulitzer Prize by simply supporting the President and his administration. . . . Truth no longer counts as long as a big sensation can be produced. . . ." As for the Washington press, they "are like a wolf pack when it comes to attacking public officials." So who did LBJ turn to for consolation? His predecessor by one hundred years, "Honest Abe" Lincoln. "I read about all the trouble Abe Lincoln had in conducting the Civil War. Yet he persevered, and history rewarded him for his perseverance."

That was the key—persevere. Stick to his guns, come what may. And in the process, Kearns has noted, "the barriers separating rational thought and delusion were crumbling." After all, Johnson figured, words were there for the defining. "No matter what anyone said," reflected LBJ in his retirement at the Ranch, "I knew that the people out there loved me a great deal. All that talk about my lack of charisma was a lot of crap. There is no such thing as charisma. It's just the creation of the press and the pollsters. Deep down I knew—I simply *knew*—that the American people loved me. After all I'd done for them and given to them, how could they help but love me?"[9]

Trouble was, it wasn't Johnson's lack of charisma that was his problem; it was his lack of honesty. And how could he be honest with others when he had so much trouble being honest with himself? Well, just in case all those voters didn't truly love him—in fact, might even try to assassinate him as they'd assassinated Kennedy—Johnson always had his bag packed for a trip to his Texas sanctuary. And he would give the press no more than an hour's notice of impending trips. Just as he cowed his aides with his increasingly frequent vitriol, so was he cowed by the thought of assassins' guns at the ready, as the Secret Service never tired of warning him.

So here was Lyndon, fulfilling the prophecy of his grandmother when she predicted the boy would end up in the penitentiary. By 1967, the White House, of all places, was his penitentiary. Locked behind the bars of the big fence surrounding the estate, Johnson fulminated against an aide one night, "What are you trying to do to me? Everybody is trying to cut me down, destroy me!" Awakened at five in the morning, Johnson listened for the distant roar of jets taking off from the Washington airport and swore they were intent on "bombing me!"

Where could he go for solace? To the East Room, where, facing the portrait of FDR, he'd quote his mentor's verse from Isaiah, "Where there is no vision the people perish." To Barbara Ward's *The Rich Nations and the*

Poor Nations, where one page was especially dog-eared, bearing the passage, "the Christian God who bade his followers to feed the hungry and heal the sick and took his parables from the homely sound of daily work gave material things his benediction." Wasn't this just what he, LBJ, was doing? Why couldn't the people understand that? There was the culprit: the press! In league with the Soviets, they were plotting against him. It was that simple and that shameful. What a difference two years made. Virtually gone was the expansive, eager, and cheerful optimist. In his place was the moody, depressed, and irritable pessimist.[10] The narcissistic President had become the paranoid President, and was, by 1967, in competition with the manic-depressive President. If no other solace could be found, there was always the trusty Cutty Sark at his elbow. Yes, he'd sworn off, when he began to fear that booze would affect his decisions on Vietnam—and result in even more body bags making their way home. But how long could he stay away from the bottle?

By the end of 1967, paranoia clearly had the upper hand. Incensed at all the unrest in America, Johnson ordered the FBI to use its "maximum resources, investigative and intelligence, to collect and report" on any hint of conspiracy to "plan, promote, or aggravate riot activities." A year later, he could take pride in "over 3,000 people reporting on their neighbors." In addition, some 1,500 Army intelligence agents were monitoring various civilian groups, ranging from the Poor People's March and the Mobilization Committee to protests by welfare mothers and classes in Black Studies.

Christmas came, but Lyndon was in no mood to play Santa Claus. He'd played Robin Hood for four years, stealing from the rich or the rich-wannabees, and giving to the poor—and losing fewer votes than he'd gained, especially among Democrats. Now, with the din of distant battle drowned out by the din of protesters surrounding his mansion, he crept from his fortified lair, bottle in hand, to climb his Mount Olympus, there to hurl rhetorical lightning bolts at his accursed enemies.

As 1968 hove into view, *Time*, having chosen Johnson as its 1967 "Man of the Year," described him as a "hill and valley" man, "Way up one day, deep down the next." Furthermore, so overbearing was he in his funks, so intolerant of questions about Vietnam—much less debate—that "many of his best lieutenants have left him, often forcing him to surround himself with less talented cronies. Increasingly his staff is becoming a projection of himself. Of his ten principal aides, six are now Texans, and few of them are known as 'no-men.' " The contrast between private self and public persona was all the more striking. In private he wallowed in depression, refusing to believe that he was responsible for the disaster that was Vietnam, pleading for someone, somewhere, to pluck him from this infernal swamp. In public he raged against his encroaching enemies, hawks and doves alike. Like a possum back at the Ranch, treed by yapping, nipping hound dogs inches away from the kill, Lyndon arched his back, bared his teeth, snarled and lashed out. As for bombing halts, there'd be no more, because Ho Chi Minh would respond by "shoving his trucks right up my ass!" As for Tet being a "psychological victory" for the Communists, that was bunk! As for Martin Luther King calling for another Nuremberg war crimes tribunal— even for American Gis—that was outrageous! When King finally met his Maker by way of another assassin's bullet, Johnson prudently dispatched his Vice-President to attend the funeral in Atlanta; after all, one couldn't be too careful. Lyndon, it seemed, didn't trust a soul—not even his wife—unless it was J. Edgar Hoover. For it was the FBI director who'd provided incontrovertible proof that Communists were behind Johnson's persecution.[11]

Whatever else it was, the Tet offensive proved to be a wake-up call for the beleaguered President, snapping him back, at least momentarily, to some semblance of reality. Still, he remained, as aides George Christian and Horace Busby noted, "a lightning rod for everything people in the country wanted to jump on." Johnson, observed Kearns, "could not rid himself of the suspicion that a mean God had set out to torture him in the cruelest manner possible. His suffering now no longer consisted of his usual melancholy; it was an acute throbbing pain, and he craved relief."

Yet he found no relief. On March 14, 1968 Clifford met with Bobby Kennedy. The new Defense Secretary had briefed LBJ on the impending meeting, and listened to him rail against the Kennedys. Be on your guard, Johnson warned Clifford, of any tricks Bobby might play. Two days later, Bobby tossed his hat in the ring. With that, Lyndon hit the ceiling: "My worst nightmare has come true. I am trapped forever between the two Kennedys!"

Lyndon Johnson *was* trapped, not by the Kennedys, but by hubris. Like so many leaders, he'd overreached. By now he was taking credit for the Great Society, ignoring the Congress which made laws out of proposals.

And by now he was shifting blame for the war to the protesters and their professors. The latter he ridiculed for believing "you can get peace by being soft and acting nice." A true believer in the geopolitical game of dominoes, he envisioned America after the "loss" of Asia and Europe, reduced to an island. Then, he exclaimed, "I'd sure hate to have to depend on the Galbraiths and that Harvard crowd to protect my property."

It was easier to vacate the Oval Office than to rid himself of his paranoia. Back on the Ranch, he continued his fulminations against the Eastern press: "They'll get me anyhow, no matter how hard I try." During his presidency he was convinced "they" were going "into town ahead of me [to] sabotage me." Now he was similarly convinced "they" were twisting future perceptions, determined to rob him of his rightful place in history as a presidential record-setter.

Pressed by Kearns in his retirement as to why he hadn't availed himself of one opportunity after another to effect a peaceful settlement of the war, Johnson exploded, "No, No, No!" he shouted. "I will *not* let you take me backward in time on Vietnam. Fifty thousand American boys are dead. Nothing we say can change that fact. Your idea that I could have chosen otherwise rests upon complete ignorance. For if I had chosen otherwise, I would have been responsible for starting World War III. . . . All that horror, as horrible as it was—and I hated it more than anyone—do you know what it's like to feel responsible for the deaths of men you love? Well, all that horror was acceptable if it prevented the far worse horror of World War III. For that would have meant the end of everything we know."[12]

This twisted, tortured former President saw the face in the mirror he'd been forewarned of in a recurring nightmare. His hair falling down over his ears and collar, his clothes disheveled, this progenitor and apotheosis of the beatnik generation was strung out on the rack of conscience—from which three packs of nicotine and a fifth or more of Cutty Sark each day were hard-pressed to relieve him.

By the time he'd drawn his last breath in January 1973, paranoia had taken its toll.

RICHARD NIXON

. . . Nixon and Clinton, who talked frequently during the year before Nixon's death on April 22 were a perfect fit. Both "came from dirt" . . . Both were closer to their mothers than to their fathers. Both operated from few core principles, but were obsessed with winning. Both lost races for Governor . . . then fought back from defeat. Both did so by reinventing themselves, Nixon as the "new Nixon," Clinton as a "new Democrat." Both survived scandals in their first major national campaign by turning in boffo TV performances.

But there's a more important similarity: an attitude of mistrust toward all Washington beyond the White House staff. This includes the press. One of the amazing aspects of Clinton's presidency is that he started with a press corps favorably disposed toward him, yet has gotten more negative coverage than George Bush, Ronald Reagan, Jimmy Carter or Nixon received in their first years. Since Clinton scarcely blames himself for this, that leaves only one other option—malevolent journalists. Obviously, there's a dash of paranoia in his attitude. But he's also persecuted. The press is out to get him. It's this mixture of paranoia and persecution that's pure Nixon.

— Fred Barnes, 1994

The Chickens Come Home to Roost

Each stage in hubris tends to lead to the next. Nixon's ambition and lust for power drove this opportunistic politician to exploit time, circumstance, and other people. This in turn resulted in a towering arrogance that caused Nixon to identify himself with the presidency, with the government, and, indeed, with the nation itself. As confrontation led him to coerce and deceive, it would in turn create enemies, real and imagined, and a full-blown paranoia. And in that paranoia, the darkening shades of melancholia would develop, just as surely, into isolation and immolation.

It was Nixon's fate, Schlesinger observed, "to carry the logic of the imperial presidency to the point of no return . . . [doing] things it never occurred to Truman or Eisenhower or Kennedy or even Johnson to attempt." Politics for Nixon was not as much the art of compromise as the art of warfare, "a succession of battles . . . to be fought against cunning and vicious foes with every weapon at hand." In the process, Schlesinger added, Nixon became "the only major American politician in our history who came to prominence by techniques which, if generally adopted, would destroy the whole fabric of mutual confidence on which our democracy rests." Our democracy is strong, and it is flexible, able to adapt to major changes, major crises. But it is not invincible. Anthony Lewis, writing in *The New York Times*, compared the nation with the corporation. Imagine a large corporation with a powerful president, one who makes it company policy to keep ultimate control of operations in his own hands. Over a year, 16 of this president's close associates are charged with serious crimes. His personal lawyer, the company's former counsel and two members of the president's staff plead guilty. So does the vice-president. Two other staff members are tried and convicted. Nine more are indicted, among them his top personal assistants and the heads of two major subsidiaries. At a stockholders' meeting the president says he knew nothing of these affairs. He deplores them, he says, but his duty is to get on with the company's business; legal questions are for the courts. When a group of his stockholders asks to see the records of his own corporate dealings, he says no—that might prejudice the trial of his associates; and besides, such disclosure is against company policy.

When there is evidence that a corporation has been in the hands of a criminal gang, we see easily enough that its president cannot escape personal responsibility. We understand that he must make an accounting to the shareholders. Is democracy more important in a corporation than in a country?

There was no event in the political career of Richard Nixon that posed just such a threat to the republic as did Watergate, the cover-up so much more than the burglary itself. As James Reston wrote in concluding his Watergate briefing book, "Watergate is fundamentally an anti-democratic event; it's an assault on democracy and democratic institutions. It was an effort to undermine free choice, free competition in one election and to undermine governmental institutions that operate only through the trust in them by the American people . . . Nixon is a fundamentally anti-democratic personality . . . his political statements over 25 years were never rooted in any deeply held political beliefs . . . he is the classic 'main-line politician' who adopts positions which mirror rather than educate the mood of the electorate and, worse, pander to and inflame the prejudice of the time. That such a figure without belief, for whom 'winning' was everything, could for a quarter of a century so dominate the political life of a country that prides itself as the greatest democracy in the world, is a stunning phenomenon of the twentieth century."

Not only was Nixon's dominance "a stunning phenomenon" but, as Reston implied, it posed a singular if not unprecedented threat to the nation. It was this that alarmed the American people and set off the firestorm of protest following the "Saturday Night Massacre." Archibald Cox put it squarely when he warned U.S. citizens that they faced a choice between a government of laws or of men. He might well have added, of laws or of anarchy.

It wasn't as though the country, had it taken the time to "stop, look, and listen"—as it was admonished to do at railroad crossings—could not have seen this accident coming down the track, bound to happen. If there is one pervasive theme running through *Six Crises*, it is that of "siege": of paranoia, of a politician so beset by enemies that, Nixon claimed, only the inner calm of his Quaker mother, combined with the resolute tenacity of his Irish father had pulled him through one crisis after another. Here was the spitting image of Archibald MacLeish's "JB," the twentieth-century Job, who, like his namesake, would issue his plaint that few were his days and those "full of trouble." Tom Wicker, reviewing *Six Crises*, lamented the pronounced lack of "any significant disclosures about Nixon the man—what he really felt, thought, believed, what he really was." Nixon seemed to be so intent on projecting his persona in preparation for his 1962 gubernatorial campaign that he almost completely ignored his person. William Costello, writing in *The New Republic*, was seething. For in the book he perceived a man "never unaware of nameless, faceless enemies, waiting to pounce." Bereft of "eloquence or elegances," the book was "surcharged with banalities, intellectual clichés, and tasteless bravado, until at last the reader averts his mind's eye in embarrassment."[1] There could be little doubt in Richard Nixon's mind that twelve years after writing *Six Crises*, his greatest crisis lay yet ahead. He leaned into the wind of impeachment, convinced that, like Job, "Man is born unto trouble." Shakespeare penned his own definition of paranoia when he wrote, "Suspicion always haunts the guilty mind."

Nixon's paranoia, which began in the green days of his early youth, became part of the larger picture of a grown boy who, unlike others, never seemed to divorce the fantasies of childhood from the realities of maturity. Gerald A. Johnson, biographer of several eminent presidents—including Jackson, Wilson, and FDR—took note of John C. Calhoun's classic *Disquisition on Government*. It had remained buried for a century, not simply because it was "dry and crabbed," but because its author lost contact with reality, and in so doing "did much to precipitate the worst disaster that has ever befallen the Republic, the Civil War, that came within a hairsbreadth of destroying the Union." It was not that Calhoun lacked a realistic grasp of practical politics. It was, rather, that he failed to realize "that the dynamics of history are not controlled by Aristotelian or any other kind of formal logic." Johnson elaborated: "His position was that what cannot happen will not happen, and when nevertheless it did happen, he flatly denied that it had occurred." Calhoun would not—perhaps could not—understand how the nation, or at least the North, "could decide, in all honesty, that the evil of slavery had become intolerable to an extent that sucked the life out of the letter of the Constitution; and he died believing that it was not an honest conviction, but an illusion created by demagogues."

In 1946—almost a century after the death of the deluded John C. Calhourn—the press discovered the ruthless Richard M. Nixon, who resorted to one trick after another, one lie after another. So vicious were Nixon's attacks, so unprincipled his ploys that, coupled with his sanctimonious, preening self-righteousness, even a jaded press recoiled in disbelief. He was alternately the savage pit bull, his teeth firmly set in the high-priced flesh of Alger Hiss, then the bleating lamb, beset by journalists hungry to reveal his glaring lack of scruple, his monumental hypocrisy.

Whatever the persona he was projecting at a given time, beneath Nixon's thin skin was a paranoia that he both reflected and exacerbated in postwar, cold-war America. Neither he, nor Eisenhower, nor Johnson detected a crisis in the verbal thunderbolts being hurled from Olympus by Mars in the form of the Wisconsin Senator McCarthy. That is, not until McCarthy targeted Ike's Army and his Secretary of Defense. From then on, it was a headlong descent into the hell of paranoia, with McCarthy answering the door of his apartment, gun in hand. Most were satisfied when, condemned in the Senate, he reaped the paranoia he'd sown across the length and breadth of the land. Yet Nixon, like Johnson—for all their close personal observation of this victim of hubris—did not seem to learn from McCarthy's downfall.

It is a telling commentary on the meteoric rise of Nixon—from freshman congressman to Vice-President in six short years—that Roy Cohn, chief aide to McCarthy, should characterize Nixon as "the most suspicious man" he'd ever met, "suspicious of everybody and everything . . . like a fellow who always thought of himself as being in a corner and trying to see who is trying to trap him." On one side were Johnson and the Democrats, intent on proving their claim that they were more loyal to Ike than his own Republicans, therefore deserving of victory at the polls and of continuing domination of Congress. On another side was Ike, that most popular of all Americans, casting, Nixon felt, a jaundiced eye at him, who had always been against him. On yet another side was Pat, indignant that she and the girls had to be dragged before millions who were watching Nixon's televised "Checkers" speech, insistent that he not only promise to quit politics but put the promise in writing. And on the last side was the infernal press, those nosy and biased reporters who, Nixon charged at a Cabinet meeting, were being "heavily influenced by the Commies." What more convincing proof was there than Herblock's outrageous caricatures in *The Washington Post* showing a filthy Nixon rising up in the street through a manhole from the sewer beneath—or from the slime of the gutter, beseeching the John Q. Public walking by, "Of course, if I had the job [as President] I'd act differently." Though Nixon canceled his subscription to the paper, he joked with Chalmer Roberts of the *Post* that he "loved the cartoons." "You know," he added, "a lot of people think I'm a prick but I'm really not."[2]

That Nixon was beset by emotional problems in the 1950s can be seen in his frequent visits to Dr. Arnold A. Hutschnecker, a psychiatrist—later dubbed, "the President's shrink." This is the same doctor who, in 1974, wrote: "Who gave the orders to defoliate the Vietnam countryside? . . . who covered-up and falsified reports on unauthorized bombings in neutral

Cambodia, lying so they would continue playing the deadly game of murder?" Who, of course, but Nixon. Was it sexual impotence that prompted Nixon's repeated visits, as campaign aide James Bassett contended? Or was it chronic insomnia, as Leonard Hall, chairman of the Republican National Committee, claimed? So keyed up was Nixon following his speeches that he'd sometimes be on the phone until three in the morning, trying to gauge his impact, leaving precious little time for sleep. Whatever the problem or combination of problems, Nixon found sufficient help from the psychiatrist that he presented the doctor with a row of ivory elephants. It is, in any case, not hard to imagine that paranoia was surfacing during Nixon's first term as Vice-President.

All in all, Nixon's was not a happy prospect as he faced 1956 and a President who was giving him the cold shoulder, if not the bum's rush. It is no wonder that rookie reporter Tom Wicker, passing the Vice-President in an empty corridor of the Capitol, was astonished by his first glimpse of Nixon: a pathetic creature "walking along rather slowly, shoulders slumped, hands jammed in his trouser pockets, head down and his eyes apparently fixed—though perhaps on nothing—on the ornate Capitol floor." His face was dark, his mind "preoccupied, brooding, gloomy, whether angry or merely disconsolate I was unable to tell." Though only a Secret Service agent was accompanying the Vice-President, Nixon gave no sign of perceiving Wicker as another human being in that long, empty corridor. Wicker concluded that Nixon's was "an unappealing presence." Another reporter, Hugh Sidey of *Time*, found Nixon, off duty as the Senate's presiding officer, "a hunched figure trying to skulk off down the back ways."

By the time of the 1960 campaign, paranoia had reached deeper into Nixon's fragile psyche, rattling his self-imposed cage. He figured he had good reason to complain. There he'd won the California delegation for Ike at the 1952 convention, yet Ike had been ready to dump him from the ticket at the first sign of Republican unease. There he'd done Ike's bidding and become his hatchet man—first making mincemeat of President Truman, presidential candidate Stevenson and Secretary of State Acheson in 1952 by labeling the three Democrats "traitors" for their cowardly failure to contain Communism; then by piling on McCarthy in 1954 to help bring about the Senate's condemnation. There he'd prudently stepped aside during Ike's near-fatal heart attack in 1955, so Ike was accusing him of lacking "administrative experience." There he'd faithfully stumped for Republican congressional candidates in 1958, and now Ike cut out the ground from beneath his own 1960 candidacy with that thoughtless "give me a week" remark. Obviously, Dwight Eisenhower was more concerned about his place in history than about his successor in the White House. As if that were not enough, there was that infernal car door that he struck with his knee, laying him up for two weeks while Kennedy was out on the hustings, building an impressive lead in the polls. Nixon, ignoring Ike's warnings, had promised to participate in three debates and to campaign in all fifty states—yet there he was, hospitalized two months before the election, losing precious time when he should be dashing around the country.

And even that was not enough. For there was the handsome, striking figure of JFK, in sharp contrast to the forlorn, exhausted, and increasingly paranoid Nixon. Given a "pass" by the obviously fawning press, Kennedy projected a persona of the ever-confident, jocular, witty, Boston Irishman who loved to banter with reporters. Sophisticated, rich, Harvard-educated, he was the very epitome of all that Nixon had come to loathe—and to envy. Though surrounded by journalists, Nixon refused to give them the time of day, holding no press conferences for seven weeks. Worn to a frazzle by the campaign's last few weeks, he made some serious blunders in the debates and on the stump, even without being baited by the jackals in the media. Ike's policy of "Peace without surrender" had become, his Vice-President rashly charged, "Peace and surrender." Furthermore, he would "make far more progress in education than . . . the past administration"— hardly the choice of words to win from Ike a rousing endorsement. Then there was his running mate, Henry Cabot Lodge Jr., who, at the close of Nixon's first debate with Kennedy, blurted, " that son-of-a-bitch just lost us the election!" It is safe to assume that there were grave doubts and consternation in the Nixon household as election day dawned.

When voters convened at the polling booths on November 8, 1960, they carried with them the image of a tanned, healthy, and confident Kennedy who in the debates had alternated serious conjecture with buoyant smiles and witty repartee. On the other hand, they couldn't forget the deer-in-the-headlights stare of the nervous, emaciated Nixon, sweat forming rivulets through the chalk powder used to cover his five o'clock shadow, a man who seemed more serious about himself than about the issues. So Americans elected the Roman Catholic—the first in the country's history—leaving Nixon choking in JFK's dust, fretting, fuming, and furious that the press had shafted him. By this time it seemed that Richard Nixon had become the favorite whipping boy of conservatives and liberals alike.[3]

One Crisis After Another

Nixon immediately took to writing *Six Crises*: the story of an all-American boy who rose by dint of bootstrap luck and pluck, only to be ground down by evil, entrenched forces—a story overlaid with a pervasive paranoia that was unrelieved by its sanctimonious homilies. This was to be both Nixon's apologia and his campaign book for 1962. Though he persuaded rich supporters to buy thousands of copies, putting it on *The New York Times* bestseller list, the book did little to rescue Nixon's ill-fated venture into California gubernatorial politics. For the common thread throughout *Six Crises* was that of a man who, like Job of old, saw himself "persecuted for righteousness sake"—suffering one cataclysm after another, sitting on a pile of ashes dressed in sackcloth, scraping his boils with a piece of potsherd, and surrounded by "friends" stabbing him with "I told you so" as they offered specious advice.

Instead of sending heavenward a resolve to remain faithful rather than to curse the Almighty, this twentieth-century Job resolved to fight to the bitter end. It was not a picture so pretty as to warm the hearts of Californians. Nixon found himself embroiled in yet a seventh crisis, and one in which he again could blame the media for his woes. His swan song to the press was, in effect, the "fat lady singing," and reporters left, convinced that they'd indeed not have Nixon "to kick around" anymore.

Repudiated by his fellow Californians, Nixon figured New York to be a more hospitable climate. But moving into an apartment in a Fifth Avenue hotel, Nixon found his upstairs neighbor, Nelson Rockefeller, no more congenial than voters on the West Coast. It seems that the liberal New York Governor felt little more than "loathing" for his fellow Republican. According to Kissinger, Nixon was "shunned by the people whose respect he might have expected . . . [he was] never invited by the 'best' families." This, Kissinger added, "rankled and compounded his already strong tendency to see himself beset by enemies." Indeed, Ambrose may have been on target when he referred to the 1963 Nixon as "the most hated and feared man in America."

In order to be admitted to the New York bar, Nixon was required to write an essay on what he believed the principles underlying the form of government of the United States to be. From his pen came forth an article that would serve as his judge and jury a few years later. He defined "decentralization, the separation of powers, and the balancing of freedom with order." Above all, "the framers of the Constitution were fearful of the concentration of power in either individuals or government." Indeed, the system devised by this Constitution was "the most effective safeguard against arbitrary power ever devised by man."

How, we are forced to ask, could this man, so aware of the threats to the republic by the abuse of power, fail prey to the madness of hubris? Was it because awareness didn't in itself constitute belief—a word rooted in the ancient Anglo-Saxon "by lief" or by life, that we believe only what we live? Or was it that, in his deepening paranoia, he felt justified in resorting to that which he knew to be illegal—later claiming that such acts weren't illegal since he was the President? Perhaps both of these entered into his riding roughshod over the very principles he'd enunciated so clearly less than a decade before. As Theodore White put it, Nixon's "ruthlessness, vengefulness, nastiness [were] the characteristics of a man who has seen himself as underdog for so long that he cannot distinguish between real and fancied enemies."

With Kennedy out of the picture by late 1963, Nixon turned his attention to Johnson, who'd determined to "stay the course" of his predecessor. The superpatriot Nixon, however, never saw a war he didn't like—and never saw a Johnson escalation he did like. By the summer of 1964, he was faulting the Kennedy/Johnson position on Vietnam as "plagued with inconsistency, improvisation, and uncertainty." Then, resurrecting MacArthur from the shadows where—as the general himself put it—"old soldiers fade away," Nixon paraphrased his hero's 1951 declaration on Korea: "there is no substitute for victory" in South Vietnam. When Fulbright, seeking to end the no-win war, suggested exploiting the growing split between China and the Soviet Union, Nixon scorned such "woolly-headed thinking" as the very thing that had "plagued U.S. policy." Never, he vowed, would he go along with the United States recognizing Red China, or pushing for its admission to the UN.[4] Yet scarcely five years later, these were Nixon's own tactics.

As long as Johnson was in the White House, Nixon played an important role in the siege that had the President hunkering down, gripped by paranoia. But after he succeeded LBJ, Nixon himself would succumb to that very paranoia—a condition that only deepened as Watergate closed in on him.

Vietnam's Path to Watergate

As his inauguration hove into view, Nixon found a number of his certainties no longer so certain. It was one thing to be on the outside looking in, castigating those occupying the Oval Office. But in 1969, he stepped into that seat of consummate power and began to see things differently. No longer was he sure that continuing escalation of the war, even resorting to nukes, would bring "peace with honor." No longer was he sure that he wouldn't be the first president to lose a war. No longer was he sure that worldwide expansion of Communism was being orchestrated in the Kremlin. No longer was he sure that China, that largest of nations, should be barred from diplomatic recognition and admission to the UN. No longer was he sure that Thieu's government resembled the free and democratic republic he'd been proclaiming. No longer was he sure the war could only be won—or lost—by the Vietnamese themselves. Finally, no longer was he sure that the war was worth the widening divisions that were giving the lie to this as the *United* States.

Having won the White House, there remained, however, one certainty, one thing of which he would make sure. It was that, as peacemaker extraordinaire, he would inherit a second term to ring in the two hundredth anniversary of the nation's founding. Everything, all those former certainties, were up for grabs—just as long as Nixon had his eyes fixed on that prize of prizes, to be won not by the slender margin that separated him from Humphrey in 1968, but by an unprecedented landslide. Here was the sole order of the day, the one goal he would bend everything and everybody to accomplish. Yet he would do it from the seclusion of his inner sanctum, by remote control, working through Kissinger in foreign affairs and the Haldeman-Ehrlichman team in domestic affairs. These and others were always at the ready, his wish their command. "For a man so constituted," Schlesinger noted, "the imperial presidency was the perfect shield and refuge."

At the same time, this imperial President would come to subvert the very constitutional democracy that he had brilliantly described five years earlier, and to which he had pledged his life at his inauguration. For in place of the Constitution he had sworn to uphold, Nixon substituted the rule of law—*his* law—the only law that would permit *his* victory over the Vietnamese Communists to coincide with *his* victory at the polls in 1972. In the process he not only corrupted his administration, but corrupted the language and the ideas that language embraced. "National security," "executive privilege"—these and other terms he prostituted, pressing them into yeoman's service to do his bidding.

With use, words resemble snowballs rolling down a hill, gathering more and more layers of meaning—until there exist at opposite sides of the big ball meanings that appear to contradict each other. Thus did the North Koreans at the 1953 Paris peace talks refer to themselves as "the People's Republic." Yet one would be hard put to find significant resemblances between that tightly closed and rigidly controlled society and the open society of the republic of the United States, with its emphasis on individual freedoms guaranteed in the Bill of Rights. But words like "republic," were fair game for the sharp eyes of Nixon and his cluster of lawyers, ever on the lookout for loopholes, for exceptions, for forcing the very Constitution into a procrustean bed—even if it meant lopping off a leg here, an arm there, or, if worse came to worse, the head itself. In this, Nixon seemed to follow the advice of President Taft: "Let anyone make the laws of the country, if I can construe them."

Bad enough that Nixon should be badgered by a Congress and a Court intent on maintaining traditional interpretations of that Constitution. But to be impaled on the spit of the media and roasted over the fire of public opinion—that was sheer agony. So Nixon, virtually abolishing the press conference as a means of informing American citizens, scripted the play himself, leaving no room for alternate wordings, interpretations, and endings. Indeed, so fearful was Nixon of the free-for-all press conferences that it wasn't unusual for him to "throw up beforehand." As a result, Schlesinger noted, Nixon "organized the executive branch and the White House to shield himself as far as humanly possible from direct question or challenge—in other words, from reality." FDR held over a thousand press conferences in his twelve years, or about two a week; Truman held about one a week, insisting that he learned more of what Americans were thinking "from the reporters' questions than they possibly could learn from me." Though Ike, JFK, and LBJ also released transcripts and resorted to TV to speak directly to the nation, they nevertheless maintained the press conference as a necessary part of informing the public. But under Nixon not only Cabinet meetings but press conferences virtually disappeared. In his first term he held just twenty-eight in four years, as many as FDR had held his first three months. As a result, Maryland Republican Senator Charles Mathias observed, President Nixon lived "in a house of mirrors in which all views and ideas tend[ed] to reflect and reinforce his own." No wonder John Dean came to feel that there was "a myth and unreality about the White House."

Whereas his press conferences dwindled to seven a year, Nixon's TV appearances burgeoned, for in that orchestrated setting there was no possibility of embarrassing questions from nosy reporters. During his first eighteen months as President, Nixon utilized prime-time TV more than Johnson, Kennedy, and Eisenhower combined. So infatuated was Nixon with this medium—the ideal propaganda tool—that when he returned from his Peking summit he laid over in Alaska for nine hours, just so he'd arrive in Washington at prime time. By minimizing his press conferences and maximizing his TV appearances, Nixon was able to control and manipulate both press and public—selecting what he wanted to say and how he wanted to say it, incorporating his own spin, his own deceptions. In this, Nixon believed he was abetted by the gullible public. After his spectacular victory in the 1972 election, the President observed that "the average American is just like a child in the family." *Father Knows Best* was a TV series he undoubtedly embraced.

Of course, there were some non-average Americans whom Nixon feared and despised. The President's counsel, John Dean, even prepared a comprehensive list of enemies, all neatly prioritized: hundreds of people Nixon wanted targeted. Nixon wasn't the first president to prepare an enemies list. John Quincy Adams had done so 150 years earlier, including on his roster such notables as Henry Clay, John C. Calhoun, Andrew Jackson, and Daniel Webster. But there was a significant difference: Adams' list was addressed only to his diary. Nixon's, however, would become public—revealing to the world that the mad dog of paranoia was on the loose in the White House.

Bob Woodward and Carl Bernstein, *Washington Post* reporters, kept turning over one rock after another, exposing all manner of political insects scurrying out from underneath. The reporters asked John Mitchell about his connection with the Watergate burglary. "All that crap you're putting in the paper," Mitchell scorned, "it's all been denied." Then he threatened that if more such stories were published, "Kate Graham [owner of the the *Post*] is gonna get her tit caught in a big fat wringer. . . ." As things turned out, it was not Graham but Mitchell who soon found himself being squeezed in "a big fat wringer."[5]

Though there is as yet no concrete proof of Nixon's ordering the Watergate burglary, and though Bob Haldeman wrote in his diary that the President was surprised to hear of it, it is well to remember that Nixon had been honing his thespian skills since high school. If not a consummate actor, he was a good one. One White House document, released in 1994, indicates that Haldeman may well have known about the burglary beforehand. And John Dean, in an interview with the BBC, concluded that, "If Haldeman knew about this, there is no doubt in my mind that Richard Nixon knew." Why the break-in? Because Nixon wanted to find out if the Democrats had learned about any number of dirty tricks that had been dreamed up in the White House; because Democratic national chairman Larry O'Brien was at the top of the White House enemies list for having poked his nose into some of Nixon's underhanded business deals; because Nixon, having lost in 1960 and barely squeaking through in 1968, wanted every advantage in 1972—and learning the Democrats' strategy would give him an edge; and because Nixon was paranoid, even about an election he *knew* was a sure thing.

Once the job was done—and bungled unmercifully—Nixon frantically tried to hide all ties to his White House. He denied any connection with the burglars, depending on "plausible deniability" to carry the day. When it was finally revealed that the Oval Office was neck-deep in the break-in and cover-up, Nixon invoked "national security" as his security blanket. It brought to mind Henry II asking his three trusted aides: "Will no one rid me of this turbulent priest?" Presto! The three rushed off to kill Archbishop Thomas á Becket in his own cathedral. So did Nixon plead to be rid of the pestiferous O'Brien. Unable to murder him, the President would at least discover what he knew and what he planned—but Nixon had to be certain there was no trace of White House complicity. Eisenhower had his "turbulent priest" in Khrushchev. That rivalry led to the President's eating crow before the world when he denied U-2 reconnaissance planes were flying over Soviet territory, only to have Khrushchev produce photographs of a captured U-2 pilot, Gary Powers. Kennedy had his "turbulent priest" in Castro. That rivalry led to the President's launching the disastrous Bay of Pigs invasion, which ended in JFK's humiliation before the world. Johnson had his "turbulent priest" in Bobby Kennedy. That rivalry led to the President's bowing out of the 1968 race. Just so, Nixon's "turbulent priest," Larry O'Brien, would in the end drink deep of the cup of satisfaction after seeing the President—despite desperate efforts at "plausible deniability" and sacrificing his lessers as sops to the Senate Watergate Committee— resign his office in disgrace.

It is also instructive that, two weeks after the break-in—dismissed by the President as "a minuscule crime unless you get something" and certainly "no blot on a man's record," Nixon turned to Chuck's Colson's imaginative notion of breaking into their own Republican National Committee headquarters, then blaming it on the Democrats. Colson: ". . . it would be very helpful if they came in one morning and found files strewn all over the floor." Nixon: "And some missing." Colson: ". . . this goes on in every campaign." Nixon: ". . . do $3,000, or $4,000 worth of damage. . . . There should be a rifling or missing files, something where it's really torn up. . . ." Then what? Nixon: "Well, I'd sue them [the Democrats]. . . ." Reported in the *San Francisco Examiner* after the release of more Nixon tapes, Kissinger assured the paper, "Nixon often said exalted [?] things that people didn't think would have to be done."

By August 1972, Nixon was turning cartwheels and doing handstands, anything to cover up the burglary and prevent it from sinking his reelection. By this time it was evident to many—especially to those on the White House staff—that it was not the Democrats, not Hanoi, not the war protesters, not even the press, but Nixon himself who was his own worst enemy. If there was any doubt about it, subsequent events would lay those doubts to rest.

As much as he tried to justify his use of the FBI, CIA, IRS, and FCC to intimidate his enemies on the basis of presidential precedent, there was no comparison between earlier occupants of the Oval Office and Richard Nixon. One of the most dramatic examples of Nixon's use of the IRS to coerce was in connection with George Wallace, the "spoiler" who could divide Democratic ranks—if he opted to run as a Democrat. Never shy about overkill, Nixon ordered no fewer than forty-seven IRS agents to descend, not on George, but on his brother and former law partner, Gerald. Were there any kickbacks? Any illegal campaign contributions? Soon Gerald was complaining that he was being hounded by IRS agents more intent on George's campaign than on Gerald's taxes. Alternating stick with carrot, Nixon invited George to take a spin aboard *Air Force One*, the flying palace. By coincidence, surely, the IRS on January 12, 1972, announced it was dropping Gerald's audit. And, coincidentally, the next day newspapers were carrying the story that George had decided to run as a Democrat, not as a third-party candidate. Quid pro quo was a political game at least as old as the Latin language. As much as he tried to justify his dirty tricks, based on the benign tricks of Democrat Dick Tuck—a political wit who specialized in bedeviling Nixon campaigns—it was a specious analogy. It was like comparing the puffs and sputters of geothermal heat in the waters of Yellowstone Park with the eruption of Mount St. Helens. Yet for his every resort to intimidation, for every dirty trick, Nixon believed he could count on retaliation, certain that his "enemies" were putting him in their crosshairs, deepening his paranoia.[6]

Separating big business—especially defense contractors and others doing business with the federal government—from their big bucks, Nixon soon had $60 million in his campaign coffers. Large corportions knew that Richard Nixon was a sound investment, because they could always count on their "quid" bringing at least as much in "quo." Nixon clearly agreed with Calvin Coolidge's contention that "the business of America is business"—and studiously ignored all those other Republican presidents who had felt quite differently. There was "Honest Abe," casting a jaundiced eye at big business: "These capitalists generally act harmoniously and in concert, to fleece the people." And Teddy Roosevelt: "There can be no effective control of corporations while their political activity remains."[7] And Dwight Eisenhower warning Americans: "beware of the military-industrial complex."

Down and Out at 1600 Pennsylvania Avenue

How ominous as well as reminiscent was the sign hanging over CREEP's secret war room: "Winning in politics isn't everything, it's the *only* thing." For twenty-six years this had been Nixon's lodestar, guiding him in what was fast becoming a star-crossed political journey. With the

Watergate break-in safely obscured from the prying press by the machinations of his trusted counsel, John Dean, Nixon coasted to an easy and overwhelming victory in November, assuring him—or so he thought—his place in celebrating the two hundredth anniversary of America's birth.

He'd beaten George McGovern—or had he? Back in the spring of 1972, some wondered if Nixon wasn't seeing himself in the mirror when he attacked his Democratic rival: "McGovern is more clever and less principled than Goldwater and will say anything to win." Yet there was the press praising McGovern for promising to hold down military expenditures, "just as Ike had." And praising the South Dakota Senator as "a prairie populist," a man of decency, compassion, and old-fashioned goodness." Learning of these offenses from his news summaries, Nixon took the sword of the pen in hand and scribbled in the margins, "Knock this down!" "Knock that down!" No action was too draconian for this Patton reincarnate.

With the election over, the bombing intensified—the continuous, overwhelming rush of every plane that could get in the air over Hanoi and Haiphong, the massive Christmas bombing of both cities that prompted outrage even from our allies—here was the 2 x 4 across the head of North Vietnam, meant not only to get its attention but its capitulation. From McGovern came the comparison of this barbarism "to Hitler's campaign to exterminate the Jews." Nixon could scarcely believe his ears. Had McGovern taken leave of his senses? Or, wondered many, had Nixon?

Had McGovern access to *The Hitler of History* by John Lukacs, not published until 1997, he might have made the comparison more detailed. For here, in the Führer, was "a talented draftsman and painter," possessed of "considerable intellectual talents," including "an astonishing memory, capable of absorbing and retaining a remarkable array of technical details, that would sometimes amaze his generals during their conferences." Furthermore, he was "courageous" and "self-assured." Indeed, "on many occasions steadfast [and] loyal to his friends" and subordinates. In addition, he was "self-disciplined and modest in his physical wants." As for accomplishments, during his first six years, "he brought prosperity and confidence" to Germany . . . "one of the world's best-educated nations. . . ." There was no question that "he was a strong man," and no question but that "a fundamental source of his strength was hatred." Here, Lukacs might have added, was a hatred based in part on the repressive reparations exacted on the Germans by the Versailles treaty. There was also no question in the mind of Lukacs that Hitler was the greatest revolutionary of the twentieth century. He noted in passing that Hitler was an orator. More than that, his hatred-based oratory so inflamed the masses that they came to truly believe he was the savior of their fatherland. Few leaders of the century have displayed Hitler's persuasive skills as he transfixed the multitudes before him. It is uncanny how many similarities there are between Adolf Hitler and Richard Nixon: the astonishing memory, the remarkable self-discipline, modest physical wants, powerful oratory, and an amazing strength rooted in man's most ancient and pervasive motivation—the fear-hatred complex.

There is no little irony—or hypocrisy—in Nixon's swan song to his staff on the morning of his resignation. He'd written *Six Crises* twelve years earlier, a book with but a rare reference to his likes, much less his loves or affections, a book revealing nothing so much as his resentments and hostilities toward the enemies he found on all sides. And over the intervening dozen years, those resentments and hostilities—like the cancer of Watergate that Dean found metastasizing in the White House—were multiplying along with his enemies. In view of this, one is hard-pressed to explain Nixon's farewell to his staff on August 9, 1974, in which he counseled, ". . . never be petty; always remember, others may hate you, but those who hate you don't win unless you hate them, and then you destroy yourself." Or was Nixon simply turning himself inside out, revealing the demon that lay at the heart of his hubris, just as it lay in the heart of Hitler? If this was, in fact, just such a self-revelation, it was the antithesis of what he'd practiced and preached since a boy. Perhaps, as political demise beckoned, he found the inner torment bursting the bonds of a highly disciplined propriety. Perhaps the greatest similarity between Nixon and Hitler lay in their inability to fend off hubris. Both ended meteoric careers by falling on their political swords and, in Hitler's case, on his physical sword. To demonize either one, to call either one a fool or a madman, as Lukacs maintains, is to excuse them from responsibility for their actions—that fundamental basis of a civilized society.[8]

The main focus of Nixon's paranoia, from the Watergate break-in until his resignation, was the media—and especially the White House press corps disbelieving Ron Ziegler's denials of White House complicity, refusing to believe that "Tricky Dick" had no hand in the burglary. On

September 29, 1972, two weeks after Dean's assurance that he'd kept the lid on Watergate, the President learned that radical McGovern supporters had burned down Nixon's campaign headquarters in Phoenix. Yet Nixon refused to note it, much less hype it, to the press. His explanation to his aides: the media "don't want to use it." At which Colson complained, "They made more news out of the fact that we were exploiting it than the fact itself."

By the middle of October, the press, while quiescent—with the exception of *The Washington Post* on Watergate—was bird-dogging Chapin and Segretti, the tricksters who were being handsomely paid by White House "treasurer" Herbert Kalmbach. The press, Haldeman complained to Nixon, was linking "all these little strings" and weaving a web to catch the President and assorted flies. At that, Nixon again retorted that the press exercised "a double standard, so I just think we've got to brazen it through . . . if there were any fairness in the press, it would be different."

Three days later, Haldeman was again griping about the press's double standard. Here it was headlining Segretti's twenty-eight phone calls to the White House solely on the basis of "just tons of innuendo, implication, and they get away with it, and it doesn't bother them a bit." On the other hand, chimed in Nixon, "They won Pulitzer prizes for the thieves who took the stuff [Pentagon Papers] out of Kissinger's office. Now what the hell is the difference. . . ?"

By October 25, Nixon was looking like a shoo-in on election day—so, feeling his oats, he determined to "screw" the *Post* for their continuing exposure of Watergate: "They don't really realize how rough I can play. I've been such a nice guy around here a lot of times, and I always play . . . on a hard-hitting basis. But when I start, I will kill them . . . they've got a radio and television station, WTOP, a CBS outlet." Colson added they had one in Miami, as well as real estate. This wasn't the first time, nor would it be the last, that Nixon threatened to use the FCC to intimidate the media.

In another week, the *Post* virtually halted coverage of Watergate—a sure sign, Nixon believed, that his threats were working. He exulted to Ehrlichman: "And now they're finished." Ehrlichman then reminded Nixon of the station's upcoming application to the FCC for renewal. Nixon: ". . . John, how do you fire a silver bullet at the *Post* without them saying you're taking the FCC and trying to get after somebody?" With that, Ehrlichman reminded Nixon that Dean Burch, head of the FCC, was one of his own appointees. Certainly, he could get away with denying the renewal.

It was somehow fitting that on Washington's birthday, February 22, 1973, Nixon learned that the five burglars, plus Liddy and Hunt, had been convicted. Would this mollify either the Ervin Committee or the press? Never, complained Nixon to the ranking minority member of the committee, Howard Baker, because "the press is after a bigger fish." The President then sought Baker's intervention on his behalf by exclaiming, "The certain thing is to have no cover-up; that's the worst that can happen. . . ."

It wasn't just the press, but particularly the Eastern liberal press, that Nixon was convinced was conspiring to get him. The hardened skepticism, the reporters with their cynical questions, he complained to George Bush, Republican National Committee chairman, were "concentrated in New York and in Washington." He insisted that "When I go to Kansas City or Cleveland or wherever, they don't ask." Therefore, he concluded, Watergate "wasn't a national issue . . . it's the *funniest* damn thing . . . outside in Kansas . . . nobody cares about it."

That was March 20. The next day John Dean broke the startling news of a cancer "close to the presidency," metastasizing exponentially. Nixon ordered Dean to buy him some time, to "keep the cap on the bottle." It was reminiscent of Thomas More's *Utopia*, written in 1516—almost twenty years before he was beheaded for his religious and political obstreperousness. There, More wrote, ". . . it will fall out as in a complication of diseases, that by applying a remedy to one sore, you will provoke another, and that which removes the one ill symptom produces others. . . ."

The skepticism rooted in the Eastern liberal press may have appeared strange, even maddening, to the increasingly paranoid Nixon. Certainly it was no longer "the *funniest* damn thing. . . ." When it came to Chappaquiddick, the press treated Ted Kennedy with kid gloves. But for Nixon they became "that bunch of vultures." Haldeman wasn't at all sure they could "satisfy the vultures when you're the first piece of meat. . . ."

Distraught that, even after he'd fired Haldeman and Ehrlichman, Ervin's committee—far from being satiated, was closing in, Nixon's paranoia by May 8 was something to behold: "I think Dean's out to kill us. . . ." Always, it seemed, it was "us" when there was blame or punishment at stake, whereas it was "The President" when there was credit or reward at stake. Of Dean, Nixon further complained to Alexander Haig, ". . . He's got a lot of cards. He's got a goddamn safe full of documents . . . this man's a consummate liar . . . is the country all crazy? Is it all crazy?" With that, Nixon mounted his soapbox. "Goddamn it . . . Haldeman must never lie, never. Ehrlichman must never lie. Nobody must lie." Ostensibly agreeing with the truthful Dean, Nixon roared. *"Goddamn it, this Goddamn thing has got to be brought out!"* So shouted the commander in chief as he pounded the table. "The President is not in it, was never in it. I've been trying to keep this son-of-a-bitch—well, it's unbelievable."

Nixon then ordered Haig, his new chief of staff, to enlist John Connally in the fight against Dean: "There's nothing more important to this country that he [Connally] could do than this, mash this son-of-a-bitch Dean . . . say, for Christ's sake, here it is, this goddamn Dean out here attacking the presidency. . . ." There were Agnew, Connally, and "those [Republican] assholes in the Senate," none of them rushing to his defense. "Good God," he told Haig, "I've got to stay out of this, Al. I mean, the thing—as you know, we've got to make some grave, very grave decisions, and I must not be, and you either, consumed by this son-of-a-bitch god-damn thing."

Haldeman was out and Haig was in, urging the President to enlist Connally to emphasize that the media was being hypercritical of Nixon in its claim that "we're in the process of inhibiting justice and truth and are involved in an orgy of very irresponsible press activity." Nixon was adamant, responding that it was not his administration that had been irre-sponsible but the media, playing "this up as being the biggest goddamn crisis. . . ." On the phone the next day, Haldeman told Nixon, ". . . I read the papers thoroughly and before I start in the morning. I just say to myself, there's going to be another pile of shit in here. . . ." To which Nixon responded by asking if Haldeman had read the latest damning *New York Times* editorial, adding his own editorial comment: "Screw it!" When Haldeman acknowledged "they got some of us out," Nixon assured him the media would settle for nothing less than destroying the presidency by insisting on "all this crap about the President should resign. . . ."[9]

That the "vultures" in the press were circling closer and closer to Nixon's high-priced flesh became evident when the President exclaimed to Ziegler on May 11: "The press has been hysterical, engaging in an orgy . . . an emotional trauma beyond belief . . . ten to fifteen minutes every night." And in all of this, Nixon bragged, ". . . I haven't given them a goddamn inch." The President was Mister Unflappable, even though, Nixon added, he knew it wasn't "really Haldeman and Ehrlichman and Mitchell, Stans and our campaign they're after." Nor, Nixon contended, was it even his administration they were after, but rather "what I stand for . . . a hard-line foreign policy, a hard-line policy of law and order..."

Incredibly, Nixon was now convinced that it wasn't Watergate—the break-in or the cover-up—but rather his "hard-line" policies that had provoked the animosity of the press. Soaring to new heights of fancy, Nixon contended, ". . . at this present time in world history, the United States has the opportunity either if you win or lose, the greatest chance that history has ever had to build a structure of peace in the world. . . ." And who would build such a structure? "*Only us*. And I'm the only man that can do it." Therefore, it was obvious that "in this larger battle where the press was just trying to kill the President . . . we must not let them do [it]." Of such grandiloquent self-importance is the Kingdom of Hubris built.

By May 14, Nixon was vowing to Rose Mary Woods, "they may kill me in the press, but they will never kill me in mind. I'm going to fight those bastards to the end." When Woods sympathized, "It's going to be very hard," Nixon responded by invoking Providence itself: "That's why we have been brought into this world." At this, Woods tried to console her boss, "God brings the hardest problems to the strongest men." Little wonder that Woods was considered to be the fifth member of the Nixon family!

Nixon *would* be strong—indeed, one of "the strongest men." Later that day, he raged against the press for being "obsessed" with Watergate. Therefore, vowed this international statesman, the only man who could bring lasting peace on earth, "Screw them! Screw them! It'll be our day . . . we're going to treat them with the contempt they deserve . . . have no illusions. These assholes are out to destroy us." Now the media was making a big deal out of the administration's "national security taps." Kennedy had 102 such wiretaps in place, Johnson 88, and Nixon only 75. But somehow of those *other* presidential taps the records had been "destroyed or can't be found." Attorney General Ruckelshaus had searched the FBI records in vain. Therefore, said the President, ". . . they're lying to protect their ass . . . I didn't know the fucking records were here, no. Nobody's ever told me a goddamn thing about the records." Yet Nixon was certain that his two predecessors had done "five times as much" tapping as he had.

Soon Connally was assuring the President that ". . . if it hadn't been a

Watergate project, it would have been something else because it was almost a rebellion in the town among the press . . . [which] is going to destroy themselves if they keep on because they're going to overplay this thing." Then Connally gave Nixon some advice, as specious as his previous advice had been obsequious: ". . . you have to restructure your staff to present a new persona."

Nixon, it appeared, needed far more than a new persona, new judges, new aides, and new arguments. As the weeks passed and his paranoia deepened, the President became ever more dependent on sycophants like Connally, Ziegler, and Haig. There was Haig assuring Nixon, "It's a hell of a lot deeper than Watergate or the Republican Party or you. . . . They [the press} don't want the right principles to survive in this country. You happen to represent that. That's just too much for them. . . . The power of your accomplishments in the past and ahead are [sic] going to swamp any of these other difficulties."

It was June 13, 1973, that the White House tapes revealed his last ringing endorsement of the press: ". . . as far as this press corps, they can go to hell." But it wasn't reporters that would be banished to Nixon's hell, for they were enjoying a feeding frenzy that stopped only when the now-former President boarded his helicopter for California. As he did so, there were some who suspected Nixon was suffering in his own hell of full-blown paranoia. John Osborne made note of Nixon's relations with the press over the last few months of his presidency: "There was a feeling that he might go bats in front of them at any time." His doctor sensed in Nixon "a death wish," while his son-in-law, David Eisenhower, was afraid that he'd take his own life. Haig, too, was concerned that Nixon might commit suicide. In one conversation during his last week in office, Nixon said to the White House Chief of Staff, "You fellows, in your business [the Army] . . . you have a way of handling problems like this. Somebody leaves a pistol in the drawer." Then, as Haig waited, wondering, Nixon added sadly, "I don't have a pistol." So worried was Haig that he ordered no pills should be given to the President, and that those Nixon already had—especially sleeping pills and tranquilizers—be taken from him. Haig also told special counsel Fred Buzhardt that he was using precautions to make sure that the Watergate debacle didn't end in Nixon's physical self-immolation.[10]

On the night of August 8, 1974—just before giving his resignation announcement to the nation—one aide described Nixon as ". . . overcome by tremendous depression at seeing everything lost in defeat. . . . He couldn't hold himself together; he had to be helped to a chair."

In Nixon's 1977 interview with David Frost he said he had to fight a war at home as well as in Vietnam. The one at home consisted of a "five-front war." He listed four: the media, the Ervin Committee, the special prosecutor's staff, and the staff of the Senate Judiciary Committee, who were all stacked against him. Given the emergency powers coincident with a war, Nixon figured, his saying "things that were not true" was fully justified. Was he "paranoiac," as he put it? "At . . . times, yes, I get angry at people." But, he reasoned, "there's a love-hate relationship in all of us. And I just hope that when they tote them all up before you go to St. Peter's or the other way down, that maybe the . . . ledger's going to come out reasonably well in that respect. . . ." Finally he came to the the fifth of his five-front war: the war protesters. He fully approved Kissinger's vow to destroy the man who leaked the 1969 Cambodian bombing to the press. "Why," Nixon asked, "do we feel this way? . . . because the people on the other side were hypocritical. They were sanctimonious." They were not intending to prolong the war, he added, but because of their dissent, the war lasted one or two years longer than it otherwise would have. "Call it paranoia," Nixon rationalized, "but paranoia for peace isn't bad."

Just as surely as Watergate and its grotesque aftermath followed from Nixon's paranoia, so do isolation and immolation—our last two steps in the path of hubris—follow from paranoia. Nixon's paranoia marked the beginning of payback time. He was getting just what he deserved.[11] The two remaining chapters will detail more fully the comeuppance of Richard Nixon.

CHAPTER 12

ISOLATION

I am casting about me to find someone who will help to enliven the solitude which surrounds the Presidency. The unfortunate incumbent of that office is the most isolated man in America.

— James A. Garfield

LYNDON JOHNSON

Here at the crowning point of my life, when I need people's help, I haven't even got the loyal here—Ken O'Donnell and Larry O'Brien, my Attorney General [RFK]. . . . People I think have mistaken judgment. They think I want great power. And what I want is a great solace—and a little love. That's all I want.

— Lyndon Johnson August 25, 1964

Isolation in the White House

Is isolation inevitable for a president? Henry Kissinger seemed to think so, contending that presidential advisers must have compassion for the isolation and responsibilities of his position and will not willfully add to his psychological burdens.

Some of our presidents seemed to agree that isolation was the lot of the incumbent. One after the other found that—for all its honor, for all those at their beck and call, for all the distinguished visitors—the presidency was a lonely place indeed.

At Wilson's inauguration on March 4, 1913, his predecessor, Taft, said he was "glad to be going—this is the loneliest place in the world." Wilson, too, found it lonely at the top: "I never dreamed such loneliness and isolation of the heart possible. . . . " Determined to forge the peace treaty with Germany by himself, Wilson found Walter Lippmann and others resigning from the American delegation. The President complained, "The more I succeed in directing things the more I am depended on for leadership and expected to do everything, make all parts straight and carry every plan to its completion." Though with other stalwarts—such as William Bullitt, Herbert Hoover, and John Maynard Keynes—at his side during the peace talks in

Paris, Wilson determined to go it alone.[1] Already he'd managed to alienate himself from T.R., who called him, "that infernal skunk in the White House," and from Taft, who felt "certain that [Wilson] would not recognize a generous impulse if he met it on the street." If Wilson could not share responsibility with his own aides, how could he possibly share responsibility with his leading Republican critic in the Senate, Henry Cabot Lodge? If Wilson found the going rough with his counterparts Lloyd-George and Clemenceau in Paris, he found it even rougher when he tried convincing the Senate to endorse the Versailles treaty. In the end, crisscrossing the nation to carry his appeal for the League of Nations directly to the voters, Wilson contracted pneumonia and died, leaving the League virtually toothless and in limbo.

It appears that Wilson, contrary to Taft, had generous impulses; he was intent on providing American financial help for prostrate Europe, such as the United States developed in the Marshall Plan after World War II. But again he ran into a stone wall in the Senate. Another world war was not only inevitable, as Wilson predicted if the League were not in place—but, in retrospect, was simply an extension of World War I.

Wilson's successor as a war president, TR's cousin, Franklin, was as much an extrovert as Wilson was an introvert. Yet for all his gregariousness, FDR complained: "It's a terrible thing to look over your shoulder when you are trying to lead—and find no one there."

Another extrovert in the White House, Eisenhower, compared presidential decision-making with "the nakedness of the battlefield when the soldier is all alone in the smoke and the clamor and the terror of the war. . . ." For in those times of decision, "one man must conscientiously, deliberately, prayerfully scrutinize every argument, every proposal, every prediction, every alternative, every probable outcome of his action and then—all alone—make a decision."[2]

This idea of the presidency, however, "with its 'awesome' responsibilities [as] the loneliest job in the world," Schlesinger ridiculed as "one of the great myths of American political folklore. No one," he explained, "could see a greater variety of people than the President or consult a wider range of opinion or tap more diversified sources of knowledge." To illustrate the failure to do so, he cited JFK in the Bay of Pigs disaster. Refusing what Schlesinger described as " uninhibited debate in advance of major decisions," Kennedy made a colossal blunder, "a salutary if costly lesson in the perils of presidential isolation."

Lyndon the Lonely

Which brings us to Lyndon Johnson. While Kennedy wore the country's mask, declared De Gaulle at his funeral in 1963, Johnson wore its real face.

From his boyhood, Schlesinger has noted, Johnson could not abide being alone. In college Lyndon would go to great lengths to make sure he was surrounded by friends. One classmate recalled, "There was never anyone that he wasn't friendly to. I don't care who it was." This testimony must have come from a good friend, for others found his braggadocio, his obsequiousness to his superiors, and his tyranny over subordinates so offensive as to alienate him from most people. As gregarious as he was by nature, loneliness was especially painful. When Lyndon was about to leave his teaching psition in Cotulla to go back for additional courses at San Marcos, he contacted roommate "Boody" Johnson, anxious that his friend would be there when he returned. Recalled Boody: "He was very lonely down there in Cotulla. *Very* lonely." There in the local cafe a waitress, Marthabelle Whitten, recalled that he was "always the life of the party." But others noticed that Lyndon occasionally would wander alone up the rise in back of town—a tall, skinny, awkward figure staring off into the endless, empty spaces outside of Cotulla.

As an aide to Kleberg, Kearns noted, Lyndon used to "roam the corridors looking for people to talk to, persuade, and learn from"—for loneliness was not so much a state of mind as the absence of people. "He could not bear to be by himself, not for an evening or for an hour." Ever the mimic, the raconteur, Lyndon enjoyed few things more as a Washington neophyte than "sitting on the floor in the middle of a circle, the center of attention." Recalled a co-worker, "He would keep us in stitches for hours. He was great company." That Johnson was driven, there can be no doubt. Nor can there be doubt that, among the major forces driving him, such as hidden terrors and gnawing insecurities, was the haunting fear of loneliness. Not only had this been expressed in Cotulla, but later when he taught in Houston. So utterly dependent was Lyndon on his mother that he wrote her, his sister Rebekah noted, "whole *stacks* of . . . letters" during the year he was there. Told that Lyndon had gained the popularity as a teacher that he'd never achieved as a student, his sister was surprised, recounting, "Lyndon was very lonely in Houston. Quite downhearted and blue."[3]

Johnson craved attention because he craved power, and he saw that the first led to the second. Even as a boy he would stop at nothing to be noticed. Did his mother try teaching him good manners at the table? Sam Houston recalled his older brother eating "with loud, slurping noises, violently cramming huge spoonfuls of food into his mouth" until Rebekah would burst into tears and order Lyndon from the table. Did his father try teaching him to respect the property of others, and not use Sam's shaving mug and ivory-handled straight razor? Straight to them would Lyndon go when Sam wasn't looking. Did Sam instruct Lyndon never to take his car without permission? It was no use. Supposedly in bed and asleep, Lyndon would crawl out the window, make for the car, and take it on a joyride with his envious pals. Did Rebekah want him in college? Lyndon balked and refused to go until he'd spent a fruitless year in California and more months with a highway crew in Texas. It wasn't just that he defied anybody telling him what to do; it was also that by displaying his fierce independence, he would attract the attention and envy of his peers.

When at last in politics for himself, Lyndon continued his independent streak—except for those who obviously could help him, like Rayburn, FDR, and the Brown brothers—until at last he entered the White House. Within three months, he was proclaiming the presidency to be "the one place where a petty temper and a narrow view can never reside." Yet ironically, it was just these two traits, his temper with his aides and his narrow view on Vietnam, that led to his increasing isolation.

Not content with a mere victory in the 1964 election, Johnson insisted that his landslide triumph meant the voters not only *liked* him but *loved* him. As he later remarked to Kearns, there were "millions upon millions of people, each one marking my name on their ballot, each one wanting me as their President. . . . For the first time in my life I truly felt loved by the American people." Never mind that, in all probability, the majority of his votes came from those believing they were choosing the lesser of two evils. FDR, his mentor, also craved attention and praise; but Roosevelt never went so far as to interpret pulling a lever or writing a name as a token of esteem—much less affection.

The mind tends to play tricks on those with power. Lord Acton talked of power tending to corrupt and absolute power as corrupting absolutely, while John Adams wrote of the "delirious tyranny" of absolute power. No wonder, then, that Madison wrote, "All power in human hands is liable to be abused." Teddy Roosevelt found that feeling "one's hand guiding great machinery" was intoxicating. The seductiveness of power was all that more persuasive, Coolidge wrote, when a president lives "in an artificial atmosphere of adulation and exaltation." He added, "sooner or later" presidential judgment is so impaired that carelessness and arrogance result. As Kennedy put it, "In the past, those who foolishly sought power by riding the back of the tiger ended up inside." Kennedy, had he ability to look ahead as well as behind, would have seen his two successors not only ending up inside the tiger, but—much worse—of opening a Pandora's box that would affect millions. It was perhaps William Henry Harrison, among our presidents, who most clearly saw the handwriting on the wall, forecasting doom for Johnson and Nixon 135 years later. "There is nothing more corrupting, nothing more destructive . . . [than] the man who, in the beginning of . . . a career, might shudder at the idea of taking away the life of a fellow-being, [yet] might soon have his conscience so scarred by the repetition of crime, that the agonies of his murdered victims become music to his soul . . . history is full of such examples."[4]

Johnson's mind played fantastical tricks on him as he became addicted to the heroin of power, craving the regular fix of continual approval and praise. When the fix was not forthcoming, Lyndon found himself in the bowels of depression.

A further trait that would rattle Johnson's cage was his obsession with simplistics. It was not, he declared, *doing* what was right, but simply *knowing* what was right. Emphasizing doing versus knowing clearly illustrates the either/or simplistics of his thinking. Just as democracy implies an open society, so does an open society imply a search—not for *right* answers, but *best* answers. Such answers are not only those that, in retrospect, seem to have worked best with a given problem, but those that arose from the kind of unfettered debate that Schlesinger found missing prior to the decision on the Bay of Pigs invasion. Whatever else characterizes the best decision, it is that decision that best represents the consensus of those participating in the discussion. For to implement the decision requires that all, or as many as time will allow, will have input. Every leader understands that it is one thing to draft a policy, but it is something else again to implement it. As Johnson and Nixon surely came to understand, the root of the protest by young people was not simply their fear of becoming casualties of war, but that they themselves had no part in the decision to wage war. The protesters might be led to slaughter, but they were determined not to go as sheep. Not only did these two presidents prevent the participation by the electorate in the form of a national referendum, they prosecuted the war without as much as notifying the representatives of the electorate sitting in Congress.

Whereas "best" implies consensus, reached invariably through compromise, "right" tends to frustrate the compromise necessary for consensus—because it implies that all other answers are necessarily wrong. Right answers are born of authoritarian institutions, best answers of democratic institutions. If Kennedy could be faulted for "groupthink," in the Bay of Pigs decision making, Johnson could be much more faulted for Vietnam decision-making—and with immeasurably worse consequences.

Beyond Criticism, Beyond Hope

We noted in chapter one that Johnson was extremely deferential in assuming the office of the presidency. He listened to one and all, even to the JFK aides who'd helped make his life miserable as Vice-President. He not only listened, but, as often as not, heeded them. But once in possession of a mandate from Congress to wage war, and of a mandate from the electorate to do anything else he saw fit, he no longer needed others' advice—especially contrarians such as George Ball and John Kenneth Galbraith.

By increasingly restricting those he would heed to only those who agreed, Johnson became not only a dictator but a tyrant in the White House—and a lonely tyrant at that, as one aide after another fled ship. What he did with his aides he did with the White House press corps and with the Congress, until, in one of the classic ironies of his presidency, Johnson became as oppressive as the Communists he so violently opposed.

Is it little wonder that, of the top ten aides by his side when he entered the Oval Office, only three remained when he turned it over to Richard Nixon? One of the three—and perhaps the most diligent understudy of Johnson's obsequiousness—was Walt Rostow. Always and everywhere, it seemed, Rostow was at the ready to assure LBJ that he was "right" in his foreign policy, that he possessed that dogged courage of a Churchill in facing down his opponents at home and abroad, and that history would acclaim him for his greatness. It was this same Walt Rostow whom JFK had once described as having ten ideas, nine of which would lead to disaster. Yet it was Rostow—"Rasputin," as another aide labeled him—who Johnson praised as "my goddamn intellectual." When Mac Bundy departed in 1966, it was Rostow who took his place as National Security Adviser. He not only sounded the alarm on affairs affecting the nation's security, but made certain by his gatekeeping at the Oval Office that his President would not be exposed to bad news. Thus did Rostow contribute ominously to isolating Johnson from the very criticism that might have rescued his presidency.

Moving beyond criticism, Johnson moved beyond hope. It was he who consented, even encouraged, Rostow to become his Chief of Staff. When other top aides—such as Ball, Moyers, Bundy, McNamara, and Clifford—turned against the war, it was Rostow who tried his best to mute, if not neutralize, the subversion.

Still, Rostow and the two others who remained faithful to the end could not keep LBJ's approval rating from plunging to 32 percent, the lowest since Truman. By this time, Goldman noted, Johnson saw himself as "the lonely, traduced figure, limned against history, resolutely doing right, grimly awaiting the verdict of the future." To White House visitors, Johnson would recite the military honor roll. There was Washington at Valley Forge, Madison in the besieged capital during the war of 1812, Lincoln at Gettysburg, Wilson at Paris, FDR in World War II, Truman in Korea, and Kennedy in the Cuban Missile Crisis. All stood tall, defying the enemy, determined to "pay any price" for the blessings of liberty. Johnson left it to his visitors to fill in the latest of these military giants. For here, in their very midst, was a hero equal to any of them—courageously defying the army of nay-sayers, confident that, as Rostow put it to Columbia professor Henry Graff in January 1968, "History will salute us!" But after his retirement, Johnson made it clear to his official biographer, Doris Kearns, that there were to be no slip-ups, and that her account was to be properly sanitized. "Goddamn it," he exploded after reading what she'd written, "I can't say this." There was a barbed comment on Wilbur Mills, head of the House Ways and Means Committee, who'd balked at Johnson's calling for a tax increase in 1968. "Get it out right now," Johnson ordered, "He may be Speaker of the House someday. And for Christ's sake, get that vulgar language of mine out of there. What do you think this is, the tale of an uneducated cowboy? It's a presidential memoir, damnit, and I've got to come out looking like a statesman, not some backwoods politician."

Here, by 1968, was the lonely, twentieth-century Elijah, wallowing in self-pity, and insisting that, of all God's people, he alone remained faithful.

Johnson entered the White House, Theodore White wrote, "one of the most friendless" of all public men, lacking most conspicuously those qualities that endeared so many to Kennedy: trust, friendship, even love. Johnson also lacked reflection, contemplation, and the ability to look either behind the present or ahead of it. He was, as are many primitive peoples, stuck to the bottom of the abstraction ladder. As a result, he was unable to reflect on the past or peer into the future. In a grim sense, he was lost. For one who is lost knows neither from whence he comes, or he could retrace his steps—nor where he is going, or he would soon find himself. Glued to the present, Lyndon was lost. Riding the helicopter to the White House from Andrews Air Force Base, White noted that "Johnson hates to be alone—his temper is not one of solitary contemplation." En route, he was engrossed, pumping information from McNamara, Ball, and Bundy. Was there any issue, he wanted to know, any urgent problem that would require his attention in the next twenty-four hours?[5] That was as far ahead as he cared to look.

Always, it seemed, Lyndon had to have others around him, whether seated on the toilet, or lying abed at night. It seemed he couldn't fall asleep without somebody in the room with him. If Lady Bird wasn't there, he'd insist on an aide being close by. Horace Busby recalled sitting with him as, exhausted, eyes sunk deep in their sockets, skin a sickly pallor, Johnson tossed and turned fitfully. Half asleep, he'd awake with a start. "Bus, are you still there?" His excuse for not wanting to be alone: "I don't like to sleep alone ever since my heart attack."

LBJ "was like a plant reaching out for water," Humphrey recalled. "His whole demeanor was one great big long reach. If you weren't there, he'd just reach a little further to get you. And if he couldn't get you physically, he'd pick up the phone and get you. And if he couldn't get you that way, he'd send an airplane and get you. He'd get you." Even, it seemed, when he was dead, "he'd get you." In 1973, speech writer Harry Middleton, standing next to the casket in which Johnson was lying in state, carefully counted those who walked by. Why, Middleton was asked, was he doing such a thing? "Because," he replied, "I have a feeling LBJ is going to ask me, someday, how many paid their respects."

By 1968, Johnson, with the help of Rostow, had managed to isolate himself in the White House, a prisoner of his own terrors—hyped by a Secret Service that took every hint of a threat seriously, which even saw threats in the young war protesters, who were actually far more hopeless than hazardous. Johnson was bewildered bythe protest movement: "I just don't understand those young people. Don't they realize I'm really one of them? I always hated cops when I was a kid, and just like them I dropped out of school and took off for California. I'm not some conformist, middle-class personality. I could never be bureaucratized."⁶ Johnson never could grasp the idea that young people regarded rightly his escalations of the war as reckless—a war for which, even under threat of imprisonment, they were unwilling to lay down their lives. So they came to deplore Johnson and to detest his policy of attrition, while he became more and more isolated from their viewpoint and even from reality.

As the chorus of opposition rose, Johnson stuffed his fingers in his ears and pulled down the window blinds so he'd neither hear the scatological chants and subversive ballads, nor see the obscene placards and desecrated flags. Luci, whose husband was serving in Vietnam, recounted walking into her father's room some nights when he'd be watching the news. "We'd just go and sit with him. He really seemed to like to have your companionship if you never said a word. Boy, you'd better know when not to say a word. He never said anything and he never needed to if you knew him, but he had looks that were like laser beams. And he'd be looking at the TV set and they'd be giving reports on fatalities that day and it was as if you were looking at a man who had a knife thrust into the pit of his stomach and turned over and over and over. He just physically looked like he was in agony." There he would sit, plagued by questions he couldn't answer, doubts he couldn't erase, insecurities he couldn't fathom.

Far from Dr. Johnson's "last refuge of scoundrels," patriotism was close to the top in Lyndon's reckoning of values. As a schoolboy he'd recited, "I have seen the glory of art and architecture. I have seen the sunrise on Mount Blanc. But the most beautiful vision that these eyes have beheld was the flag of my country in a foreign land." Later, as President, Johnson would mount a platform, point to Old Glory and shout, "Where American citizens go, that flag goes with them to protect them."

And yet here were these war protesters desecrating that very flag, wearing it on their chests, on their hands, even on their backsides! By 1968, this oversized Texan with the oversized ego was hunkering down in the oversized White House, sitting in his oversized chair in the Oval Office, fuming and fretting over the misery of his loneliness, made all that more insufferable for his expansive gregariousness. Some called his brand of patriotism "cornball jingoism." But Johnson called it the blessing of the Almighty on these, his chosen people.

In the end, Reedy concluded, Johnson remained a lonely, isolated President "largely because everything and everybody he always used to further his own goals and to feather his own nest." As he listened to fewer and fewer, deferred to even fewer of those, Johnson found himself, in the end, almost totally alone. He confided to Kearns in his retirement, "I was always very lonely."[7] Which is to be interpreted, "no matter how often and how many were the assurances of my greatness, they were never enough." Lyndon Baines Johnson was a towering egomaniac and an insecure cowpoke, a detestable sycophant and a raging bully, a clever, sly politician and a bumbling, fumbling worrywart—all rolled into one.

Still ahead is the final chapter in this tale of a tragic President, who was drawn like a moth to the flame that would immolate him.

RICHARD NIXON

God will give you the strength to take this terrible . . . burden of the presidency .
. . the awful loneliness.

— Rose Mary Woods to Nixon, June 12, 1973

. . . Nixon was really the most unisolated President in history . . . our staffing sys-
tem gave him the opportunity to control his time and his access to his advisers he
knew would be most useful.

— H.R. Haldeman, *Ends of Power*, 1978

No Buddy-Buddy Boy

If there was any American constitutionally unfit to be a politician,
much less to occupy the highest office in the land, it was the introvert, the
loner, the furtive Richard Nixon. As Helen Thomas, UPI reporter, later put
it, "Nixon is and always has been a private man—shy, reserved, isolated."
Nixon's cousin, Merle West, recalled him as a boy, secluding himself in a
room above his garage, there to read, there to study, there to dream, away
from other youngsters playing ball or otherwise engaged in the games
children play.

Insecure—pathetically insecure—Nixon grew up suspecting that few,
if anybody, really liked him. Never did it seem to occur to him that friendship was a reciprocal arrangement, that to win friends he had to be a
friend, to extend himself to others, to listen to others, to empathize with
others. Deadly serious, Nixon forever obeyed—even as Pat would obey—
the call of duty.

Dick had little time for anybody else, recalled brother Don, but "used to go up into the bell tower [of the church they'd converted into a store], which was the store's office, to study by himself at night." And it wasn't just the evening, or until midnight that he'd be studying. "Many's the time," Don recounted, "the delivery man who came before dawn would find [Dick] with his light still on, after studying all night." Outside, Dick was fond of lying on the grass and daydreaming. When walking along a sidewalk, he'd be so engrossed in his own thoughts that he'd pass people without seeing them, much less greeting them or listening to them. When it came to family picnics, Don could count on finding Dick "off by himself." When others joined them for the picnics, Dick always insisted on riding in a car "with friends or members of his family," Don remembered, "because we know he doesn't want to waste time talking. He can't stand small talk."

Dick grew up loving mankind, but not able to stand people. He learned to love to talk—when he had an audience of upturned faces before him. But rarely did Don remember Dick talking with customers in the family store. Indeed, his entire boyhood seemed to constitute an embarrassment to him. Garry Wills pointed out that in 1968, when Nixon returned to his birthplace at Yorba Linda—the small, white clapboard house that father Frank had built with his own hands—he "scuffed the floor in embarrassment, ducked his head dutifully into this hole and that corner as if each were a trap, and left like one released." As his PR man in 1960, Roger Ailes found him not only "dull," but "a bore, a pain in the ass," one "who was forty-two years old the day he was born."[1] He not only preferred people at arm's length, he preferred them out in left field.

Nixon, of course, always had a reason—however strained, however distorted—for behavior not quite normal. In a 1990 interview he couldn't recall an occasion when his mother told him, "I love you." "This," he explained, "she considered to be very private and very sacred." One is left to wonder if mother and son *ever* shared "very private" or "very sacred" moments together. Like mother, like son, in this case, for Pat was hard-pressed to remember her husband ever saying, "I love you." It was as if love, or at least the expression of that love, was one of the seven deadly sins. In the same 1990 interview he noted, "I don't say, 'God bless you,' 'I love you,' and the rest . . . that's just the way I was raised. . . ." So fearful was Nixon of appearing effusive that he dared not show affection, even to his family. Leaving San Clemente for the capital one day, his good-bye to

Tricia came, she recounted, "as close to outward emotion as he ever does when he said how much it meant to him for us to be in California with him." Nixon looked with contempt on Johnson's "treatment"—his bear-hugging and excessive sentimentality—as "buddy-buddy" baloney.

One would think four years in the Navy would do something for "Nick"—his moniker with fellow officers—that college, law school, and a stint at private practice hadn't seemed to do. There he was, evening after evening, in the poker games, a welcome respite from what he called "the oppressive monotony" of a "lonely war . . . filled with seemingly interminable periods of waiting." To fill the hours, Nixon would later remember, he "devoured the copies of *Life* magazine . . . read and reread [his] old illustrated Bible . . . [and] wrote to Pat every day during the fourteen months [he] was away." Finally, "in the intense loneliness and boredom of the South Pacific," he took to the game he mastered, playing "with a true poker face." He appeared to possess a congenital inability to disclose himself to others; to do so would be a gross violation of his inner sanctity.

A fellow officer saw Nixon as "a solitary type, a loner . . . afraid of being involved with anyone, even as a friend, because then he would have to reveal something of himself." In life, as in poker, he invariably kept his cards close to his chest. Another officer saw Nixon as never able or willing to maintain a friendship after his original reason for its existence had passed. A friend was a friend because the person could be of help to Nixon; but once no longer of any use, the friend was discarded. Here was the basic root of Nixon's exploitation of others, and the basic root of his isolation. It is of more than passing interest that not one person from Nixon's youth, through college, law school, and the Navy, ever played a significant role in his political rise. These relationships he regarded as obsolete, as excess baggage, as encumbrances that could shackle him in his race for the White House. Once he'd set his sights on 1600 Pennsylvania Avenue, there was no turning back.[2]

A Heartbeat from the Oval Office

As Vice-President, not only was Nixon a loner by instinct, but he was kept at arm's length by those who feared his slashing attacks. Ike himself kept his distance for eight years. He rarely invited Nixon to golf with him or to use the White House swimming pool, and never invited the Vice-President to his family living quarters in the White House or inside his

Gettysburg farm. Though Nixon chalked up these snubs to Ike's natural aloofness, most of his aides and friends found the General's easy smile a sure sign of his congeniality. He was far from the cold fish that so many discovered in the Vice-President. Undoubtedly Pat's unflagging generosity of spirit, especially on overseas trips, did much to offset Nixon's obtuseness, his abrasiveness, his furtiveness.

Pat could help to neutralize her obnoxious husband in their trips abroad, but at home, except during campaigns, she insisted on being with her children as much as possible—especially since Dick was even less a dutiful father than a caring husband. As President, Eisenhower needed the support of Democrats and Independents to stay afloat. But at campaign time, Ike appreciated the verbal thunderbolts that Jove Nixon would hurl at the Democrats from what he was confident was the pristine atmosphere of Olympus. Yet once the campaign ended, Ike would extend a hand to the fallen foe, while Nixon seemed to relish kicking the fellow when he was down. This did little to endear him to Ike or anybody else.

In the fall of 1954 Nixon crisscrossed the country on behalf of Republican congressional candidates, and was virtually alone in doing so. Just how alone he was, and wanted to be, can be seen in a layover at a hotel because of inclement weather. Nixon's staff and accompanying press took to the hotel pool for a swim. Suddenly there was Nixon, diving in, swimming several laps, then emerging to grab his towel and make off for his room. Not a word did he speak; not once did he give so much as a nod of recognition to anyone. It was just this sort of aloofness and obtuseness, coupled with his public swashbuckling, that prompted the Duke faculty to vote against conferring on him an honorary degree, and the president at Whittier College to call for two reception lines following Nixon's commencement address—one for those unwilling to shake his hand.

His was efficiency, albeit a cold efficiency. In his 1956 campaign, Nixon won plaudits from TV newscaster David Brinkley. He wrote Leonard Hall, RNC chairman, "I've just spent nine days scurrying around the country on the Dick Nixon special. And in my fifteen years of covering presidential politics and candidates on trains, planes, cars, buses, and helicopters, this is the best operation I've ever seen." As for Nixon himself, he "is a splendid campaigner." This despite the fact that, apart from strictly business events, and with the exception of Pat, he was always alone.

There was but one person, apart from his wife with whom Nixon seemed to relax and to let his hair down: Bebe Rebozo. Ever the congenial and generous host, Rebozo knew when to use his mouth, when to use his ears, and when to open his wallet. Whatever the occasion—fishing, swimming, golf, or just relaxing over a drink, Rebozo was always there, ready to listen, ready to pick up the tab. And he could always be counted on not to betray confidences. With a friend like that, it was no surprise that Nixon wrote him in 1952, "We have put your name at the top of the list for the Inauguration ceremonies." One of Rebozo's natural talents was his reticence, especially his reluctance to challenge Nixon in any of what must have been many outlandish statements. Bebe just seemed to blend in with the rest of the furniture, so much so that one mutual acquaintance noted, "Nixon likes to be alone, and with Bebe along, he is." As Vice-President, Nixon opened up more than usual to the sympathetic journalist, Stewart Alsop. Not only was any "major public figure [necessarily] a lonely man [but a] President very much more so." In his job, Nixon insisted, he simply couldn't "enjoy the luxury of intimate personal friendship." He couldn't "confide absolutely in anyone." Personal plans, feelings— these were a matter of "keeping [his] own counsel."

Then Nixon revealed a bit more of himself. Yes, he recognized there was an image of him as "cold or withdrawn." But, of course, that was "false." He was just "fundamentally relatively shy," and when he met people, he sought out "the shy ones." In the last analysis, he simply couldn't "really let [his] hair down with anyone . . . not . . . with old friends . . . not even with family."[3]

By early 1958, Nixon was planning for his run for the presidency two years later. Cherishing the solitude he needed to contemplate his future, he found no more relaxing spot than Rebozo's home in Key Biscayne, Florida. There he swam, he fished, but mainly he walked the beach, alone. Yes, Bebe was around if needed, but he could also disappear when Nixon was given to contemplation: planning, brooding, meditating. For Nixon seemed never so confortable as when he was alone, solitude his companion, only himself to argue with. No politician ever enjoyed his own company more than he. No insolent reporters, no bureaucratic foul-ups, no back-talk, no hassle—it was just what the doctor ordered for this most reclusive of public men. Indeed, by 1960, surrounded by campaign aides, supporters, and reporters, Nixon was, as Ambrose put it, "one of the loneliest men in the United States. He was never close enough to any of his staff—regardless of their dedication—to confide in them, and would not tolerate any of them in the studio when he was broadcasting. In addition, though as president of the Senate he knew every senator on a first-name basis, and appeared to get along well with most of them, none were close friends." In an interview with Joseph Alsop, Nixon confessed, "In my job, you can't afford to have friends; you can never afford to open yourself up." He was, in short, his own man, the apotheosis of Emerson's classic essay, "Self-Reliance." So reliant on himself had Nixon become, so independent of any and all who would advise him—including Eisenhower—that he bungled his campaign unmercifully.

Ike's visit to Nixon at Walter Reed Hospital after the collision of his knee against the car door was revealing. Afterward Ike told Ann Whitman, his secretary, "There was some lack of warmth." Ike also observed that Nixon had few personal friends, something he couldn't understand; for how could a man live without friends? Whitman gave part of the answer in her diary as she compared the two men. "The President is a man of integrity and sincere in his every action. . . . He radiates this, everybody knows it, everybody trusts and loves him." If no man is a hero to his butler, Ike was certainly the hero to his secretary. Yet even accounting for Whitman's puffery, it is noteworthy that to her, Nixon, by contrast, "sometimes seems like a man who is acting like a nice man rather than being one." Here it was in a nutshell. Nixon's persona was the deliberate, contrived expression of a man who valued appearance above substance, whose person he disliked so intensely that he would permit only a camouflage job for the public. Ike and JFK could afford to relax, to be themselves. Not Nixon. He was forever tinkering with his image, modifying this part, burnishing that part—the PR manual always at his side.

Following the 1970 congressional campaign, in which both Nixon and Agnew had worked vigorously and unavailingly for Republican candidates, Nixon decided to take the suggestion of *The New York Times* and reconsider his strategy. It was time for introspection—more introspection—something that absorbed him as little else. He would shore up his communication bridges. His persona had to emanate compassion, humanness, warmth, nobility, hope, confidence, optimism, courage. As if these were not enough, he added candor, honesty, openness, and trust, surely the most difficult for this most deceitful of men. But he would also, in this sweeping remake of himself, continue to "fight for what [I] believe."

Did it work? For a time, yes. Robert Semple of *The New York Times* detected "a new mood. . . . His oratory has become more conciliatory, his approaches to the press and the Congress more open." Why, he even began the new year, 1971, by granting an interview with four reporters, telling them he was now ready to "wear my hat as President of the United States." But what with the war dragging on and his approval rating dropping, Nixon had, within days, reverted to the "Tricky Dick" of old. It would have been easier to change a leopard's spots than change this fifty-seven-year-old President.

Perhaps Nixon's loneliness resulted from the fact that he, in short, was just not a likable man. His furtiveness and his secrecy, his sulking and his skulking, his trickery and his deviousness, his belligerence and his vindictiveness—these were hardly qualities that would endear him to anyone.They obviously hadn't endeared him to the voters in 1960. Despite JFK's being rich, a member of Boston's elite, a graduate of Harvard, and an Irish Catholic, he carried the day. Nixon was left to retreat to his lair, there to try and extricate himself from six successive crises. As Nixon withdrew into the shadows to consult with Haldeman over the manuscript, he left behind seasoned presidential watchers like Theodore White, who chalked up the Republican candidate's defeat to quite different factors than Nixon emphasized in his book. Here, White emphasized, was "a brooding, moody man, given to long stretches of introspection." He trusted no one save his wife, and conferred with only "the smallest number of people." What's more, "No other candidate . . . operated in 1960 with fewer personnel or kept more of the critical decisions in his own hands. Nixon is a man of major talent—but a man of solitary, uncertain impulse." Psychobiographer David Abrahamsen put it differently: "His public posture became a facade to mask the turbulent inner life which he guarded jealously because he did not and could not share his feelings with anyone."[4]

It appeared that Nixon, from time to time, receded into the mists of his own thoughts, secluding himself like one of the ancient Hebrew prophets, then emerging as though baptized with a revelation from on high. At other times it appeared as though he simply enjoyed the pleasure of his own company.

The Luxurious Loneliness of the White House, 1969-72

If there was any question that Nixon, as a major public figure, was entitled to solitude in 1960, there could be no doubt that he granted himself that entitlement when he was elected president in 1968.

For twenty-two years Nixon had clawed his way to the top of the pile, and now he was "King of the Mountain." Just as in the game, he would fight to retain that position, tossing others back as they ventured too close. The Mountain, in this case, was the White House. When Nixon was aboard his magic carpet, *Air Force One*, it was his cocoon, where he was hermetically sealed off from his aides, his family, and from the press. When he was entrenched in one of his three hideaways—Camp David, Key Biscayne, or San Clemente—the same protection availed. Just as Nixon had been excluded from Eisenhower's inner circle, just as he had been excluded from Rockefeller's embrace when living in the same apartment house in New York, so would he now give his lessers similar treatment. Here was one important way of knowing he'd arrived—he could form that most exclusive club in all the world, even more exclusive than the one hundred-member Senate—the club that excluded all others but himself. Nixon relished every minute of it. He could be kind on occasion, and he could be cruel. But the two qualities that left the most lasting impression on Theodore White were his fatalism and his melancholy, both nourished by his compulsive solitariness.

Of course from time to time Nixon had to communicate with others. Most of this he did with copious memos, addressed primarily to Haldeman in the form of orders. When Nixon did unlatch the door to his inner sanctum, it was only under the most restrictive circumstances. The rhetoric was there, but not the reality. In this respect he was following in the footsteps of perhaps his favorite President, Woodrow Wilson. It was Wilson who, reelected in 1916 on the campaign slogan, "He Kept Us Out of War," took the nation into war within a month of his second term. It was the same Wilson who called for "an open world—a world of open doors, open hearts, open minds. . . ." And it was the same Wilson who excluded any and all Republicans, especially Senator Henry Cabot Lodge, from contributing to the League of Nations plan—much less accompanying the President to Paris to fend for it. It was the same Wilson who, relishing the epiphany of being hailed the conquering hero as he paraded down the Arc de Triumph in Paris, sealed himself off from his aides, determined to go it alone in confronting Lloyd George and Clemenceau. Little wonder that, returning home, he was a broken man, his League in tatters. And when Wilson tried to push the remnants through the Senate for confirmation, there was Lodge standing squarely in his path. So, as we have noted, he hit the open road, to take his case to the people, contracted pneumonia, and died.

Nixon knew this—all this and more—when he entered the White House fifty years later. He knew it, but he could not—would not—learn from it. Studying Nixon's first term, one can almost hear the echo of Wilson's voice reverberating down the corridors of time. It sounded like the voice of a prophet, ringing with certainty, absolutes firmly in place, half-measures not to be tolerated. "*Every* arbitrary power *anywhere*" must be destroyed. "*Every* question" must be settled. "*All* nations" must consent. "*Every* invasion of right was *certain*" to be checked by the League.

Here was the message Wilson took to Versailles. Here was the message the Scotch Presbyterian Covenanter had received from on high, a revelation that would brook no compromise. That, Lloyd George and Clemenceau in effect told Wilson, was the stuff of sacred books but not of the real world, a world in which Germany had to suffer for its laying waste to France and impoverishing Britain. In his solitude, Wilson had hatched a plan to save the world from the scourge of future wars. In his discussion with his peers, leaders of allied nations, he had to retreat, to grant one concession after another until he left for Washington, disheartened, with but a shadow of the League intact.

Nixon, like Wilson, relished the luxury of isolation, there to think the lofty thoughts that would elude him if he had to deal with the everyday nitty-gritty. Nixon, however, had neither the intellectual acumen of a Wilson nor the vision of a statesman. In addition, he was burdened with the albatross of an undeclared war around his neck. It was a distant war in an impoverished, third-world nation of peasants who lived as their ancestors had for thousands of years, caught in a time warp from which only the devastation of war would separate them. It was a war Nixon could not win and dared not lose. There appeared but one way out: "Peace with honor," and that meant handing the fighting back to the South Vietnamese. And that, in turn, meant surrender, the "surrender on the installment plan" he'd been castigating for years before entering the White House. So Nixon, ostensibly holding fast to his goal of "Peace with honor," compromised and compromised again until, on January 31, 1973, he announced that he'd at last won "Peace with honor." But the press corps, as well as the millions who read their dispatches, refused to believe their President. Just as a U.S. officer had explained that he'd had to destroy a village in order to save it, so did many Americans believe we'd committed the ultimate atrocity of destroying a nation in order to save it—or to save our "honor"—or to save future generations from World War III. Worse, White House reporters and others close to the situation knew that Nixon had wrought destruction on Indochina primarily to save his reelection and his place in the history books. That constituted a barbarism more heinous than any. And Nixon, like Johnson before him, would pay for his hubris.

Not only did Nixon prolong the war unnecessarily, simply to assure his second term—emerging with a peace no better than he would have gotten within a month of his inauguration—but he stretched and distended the limits of the Constitution, subverting the purposes of the nation's Founders and endangering the very system of checks and balances that served to impede the abuse of power. Both Vietnam and Watergate, leading ultimately to Nixon's resignation in disgrace, were in no small part a product of his obsession with isolation.

Nixon craved the cold efficiency that at the time could have been found in one authoritarian government after another. Along with press conferences, he virtually abolished the Cabinet, depending instead on a small circle of intimate aides more loyal than competent. None of these had ever run for elected office and were thus not answerable to the electorate. So Nixon got his efficiency—at least a measure of it—but at the cost of disillusionment among Cabinet members who resigned in dismay, and at the cost of alienating a press, a Congress, and an electorate.

Though Nixon prized his solitude even more than his rectitude—posting Haldeman as a resolute gatekeeper to the Oval Office—he occasionally complained, as he did in 1967, that "the road to another presidential primary had at times been unbearably lonely." Was it because his solitude was so unbearable that, within a year after entering office, he declared "the goal of this administration is a free and open society?" Or was it simply camouflage for further evasions and secret actions in Vietnam? Did he really mean it when, during his inaugural address in 1969, he proclaimed to all nations that "during this administration our lines of communication will be open"? Or was this concocted out of thin air like so many of his campaign promises, meant to soothe a public sickened by chaos at home and abroad?

Open doors, open lines of communication, a free and open society— always the rhetoric outran the reality. The Oval Office became in effect a medieval fortress, with Haldeman guarding the door against all intruders. He wasn't simply a sentry on duty, calling out, "Who goes there?" He was, in addition, demanding, "What do you want?" "Where is your agenda?" "Can't somebody else handle that?" or "Put it in writing." For Nixon had made it clear to his Chief of Staff: the President wanted to be consulted only on the *big* issues.[5]

So secluded did Nixon become during his first term that RNC Chairman Bob Dole, after weeks of trying to see the President—and instead being shunted aside to a Haldeman aide—finally gave up in disgust. Transportation Secretary John Volpe likewise tried for months to talk with Nixon, but in vain. Rather than quit, however, he waited outside the Oval Office and latched onto the coattails of a visiting foreign archbishop, thus escaping the eagle eye of Haldeman. Others would forsake their churches on Sunday in order to catch Nixon unaware as he emerged from his own church. At such times Nixon would give the appearance of interest, only to promptly forget it. One little girl at an airport stop, however, did manage to catch Nixon's attention as she waved and shouted, "How is Smokey the Bear?" When the President smiled and turned away she persisted, waving and repeating the question until Nixon turned to an aide to ask what she was saying. The aide explained, "Smokey the Bear, Washington Zoo," whereupon the President walked over to the girl and extended his hand: "How do you do, Miss Bear."

It was during the 1968 campaign that Dan Rather took note of the crisp, martial bearing of the watchdog Haldeman, alert and dutiful in protecting his boss so Nixon could relax. It was relaxation, Haldeman insisted, that was "the key to an effective Richard Nixon." Having watched Nixon exhaust himself and his staff on the 1960 campaign trail, having seen Nixon appear for the presidential debate in Chicago bedraggled and gaunt—in sharp contrast to the relaxed and confident Kennedy— Haldeman resolved that there would be no repetition of this eight years later. But, Rather asked, how then did someone get in to talk with the man who would be president? Rather answered his own question: very few people *would* be granted admittance. "Certainly not those who incurred Haldeman's displeasure. And not relative newcomers on Nixon's campaign staff, and certainly not those who drank and socialized with the press. And not those who tried to circumvent Haldeman and make direct contact with Nixon. They were to state their business in writing, they were crisply told, for the candidate was too busy or resting."

By the time Nixon was in the Oval Office and Haldeman posted guard at the door, not even congressmen were allowed in. As far as Haldeman was concerned, they were a breed apart, members of a foreign branch of government. His explanation, "I don't think Congress is supposed to work with the White House," was as empty as his additional argument that Congress "is a different organization and, under the Constitution, I don't think we should expect agreement. " With the President's Chief of Staff trying to justify his tight monitoring of the Oval Office on such flimsy pretexts, it is understandable how Nixon became increasingly cut off from reality.

Kissinger noted that Haldeman's staff system isolated Nixon because the President insisted on being isolated. Haldeman agreed, contending that Nixon secluded himself because of his "poor self-image," the result of an impoverished emotional life—and that this, in turn, led to "a deep inner sense of alienation."[6] Kissinger, however, believed that the President's isolation kept him free from distraction and enabled him to consider thoughtfully various options in decision-making.

Nixon himself eventually came to see his mistake in letting Haldeman sequester him. But by then it was too late. He'd already resigned—partly due to his determination to cut himself off from all but a handful of people. So his plaint rang hollow when he said, blaming Haldeman, "I didn't realize that I was being isolated."

Having jumped out of the frying pan of Vietnam, Nixon found himself in the fire of Watergate. There was "Dr." John Dean, on March 21, 1973, diagnosing a cancer near the presidency. Before Sam Ervin's Watergate Committee, Dean was asked by Georgia Democrat Herman Talmadge why, after he knew about the cover-up, he didn't tell Nixon what was happening. Dean's answer astonished Talmadge and the rest of the Committee. "Senator, I did not have access to the President." "You mean you were counsel to the President of the United States and you could not get access to him if you wanted to?" Talmadge didn't think it possible.

Dean later wrote, "There were hundreds of stories I might have offered to show that I could not have gotten a piece of paper into the Oval Office, much less my body."

One person who did have access to Nixon was a Greek-American businessman, Thomas Pappas, who was generous enough to provide the "hush money" to buy the silence of the Watergate burglars. Nixon was certainly appreciative as he met Pappas in the Oval Office: "I'm aware of what you're doing to help out in some of these things that Maury's people [a reference to Maurice Stans] and others are involved in. I won't say anything further, but it's very seldom you find a friend like that." With the pendulum of Watergate circling closer and closer to his neck, Nixon, in as black a pit imaginable, needed all the friends he could muster.

Nixon's isolation, he claimed, was an utter necessity for the kind of concentration he needed to wrestle with great decisions. But Magruder has pointed out that not all presidential revelations came from on high. "We had been seeking our 'New Frontier' for two years when in January 1971, Nixon was waiting to speak at the dedication of the Eisenhower Republican Center in the Capital. Then he noticed an open door in the back of the hall. Suddenly a great idea grabbed him and he couldn't let go. Abandoning his prepared text, he spoke instead on the need of the party to be 'the party of the open door.'" The next day in the White House, Nixon gave marching orders to his troops: use the "Open Door" idea as often as possible. Call the meetings with congressional members "Open Door Sessions." Show by the statistics that Nixon is the most "Open Door" President in history. It wasn't long before 3,000 Republican headquarters across the country were sporting engraved, framed copies of their new motto: "The Party of the Open Door."

It was obvious that the President understood the importance of PR, regardless of reality. And the reality, as far as Theodore White was concerned, was that Nixon lived "behind a palisade of privacy more impenetrable than had any President in living memory."[7]

Nixon's biggest surprise during his first year in office was "the paradoxical combination of loss of privacy and sense of isolation. . . ." Indeed, as he stated in his *Memoirs,* he had "discovered how isolated from the reality of American life a president can feel in the White House." Yet having discovered that, it appears that Nixon took no pains to counteract it, other than his PR ploy to capitalize on the "Open Door." Over the next four years, his sense of isolation would only deepen and become more threatening to his presidency.

Kissinger wrote of Nixon's increasing disassociation in revealing detail. "The White House is both a goldfish bowl and an isolation ward: the fish swim in a vessel whose walls are opaque one way. They can be observed if not necessarily understood; they themselves see nothing. Cut off from the outside world, the [fish] . . . live by the rules of their internal coexistence or by imagining what the outside world is like. This in the Nixon White House became increasingly at variance with reality until suddenly the incommensurability between the two worlds grew intolerable; the bowl burst and its inhabitants found themselves gasping in a hostile atmosphere."

For almost six years, Nixon's view of reality had become increasingly blurred. He'd ridiculed Johnson for hunkering down in the White House to protect himself as war protesters laid siege to 1600 Pennsylvania Avenue. He, Nixon, was no Johnson. He would never humiliate himself with such cowardly behavior! It wasn't only the taunting calls of the protesters but the miserable results in the polls that had driven Johnson to distraction. He, Nixon, would let neither protesters nor polls intimidate him! In fact, as he wrote later—in a dramatic example of circular reasoning—"I don't give a damn what the polls say insofar as affecting my decisions. I only care about them because they may affect my ability to lead, since politicians do pay attention to them." But by 1972 his bravado was wearing thin as he began selecting only "safe" audiences, such as military posts, where he could count on friendly faces: spontaneous from the top brass, coerced from the enlisted men and low-level officers who'd been to the Vietnam front, or who were still in line to go.

However friendly those faces, Nixon's own countenance, once out of the limelight, was seldom amiable. But he would resolve to make it so after an incident at one of the inaugural balls in January 1973, when he was confronted by an hysterical girl crying, "I love and respect you so much!" "Even though we were leaving," Nixon recounted, "I danced with her for a few minutes." Those few minutes, recalled the wistful President, "was the great hit of the evening . . . the girls and even some of the boys were crying. . . ." How much of this was selective memory, how much sheer hype, one is left to wonder. But Nixon recounted his resolve "to get across more of what Rossiter has called 'affability.' The staff just hasn't been able to get it across and so I'm going to have to do all these things publicly which demonstrates [sic] that." Of course, Nixon himelf was, by nature, an "affable" person; it was just that his incompetent staff had failed to project that image of their President.

But try as they might, the staff could not accomplish the impossible. And affability, congeniality, gregariousness—these were simply not in Nixon's blood. Writing in his diary over Christmas 1972, while his barbaric devastation of North Vietnam by waves of B-52 bombers was underway, Nixon apparently found comfort—however cold it must have been—by musing, "It is inevitable that not only the President but the First Lady become more and more lonely individuals. . . . It is a question not of too many friends but really too few—one of the inevitable consequences of this position."[8] It apparently didn't cross his mind that his calamitous decision to wreak untold hardship on millions of North Vietnamese civilians, which triggered a barrage of caustic criticism from around the world, might have had something to do with his sense of isolation.

The Anguish of Seclusion, 1973-74

By 1973 Nixon was increasingly cut off from his aides, with the exception of Haldeman, Ehrlichman, Kissinger, and Dean. It is in his relationship with Dean that we see most clearly Nixon's treatment of others as disposable Kleenex, no longer useful once they'd served their purpose—thereby isolating himself from reality, just as he isolated himself from everyone except sycophants and family.

By August 15, 1972, about two months after the Watergate break-in, Nixon was convinced—on the basis of "500 or 600 cases" he had faced with the House Un-American Activities Committee—that he'd "won the fucking public relations matter," and that he "didn't give a goddamn what happened in court." That was what mattered: PR—getting his name out before the public in a favorable light. John Dean understood that. In another month, he was assuring his President that he had the lid on everything and that, on election day ". . . nothing will come crashing down to our . . . surprise." Nixon, exhilarated at the good news, commended Dean on "putting [his] finger in the dikes every time that leaks have sprung here and sprung there. . . ." As Nixon had insisted all along, this was just a matter of "public relations."

Dean was right. Except for the *Post*'s Woodward and Bernstein digging in the woodpile, the media was saying almost nothing about Watergate, and Nixon breezed through to his reelection. Still, by November 24, the President was aware that when Congress reconvened in January with a Democratic majority, he'd be vulnerable. So he made it clear—once again—to Haldeman: "The main thing you've got to protect is the presidency . . . we need a simple, clear statement and we need it early, which simply says again what we've already said by the Dean report to the President: '. . . there is no present member of the White House staff who had any knowledge of, or was involved in, the . . . Watergate matter' . . . I want him [Dean] to say it again . . . it's got to come from Dean, that I have conducted an investigation. . . . Yet there was Ehrlichman, and maybe Dean too, suggesting, '. . . let it all come out and it will be clear that the President was not involved.' That won't do it. This is a public relations exercise. . . . Dean has got to report that, pursuant to my direction, he has conducted a thoroughgoing investigation . . . have Dean write out that nice little statement so that I can mail it to all my friends."

On February 3—just four days before the Senate voted unanimously to authorize a select committee under Sam Ervin to investigate 1972 campaign practices, particularly Watergate—the Watergate jury in Judge Sirica's court had convicted Hunt, Liddy, and McCord. On February 7, the five burglars pleaded guilty. Now Ervin was determined to draw the net around the White House.

By March 1 it was evident that Nixon was leaning increasingly on his thirty-two year-old counsel to protect him. Nixon reminded the Attorney General that "this administration is being more cooperative than anybody else," and if Kleindienst had to talk about Watergate, ". . . Dean is the only other fellow you should talk to except for me." But, he added, "I should stay out of the damn thing." Why limit Kleindienst to him or to Dean? Nixon: "Because you have confidence in him, he never opens his mouth. . . ." And for that Nixon was so grateful that, the next day, he told Haldeman. "Hell, I'm convinced that Dean is a pretty good gem . . . he's awfully smart . . . he thinks things through. . . . He's not cocky. . . . I'm not talking to anybody but Dean. . . ."

The President was scrambling to steer clear of "the damned thing." But by mid-March, it was obvious that Nixon's claim of "executive privilege" in refusing to submit evidence to the Senate committee was becoming a PR disaster—for Americans now suspected that their President had something to hide. Just as bad, Nixon learned that both Mitchell and Haldeman had known about the break-in beforehand. Therefore, Ehrlichman pointed out to the President, "Haldeman's got a problem."

But if Haldeman had "a problem," so did Nixon—for the Chief of Staff would never have kept such a thing from his boss. By March 20 Nixon was so unsettled that he thought the roof would cave in at any moment. Dean, the President told Ehrlichman, should brief Republican congressional leaders, so that they didn't "get caught with their pants down." Nixon also assured Ehrlichman that Dean had a "confidential relationship with everyone he talked to," thus assuring attorney-client privilege. "So," added the President, "he's not telling me everything. He's telling me everything I need to know. . . ."

The next day Dean decided that Nixon needed to know about the "cancer within—close to the presidency—that's growing. It's growing daily. It's compounding. It grows geometrically now. . . ." Despite Dean's heroic efforts, he no longer had enough fingers to plug all the leaks in the dike. Back in January 1972, learning of the Plumbers, Dean had called their shenanigans "a growing disaster on our hands. . . . The White House has got to stay out of this and I, frankly, am not going to be involved in it." But he was involved, and now, more than a year later, he would do almost anything for his President—except perjure himself. At the close of their lengthy conversation, during which Dean had laid it all out, he told Nixon, "We cannot let you be tarnished by that situation."

Later that day Nixon pointed out to Haldeman, "we've obviously overloaded Dean . . . now we've really got to step in there. . . ." Apparently the administration's hush-money raiser, Fred LaRue, had not been effective in pulling together the kind of cash that Dean needed to buy the silence of the eight convicted men, so—as Haldeman put it to Nixon—"Dean finally just goes running pretty much to Mitchell and said 'I've got to have some money. You guys know I just can't go asking. . . .' " At this, Nixon warned his Chief of Staff to "Put it on the shelf." It was beginning to smell like "obstruction of justice, [and] . . . we are all in it. . . ." The money, Nixon explained—having just talked to Rose Mary Woods, who was holding it in her safe—was "available . . . in cash in $100 bills. . . . I can get it." But as part of his campaign funds, it was traceable, Nixon told Haldeman so, "I cannot consider it unless there is an effective change. . . ." At this, Haldeman informed the President that Dean had "learned a lot about this stuff now . . . the easy way [to launder the money] is to pay it to Vegas and run it through [the casinos] out there and it gets lost pretty easy in there. . . ."[9]

"Dean's right," Nixon replied, "you've got to fight this thing. But I don't know how much time we've got to fight it." All those aides—Kleindienst, Mitchell, and others, even Krogh—were susceptible to blowing the cover story, Nixon complained. "The guy says: 'Oh Christ, they're abandoning me.'" Furthermore, ". . . whether it's Mitchell, Chuck [Colson], you [Haldeman], Ehrlichman, Dean, Magruder, the rest, the tendency in a case like this, you know, is for people to say: 'Well, I didn't, but he did,' and so on and so on and so on." Why did the President include even Dean, whom he still believed was the White House linchpin on Watergate? There we were, Nixon commented, "trying our best. . . " and Dean was "an absolutely innocent accomplice in the whole thing. Dean, he gave good advice. . . . He was just holding the pieces together because he thought that was his job."

Having heard from Dean later that day that he'd had "a terrible breakdown in communication with both the committees and . . . the grand jury," Haldeman relayed the bad news to Nixon. Furthermore, there was Mitchell, insisting to Dean that his story had better jibe with Mitchell's. Dean replied, ". . . I cannot go to the grand jury and not tell the truth . . . if I start doing that, my hands will start trembling and my voice will shake. . . . I can't get away with it. . . . I will do the best I can, but I will not change the facts. . . ." Later that evening, Haldeman reminded the President that his counsel had "immunity, at least until he's fired. He doesn't go to jail and he isn't disbarred." When they discussed the various aides that Watergate might "touch," the list included Dean. Then, more prescient than he realized, the Chief of Staff predicted, "If you fire everybody now, in effect you send them to jail . . . and that's the danger of throwing any baby to the wolves, is you always just make the wolves more hungry and prove to them that you've got some more babies."

The next day, March 28, was just a week after Dean's "cancer" news to Nixon, and just a day before Dean decided to retain a lawyer. Nixon, however, was still convinced, as he put it to Haldeman, that "Dean is a damn good thing here . . . I personally would stand back of him on it, that the White House counsel simply can't talk [even though] . . . the difficulty in Dean's case is that . . . he can hire a criminal lawyer. . . ." But, Haldeman protested, "If he's charged directly [before the grand jury], unless he takes the Fifth, and then you've got to fire him . . . [for] Dean's capable of talking just like Magruder is, if you undercut him very far too." At this, Nixon was resolute: "Oh, Christ, I wouldn't think of undercutting him. Never. He's been a hero, really . . . he's been a sturdy, like a giant . . . be sure he knows . . . that he's backed to the hilt."

The next day Haldeman broke the news to Nixon that McCord had implicated not only Mitchell and Magruder before Ervin's Committee, but also Dean. His counsel, Nixon predicted, "can't avoid this grand jury." His problem was, "Mitchell in effect is asking Dean to commit perjury."

Seeing Dean becoming increasingly vulnerable, Nixon desperately tried to distance himself from his counsel, insisting to Haldeman, "I never saw Dean, I know that. I never saw Dean or Magruder until after the goddamned election." Both the President and his Chief of Staff were fully aware by this time, if not a year before, that Dean was present when Liddy came before Mitchell and the Plumbers with plans for Operation Gemstone—a series of ridiculous schemes to sabotage the Democrats' national campaign—which Dean and Mitchell agreed were too expensive.

By March 30 Nixon's premonition that his aides would end up blaming each other seems to have happened, as Haldeman informed him of the latest maneuvering. "It's funny. Boy, the raw human stuff . . . as you grind people against the wall, it starts coming out . . . Mitchell says that Dean doesn't trust Ehrlichman, he thinks Ehrlichman is maneuvering to sink Dean. Now Dean thinks Mitchell and Magruder are maneuvering to sink him. Ehrlichman will maneuver to keep himself clear." Nixon: "You're damn right he will, and everybody does." Had Nixon been in a truth-telling mode, he might have added—"especially me."

On April 10 Nixon told Ehrlichman, "I better not talk to Dean. It is not necessary. Dean knows that I care about him." Two days later, Nixon was convinced by Ehrlichman—less than three weeks before Ehrlichman himself would be fired—that Dean "should take a leave [of absence]." This, Nixon assured Ehrlichman, is "the only decent thing to do."

By April 13 Haldeman and Nixon were aware that Dean was spilling all to the grand jury and that the cover-up was fast crumbling. The President complained to Ehrlichman, "If they're [Nixon's aides] going to piss on the White House, that's what I'm worried about." Two days later, Nixon learned that Dean intended to pull Haldeman and Ehrlichman down with him. At the same time, Dean passed on a message to Haldeman that he hoped "you understand that my actions are motivated totally out of loyalty to you and the President."

On April 17 Nixon, still believing Dean could be useful, asked him to check on the constitutionality of one of Sirica's requests. He concluded their conversation on a sentimental note. ". . . God, you know, it's tough for everybody, John. All of you are good friends . . . you have fought the good fight"— quoting, of all people, the apostle Paul—"and you'll live to fight another one. That's the important thing."

That evening, however, Nixon began having second thoughts. "Dean is the real, the fellow that's really going to be the loose cannon, because he's trying to save his ass, trying to get immunity," the president told Haldeman and Ehrlichman. "He has goddamn little credibility. . . . He was the one that said there was no [White House] involvement, and that's what we relied on . . . nobody really will know what they put a President through on a thing like this."[10]

By April 25 Nixon was beginning to panic that John Dean might break ranks. In a conversation with Attorney General Kleindienst, the President said that the break-in of Dr. Fielding's office in Los Angeles by "these crazy fools" turned out to be "a dry hole." And who ordered it? "Dean was the one that implemented the whole thing . . . he carried it out. . . . Shit, it's the dumbest goddamn thing I've heard of. . . ." Kleindienst: "Do you think he [Dean] would not try to implicate you? Nixon: "I think he would implicate anybody. . . . I haven't seen Dean until February. I never had a conversation." Kleindienst: ". . . a trump card of Dean would be that I'm going to implicate the President, and I told Henry at that point you have to tell Dean to go fuck himself. You're not going to blackmail the government of the United States and implicate the President. . . ." Nixon: "He's [Dean] clever as shit . . . you know him better than I do, Dick . . . but you've always trusted him, haven't you?" Kleindienst: "I trusted him . . . up until two weeks ago. I thought he was one of the most able, fine, decent, honest, sensible young kids." Nixon: "All our people around here did . . . they set Dean in charge of this *whole goddamn thing* . . . he was involved in the subornation of perjury with Magruder . . . he was involved in the payoffs . . . [and] he's still trying to make a deal. . . . I will not be in a position of having the President of the United States blackmailed by anybody. I've been trying to get to the bottom of this thing, believe me." Kleindienst: "Nobody else implicates the President of the United States except John Dean, and John Dean turns out to be the very, very weak, selfish, self-directed . . . link in the whole operation . . . if he can't work this [immunity] out that he wants to talk to Henry Petersen and play his final trump card. . . . But I told [Henry] . . . that at that point if it's you, just tell the sonofabitch to get his fucking ass out. . . . You can't let a little guy like this for his very intense, deep, selfish motives—you know, blackmail . . . people who are innocent of this goddamn thing. . . ."

That evening, Nixon was back on the phone to Kleindienst to remind him that it was "important to let the prosecutor know . . . this [Watergate] was a national security investigation of very great sensitivity. . . . You can give absolute assurances on that . . . and I think the judge should know that, too." That same night, Nixon learned from Petersen that Dean had exposed [acting FBI director] Gray's destruction of "fraudulent cables from the State Department purporting to link JFK with the murder of Diem . . . [documents] concocted out of whole cloth." Nixon insisted that certainly he wasn't the culprit behind any of these offenses: "If there was one person that had really no knowledge whatsoever about Watergate, it was I." As for Dean, "He is the man that had the responsibility . . . [and] he didn't tell me [until] March 21. . . . I said, write a report on this thing, take it to the Cabinet, take it to the congressional leaders as to what the hell this is all about. I said, let it hang out, whatever it is . . . that was the date I started my personal investigation. . . . Henry, he can't make the immunity thing on the basis of blackmailing the President." As far as getting money for the defendants was concerned, Nixon added, "I want you to know that he was told that this is a road you can't go down, and if you don't believe me on this—understand I don't ask you to believe me any more than anybody else. I don't lie to people. . . . We cannot let this stinking damn thing kill the presidency. . . ."

During a five-hour meeting with Haldeman the next day, Nixon fingered Dean as "basically what the problem is . . . a desperate man who has misled . . . and there's an old story: You don't strike a king unless you kill him. . . . On March 21 . . . he informed [me] . . . that Hunt's people were requiring money, which was my first knowledge of it, believe me, of the whole thing."

Later the same evening, Nixon phoned Kleindienst to insist, "I never saw him [Dean] personally till . . . February 22." When Kleindienst—

remembering Nixon's earlier mention of his conversation with Dean on March 21—questioned that date, Nixon changed it to February 27. Kleindienst: "You mean he was not in your office?" Nixon: "Never, except one time, to sign my wills." Kleindienst: "You know, to listen to this little bastard, he's in there talking to you four times a day . . . even last summer, you know." Nixon: ". . . let's get one thing straight. *I, the President, never saw John Dean once except for the signing of the wills* [spoken with emphasis, pausing between words]. And that was on August 14. . . . That's the only time I ever saw him. . . ."

Before providing a virtual affidavit to his Attorney General, Nixon called Kleindienst's assistant, Petersen, about Gray's destruction of evidence. Gray, it seems, was told by Dean—who, in turn, was told by Ehrlichman—to "deep six" incriminating documents. Dean wasn't about to personally destroy evidence, so he asked Gray, who had the papers in his safe, to get rid of them. Now was he going to lie under oath? "Goddamn it," vowed Dean, "I wouldn't lie for Ehrlichman, whatever I might do for the President"—clearly implying that Nixon himself had given the initial command, though he would never admit it. In fact, Nixon pressed the point to his assistant attorney general, ". . . the destruction of the documents story, even though it was done with no venal intent, this is stupidity of an unbelievable degree." Would—could—the President be guilty of such stupidity? Of course not. Thus did Nixon attempt to prove "plausible deniability." Petersen, in turn, assured the President, ". . . we're trying to bring Dean around to the point where he'll plead [guilty]." Nixon was caught in a bind, for if Dean were to testily, Nixon feared that he'd further implicate Haldeman and Ehrlichman and—inevitably—the President. Naturally, then, he maintained that Dean "has got about as much credibility as Magruder. . . ."

The next day, April 27, Petersen finally convinced Nixon ". . . you cannot jeopardize our position with Dean by anything you might do now." At that, the President offered, ". . . he's in effect saying that he goes provided the other guys go. . . ." Petersen: ". . . the longer you wait [to rid yourself of all of them], the worse it gets." That evening, convinced he would have to jettison both Haldeman and Ehrlichman as well as Dean, Nixon took Ziegler into his confidence: "Christ, impeach the President on . . . John Dean's word. . . . He claims he's got some documentary stuff. You know, it must be some goddamn memos from that fucking Colson." And, once again, Nixon insisted that Dean never talked to him about Watergate "until March 21." Yes, he admitted, ". . . Dean was nothing short of magic. You've got to give him credit. We all said he did a helluva good job." But his trouble was in making "payments to the defendants . . . [getting] involved with Mitchell . . . protecting [him], not the White House."

Aware of the ugly box he now found himself in, Nixon's blood pressure was rising: "We're trying to contain the goddamn thing, because we've got to remember this is a continuing battle. Look, if we went in sackcloth and ashes and fired the whole White House staff, [Speechwriter Raymond] Price must realize that isn't going to satisfy these goddamn cannibals. . . . Hell, they're not after Haldeman or Ehrlichman or Dean; *they're after me*, the President."

With so much at stake, namely his own hide, Nixon had no other choice but to rid himself of his "pestiferous priests": Haldeman Ehrlichman, and Dean—especially Dean. That "loose cannon," Nixon complained to Ziegler. "He's going to raise hell, but I don't think he's going to have that much credibility." There would be no leaves of absence, as Nixon had earlier promised the three men. It was simply resign or be fired.

So out they went, one aide after another, including, of course, his counsel—the man Nixon once couldn't praise enough, until Dean insisted he'd not perjure himself, even for the President. In this "blowing hot and cold," as J. Edgar Hoover described Nixon's attitude toward those around him, lay the key to his relationships with others. In the final analysis, all were expendable, and none more so than John Dean. The President could rid himself of his aides, but the one person he could not be rid of was Richard Nixon. That would be, above all, his punishment for presidential presumption, for presuming that the White House lay astride the globe, if not Mount Olympus itself. And his purgatory would be that he had to abide forever with Richard Nixon living beneath his skin.

The details of the last few weeks of his presidency we leave to our final chapter, when hubris had at last run its reckless and devastating course. Richard Nixon had come to know isolation as the most lonely of presidents. His was not "the loneliness of the long-distance runner," but the loneliness of one who, never having come to grips with himself, never having accepted his self-worth as a human being, could never accept the worth of those around him. With no solid foundation beneath him, he lacked the stability to reach out and embrace others, including his own family.

In the end, he found himself isolated and alienated, a man without a country. He was no longer the indispensable President, the man who'd identified himself with the office and with the nation. He was, in fact, the most dispensable of men.

On January 1, 1975 John Dean, languishing in prison—"escaping my loneliness" as he put it—was reading Somerset Maugham's *The Summing Up*, undoubtedly pondering just how his own life would sum up. And there he came across a telling passage: "We are shocked when we discover that great men were weak and petty, dishonest or selfish, sexually vicious, vain or intemperate; and many people think it disgraceful to disclose to the public its heroes' failings. There is not much to choose between men. They are all a hotchpotch of greatness and littleness, of virtue and vice, of nobility and baseness. . . . I do not think I am any better or any worse than most people, but I know if I set down every action in my life and every thought that has crossed my mind the world would consider me a monster of depravity."

A week later Dean got unexpected good news. Judge Sirica had limited his imprisonment to time served. He was a free man, and he had trouble believing it. Looking out the window, he murmured, "The nightmare is over." Dean described that moment in *Blind Ambition*, reflections on his White House years. "I couldn't stop shaking my head as I gazed out the window, nor could I stop the tears. Everything is different now."[11]

As far as Nixon was concerned, he would not have John Dean "to kick around anymore." Here, in the President's treatment of his once-trusted counsel, can be seen a major reason for Nixon's isolation. It was the loneliness of a man unable, if willing, to sympathize with others, to extend to them a helping hand, to give them the benefit of the doubt. Now it was but a brief step to self-immolation, the last of the stages in hubris.

CHAPTER 13

IMMOLATION

The longest war [Vietnam] had come to an end. Faintly from a distance of 200 years might have been heard Chatham's summary of a nation's self-betrayal: "by the arts of imposition, by its own credibility, through the means of false hope, false pride and promised advantages of the most romantic and improbable nature.

— Barbara Tuchman, *The March of Folly*

There was no way I could say that what had happened was in their interest or in the national interest or in anyone's interest.

— Congressman Donald Riegle, vainly trying to justify the death in Vietnam of the son of one of his constituents.

LYNDON JOHNSON

Down in my heart of hearts I knew—I simply knew—that the American people loved me.

— Lyndon Johnson in Retirement.

There is nothing that I would change, as I look back, of any consequence that I have done.

— Lyndon Johnson, January 1969.

For a fellow like Lyndon Johnson to announce that he's not going to stand for reelection, this is an act of self-immolation.

— Harry Ashmore

Whom the Gods Would Destroy

There is nothing that feeds hubris like pride—wanton pride. Pride that becomes increasingly selective of to whom it defers, and shuts out those who disagree or refuse to pay homage. Pride that, having won power by ingratiating itself with higher-ups, turns on subordinates and tyrannizes them. Pride that brings to bear every strength, every device, every resort to expand the power already gained. Pride that seizes each opportunity, regardless of intellectual honesty, to aggrandize itself. Pride that exploits fellow human beings, manipulating them to serve its own ends. Pride that reeks of arrogance, arrogating to itself that to which it has no rightful claim. Pride that identifies itself with institutions—and when advantageous, insists it is indispensable to those institutions. Pride that confuses confrontation with courage: wheedling superior forces, procrastinating equivalent forces, bullying inferior forces. Pride that coerces others, deceives others, depriving them of liberty, if not life itself. Pride that, having invited retaliation, whimpers with its back to the wall that its enemies are out to subvert it. Pride that, having used and abused everyone in its path, finds itself, at long last, alone—isolated even from those who were closest. It is only fitting, then, that such pride, having destroyed the peace, the hopes, the lives of so many, should, in the end, destroy itself.

Thus does hubris run its course. Thus does power, once abused, turn on its abusers. Thus are the mighty brought low. Many of those closest to Johnson saw there tragedy incarnate. Eric Goldman's *The Tragedy of Lyndon Johnson*, Joseph Califano's *The Triumph and Tragedy of Lyndon Johnson*, and Robert McNamara's *In Retrospect, The Tragedy and Lessons of Vietnam*—all have caught in their titles the essential truth that Lyndon Johnson, entering the White House in the wake of a tragedy, was a tragedy waiting to happen.

Yet the greater tragedy, by far, lies not in what happened to Johnson—whom the gods first made mad before destroying—but in what he inflicted on countless others. It is this, the devastation he wrought not only in America but on a small, struggling nation, turning it into a vale of tears. It is this that remains the legacy of hubris.

A fitting epitaph for Johnson were the words penned by Matthew Arnold, British poet and literary critic. "Most men eddy about/Here and there—eat and drink/Chatter and love and hate/Gather and squander, are raised/aloft, are hurl'd in the dust/Striving blindly, achieving/Nothing and then they die."

Shakespeare introduced some forerunners of Lyndon Johnson with the likes of Hamlet, Julius Caesar, Richard III, and Henry VIII. Of them he wrote: "But man, Proud man/Drest in a little brief authority/Most ignorant of what he's most assured/His glassy essence like an angry ape/Plays such fantastic tricks before high heaven/As make the angels weep."

Henry VIII prefigured Johnson when he exclaimed, "I have touched the highest point of my greatness/And from that full meridian of my glory/I haste now to my setting; I shall fall/Like a bright exhalation in the evening/And no man see me more."[1]

The autumn of 1967 found the thirty-sixth President mean and miserable, suffering the pangs of hubris in its final stage. Like Icarus, he was drawn to the brightness of the sun, the zenith of power. Circling ever closer, in defiance of Daedalus—the electorate—the wax on those wings that had borne him aloft was melting, and he was about to plunge to his political demise, there to writhe for four years until physical death finally gave him respite.

It was not long after this "accidental" President stumbled into the White House that Bill Moyers noted, "The war would destroy [LBJ] politically and wreck his presidency. He was a miserable man." By 1967, he was being jabbed with roundhouses from both the left and the right, until punch-drunk, he was staggering in the political ring. So desperate was Johnson by autumn—and so certain that no matter what he did, World War III was beckoning—that he announced his decision to build a partial defense system against nuclear missile attack, prefiguring Reagan's later, futile, and enormously costly "Star Wars." Yet *Time* named LBJ its 1967 "Man of the Year"—calling him the odds-on favorite to win the 1968 Democratic nomination, if not the election itself, and citing a survey of 1964 convention delegates that showed an astounding 87 percent still backing Johnson. The campaign, *Time* continued, "would be a spectacle to behold. . . . If there is one thing that Lyndon Johnson enjoys as much as being President, it is running for President."

Alas, it was not to be. The first offensive against that candidacy was the broad, coordinated attack by the Communists during Tet, the Asian New Year, at the end of January. The gloss of Tet as a "resounding victory"—hyped by Westmoreland and then by LBJ—did little to alleviate the cold, hard truth: it was costing the United States $9.00 for every $1.00 of damage inflicted on the enemy. What's more, a CIA analysis found that there was no level of damage America could inflict in its "war of attrition" that would be intolerable enough to make the Communists stop fighting.

By this time the President's lethal bombing policy had taken on a life of its own. Faced with brutal "cognitive dissonance," Johnson nevertheless clung desperately to the conviction that, ultimately, his policy would prevail and he would be vindicated. In this, he was virtually alone. An Australian journalist, visiting Hanoi, declared publicly, "I know of no leader who believes that President Johnson is sincere in stating that he really wants to end the war on terms that would leave the Vietnamese free to settle their own affairs."

In November 1967, *The Saturday Evening Post* asserted, "The war on Vietnam is Johnson's mistake." By 1968, *The Wall Street Journal* was even more dire: "We think the American people should be getting ready to accept . . . the prospect that the whole Vietnam effort may be doomed."

Tet having taken its toll, Johnson dispatched a group that included Clifford, Rusk, Rostow, and Taylor to assess the Vietnam situation. But only Clifford appeared able to gauge the grimness of it all. As for the others, the intellectual war critic George Kennan wrote, "They were like men in a dream, incapable of any realistic assessment of the effects of their own acts." Backing Clifford, however, was the CIA: "Despite the massive influx of 500,000 troops, 1.5 million tons of bombs a year, 400,000 attack sorties a year, 200,000 of the enemy killed in action in 3 years . . . our control of the countryside and urban areas remains at pre-1965 levels." Having learned the previous summer that there would be no help forthcoming from SEATO allies, Clifford concluded, "The military course we are pursuing is not only endless but hopeless."[2]

The sole way to avert a bloodbath at the polls in November, 300 California Democrats wrote, was "an immediate all-out effort to secure a non-military settlement. . . ." For five years Johnson had fiercely resisted this, convinced it was tantamount to surrender. He was not about to reverse course. Then the polls revealed that LBJ was trailing all six Republican candidates. Worse, after returning from an inspection trip of Vietnam, America's "most trusted journalist," Walter Cronkite, went on national TV, to tell of the "burned, blasted, and weary land" laid waste by the Tet offensive and the U.S. counteroffensive. There were 470,000 new refugees to add to the 800,000 already fighting to survive in the "unbelievable squalor" of South Vietnamese shantytowns. The only rational solution, Cronkite concluded, was to negotiate without trying to dictate terms. "If I've lost Walter," moaned Johnson, "I've lost middle America."

A week later, Fulbright weighed in. His Foreign Relations Committee had taken another look at the Tonkin Gulf Resolution and concluded that Johnson had gotten it through outright "misrepresentation" of the facts. Therefore, the Resolution was "null and void." No wonder, Fulbright declared publicly, that so many young people had engaged in a "spiritual rebellion" against this betrayal of "traditional American values." Fulbright, backed by the rest of the Senate, was openly questioning Johnson's authority to expand the war without congressional approval.

By March 1968 Johnson's rollercoaster presidency had already hit the top, leveled off, and was now plummeting down the slippery slope of hubris to its demise. Eugene McCarthy, running on an antiwar platform, carryied no less than 42 percent of the vote in the New Hampshire primary. Then Bobby tossed his hat in the ring, and Johnson saw his chances of even being nominated dwindling to the vanishing point. Lyndon's mirror of invulnerability, polished by Rusk, Rostow, et al, was cracking—revealing a policy that was not only bankrupt, but threatening to bankrupt the nation. The catch-22 was agonizing to LBJ: "If I left the woman I really loved, the Great Society, in order to get involved in that bitch of a war on the other side of the world, then I'd lose everything at home . . . but if I left the war and let the Communists take over South Vietnam, then I'd be seen as a coward and my nation would be seen as appeaser and we'd both find it impossible to accomplish anything for anybody anywhere on the entire globe."

Such reasoning is why the cells of mental institutions are padded. For here, all rolled into one, were stretched metaphor, simplistics, polarization, and monumental hyperbole. And it was compounded, Wicker emphasized, by "his vanity, his overbearing manner, occasional crudity, glowering presence and reputation for crafty maneuvering. . . ." Even Johnson's friend, the Pulitzer Prize winning biographer William S. White, noted that LBJ had become "too nearly an object of fear to permit him the popularity with which he'd begun the White House."[3]

1968 and the Moment of Truth

By 1968, "credibility gap" fit no one, it seemed, as much as the President. It stood as "a symbol of evasion, half-truth, deception, and expedience," on behalf of a war "never declared, stealthily executed, of no vital interest to this country, and cruelly devastating to Vietnam," wrote Wicker. In short, he added, "Johnson's war made a mockery of both justice and democracy." On October 31, 1967, Wicker wondered in *The New York Times* if the Democrats would repudiate Johnson in favor of Robert Kennedy. "It is possible," Wicker conjectured, "that Johnson will withdraw." Then he concluded that it was "about as likely as it is that Dick Nixon will stop running. . . ."

Less than a year after entering the White House, LBJ had been making noises as though he would not run in 1968. Encountering increasing flak in Congress, Johnson, when asked why he was pursuing such a frantic pace with his legislation, answered, "I have so little time." His honeymoon with Congress was soon over, despite his landslide victory in 1964. Again and again over the next four years, Johnson—in a funk about the progress of the war, about the mounting protest at home, about the prospects for his Great Society, and about a dozen other lesser travails—threatened to bypass the 1968 race. However, there were always his aides, loyal to a fault, ready to bolster his sagging morale, to insist that he, and only he, could see the nation through to victory in Vietnam; that only he could pump new blood into his anemic Great Society.

And it needed it. Some thirty-one months after Johnson had hailed this new monument that was to have fixed his place in history, *Time* was carping, "its impact has been disappointingly slight." It was not because Congress hadn't heeded LBJ's call. Soon it had responded with no less than 21 different health provisions, 17 education programs, and 15 economic initiatives—as well as 12 measures to deal with urban crises, 4 to shore up manpower training, and 17 to preserve natural resources. In addition, Congress created two new Cabinet posts to deal with urban problems and transportation. Yet by the end of 1966, Budget Director Charles Schultze was at his wit's end trying to create order out of chaos. For with all the new legislation came $15 billion to be distributed among 170 different programs, funded by 400 different appropriations, administered by 21 departments and agencies, and assisted by 159 bureaus. Some indication of the resulting confusion can be seen in Attorney General Nicholas Katzenbach's appearance before a Senate hearing. When he was asked how much federal aid was available to cities, Katzenbach replied: $13 billion. Yet the next day Robert Weaver, HUD Secretary, gave the figure at $28 billion. Meanwhile, state and municipal governments found themselves trying to tunnel out from the deluge of paperwork flooding their offices. In Oakland, California, for example, city officials had to keep separate account books for 140 federal grant programs. Asked about the chaos, one of Johnson's top aides explained: "Maybe Lyndon Johnson had to do what John Kennedy could not do—pass the bills. And maybe someone else had to do what Lyndon Johnson cannot do—make it all work." In any case, Vietnam was preempting Johnson's time and attention. And the Great Society, which the President had once claimed would be bent "to the hopes of man," was left simply bent.

On November 1, 1967, Nixon was ahead of Johnson in the polls by 49 percent to 45 percent. And five months later, on March 31, 1968, Tom Wicker's prediction was to be proven wrong. For that night LBJ went on national television to announce that he was ordering a cease-fire. Then he appended that statement with a lot of platitudes that sounded much like the platitudes he'd been uttering for the past four years. Johnson said he prayed for God's help "to keep the American commitment. . . . United we have kept that commitment. United we have enlarged that commitment." There is a major dose of irony alloyed with folderol in this business of commitment and a united front. The commitment had to do with our pledge to assist all other SEATO members under attack. Since South Vietnam was not a nation, it could not be a member of SEATO. The conflict there was nothing but a civil war. Furthermore, other SEATO members were not committed to this venture—nor were Americans "united" in waging a war for South Vietnam. It is also questionable just how "committed" John F. Kennedy had been to the effort, especially in view of his intention, stated on at least three separate occasions, to withdraw all U.S. troops by the end of 1965. And there was most assuredly no "united" front behind America's escalation of the war. Indeed, it was because any announcement of major escalation would have sparked an uproar in Congress and across the nation that Johnson jiggered the war, by fits and starts, but always on the sly.

The U.S. involvement in Vietnam was such a peripheral issue for the electorate when Johnson assumed office that he made no mention of it during his first State of the Union address in 1964. Few Americans had any idea where Vietnam was, and fewer still knew why we were there. Though it remains debatable how JFK, had he lived, would have pursued America's undertaking in Vietnam, there is no doubt that Kennedy's successor misrepresented the facts in filching from Congress the Tonkin Gulf Resolution. Nor can there be any doubt that Johnson escalated the war while concealing that process from Congress, the press, and the electorate. But 1968 was pay-back time. As New York Senator Daniel Patrick Moynihan put it, "Johnson was the first American president to be toppled by a mob. No matter that it was a mob of college professors, millionaires, flower children, and Radcliffe girls." Indeed, Moynihan was seeing in those times of trouble what Yeats had seen in turn-of-the-century Ireland: "Things fall apart: the centre cannot hold; mere anarchy is loosed upon the world . . . worse, the best lack all conviction, while the worst are full of passionate intensity"

So, as Johnson stood before the TV cameras on March 31, viewers were looking at a dissembler, an evader—a man not to be believed, no matter how sincere he might appear. But that night, there was a certain unctuousness, larded with a sanctimoniousness, that only compounded his stunning announcement. Taking the high road, LBJ preached what he'd not practiced during his five years in the White House: "This country's ultimate strength lies in the unity of our people. There is divisiveness among us all tonight. And holding the trust that is mine, as President of all the people, I cannot disregard the peril to the progress of the American people and the hope and prospects of peace for all people. . . . With America's sons in the fields far away, with America's future under challenge right here at home . . . I do not believe that I should devote an hour or a day of my time to any personal partisan causes. . . . Accordingly, I shall not seek, and will not accept, the nomination of my party for another term as your President."

It was as if the blackness of a seemingly endless night had at last given way to the first signs of dawn. Euphoria gripped the capital the next day, and Johnson's standing in the polls bounded upward. Once again he could venture out beyond the carefully controlled military installations to speak. Some crowds were even cheering him again. Hanoi was soon making noises about wanting to go to Paris to negotiate. If a burden had been lifted from Johnson, it had also been lifted from the American people. There is no little irony that Johnson's immolation—his withdrawal from the field of political battle that he'd cherished over the years—would cause both him and the nation he'd led so miserably to breathe a huge sigh of relief.[4]

If the most convincing testimony is reluctant testimony—that is, testimony in which the speaker has nothing obvious to gain and perhaps much to lose—Johnson should have, in one fell swoop, bridged the pervasive credibility gap that had plagued his presidency. And apparently almost everyone did believe LBJ's statement that he was withdrawing from the race. But some—those who knew him best, his staff—weren't so sure. Many, like Reedy, saw not only "a son of a bitch," but "a colossal son of a bitch," yet one who insisted to Kearns, "If the American people don't love me, their descendants will."

But Johnson's aides had seen the same man they'd become inured to over five years of use and abuse. That was the LBJ who, ever conscious of making the right impression, went through twelve drafts to be certain his person would project the persona of a selfless President, bowing out for the welfare of the party, of the country—of everybody but himself. It all sounded too good to be true. And it was. Subsequent events, leading up to the Democratic National Convention in August, showed that LBJ's staff had good reason to be skeptical.

If Johnson didn't throw himself on his political sword as a noble sacrifice for his country, then why did he? The reasons are as many, as vague, and as contradictory as those he and his administration gave for our involvement in Vietnam. Those reasons depended on who did the asking, and when, where, and why they were asking. And that suggested the first reason. If there was any venture that epitomized Murphy's Law, it was Johnson's ill-starred enterprise in Vietnam. Within a few months of General Westmoreland's trumpeting that victory was in our grasp, there he was, calling for more than 200,000 additional troops—an expansion of U.S. forces that would require mobilizing the reserves and hitting up Congress for a major tax increase. Then, too, there was McNamara bowing out as Defense Secretary and being replaced with "bad news" Clifford, who told Johnson that neither other SEATO members nor his own senior advisory group were for continuing the war.

And then, of course, there was LBJ's perpetual antagonist, Bobby Kennedy, deriding the war effort. There were, Kennedy said scathingly, 500,000 American troops plus 700,000 South Vietnamese troops, "with total command of the air, total command of the sea, backed by huge resources and the most modern weapons . . . unable to secure even a single city from the attacks of an enemy whose total strength is about 250,000." It would be ludicrous if it weren't so pathetic. Bobby, the "peace" candidate, offered to stay out of the race if LBJ would appoint a commission to take a hard look at the war—only to announce his candidacy two days later when Johnson labeled the proposal "blackmail." And, to make matters worse, the press and the public seemed to be swinging to RFK's side. Wicker, for example, wrote that Kennedy's was "the most sweeping and detailed indictment of the war and the administration's policy yet heard from any leading figure in either party." Meanwhile, the polls were disclosing that 49 percent of Americans believed deploying our troops in Vietnam was a mistake, while 61 percent believed we were losing the war, or at least not winning it.

There can be little question but that Johnson's decision not to run was centered much more on the war than any other issue. He'd tossed all his chips on the Vietnam poker table and was left with a pair of deuces—so now it was better to abandon the game than the war. If he withdrew from

Vietnam, he'd be labeled a traitor. And that left only withdrawal from the politics that had been his lifeblood for over thirty years.

The political considerations were also very much a part of the issue. Contrary to Kearns, Johnson was no shoo-in as the party's candidate. After Bobby's late entry into the race, LBJ met with Larry O'Brien, Democratic National Committee chairman—who predicted that Johnson would do well to garner even 35 percent of the vote in the Wisconsin primary.[5]

Another issue was Johnson's safety. With one death threat after another against their President, the Secret Service was fearful that LBJ would end up as Jack Kennedy had. They counseled Johnson to avoid the hustings, stick to military bases—or better yet, to the White House—and let others do the campaigning. Johnson dispatched Cabinet members to beat the drums and organize local headquarters, particularly in Wisconsin and California, but it was no use. Volunteers were staying away in droves. Johnson was at the end of his political tether. He knew it, and so did Congress, many of whom—up for reelection in November—were leaving more and more space between themselves and this presidential albatross. So when LBJ opened his fateful March 31 speech, he noted, "I was thinking as I was walking down the aisle tonight of what Sam Rayburn told me many years ago. The Congress always extends a warm welcome to the President—as he comes in."

Apart from the issue of security, there was the matter of Johnson's health. He did nothing to scotch rumors that this was the paramount reason for his withdrawing from the race. Long before he acknowledged to Goldwater in January 1969 that "This job is a killer," he'd come to understand that politics, especially at the national level, could exact a frightful toll. His succession of illnesses, some of them near-fatal, were grim testimony to that toll. Theodore Roosevelt, sickly as a child, had, through a strict regimen of outdoor exercise, developed such a constitution that, in 1912, he declared himself "fit as a bull moose!" Lyndon, by contrast, was born with a rugged constitution, yet repeatedly complained of his haunting premonition that he, like his father and other male predecessors, would die prematurely. This foreboding, however, seemed to have little effect on the witches' brew of bad habits that would plague his political years.

Perhaps, in considering his withdrawal, LBJ recalled the words of Truman's similar decision on July 27, 1952: "I have served my time. . . . I don't want to be carried out of the White House in a pine box." Beyond

that, Clifford made note of the striking similarities between the with-
drawals of both presidents. Both were "accidental" presidents. Both left
office in the midst of land wars in Asia that were dividing the nation. And
both suffered political setbacks in New Hampshire.[6] But whereas Truman
disciplined himself, remaining fit and living another twenty years,
Johnson returned to his bad habits and died four years later.

One of the reasons LBJ settled for the vice-presidential slot in 1960, he
explained to aide Bobby Baker, was his poor health. "Bobby," he said, "you
never had a heart attack. Every night I go to bed and I never know if I'm
going to wake up alive the next morning. I'm just not physically capable
of running for the presidency." When economist Elliot Janeway encouraged him to get in the race quickly—for time was short and JFK already
had a commanding lead—Johnson demurred. But Janeway persisted until
LBJ protested, "What are you trying to do, destroy me?"

It wasn't Janeway who would destroy him, or the other reasons he
gave, or others he might have given. It was rather that hubris had run its
course. One step had led to another, not inevitably but willfully, until there
was no other recourse than to touch a match to his own political funeral
pyre.

Yet the question persisted: did he really mean it about withdrawing?
Shortly before his announcement, LBJ had complained to Califano, "Ho
Chi Minh and Fulbright don't believe anything I say about ending the
war." Now few if any of his aides thought he was sincere about bowing out
of the race. Even Lady Bird wasn't sure he meant it. If it took one master
of deception to recognize another, Nixon was well qualified when he concluded that his predecessor, in failing to level with the public, "failed in the
end and was driven out of public office."[7] At the same time, the press was
insisting that it was the Tet offensive that drove him from office. Johnson
was outraged. No one, he insisted to Kearns, had ever *forced* him to do anything. It was his decision and his alone. Many times during his presidency
he'd threatened to quit, although few believed him. Moyers, for one, had
listened to him curse, ruing the day he'd entered office, claiming he simply couldn't wait to leave.

Now he had. Or had he? Always, it seems, Lyndon Johnson hedged
his bets, refusing to close out any options—just in case. That's the reason,
having fallen to JFK, he agreed to be his running mate, despite his view
that Kennedy should have been *his* running mate; despite his vow not to

join the Kennedy ticket, on the advice of his staff; despite his knowledge that nobody on Kennedy's staff wanted him; and despite his own window dressing for the benefit of Bobby Baker, that he was "just not physically capable of running for the presidency."

Now he'd proclaimed to one and all he'd not seek, nor accept, the nomination. What could be simpler than that? Trouble was, Johnson's "credibility gap" was mute testimony to the fact that he'd never be that simple. For there, at the convention in Chicago, was the wisp of a forlorn hope that the nomination would deadlock—that the delegates would come to their senses and draft this elder statesman. It was the same strategy that he'd used in 1960, prompting him to enter the race only at the last minute. But it didn't work then, and it wouldn't work now.

One of the first clues that Johnson didn't really mean his March 31 statement was his appointment of aide Marvin Watson to be Postmaster General, a traditional springboard for campaign manager. At his Ranch that August, LBJ stayed in constant touch with Watson in Chicago, eager for a blow-by-blow description of the anarchy within and without the auditorium. Waiting in the Hill Country wings was the great peacemaker who would calm the unruly masses. He was like John Barrymore, who, taking a curtain call, detected a persistent hiss amid the applause—and, turning to the miscreant, asked, "I agree with you, but then, who are you and I against all this crowd?"

Everything would be in readiness when the call came. A special phone line connected Johnson to Watson in his hotel. In a nearby room, an advance man and Secret Service agents were primed. Gulley, LBJ's military aide, had *Air Force One* and its crew on standby. And then the fateful call came as Johnson was in his swimming pool. His face fell. He heaved the phone across the pool, stomped out of the water, and found refuge in a funk, isolating himself for the rest of the day.[8]

There was no longer any question. Johnson was out of the race. Now his focus was on his place in the history books, which would certainly highlight his upcoming summit in Leningrad, the first such visit for an American president. So fixated was he on this meeting to discuss strategic arms limitations with Soviet leader Leonid Brezhnev that he scarcely heard a word Brezhnev's ambassador, Anatoly Dobrynin, was saying: that the USSR planned to invade Czechoslovakia to put down an insurrection. There, noted the astonished Dobrynin, was the U.S. President, appearing to pay attention—yet he "did not react to it at all; just thanked me for the information."

With that, Johnson moved on to the subject closest to his heart. He was still waiting for the Soviet response to his proposed trip to the USSR. "Utterly oblivious to the impact of what was happening in Prague," recalled Dobrynin, "Johnson asked us to give him a reply about his visit to Moscow no later than between 8 and 9 A.M."

Taking his leave, Dobrynin phoned Brezhnev of LBJ's seeming in-difference to the decision to quash the Prague rebellion. On Wednesday, August 21, Johnson's upcoming trip to the Soviet Union was to be announced simultaneously by Washington and Moscow. But the night before, Soviet tanks rolled into Czechoslovakia.

Testifying before the platform committee of the Democrats, Rusk was interrupted by an aide handing him a note, informing him of the invasion. Immediately he phoned Dobrynin to protest that "the Soviet action was like throwing a dead fish in the President's face." With that, Rusk insisted that Dobrynin phone Moscow and cancel LBJ's proposed summit. Any refusal to cancel he observed, "would have been interpreted worldwide as the United States' condoning the Soviet march into Czechoslovakia." Three weeks earlier, Dobrynin had assured Rusk that no such invasion was planned. But it was clear Johnson had been told in advance—and that LBJ's attitude was, well, he had his own future to worry about. As a result, Dobrynin later commented, Brezhnev "interpreted this indifference to its aggression as evidence that the West would not engage militarily on Warsaw Pact territory." The USSR stamped its heel on the Czechs and, a decade later, sent its military into Afghanistan.

There is some irony in the fact that it was April Fool's Day when Johnson told Larry O'Brien that, by withdrawing from the presidential race, he was trying to restore America's confidence in him. But it was soon evident that America had instead breathed a sigh of relief when LBJ bowed out—and that it had no intention of reelecting him. Hubris had run its course. To Walter Lippmann, Johnson's troubles were rooted in pride, "a stubborn refusal to recognize the country's limitations or his own." To George Reedy, if it hadn't been Vietnam, it would have been something else—for it wasn't so much the issue as Johnson's approach to the issue. To Kearns, it was Johnson's inability to live up to his own definition of a true leader: one "who can get people to work together on points on which they agree and who can persuade others that when they disagree there are peaceful methods to settle their differences."⁹

There is truth in each of these explanations. Yet the one that comes closest to the theme of this chapter was the one enunciated by Harry Ashmore, a newspaper editor who, as senior fellow at Robert Hutchins' Center for the Study of Democratic Institutions, was in Hanoi at the time of Johnson's swan song. Wrote Ashmore, "For a fellow like Lyndon Johnson to announce that he's not going to stand for reelection, this is an act of political self-immolation."

So here was this larger-than-life Texan with the carefully nurtured persona of a superman, turning out to have, like the Hebrew Samson of old, feet of clay. In both cases those feet trod the tragic cycle of hubris. Samson ended up, the blind beast of the Philistines, grinding corn like an ox until he pulled down the temple upon them all. As for Lyndon Johnson, he declared in January 1969, "There is nothing that I would change, as I look back, of any consequence that I have done." For the next four miserable years, he lived this further lie, seeking all manner of rationalization for the grave mistakes he'd made, hiring Kearns to do his official biography in hopes she'd perpetuate the superman persona for future generations. One rationalization he gave Kearns in 1971 was the same one that Moyers and Goodwin had heard as early as 1965, when Johnson tried to link academia and the press in a grand conspiracy: "Two or three intellectuals started it all, you know. They produced all the doubt, they and the columnists on *The Washington Post*, *The New York Times*, *Newsweek*, and *Life*. And it spread and spread until it appeared as if the people were against the war. Then Bobby began taking it up as his cause, and with Martin Luther King on the payroll, he went around stirring up the Negroes and telling them that if they came out in the streets they'd get more. Then the Communists stepped in. They control the three networks, you know, and the forty major outlets of communication." And where had Johnson gleaned all this startling information? From the one person in Washington he had learned to trust, J. Edgar Hoover. LBJ gave credit where credit was due. "It's all in the FBI reports. They prove everything. Not just about the reporters but about the professors, too."

Down in his heart of hearts, he insisted to Kearns, "I knew—I simply knew—that the American people loved me." He desperately clung to the illusion. Yet in the end, his electorate not only came to distrust but to despise this political animal who was all too eager to show every voter the face he imagined each wanted to see.

It is to Kearns' credit she did not collaborate in the deception. In her postscript she concluded, ". . . the war in Vietnam became Lyndon Johnson's war; he personally was dropping the bombs, disrupting the economy, making prices rise, setting back the progress of black and poor." LBJ was, she contended, neither a hero for his success in the Great Society nor a villain for his failure in Vietnam. Johnson's hyping of his personal powers, echoed in the press, were bound to fall short of expectation, dashing his hopes and dreams, "producing," Kearns summarized, "a destructive cycle for the man, the office, and the nation."[10]

Were that the sum and substance of the tragedy—what it did to America—the dimensions would be enough to reduce LBJ to pygmy size among U.S. presidents. But when one considers the gruesome destruction of Vietnam and partial destruction of Cambodia and Laos; the incalculable grief and misery inflicted on millions of homeless refugees; the carnage that left millions severely wounded or dead, 90 percent of whom were civilians and most of these women and children; the havoc caused by millions of land mines that continue to take their toll in death and dismemberment, mainly on children; and the economic sanctions America imposed on Vietnam; then the legacy of Lyndon Johnson reduces him to the level of near-worst, if not *the* worst of U.S. Presidents. His is the legacy of which future generations will not boast. And, lest we, like Kearns, come to think of the Great Society as a success, it is well to note: what the Vietnam War did to near-bankrupt the nation, the Great Society almost completed. A $5 trillion plus millstone of debt around our necks and the necks of our children will serve to remind us that hubris can exact a lasting as well as a frightful toll.

RICHARD NIXON

Out of pride and sycophancy there was born a monstrous fraud. Contempt for others fostered the belief that lies and tricks would work even as mounting evidence showed the truth would out. In the end, Mr. Nixon was alone, divorced from friends and reality in a psychic bunker of his own making.

His end was implicit in his beginning and in his middle. At all stages, in its good parts and its bad, his presidency announces a single warning. It announces the danger of hubris. It proclaims anew the deathless message that those blinded by pride and cut off from reality rush headlong to their own doom.

— Joseph Kraft

Rhetoric v. Reality

"God bless you both." With that benediction, Nixon took leave of Haldeman and Ehrlichman. Having just demanded their resignations at Camp David on Sunday, April 29, 1973, Nixon sought their sympathy as he moaned that it was "like cutting off my arms" to have to fire them. Whether God blessed the pair is problematic, at best. Whether Nixon did was clear. Returning to the White House that evening, he announced to the nation the resignations of "two of the finest servants it's been my privilege to know." High praise indeed from the one who, obtaining a pardon from his successor within a month of his own resignation, refused even to consider pardoning these two men whose crime was having been all too loyal to their President. They'd obeyed virtually every order without question, without hesitation, the picture of resolute fealty.

Of course not all, especially those on Nixon's staff, agreed with the

President's towering appraisal of his two top aides. TV commentator John Chancellor, for example, called them "by far the most unpopular of the two and a half million federal employees," and quoted a member of Congress who claimed that there was "dancing in the halls" after their fall from grace. Given the contempt with which the pair regarded Congress, this was well-earned reciprocity. To recognize just how lopsided the President's thinking was becoming, his proposed defense for them before the grand jury was that, whatever the press wrote about Haldeman and Ehrlichman, "their *motives* were never criminal." Nixon declared in his *Memoirs*, "from that day on the presidency lost all joy for me."

The countdown to Nixon's self-immolation had begun. There could be no turning back. The final, tragic step of hubris seemed to beckon with an inevitability that was as certain as was the complexity of the factors leading to it. In Kissinger's opinion, it was all downhill from then on: ". . . in the final analysis Nixon's fate was ordained once the White House staff began to fall apart and to turn on him."

For some time an astute observer could have detected the end of the reign of King Richard and his imperial court. Hanna Rosin put it well. "There are always signs that a reign is ending, and they are usually spotted not in the king himself but in his court. In the inner circle, latent jealousies between advisors spill into open conflict as they angrily debate who is to blame for the calamity, chewing over each other's past errors and pointing the finger at old and nascent enemies. . . . The ingrained habits of reverence toward the great one—the averted eyes, the bowed head, the devotion to every word as received truth—break down. The subjects no longer regard the king as divine; they begin to speak of him as all too human: one of them, perhaps not even much of an example of one of them. They hang on his every word for an altogether different reason now: to spot the next stumble, record the growing list of regal follies and delusions."[1]

Having fired Haldeman and Ehrlichman, the enigmatic Nixon wallowed in self-pity. To Ray Price, who was drafting a presidential speech, Nixon said mournfully, "Ray, you're the most honest, cool, objective man I know. If you feel I should resign, I am ready to do so. You won't have to tell me. You should just put it in the next draft." Price refused to include it and Nixon heaved a sigh of relief—not that he'd have stuck to this promise any more than the hundreds of others he'd reneged on throughout his political career. Deception—habitual deception—was just one of many corrosives that had eaten away at the foundations of his presidency. It had happened in Britain centuries before, when Lord Acton noted that power tended to corrupt. John Adams had elaborated: "When a government [Britain's] becomes totally corrupted, the system of God almighty in the government of the world, and the rules of all good government upon earth will be reversed, and virtue, integrity, and ability will become the objects of malice, hatred, and revenge of the men in power, and folly, vice, and villainy will be cherished and supported." The remedy: ". . . throw the rich and the proud into one group, in a separate assembly, and tie their hands [as in Britain's House of Lords, a house as devoted to ceremony as is royalty itself] . . . if you give them scope with the people at large on their representation," Adams continued, "they will destroy all equality and liberty, with the consent and acclamations of the people themselves."

Andrew Jackson shed more light on the temptations of hubris when he wrote that few were the men able to "enjoy office and power for any length of time without acquiring a habit of looking with indifference upon the public interests and of tolerating conduct from which an unpracticed man would revolt."

These words might have been written by Nixon himself, so intellectually aware was he of the folly of hubris. Some twenty years earlier, he'd been pushing, like the blinded, weak-kneed Samson of old, at the twin pillars that hold up the foundation of any administration: integrity and responsibility. To the press in 1956, Nixon declared there were just three "surefire issues that would sink an administration: failures in foreign policy leading to war, failures in domestic policy leading to depression, and failures in administration leading to corruption." One sure thing about politics, Nixon had observed, "what goes up comes down."

It took Joe McCarthy four years to learn the lesson as he drank himself to death. It took both Johnson and Nixon five and a half years to learn the same lesson.

It wasn't that the rhetoric was absent. During his last campaign speech in 1968 Nixon roused the audience with, "Let's make the next four years the best in American history!" It wasn't the fault of American history that it had to settle for four of its *worst* years, to be followed by another eighteen months of calamity. The gaping hypocrisy wouldn't have been quite so bad had Nixon's pretenses not been quite so inflated. By June 1969, he had the audacity to compare Americans with Athenians during the Golden Age of Greece, and with the Italians during the Renaissance. All we needed, he declared, was "a resurgence of American idealism [to] bring about a modern miracle in a world order of peace and justice."[2]

Part of Nixon's problem was that he failed to see there was no such thing as lasting peace or lasting justice, that the most we could hope for, or strive for, was a temporary accommodation to peace, a resort to negotiation in order to gain some semblance of equity in the distribution of the world's goods and services. That peace and justice were ideals, like liberty and equality, for which we must strive, knowing we shall never attain them. That, like truth itself, the best we can hope for is approximation, a gaining of a bit more proximity as we pass the truth from one generation to the next. That a measure of justice, a sense of fair play, must ever be achieved to realize a semblance of peace. But then, Nixon would have probably rationalized that the public would fail to grasp, much less tolerate, this hedging notion of idealism, this muffling of the trumpet sounding the clarion call to action, this shackling of the helmsman's arms as he tries to steer the ship of state in the "right" direction. After all, it is enthusiasm that has galvanized the multitudes to respond in unison to accomplish near-impossible tasks. And enthusiasm has forever been founded in certitude, not in hesitation; in slogans, not in caveats.

As G.W.N. Sullivan, former science editor for *The New York Times*, has written: "On all matters where their passions are strongly engaged, men prize certitude and fear knowledge. From certitude can come purpose and a feeling of strength. It breeds courage and action, and is a ready means of ensuring that most desired of all things, an increased sense of vitality. Only the man of strong convictions can be a popular leader of mankind. For most men in most matters, whether it be the justice of a war, the rightness of a political creed, the guilt of a criminal, or the wholesomeness of apples, certitude, in the entire absence of adequate evidence, is easily arrived at and passionately welcomed." Therefore, Sullivan concluded, "A politician who was impatient with misleading catchwords, who really tried to think things out, would probably find his 'usefulness' destroyed, since he might become incapable of simulating that degree of conviction and moral fervor which is necessary to sway large audiences."

So Nixon did what Nixon did best. He mounted podium after podium, addressing the thousands in live audiences, the millions on TV, there to summon one and all to a vision of service, of sacrifice, just as Kennedy had done in 1961. But Richard Nixon was not John Kennedy. JFK, born and raised an aristocrat, rallied the multitudes to support his Peace Corps, his Vista volunteers, his landing of a man on the moon before the decade was out. Nixon, born and raised in comparative poverty, could rally the Republican troops for the short season of a campaign, before they realized that this politician was long on rhetoric and short on reality. The rhetoric: He would end the war in six months with a secret plan that national security would not permit him to divulge. The reality: He extended the war and escalated the bombing, trying desperately to time its conclusion with his reelection. The rhetoric: He would bring the nation together, healing the gaping wounds of a fractured and fractious public. The reality: He drove the wedges ever deeper, dividing the nation as it had not been for a century. The rhetoric: He would leave as his legacy for the history books an image of peacemaker extraordinaire. The reality: He left as his legacy the face of a tyrant who sacrificed Americans and Indochinese alike on the altar of self-aggrandizement.

In 1974, with the release of transcripts of Nixon's White House tapes, the public began to grasp the yawning chasm between rhetoric and reality, between the persona he'd tried to project for twenty-eight years as a skilled actor and the person, the private Nixon, he went to so much trouble to hide.

But Nixon would continue the pretense, serving only to exacerbate the hypocrisy. When Ehrlichman, about to be fired, told Nixon it would do no good, because impeachment was possible if not probable, Nixon pretended to be shocked. The impression he sought to leave was that even the thought of impeachment had never crossed his mind. Yet three months earlier, in January 1973, Nixon the bean counter had, through his intelligence network in the House, arrived at a figure of from 74 to 125 congressmen who would vote there against his impeachment.

High Crimes and Misdemeanors

Little, apparently, did Nixon understand the nature and necessity of the impeachment process. While Jefferson considered impeachment "not even a scare crow," others of the Founding Fathers considered it the single most effective recourse for the abuse of power, short of assassination.

When George Mason stood to address the Constitutional Convention in Philadelphia, he declared, "No point is of more importance than that the right of impeachment should be continued. Shall any man be above justice? Above all, shall that man be above it who [as President] can commit the most extensive injustice?"

The basis for impeachment, the commission of "high crimes and misdemeanors," was not intended to distinguish, as we do today, between felonies and misdemeanors, but was taken directly from British law, implying offenses against the state. James Madison, "Father of the Constitution," was every bit as emphatic as was Mason on the necessity of impeachment. It was "indispensable. . . . For defending the community against the incapacity, negligence or perfidy of the Chief Magistrate." The genius of impeachment, Schlesinger observed, "lay in the fact that it would punish the man without punishing the office."[3]

Repeatedly, as we have noted, Nixon tried to identify the person, the president, with the office, the presidency. By so doing he hoped to frighten the nation, and in turn Congress, into avoiding the drastic action of impeachment, lest the presidency itself be impaired—indeed, lest the government itself be transformed into a parliamentary democracy such as Britain's, where the prime minister, once he loses a vote of confidence, is replaced.

In our nation, presidential impeachment had been tried but once before, 106 years earlier, in the case of Andrew Johnson. It took but three months to impeach, then to try Johnson in the Senate. By the margin of a single vote, it decided he was not guilty of "high crimes and misdemeanors," or, as Mason put it, "great and dangerous offenses." Johnson's offense: he removed his Secretary of War, Edwin Stanton, rump leader of radical Republicans who believed Johnson was trying to "sabotage" Reconstruction. Now Stanton—whom some historians since have implicated in the assassination of Lincoln—was out to impeach Johnson, Lincoln's successor. His crime: trying to "bind up the wounds" left by the war between the states. Stanton was more interested in reparation than reconciliation, a foretaste of Wilson's dilemma at Versailles. This, the impeachment of Johnson, was a slick political maneuver—and certainly not to be compared with the impending impeachment of Nixon, however much he tried to brand it simply "politics as usual." Even Barry Goldwater, an ardent Nixon supporter, was changing his mind. In the

Christian Science Monitor of April 11, 1973, the Arizona senator was quoted, "The Watergate, the Watergate—It's beginning to be like the Teapot Dome. I mean there's a smell to it. Let's get rid of the smell."

The Articles of Impeachment brought against Richard Nixon, divided into three categories, included no less than eighty-three separate "crimes and misdemeanors" against the state, any one of which would have sufficed to impeach him. Andrew Johnson emerged, barely, as not guilty to a charge so patently political that, in retrospect, it appears a farce, a blot on our history. By contrast, the impending impeachment of Nixon was as justified as it was certain.

Had the nation adhered to its pledge to abide by the rules of the United Nations, Nixon and Lyndon Johnson would, in all probability, have been hauled before a war crimes tribunal and been branded as war criminals. For theirs was a war in which America thumbed its nose at the UN and thwarted every effort of that body to negotiate a peaceful end to the conflict, a war as unconscionable as it was interminable: the tragedy of Vietnam. Had Hitler not taken his own life, a war crimes tribunal would undoubtedly have taken it—an inadequate retribution for the millions he methodically butchered in the Holocaust. Had the Indochinese the clout that America wielded as the single most powerful nation on earth, they might well have summoned a similar war crimes tribunal, with Johnson and Nixon first on the docket.

Alas, the power of the three nations making up Indochina couldn't compare with America's power—so after more than a quarter-century, its people continue bearing the scars of war, and falling victim to the millions of land mines strewn across their fields and forests. Meanwhile, the United States, "the land of the free and the brave," has turned to new pages in its ongoing saga. Vietnam, like Korea, has been relegated to the cobwebbed past in the minds of most Americans alive at the time.

By dint of our international dominance, Nixon escaped the hangman's noose or the firing squad's bullet. But he had no way of escaping impeachment, a trial by the Senate, certain conviction, and probable imprisonment. So the idea of his resignation seemed like a masterstroke. It would not only avoid the ignominy of impeachment and imprisonment, but would provide him the opportunity both to secure a pardon and to retain his pension and perks, just as if he'd simply been turned out of office in an election. As the good Doctor Samuel Johnson put it, one's impending execution does wonders in concentrating the mind; so did the thought of impeachment come to concentrate Nixon's mind.

During the countdown he squirmed, like a fish on a hook, trying to save his political hide—while it simultaneously became apparent that he cared not a fig for the welfare of those who had served him loyally, if not well.

Colson's loyalty may have been extreme—though not by much—when, eight weeks after the Watergate break-in, he addressed Nixon's staff: "Think to yourself at the beginning of each day, 'What am I going to do to help the President's reelection today?' And then at the end of each day, think what you did in fact do to help the President's reelection. Just so you understand me, let me point out that the statement in last week's UPI story that I was once reported to have said that I would walk over my grandmother if necessary [for Nixon] is absolutely accurate." The President understood the need for such loyalty, and he appreciated it—to a point. And that point was where he would deign to pardon any before resigning.

Then there was Congress, increasingly suspect of Nixon's call for more and more money either to prosecute the war or to initiate projects at home. So the President simply shifted funds from one account to another—book-keeper's sleight-of-hand. If, however, Congress appropriated money for something Nixon disapproved of, he simply impounded the money, refusing to spend it. These and other abuses at home and abroad were perpetrated at the direction of a President who would be King, commanding a small coterie of unelected aides who were responsible to no one but Nixon. Under a shroud of secrecy, this group perpetrated innumerable illegal acts of planting wire-taps and bugs, of burglaries, conspiracies, and—once caught—perjuries and other means of obstructing justice, all laid at the feet of the one who'd pledged to uphold the laws of the nation, who rode into power on his white horse, proclaiming law and order.

Again and again Nixon pledged to root out the villains, after ridding himself of his Chief of Staff, his Domestic Adviser, and his Attorney General. He insisted on denying any personal involvement in either the break-in or the cover-up. In May, 1973, reporter Helen Thomas noted Nixon's voice quivering and his hands shaking as he declared, "This President solemnly pledges that justice will be pursued, fairly, fully, and impartially, no matter who is involved." That is, unless it be the President.

No surprise to Thomas, Nixon then "almost disappeared from public view." When he did finally reappear, the President was "very downcast, seeking solace from his family and his closest friends. All the while he vowed he'd neither be impeached nor would he resign, regardless 'how rough the going may be.'" Nixon prided himself, as he told David Frost, on being "a pretty tough guy." Indeed, he repeated this to make the point, even though he added unctuously, "When it comes to people . . . I feel for 'em."

For the next fifteen months, the President was so engrossed in avoiding immolation that he virtually ignored problems at home and abroad. While Nixon twisted and turned, Kissinger was "filled with foreboding," as he put it, because the nation, in a "suicidal mood," could suffer "irreparable damage" during the Watergate trials. However, the "rot" they explored "was real enough." Furthermore, "Once Watergate erupted, it was impossible to arrest its course."[4]

Meanwhile, Soviet Ambassador Dobrynin, who was making plans for Brezhnev to visit the United States in June 1973, told Kissinger he was utterly dismayed by the endless fulminating of Americans over the Watergate "mess." No other country, he insisted, would allow itself the luxury of tearing itself to pieces in public. What Dobrynin couldn't seen to grasp was that this country was unlike any other country—and markedly different from the Soviet Union, where Khrushchev had been summarily removed from office for besmirching the honor of the nation in the Cuban Missile Crisis. Brezhnev arrived on June 18, to be greeted by a prediction in *The Washington Post* that Nixon would utterly abandon Haldeman and Ehrlichman, having already fired them, in a last-ditch stand to save his own neck. What he said of this to Brezhnev is unknown. What he wrote in his diary is known: "The story was absolute fiction, but . . . it contributed to the impression that the Nixon White House was a viciously cynical place where I'd turn on my closest aides to save myself." Having written that, Nixon did just that—hanging the two men out to dry with no leave of absence and no prospect of a pardon.

On July 11 Alexander Butterfield, Haldeman's former assistant, helped grease the slope of Nixon's steepening decline by disclosing the White House taping system to Ervin's Committee. That was exactly the break it needed. Immediately Nixon retreated to his fall-back position of executive privilege, claiming that George Washington himself had "refused to surrender executive branch documents to the House. . . .

"What's more, Nixon further claimed, Ervin had argued "that one branch should not be allowed to compel testimony about the internal affairs of another branch"—yet here was the same Ervin denouncing the President's "abstruse arguments about separation of powers and executive privilege."

If Nixon thought he was going to get anywhere with that argument, he was wrong.

Whistling in the Dark

Why did Nixon tape? The claim: "If I'd discussed illegal action, I'd not have taped . . . and if I had taped, I'd have destroyed the tapes once the investigation had begun." So why *did* he tape? For "protection, in case others turned against me." The fact: Nixon started taping long before the Watergate break-in. He did tape his discussion of illegal action, apparently forgetting the machine was recording. In all probability, it was Nixon who bungled the job of trying to erase incriminating parts of one of these tapes—an act for which he blamed Rose Mary Woods, even as Haig blamed "some mysterious force." The President's statement that he would have destroyed the tapes if he'd recorded illegal actions only added credence to the opinion of others, including the experts, that it was Nixon himself who'd tampered with the tapes. Haldeman was certain that it had indeed been his President who had failed in an attempt to conceal or alter the evidence.

On August 7 Tuchman contended that "enough illegal, unconstitutional, and immoral acts have already been revealed and even acknowledged to constitute impeachable grounds." Furthermore, because of the closed societies in the other two major world powers, China and the Soviet Union, it was imperative "to preserve and restore to the original principles our constitutional structure." Therefore, she concluded, "we should grasp the nettle of impeachment if we must." One *Washington Post* reporter went so far as to predict that the percentage of Americans "supporting impeachment would grow dramatically as the case started to be made and the facts organized."

On November 15, Congress allocated $1 million to start impeachment proceedings. By now, Len Garment and Fred Buzhardt had quit, disgusted that Nixon not only refused to level with them, his lawyers, but even to give them the time of day when they tried to convince him to resign.

Members of the House were urging Nixon to go before a Joint Session of Congress, both to lay his case before the legislators and to answer their questions. Never! His explanation: "If I gave a speech and said 'I didn't do it!' the Democrats would say, 'The son of a bitch is lying,' and the Republicans would say, 'Ho hum, he is probably lying but he is our son of a bitch.'" Then Nixon resolved, "I will go down—and I will go down gracefully—but I will not resign. . . . You are wondering why in hell the President can't clear it up. . . . But I know that in the history books twenty-five years from now what will really matter is the fact that the President of the United States in the period from 1969 to 1976 changed the world."[5] No small boast, that.

It was evident that Nixon himself, as well as his case, was coming apart at the seams. Why not go before the people and bare all, including his own mistakes as well as those of his overzealous aides? Why not seek forgiveness in contrition and pledge to turn over a new leaf? Here was what Haig and Kissinger were suggesting. "Bullshit!" was Nixon's response, as communicated by his ever-faithful Ziegler.

Pat Buchanan, a presidential assistant and speech writer, listened to the tapes and concluded that with proper PR, Nixon would be exonerated. Harlow listened to the tapes and concluded, "Those tapes will destroy the President. They'll kill him." Jaworski listened to the tapes and urged Haig to get Nixon "the best criminal lawyer available. . . ." Sirica listened to the tapes and was aghast at Nixon's nefarious hypocritical double-dealing to thwart the long arm of the law. Especially offensive to the judge was the incriminating tape of March 22, 1973—the day after Dean had announced to Nixon that there was a cancer near the presidency. Nixon was nothing if not direct as he gave orders to his aides: "I don't give a shit what happens. I want you all to stonewall it; let them plead the Fifth Amendment, cover-up, or anything else if it'll save the plan." The "plan," of course, was to guarantee "plausible deniability" to keep the cancer from invading the Oval Office itself.

Sirica's perspective after seven more months of Nixon in the White House was that there was an "an inevitable progression of events leading to his resignation in early August." Had Sirica viewed the long stretch from 1946 to 1974, he'd have perceived, step-by-step, the inexorability of Nixon's meteoric career endiing in the ashes of hubris. The last step, immolation, was the grim finale of a political life lived below the thin veneer separating civilized behavior from barbarism. And it came to its climax in 1974.

At the end of that January, Steward Mott, a major McGovern contributor, published what Nixon called "a broadside accusing [me] of twenty-eight indictable crimes ranging from the war in Vietnam to the Watergate break-in." Yet the President was determined to fight on, rationalizing that "although the *case* was badly flawed . . . the *cause* was noble and important." Again he summoned the ghost of Churchill to speak on his behalf: "The longer one lives, the more one realizes that everything depends upon chance. If anyone will look back over the course of even ten years' experience, he will see that tiny incidents, utterly unimportant in themselves, have in fact governed the whole of his fortune and career." The major problem with this explanation, of course, is that it tends to exonerate one of one's mistakes, minimizes volition and, with it, responsibility—the basis not only of a democratic republic but of civilization itself.

In his State of the Union speech to a joint session of Congress on January 30, 1974, Nixon appeared jubilant as he recounted what he considered to be his accomplishments over the previous five years. The President then laid out ten more "landmark accomplishments" he planned for 1974—if "the opposition" would allow him to carry on with "the job that the people elected [me] to do." Then he vowed never to do "anything that weakens the office of the President of the United States or impairs the ability of the presidents of the future to make great decisions that are so essential to the nation and to the world." Such as resigning, he might have added. His rhetoric was as loftily self-serving as his promises were threadbare. But Nixon had his ear tuned to the sound of applause, interrupting him again and again, by a small but fervent group of die-hard Republicans who were convinced that their President was innocent of all charges. Most congressional members, however, felt skeptical, if not downright cynical, about the manipulator who stood before them.

With March came spring, but it brought precious little new life to the besieged presidency. Even the *Washington Star-News*—a Nixon bulwark in his 1972 campaign—had done an about-face, and was now describing his administration as "shot through with moral corruption." William Buckley's brother James, a Senator from New York, called for Nixon's resignation "to spare the nation the agony of a trial in the Senate which might disgrace us in the outside world." Meanwhile, the House Judiciary

Committee contended that Nixon committed "grave misconduct," injuring or abusing "our constitutional institutions and our form of government," and was therefore subject to impeachment. Then, to clarify the difference between impeachment and criminal indictment, the committee defined impeachment as "the first step in the remedial process of removal from office and possible disqualification from holding future office." Its purpose was "not personal punishment" as under criminal law, but simply "to maintain constitutional government."

On April 11, committee chairman Rodino issued a subpoena for 42 more tapes. The President stalled, even as his staff prepared the 1,308 pages of transcripts that Nixon, on national TV, would soon announce he was releasing. Less than three weeks later, the President, with smarmy earnestness, gazed into the cameras and proclaimed he was confident that the American people, if not the Judiciary Committee, would accept the transcripts, "blemished and all," in the spirit in which he was "donating" them. Then, in a redux of "Checkers" 22 years earlier, Nixon said he placed his "trust in the basic fairness of the American people." It was grandstanding at its best. Secretly, Nixon was confident he could perform an end run around the Judiciary Committee, much like he'd done around Eisenhower in 1952. Clothed in the robes of self-righteousness, he counted on the public pressuring the committee to back off, just as he'd gotten the public to pressure Eisenhower to retain him on the ticket.

But Nixon had made a monumental misjudgment. Senate Minority Leader Hugh Scott said the transcripts exhibited "a deplorable, shabby, disgusting, and immoral performance."[6] Vice-President Gerald Ford pronounced Nixon's authority "crippled," while Sirica called the carefully edited transcripts Nixon's "last big lie." Furthermore, by publishing the transcripts, the President forfeited any claim of executive privilege to protect his confidentiality. Then came another bombshell, when the grand jury secretly named Nixon "an unindicted co-conspirator." This meant he was as guilty as the rest in obstructing justice—but he was not indicted because the Constitution didn't seem clear about impeachment proceedings in a case such as this. With the grand jury's pronouncement, Sirica concluded, "The President is doomed."

On May 15, Rodino issued a second subpoena, giving Nixon a week to comply. Seven days later, Nixon responded that he would *not* comply; he'd already done so by releasing the transcripts, "so that a record of any knowledge and action in the Watergate matter would be fully disclosed, once and for all." To ask for more constituted "a never-ending process" that would "fatally compromise" the "institution of the presidency." Therefore, he would not submit to the committee's subpoenas.

Rodino issued yet a third subpoena on May 30, warning Nixon that his refusal to comply, far from trying to protect "the presidency," was a transparent attempt to subvert the wheels of justice by withholding evidence he knew would destroy him. Listening to the "smoking gun" tape of June 23, 1972—in which the President had approved an attempt to cover up Watergate—Nixon was more determined than ever that no one on the Committee would be privy to it.

If Nixon couldn't convince the public that he was the innocent victim of a partisan political attack, he would do the next best thing: demonstrate that he was indispensable to the conduct of foreign policy, which he'd argued was the only important function of the presidency. So, having made plans to visit the hornet's nest of the Middle East, he set off on June 10, 1974. Reporters Evans and Novak, having learned of these plans earlier in the spring, warned that Nixon was playing a dangerous game: "Beleaguered in his White House redoubt and surrounded by fanatic loyalists, the President obviously hopes that during the long delays, the obfuscations and possible court battles ahead, he can recover his political power by brilliant successes in Moscow, the Middle East, and other exotic climes, and ride out the impeachment storm."

Nixon received a lift when, on the eve of his departure, Rabbi Korff's National Citizens Committee for Fairness to the Presidency rounded up 1,400 well-wishers at the Shoreham Hotel Regency Ballroom to give the President a rousing send-off. The group, true believers all, cheered lustily as Republican Senator Carl Curtis of Nebraska predicted, "The get-Nixon crowd, including those who conduct a trial by press, are in for a big surprise." Tricia was even more specific, assuring the audience, "You will be in our hearts all the days of my father's presidency—965 more days." Unfortunately, she would find she was off by 904 days. But the crowd ate it up. When Nixon took his turn at the podium, he began reciting his many accomplishments, only to be interrupted respectfully by applause, cheers, and shouts of "God Bless Nixon." Then the President quoted from a letter he'd gotten from one of his few remaining staff who were not heading to jail: "we shall leave heads high on January 20, 1977"—when

Nixon's second term would end. It all sounded like whistling in the enveloping darkness to which the President had become accustomed. Even with his earthshaking trips to the Middle East and Moscow ahead of him, Nixon was certain "the press will be more obsessed with the minuscule problems involved in Watergate than in the momentous stakes involved in what I'll be doing and saying in the Middle East."[7]

In Cairo, Nixon's hopes soared when he saw more than one million Egyptians lining the streets to greet his motorcade, waving signs that claimed, "We trust Nixon." And well they should, reasoned Egypt's president, Anwar Sadat, thanks to the bountiful largesse that had flowed their way, courtesy of U.S. foreign aid. Possibly more than a little of this largesse had made its way into the personal coffers of Sadat and Nasser before him. In any event, despite over $20 billion in aid from the United States in as many years, the average Egyptian citizen was worse off in 1970 than in 1950. America's generosity had merely served to fulfill Thomas Malthus' dire predictions: enabling children who would have died in infancy to live long enough to reproduce. And they did so in such numbers as to double the size of the population.

Now much of that population had turned out, at Sadat's bidding, to give Nixon what he described in his *Memoirs* as "perhaps the most tumultuous welcome any American president has ever received anywhere in the world." Always, everywhere, Nixon was on the lookout to assure his name in the political "Guinness Book of World Records," if not emblazoned among the great in our history books.

To show his appreciation to the multitudes, Nixon stopped his caravan often, stepping out to press the flesh of startled but eager Egyptians. At the same time Dick Kaiser, heading up the Secret Service contingent, gasped in disbelief: "You can't protect a President who wants to kill himself." It was the same way with his phlebitis. His personal physician, Walter Tkach, had pleaded with him to postpone, if not cancel the trip. No way. Well, keep off your feet. No way. If the phlebitis didn't get him, maybe an assassin's bullet would. Then he'd be able to take his place alongside Lincoln, Kennedy, and other immortals whose devotees could be counted on to continue burnishing their halos. In any event, he told Tkach, this trip was "more important than my life." Therefore, he would not postpone it, much less cancel it. And he would not simply sit, his leg propped up. He would stand; he would walk; he would press the flesh when the spirit moved him. As his leg swelled and inflamed, Nixon refused to be hospitalized, refused to cut short his trip, refused even to wear support hose. The one concession he did make was to have his left leg wrapped in hot towels four times daily and keep it elevated when possible. All that Tkach could conclude was, "The President has a death wish." Well, perhaps so; he'd expressed this on more than one occasion. Yet Abrahamsen believed that Nixon was "too much in love with himself to commit suicide, [seeing] to place himself at the center of the universe."

Back in Washington, Nixon found that Rodino and his committee had finished hearing testimony on all the charges—filling 7,000 pages in 38 volumes. The President, as might be expected, dismissed the evidence as "weak," with most having "little or no direct bearing on my own actions." By June 22, Nixon figured he had 70 Democratic votes in the House on his side, so he needed only 150 Republicans to derail the train of impeachment racing down the track. It was, Nixon marveled in his diary, "just miraculous that we are still in the game at all."[8]

Resting up as best he could at Camp David, Nixon was off again, this time for Moscow. Brezhnev, ever the congenial host, made sure the route from the airport was lined with well-wishers, waving Soviet and American flags. The Soviet press, too, was congenial, scarcely mentioning the Watergate scandal, or treating it as a plot by Nixon's opponents who were out to subvert détente. But the nightmare of Watergate was haunting the President, eroding his power, leaving him in a poor bargaining position to follow through with SALT II negotiations. Worse—at least from Henry Kissinger's viewpoint—Nixon insisted on closeting himself alone with Brezhnev in the Soviet leader's dacha at Yalta. Kissinger, only too aware of FDR's "sellout" to Stalin there in 1945, worried that Nixon would be no match for Brezhnev—especially since he'd excluded his Secretary of State from the meeting. Only after two hours did the President invite Kissinger, armed with the technical details Nixon lacked, to join them. But it was useless. Both sides had reached an impasse over offensive weapons, and the superpowers issued a joint statement, essentially agreeing to disagree.

This was not, however, the way Nixon wanted to spin it. So he had Ziegler hype it as a treaty of "historic proportions." A few people even bought the story. Vice-President Ford, greeting Nixon on his return to the United States, pronounced the benediction on this magnificent achievement: "I cannot escape the conclusion that the Biblical injunction, 'Blessed are the peacemakers,' has again been confirmed."

Soon this "peacemaker" figured he'd put Rodino in his place. So to Allenwood Prison Camp in Pennsylvania Nixon dispatched aides, there to strike a deal with Cornelius Gallagher, a New Jersey Congressman doing time for income tax evasion. Would he like an early release? Certainly, but what would he have to do? Well, word had it that Peter Rodino occasionally kept company with some unseemly Italians, members of the Mafia. Now if Gallagher would "cooperate" and testify to that, he would find an early release forthcoming. It was a deal he just couldn't refuse, thought Nixon. But in fact Gallagher *did* refuse and instead phoned his congressman—who, in turn, phoned Majority Leader "Tip" O'Neill—who immediately got in touch with Rodino. Was there anything that "could come out of the woodwork on us?" Rodino didn't think so. O'Neill breathed easier. "Thank goodness! There's too much riding on this impeachment process." Then O'Neill quoted Justice Brandeis: "Decency, security, and liberty alike depend on a system in which no man is above the law."

By the end of July, Nixon's approval rating had plummeted to an abysmal 13 percent, the lowest since the polling had begun. Impeachment was imminent, its processes lined out in the Constitution. Having gotten the motion to impeach from Rodino's committee, the House, by a simply majority, could vote to impeach. A sort of grand jury at the national level, it would accuse Nixon of specific charges. If impeached, Nixon would have to stand trial in the Senate, presided over by Chief Justice Rehnquest. It would take a two-thirds vote to remove Nixon from office. Then he would be subject to both criminal and civil suits, and would forfeit his presidential pension and perks.

The question facing Nixon was: did he prefer the calamity of resignation in disgrace, with even a pardon from his successor a tacit admission of guilt? Or did he prefer the catastrophe of an impeachment, a trial, and probable imprisonment? "If at all possible," wrote Kissinger, "he has to resign because his own personal judgment of the national interest dictated it." Nixon would indeed resign, but "the national interest" had little to do with it. He figured saving his own skin was a good trade-off for losing face.

It had been fifteen months since the publication of Leonard Lurie's *The Impeachment of Richard Nixon: A Call to Action Now.* "It was time," Lurie concluded in his widely circulated paperback, "for Richard Nixon to join those men he had sent on ahead for judgment and face the consequences for the 'high crimes and misdemeanors' he had committed against his countrymen."[9] Yes, it was almost time.

On July 11 John Dean appeared before the House Judiciary Committee. Nixon called him a "tricky conniver" and Joe Alsop called him a "bottom-dwelling slug." But Dean was there, not to trade aspersions, but to finger his former boss. Presidential lawyer James St. Clair repeatedly made factual mistakes, and Dean repeatedly corrected him, his remarkable memory intact and not swayed by the occasion. In the end, St. Clair's rope was badly frayed, with Nixon hanging at the end.

Finally, on July 12, Rodino's committee issued its report, all 3,888 pages of it, replete with one abuse after another of presidential power. Nevertheless, Ziegler, loyal to the last, said he felt "strongly that the House will not vote impeachment"—more wishful thinking to buoy the spirits of a President that, Haig confided to Jaworski, was "out of control." Jaworski had his own problems. Assuming the House voted to impeach, and the Senate found Nixon guilty, how could the Special Prosecutor find an impartial jury that autumn when the cover-up defendants were scheduled for trial? Somehow Jaworski would have to work out a plea-bargain with the President.

Nixon had his eyes focused not so much on the House, the Senate, or even Jaworski. He was eyeing the Supreme Court, which had four members he himself had named. Surely they would appreciate this prestigious appointment to the highest court in the land and rule for executive privilege and presidential privacy. Yet there was *The Washington Post*, poisoning the well of the justices with its anti-Nixon stories. So the President figured it would be a close call.

By July 17 Minority Leader Scott and Majority Leader Mansfield agreed the Senate had better start preparing for a trial. Scott, less than sad at the prospect, had good reason to feel that way. For he'd gotten a phone call from Haldeman following Nixon's 1972 landslide, telling him that the President intended to replace him as Minority Leader in the Senate. Scott had been thunderstruck. Why? "Because you are not measuring up." Furious at this brazen attempt to usurp the power of the Congress, Scott asked Haldeman if this was Nixon's decision. Haldeman gave no answer, but Scott knew this was not a move the Chief of Staff would have made on his own. Yet despite the White House opposition, Scott was reelected to his position by Senate Republicans. Now it was pay-back time, and Nixon wasn't at all sure he could count on the Minority Leader.

Scott, along with countless others, must have wondered why the President had chosen to cover up the bungled burglary in the first place. For doing that was like opening Fibber McGee's closet on the radio show so popular in the forties. Once opened, pandemonium would break loose. Out would plummet the forged cables Nixon had ordered in hopes of implicating JFK in the death of Diem. Out would tumble the lavish bribes from big businesses. Further, out would fall the burglary of Dr. Fielding's office, in the hopes of discrediting Daniel Ellsberg; the plan to put White House aide Tom Huston in charge of wire-taps, illegal entry, and other intelligence-gathering operations; the Plumbers, who had conducted electronic surveillance on journalists and government officials—in short, the whole kit and caboodle of dirty tricks Nixon had been playing since 1968. The imperial President, the emperor indeed, was to be revealed in all his nakedness, a man without clothes. Even the fig leaf of "Operation Candor"—which reporters dubbed Nixon's repeated assurances that he'd told the whole truth about Watergate—was blatantly transparent. The furtive, secretive Nixon, the President who turned somersaults to secure his "plausible deniability," was at last to be exposed as the forgery he was. The private person was, at long last, to give the lie to the crafted persona he'd been careful to project for twenty-eight years. His self-immolation was as imminent as it was humiliating.

Hubris was about to run its course. The only question the nation had was: which course—impeachment or resignation? A half-dozen times, Nixon later recounted, Kissinger had urged him to resign, but the President refused "to quit." Nixon enjoyed contrasting Kissinger's weak backbone with his own courageous stand in adversity.[10] Now, facing virtually certain impeachment, he vowed to "fight . . . like hell."

July 23, 1974 was, Nixon moaned to Haig, his "lowest day in the presidency," the day when in "a sense of hopeless loss and despair," he laid out his two options. He could "voluntarily" resign, or subject the nation to "six months of having the President on trial in the Senate." If he resigned, he'd be "besieged by lawsuits costing millions of dollars and taking years to fight." Then, to make sure that Haig understood just how lofty were his intentions, Nixon insisted that "personal factors must not be the deciding ones;" instead, the deciding factor would be the welfare of the nation. Then, ever adept at giving the lie to his own statements, Nixon turned again to count noses on the Hill. To his dismay, he found he'd lost all three Southern Democrats on the Judiciary Committee. Here was a blow to the solar plexus. Yes, he'd been "prepared to lose one and had steeled [himself] for losing two." But losing all three meant certain defeat on the House floor. It meant impeachment.

Nixon was down, the wind knocked out of him. But he wasn't out—not by a long shot. To the phone he hustled. Would Flowers change his vote? No. Would George Wallace? No. Would James Allen? No. Would Joe Waggoner? No. "Well, Al," complained the President to his Chief of Staff, "there goes the presidency." Not exactly. There goes the *President* would be more like it. But then, identification had always been a useful ploy for Nixon.

If that had been Nixon's "worst day," July 24 would be little better. For that morning the Supreme Court handed down its verdict, ruling in favor of congressional subpoena power and against executive privilege—unanimously. Nixon's verdict: ". . . The United States has lost. . . . The presidency itself was a casualty of this ruling." He would now have to turn over—"voluntarily," of course—all sixty-four tapes subpoenaed by Rodino's committee.

With the remaining tapes at last surrendered, the committee, the press, and the nation soon learned of the incriminating evidence of obstructing justice in the "smoking gun" tape. It proved to be the last nail in his impeachment coffin. On July 27 Republican National Committee chairman Dole saw that Nixon was no Midas. Instead of everything the President touched turning to gold, it all turned to ashes. For on that day the Judiciary Committee approved, 27 to 11, the first article of impeachment, stating that Nixon had engaged in a "course of conduct" designated to obstruct the investigation. All the proof they needed was on that June 23, 1972 tape. Some of Nixon's counterparts across the world were "shocked" by this nation's treatment of its President. Other world leaders tended to see Nixon as David Frost described him: "a tragic figure in the classic sense—a man of limited character who had striven valiantly to rise above his own limitations, succeeding for a while but destroyed in the end by his own inherent flaws."

Nixon, returning from his Western White House two days later, was "shocked to see . . . impeachment hysteria had taken over the city," in the wake of the issuing of the second article of impeachment. It charged, Nixon wrote, "That I had committed an impeachable offense by abusing the powers of the presidency." The next day came the third: "That I had committed an impeachable offense by defying the committee's subpoenas for tapes and documents." Debate on impeachment was scheduled to begin in the House on August 19.

The same day, July 30, Nixon got lawyer Fred Buzhardt to listen to the June 23, 1972 tape of him conversing with Haldeman on two occasions. Buzhardt was insistent that the two were corroborating the cover-up plans they'd agreed upon earlier that day, including the use of the CIA to stop the FBI's investigation for political reasons. But, Nixon protested, didn't the tapes show clearly that national security was the overriding issue? No. All the tapes did, Buzhardt contended, was to "make it clear that the security business was the cover story." Nixon was vehement, almost shouting, "I know what I meant, and regardless of what's on the tapes, it was done for national security reasons." Buzhardt wanted particulars: "What were they?" Nixon refused to reply. Buzhardt then figured that fellow attorney James St. Clair should judge for himself. St. Clair listened to the damning tape three times and concluded that he'd misinformed the Judiciary Committee. The implication was as clear as the evidence: For two years, Nixon had been lying about national security being his sole motive for the CIA to squelch the investigation. It was patently a political ploy.

If Nixon and Buzhardt were upset, St. Clair was more so. For if a client lied to his attorney or withheld evidence, it was the lawyer's obligation either to reveal it or to persuade the client to change his plea. The one option left, St. Clair insisted to the President, was resignation. But Nixon was deaf to the idea. He'd stay and fight. He was no quitter. He'd fight to the finish![11]

Even Nixon's son-in-law, David Eisenhower, was by this time convinced that the President had been lying all along. The transcripts did it. Julie's father, David suggested to his wife, should "admit his participation" in the cover-up and acknowledge he was guilty of woeful mismanagement—although not of criminal conduct. Julie was furious. How could her husband even suggest such a thing?

On August 1 Nixon told his Chief of Staff that he'd changed his mind: he *would* resign. But, the President insisted, he'd also end his career "as a fighter . . . the way it had begun." His "instincts," always reliable, had told him the night before that this was "the right thing to do." Yet resignation seemed tantamount to the victim of a mugger forking over his wallet when, with a gun in his ribs, he was given the option, "Your money or your life!"

Calamity was staring Nixon in the face. There was St. Clair, upset that his client had consistently and deliberately lied to him, and let him misinform Rodino's Committee. There was Haig, upset at the stark contradiction between Nixon's plea of innocence and his actual words with Haldeman on June 23, 1972. In fact, Haig told Nixon, the tape was probably fatal. Not so, insisted the President, it was all in the testimony—national security, pure and simple. "Goddammit," shouted the frustrated Haig, "it's not all in the testimony." This tape contained new, different, and insurmountable evidence. Then, with the forced calmness of a teacher trying to explain the ABCs to the class dunce, Nixon tried to show Haig the facts. Around and around they went, until the President at last conceded that Haig might have a point. Reaching a new low, Nixon then asked Haig to construct a list of options. He and Buzhardt came up with a half-dozen, the last one to "resign and hope that Ford would pardon him."

It was time for Haig to consult with Ford, who asked him about the power of a president to pardon. Haig assured him that he had the unrestricted right to do so—and before any criminal charges were brought against Nixon. Well, Ford acknowledged, he'd have to think it over, talk to his wife, and consult with St. Clair.

Now that he knew Nixon's days were numbered, Ford met with the transition team he was putting in place. Ford made it clear tht there was not to be even a hint of a deal struck between him and Nixon.

Judge Sirica was disgusted at the news that Nixon might resign to avoid the wheels of justice. "I would have sent him to jail," vowed the judge, had Nixon remained in his court. Sirica noted that the President had not even answered the pleas of Haldeman and Ehrlichman for a pardon, yet now he was banking on the leniency of Gerald Ford to pardon his own far worse crimes.

This is no little irony and a lion's share of hypocrisy in the fact that Nixon's meteoric rise to power as Vice-President was predicated on his finding Hiss guilty of perjury. Now, twenty-five years later, Nixon's plunge into the abyss of hubris stemmed in large part from his own lying.

Buchanan, one of the last of Nixon's loyalists, listened to the June 23, 1972 tape, and, in his inimitable way, declared on August 5, "All I can conclude is that the old man has been shitting us."[12]

For Whom the Bells Toll

Were all the church bells across the land to have tolled, simultaneously, eighty-three times—one for each of Nixon's "high crimes and misdemeanors" lumped under the three articles of impeachment, perhaps the public would have fully grasped the seriousness of what Theodore White declared to be, "The greatest scandal in American political history." Or, as Leon Jaworski put it, Nixon's hoisting the flag of national security over his misdeeds may have given them "a deceptively compelling ring," yet they ultimately represented a "wholesale rejection of the rule of law."

Before the Supreme Court, St. Clair dragged out Nixon's threadbare argument that this was partisan politics, pure and simple, and as such should be settled between the White House and Capitol Hill. The Supreme Court disagreed, and rang down the curtain on Nixon's last plea. Still the drowning President held on, clutching at every straw of rationalization. His resignation was just days away, yet the President continued to ask, "*What* wrongdoing?" Almost two years later, Nixon, talking to a former schoolmate, never so much as hinted that he'd done anything wrong—and certainly nothing deserving impeachment! That same month, talking with old friend Bob Finch, he did acknowledge, "*We* made some mistakes." Not, a surprised Finch noted, "*I* made a mistake."

On July 27, when the Judiciary Committee approved the first article of impeachment, George Will predicted that not only would Nixon take the escape hatch of resignation, but would utter his swan song, "with a sincerity at once grotesque and pathetic, that he'd done no serious wrong."

President Calvin Coolidge had once written, "For a man not to recognize the truth, not to be obedient to law, not to render allegiance to the state, is for him to be at war with his own nature, to commit suicide." Nixon would do just that, albeit political suicide.

Far from having "suffered enough," as Ford put it in pardoning Nixon, he scarcely felt the lash of justice that seventy of his aides suffered: men who had done his bidding, directly or indirectly, or who had acted as they did, thinking it was in the best interests of their President.

By resigning and being pardoned, Nixon received the same benefits—including pension, expenses, staff, and Secret Service protection—as other former presidents."[13]

Nixon, inflaming passions and inflicting pain, held to a course, as Frost noted, that—reduced to basics—was meant to serve only himself. The President first dismissed Watergate, that tiny cloud on the horizon, as "a third-rate burglary," perpetuated by a bunch of bungling amateurs. As the cloud grew and approached, Nixon acknowledged it might be "a blip on history." When it moved ever closer, punctuated with lightning on the horizon and the low rumbling of distant thunder, Nixon decided it might become "the broadest and thinnest scandal in the history of American politics." And now the twentieth-century Elijah ordered speech writer Ray Price to prepare his last public words as President—vintage Nixon all. Instead of acknowledging the maelstrom in which he'd finally been caught, instead of owning up to the repeated violations of the law he'd sworn to uphold, instead of recognizing the eighty-three separate offenses, any one of which was enough to impeach him—he sounded, in Frost's words, more like a chief executive who'd lost a close vote over dam projects. He was resigning, subjecting himself to "voluntary impeachment," Nixon said, "because it has become evident to me that I no longer have a strong enough political base in Congress to justify continuing that effort." It was as if the last words of a serial killer, facing the hangman's noose, had been, "I do this because I lost my support in the jury that convicted me."

By this time Barry Goldwater was determined Nixon should resign. "There are only so many lies you can take and now there has been one too many. Nixon should get his ass out of the White house—today!" On August 7, a trio of Republicans—Senators Goldwater, Scott, and House Minority Leader John Rhodes—met with Nixon, who was still counting votes on Capitol Hill. Could he muster ten in the House, Nixon asked Rhodes sarcastically. Before Rhodes could answer, the President turned to Goldwater, who painted a picture more grim than Nixon had imagined: he didn't have half of the thirty-four votes he needed in the Senate. Scott chimed in that there were maybe fifteen, "and they're not very firm." In fact, he added, when push came to shove, the most Nixon could count on were four.

The next night, while Kissinger was consoling Nixon—distraught for all the front he'd managed to muster—Rose Mary Woods was trying to console the girls after informing them that their father was resigning. Suddenly Nixon walked in and announced, "We're going back to California." The girls broke down. But not Pat; she seemed to have no more tears to shed. When White House photographer Ollie Atkins entered to take some final pictures, Pat objected, but her husband, as usual, prevailed. When Atkins left, father and Julie fell in each other's arms, while Tricia began to weep.

With Kissinger, Nixon had been more talkative—but it all had to do with him: with his place in history, with a recital of his accomplishments, with what he and Kissinger had done together. On this night before his resignation, there was no concern expressed about his family, his aides, or his Republican colleagues. Nixon made no mention of some 25,000 Americans who had lost their lives in Vietnam during his administration, no mention of the million or more Indochinese killed, no mention of the savagely wounded, no mention of the grieving families on both sides of the ocean. There was nothing of the million or more land mines planted by U.S. troops, which would still be taking their toll a quarter-century later. Nothing of the fields and forests devastated by Agent Orange, nothing of the cities and hamlets left in ruins, nothing of the millions of hapless refugees in makeshift, squalid camps, desperately clinging to life day by day. And, finally, there was nothing of the hundreds of POWs, many of them tortured and starved, or the hundreds of thousands of GI's returning home, many of them strung out on drugs, the anesthetic of choice when facing a thankless and carping public.

This was the ultimate obscenity. None of these larger concerns occupied Nixon's mind, for, as Kissinger noted, the fallen President was "hardly [able to] bear the thought of the indignity of a criminal trial. . . ." When Kissinger tried to console Nixon over brandy, insisting that history would "remember his major achievements," the President answered, "It depends who writes the history." As the evening ended, Nixon the Quaker asked Kissinger the Jew to pray with him. Kissinger "was filled," he wrote, "with a deep sense of awe"—and at a loss as to "exactly what to pray for."

The next day, Kissinger met with Ford, and after ninety minutes, left realizing "that for the first time in years after a presidential meeting, I was free of tension." And how did he explain it? "It was impossible to talk to Nixon without wondering afterward what other game he might be engaged in at the moment. Of one thing you could be sure: no single conversation with Nixon ever encapsulated the totality of his purposes. It was exciting, but also draining, even slightly menacing."

Another Nixon aide, unidentified by Frost, told him that in all the years he'd worked with Nixon, "I never heard him utter a profane word." Yet now, he added, "The memory of Nixon tortures me . . . I feel raped, betrayed. I have had nightmares—screaming nightmares—about him." America's long nightmare under its thirty-seventh President was about to end. Hubris had run its course, claiming not simply this one victim, but the many millions more affected by his decisions. The persona of the international statesman, whose fascination with global issues preoccupied his presidency, was now in a dramatic clash with the person, the private man—the man one policy adviser described as a "frighteningly insecure political thug," the man Americans discovered in the transcripts, "sanitized" though they were.[14]

Nixon went to great pains on his last address as President. His speech, he told Price, had to be letter-perfect. Indeed, Nixon had awakened Price at 4:15 that morning to give him further suggestions. The President's appearance also had to be perfect. In came Milton Pitts, his barber, to give him a shampoo, blend his hair with a razor, and blow-dry it, Pitts said, for a "softer, more natural look." Finally, Nixon checked to make sure there was a back-up TV camera, that the lights showed him at his very best, that the microphone was carrying his voice just right. But he had a problem with his collar. "Would you mind checking my collar? Is it . . . it's not ruffled up?" He coughed. He cleared his throat. Everything had to be just so. Persona again. It is monumentally ironic that this President—charged with no less than eighty-three "crimes and misdemeanors," facing certain impeachment, a certain guilty verdict in the Senate, and possible prison—would be so preoccupied with himself and his place in history one night, and so preoccupied with his appearance on television the next night. But that was Richard Nixon: obsessed with the image, it was all PR. How would it play in Peoria? Style over substance. Persona over person. He'd spent a political lifetime manicuring, buffing, polishing his persona. Yet beneath the veneer was a character as morally bankrupt as any occupant of the White House before or since. Now, in that palace of his dreams, Nixon was about to take his leave—not willingly, but because the American people were finally fed up with this egomaniac.

As offensive as was Nixon's fixation on the trivia of his persona, the next sixteen minutes capped even that. In some respects it was a redux of "Checkers," twenty-two years earlier. Peter Rodino shook his head in disgust as the President claimed the lack of "a strong enough political base in the Congress" was his reason for resigning.

The closest Nixon came to contrition was, "I regret deeply any injuries that may have been done in the course of events that led to this decision. I would say only that if some of my judgments were wrong, they were made in what I believed at the time to be the best interest of the nation." Leon Jaworski was seething as he listened. "Here would have been a good resignation speech for a President leaving office because of illness, or for one who had lost congressional support because of differences over policies. It was not the speech of a President who had violated his Constitutional oath and duty by obstructing justice, by abusing the power of his office, by transforming the Oval Office into a mean den where perjury and low scheming became a way of life." Jaworski concluded that Nixon "hadn't given Congress even a crumb of remorse to chew on."

Concluding his speech, Nixon started to walk to his living quarters when he heard chanting outside. At first misunderstanding, Pat steered her husband to the window to look out at the crowd. But it was not the group of supporters the Nixons had hoped to see, and their shout was not "Hail to the Chief" but "Jail to the Chief." Those few protesters were speaking for the great majority of their countrymen—who were sick of Nixon's Vietnam, sick of Nixon's "peace with honor," and sick of Nixon's complicity in the Watergate cover-up.

Painfully, they had come to realize that the President's worst enemy was not the press, or Congress, or the Democrats, or any of the 101 other enemies he was so obsessed with cataloging. Instead, it was the President himself. As Theodore White put it, ". . . Richard Nixon alone had been able to destroy Richard Nixon. . . .for his perception of power, at which he thought himself a master, was flawed, as his character was flawed."

The next morning Nixon said his good-byes to his White House staff, disturbed that he had to wear his glasses for the first time in public. Persona again. With that, Nixon signed the single sentence handed him by Haig: "I hereby resign the Office of President of The United States." It was 11:35 A.M., August 9, 1974, the 2,027th—and final—day of his presidency. Little good it had done for his grandmother to present him, at the age of 13, a picture of Lincoln, her idol, inscribed with the lines from Longfellow:

"lives of great men oft remind us/We can make our lives sublime/And, departing, leave behind us/Footprints on the sands of time."[15]

Richard Nixon left footprints, but hardly as a "great man." As Fawn M. Brodie put it: "The sense of national humiliation and betrayal affected everyone; those who voted for him felt shame, and those who did not were ashamed for their country. In his fall he was pelted with epithets: '. . . shabby, foul-mouthed, conspiratorial, manipulative, synthetic, power-hungry, and morally bankrupt.'" He displayed, John Kenneth Galbraith wrote, "a deeply bogus streak." Arthur Miller saw that he'd "marched instinctively down the crooked path." As far as Henry Steele Commager was concerned, Nixon was "the first dangerous and wicked president," while Arthur Schlesinger believed his resignation had saved the office "from the man who did more to discredit and endanger it than any other President in our history." George McGovern added, "I have to live with the knowledge that, not only did I lose the election, but I lost it to the most discredited man ever to occupy the White House."

Though Nixon had been vanquished, the Constitution had been vindicated, and with it the wisdom of the nation's Founding Fathers. As Commager has reminded us, the brilliant, mercurial Alexander Hamilton gave but half-hearted support to that new Constitution, branding it "a frail and worthless fabric." He had little confidence in such a document, with no historical precedent, that had been cobbled together by men widely separated in vital beliefs and values. Moreover, it was attempting to devise a federal system and elect a president for the first time in history. Beyond that, it was incorporating not only the separation of three powers within government, but authorizing each to keep a rein on the other. Finally, it was attempting to devise a balance between the rights of the states and those of the federal government on the one hand, and a balance between the rights of individuals and the federal government on the other. It was indeed a tall order; no wonder Hamilton held out scant hope for it. Incredibly, however, it worked—and has continued to work, not only for Americans, but as a beacon to other nations attempting to devise representative governments. Tom Paine put it well: "Where then is the king of America? Know that in America the Constitution is king."[16]

"Have a nice day," said Betty Ford as Nixon and his wife boarded a helicopter on the South Lawn. Never forgetting the vital importance of projecting the persona he'd polished for twenty-six years, Nixon stood in the doorway of the helicopter and, with arms held high, effected the picture of a fighter to the end, suffering the torments of the damned because his innumerable enemies were all linked in some vast conspiracy. He was the dogged hero, upholding integrity and honor, sure to be vindicated by history as statesman extraordinaire. Still, Betty Ford's farewell was a tall order. Not only had he resigned in the humiliation of perpetrating the greatest scandal of the American presidency. Even his phlebitis began acting up again, leaving him almost dead after surgery that October. He was also plagued by debt, owing more than $460,000 in back taxes, as well as sky-high legal and medical bills—all on a pension of $60,000, which came to about $500 a week after state and federal taxes were subtracted. In addition, he'd been reduced to a staff of four secretaries to handle over a million pieces of accumulated mail, and the government allotment for that staff would end on July 1, 1975. It would take some doing to "have a nice day," or week, or month, or year, even with Ford's pardon. Hubris had run its fateful course and the President—now ex-President—would have twenty years to reflect, to rationalize, to emerge again and again in desperate attempts to resurrect his persona: the peripatetic phoenix rising from the ashes.

Not for another year would Nixon even come close to a *mea culpa*. After receiving his pardon in September 1974, he mustered only this: "No words can describe the depth of my regret and pain at the anguish my mistakes over Watergate have caused this nation. . . ." Still no admission of wrongdoing, of violating the inaugural pledge he'd taken to uphold the law, and especially the Constitution.

Almost three years later, in a series of discussions with British journalist David Frost, Nixon was still holding tenaciously to his innocence. Back in 1968, Frost had interviewed Nixon—and, asked how he'd like to be remembered if he were president, he responded, "As having made some contribution to a kind of world in which we can have peace in the last third of this century." Nine years later, his presidency in tatters, desperate for the $600,000 Frost was paying him so he could meet his legal bills, Nixon was less than candid. The only way in which he'd "brought us together" was in the near-unanimous conviction that he was, indeed, guilty of high crimes and misdemeanors, and therefore fully deserving of being flushed from office.

Asked about his significant contributions as president, Nixon was as candid and clear-thinking as he was unhesitating. Asked about shortcomings, he hemmed and hawed, resorting to vagueness, circumlocution, and dissembling. He would admit nothing, no questionable—much less criminal—activities. How did Nixon justify lying to the American people about his secret bombing of Cambodia within three months of inheriting the White House? Well, Ike had done the same in putting out false leaks "of where we might attack" before going into Normandy. Nixon saw no difference in deceiving an enemy in wartime as a justifiable tactical maneuver, and deceiving the American electorate to whom he was ultimately responsible.

Did Nixon have any regrets about the emergence of Pol Pot and his Khmer Rouge, with their genocidal rampage in Cambodia? Didn't the United States, in fact, create the Khmer Rouge with its indiscriminate bombing there? Nixon: "It was never the policy of the U.S. to kill civilians. That was the enemy's way." It was pitiful, Nixon maintained: After ordering "the biggest strike of the war" over Christmas 1972, and forcing Hanoi to the bargaining table within the month so that Nixon could at last have his "peace with honor," Congress blew it by shutting off funds for the war. There was no doubt about it in Nixon's mind. "Congress lost [Vietnam]. And that's the tragedy and they have to take responsibility for it." Nixon made no mention of his secret $3 billion pledge in reparations to bribe the North Vietnamese to negotiate, or of congressional unwillingness to part with more than a tenth of that.

Throughout the twenty-two hours of interviewing, the closest Nixon came to an admission of guilt was when Frost asked if it wouldn't have been better to fight his political enemies lawfully—rather than resorting to the illegal and thus "adding another crime to the list." In theory, Nixon insisted, Frost's proposition was "perfect." However, "in practice it won't work." But, Frost persisted, trying to explain his actions on the basis of what he considered in the interests of the country, how could Nixon justify illegalities? Nixon's answer will probably resonate throughout history as the epitome of a hubristic president: "Well, when the president does it, that means it is not illegal."

It is little wonder then, that after assuming office, President Gerald Ford announced, "Our long national nightmare is over. Our Constitution works; our great Republic is a government of laws and not of men; here the people rule."[17]

EPILOGUE

Progress, far from consisting in change, depends on retentiveness. . . . Those who cannot remember the past are condemned to fulfill it.

— Santayana

Johnson and Nixon: An Evaluation

Hedley Donovan, former editor-in-chief of *Time* and senior advisor to Jimmy Carter, suggested in 1982 some thirty-one characteristics of a good president. Among them was Truman's insistence that "the principal power that the President has is to bring people in and try to persuade them to do what they ought to do without persuasion."

One of the flaws of both Johnson and Nixon was the impression they left on their audiences. Where Johnson read his speeches as if he were on the stump back in Texas, Nixon was alternately the cold fish, the pugnacious campaigner, or the self-righteous Job, set upon by unspeakable enemies. Neither of them wanted to level with the voters, both tried to patronize them, and, in the end, both failed in their attempts to seduce the muse of history.

The ability of a leader to effect change, that is, substantial change for the best, is perhaps the hallmark of a president's standing. Through his indomitable courage and steadfast commitment, Washington led the colonies to their independence from Britain. More importantly, with others at his side, he helped secure the foundations of a new nation. "Four score and seven" years later, Lincoln engaged in a "great civil war, testing whether that nation . . . can long endure," as many states seceded to form a separate country. By dint of the same courage and commitment

Washington had displayed, and in the face of repugnant and incessant criticism, North and South, Lincoln succeeded in holding America together. In another fifty years, Wilson led the nation into its First World War, armed with his vision of a League of Nations designed to "make the world safe for democracy." Twenty years later, Roosevelt led the nation into another World War, and from it sprang the seeds of a new world order, the United Nations—bringing at last to fruition Wilson's dream. It is instructive that all four of these presidents place in the top ten of virtually every ranking of U.S. presidents. It is also instructive that all were war presidents, consumed with their vision of sweeping and auspicious changes: the first with founding a new nation, the second with holding it together, and the third and fourth with founding a new world order in which peaceful negotiation would replace military confrontation. The magnitude of the changes wrought, and the transparent good—for the nation and for the world of nations—can only add to the luster of these four presidents.

This is not to say that their four wars were necessary, much less noble. Amost certainly, all four conflicts—and the resultant huge loss of life—were preventable. But perhaps they were also illustrative of the axiom of philosopher Alfred North Whitehead: that momentous advances in civilization invariably come at the cost of virtually wrecking the societies in which they occur.

Not that these presidents were flawless. Yet if we were to wait for saints to come marching in to effect necessary transformations, we would have a long wait. These men, striving to extend their reach beyond their grasp, invariably stretched from precarious feet of clay, amid swelling tides of criticism. And the greater the change, the greater the criticism. As Wilson put it, "If you want to make enemies, try to change something." He made this observation just months before introducing the catastrophic change of leading the nation into war. Less than twenty-five years later, not long before he led the United States into World War II, FDR also spoke of change. "Since the beginning of our American history we have been engaged in change—in a perpetual peaceful revolution—a revolution which goes on steadily, quietly adjusting itself to changing conditions—without the concentration camp or the quick-lime in the ditch." The change wrought by this second global carnage was neither quiet nor peaceful. But from its ashes rose the dream of Wilson and Roosevelt: a world body encouraging nations to resolve their differences peacefully.

Under these four presidents great goals were proposed, great risks taken, and great transformations effected.

And what of Johnson and Nixon? Each was aware of change as vital to survival. "We must change to master change," said Johnson. "The people's right to change what does not work," wrote Nixon, "is one of our greatest principles of our system of government."[1] Both undertook radical change: Johnson in his domestic programs, as he tried building his "Great Society"; Nixon in his foreign programs, such as opening up xenophobic China "to the family of nations." Both, however, fell prey to the Vietnam War and, in Nixon's case, the extension of that into Watergate. Had it not been these obstacles, it would have been others—mileposts along the fateful path of hubris.

Not only must presidents attempt profound change, but take great risks in doing so. Though "prudence," wrote Jefferson of Washington, "was perhaps the strongest feature in [his] character . . . once decided, he went through with his purpose, whatever obstacles opposed." Lincoln was assassinated for the momentous risks he took to hold the nation together. While few could express it so well, many agreed with Walt Whitman that his "captain" had steadied the keel of "the vessel grim and daring" before being slain. Wilson, too, took great risks in reneging on his promise to keep us out of war, then in fashioning a League of Nations, paying for his relentless advocacy of it with his life. As for Roosevelt, made a paraplegic by polio, he was, in the words of Lyndon Johnson "the only person I ever knew—anywhere—who was never afraid." Johnson and Nixon both took substantial risks, yet neither persuaded the American people that the risks were worth the goal, partly because neither tried hard enough, partly because their penchant for deception undercut their credibility.

All four of our greatest presidents fixed their eyes on great goals and risked much to reach them, striving mightily in the process. The same indefatigable industry that drove Washington from tent to tent at Valley Forge to bolster the courage of his men carried through his presidency. Night after night, Lincoln burned the midnight oil as he pursued the long, arduous, and bloody war to a successful conclusion. It was Wilson's unflagging determination to go beyond the nay-sayers in the Senate and take his case for the League directly to the people that led to his fatal illness. Roosevelt, despite crutches and wheelchair, threw himself into "the joy and stimulation of work" in rousing a nation from the depths of a searing depression and leading it into a world war. No other president worked harder to over-come a major affliction. His reasoning: "If you have spent two years in bed trying to wiggle your big toe, everything else seems easy." As for Johnson and Nixon, few could criticize them for lack of commitment as they drove themselves, their wives, and their staff. At times it appeared that the only respite from their exhaustion would be the deathbed itself.

The goal, the risk, the effort—none would mean much without the master switch of an intelligent mind directing them. Of Washington, Jefferson wrote, "His mind was great and powerful, without being of the very first order; his penetration strong. . . ." But it was his judgment that Jefferson scored at the top: "No judgment was ever sounder." Of Lincoln, Wilson wrote, "Lincoln was a very normal man with very normal gifts, but all upon a grand scale, all knit together in loose and natural form, like the great frame in which he moved and dwelt."[2] Wilson himself, as president of Princeton, was one of the few true intellectuals to be admitted to the White House. FDR, while but an average student at Groton School in Massachusetts, went on to Harvard—where he edited *The Crimson*—and then to Columbia for his law degree. There can be little doubt that both Johnson and Nixon were quick studies, possessed of remarkable memories, particularly when it came to facts, names, and faces that could boost their political stature. While neither thought of himself as an intellectual, it is evident from Nixon's seven books that he was articulate. Yet if judgment remains a critical mark of intelligence, both men fell well below the mark of our great presidents.

In 1788, before Washington took office, Alexander Hamilton predicted that office would "never fall to the lot of any man who is not in an eminent degree endowed with the requisite qualifications." Above all, he foresaw in that office men "prominent for ability and virtue." And it was there, in the realm of character, that both Johnson and Nixon came up dramatically short. We need not resort to the legend of the cherry tree to attest to Washington's integrity. Jefferson described it as "most pure." Indeed, "He was . . . in every sense of the word, a wise, a good, and a great man." Lincoln, for his part, thought the name of Washington as "mightiest in moral reformation."

Other presidents, in turn, paid tribute to Lincoln's character. Benjamin Harrison praised him for his "ability to endure the impatience of others." Grant, on the other hand, wrote of his "generous and kindly spirit toward the Southern people, never [having] heard him abuse an enemy." These and similar tributes to Lincoln's character were shared widely enough at the time of his assassination that, in calling for a day of mourning, Andrew Johnson urged the nation to contemplate his virtues.

Wilson, whose admiration of Lincoln persisted despite his being raised in Georgia—scene of Sherman's devastating "March to the Sea," and the painful years of Reconstruction—was the son of a Presbyterian minister, and no slouch when it came to character. Elected governor of New Jersey in part by the Democratic bosses, he nevertheless pushed through laws to curb their corruption. Once in the White House, Wilson was the first president to initiate press conferences, convinced that Jefferson was right when he wrote, "If a state expects to be ignorant and free, in a state of civilization, it expects what never was and never will be."[3]

Perhaps the most outstanding example of personal courage in an American leader occurred on June 26, 1924, when FDR—leg braces barely supporting his 6'4" frame that had been wracked with polio—stood without his crutches, then step by painful step made his way to the podium to nominate Al Smith for president. Gripping it, he tossed back his head and broke into an infectious smile that later became his trademark throughout thirteen years in the Oval Office. Delegates responded that June afternoon with a roar of acclamation that would echo and re-echo down the corridors of time as a nation, paralyzed with the polio of a searing depression, roused itself to follow the lead of the man who said the only thing to fear was fear itself. If there was any man who wore the badge of courage in the White House, it was Franklin D. Roosevelt.

Inasmuch as character affects judgment, and judgment is the basis of the decisions presidents make and the accomplishments they leave behind, it is clear that Johnson and Nixon both failed to pass the test. Part of the reason Americans are increasingly concerned about a president's character is that, as the indisputable leader of the world, his moral example affects so many. Without doubt, Henry Graff, Columbia University historian, was right in contrasting the problems of the present day with those of the thirties. "In the Great Depression, great ideas were generated," but given the present climate, "problems come at you from left and right, and the public knows there is no quick answer." It is not just the frequency of the problems; it is also their complexity. As Mitroff and Bennis have emphasized, "It is not that the nation lacks problems, but that the problems are so complex and interrelated that it is next to impossible for candidates to propose solutions that are both appealing and credible." In 1976, for example, *The Yearbook of World Problems and Human Potential* identified no less than 2,653 distinct, widespread problems—not counting natural disasters—together with 3,300 international agencies dedicated to coping with them. Such a welter of issues, and America's standing as the world's preeminent nation, are all the more reason the electorate has come to place such emphasis on judgment: judgment in which character plays no small part.

In the cases of Johnson and Nixon, it is arguable that there is nothing in the way of long-standing, significant accomplishment—no achievement sufficient enough to offset the sheer deadweight of the disasters they both wrought. Johnson's "Great Society" has proven to be far less than meets the eye. Whereas Eisenhower presided over forty-five social programs, Johnson developed no fewer than four hundred. Here indeed was quantity, and in LBJ's judgment, more was better. Clinton Rossiter has classed presidents as either "earth shakers" or "earth smoothers." In Johnson's case, as a Majority Leader bent on achieving consensus through conciliation, he was the "smoother" extraordinaire. But once in the White House, he became a "shaker," bent on leaving a trail of Texas dust in his wake. "No president," maintained *Time* in January 1968, "has ever laid his prestige so squarely on the line in behalf of the Negro. None has tried so persistently to persuade the wealthiest nation on earth of the need to uproot poverty. None has achieved more for the advancement of education and health." Johnson confided in Schlesinger his strategy: "The country wants to be comfortable. It doesn't want to be stirred up. Have a revolution all right, but don't say anything about it until you are entrenched in office. That's the way Roosevelt did it."

That was 1968. Thirty years later, Johnson's "War on Poverty" had evolved into seventy-eight programs. Aid to Families with Dependent Children beneficiaries, for instance, were receiving cash payments ranging from $200 to $1,000 per month, in addition to Medicaid, food stamps, and rent subsidies. In keeping with the axiom that whatever the government subsidizes is bound to grow—often exponentially—it was no surprise that in 1995, some 48 percent of those giving birth in the United States were single mothers. In addition, studies also showed that welfare children were two to three times more likely to use drugs and turn to crime than children in two-parent homes of corresponding economic status. Worse, children from these dysfunctional families were more apt to have illegitimate children and depend on welfare—the cycle perpetuating itself.

As it turned out, Johnson's trumpeted "War on Poverty"—for which he'd asked Congress in 1964 to pony up only $962.5 million has cost taxpayers some $5 trillion over 3 decades, has left more than ever below the poverty line, and has added substantially to the federal deficit that today surpasses that $5 trillion. Other Johnson programs have either foundered or fared little better, with the possible exception of Head Start. What makes the cost of all those programs even more galling was the vow LBJ made in his first presidential speech to Congress: "I pledge that the expenditures of your government will be administered with the utmost thrift and frugality. I will insist that the government get a dollar's value for a dollar spent. The government will set an example of prudence and economy."[4]

Nixon's trumpeted accomplishment, the opening of China's door, must be set against what preceded and what has followed. For over twenty years before his 1972 summit in Beijing, it must be remembered that there was no political figure more intent on driving our two nations apart. By 1971, he had reversed himself not only on Vietnam but on China, coming to realize that going there to talk with Mao might very well prove to be the "monument" he was desperately seeking to assure his reelection.

Seventeen years later, the world gasped in horror at the brutal quashing of the pro-democracy demonstration in Beijing. Never mind, we were told, for China's billion people would provide fantastic new markets for our exports. Yet in 1996, our exports to China were less than $12 billion, placing it behind Japan, South Korea, Taiwan, and Singapore, despite the torrid growth of China's economy. Who, then, has stood to gain from the opening of China to the West, and particularly to the United States? Primarily, Henry Kissinger and his long-term protégé, Alexander Haig. Kissinger has succeeded, through his international influence-peddling firm, Kissinger Associates, to win access to China's markets for a number of his firm's clients, including GTE. In 1987, at the behest of China's ambassador to the United States, Kissinger founded the American China Society, and he is widely recognized as the Chinese government's staunchest and most prestigious defender in the West. Haig, after resigning as Reagan's Secretary of State in 1982, took a cue from his former mentor and founded Worldwide Associates—with one of his main clients United Technologies, of which he was formerly chief operating officer and president. No surprise, Haig has been successful in wangling billion-dollar contracts with China for United Technologies.

Though Nixon's foreign policy usually draws kudos from those searching for a lasting legacy, it is important that we recognize his role as the Great Regulator. The list includes the National Environmental Policy Act, the Poison Prevention Packaging Act, the Clean Air Amendments, and the Occupational Safety and Health Act, all of which were passed in 1969–1971. To these were added, in 1972–1974, the Consumer Product Safety Act, the Federal Water Pollution Control Act, the Vocational Rehabilitation Act, the Safe Drinking Water Act, and the Hazardous Materials Transportation Act.

Under Nixon, the number of pages in the Federal Register jumped from 20,000 per year to three times that—where it has stayed ever since. Additions to the government bureaucracy that were needed to regulate all this legislation have included the Environmental Protection Agency (EPA), the Consumer Product Safety Commission (CPSC), and the Occupational Safety and Health Administration (OSHA). In all, by 1995 these regulations had cost some $5 trillion, or about $5,000 per household. There are many who see this as Nixon's lasting legacy, with the good arguably outweighing the bad.

But it is Nixon's Vietnam disaster, from which Watergate emerged, that overwhelmingly outweights any of his accomplishments. His dallying in Vietnam, and his broadening the war into Laos and Cambodia, left more than 25,000 additional Americans dead—to say nothing of the more than 500,000 Asians. The war tore the United States apart as it had not been in a century, and since extending of the war into Cambodia prepared the ground for the grisly genocide of Pol Pot and the Khmer Rouge, it is vital that we recognize that Nixon's "peace with honor"—proclaimed in January 1973, and larded with the promise of $3 billion in war reparations—was not essentially different from a settlement he could have negotiated in 1969.

When LBJ lay on his deathbed in 1973, Nixon assured him that the upcoming "victory" would secure Johnson's place in history. When Nixon himself died in April, 1994, Billy Graham assured an audience, "A great man has fallen . . . a great statesman . . . the most important figure in the postwar era. His beloved Pat has gone to heaven. . . . I believe Richard Nixon is in heaven right now with Pat." It seemed that Graham knew something most Americans didn't know—and didn't believe. In truth, most Americans, twenty-five years after Watergate and the Vietnam War, would probably be more apt to agree with Jonathan Rauch: "In the end, Nixon committed about as long a chain of devastating mistakes as it is possible for a single president to make, even in six years of trying hard. Worse . . . we have spent the last two decades struggling to undo his errors, and may spend another two this way. He left behind an embittered, polarized country, a nation disillusioned with its government, unsure of its place in the world, whiplashed by its economy and condemned to years of fiscal strife. If a good president builds confidence without making any mistakes, Nixon was as bad as they get." Rauch concluded, "That a politician as astute as Nixon would carry on a losing war in open defiance of a public mandate to end it beggars belief. Nixon's secret bombings, his wartime lies, his betrayal of the voters, all taught millions of Americans that government could not be trusted . . . that the government itself was a fountain of lies."

When considering the appalling legacy of the Vietnam War, one is reminded of Tuchman's three criteria of governmental folly: "It must have been perceived as counterproductive in its own time, not merely by hindsight . . . a feasible alternative course of action must have been available . . . [and] the policy in question must be that of a group, not an individual ruler, and shouldn't persist beyond any one political lifetime." Of Vietnam, Tuchman was more specific. There was no "ignorance of the contra-indications. . . . All the conditions and reasons precluding a successful outcome were recognized or foreseen at one time or another during the thirty years of our involvement. . . . At no time were policymakers unaware of the hazards, obstacles, and negative developments. The folly consisted in the pursuit [of that war] . . . despite accumulating evidence that the goal was unattainable [or even understood], and the effect disproportionate to the American interest and eventually damaging to American society, reputation, and disposable power in the world."

Why, then, did the Johnson and Nixon administrations insist on pursuing this war, closing their minds to the evidence and its implications? Tuchman's answer is that "This is the classic symptom of folly: refusal to draw conclusions from the evidence, addiction to the counterproductive."

Johnson, Nixon, and their aides could well have wished for the two virtues Lady Bird craved: elasticity and compassion.[5]

Perhaps, in the end, the most that Johnson and Nixon did for the country was to reflect as well as to exacerbate its own hubris—to show that even an economic and military giant could still be vulnerable. We came to understand something of our own limitations, and it was a sobering experience. As unintended as this was, it was also unintended that both presidents, in leaving behind hundreds of hours of taped conversations, opened wide the door of the Oval Office and its extensions to afford a view of the White House that, while disillusioning, helped to neutralize the appalling naiveté of so many of us as to how government operates. In the figures of Johnson and Nixon, we can grasp something of the painful nettle of political machinations and acknowledge, "There, but for the grace of God, go I."

Checks on Power

In the middle of the nineteenth century the Swiss examined the U.S. Constitution as a possible model for their own 1848 charter, and rejected it on the grounds that the presidency was a "matrix for dictatorship." Nonetheless, even the most expansive presidents have had to tuck in their wings. "Lincoln," FDR noted, "was a sad man because he couldn't get it all at once. And nobody can," not even Roosevelt himself, as the Supreme Court reminded him after the start of his second term. FDR's successor, Harry Truman, growled over bourbon and water one day, "They talk about the power of the President, how I can just push a button to get things done. Why, I spend most of my time kissing somebody's ass." Johnson, as we have seen, understood the awkwardness of that position and roared one day, "Power? The only power I've got is nuclear—and I can't use that."

That Johnson expanded the powers of his presidency, far more than 90 percent of his predecessors, is as obvious as his abuse of that power. Paul D. Zimmerman has made note of the striking parallel between the rambling, distracted Johnson, long hair flowing down to his shoulders, looking like a superannuated refugee from the "hippies" who'd bedeviled him about the war, and Nixon's distraught, harried, and incoherent frenzy as he tried every twist and turn to escape impending impeachment.

Zimmerman then asked, "What institution ought to be in place to prevent private demonology from determining public policy?"

Zimmerman underscored two points that we need to address. The first is that there is a sore temptation to demonize both Johnson and Nixon, to castigate them simply as evil men, and thus not responsible for their actions. Parallel with this is the temptation to presume that Divine Providence has simply used them as a scourge to punish the world for its sin, again inoculating them against personal responsibility. In reality, they were, as Wicker has observed, men like us. Only by recognizing this can we grant them the measure of humanity we grant each other and ourselves. Only then can we empathize with them enough to attempt some measure of forgiveness. The second point of Zimmerman's is that there are, indeed, institutions that serve as checks on the awesome power of the presidency. And to these we'll turn, but only after considering some internal checks that presidents themselves can use to rein in the temptation to abuse their power.

Internal Checks—Step-by-Step

In terms of deference, the temptation for a president is to defer to as many as possible at the outset, even to those of the opposition party—then to gradually narrow that focus to those who agree with him or, better still, applaud his policies. With Johnson and Nixon, no degree of flattery, of sycophancy, ever seemed excessive. In the end, both presidents had so alienated their staffs—with the conspicuous exception of a few die-hard loyalists—that almost all had forsaken them. Though both presidents were repelled at the thought of "kissing ass," they seldom if ever refused the sycophancy of others. An honest and modest deference to others is an integral part of the social order. The unrelenting temptation is to defer extravagantly to our superiors, to be minimally cool to our equals, and to ignore our subordinates. Ralph Waldo Emerson considered every man he met to be his superior in some way, "and in that way I learn of him."

If there is any man for whom time is of the essence, it is the president. There are only so many hours in the day he can listen to others. But to narrow those to whom he listens to only those who agree with him is to do himself, and the nation he attempts to lead, a disservice. Another temptation to which Johnson was especially vulnerable was to defer, and to defer extravagantly, to a potential aide in order to recruit him, then to ignore him once he was aboard.

We have noted that both Johnson and Nixon looked up to certain models, including their predecessors, on which to pattern their behavior. Few, if any, served the nation with greater distinction than its first president. A man of rather common parts, Washington could speak no foreign languages, while Jefferson spoke five. Where Franklin, Adams, and Jefferson were well traveled in Europe, Washington never set foot on the continent. Where others, notably Patrick Henry, were accomplished public speakers, Washington, like Lyndon Johnson, was drab. Benedict Arnold was hailed as a genius when it came to military tactics, whereas Washington won his battles through sheer determination and perseverance, regardless of the odds. Where others, like Franklin and Jefferson, were extroverts, outgoing, the picture of bonhomie, Washington kept his cool and kept his distance, removing the hand of friend Gouverneur Morris from his shoulder when Morris became overly familiar. While others, like Jefferson and Hamilton, were well-read in the classics, Washington preferred "how to" books on managing his estate. Scholars examining the life of our first President remain baffled by how a man of meager, pedestrian qualities emerged the giant among us, casting a lengthening shadow across the pages of our history books for more than two centuries. Hugh Sidey thought he recognized the key in the simple yet profound word, character. Like obscenity, character may be hard to define and harder to measure, but we usually "know it when we see it."

Perhaps that is the reason we are suspicious of politicians who seek the highest office in the land, who long for it, yearn for it, lust after it—and do anything, say anything, to get it. Washington, as we have seen, was virtually shanghaied into assumiing the presidency, which meant leaving his beloved Mount Vernon. One potential candidate after another has begged off, citing their own inability to fulfill the awesome task. Johnson and Nixon had no such problem. Modesty and self-deprecation were scarcely a part of their makeup. Having failed to reach the White House on their first try, both came to crave the office and the power it bestowed as few others ever had. Indeed, their actions, their words in achieving the position from which they could make a run for the presidency, were such that alarm bells should have been ringing long before they took up residence at 1600

Pennsylvania Avenue. The American people had ample warning—but chose twice to ignore it.

The last president to have been virtually dragooned to run for the office was Dwight Eisenhower. No coincidence that, concluding his eight years, he was not only the most popular person in the country, but in the world. His had been no false modesty when he initially begged off; he knew enough about military leadership to earn an unprecedented five stars, but he also knew himself to be politically naive. Yet those who lived through his eight years, Democrats and Independents as well as Republicans, found the contrast with both Johnson and Nixon so stark that they came to yearn for the "good old days": those eight years of relative peace and prosperity, when Americans had confidence in their president and their government. Despite the U-2 incident—excused because most believed that Ike dissembled in the name of national security—a majority of Americans felt that Ike displayed a proper modesty and deference. With all his mistakes, many because he was a political neophyte, Ike was, for the most part, Mister Integrity. In this respect he was perhaps closest to that other General of the Army, George Washington, to whom he paid tribute: "When I compare the weak, inconsequential things said about me, compared to what they said about the man who I think is the greatest human the English-speaking race has produced, then I can be quite philosophical about it."

As for the second stage in hubris, delegation, many presidents have complained of friends and party members besieging them for jobs. The temptation has been for the president to surround himself with flunkies— loyal flunkies, but flunkies nonetheless. Even Machiavelli cautioned his Prince to avoid flattery, to seek out the truth. A study of a president's aides is in no small part a measure of him and his administration.

It wasn't that Johnson and Nixon did not assemble around them men of distinction. They may not have been "the best and the brightest"—a tongue-in-cheeck phrase invented by David Halberstam to describe the men Kennedy recruited as aides—but they were, for the most part, men to whom these two presidents should have listened. Instead, more often than not, both Johnson and Nixon went to great lengths to recruit them, hailed them publicly for their political astuteness, then promptly ignored them. As a result these two presidents found themselves making vest-pocket decisions, consulting only with themselves or with a select few who were little more than yes-men. By doing so, they deprived themselves of the very basis of intelligent decision-making: selecting the best alternative or combination of alternatives from the arena of open debate.

There can be little doubt but that "her majesty's loyal opposition" is a legacy from the British that we should continue to honor. In the middle of the nineteenth century, Englishman John Bright took a look at the U.S. presidency and was smitten. "I think the whole world offers no finer spectacle than this; it offers no higher dignity; and there is no greater object of ambition on the political stage on which men are permitted to move . . . to my mind there is nothing more sacred . . . than the authority of the freely chosen magistrate of a great and free people; and if there be on earth and amongst men the divine right to govern, surely it rests with a ruler so chosen and so appointed."[6]

If this is true—and most Americans would agree that it is—then it behooves a president to gather about him the very best people he can to safeguard the decision-making process. This presumes that, having recruited the best, a president will avail himself of their collective intelligence; not simply tolerating, but honoring, and at times deferring to those who disagree with him. The Brights of the world may rightly envy our constitutional government and the presidency it produces. Indeed, it is such a treasure that it must be protected by calling upon a president to delegate his power carefully, assuring that—as D'Israeli noted—the best decisions arise from the best information. Both Johnson and Nixon would have done well to have heeded Washington's concern not to be criticized for "a supposed partiality for friends or relatives" and—one might add—sycophants.

As for expansion, our third step along the path of hubris, we can do no better than to turn once again to our first president. He observed in a letter to Alexander Hamilton, "The powers of the Executive of the U. States are more definite, and better understood perhaps than those of almost any other country; and my aim has been, and will continue to be, neither to stretch, nor relax from them in any instance whatsoever unless imperious circumstances should render the measure indispensable."

After all, his reluctance to take the office pressed on him by his contemporaries derived in part from "the magnitude and the difficulty of the trust to which the voice of my country called me," and in part from his being "particularly conscious of my own deficiencies." Indeed,

Washington wrote, ". . . I feel an insuperable diffidence in my own abilities . . . in the execution of the duties of my arduous Office, how much I shall stand in need of the continence and aid of every friend to the Revolution, and of every lover of good government."

Jefferson, so gifted with the pen that he was called upon to draft the Declaration of Independence, was equally reluctant to become our third president. "I have no ambition to govern men," he wrote. "It is but a painful and thankless office." In another letter he stated, "The second office of the government [the vice-presidency] is honorable and easy; the first is but a splendid misery."

Lyndon Johnson's judgment was a complete reversal of Jefferson's. The vice-presidency he found miserable indeed, because Jack Kennedy— his junior by nine years, the boy Senator who'd come to the minority leader in 1953 for an office, for a staff, and for committee assignments— outfoxed him in 1960 to become the Democratic nominee, leaving Lyndon choking in the dust of humiliation as Kennedy's Vice-President. Merle Miller aptly described LBJ's swearing-in on January 21, 1961, "He had never wanted the vice-presidency; he did not now, and there is no evidence that in his few years in that position he changed his mind." Still, Lyndon had spent much of that December at his Ranch, contemplating "an answer to the question that now most plagued him—how to circumvent the traditional powerlessness of the vice-presidency."[7]

Richard Nixon, unlike his predecessor, thoroughly enjoyed his vice-presidency. After all, six years after entering Congress as a green freshman, he was, in 1952, just a heartbeat away from the Oval Office! Crushed by his 1960 defeat at the hands of Kennedy, he, too, bided his time until it came eight years later. Like Johnson, Nixon at last grasped the brass ring at the age of fifty-five.

By 1974 the picture had changed—dramatically. Nixon, like his predecessor, exceeded the authority of his office in an attempt to usurp the powers of both Congress and the Court. When it came to expansion, neither Johnson nor Nixon resolved, as Washington had, "neither to stretch— nor relax" his powers, "unless imperious circumstances" should intervene. That was the first President's only caveat. No doubt he had in mind a further conflict with Britain, which did happen twenty years later. In the case of the thirty-sixth and thirty-seventh presidents, the fig leaf of "national security" provided the pretext for expanding their control, until both found themselves plunging toward political self-destruction. So towering were their egos, so far-reaching their ambitions, that the two became the black holes into which all about them was sucked—until, in the end, their expansion foundered on the rock of hubris.

The most successful presidents have sought goals which, if not identical with those of ordinary U.S. citizens, at least ran parallel to them. It is the prudent president who pauses, from time to time, to take a reading on the proximity of his goals to those of his constituents. So intent were Johnson and Nixon on their own aggrandizement that they never deigned to probe the hopes of America's people.

Opportunism, our fourth step, is a law of cultural as well as biological evolution. Let a niche occur in the social order, and any one of a number of entrepreneurs will be rushing to fill it . The question posed for a president who would avoid hubris is, at what cost? At the cost of compromising one's integrity? The illegitimate opportunist disregards what he has said or done in order to "seize the moment"—as Nixon was fond of quoting Mao Zedong, especially in his presence.

The speaker's credibility, Aristotle wrote over 2,300 years ago, stems in part from his intelligence, in part from his good will, but mostly from his integrity. Taken from integer, or a whole number, integrity implies wholeness, a coherence among the varied parts of the speaker's character. It implies that there is a consistency not simply between successive speeches, but between those speeches and the speaker's actions. Lacking that, no president can fulfill what Truman saw as the most important power of the office: to persuade people to do what they ought to do, without persuasion.

Well might Johnson and Nixon have followed the example of our fifth president, James Monroe, who refused to take advantage of a "thousand opportunities" to enrich himself in office, especially when he could have "escaped detection." But they did not. And it was not lost on the American people that both Johnson and Nixon, having entered politics with little more than the shirts on their backs, left the White House as multimillionaires.

Obviously, both men had chosen to ignore the wisdom of Lincoln, who resolved "to conduct the affairs of this administration that if at the end, when I come to lay down the reins of power, I shall at least have one friend left, and that friend shall be down inside of me."

In the case of exploitation, the fifth step in hubris, we have noted that it is one thing to exploit time and circumstance, or technology and learning. It is exploitation of a different order to exploit people. As often as not, a president and his aides, friends, colleagues, and even family members will find themselves in a mutual exploitation, a symbiotic relationship in which one feeds off the other. When the symbiosis breaks down, however, the relationship starts to unravel. This was what happened with Johnson and his Secretary of Defense. Once McNamara could no longer endorse the war that LBJ had come to claim as his own, the Secretary's conscience forced him to back off and eventually bow out. The same happened with Nixon and his Watergate lawyers. Once they found out their client was not leveling with them—even though he was a lawyer himself—they headed for the door, leaving him alone and isolated in the Oval Office.

Both Johnson and Nixon were utterly ruthless in their exploitation of their aides. Tolerating nothing less than one hundred percent loyalty, nothing less than complete and immediate obedience, nothing less than twelve to fourteen hour days, and nothing less than being available twenty-four hours a day and seven days a week—it is little wonder that neither was able to hold onto his White House staff.

Arrogance, step number six, implies arrogating to oneself something that doesn't belong to one. We have noted under opportunism the enriching of both presidents while in political office. But here was not simply an arrogating of riches, but an arrogating of power. For as long as men can be bought, riches brings power.

In addition to their indirect arrogating of power, Johnson and Nixon arrogated direct power that rightfully belonged to Congress and to the Court. Lincoln, Wilson, FDR, all wartime presidents, exercised a bona fide claim of national security to stretch their powers—as long as they maintained the confidence of the electorate. Lincoln resolved to "go just as fast and only as fast as I think I'm right and the people are ready for the step."

Johnson and Nixon exercised no such caution. Both invoked a spurious claim of national security regarding a war that was never declared, a war that had no clear goal or goals, a war without a clear definition of what would constitute victory or defeat, a war that was Vietnam's to fight. With sheer bullying arrogance, America repeatedly violated the Geneva Accords and falsely branded North Vietnam as the aggressor. In essence, the United States was in the wrong place at the wrong time, fighting the wrong war for the wrong reasons. Here was the world's preeminent economic and military power, devastating a poor, third-world nation on the other side of the world in a show of force meant to intimidate one and all—especially China and the Soviet Union.

What both presidents succeeded in doing, though neither intended to, was to ring down the curtain, at least temporarily, on the nation's arrogance. Lippmann described it well in 1973, as Nixon began his second term. "His role," wrote Lippmann, "has been that of a man who had to liquidate, defuse, deflate the exaggerations of the romantic period of American imperialism and American inflation. Inflation of promises, inflation of hopes, the Great Society, American supremacy—all that had to be deflated because it was all beyond our power."

Theodore White put it a bit differently: ". . . The most deceptive inherited social myth" in the postwar period, "was of American power. The virulence of that myth was fresh—and rested on the fleeting dominance of American arms as they spread triumphant over the entire globe in 1945. . . ." Indeed, ". . . no plane flew the globe except under the surveillance or with the permission of American might." Worse, we fought our wars with a singular moral ferocity "that was the terror of our enemies. The result: we estranged entire social groups; we choked free discussion as we ferreted out enemies in the shadows among us; and we, through our representatives in Congress, granted dictatorial powers to our commanders in chief."[8]

Johnson and Nixon came to know and practice arrogance as few other presidents. Through deception LBJ arrogated to himself the paramount power of Congress to declare and wage war, then surreptitiously escalated the conflict in bold defiance of his promise to consult with Congress before using the Tonkin Gulf Resolution. Nixon, also through deception, reneged on his promise to end the war in six months, and instead, on the sly, expanded the conflict into Cambodia and Laos. When Congress finally took back its power—first by revoking the Tonkin Gulf Resolution, then by cutting off further funds for America's misadventure in Southeast Asia—Nixon and Kissinger proceeded to blame Congress for losing the war.

Yet a seventh step, following hard on the heels of arrogance, is identification. Presidents are prone to identify themselves with their party, with their office, with the nation, with the "free"world," and with the world itself. Seldom is the statement as bold as that made by DeGaulle who, copying Louis XIV, claimed, the state is me [or I]. More often it is reflected in the president's feeling increasingly indispensable to each one of these larger entities—until he finally decides that they cannot operate, or operate effectively, without him.

Johnson simply could not believe that anybody—certainly neither Humphrey nor Nixon—could replace him in the White House. It was only he who could micromanage the war from the Ready Room. It was only he who could end the war at the negotiating table. And it was only with greatest reluctance that he followed Humphrey's lead in "taking a risk for peace" by calling for a complete cease-fire just before the 1968 election. His greatest regret was that the likes of Richard Nixon should succeed him. Nixon, for his part, envisioned himself as the only statesman capable of dealing effectively with foreign policy—and predicted that America's representative democracy would be replaced by Britain's parliamentary democracy if he was impeached.

Each saw himself as indispensable to the conduct of domestic and foreign policy. The prudent leader will go out of his way to maintain a distinction between himself and larger entities, realizing he will become dispensable after leaving office. There can be little doubt that all presidents have contributed something during their time in the White House; not all, however, have contributed enough to offset their mistakes. Even fewer have been valuable to the office, and fewer still have been vital. None, however—not even Washington—was indispensable.

A president's dependence on the external trappings of his position is in direct proportion to his sense of insecurity. Thus did Nixon wrap himself in the semantic cloak of "The President" rather than simply saying "I" when giving an order. Thus did he attempt to costume his White House guards in the extravagant garb traditionally belonging to royalty. And thus did he cater to every nuance of protocol, insisting, for example, that he walk to the left of the newly elected Kennedy. Once in office himself, he expected all would come before him only when summoned, or only when passing the rigorous inspection of his gatekeeper, Haldeman. Of such folderol is insecurity, if not mediocrity, revealed.

At one time or another, every president finds himself in the stage of confrontation. Indeed, open and honest confrontation, lubricated by tact and civility, is indispensable to the discussion that is the bedrock of a democratic government. John Stuart Mill, perhaps the preeminent American genius of the mid-nineteenth century, envisioned a market place of ideas in his classic essay, "On Liberty," in which proponents would discuss, even argue, but in the end discover the "best"—that answer most easily implemented as a result of compromise and consensus. Neither the public nor the press was allowed to witness the Constitutional Convention, lest they witness, or even be drawn into, the debates—some of them heated—that provided the furnace of disputation from which could emerge a Constitution that might be ratified by at least nine of the thirteen colonies.

Was it Churchill who remarked that democracy was a terrible form of government—with its dissension, confusion, even rancor, not to mention its cost in time and expense—until you consider all the rest?

It was Jefferson who placed his faith in an educated and informed citizenry as the logical means of avoiding violence and bloodshed in the course of confronting differences. That remains the basis not only for an increasing number of the world's two hundred nations—but lies at the heart of the United Nations, which is resolved to settle disputes peacefully.

It would make sense, then, that every president perfect not only his speaking skills, but his skills in moderating discussion, in listening, in summarizing and in discovering and exploring commonalties rather than differences, among disputants. Without the ability to resolve confrontation amicably, a president can easily find himself resorting to coercion. Both Johnson and Nixon came to think of themselves not so much as duly elected presidents, accountable to the people, but as parents lording over their children. Treating voters on a "need-to-know" basis, they each withheld information from the public—information that Americans needed in order to gauge their president's effectiveness. Parents, we have come to understand, do no service for their children by expecting little from them; it is high expectations that produce achievers. Presidents, too, have a responsibility to expect much of their constituents—just as they, in turn, have a responsibility to expect much from their presidents.

One of the great mistakes both Johnson and Nixon made was their patronizing of voters, their attitude of condescension, even contempt. The two most effective and onerous means of coercion that presidents bring to bear on citizens are taxation and conscription. It was only when business rebelled against the increasing taxes needed to fight the war, and young men rebelled against conscription, that Congress finally demanded the troops be withdrawn and the war brought to a close.

Of coercion—the violation of the rights of others—one thing we can be certain: it is invariably counterproductive. As a result, the war gripped America in a social schizophrenia, dividing the country as it had not been for a century. The heavy hand of coercion has no place in a representative democracy, and a president must beware when he resorts to it.

Deception, the tenth step on the path of hubris, is a more subtle form of coercion because it deprives people of the facts they need to form intelligent decisions. In this respect it is also dangerous since it violates that most basic of freedoms: the freedom to choose. Intelligent choice depends on accurate sources of information. To violate that freedom is to reduce voters to automatons, to unthinking, genuflecting robots who, like Al Capp's "Lil Abner," pay homage to the president simply because he *is* the president.

Of the plethora of mistakes that hounded the presidencies of Johnson and Nixon, none were more execrable than their determination to deceive the press, the Congress, the Court, and the public. Neither seemed to feel as Jackson did when he wrote, "That if the president speaks to Congress, it must be in the language of truth." Indeed, so habitual became their many obfuscations, misrepresentations, equivocations and prevarications; their mendacity, dishonesty, and hyperbole, that in the end there were few who would take them at their word—on any subject.

Worse, their repeated deceptions were done not on behalf of others, not to confound an enemy in war, but ultimately to mislead the public to whom they were accountable—either to ensure their reelection or their place in history. Not only were their means reprehensible, but so were their motives. Both, in the end, held desperately to the wisp of a hope that a miracle would intervene to save them from their own destruction.

By the time these two presidents arrived at step number eleven, paranoia, they were on a slope so steep and slippery that there was no turning back. Isolation and immolation became inevitable. They had reached the point of no return. Their predicament could only worsen, and in both cases it did, leaving them to witness the horror of their own political demise—by their own hand. That, in the end, constituted the ultimate humiliation.

Perhaps the capstone of internal checks on hubris is to be found in the nature of the task to which presidents are elected. Their job is to administer the laws enacted by Congress—implying "minister"—and their overriding concern must be for the welfare of the people. Their job is to serve, and one who serves is, by definition, a servant. Thus presidents should minister to and serve the body politic, ever vigilant to maintain its robust health. There is yet another facet that rounds out the job of the president, and it is undoubtedly the most difficult: to lead. The president must go before the people and lead them to even greater freedom, so that they may fulfill their potential. Here, as Fromm has reminded us, is the highest degree of freedom, commensurate with an emphasis on interdependence rather than simply independence.

Robert Greenleaf, one of the most influential management theorists of the past forty years, introduced the idea of the leader as servant in the 1960s. His notion was a major assault on the conventional wisdom of that decade, but it is currently taught in leading business schools across the country—laying the foundation for the theories of a whole generation of today's management thinkers.

External Checks: Family and Friends

One would think that family and friends constitute the first line of defense against hubris. Unfortunately, this is seldom so, and did not occur with either Johnson or Nixon. Not only their close friends but their wives and daughters remained faithful to the bitter end, true believers who found it inconceivable that their intimate friends, their husbands, their fathers could conceivably have stooped to activities that plummeted them to purgatory from their presidential heaven.

The Congress

While family and friends have no constitutional responsibility to ride hard on presidents, Congress does. Indeed, theirs is the first and most readily available check on the powers of the president. Suspicious of power concentrated in any one person—be it the king of England or the president of the United States, the Founding Fathers apparently intended that Congress should run the government, while the president would execute the laws that Congress passed. Throughout the Constitution and its many amendments, there appears an overriding concern to keep the president in his place. No doubt the flagrant abuse of power by George III stirred their sensitivity to the awful consequences of such abuse.

There is no little irony in that both Johnson and Nixon, as former congressmen and senators, spoke out in favor of the legislative branch exercising dominion. Yet once in the White House, both did their best to erode the power of what by then they considered their natural enemy. This seems astounding, given that for eight years Lyndon served first as Minority Leader, then Majority Leader of the Senate, while Richard presided over it.

It is instructive that those presidents who defied or dominated Congress—including Jefferson, Jackson, Lincoln, both Roosevelts, Wilson, and Truman—are usually considered among the top fifteen presidents. On the other hand, those presidents dominated by Congress—Van Buren, W.H. Harrison, Tyler, Polk, Taylor, Fillmore, Pierce, Buchanan, A. Johnson, Hayes, B. Harrison, Harding, Coolidge, and Ford—have settled at the bottom of the rankings. What appears to occur is a tug-of-war for power, with the stakes going to the president perhaps half the time, especially during war, when he can justifiably call for emergency powers: powers taken from the Congress or the judiciary or both.

It is precisely in the area of foreign policy that congressional checks seem most powerless. Francis Wilcox, Dean of the School of Advanced Studies at Johns Hopkins, warned in 1970 that "The most significant development in the government of the U.S. during the past 30 years has been the formidable expansion of presidential authority. One by one," he emphasized, "the powers of Congress have fallen into disuse. One by one they have been whittled away. Slowly but surely the president has taken a larger slice of the foreign-policy pie."

With the advent of the Cold War, major foreign-policy initiatives originated not with Congress, but with the Truman administration: the organization of the UN, the Marshall Plan, the Truman Doctrine, NATO, and SEATO. It was left to the Senate Foreign Relations Committee simply to monitor presidential powers during the Korean War, the Berlin Blockade, the Middle East and Hungarian crises, the Bay of Pigs, the Cuban Missile Crisis, and the Vietnam War. Invariably, the initiatives arose not on the Hill, but in the White House.

What holds true with foreign policy appears increasingly true of domestic policy. As we noted in evaluating Nixon's presidency, he was the Great Regulator, putting in place one regulation after another, one agency after another. In effect, his administration served as legislator, executor, and judge in each of these regulations. In addition, as Roscoe Drummond pointed out, "Congress has lost control of the budget. It is not an adequate monitor of the administration. It is so burdened with trivia that it is rarely able to give priority to crucial legislation. At most points it is so under-staffed with its own experts that, more often than not, it cannot give inde-pendent study to presidential proposals."

It was not until 1976 that Congress took far-reaching measures to curb the power of the presidency, particularly in times of emergency. Until then, simply by declaring a national emergency—as FDR did in 1933, as Truman did in 1950, and as Nixon did in 1970 and 1971—the president had the power to:

1. Seize private property and commodities;
2. Control all transportation and communications;
3. Control the means of production;
4. Assign the military overseas and to other nations;
5. Impose martial law;
6. Restrict travel at home and abroad.

With the passage of the National Emergencies Act, however, a presi-dent must notify Congress in advance, spelling out those laws he intends to use. Any emergency would automatically end after six months, although the president could declare it again for six additional months. Finally, a majority vote in both House and Senate would end the emer-gency at any time.

Especially significant was the explanation for this new act by the Senate Government Operations Committee: "At a time when governments throughout the world are turning with increasing desperation to an all-powerful executive, the legislation is designed to insure that the United States travels a road marked by carefully constructed legal safeguards." The new legislation did leave intact the 1973 War Powers Act, enabling the president to commit combat troops for a ninety-day period without prior congressional approval. It also left intact the Trading With the Enemy Act of World War I, permitting the president to impose controls on credit, hold assets of enemy nations, and take similar economic steps.[9]

Again and again, one finds presidents railing against Congress and its constitutional checks. John Adams ridiculed Congress for presuming that each member was an expert on everything. Of all the powers lodged in the Constitution, Adams judged those given the Senate to be the most dan-gerous. It was therefore the president's task to be "the indispensable guardian of [the people's] rights." That Congress was a sore trial for the besieged Adams is seen in his complaint, ". . . I was turned out of office, degraded and disgraced by my country," despite the fact that "I left my country in peace and harmony with all the world . . . I left navy yards, fortifications, frigates, timber, naval stores, manufactories of cannon and arms, and a treasury full of five millions of dollars." Yet here was Congress badgering him with "perpetual oppositions, clamors and reproaches such as no other president ever had to encounter. . . ."

Adams was not alone in begrudging Congress its constitutional restraints. Jefferson complained of "the tyranny of the legislators [as] the most formidable dread." Tyler resented the attempt by Congress "to break down the undoubted constitutional power" of his office "without a solemn amendment of that fundamental law." And Jackson thought it axiomatic "that the greatest wrongs inflicted upon people are caused by unjust and arbitrary legislation." The reason? Congress was "seeking the welfare of a single interest at the expense of many and varied interests. . . ."[10]

It is just this dominance of a "single interest" or a "special interest" that dogs congressmen to this day, as they kowtow to such interests to seek financing for their reelections. Not until campaign finance reform becomes law—stipulating that Congress will be funded publicly and putting a cap on such spending—will legislators be freed from the humiliating and time-consuming task of going, hat in hand, to one special interest after another to finance their campaigns. Meanwhile, not only is a congressman's principal duty of drafting intelligent legislation given short shrift, but the contributions he receives from special interests amount to little more than outright bribery. Indeed, the average taxpayer would be aghast at how many laws are written by lobbyists and others employed by these special interests—with the tacit approval of legislators.

We have already noted how Congress virtually rolled over and played dead when Johnson went before it to extract the Tonkin Gulf Resolution, handing him its constitutional right to declare and to wage war. It took Vietnam and Watergate to rouse Congress to drastic action to curb the power of Richard Nixon. Not until May 1969, did Congress—lagging, as usual, behind its constituents—pass a law, in this case the Cooper-Church Amendment, to restrict the movements of the president in Indochina. And not until August 1973, some seven months after the United States concluded the peace agreement with Hanoi, did Congress shut off the money spigot for Vietnam. But it was Watergate that finally drove Congress to exercise its most critical check on the powers of the president: his removal from office. When the Senate appointed Sam Ervin to head up an investigating committee in January 1973, Connally reported to Nixon that the mood on the Hill was "the most vicious thing I've ever seen." To this, Nixon responded that Congress was "cumbersome, undisciplined, isolationist, fiscally irresponsible, overly vulnerable to pressures from organized minorities, and too dominated by the media."

One other factor should be noted regarding congressional oversight of presidential power. That has to do with the increasing complexity of the task confronting the average member of the Hill. Harking back to his first year in Congress in 1947, Nixon recalled that "it was still possible for a congressman to run his office, do his homework, keep in touch with his constituents, and have his eye on his political fortunes." But twenty-six years later, it was a different story. By then, "the federal government had become so big and the business of government so extensive that even the most conscientious congressman had to delegate a large part of his responsibilities to the personnel and committee staffs that had correspondingly swelled in size and influence."

By that time, Nixon was complaining repeatedly of the restraining power of the "iron triangle," which he described as a three-sided set of relationships composed of congressional lobbyists, congressional committee and subcommittee members and their staffs, and the bureaucracy.

It is vital to note that Congress itself is vulnerable to the seductive songs of the nymphs of hubris. In 1774, John Adams found the business of Congress "tedious beyond expression," with every man "a great man, an orator, critic, a statesman. . . ." Therefore, concluded Adams, "every man upon every question must show his oratory, his criticism, and his political abilities." Years later, our second President was no less critical of senators and representatives, who he claimed were just "as fond of power as a president. . . ." Indeed, Adams asked, "Are not ambition and favoritism and all other vicious passions and sinister interests, as strong and active in a senator or a representative as in a president?"

Subsequent presidents sensed hubris settling over Congress. In 1846, Polk noted "There is more selfishness and less principle among members of Congress . . . than I had any conception of, before I became President. . . ."

A century later, Truman denounced the "do-nothing" Eightieth Congress in no uncertain terms: "If you tell [them] anything about the world situation, they get hysterical. If you tell them nothing, they go fishing."[11]

Yet with all of its sins, there can be little doubt that Congress remains, constitutionally and realistically, the major institution meant to check the powers of the presidency.

The Courts

Just as Congress drafts the laws the president is sworn to execute, so is the judiciary both the official interpreter of those laws and the official arbiter among conflicting interests. The courts are empowered by the Constitution to provide a rein on presidential power second only to that of Congress. In their wisdom, the Founding Fathers went back to Locke and Hobbes in England and Rousseau and Montesquieu in France, who in turn went back to the ancient Greeks with their first experiment in democracy—back to Pericles, Socrates, Plato, and Aristotle. Well-versed in learning, especially about the Golden Age of Greece, the leaders of the Renaissance drew from that rich intellectual heritage the wisdom of the ages. Those who drafted our Declaration of Independence, our Constitution, and our Bill of Rights, knew all too well what happens to men, to institutions, and to nations when, afflicted with hubris, they destroyed themselves. The Federalist Papers, as no other documents, provided the soil from which the tree of liberty would spring. "Had the Greeks been as wise as they were courageous," wrote Madison and Hamilton, "they would have been admonished by experience of the necessity of a closer union, and would have availed themselves of the peace which followed their success against the Persian arms, to establish such a reformation." But they fell victim to hubris, and "instead of this obvious policy, Athens and Sparta, inflated with the victories and the glory they had acquired, became first rivals, then enemies; and did each other infinitely more mischief than they had suffered from Xerxes. Their mutual jealousies, fears, hatreds, and injuries ended in the celebrated Peloponnesian War, which itself ended in the ruin and slavery of the Athenians who had begun it."

With this example of city-states hovering over them from the distant past, and with the example of King George III hovering over them from the very recent past—during which the colonies had wrested their independence from the crown—Madison became the chief architect of a Constitution that would turn out to be the envy of the world. It was founded on the firm belief that concentrated power was inherently dangerous, and that hubris was almost invariably its handmaiden. So Madison took great pains to circumscribe that power, especially when concentrated in the single person of the chief executive. If suspicion of power motivated the Founding Fathers so to circumscribe presidential power, then the major question to which they addressed themselves was "whether societies of men are really capable or not of establishing good government from reflection and choice," or whether they are forever destined to depend "for their political constitutions on accident and force." Good government, then, clearly derived from hedging in the president with a system of checks and balances, primarily employed by the Congress and the courts. Only then could the people be protected from arbitrary use of power.

When at last the Constitution was completed, hammered out on the hard anvil of open and free discussion, Washington affixed his signature, exclaiming, "A Miracle has been wrought." Perhaps the most important aspect of that miracle remains the ability of the people to replace one administration with another in peaceful transition. That was dependent on the ability of the system of checks and balances to keep hubris at bay, so that continuity could be maintained somewhere between tyranny and anarchy. With this "miracle" of a Constitution, the judiciary could offer a second curb on the presidential powers.

It is a tribute to that Constitution, and its basis in free and open discussion, that while Washington was praising it, Jefferson—even though calling it "unquestionably the wisest ever yet presented to men"—railed against the judiciary, particularly federal judges, for "sapping little by little the foundations of the Constitution. . . ." Indeed, retiring from office in 1809, Jefferson labeled the judiciary a "subtle corps of sappers and miners constantly working underground to undermine the foundations of our confederate fabric." Judges, Jefferson assumed, "are as honest as other men, and not more so. They have, with others, the same passions for party, for power, and the privilege of their corps."

A century later, Theodore Roosevelt warned, "I may not know much about law, but I do know one can put the fear of God into judges." Nixon, on the other hand, emphasized the power of the Supreme Court justices as having "probably . . . more profound and lasting influence on their times and on the direction of the nation than most presidents have had." Five years later, Nixon came to understand and appreciate the restraining hand of the Court when, in 1974, it ruled against him and his claim of executive privilege—forcing him to relinquish the tapes that would quickly leave his political career in shambles. With that decision, Nixon wrote, the country had not triumphed, as one reporter had put it, but lost. "I felt that the presidency itself was a casualty of this ruling."

Down through the years the Court has often been divided, sometimes sharply so, reflecting the primacy of democracy working within the judiciary. Yet in the case of *United States* v. *Nixon*, it was unanimous. The Court had succeeded in upholding the right of Congress to overturn Nixon's plea of confidentiality and executive privilege, and ruled that his accountability to Congress and the country it represented was far more important than presidential privacy—especially when that privacy appeared to reflect the overreaching of the President in violating the laws he had sworn to uphold.[12]

The Media

It is the media that serves as a crucial link between American presidents and their constituents. As early as 1765, John Adams wrote, "None of the means of information are more sacred, or have been cherished with more tenderness and care by the settlers of America, than the press." Therefore Adams warned the colonists not "to be wheedled out of your liberty by any pretenses of politeness, delicacy, or decency. These, as they are often used, are but three different names for hypocrisy, chicanery, and cowardice." How to arm ourselves, to be on guard? Adams suggested, "Let us dare to read, think, speak and write."

Jefferson, while disagreeing with Adams on other vital issues, agreed with him that "Our liberty depends on the freedom of the press, and that cannot be limited without being lost." So strongly did he feel about the press that "Were it left to me to decide whether we should have a government without newspapers, or newspapers without government, I should not hesitate a moment to prefer the latter." Toward the end of his second term, Washington, exasperated with the constant carping of the press, told

Jefferson, "I had no conception . . . that every act of my administration would be tortured . . . in such exaggerated form and indecent terms as could scarcely be applied to a Nero, a notorious defaulter, or even a common pickpocket." Nevertheless, even with such abuses by the press, Jefferson wrote in 1799, "The world is indebted for all the triumphs which have been gained by reason and humanity over error and oppression."[13]

Once Adams and Jefferson had served their terms and been the target of criticism from the press, they, like Washington, thought less kindly of it. Adams concluded that "If I am to judge by the newspapers and pamphlets that have been printed in America for twenty years past, I should think that both believed me the meanest villain in the world." Jefferson, in the same mood, complained, "The man who never looks into a newspaper is better informed than he who reads them, inasmuch as he who knows nothing is nearer the truth than he whose mind is filled with falsehoods and errors." Still, Jefferson acknowledged in 1816 that "Where the press is free and every man able to read, all is safe." Two years before his death in 1825, Jefferson touted the press as "the best instrument for enlightening the mind of man, and improving him as a rational, moral, and social being." Madison figured if "every newspaper, when printed on one side should be handed over to the press of an adversary, to be printed on the other, thus presenting to every reader both sides of every question, truth will always have a fair chance. But such a remedy is ideal." These Founding Fathers, however critical of the press from time to time, recognized that it and it alone was necessary—albeit at times a necessary evil—to curb the power of the government, and particularly that of the president. So much did they believe this that they made provision in the very first amendment of the Bill of Rights for freedom of the press. "Congress," they agreed, "shall make no law abridging the freedom of . . . the press. . . ."[14]

By the twentieth century, Theodore Roosevelt was castigating the "Man with the Muck-rake . . . as one of the most potent forces for evil." Hoover, on the other hand, figured a president would have to be dead for twenty years before he "could satisfy the press. . . ." FDR, who was mauled by the press as much as any president, acknowledged after eight years in office that, "Freedom of conscience, of education, of speech, of assembly . . . would be nullified should freedom of the press ever be successfully challenged." Truman told a conference of editors, "When you read what the press had to say about Washington, Jefferson, and Lincoln, and the other presidents, you would think we never had a decent man in the office since the country began." Eisenhower, however, at his first news conference, gave the press the benefit of the doubt, having "found nothing but a desire to dig at the truth . . . and be open headed and forthright about it"[15]

Recognizing that Americans had "come to think of the president as an institution rather than a person, [thus] shielding the president from accountability," Herb Block of The *Washington Post* set about rectifying the situation. He went after Nixon in the fifties as a result of Nixon's smears against Voorhis and Douglas, his subsequent "Checkers" mess, his branding of the Democratic Party as the "party of treason" for having "lost China," then for getting us into a war with Korea and "losing" it as well. It was the same *Post*, through its intrepid young reporters, Woodward and Bernstein, who continued to nip at Nixon's heels after the Watergate break-in—when all other papers had called off the hunt—that finally brought about the President's resignation.

It is arguable that two photographs—one of a nine year-old Vietnamese girl, naked and fleeing in terror from a napalm bombing attack; the other of an American college student, kneeling on the sidewalk at Kent State, and crying in anguish over her slain comrade—did as much as anything in print to end the war. The first picture helped to end Johnson's political career, the second to end Nixon's.

Senator Bill Bradley, thoroughly disenchanted with the Senate and about to leave office, was similarly disenchanted with a press "obsessed with the trivial and the lurid." David Eisenhower in 1968 faulted the press for the "simple country bumpkin, sweet old general" view of his grandfather pervasive at the time. In 1961, however, Ike, asked if he thought the press had been fair to him over the years, responded, "Well, when you come down to it, I don't see that a reporter could do much to a president, do you?"

When, at long last, the final curtain rang down on the checkered career of Nixon in 1974, it was, once again, the media that was to blame. In 1977, in his last meeting with David Frost, Nixon suggested that Frost had probably cut out "the most important thing I said in the interviews. . . ." Frost asked, "What's that?" Nixon answered, "About where power lies today. In the media. With no checks and balances."[16]

If it is true that the power brokers in the preindustrial age were those who owned the land and thus the means of agricultural production, and that the power brokers in the industrial age were those who owned the means of manufacturing, then it follows that in this postindustrial era known as the information age, the power brokers are those who control the media.

With all its faults, and there are many—obsession with the bottom line, and a preoccupation with the banal, the trivial, the scandalous—the media nevertheless serves an indispensable function in checking the power of the Congress, the judiciary, and especially the chief executive.

The Bureaucracy

What is so often maligned as the bureaucracy, consisting of "faceless bureaucrats," is none other than the people who keep the government running regardless of changes of the guard. It was Chester Arthur who instituted civil service in order to avoid patronage and to provide a more permanent sinecure for competent people in government. In a sense the bureaucracy of government represents a great flywheel, keeping all the machinery working, regardless of who is elected to office. Taft in 1916 wrote, "Presidents may go to the seashore or to the mountains, Cabinet officers may go about the country explaining how fortunate the country is in having such an administrator, but the machinery at Washington continues to operate under the army of faithful noncommissioned officers, and the great mass of government business is uninterrupted." The bureaucracy, then, is a conservative force, protecting tradition by eschewing change. With conservative presidents, generally the weaker of the lot, conflict with the bureaucracy is minimized. Given activist presidents, however, men such as those at the top of the rankings, it is another case indeed. As early as 1816, Jefferson was complaining of "more machinery of government than is necessary, too many parasites living on the labor of the industrious." When Ford opened the centennial time capsule in 1976, he discovered that a century earlier there had been fewer than 100,000 on the federal payroll, as opposed to over 2,000,000 during his tenure. Hoover warned, "Whenever you increase the numbers of political bureaucracy, you not only have to pay them, but they are veritable research laboratories for new inventions in spending money." By 1930, FDR warned, "If we do not halt this steady process of building commissions and regulatory bodies and special legislations like huge inverted pyramids over every one of the simple constitutional provisions, we shall soon be spending billions of dollars more." Yet despite Roosevelt's warning, his predecessor, Herbert Hoover, reported in 1955—when he was serving as Chairman of the Commission on Organizing the Executive Branch—that the federal government had grown by fourteen times in just the previous twenty years.[17]

By the time of the Johnson and Nixon administrations, there was not simply a great increase in the federal bureaucracy, but in the complaints of those two activist presidents who saw themselves as set upon. Johnson's Secretary of State, Dean Rusk, noted that our constitutional and political system is the most complicated in the world, in large part to provide an effective brake on power. He then quoted Chief Justice Earl Warren, "If any branch of the federal government pursued its own constitutional powers to the end of the trail, our system simply could not function. It would freeze up, like an engine without oil." Helping to prevent that are the bureaucrats—which was reason enough, Johnson and Nixon figured, to lambaste them.

Asked by Kearns if he ever felt imprisoned by the bureaucrats, as he appeared to be by the war protesters, Johnson answered, "Yes, but not for the reasons you think. My problem was not bureaucracy with a capital B, but a few self-satisfied bureaucrats in the Defense Department who thought they knew what was going on better than the president. I barely knew or saw them, yet there they were disagreeing with my policy and leaking materials to the press. It was a real problem all right. A president is entitled to people who'll execute his views." This was, of course Adolf Eichmann's defense at his 1961 trial in Jerusalem: he had simply been carrying out the orders of his Führer in rounding up and executing Jews. Undoubtedly many in the Johnson administration, some of them bureaucrats, believed that LBJ was not getting an accurate picture of the situation in Vietnam. As a result, they undoubtedly felt that he had established his ruinous policy because it was founded on inaccurate information. They probably also felt it was their duty to oppose the President's course of action in whatever ways they could. Daniel Ellsberg was only one of many who concluded that Johnson had betrayed the American people—just as Nixon maintained that Ellsberg had betrayed the nation in 1971, when he leaked the Pentagon Papers to *The New York Times*.

What had been a soft-pedaling of the bureaucracy under Johnson became a tirade under Nixon. The bureaucracy, the third side of his "iron triangle," was yet another obstacle in his path toward total control. This, of course, was not the way Nixon put it. In his *Memoirs,* he wrote that as president-elect, he wanted to "break the hammerlock" that Washington held "over the money and decisions that affect American lives." He intended to "break open the triangle" by "turning money and power back to the states and cities," and to "throw the red tape out the window." Once in office, Nixon urged his new Cabinet members to replace quickly holdover bureaucrats with people who believed "in what we are trying to do." He warned that if they did not act immediately, they would become "captives of the bureaucracy they were trying to change." As for Eastern liberals, Nixon ordered them not to "recruit any more"—apparently exempting Kissinger—and "get rid of those people [who] will either sabotage us from within, or they'll just sit back on their well-paid asses and wait for the next election to bring back their old bosses."

Nixon, of course, had a point in criticizing the Democrats under Kennedy and Johnson for their "politics of expectation," as Henry Fairlie called it: the promise that the federal government could solve poverty and racial discrimination. Consequently, welfare benefits had nearly tripled between 1960 and 1969, while LBJ spent $250 billion for his "War on Poverty" between 1964 and 1969. What Nixon failed to mention, however, were the inherent problems in turning money and power back to the states by cutting taxes, then letting the states pick up the tab for social programs. Furthermore, it is interesting, if not hypocritical, that Nixon should fault his predecessors for cadging votes through these and other spending programs—when he anticipated support for his own administration from the thousands of governors, mayors, city councilmen, and town selectmen to whom he would return the largesse. Enacted into law in 1971, this "New Federalism," or "Second American Revolution," continued for 15 years, with the federal spigot gushing some $83 billion back to 37,000 political entities—before Reagan, running out of money, shut the spigot off. It may well have been that Congress would have turned thumbs down on any drastic reduction in taxes and programs, but there is no evidence that Nixon even tried to take the more sensible route of decentralization. It was also something less than forthright for Nixon to show first such confidence in his Cabinet by telling them "to do more than we can promise," then to promptly ignore and/or circumvent them so that most Cabinet members had quit by the end of his first term.

Nixon's prize "eastern liberal," direct from the elitist school he both envied and loathed, was Henry Kissinger, who was as fearful of bureaucracy as Nixon was of Harvard. For, Kissinger wrote, "a large bureaucracy. . . tends to stifle creativity. It confuses wise policy with smooth administration . . . . More time is spent in running [it] than in defining [its] purposes." Furthermore, "A complex bureaucracy has an incentive to exaggerate technical complexity and minimize the scope of importance of political judgment; it favors the status quo, however arrived at, because short of an unambiguous catastrophe, the status quo has the advantage of familiarity and it is never possible to prove that another course would yield superior results." Kissinger did admit, "The complexity of modern government makes large bureaucracies essential."[18] Yet he seemed to have ignored an equally important reason for that bureaucracy's esistence: to check the power of the chief executive.

If we can include Haldeman and Kissinger himself as bureaucrats, it becomes readily apparent how a bureaucracy can check the abuses of power to which Nixon was prone. There were several occasions on which Haldeman procrastinated, or outright refused, an order from his boss. In most cases, Nixon came around to seeing the rashness of his order, given in the heat of one of the many times he was furious or frustrated.

Another instance of the bureaucracy being the pebble on which Johnson and Nixon, in their pell-mell rush to greatness, stubbed their toes was the Pentagon Papers case. The study had been commissioned by McNamara in 1967, at a time when he was casting a jaundiced eye at Johnson's useless escalations, and was very probably meant to show that this was LBJ's, not McNamara's, war. Some thirty-six "bureaucrats" were appointed to investigate America's relationship with Vietnam since World War II. When the history was completed, in 1971, one of those "bureaucrats," Daniel Ellsberg—seeing, that Nixon was more interested in expanding than in ending the war—leaked the papers to *The New York Times*, precipitating both the end of the war in 1973 and the end of Nixon's administration in 1974.

Granting all the problems that presidents and their staffs have had with the federal bureaucracy, it nevertheless performs an invaluable service by checking abuses of power in the White House. Jonathan Schell has pointed out more than one instance in which the bureaucracy served as a safeguard against Nixon's overreaching his authority. In 1969, Justice Department bureaucrats fought presidential attempts to thwart civil rights laws. A year later, bureaucrats at State and HEW participated in a group protest against Nixon's invasion of Cambodia. In 1972, Nixon ordered the CIA to squelch an FBI investigation of the Watergate break-in, only to have, as Schell pointed out, "a small rebellion" among bureaucrats at both agencies, prompting FBI acting director L. Patrick Gray and CIA deputy director Vernon Walters to resign rather than submit to White House pressure.

Schell concluded: "The executive bureaucracy was one source of the President's great power, but it was also acting as a check on his power. In some ways, it served this function more effectively than the checks provided by the Constitution for, unlike the other institutions of government, it at least had some idea of what was going on." With no public voice and unable to sway public opinion, bureaucrats were castigated as "faceless," "briefcase-toting," "red-tape addicts." Their only answer—and an effective one—was to resort to passive weapons: procrastination, obfuscation, concealment, and the leaking of "classified" information and sensitive documents.

In short, the massive federal bureaucracy has served not only to keep the wheels of government running, regardless of who is elected, but has served a subtle yet powerful curb on presidential power. Gerald Ford wrote, "One of the endearing truths of the nation's capitol is that bureaucrats *survive*."[19] We might add, "And a good thing they do."

The Public

If the Congress serves as a first line of defense against presidential abuse of power, the people themselves serve as the last and ultimate line of defense. Once that defense fails, anarchy or tyranny looms. In ancient Greece, each city-state constructed an amphitheater capable of seating all its voting citizens. It was just such an assembly that Socrates himself appeared before in his famous defense against the charge of corrupting the youth of Athens.

The wresting of power from the ruler—starting with the Magna Carta of 1215 in England, proceeding through the Middle Ages and the Renaissance, and on to the founding of our own nation—constitutes a continuing battle for the rights of man. Gradually the divine right of kings has shifted to the divine right of the people, as Jefferson emphasized in the Declaration of Independence.

Regardless of the particular form of democracy, whether representative as in the United States, parliamentary as in Britain, or social as in many European countries, democracy requires eternal vigilance. Vigilance, in turn, requires alertness, education, a free flow of information between leaders and their constituents, and the ability of the public to understand that information and act on it.

The Constitution, Jefferson wrote in 1816, was not "the Ark of the Covenant, too sacred to be touched. Some men . . . ascribe to the men of the preceding age a wisdom more than human . . . I know that age well; I belonged to it, and labored with it. It was very like the present. . . ." Earlier he'd praised the Constitution as "the wisest ever yet presented to men." Just so, and its wisdom derived in no small part to its restricting the concentration of presidential power. "In questions of power," Jefferson wrote in 1798, three years before he himself became president, "let no more be heard of confidence in man, but bind him down from mischief by the chains of the Constitution."

Here were no divinely appointed and infallible kings or popes, only fallible colonists, doing their best to prevent being oppressed as they had been by George III and his minions. Their leaders, for the most part, were well educated. One has but to tour Jefferson's Monticello to be impressed by his wide-ranging intellect and his innate, boundless curiosity about both the arts and sciences. Returning home after eight years in the presidency, Jefferson labored to bring forth the University of Virginia in 1819. "Knowledge," he wrote, "is power . . . knowledge is safety . . . knowledge is happiness." As for books, they were capital. "A library book lasts as long as a house, for hundreds of years. It is not, then, an article of mere consumption but fairly of capital. . . ."

Madison was equally certain that the nation was only in good hands with an educated electorate: ". . . a well-instructed people alone," he said in 1810, "can be a permanently free people." Fifteen years later, he was no less convinced: "The diffusion of knowledge is the only guardian of true liberty." In 1822, Madison had spelled out more completely this point: "A popular government without popular information, or the means of acquiring it, is but a prologue to a Farce or a Tragedy, or perhaps both. Knowledge will forever govern ignorance; and a people who mean to be their own Governors must arm themselves with the power which knowledge gives."[20]

The recent and disheartening comparisons of our schools with other industrial nations only serve to emphasize the importance of an educated electorate, particularly when it comes to the three branches of government. Not only must the electorate be educated, but it must be kept informed of all three branches of government. Johnson and Nixon, however, tried one ruse after another to prevent the public from knowing what was going on during their administrations. This was done by furtive, backdoor decision-making, keeping Congress, as often as not, in the dark. It was also done by circumventing press conferences, using instead prepared news releases and television talks so as to avoid the scrutiny and questions of curious reporters. A third strategem was to classify arbitrarily and recklessly documents in the name of "national security"—although this ploy could have been more properly labeled *"presidential* security."

The abuse of classification has continued since the seventies. In 1982, President Reagan issued an executive order clamping down on the release of government information and giving federal officials even more leeway in stamping records, "Classified" or "Secret" or "Top Secret." Republican Senator David Durenberger was stunned. "I never thought I would have to do this with Ronald Reagan as President," he exclaimed when he introduced legislation to free up at least some of the mountain of information being classified. Durenberger saw Reagan's pretext of "national security" as defying the "public's right to know what the government is doing." Subsequent events in the Reagan administration—notably the Iran-Contra scandal—fully justified Durenberger's skepticism.

When the issue of the release of the Pentagon Papers to *The New York Times* was being decided by the Supreme Court, Justice Potter Stewart stated, "The hallmark of a truly effective internal security system would be the maximum possible disclosure, recognizing that secrecy can best be preserved only when credibility is truly maintained."

To maintain credibility is no easy task for a president who recognizes that in some affairs secrecy is mandatory; that in other affairs it is necessary for a period of time; and that in still other affairs—and most affairs—there is no need for it. Fraudulent claims of "national security" under Johnson and Nixon were nothing but security blankets for themselves, under which they sought to perpetuate one abuse of power after another. It came as no surprise when the ruse proved counterproductive, serving only to grease the slide down a precipice to self-destruction.

On the public's side of the information equation, there have been at least three disturbing trends that threaten the democracy—the freedom—for which so many have paid with their lives. The first is the deteriorating standards of our educational system, particularly public education, K–12. If Whitehead was right, and ours is a race between catastrophe and survival, between barbarism and civilization, then we must always remember that civilization arose with the development of writing. Literacy is rightly the hallmark of a civilized society. Whether our information comes from the Internet or from the page of a book, we must be able to read and to comprehend. Almost without exception, those nations with the lowest literacy rates are those that remain largely undeveloped, poor by virtually every standard.

The second disturbing trend is America's growing addiction to consumption. Seduced by increasingly sophisticated advertising, we have come to identify the man of distinction with the man of consumption. Other roles that we have traditionally prized, as parents, as neighbors, as colleagues, as citizens, or simply as human beings, are being eclipsed by the one dominant role that promises to bring us happiness: that of consumers.

As a result of this trend, a third trend threatens our societal well-being. We allot so much time to earning enough money to become conspicuous consumers, then spend so much time using and caring for the products we consume, that we have almost no time to devote to our other roles—particularly to the role of citizen. As a result, we are deluged with bite-sized political ads on television and radio, thirty-second spots that reveal little more about a candidate than can be gleaned from a bumper sticker. Our attention spans have become so truncated that any attempt to deal comprehensively with issues, even issues vital to our welfare, are usually ignored. The only time that we seem to give prolonged attention to political issues is when there is a scandal—especially a sexual scandal—in the private life of a politician. Our bumper-sticker mentality has been coupled with a tabloid mentality that deprives us of just the responsibility that makes freedom meaningful in our lives.

Eisenhower put it well when he declared, ". . . failure to fulfill the recognized responsibilities of citizenship . . . is the worst form of laziness and leads, inevitably, to centralization of power." Dean Rusk later wrote, ". . . our system ultimately depends upon the intelligence, integrity, and good faith of the people in the government." In large part, politicians but represent and reflect the same values of the electorate from which they come.

It is America's increasing cynicism with government that, in part, prompted McNamara to publish his *mea culpa* in 1995. "I have grown sick at heart," he wrote, "witnessing the cynicism and even contempt with which so many people view our political institutions and leaders." Little wonder. As he was quick to confess in his preface, "We of the Kennedy and Johnson administrations . . . acted according to what we thought were the principles and traditions of this nation. . . . Yet we were wrong, terribly wrong." When the calamity of Vietnam is followed by the further outrage of Watergate and its deliberate cover-up, we can be thankful for any residue of good will and faith in government that persists now that we have entered a new century and a new millennium.

William Henry Harrison, writing in 1829 to Simon Bolivar, the heroic Latin American revolutionary, sounded a warning to North Americans as well: "The chains of military despotism, once fastened upon a nation, ages might pass away before they can be shaken off." One of the conspicuous ironies—even hypocrisies—of the Johnson and Nixon administrations was their determination to continue the war lest they break faith with those thousands who had already given their lives in Indochina. Yet their conduct of the war and the subsequent revelations of Watergate constituted, in the words of Theodore White's apt title, an egregious *Breach of Faith*—not simply with those who fought and died in Vietnam, Cambodia, and Laos, but on the battlefields of all our wars for two centuries.

It remains for us, if we are intelligent enough and caring enough, to keep faith with those who have bought our freedom with their lives. It is "we the people" who constitute the last line of defense against hubris in our politicians, and particularly our presidents. Just weeks after Nixon's resignation, Winton Blount, former postmaster general, emphasized our responsibility. We must "find a way to restore a human dimension to the [presidency] or we are going to stagger along from one crisis of leadership to the next. . . . If [the president] cannot maintain the confidence of a majority of Americans for more than four years, for whatever reasons, then we stand a very good chance of ending up as the world's most powerful banana republic."

Blount then elaborated, "In the past fourteen years [since 1960] we have had one president assassinated, one hounded out of office, and one forced out of office in disgrace. . . . We have the right to expect our president to be a good and an honorable man who does the best he can as he is given the wisdom to do it. It is as much as we could expect of ourselves. Instead, we want a man who has the courage of David, the wisdom of Solomon, the probity of Lincoln, the patience of Job, and the looks of Tyrone Power. We want what has never been and never will be, and if we persist in demanding this media-manufactured notion of what a president ought to be, we're going to end up with a president whose chief advisors are his make-up man, his tailor, and his barber. . . . The simple fact . . . is that in spite of all the power of the office, the future of the presidency is in our hands."

In the final analysis, as Gerald W. Johnson has put it, "The capacity for being properly led is one of the measures of a great people."[21]

END NOTES

Introduction and Prologue

(Abbreviation: GBWW – *Great Books of the Western World*, Chicago: Encyclopedia Britannica, 1952)

1. de Toqueville, Alexis, *Democracy in America,* 1835, from *Great Ideas Today,* Chicago: Encyclopedia Britannica, 1996.
2. Ambrose, Vol. 2, 507–9; *World Almanac and Book of Facts,* 1993, NY: The Sun, 572–7; *Great Ideas Today,* 1998, 260–264.
3. Ferm, 607; Old Testament, Proverbs 16:18; Welles, 16, 21; New Testament, Revelation, Ch. 6.
4. New Testament, Romans 13:1, 2; Hook, xii.
5. Marcus and Flannery, reviewed in *Science,* August 30, 1996, 1178–9.
6. White. T. H., "DeGaulle: Savior of the Republic or Assassin?" *Saturday Review,* June, 1958, 17; Salisbury, Harrison E., *New York Times,* November 25, 1964; Edwards and Wayne, 1.
7. Washington, letter to Benjamin Lincoln, Oct. 26, 1788; First Inaugural Address, April 30, 1789; letter, 1789; Garfield, journal, Mar. 16, 1881; Lincoln, letter to T.J. Pickett, April, 1859. All cited in Frost, E., 174, 178, 180.
8. White, T. H., *1972,* 383; Sidey, H., "The Presidency," *Life,* Jan. 1968.
9. Reston, J., "Stevenson, Objective Man of Thought, Never Expected to Be President," *New York Times,* July 15, 1965.
10. White, T. H., *1972,* 389; Bell, 459, 464.
11. Lincoln, comment to Senator Henry Wilson, c. 1863; Jackson, letter to T.J.R. Chester, November 30, 1839; Truman, diary, April 12, 1945; Press Conference, April 13, 1945; Memoirs, 1948; Kennedy, speech honoring his 44th birthday, May 27, 1961; Coolidge, *Autobiography,* 1929; Taft, from Tourtellet, Arthur B., *The Presidents on the Presidency;*

Taylor, letter to J. R. Ingersoll; Adems, John, letter to Monroe, Jan., 1809; Jefferson, letter to John Dickerson, Jan. 13, 1807; Garfield, speech, Mar. 3, 1881; Jefferson, letter to Eldridge Gerry. —all cited in Frost, E., 126, 175, 177–8, 180, 184–7, 195; White, T. H., *1972*, 389–390; Bell, J., 459–460, 464.

12. Barclay, 41; Ambrose, Vol. 2, 244; Bell, J., 424–5; Kessler, *Inside the White House,* 8, 75, 254; Gulley, 19–20.

13. New Testament, Matthew 13:57, 14:36; Kessler, *Inside the White House,* 7–8.

Chapter 1 (LBJ) *Deference*

1. Machiavelli, *The Prince,* GBWW, Vol. 23, 34; Washington, letter to E. Rutledge, May 5, 1789. Cited in Frost, E., 174–5.

2. Caro, *Path,* 761–2; Reedy, 152–3.

3. Halberstam, 448–9.

4. Washington, letter to E. Rutledge, May 5, 1789; Jefferson, "The Rights of British America," 1774; "Notes on Virginia," 1781. —all cited in Frost, E., 79, 85, 174–5; Schlesinger, 332, 407.

5. Caro, *Path,* 109–111, 151, 153, 160; Old Testament, Proverbs 25:11; Kearns, 26; Dallek, 34, 41.

6. Johnson, Alfred B "Boody," quoted in Miller, 28; Dallek, 65, 66, 70; Caro, *Path,* 143, 145–6, 153, 158–9; Johnson, Sam H., 26.

7. Caro, *Path,* 219, 224–5, 256; Fleming, Robert, *LBJ,* and Humphrey, all quoted in Miller, 38, 43; Kearns, 78–9.

8. Kearns, 84, 89; Miller, 56–7, 62–3; Trohan, Walter, quoted in Miller, 63; New Testament, Matthew 14:17.

9. Caro, *Path,* 448–9; PBS Home Video, "LBJ"; Lerner, Max, "Correcting a Canon," *The New Republic,* July 14, 21, 1986, 38.

10. Evans and Novak, *LBJ,* 24–5, 28, 788–790; Bush, Horace, quoted in Miller, 116; Baker, Bobby, guoted in Miller, 142; Kearns, 104–5.

11. Evans and Novak, *LBJ,* 33, 88–9; Huitt, Ralph, Bobby Baker, and Hubert Humphrey, all quoted in Miller, 154; Miller, 154–5; Kearns, 107–8, 110, 112; Dallek, 424–5.

12. Rusk, Dean, quoted in Miller, 279; Miller, 335–6; Johnson, L. B., 28–33; Beschloss, 17–8, 20, 39–41.

13. Miller, 338–340; Evans and Novak, *LBJ,* 349–350; Kearns, 175; Beschloss, 36–7; Goldman, 6–10; Johnson, Sam H., 130–1; White, T.H.,

1964, 45.

14. Beschloss, 71, 117, 178, 230, 396; Califano, 36, 155, 207.
15. Evans and Novak, *LBJ*, 358–9, 411~2; Schlesinger, 88; Beschloss, 65, 298.

Chapter 1 (RMN) *Deference*

1. Rather and Gates, 76–7; Schell, 40–1; Parmet, 620.
2. Ambrose, Vol. I, 25, 30–1, 49; Brodie, 38–40, Ch. 5; Abrahamsen, 58, 73, 218; Gardner, 55.
3. Brodie, 258; Yoder, 13; Rather and Gates, 75; Wicker, 198.
4. Nixon, *Memoirs*, 177; Wicker, 181, 197–8, 224–5; Brodie, 356; Ambrose, Vol. I, 408, 411–2, 552, 555, 559; Goldwater, 73.
5. Brodie, 432–4; Ambrose, Vol. I, 227, 557–8; Vol. II, 165–9.
6. *New York Times*, Sept. 23, 1968; Ambrose, Vol. I, 140; Nixon, *Memoirs*, 305; Schlesinger, 219; Frost, D., 12.
7. Gulley, 234–5; Schell, 30; Rather and Gates, 76–7.
8. Gulley, 242; Kissinger, Vol. II, 386; Nixon, *Memoirs*, 674–5; Ambrose, Vol. II, 133; Rather and Gates, 207–8.
9. Frost, D., 90; White, T. H., *1972*, 234; Kissinger, Vol. I, 180; Ambrose, Vol. II, 184–5; Evans and Novak, *RMN*, 344–5.
10. Parmet, 620–2; Nixon, *Memoirs*, 545–6, 548, 550, 552; Kissinger, Vol. I, 757–9.
11. Gulley, 242; Kissinger, Vol. I, 752, 756–7, 1054; Nixon, *Memoirs*, 559.
12. Ambrose, Vol. II, 511; Kissinger, Vol. I, 1058; Parmet, 620; Nixon, *Memoirs*, 557–8.
13. Kutler, *Abuse of Power*, 124, 351, 381–2; Haldeman, *Ends of Power*, dedication page.
14. Nixon, *Memoirs*, 601–2; Smith, Gerard, 376; Hersh, 530; *New York Times*, June 2, 1972.
15. Kissinger, Vol. II, 134; Ambrose, Vol. I, 546; Zumwalt, 407; Janis, *Groupthink*, 2nd ed., 210–1.

Chapter 2 (LBJ) *Delegation*

1. Machiavelli, GBWW, Vol. 23, 33; Jefferson, letter to Trenche Coxe, 1820; Lincoln, Washington, D.C., 1865. —both cited in Frost, E., 9, 11; Eisenhower, D., 456; Beschloss, 116–7; Rather and Gates, 21.
2. Coolidge, *Autobiography*, 1929; Eisenhower, D., diary, Jan. 1, 1953;

Harrison, B, *This Country of Ours*, 1897; Cleveland, n.d.; Lincoln, letter to W. H. Henderson, 1861; Polk, *Diary*, April 6, 1848. All cited in Frost, E., 10–13, 163, 184.

3. Adams, ,John, letter to John Quincy Adams, Feb. 18, 1811; Washington, letter to Bushrod Washington, July 27, 1789; Jackson, n.d.; Coolidge, *Autobiography*, 1929; Truman, n.d. —all cited in Frost, E., 149, 167, 172, 175, 186; Sorensen, 288.

4. *Indianapolis Star*, April 28, 1995; Kearns, 163; Adams, John, letter to Josiah Quincy, Feb. 14, 1825. Cited in Frost, E., 176.

5. Rather and Gates, 14, 18; Caro, *Path*, 41.

6. Beschloss, 25; Halberstam, *Best and Brightest*, 40–1; Evans and Novak, *LBJ*, 341–2, 346–7.

7. Evans and Novak, *LBJ*, 506–7; Alsop, S., "LBJ. How?" 14; Allen, Robert S., quoted in Miller, 175; Johnson, Sam H., 168–170.

8. Beschloss, 340, 471, 486–7; Johnson, Sam H., 92.

9. Halberstam, *Best and Brightest*, 434, 533; Beschloss, 113–4; Califano, 113; Reedy, 157; Caro, *Path*, 302.

10. McNamara, 15–6; Johnson, Sam H., 114–5, 117; Caro, *Means*, 117–8; Cormier, 79.

11. Beschloss, 148; Sidey, *Personal Presidency*, 188.

12. Johnson, Sam H., 68; Evans and Novak, *LBJ*, 108; Sidey, *Personal Presidency*, 156–8.

13. Califano, 26, 28–9, 162; Mooney, 185.

14. White, T. H., *1964*, 284; Beschloss, 535; Roche, John P., quoted in Miller, 421; Steinberg, 632, 735; Halberstam, *Best and Brightest*, 517–8.

15. Gulley, 56–7, 59, 113–4; Steinberg, 632; Kessler, *Inside the White House*, 25, 30; Adler, 197.

16. Califano, 169–170; Gulley, 66–8, 92; Tuchman, 283; Halberstam, *Best and Brightest*, 437–8.

17. Janis, *Victims*, 3, 105, 197–8; Tuchman, 380; McNamara, 95.

Chapter 2 (RMN) *Delegation*

1. Haldeman, *Ends of Power*, 405.

2. Ambrose, *Best and Worst*, 68; Vol. II, 236–8; *Time*, Jan. 5, 1968, 22; Schlesinger, 220; White, T. H., *Breach of Faith*, 412; Viorst, 72.

3. Nixon, *Memoirs*, 26; Viorst, 76; Schlesinger, 221.

4. Ambrose, Vol. II, 489–491; Ehrlichman, 306; *U.S. News & World*

Report, Sept. 16, 1996, 62; Hersh, *Price of Power*, 475; Stoessinger, 37. In August 1966, Kissinger gave his assessment of the Vietnam War to *Look* magazine: "Withdrawal would be disastrous and negotiations are inevitable. Therefore we should stay in there, fighting to gain enough territory to enable us to negotiate from strength. Whatever we do we can't withdraw, for that would 'strengthen' the hand of our adversaries, 'demoralize' our allies, and 'lessen [our] credibility,' causing other nations to shift their allegiance to the U.S.S.R." A year later Kissinger was aboard LBJ's team negotiating in Paris, trying to convince the President about a certain plan. Growled Johnson, "I'm going to give it one more try, and if it doesn't work, I'm going to come up to Cambridge and cut off your balls." As unnerving as this threat was to his manhood, Kissinger was just as upset when LBJ kept addressing him as "Professor Schlesinger." Isaacson, Walter, *Kissinger: A Biography*, 120, 122.

5.   Ehrlichman, 17, 20; Rather and Gates, 148–9, 227, 230, 232; Kissinger, Vol. II, 93–4. Whalen was the speech writer to whom candidate Nixon leveled in March 1968: "There's no way to win this war. But we can't say that, of course. In fact, we have to seem to say just the opposite, just to keep some degree of bargaining leverage." Isaacson, Walter, *Kissinger: A Biography*, 159–160.

6.   Nixon, *Memoirs*, 774; Ehrlichman, 386–393; Rather and Gates, 219. Thompson recounts, "Whenever Ervin scored points or made a clever comment . . . the audience applauded. Ehrlichman's responses were met with moans, groans, and hisses. Each morning, as Ervin entered the hearing room, the crowd applauded as he walked to his seat." Thompson, 99–101.

7.   Ehrlichman, 402, 407–410; Parmet, 638.

8.   Mazo, 284–5; Haldeman, *Ends of Power*, 13, 20; Mankiewicz, *Perfectly Clear*, 72–5.

9.   Rather and Gates, 49, 142–3, 161, 277; Kissinger, Vol. I, 483; Vol. II, 124–5.

10.   Ambrose, Vol. II, 475; Sidey, *LBJ*, 95; Gulley, 156; Rather and Gates, 155, 236, 238.

11.   Haldeman, 20–1; Rather and Gates, 238–9, 249; Nixon, *Memoirs*, 812, 1071; Frost, D., 277; Abrahamsen, 201.

12.   Kutler, *Abuse of Power*, 410, 347, 373, 380–1, 483, 496, 604–5, 233, 407,

550, 286, 632–3; 232–3; 399, 447–8, 274, 310.

13. Janis, *Victims*, 3; Conant, 36*ff*; Kissinger, Vol. II, 491; White, T. H., *1972*, 530; Sirica, 281; Nixon, *Memoirs*, 826.

14. Kutler, *Abuse of Power*, 380; Nixon, *Memoirs*, 832; White, T. H., *Breach of Faith*, 433; Machiavelli, GBWW, Vol. 23, 33–4.

Chapter 3 (LBJ) *Expansion*

1. Godkin, E. L., "The Moral of Tweed's Career," *The Nation*, April 18, 1878; Kearns, 44, 322; Miller, 562, 3

2. Blount, 64; Madison, to the Virginia Convention, June 20, 1788; Washington, letter to Alexander Hamilton, July 2, 1794; Farewell Address, November 17, 1798. All cited in Frost, E., 86–7, 125, 210.

3. Schlesinger, 3–4, 6, 9; Kearns, 214; Kissinger, Vol. I, 17; Miller, xiv.

4. Cohen, Reedy, Connally, Neustadt, and Humphrey, all quoted in Miller, xv–xxii; Sidey, *LBJ*, 72; Taylor, letter to his brother, June 11, 1846. Cited in Frost, E., 177.

5. Kearns, 44, 53, 62; Halberstam, *Best and Brightest*, 443–4; Ambrose, Vol. I, 147; Sidey, *LBJ*, 13.

6. Dallek, 53; Beschloss, 19–21.

7. Provence, 35; Dallek, 79, 89; Kearns, 72–3.

8. Caro, *Path*, 340, 350–2, 405–9, 423–5; Lee, Ray E., quoted in Miller, 61; Johnson, Sam H., 147; Steinberg, 134, 360.

9. Rusk, 276; McPherson, Harry, quoted in Miller, 305; Reedy, 46, 50.

10. Wilson, *Fortnightly Review*, Feb., 1913. —cited in Frost, E., 164; Tabori, 15; Tuchman, 311.

11. Sidey, "Deep Grow the Roots of the Alamo," *Life*, May, 1968, 32; Gasset, "The Barbarism of Specialization "; Beschloss, 105, 145; Jefferson, letter to Samuel Kercheval, July 12, 1816. —cited in Frost, E., 44; White, T. H., *1964*, 19–20.

12. Caro, *Path*, 155–6; Kearns, 185; Califano, 308; Boorstin, "Yes, We Should," 8; Beschloss, 372, 440.

13. Reedy, 23, 26; Fvans and Novak, *LBJ*, 328, 556; Conant, James B., "The University in a Free Society," *Modern Minds*, ed. by H. M. Jones, Boston: Heath and Co., 1949, 36*ff*.

14. "McNamara Seen Now, Full Length," *Life*, Oct., 1968; Wicker, "LBJ Can't Corral Intellectuals," *New York Times*, 1967; Kearns, 53; Sidey, *LBJ*, 201.

15. See assorted quotes in Miller, 149, 175; Reedy, 107–8; Evans and Novak, *LBJ*, 160, 166; Tuchman, 234; White. T. H., *1960*, 20; Beschloss, 177–8; Jefferson, letter to Eldridge Garry, 1797. Cited in Frost, E., 175.

16. Reedy, 21; Kennedy, conferring honorary citizenship on Churchill, April 9, 1963. —cited in Frost, E., 101; Bell, 155, 321; Miller, 24.

17. Keach, Carroll, and Benjamin C. Bradlee, quoted in Miller, 59–60, 174; Caro, *Path*, 414; Evans and Novak, *LBJ*, 274; Dallek, 573–4; White, T. H., *1960*, 100, 154–5, 157; Goldwater, 191–2; Califano, 51–2, 55; Johnson, Sam.H., 134.

18. Evans and Novak, *LBJ*, 348; Waldron, Robert, and Hubert Humphrey, both quoted in Miller, 338, 345–6; Miller, 340. This is the same Dick Gregory who described Hubert Humphrey as looking like one "who'd buy a used car from Nixon," and Geoge Wallace as one "who'd steal it!" Kutler, *Wars of Watergate*, 66.

Chapter 3 (RMN) *Expansion*

1. Matthews, 144–5; Wills, 175; Bell, 191; Tuchman, 358.

2. Abrahamsen, 77, 98, 103–4; Schlesinger, 406; White, T. H., *1964*, 215; Goldwater, 76, 190; Morrow, Lance, "Kennedy Going on Nixon," *Time*, May 18, 1987, 90; Brodie, 89–90.

3. Wicker, xiv–xv; "Making Things Git," book review, *Time*, Mar. 14, 1969, 103; Woodward and Bernstein, *Final Days*, 168; Kissinger, Vol. I, 46, 12; Haldeman, *Ends of Power*, 21, 96, 99.

4. Parmet, 641; Oudes, xlii; Wicker, xiii–xiv, 418; Frost, D., 275; Aitken, 2.

5. Nixon, *Memoirs*, 3–4, 9; Dean, 13; Adams, John, letter to John Quincy Adams, Jan. 3, 1794; Adams, John Quincy, *Parties in the U.S.*, c. January, 1822. —both cited in Frost, E., 114; Bell, 417, 422.

6. Abrahamsen, 179; Nixon, *Memoirs*, 208–9, 292; Safire, 690; Dean, 18–19; Ambrose, Vol. II, 38; Wicker, 421–2, 429.

7. Wicker, 427–8; Kutler, *Abuse of Power*, 477; *Parade Magazine*, Feb. 11, 1996, 8; Kissinger, Vol. I, 944, 1395.

8. Wills, 172, 177–8; Ambrose, Vol. I, 35; Nixon, *Memoirs*, 5, 20; Wicker, 9.

9. Nixon, *Memoirs*, 223; *Six Crises*, 426; Kissinger, Vol. I, 943.

10. Madison, letter to Samuel H. Smith, Nov., 1826; Jefferson, letter to Col. Charles Yancy, Jan. 6, 1816. —both cited in Frost, E., 107, 114; Parmet, 71; Ambrose, Vol. I, 91; Kissinger, Vol. I, 79.

11. Nixon, *Memoirs*, 15, 252–3, 724; Mazo, 293, 108; Bell, 444; Lincoln, c. 1859. Cited in Frost, E., 178. Aitken, a member of Britain's Parliament, was one of the few foreigners to write a biography of Nixon. After a two-hour interview with Nixon at San Clemente in 1975, Aitken was impressed. "His grasp of the international scene was still formidable. He had a striking gift for tying all the threads of a long, analytical discourse neatly together in a precise and authoritative conclusion." Aitken, 2–3.

12. Parmet, 496; White, T. H. *1972*, 435–6; Kissinger, Vol. I, 65; Skinner, B.F., *Beyond Freedom and Dignity*, NY: Bantam, 1971; Taft, *The President and His Powers*, 1916. Cited in Frost, E., 183.

13. Ambrose, Vol. II, 412; White, T. H., *Breach of Faith*, 435–6; Ambrose, *Best and Worst*, 68; Adams, John, letter to John Taylor, April 15, 1814. Cited in Frost, E., 135; Magruder, 106; Kissinger, Vol. II, 180.

14. Parmet, 399, 642; Sirica, 204, 299, 313*ff*; Ambrose, Vol. II, 552; Wicker, 26–7. See also *The White House Transcripts*.

15. Kutler, *Abuse of Power*, 416, 561, 615; Haldeman, *Ends of Power*, 273; Kissinger, Vol. I, 12–5; Brodie, 106–8.

16. Ambrose, Vol. I, 131–7, 216–6; Parmet, 110–3, 103, 192, 198–9.

17. Nixon, *Six Crises*, 118–9; Parmet, 246–7; Nixon, speech to Sales Executive Club of New York, Jan. 26, 1965. —cited in Frost, E., 39; Ambrose, Vol. II, 345–6; Nixon, *Memoirs*, 451–3.

18. Abrahamsen, 120; Sirica, 203–4; Nixon, *Memoirs*, 879; Ambrose, Vol. II, 419; Wicker, 27.

19. Nixon, *Memoirs*, 18; Mazo, 23; Abrahamsen, 110; Parmet, 57, 70.

20. Bell, 280; Wicker, xiii, 24, 26, 366; Halberstam, *Best and Brightest*, 98.

21. Abrahamsen, 182; Sevareid, 10; Parmet, 360–1.

22. Hughes, *Political Memoir*, 316–7; Nixon, *Six Crises*, 422; Wicker, 357; Ambrose, Vol. I, 457.

23. Oudes, xv; McGinniss, 27–8; Abrahamsen, 192; Osborne, 25.

24. McGinniss, 29–30; Wicker, 344, 364–5; Kessler, *Inside the White House*, 63–4; Sheehan, 31–5.

25. Mazo, 24; Abrahamsen, 59, 97–112; Ambrose, Vol. I, 65–6. Aitken's biography carries a photo of Ola-Florence Welch, once she had been engaged to Nixon on June 10, 1933. Aitken, 338.

26. Abrahamsen, 103, 105, 116; Ambrose, Vol. I, 65-7, 81–3; Alsop, S., *Nixon and Rockefeller*, 237–8.

27. Ambrose, Vol. II, 403, 409; White, T. H, *1960*, 339; *U.S. News & World Report* Jan. 8, 1996, 23; Breslin, 51; Kutler, *Abuse of Power*, 559, 565, 584, 586, 611, 628, 651.

28. Haldeman, 105; Nixon, *Memoirs*, 649, 670; Sirica, 230, 233–5; Parmet, 278; Woodward and Bernstein, *Final Days*,169; Ambrose, Vol. II, 272–3.

29. Parmet, 394–5, 632–3; Kissinger, Vol. II, 1125, 1136; Woodward and Bernstein, *Final Days*, 101–2; Nixon, *Memoirs*, 973.

30. Goldwater, 287; Kissinger, Vol. I, 78; McGinniss, 103, 161; Abrahamsen, 209; *Impeachment Report*, x; Haldeman, *Ends of Power* 107.

Chapter 4 (LBJ) *Opportunism*

1. Gordon, John Steele, "The Freedman's Bank," *American Heritage*, Dec. 1993, 20; Monroe, letter to General "Stonewall" Jackson, July 3, 1825 —cited in Frost, E., 177; Sherrill, 71; Beschloss, 353; Kearns, 49.

2. Dobzhansky, *Biological Basis*, 239; Beschloss, 443; Johnson, L. B., speech to the University of Michigan, May 22, 1964; speech to the National Urban League Conference, Dec. 1964. —both cited in Frost, E., 228; Provence, 54.

3. Caro, *Path*, 112–4, 161–3, 284–5, 294-9, 372–3; Dallek, 81, 120–1; Miller, 49.

4. Dallek, 140–5, 154–5; Miller, 57–8; Machiavelli, 25.

5. Caro, *Path*, 273–5; Roosevelt, T, n.d.; Harrison, W. H., speech, Oct. 1, 1840. —both cited in Frost, E., 16, 163; Caro, *Means*, 80.

6. Dallek, 174–5; Caro, *Path*, 467–9; *Means*, 80–1; Busby, H., quoted in Miller, 116.

7. Evans and Novak, *LBJ*, 10, 21; Caro, *Means*, 81–2; Caro, *Path*, 765–7.

8. Miller, 105–6, 107–8, 111, 114–5, 122; Dallek, 249–251, 279–280, 288; Caro, *Means*, 101.

9. Kearns, 99–100; Webber, P., quoted in Miller, 299–300; Beschloss, 75, 93, 160–1, 179, 352–3, 385.

10. Clifford, 390–1; Beschloss, 74–5, 242.

11. Caro, *Means*, 88, 90; Dallek, 251–2, 409–410, 412–3, 415; Beschloss, 217, 290.

12. Caro, *Means*, 113; Sidey, H. quoted in Miller, 304; Beschloss, 235, 241, 314–5, 324–5.

13. Durr, V., quoted in Miller, 214; Finder, 35, 38; Dallek, 412–3;

Beschloss, 115–6. Note: *Ramparts* magazine ran an article in the late sixties more fully documenting the fortunes of Brown and Root in Vietnam.

Chapter 4 (RMN) *Opportunism*

1. Kissinger, Vol. I, 6; Kutler, *Abuse of Power*, 20, 254.
2. Ambrose, Vol. II, 187–9; Kissinger, Vol. I, 171; Mazo, 21, 23–8; Parmet, 79, 100; Abrahamsen, 166; Morris, 671*ff.*
3. Parmet, 361, 386; Schell, 111; White, T.H. *Breach of Faith*, 15, 34; Goldwater, 262; Bell, 52; Mazo, 275; Costello, 24.
4. Kutler, *Abuse of Power*, 4, 42, 165–6; Schell, 211–2; Ambrose, Vol. II, 551, 557; Finder, 38.
5. Ambrose, Vol. I, 272; Vol. II, 514; Parmet, 56; Nixon, *Memoirs*, 4; de Toledano, 16; Abrahamsen, 51–2; Nixon, *Self–Portrait*, 7.
6. Wills, 23; Nixon, *Memoirs*, 231; Ambrose, Vol. I, 427.
7. Parmet, 393, 401; Abrahamsen, 209–210; Mankiewicz, *Perfectly Clear*, 62; Morris, 655.
8. Parmet, 396, 401–2, 640; Brodie, 385, Wicker, 667–9; Nixon, *Memoirs*, 489–490; White, T. H., *Breach of Faith*, 258
9. Parmet, 395; Ambrose, Vol. I, 597–8, 662–3; Kutler, *Abuse of Power*, 118–9.
10. Ambrose, Vol. II, 585; Parmet, 394–5; Kutler, *Abuse of Power*, 218, 301–2, 378; Wicker, 390–1.
11. Nixon, *Memoirs*, 961–2; Brodie, 447; Ambrose, Vol. II, 227; Kutler, *Abuse of Power*, 493–6, 620
12. Brodie, 620; Sidey Hugh, "The Mandate to Live Well," *Time*, April 5, 1974, 17; Woodward and Bernstein, *Final Days*, 454; Abrahamsen, 217; Rauch, 30.

Chapter 5 (LBJ) *Exploitation*

1. Adams, John, to J. H. Tiffany, Mar. 31, 1819; Adams, John Quincy, 1821; Jefferson, letter to Edward Carrington, 1788. —all cited in Frost, E., 129–131; Caro, *Path*, 607; Dallek, 123; Johnson, Lady Bird, 231.
2. Caro, *Means*, 368; Reedy, 44–5; Caro, *Path*, 607; Johnson, Sam H., 173; Jefferson, letter to A. L. C. Destutt de Tracy, Jan. 26, 1811. —cited in Frost, E., 170.
3. Caro, *Path*, 675–6, 678–680; Dallek, 217–221.

4. Caro, *Path*, 675–6, 693–4; Dallek, 218–9; Miller, 83–5; Jenkins, Walter, Joe Mashman, and Thomas G. Corcoran, all quoted in Miller, 119–120.
5. Caro, *Means*, 249; Goldman, 475; Beschloss, 26–7; Johnson, Sam H., 35–6.
6. Dallek, 482–3; Davidson, Bill, and William Theis, both quoted in Miller, 180, 220; Kearns, 136–7; Acheson, Dean, *New York Times*, August 13, 1957; *New York Times*, July 13, 1956.
7. Beschloss, 171, 313, 319–320; Sparkman, John, Bill Moyers, and Philip Graham, all quoted in Miller, 249, 417–8; Sidey, *LBJ*, 268; Evans and Novak, *LBJ*, 411; White, T. H., *1964*, 409.
8. Sidey, *LBJ*, 133, 175; Evans and Novak, *LBJ*, 541; Tuchman, 327–8; Kearns, 313–5; Taft, 228.
9. Washington, letter to Robert Howe, Aug. 17, 1779; "Goldman's Variations," *Time*, Mar. 14, 1969, 104; Miller, 76; Dallek, 192, 194–5; Caro, *Path*, 568, 571.
10. Caro, *Path*, 590–1, 593; Dallek, 196; Roberts, Jay, quoted in Miller, 76.
11. Caro, *Path*, 300–4; Kearns, 83; Steinberg, 128; Dallek, quoted in TV series, "Lady Bird Johnson," Mar. 30, 1998.
12. Caro, *Path*, 304–5, 476–7, 483; Miller, 58; Pickle, Joe, quoted in Miller, 94; Beschloss, 251.
13. Beschloss, 137, 251, 268, 446; Califano, 387; Redman, Coates, quoted in Miller, 444; Reedy, 142–3; Sullivanr 181.
14. Quoted in TV series, "Lady Bird Johnson," Mar. 30, 1998; Kessler, 1–2, 12–4, 37; Beschloss, 146–7; Miller, 445.
15. Miller, 445; Geovannatti, Lenny, Liz Carpenter, Lady Bird Johnson, and "Scooter" Miller, all quoted in Miller, 396, 445; Beschloss, 245, 405.
16. Beschloss, 268–9; Sidey, *LBJ*, 19; New Testament, I Corinthians 13; TV Series, "Lady Bird Johnson," Mar. 30, 1998.

Chapter 5 (RMN) *Exploitation*

1. Kutler, *Abuse of Power*, 266, 302–3, 356, 384, 407, 420, 463, 472, 487, 494, 639
2. Ambrose, Vol. I, 122; Costello, 52; Brodie, 157; Nixon, Six *Crises*, 113–7; Abrahamsen, 144; Spalding, 136.
3. Ambrose, Vol. I, 87–9, 128–9; Parmet, 89–93; Brodie, 172, 175; Wicker,

33–45; Nixon, *Six Crises*, 134. Morris has a fuller account of Nixon's malfeasance in his Whittier law firm. Morris, 189–192.

4. Brodie, 158, 172; Kornitzer, 149, 160–1; Mazo, 44.

5. Brodie, 173; Alsop, S., 187–8; Nixon, *Memoirs*, 40; de Toledano, 44; Costello, *Facts*, 44, 46; Wills, 75, 78.

6. Parmet, 95; Wicker, 40; Brodie, 180–1; Bullock, 263, 266, 273.

7. de Toledano, 44; Wicker, 34; Ambrose, Vol. I, 132; Allen, 424; Brodie, 179.

8. Brodie, 357; White, T. H., *1960*, 98; Eisenhower, J. N., 126; *Indianapolis Star*, Nov. 9, 1997: review of *The Dark Side of Camelot*, by Seymour Hersh. It was the same Giancana who shared his mistress, Judith Exner, with JFK, starting in March 1960. Having contracted gonorrhea while a student at Harvard, Jack had enjoyed his share of sexploits and Exner was no exception. Indeed, after entering the White House in 1961, phone logs recorded some 70 calls between JFK and his tall, black-haired, blue eyed beauty, a former actress at the Sands Hotel in Las Vegas. Kessler, *The Sins of the Father*, 375–6, 381.

9. Ambrose, Vol. I, 93–4; Eisenhower, J. N., 17–8, 21–7, 54–69, 74–87; Brodie, 150–5, 170–1.

10. Eisenhower, J. N., 86–9; Ambrose, Vol. 1, 118, 462; Brodie, 178–9, 235; White, T. H., *1960*, 207.

11. Eisenhower, J. N., 110–2, 171; Ambrose, Vol. I, 225–9, 246; Brodie, 466; Nixon, *Memoirs*, 78.

12. Ambrose, Vol. I, 244, 264; Eisenhower, J. N., 115; Nixon, *Memoirs*, 86; David, 94; *New York Times*, July 12, 1952.

13. Ambrose, Vol. I, 245–6, 247–8; Brodie, 235, 238; Nixon, *Memoirs*, 111.

14. Nixon, *Memoirs*, 107; Machiavelli, 27; Parmet, 288; Ambrose, Vol. I, 359; Eisenhower, J. N. 133, 145, 159, 167, 218; Abrahamsen, 134.

15. Eisenhower, J. N., 178; Halberstam, *Best and Brightest*, 97; Brodie, Ch. 11; Ambrose, Vol. I, 585–6; Nixon, *Six Crises*, 205, 209, 228, 231; Alsop, S., 59; Brodie, 141; *Newsweek*, Feb. 22, 1960, 28.

16. Ambrose, Vol. I, 644, 646–8; Vol. II, 111; Nixon, *Memoirs*, 236–7; Eisenhower, J. N., 206; Woodward and Bernstein, *Final Days*, 165; Abrahamsen, 237; Parmet, 14.

17. Eisenhower, J. N., 131; Wicker, 422–3; Woodward and Bernstein, *Final Days*, 166; Kessler, *Inside the White House*, 39; Nixon, *Memoirs*, 753.

18. Brodie, 144–5; Smith, H. M., 129, 133.

19. Kornitzer, 134; Brodie, 143, 147; Nixon, *Memoirs*, 23; Parmet, 288.

Chapter 6 (LBJ) *Arrogance*

1. Sophocles, *Oedipus the King*, GBWW, Vol. 5, 107; Plato, *The Republic*, Book I, GBWW, Vol. 7, 304; Machiavelli, *The Prince*, GBWW, Vol 23, 24; Shakespeare, *Henry VIII*, Act III, Scene 2.
2. Kearns, 354; Miller, 49; Caro, *Means*, 192.
3. Karnow, 13–4; Caro, *Path*, 500–1; Kennedy, Paul, 372; Sorensen, 276–8; Fulbright, 3.
4. Goldman, Ch. 1; Kearns, 156, 241; Miller, 280; Caro, *Path*, 335, 338.
5. Caro, *Path*, 107–8; *Means*, 24, 26–7, 30–1, 32, 37; Kearns, 95; Califano, 337; Dallek, 231.
6. Dallek, 230–1, 236–7; Caro, *Msans*, 32; Miller, 93; Evans and Novak, *LBJ*, 192–3.
7. Miller, 96; Barin, Cpl. Harry G. and Sgt. Claude A. McCredie, both quoted in Miller, 97; Caro, *Means*, 40–1.
8. Johnson, L. B., diary, and Cpl. Lillis Walker, both quoted in Miller, 95–6, 97–8; Johnson, L. B., letter, quoted in Miller, 99; Dallek, 62–3, 239–241; Miller, 98; Caro, *Means*, 38–9, 99.
9. Kearns, 94, 99; Dallek, 240–2; Johnson, L. B., letter, quoted in Miller, 99; Caro, *Means*, 51.
10. Caro, *Means*, 45, 49–52; Miller, 101.
11. Grant, *Personal Memoirs*, 1886, cited in Frost, E., 255; Caro, *Means*, 52–3; *The New Republic*, June 9, 1997, 8; Beschloss, 111; Dallek, 232
12. Caro, *Means*, 129, 179; Dallek, 158, 209; Kearns, 100; Busby, H., quoted in Miller, 116.
13. Caro, *Means*, Ch. 8; Dallek, 299–300, 315; Clark, Ramsey, and Paul H. Douglas, both quoted in Miller, 118, 147; Miller, 117.
14. Connally, John, and Walter Jenkins, both quoted in Miller, 118–9, 121; Dallek, 305–6, 309.
15. Caro, *Means*, 181–3, 185, 189–190; Dibrell, T. K., George Reedy, and Callan Graham, all quoted in Miller, 125–6; Miller, 121–2.
16. Miller, 121–2; Jenkins, Walter, George Reedy, Jake Pickle, T. K. Dibrell, and Allan Shivers, all quoted in Miller, 124.
17. Miller, 126–8, 130–1; Graham, Callan, Bryan Skelton, Walter Jenkins, and Abe Fortas, all quoted in Miller, 128–9.
18. Porter, Paul and Abe Fortas, both quoted in Miller, 133; Miller, 134–5;

Dallek, 561.

19. Miller, 136; Adams, John, letters to Jefferson, Dec. 6, 1787 and April 6, 1796, cited in Frost, E., 75; Beschloss, 242, 442.

Chapter 6 (RMN) *Arrogance*

1. Nixon quoted on "McNeil–Lehrer News Hour," April 29, 1994; Kutler, *Abuse of Power*, 549; Wicker, 89; Schlesinger, 467.
2. Schlesinger, 406; Kornitzer, 176; Abrahamsen, 122–5; Brodie, Ch. 10; Wills, 133–9, 207.
3. Ambrose, Vol. I, 556–7, 565; Wicker, 175, Nixon, *Six Crises*, 400–1; Wills, 144–6, 149.
4. Nixon, *Memoirs*, 300, 1080, 1083, 1089; Wills, 207.
5. Schell, 246–7; White, T.H., *1972*, 357, 396; Nixon, *Six Crises*, 426; Nixon, *Memoirs*, 825.
6. Nixon, *Memoirs*, 454–5, 456–7; Ambrose, Vol. I, 562; Vol. II, 325; Wills, 145, 149.
7. Kalb, Marvin, *Nixon Memo*, 199–200, 209–210; White, T. H., *1972*, 50; Dean, 201; Nixon, *Memoirs*, 756–7.
8. Schlesinger, 299; Fulbright, 257–8.
9. Kutler, *Abuse of Power*, 100; 226, 292, 504, 85, 116, 147, 175, 226, 292, 381, 44, 48, 50, 88, 98, 106, 43, 55, 148–9, 392, 448, 460, 505, 516, 324, 130, 151, 178, 505, 591, 608, 148, 253.
10. Kutler, *Abuse of Power*, 174, 53–5, 72, 81, 380–1; Goldwater, 245; Nixon, *Memoirs*, 717.
11. Kutler, *Abuse of Power*, 382, 384–5, 376, 386, 204–5; Schell, 309–310; Breslin, 108–9, 114–5.

Chapter 7 (LBJ) *Identification*

1. Washington, letter to Alexander Hamilton, July 2, 1794; Jefferson, announcing he would not run for a third term; both cited in Frost, E., 175; Sidey, *Mandate*, 17; White, T. H., *1960*, 155.
2. Sidey, *LBJ*, 98; Miller, 470; Johnson, Sam H., 210; See Curtis, *Evolution or Extinction*, Ch. 5, for further elaboration.
3. Dallek, 64; White, T. H., *1964*, 54, 64; *Chicago Tribune*, Mar. 9, Dec. 21, 1958; Steinberg, 565–6; Miller, 264; PBS Documentary, "Liberty," Nov. 25, 1997; Taylor, Alan, review of *George Washington: Writings* in *The New Republic*, Jan. 19, 1998, 38.

4. Califano, 94, 169; Symington, James, quoted in Miller, 455–6; Johnson, Sam H., 214; Sidey, *LBJ*, 141–3, 153–5, 250; Old Testament, Ecclesiastes, 1:2.

5. Sidey, *LBJ*, 152, 261; Johnson, Sam H., 214; Moyers, Bill, quoted in Miller, 441; *Time*, January 5, 1968, 21.

6. Busby, Horace, Thomas G. Corcoran, Harry McPherson, and D. B. Hardeman, all quoted in Miller, 78, 203–4; Evans and Novak, *LBJ*, 119, 141–2.

7. Evans and Novak, *LBJ*, 100, 104–5, 161, 168, 223; Truman and Coolidge, cited in Frost, E., 185; Cormier, 34.

8. Karnow, 410, 412–5; Halberstam, *Best and Brightest*, 624; Clifford, 381; Miller, 488; Moyers, Bill, quoted in Miller, 488–9; Hamilton, Roultec, "Johnson Powers Show Success," *Columbus* (Ohio) *Dispatch*, Mar. 10, 1968.

9. Sidey, *LBJ*, 80; Cohen, Wilbur J., quoted in Miller, 490; Johnson, Sam H., 202–3; Karnow, 558, 559–560; Beschloss, 135.

10. Karnow, 559–560; Sidey, *LBJ*, 47, 80, 144; Evans and Novak, *LBJ*, 4; Schell, 20.

Chapter 7 (RMN) *Identification*

1. Kutler, *Abuse of Power*, 525, 546, 376; Kissinger, Vol. II, 470; Nixon, *Memoirs*, 80–2, 88; Parmet, 21; Brodie, 162; Ambrose, Vol. I, 322–3.

2. Safire, 183; Brodie, 271; Kissinger, Vol. I, 107, 780; Wicker, 585; *Los Angeles Times*, Dec. 4, 1978; Parmet, 300; Evans and Novak, *RMN*, 93. Another with whom Nixon liked to identify was Britain's 19th century prime minister, Benjamin D'Israeli. Both, Nixon believed, had been humbly born as outsiders but who rose by force of sheer intellect and perseverance to become outstanding, albeit controversial, conservative leaders of their respective nations. Aitken, 7.

3. Abrahamsen, 170; Mazo; 277 Ambrose, Vol. II, 643; Schlesinger, 410; Nixon *Memoirs*, 651; Sirica, 261.

4. Nixon, *Memoirs*, 773, 833–4, 981; Kutler, *Abuse of Power*, 239, 247, 321; Dean, 201.

5. Kutler, *Abuse of Power*, 338, 353, 363, 393, 406, 409, 420, 453, 460, 495; Janis, *Groupthink*, 232. Whatever else Haig had done, he'd polished the art of sycophancy to such a luster that astonished his 240 senior officers he leap-frogged over, as Kissinger's aide, to exchange his

silver lieutenant-colonel's leaf for the four stars of a full general in five short years. And this from one who graduated 214th out of 310 in his West Point class. It is noteworthy that, far from pleading a lack of fitness for the presidency, when Ronald Reagan was shot in 1981, it was Haig who stepped in to announce airily, "I'm in charge here!" Kutler, *Wars of Watergate*, 326–327.

6. Ambrose, Vol. II, 659 Woodward and Bernstein, *Final Days*, 61, 104, 111, 157; Mankiewicz, *Final Crisis*, 220.

7.   Kessler *Inside the White House*, 45–6, 258-9; Nixon, *Memoirs*, 994–6; Rather and Gates, 162–3, 232.

8. Lurie, 262; Kutler, *Abuse of Power* 413–4; Woodward and Bernstein, *Final Days*, 255–6, 213; Mankiewicz, *Final Crisis*, 136.

9. Kissinger, Vol. I, 93, 904; Vol. II, 227; Ambrose, Vol. II, 643, 650; Kutler, *Abuse of Power*, 349–350. So little did Nixon regard his Vice-President that Agnew later complained, "I never engaged Nixon in a substantive conversation!" When they did talk, Agnew added, "Nixon would ramble on in a monologue, skirting substantive topics." Kutler, *Wars of Watergate*, 393.

Chapter 8 (LBJ) *Confrontation*

1. Wilson, *Life and Letters*, cited in Frost, E., 184; Rather and Gates, 12; Evans and Novak, *LBJ*, 447–8; Reedy, 66.

2. White, W. S., 191–2; Evans and Novak, *LBJ*, 65–7, 161, 168, 263, 221; Birkhead, Kenneth, quoted in Miller, 159–160.

3. Johnson, L. B., 3; Johnson, Sam H., 102, 154; Kearns, 201; Evans and Novak, *LBJ*, 238–9; White, T. H., *1960*, 56, 160.

4. Krock, Arthur, quoted in Miller, 240; Dallek, 559, 561, 566; Evans and Novak, *LBJ*, 261; Johnson, Sam H., 106; Miller, 306; Kearns, 160. It was the same Krock who asked Joe Kennedy if his son would consider running as Vice-President if he was not nominated for the top spot in 1960. Nothing doing. "For the Kennedys, it's the castle or the outhouse. Nothing in between." Jack, of course, took the nomination on the first ballot on July 13, and Joe continued to use his money—lots of money—to lubricate Jack's slide to the White House. Having been elected president of Columbia Trust at 25, Joe was the youngest bank president in the country. Ten years later, in 1924, with the Volstead Act the law of the land for four years, Joe turned to

bartending on a massive scale: becoming the largest distributor of Scotch whiskey in the country. By the end of the decade, he was neck deep in the movie business, and selling short in a plunging stock market. By these and similar means Joe Kennedy would see that son Jack would wind up in the White House. Kessler, *The Sins of the Father*, 383, 28, 36, 55–6, 81–2.

5. White, T. H., *1960*, 57–8, 60, 67, 153, 199; Johnson, Sam H., 103; Reedy, 66; Evans and Novak, *LBJ*, 257, 263; Sidey, Hugh, quoted in Miller, 241.

6. Evans and Novak, *LBJ*, 263–5, 266; Dallek, 570, 572–3; White, T. H., *1960*, 157; Sidey, *LBJ*, 169.

7. Evans and Novak, *LBJ*, 277–8; Dallek, 574–6; Johnson, Sam H., 107; White, T. H., *1960*, 199–200, 202; Goldwater, 121.

8. Johnson, Sam H., 107; Adams, John, written as Vice–President, 1789, and Coolidge, Nov., 1920, both cited in Frost, E., 248; Evans and Novak, *LBJ*, 282, 284–7.

9. Miller, quoting various witnesses, 258–260; Rowe, James and Luther Holcomb, both quoted in Miller, 261–2; Evans and Novak, *LBJ*, 278, 285; Goldwater, 122.

10. Evans and Novak, *LBJ*, 267–8, 291–4, 298; White, T. H., *1960*, 168, 204; Rowe, James, and James Blundell, both quoted in Miller, 267–8.

11. Evans and Novak, *LBJ*, 305, 309–310, 313; Kearns, 164–5; Beschloss, 213; Schlesinger, *JFK*, 646.

12. Evans and Novak, *LBJ*, 315–9; Bell, Jack, quoted in Miller, 305.

13. Beschloss, 400; PBS Documentary, "The Man Who Killed Kennedy," Feb. 15, 1998; Karnow, 485; Kearns, 253; Miller, 506–7; Clifford, 502–5; Sidey, *LBJ*, 293–4. According to Russell, "No less than four of the past six presidents . . . either expressed doubts about the Warren Commission's conclusions or had some kind of direct role in post-assassination events." Even LBJ was convinced by 1967 that in some way the CIA was involved. Russell, 709–710. By 1968 Johnson could back up his claim to Clifford, "I know where to look for [power]." Less forthcoming was his next part of the claim, "and how to use it." Indeed, it wasn't long before he'd be shorn of his power, bowing out of the presidential race because the nation, through its representatives in Congress, was calling for him to step down. Kutler, *Wars of Watergate*, 59.

14. Miller, 519; Califano, 297–300; Johnson, Sam H., 259; Clifford, 300, 545.

15. Clifford, 301, 546; White, W. S., 166; Kearns, 39; McConnell, 203; *Modern Maturity*, March, 1997.

Chapter 8 (RMN) *Confrontation*

1. Kutler, *Abuse of Power*, 448, 629; Haldeman, *Ends of Power*, 81, 107; Bell, 179; Sirica, 143.

2. White, T. H., *1964*, 151–3; Kissinger, Vol. I, 10–12, 29, 108–9, 142, 481; Kutler, *Abuse of Power*, 181, 347–9, 375–8, 388. It is significant that, just prior to Nixon's run for the presidency in 1960, Ike castigated his Vice-President with "Goddammit, he looks like a loser to me!" Kutler, *Wars of Watergate*, 51.

3. Kissinger, Vol. I, 95–6; Schell, 57–8; Kutler, *Abuse of Power*, 638; Ambrose, Vol. I, 186, 237–8, 332–3; Vol. II, 269–271; Nixon *Memoirs*, 138–9, 143–8; Brodie, 297–8.

4. Ambrose, Vol. I, 334–5, 337–8, 340; Brodie, 300–1; Nixon, *Memoirs*, 159.

5. Parmet, 124–5, 141–2, 143; Wicker, 49; Nixon, *Six Crises*, 3, 6–9. By the nineties it was evident that Nixon, interviewed by Crowley, was becoming increasingly selective as he sought to spin his career for the benefit of historians. Thus he beat Voorhis in 1946 because this incumbent Congressman, voted the fifth most intelligent in Congress, was "too sappy." As for Hiss, Nixon drove his critics "crazy" because he dared to "hit at the heart of the [Eastern liberal] establishment." As for his whipping of Douglas in 1950, she deserved it because she was "closely associated with the Communist-front organization." Crowley, 146–7.

6. Nixon, *Six Crises*, 10–11; Ambrose, Vol. I, 173; Parmet, 150–1, 168–170; Wicker, 64–6, 173.

7. Mankiewicz, *Perfectly Clear*, 48; Parmet, 174; Wicker, 54, 57, 66–7; Ambrose, Vol. I, 167, 169, 171, 192.

8. Ambrose, Vol. I, 164, 174; Wicker, 51–2, 69; Mazo, 284–5. Weinstein's *Perjury: The Hiss-Chambers Case* is probably the most comprehensive account of Nixon's bout with Hiss. He confirms the misdating of the Kodak microfilm by Stripling.

9. Nixon, *Six Crises* , 69–70, 250; Brodie, 383–7; Evans and Novak, *RMN*,

256–7; Ambrose, Vol. I, 177; Kutler, *Abuse of Power*, 520, 609, 635. Butterfield was at UCLA with Haldeman and Ehrlichman in the late forties, having served as a fighter pilot in World War II and subsequently a member of a jet aerobatics team, before becoming appointment secretary for Nixon. Kutler, *Wars of Watergate*, 367.

Chapter 9 (LBJ) *Coercion*

1. Machiavelli, 25; Powell, 20-1, Beschloss, 377; Halberstam, *Best and Brightest*, 512, 633; Water, Elizabeth in *The Indianapolis Star*, Mar. 15, 1998.
2. Caro, *Path*, 134–5; White, W. S., 62; Sidey, H., "Locking Eyes at the Top," Time, Nov. 22, 1982, 75; New Testament, Matthew 24:6; Machiavelli, 21, 24; Henry, 244.
3. Old Testament, II Kings 2:8–15; Reedy, 161; Karnow, 249; Evans and Novak, *LBJ*, 538. McMaster challenges McNamara's claim that he and other policy makers in the Johnson administration were effectually prisoners of the ideology of containment of Communism and therefore should be absolved of the responsibility for Vietnam's final outcome. All well and good. Yet McMaster, a military officer himself, blames these civilians for ignoring the JCS when, in fact—as this chapter develops—the JCS were constantly egging on these civilians to escalate, regardless of their own wargames and the CIA showing there was no way they could win the war, regardless of the most massive escalations, without resorting to nuclear weapons with its threat of igniting yet a larger war, World War III. In fairness to McMaster he concludes that the Vietnam disaster was a result of both military and civilian advisers. "The failures were many and reinforcing: arrogance, weakness, lying in pursuit of self-interest and, above all, abdication of responsibility to the American people." McMaster, 1, 333–4.
4. Halberstam, 175, 483; Karnow, 9; Shelton, 18–9; Reedy, 160, 162; Tuchman, 311.
5. Kessler, *Inside the White House*, 27; Farrell and Smith, 124–5; Beschloss, 210, 226, 258.
6. Farrell and Smith, 129–137; Kearns 196–7; *The Indianapolis Star*, Feb. 15, 1997; Beschloss, 363; Evans and Novak, *LBJ*, 477; Karnow, 472–3; Fulbright, ix–x, 15.

8. McNamara, 306–310; Califano, 122; Cousins, Norman, "On the Subject of Pain," *Saturday Review*, Dec. 23, 1967, 22; Karnow, 455–6; Kearns, 268.

9. NcNamara, 32–3; Steele, John L., "Historical Generalizations," *Time*, Jan. 5, 1968, 13–5; Karnow, 533, 545; Clifford, 474, 476, 547, 549, 550; "Man of the Year," *Time*, Jan. 5, 1968, 13–22.

10. Karnow, 549; Clifford, 449, 485, 513; Beschloss, 401–2. At the same time Westmoreland was calling for an additional 205,000 U.S. troops, Saigon's ARVN had grown to "a well-equipped force of 850,000, yet continued to suffer from low morale, corruption, and leadership rivalries." To add 205,000 to our 550,000 already there, and add Saigon's 850,000, in addition to several thousand more from South Korea, Australia, and New Zealand, meant the combined allies would be fielding no less than 1,600,000 men, together with uncontested power in the air and on the seas. Given the strength of the NVA at the time of Tet at 175,000 (the high figure given by the JCS), and it appears that the Allies constituted Goliath and Ho's NVA constituted David. Hunt, 112.

11. Kearns, 339; Clifford, 507, 513-4; Karnow, 554-6; Califano, 47.

12. McNamara, 253–4, 254–6, 257–8, 260–1, 280–1; Beschloss, 377 Halberstam, *Best and Brightest*, 633; Kutler, *Abuse of Power*, 1–2; Karnow, 507.

Chapter 9 (RMN) *Coercion*

1. Kutler, *Abuse of Power*, 3, 5, 6, 8.

2. Nixon, *Memoirs*, 348–9; Parmet, 625; Barr, 39–50; Murray, 64–76; Ambrose, Vol. II, 533, 536–7; Hersh, *Price of Power*, 503.

3. Tuchman, 369–370; Ambrose, Vol. II, 536, 539, 540, 547; Karnow, 630–1, 641, 643–6.

4. Ambrose, Vol. II, 547, 549–551, 612–3; Tuchman, 371; Nixon, *Memoirs*, 614, 689–693.

5. Kissinger, Vol. I, 1336–7, 1345–6, 1359; Ambrose, Vol. II, 627–8; Nixon, *Memoirs*, 691–3, 694–5.

6. Ambrose, Vol. II, 629–630; Hersh, *Price of Power*, 585–6; Cousins, Norman, "Notes on a 1963 Visit with Nikita Kruschev," *Saturday Review*, Nov. 7, 1964, 16–21. Cousin's account is a chilling reminder of how close the U.S. got to nuclear war during the Cold War.

7. Ambrose, Vol. II, 631–2, 633–4, 636–7, 642; Nixon, *Memoirs*, 690, 697–8, 701–3, 705; Kissinger, Vol. II, 84; Vol. I., 1398–1400; *Newsweek* , Nov. 6, 1972, 33; Hersh, *Price of Power*, 582; Ehrlichman, "Where's the Man I Know?" 7; Herring, 253.

8. Kissinger, Vol. I, 1401; Vol. II, 307; Ambrose, Vol. II, 643–5, 648–9, 662; Nixon, *Memoirs*, 706, 716–7; Hersh, *Price of Power*, 603, 612.

9. Frost, D., 119–120; Hersh, *Price of Power*, 612–4, 620, 624–5, 630; Nixon, *Memoirs*, 733–4, 739; Parmet, 625; Tuchman, 372; Karnow, 653–4.

10. Nixon, *Memoirs*, 737–8; Hersh, *Price of Power*, 623; Karnow, 652–3; White, T. H., *1972*, 356; Frost, D., 121; Woodward and Bernstein, *Final Days*, 103–4; Catton, Bruce, *Grant Takes Command*, reviewed in *Time*, Mar. 14, 1969, 103.

11. Nixon, *Memoirs*, 737, 740–3, 746–8, 751; Tuchrnan, 373; Kissinger, Vol. I, 1461, 1464.

12, Karnow, 655; Nixon, *Memoirs*, 763; Green, Peter, review of *Alexander the Great* by Richard Stoneman in *The New Republic*, Dec. 29, 1997; PBS Documentary, July 8, 1996.

13. Wicker, 110–1, 610; Frost, D., 123–4; Karnow, 660–1; Tuchman, 373; Nixon, *Memoirs*, 889.

14. Gelb, Leslie, "Today's Lessons," 35–6; Frost, D., 119–120; Hinckle and Turner, xxxvi, 25; *The Indianapolis Star*, Nov. 9, 1997; ABC Evening News, Mar. 26, 1997.

15. ABC Evening News, Apr. 16, 1998; Sheehan, 746; Steel, Ronald, "Blind Contrition," review of McNamara's *In Retrospect* in *The New Republic*, June 5, 1995; *The Indianapolis Star*, Dec. 15, 1997. One of the most dreadful consequences of Nixon's "incursion" into Cambodia was the murderous rampage of the Khmer Rouge, its army swollen by enlistees who had suffered in the American attack. Conkin, 286.

Chapter 10 (LBJ) *Deception*

1. Machiavelli, 25; Shakespeare, *Hamlet*, Act II, Scene 3, Scene 5; Berkowitz, Peter, "The Political Moralist," *The New Republic*, Sept. 1, 1997, 40; Johnson, L. B., Commencement Address, Howard University, June 4, 1965, cited in Frost, E., 141.

2. Sendel, Michael J., "White Lies," *The New Republic*, Mar. 2, 1998, 10; Reedy, 3, 12; Ball, George, quoted in Miller, 413; Califano, 249; Tuchman, 320–1, 328–9, 338; McNamara, 156–8; Scott, Sir Walter, *The*

Lay of the Last Minstrel, Canto 6, Stanza 17.

3. Washington, Farewell Address, Sept. 17, 1796; Lincoln, 1842; Eisenhower, D., Aug. 7, 1957; Adams, John, letter to William Eustis, June 22, 1809. —all cited in Frost, E., 95, 104, 262; Tuchman, 340; Rapoport, 139–140.

4. Fromm, *Escape from Freedom*. Its thrust is a necessary corrective for the over-emphasis on negative freedom, or freedom *from* rather than the positive freedom *to*; Tuchman, 311; Sheehan's book is aptly titled; Kearns, 15; Johnson, L. B., news conference, Feb. 29, 1964, cited in Frost, E., 187; Reedy, 19, 55–6, 68; Shakespeare, *Measure for Measure*, Act IV, Scene 2; Karnow, 22.

5. Halberstam, *Best and Brightest*, 403–4, 409; Tuchman, 313; Kearns, 198; Beschloss, 380; Karnow, 362; McNamara, 140; "The Federalist," Number 63. GBWW, Vol. 43, 192.

6. Halberstam, *Best and Brightest*, 409; *New York Times Magazine*, Aug. 10, 1997, interview with the director of the Institute of Military History in Hanoi; Beschloss, 493–4, 496–7.

7. Evans and Novak, *LBJ*, 532; McNamara, 131, 133, 135–6; Karnow, 366, 370–1; Beschloss, 498; "Air Combat," TV series, History Channel, July 24, 1997; Tuchman, 316; Califano, 31–2; Goldman, 175–6; Rusk, 384.

8. Beschloss, 499–502, 504; Evans and Novak, *LBJ*, 534; McNamara, 134–5; Karnow, 371–2; Rusk, 385; Halberstam, *Best and Brightest*, 413–4.

9. Goldman, 175; Evans and Novak, *LBJ*, 534; *Washington Post*, Nov. 11, 1995; Beschloss, 505–6; MoNamara, 137.

10. Kearns, 313; Tuchman, 316; Halberstam, *Best and Brightest*, 416–8; McNamara, 136–7; Gruening, Ernest, quoted in Miller, 487; Karnow, 375; Beschloss, 508.

11. McNamara, 137–8; Beschloss, 506; Karnow, 374, 376; Tuchman, 316–7; Halberstam, *Best and Brightest*, 419.

12. McNamara, 39; Kearns, 198–9; Halberstam, *Best and Brightest*, 423; *The Nation, 1865–1990,* Anthology, 112; Sullivan, G. W. N., 173; Tuchman, 319.

Chapter 10 (RMN) *Deception*

1. Quotation from "Washington Week in Review," PBS News Program, Apr. 30, 1994; Kutler, *Abuse of Power*, 397, 584; Nixon, *Six Crises*, 406; Karnow, 21–2.

2. Jefferson, July 4, 1776, cited in Frost, E., 198; Whitehead, 36; Shakespeare, *Romeo and Juliet*, Act III, Scene 2, *Hamlet*, Act I, Scene 3; Nixon, *Memoirs*, 1020; Abrahamsen, 172; Kessler, *Inside the White House*, 56.

3. Wills, 94; Brodie, 353, 452–9; Parmet, 406, 494–5.

4. Ambrose, Vol. II, 190–1, 196–8; Hersh, Ch. 1; Kagen, Donald, reviewed by Lawrence Freedman, "The Power of Balance," in *The New Republic*, June 19, 1995, 45; Clifford, 571–2; Parmet, 518–9, 566. According to Clifford, Moscow sent a secret message to LBJ just three weeks before election day, proposing that "If the U.S. stopped bombing the North, Hanoi would agree to the participation of Saigon's government in negotiations that would follow immediately." Why? Because the USSR was determined to keep cold warrior Nixon out of the White House. LBJ agreed, on condition "that negotiations begin within 24 hours after the bombing ceased." This in order to have maximum effect on the election. Aitken, 362–3.

5. Hersh, 19–22; Ambrose, Vol. II, 196–200, 206; Parmet, 519–520; Clifford, 577–8, 581–2; Kutler, *Abuse of Power*, 198–9.

6. Ambrose, Vol. II, 209–210; Clifford, 579–581; Hersh, 20–2; Parmet, 519; Nixon, *Memoirs*, 323.

7. Ambrose, Vol. II, 211–4; Clifford, 592, 594; Parmet, 519, 521, Nixon, *Memoirs*, 328–9.

8. Nixon, *Memoirs*, 329, 717–751; Ambrose, Vol. II, 215–8; Clifford, 593; Parmet, 520–3.

9. Nixon, *Memoirs*, 340–1; Ambrose, Vol. II, 216–7, 221; Clifford, 595, 600; Abrahamsen, 194.

Chapter 11 (LBJ) *Paranoia*

1. Shakespeare, *King Henry IV*, Act V, Scene 6; Hoover, speech to Gridiron Club, Washington, D.C., Dec. 14, 1929, and Truman, speech to the United Nations, Oct. 24, 1950. —both cited in Frost, E., 49; Beschloss, 530.

2. Sherrill, 35; Plato, *Gorgias*, GBWW, Vol. 7, 265; Farrell and Smith, 2–3; Goldman, 222; Evans and Novak, *LBJ*, 446–8; Johnson, Sam H., 167–8.

3. Jefferson, letter to Wilson C. Nicholas, 1809; Washington, letter to W. Gordon, Oct. 15, 1789; Grant, comment to Adam Badeau; Roosevelt,

T., to Kermit Roosevelt, Oct. 2, 1908; Coolidge, *Autobiography*; and Lincoln, last public address, Apr. 11, 1865; all cited in Frost, E., 31, 175, 14, 48, 49, 43.

4. Bunyan, John, *Pilgrim's Progress*, NY: P. F. Collier, 1909; Beschloss, 188, 274–5, 300, 328. According to Small, whenever LBJ became apoplectic about criticism in the media, Valenti flew to the rescue, assuring the despondent President that *all* Americans loved him. After all, he would say, "Who gives a shit about William Sloan Coffin [Yale University chaplain]?" Small, 19.

5. Reedy, 73, 75; McNamara, 186, 191; Machiavelli, 27; Hobbes, 68; Karnow, 324–5; Goldman, 498–500.

6. Goldman, 500–502; Gulley, 88–9; Karnow, 324 5; Busby, Horace, and William Jordan, both quoted in Miller, 535.

7. Rapoport, Ch. 7; Kearns, 329; Johnson, Sam H., 269, 435–6; Reedy, 73; Jordan, William, quoted in Miller, 535. Organized protest against the war began in 1965, with LBJ's massive escalation in July, exhibiting itself in college "teach-ins" in which college students, numbering about 7 million by 1968, goaded by their faculty, made it known to Johnson that this was his war, not theirs. Small, 22.

8. Schell, 60; Reedy, 142; Karnow, 513; Reedy, George, and Virginia Durr, both quoted in Miller, 375, 489; White, W. S., 21.

9. Dallek, 9; Reedy, 142, 162; Humphrey, Hubert, *The Education of a Public Man*, 348–9; Karnow, 513; Kearns, 313–5.

10. Halberstam, *Best and Brightest*, 639–640; Johnson, Sam H., 11; Sidey, *LBJ*, 46, 210; 269, 290–1.

11. Nixon, *Memoirs*, 473; Sidey, *LBJ*, 83–4; Halberstam, *Best and Brightest*, 624; *Time*, Jan. 5, 1968, 21; Califano, 277.

12. Christian, George, quoted in Miller, 498; Kearns, 310–1, 313, 342; Clifford, 505.

Chapter 11 (RMN) *Paranoia*

1. Barnes, 11; Schlesinger, 217, Mankiewicz, *Final Crisis*, 133–4; Frost, D, 66; Costello, William, *The New Republic*, Apr. 9, 1962.

2. Shakespeare, *Henry IV*, Part 2, Act V, Scene 6; Johnson, Gerald W., 9; Abrahamsen, 227; Brodie, 302; Ambrose, Vol. I, 348, 351, 388, 460; *Washington Post*, Oct. 16, 1958; Halberstam, *The Powers That Be*, 604.

3. Hutschnecker, 16, 35–6, 48, 55, 84, 132, 198, 266, 296, 301–2; Wicker,

xii–xiii, 228–9, 438–440; *Washington Post* , Nov. 23, 1996; Nixon, *Six Crises*, 335, 339, 361; Ickes, 325–6; White, T. H., *1960*, 61.

4. Kissinger, Vol. I, 6–7; Nixon, *Memoirs*, 266; Ambrose, Vol. II, 22, 25, 43–4; Brodie, 478–9; White, T. H., *Breach of Faith*, 423. So convinced were Nixon and Kissinger that it was China, not the Soviet Union, that was behind the North Vietnam "aggression" against the South that in March 1965 Nixon publicly challenged Johnson to bomb China. Kutler, *Wars of Watergate*, 23; Isaacson, Walter, *Kissinger: A Biography*, 123.

5. Parmet, 442–3; Schlesinger, 216, 222–3, 224–5, 229–230, 231–2; Taft, *The President and His Powers*, cited in Frost, E., 125; Wicker, 444–5.

6. Shank, 25, 28; Ambrose, Vol. II, 360–1, 499–500; Otto, 98; Kutler, 81, 90; *The Indianapolis Star*, Feb. 15, 1997; White, T. H., *Breach of Faith*, 201–2, 206. That Dean was right in suggesting that, since Haldeman knew of the Watergate burglary in advance, then so would Nixon, is borne out by Alexander Butterfield and Harry Dent claiming that Nixon was always in control of his White House. He was, in their words, "master of his house." When this is coupled with Nixon's obsessive attention to details, even to minutiae, and to Haldeman's doing absolutely nothing without Nixon's knowledge, then it appears that, indeed, Nixon *had* to know of the break-in in advance. Kutler, *Wars of Watergate*, 84–5, 216.

7. Coolidge, speech to the Society of Newspaper Editors, Jan., 1925; Lincoln, speech to Illinois Legislature, Jan., 1837; Roosevelt, T. "The New Nationalism," 1910; all cited in Frost, E., 24. Apparently yet another reason for the Watergate burglary was to discover how much Larry O'Brien knew of the "Greek connection," already noted by Elias Demetracopoulos. Kutler, *Wars of Watergate*, 207–8.

8. White, T. H. *Breach of Faith*, 200, 554; Nixon, *Memoirs*, 1089; Deak, 37–42.

9. Kutler, *Abuse of Power*, 156, 159, 169, 173–5, 212–3; 242; Quotation from *Science*, Nov. 28, 1997, 1545; Kutler, *Abuse of Power*, 246, 285, 420, 424, 448.

10. Kutler, *Abuse of Power*, 451–2, 452–3, 488, 490–1, 505–6, 556–7, 608; Osborne, 5; Woodward and Bernstein, *Final Days*, 214, 343, 403–4, 436.

11. Abrahamsen, 244–5; Frost, D., 241, 258–9; Old Testament, Hosea 8:7.

Chapter 12 (LBJ) *Isolation*

1. Garfield, letter to John Hay; Taft, comment to Wilson, Mar. 4, 1913; Wilson, letter to M. Poindexter, May 22, 1918; all cited in Frost, E., 180, 184, 264; Beschloss, 531; Kissinger, Vol. I, 502; Taft, John, 21–2.

2. Roosevelt, T., c. 1914–5; Taft, from *William Howard Taft* by A. T. Mason; Roosevelt, F. D., comment to friend, 1937; Eisenhower, D., political address, Nov. 4, 1960; all cited in Frost, F., 127, 186, 264; Taft, John, 24–5; Schlesinger, 214–5.

3. Dallek, 7, 52, 54–6; Schlesinger, 215; Caro, *Path*, 172, 212–3; Kearns, 7–8.

4. Johnson, L. B., addressing Democratic Party dinner, Feb. 27, 1964; Adams, John, from "A Defense of the Constitution of Government of the United States of America," 1787–8; Madison, letter to Thomas Ritchie, Dec. 18, 1825; Roosevelt, T., from *The Rise of Theodore Roosevelt* by Edmond Morris; Coolidge, from his *Autobiography*; Kennedy, Inaugural Address, Jan. 20, 1961; Harrison, W. H., letter to Simon Bolivar, Sept. 27, 1829; all cited in Frost, E., 170–2, 187.

5. Halberstam, *Best and Brightest*, 627–8, 637–8; Goldman, 511; Janis, *Groupthink*, 120; Kearns, 355; White, T. H., *1964*, 83–5.

6. Califano, 29; Humphrey, quoted in Miller, 420; Dallek, 6; Kearns, 333–4.

7. Dallek, 51–2; Caro, *Path*, 411–432; Sidey, *LBJ*, 214; Reedy, 171; Kearns, 79.

Chapter 12 (RMN) *Isolation*

1. Kutler, *Abuse of Power*, 602; Haldeman, *Ends of Power*, 90; Thomas, *Impeachment Report*; Wicker, 648–9; Wills, 170–1; McGinniss, 103.

2. Wicker, 651; Nixon, *Memoirs*, 29; Abrahamsen, 145; Ambrose, Vol. I, 115, 430–1. Nixon revealed to Aitken in 1975 that "mother never indulged in the present day custom, which I find nauseating, of hugging and kissing her children." Indeed, he never recalled her saying, "I love you." Why? Because, Nixon insisted, "she didn't have to." Aitken, 14.

3. Parmet, 311–3; Abrahamsen, 168; Ambrose, Vol. I, 305, 347, 361, 412; Lainster, Colin, *Life*, July 31, 1970; Alsop, S., 195, 200–1.

4. Ambrose, Vol. I, 431,456, 564; Ambrose, *Best and Worst*, 67; Parmet, 614–5; *New York Times*, Jan. 5 and 21, 1971; White, T. H., *1960*, 81; Abrahamsen, 172–3.

5. White, T. H., *1972*, 240; Wills, 456–8; Nixon, *Memoirs*, 292; Kissinger, Vol. I, 50.

6. Rather and Gates, 145–6, 239–240; Woodward and Bernstein, *Final Days*, 200; Kissinger, Vol. I, 48; Abrahamsen, 230.

7. Gulley, 285; Dean, 314–5; *The Indianapolis Star*, Nov. 1, 1997; Magruder, 139–140; White, T. H., *1972*, 233. Elias Demetracopoulos, an award-winning Greek-American journalist, contends that Nixon had good reason to be grateful to Pappas. For the three Greek colonels who had overthrown the legitimate government of Greece siphoned off $549,000 of American aid and returned it to CREEP as a thank-you note to the Republican Party. Although "donated" by the Greek KYP intelligence service, founded and subsidized by the CIA, and with the knowledge of CIA Director Richard Helms, the moving spirit behind the Greeks' generosity was none other than Pappas, the same Pappas who helped convince Nixon to put Agnew on his ticket in 1968. Having fled Greece for America when the Greek junta assumed power in 1967, Demetracopoulos has for more than thirty years been a staunch advocate for the nation that gave birth to democracy during its "Golden Age." For his trouble he has been hounded by the FBI as well as the CIA, and almost deported back to his native soil in 1971, where the junta would have slapped him behind bars—or worse. See "Minority Report" by Christopher Hitchens, *The Nation*, June 30, 1984; *The Phoenix Gazette*, December 26, 1985; *The Boston Globe*, November 10, 1997. See also Kutler, *The Wars of Watergate*, 205–8, 276; Haldeman, *Diaries*, 13. Aitken also tied in Vietnam with Watergate, insisting that "without the war, Watergate would never have happened." Except that it was simply the "political climate . . . severely polluted by mutual bitterness" that blew "so minor a scandal . . . into so momentous a catastrophe. . . ." And who convinced him of this? None other than Nixon himself, in 1975. Aitken, 525.

8. Nixon, *Memoirs*, 434, 740, 752–4; Kissinger, Vol. II, 98.

9. Kutler, *Abuse of Power*, 130–1, 148–151, 177–9, 204–211, 215–9, 233–4; 236–7; 243, 245, 249, 257–9.

10. Kutler, *Abuse of Power*, 271–4, 281–2, 291, 298–301, 317, 320–3.

11. Kutler, *Abuse of Power*, 331–4, 336–8, 340–4, 344–6, 347–351, 366; Dean, 395–8. So fearful was Nixon of Dean's testimony that he

assigned Ziegler's assistant, Diane Sawyer, to his attorney, Buzhardt, in an attempt to prove Dean was lying. Kutler, *The Wars of Watergate*, 361, 452. So obsessed was Nixon with Dean's turning on him that he insisted to Aitken that Dean actually ordered the Watergate break-in because he was "desperately anxious to acquire hard information on leading Democrats sleeping with call girls." Aitken, 470.

Chapter 13 (LBJ) *Immolation*

1. Tuchman, 377; Johnson, L. B., quoted in Kearns, 18; Johnson, L. B., quoted in Miller, 19, 529; Ashmore, Harry, quoted in Miller, 518; Bartlett, 12; Shakespeare, *Measure for Measure*, Act II, Scene 2; *Henry VIII*, Act III, Scene 2.
2. White, T. H., *1964*, 287; *Time*, Jan. 5, 1968, 22; Tuchman, 347–350; Clifford, 349, 473–5, 495; Johnson, L. B., 32.
3. Tuchman, 351; Karnow, 566; Kearns, 338; Clifford, 351; Johnson, Sam H., 238–9; Janis, *Victims*, 124–5; Johnson, L. B., 416–8; Goldman, 499–500; Wicker, 293; White, W. S., quoted in Miller, 543,
4. Wicker, 294; *The Indianapolis Star*, Jan. 2, 1966; *Time*, Dec. 9, 1966, 25; Rather and Gates, 72; Kearns, 348–9.
5. Reedy, 172; Kearns, 334, 344; Clifford, 502–5; Wicker, 303; Miller, 498, 510.
6. Sidey, *LBJ*, 296; Miller, 498; Goldwater, 209; Roosevelt, T., to reporter, Aug. 7, 1912, and Truman, July 27, 1952, both cited in Frost, E., 28, 186; Clifford, 284.
7. Baker, Bobby, quoted in Miller, 236; Evans and Novak, *LBJ*, 228; Califano, 268; Gulley, 104–5; Sidey, *LBJ*, 284; Nixon, *Memoirs*, 754.
8. Kearns, 355–6; Moyers, Bill, Bobby Baker, and Larry O'Brien, all quoted in Miller, 236, 496, 523; Gulley, 106–7.
9. Rusk, 294–5; Schell, 19; Reedy, 160; Kearns, 156.
10. Ashmore, Harry, and Johnson, L. B., both quoted in Miller, 518, 529; Kearns, 18, 395–400.

Chapter 13 (RMN) *Immolation*

1   Kraft, Joseph, "The Nixon Presidency," *The Indianapolis Star*, Aug. 12, 1974; Ehrlichman, 390; Nixon, *Memoirs*, 848–9, 854; Kissinger, Vol. II, 126; Rosin, 23. In Haldeman's account of Nixon's firing him at Camp David on April 29, 1973, he notes that Nixon "shook hands with me,

which is the first time he's ever done that." Nixon then proceeded to assure Haldeman that the President's decision to fire him came from on high, for not only had he "prayed on his knees every night that [he'd] been in the Presidential office," but he'd prayed especially "hard over this decision, and it's the toughest decision [he'd] ever made." Haldeman, *Diaries*, 672.

2. Nixon, *Memoirs*, 849; Adams, John, c. 1770–1, and Jackson, First Annual Message to Congress, Dec. 4, 1829, both cited in Frost, E., 46; Bell, 458; Wicker, 1; Ambrose, Vol. II, 650; Wills, 493–4

3. Sullivan, 173–4; Nixon, *Memoirs*, 1002; Schlesinger, 414–5; Lurie, 203–4.

4. Barclay, 183, 185; Lurie, 195, 205–6; Frost, D., 236; Thomas, *The Impeachment Report*, xi–xii; Kissinger, Vol. II, 125.

5. Nixon, *Memoirs*, 498, 877, 897–8; Mankiewicz, *Final Crisis*, 176; Abrahamsen, 239.

6. Woodward and Bernstein, *Final Days*, 106–110; Mankiewicz, *Final Crisis*, 205, 209, 217; Nixon, *Memoirs*, 974–6; Sirica, 221.

7. Anderson, Jack, "Tyrants Pamper Washington Politicians," *The Indianapolis Star*, Nov. 14, 1976; Nixon, *Memoirs*, 996–8, 1008; Sirica, 228–30; Mankiewicz, *Final Crisis* , 127, 229–232; Woodward and Bernstein, *Final Days*, 208–9.

8. Curtis,. *Evolution or Extinction*. Ch. 6. See also Poston, Richard W., *Democracy Speaks Many Tongues*; Abrahamsen, 241; Woodward and Bernstein, *Final Days*, 213; Nixon, *Memoirs*, 1000, 1019–1020.

9. Woodward and Bernstein, *Final Days*, 221–3, 225–8; Breslin, 141–2, 154; Kissinger, Vol. II, 1187, 1197; Lurie, 195.

10. Dean, 332–3; Woodward and Bernstein, *Final Days*, 248–250; Rather and Gates, 303–4, 308–311; Jaworski, Ch. 11; Frost, D., 147.

11. Nixon, *Memoirs*, 1049–1052, 1053–5; Woodward and Bernstein, *Final Days*, 308–9, 311–2.

12. Woodward and Bernstein, *Final Days*, 215, 320, 324–5, 326–7; Nixon, *Memoirs*, 1056–7; Sirica, 230, 235–6; Oudes, lix. Because of his harsh treatment of criminals, it was just as inevitable that, had Nixon landed in Sirica's court, he'd have received "the max" from "Maximum John" Sirica, *Time's* Man of the Year in 1974. Kutler, *Wars of Watergate*, 253; Emery, 419.

13. White, T. H., *Breach of Faith*, 141; Jaworski, 23, 211; Abrahamsen, 231;

Mankiewicz, *Final Crisis*, 2–6, 140; Coolidge, *Autobiography*, cited in Frost, E., 231.

14 Frost, D., 12, 14, 60, 153, 243, 245, 274; Lukas, 559; Woodward and Bernstein, *Final Days*, 421; Kissinger, Vol. II, 1210, 1212. Eight months before Nixon's resignation in disgrace he had assured his family "that there was nothing damaging in the tapes." Then he appeared to contradict himself when he warned them that he "might be impeached because of their content." Reasoned Tricia, "Knowing Daddy, the latter is the way he really feels." Emery, 419.

15. Woodward and Bernstein, *Final Days*, 425, 428; Jaworski, 220; Nixon, *Memoirs*, 1084–5; White, T. H., *Breach of Faith*, 50; Kornitzer, 41.

16. Brodie, 17; Miller, Arthur, "The Limited Hang-out," *Harpers*, Sept., 1974; Quotation in McCurdy, Jack, "Scholars' Opinions Bode Ill for Nixon's Place in History," *Los Angeles Times*, Oct. 20, 1974; Lewis, Michael, "Silver Medalists," *The New Republic*, Oct. 21, 1996, 16; Commager, *Defeat*, 153–4.

17. Ford, G., 37; White, T. E., *Breach of Faith*, 170, 434; Frost, D., 12, 21, 62–3, 90, 92–4, 96, 106, 110, 120–4, 163–4.

Epilogue

1 Santayana, quoted in "The Freedman's Bank," by John Steele Gordon, *American Heritage*, Dec. 1993, 20; Donovan, 20–1; Whitehead, 63; Wilson, speech at Detroit, July 10, 1916; Roosevelt, F.D., Four Freedom Speech, Jan. 6, 1941; Johnson, L. B., State of the Union Address, Jan. 12, 1966; Nixon, "Manpower Report of the President,", Mar. 1972; all cited in Frost, E., 30–1.

2. Jefferson, letter to Dr. Walter Jones, Jan. 2, 1814; LBJ, n.d.; Roosevelt, F. D., First Inaugural Address, Mar. 4, 1933; Wilson, speech at Chicago, Feb. 2, 1909; all cited in Frost, E., 132, 209, 262, 266; Whitman, Walt, quoted in Henry, 134; Roosevelt, F. D., quoted in Barclay, 327.

3. Borden, v; Jefferson, letter to Dr. Walter Jones, Jan. 2, 1814; Lincoln, 1842; Harrison, B, *Views of an Ex–President*, 1901; Grant, *Personal Memoirs*; Johnson, A., "A Proclamation of Mourning," Apr. 25, 1865; Jefferson, letter to Col. Charles Yancy, Jan. 6, 1816; all cited in Frost, E., 107, 132, 262.

4. Mitroff and Bennis, 169; Curtis, *Evolution or Extinction*, Ch. 2, "Global

Issues"; Beard, 127; *Time*, Jan. 5, 1968, 22; *The Indianapolis Star*, Nov. 22, 1996; Beschloss, 131, 324.

5. Moggs, 15–17; Judas, 17–20; *The Indianapolis Star*. Apr. 26, 1994; Rauch, Jonathan, "What Nixon Wrought," *The New Republic*, May 16, 1994, 28, 31; Tuchman, 5, 234; Beschloss, 133.

6. Zimmerman, Paul D, 69–70; Eisenhower, D., Aug. 7, 1957, cited in Frost, E., 262; Machiavelli, 33–4; Sidey, Hugh, "The Presidency," *Life*, Jan. 5, 1968.

7. Washington, letter to Bushrod Washington, July 27, 1789; letter to Alexander Hamilton, July 2, 1794; First Inaugural Address, Apr. 30, 1789; letter to E. Rutledge, May 5, 1789; Jefferson, letter to John Adams, 1796; letter to Eldridge Gerry, 1797; all cited in Frost, E., 174–5; Miller, 275–6.

8. Monroe, letter to General "Stonewall" Jackson, July 3, 1825; Lincoln, reply to Missouri Committee of Seventy, 1864; letter to H. Maynard; all cited in Frost, E., 177, 179; Ambrose, Vol. I, 251; White, T. H., *Breach of Faith*, 418.

9. Frick and Spears, eds.; Fromm, Eric, *Escape from Freedom*; Bell, 42; Tobin, 28; *U.S News & World Report*, Sept. 27, 1976, 76.

10. Adams, John, letter to *The Boston Patriot*, 1809; letter to James Lloyd, Mar. 31, 1815; Jefferson, letter to James Madison, 1789; Tyler, protest to the House of Representatives, Aug. 30, 1842; Johnson, A., Fourth Annual Message to Congress, Dec. 19, 1868; Comments on his veto of the Tariff Act, Feb. 22, 1869; all cited in Frost, E., 128, 176–7.

11. Karnow, 491; Nixon, *Memoirs*, 770–1; Adams, John, review of propositions to amend the Constitution, 1808; Polk, *The Diary of James K. Polk*, Dec. 18, 1846; Truman, comment, July 17, 1950; all cited in Frost, E., 39–41. For their trouble in trying to block Johnson's Tonkin Gulf Resolution, both Morse and Gruening were defeated for reelection in 1968, this after LBJ had ordered the FBI to investigate Morse supporters in Oregon. Kutler, *Wars of Watergate*, 16.

12. *Federalist Papers*, #1, 18, GBWW, Vol. 43, 29, 71; Washington, summer, 1787; Jefferson, letter to David Humphries, Mar. 1789; Jefferson, after returning from office, 1809; letter to William C. Jarvis, 1870; Roosevelt, T., remarking on judicial excess to William B. Harbaugh, 1912; Nixon, TV broadcast, May 21, 1969; all cited in Frost, E., 43, 116–7; Nixon, *Memoirs*, 1051.

13. Adams, John, "Dissertation on the Canon and Feudal Law," 1765; Jefferson, letter to Col. Edward Carrington, 1787; Jefferson, Virginia and Kentucky Resolutions, 1799; all cited in Frost, E., 189; Safire, William, *Indianapolis Star*, Jan. 20, 1996.

14. Adams, John, letter to Benjamin Rush, Aug. 28, 1811; Jefferson, letter to John Norvell, June 11, 1807; letter to Charles Yancy, 1816; letter to M. Coray, 1823; Madison, letter to N. P. Trist, Apr. 23, 1828; all cited in Frost, E., 190; GBWW, Vol. 43, 17.

15. Roosevelt, T., speech to Gridiron Club, Jan., 1906; Hoover, speech to Gridiron Club, Dec. 12, 1913; Roosevelt, F. D., letter to W. H. Hardy, Sept. 4, 1940; Truman, speech to Conference of Editors of Business and Trade Papers, Apr. 23, 1948; all cited in Frost, E., 191–2.

16. TV Interview, Jan. 24, 1996; Nixon, *Memoirs*, 293; Ambrose,Vol. II, 229; Frost, D. 286.

17. Taft, *The President and His Powers*, 1916; Jefferson, letter to James Madison, 1796; Hoover, n.d.; Roosevelt, F. D. Radio Address, Mar. 2, 1930; all cited in Frost, E., 22–3; Parmet, 646; Interview with Herbert Hoover, *U.S. News & World Report*, Aug. 5, 1955, 48.

18. Rusk, 471; Kearns, 299; Nixon, *Memoirs*, 353, 525.

19. Kissinger, Vol. I, 39; Schell, 263–4; Ford, *A Time to Heal*, 1982, cited in Frost, E., 23.

20. Jefferson, letter to Samuel Kercheval, July 12, 1816; Kentucky Resolutions, Nov., 1798; letter to George Ticknor, Nov. 25, 1817; letter to James Madison, Sept. 16, 1821; Madison, Second Annual Message to Congress, Dec. 5, 1810; letter to George Thompson, June 30, 1825; letter to W. T. Barry, Aug. 4, 1822; all cited in Frost, E., 43–4, 72–3.

21. Weinberg, 28–9; Eisenhower, D., *New York Times* , Sept. 11, 1959; Rusk, 481; McNamara, xvi; Blount, 63–4; Johnson, Gerald W., 31. According to Nixon aide Robert C. Mardian "maybe 95% of the Pentagon Papers could be declassified." In addition, Mardian concluded that the Plumbers got their start, leading to the Watergate break-in, when he, Mardian, was unable to "get" Ellsberg. When Mardian confessed this in answer to Haldeman's questioning, Haldeman blurted out, "Mardian, you never come up with the right answers!" Strober, 49, 209.

BIBLIOGRAPHY

Abrahamsen, David. *Nixon vs. Nixon: An Emotional Tragedy.* New York: Farrar, Straus and Giroux, 1977.

Adler, Bill, ed. *The Washington Wits.* New York: Harper & Row, 1967.

Aitken, Jonathan. *Nixon. A Life.* Washington DC: Regnery, 1993.

Allen, Gary. *Nixon: The Man Behind the Mask.* Boston: Western Island Press, 1971.

Alsop, Stewart. "How Does He Do It?" *Saturday Evening Post,* January 24, 1959, 14.

———. *Nixon and Rockefeller: A Double Portrait.* Garden City, NY: Doubleday, 1960.

Ambrose, Stephen. "The Best and Worst of Presidents." *U.S. News & World Report,* May 4, 1987, 67–68.

———. *The Education of a Politician.* New York: Simon and Schuster, 1987.

———. *The Triumph of a Politician.* New York: Simon and Schuster, 1989.

American Experience, The. PBS Documentary, January 8, 1996.

Barclay, Barbara. *Our Presidents,* Bicentennial Edition. Promontory Press, 1976.

Barnes, Fred. "Clinton's the One!" *The New Republic,* May 16, 1994.

Barr, Stringfellow. "Second Edition/Consulting the Romans." *Center Magazine,* January 1970.

Bartlett, John. *The Shorter Bartlett's Familiar Quotations.* Garden City, NY: Permabooks, 1953.

Beard, Charles, updated by William Beard. *Mr. President: The Presidents in American History.* New York: Julian Messner, 1977.

Bell, Jack. *The Splendid Misery: The Story of the Presidency and Power Politics at Close Range.* Garden City, NY: Doubleday, 1960.

Bernstein, Carl, and Bob Woodward. *All the President's Men.* New York: Simon and Schuster, 1974.

Beschloss, Michael R., ed. *Taking Charge: The Johnson White House Tapes, 1963–1964.* New York: Simon and Schuster, 1997.

Blount, Winton. "The Presidency in Perspective." *Vital Speeches of the Day,* November 1, 1974, 63–64.

Boller, Paul E. *Presidential Anecdotes.* New York: Penguin Books, 1982.

Boorstin, Daniel J. *Democracy and Its Discontents.* New York: Vintage Books, 1974.

———. "Yes, We Should." *Parade Magazine,* February 11, 1996, 8.

Borden, Morton. *America's Eleven Greatest Presidents,* 3rd ed. Chicago: Rand, McNally, 1971.

Boulding, Kenneth E. *Ecodynamics: A New Theory of Social Evolution.* Beverly Hills, CA: Sage, 1978.

Breslin, Jimmy. *How the Good Guys Finally Won: Notes from an Impeachment Summer.* New York: Ballantine Books, 1975.

Brodie, Fawn M. *Richard Nixon: The Shaping of His Character.* Cambridge, MA: Harvard University Press, 1983.

Bullock, Paul. *Jerry Voorhis: The Idealist as Politician.* New York: Vantage, 1978.

Califano, Joseph, Jr. *The Triumph and Tragedy of Lyndon Johnson.* New York: Simon and Schuster, 1991.

Caro, Robert. *The Years of Lyndon Johnson: The Path to Power.* New York: Alfred A. Knopf, 1982.

———. *The Years of Lyndon Johnson: Means of Ascent.* New York: Alfred A. Knopf, 1990.

Catton, Bruce. "Learn to Say 'NO!' " *This Week,* January 13, 1957, 2.

Chase, Stuart. "The Luxury of Integrity." *The Nemesis of American Business and Other Essays.* New York: Macmillan, 1931.

Clifford, Clark, with Richard Holbrooke. *Counsel to the President: A Memoir.* New York: Random House, 1991.

Commager, Henry Steele. *Freedom and Order.* New York: Braziller, 1966.

———. *The Defeat of America: Presidential Power and the National Character.* New York: Simon and Schuster, 1974.

Conant, James B. "The University in a Free Society." *Modern Minds. An Anthology of Ideas.* Howard M. Jones, et al, eds. Boston: D.C. Heath, 1949, 36ff.

Conkin, Paul K. *Big Daddy from the Padernales. Lyndon Baines Johnson.* Boston: Twayne Publishers, 1986.

Cormier, Frank. *Lyndon Baines Johnson: The Way He Was.* Garden City, NY: Doubleday, 1977.

Costello, William. *The Facts About Nixon.* New York: Viking, 1960.

————. "The New Republic." *The New Republic*, November 7, 1960.

Cousins, Norman. "American Traditions and Secret Police." *The Saturday Review*, August 9, 1975, 4.

Crowley, Monica. *Nixon off the Record. His Central Commentary on People and Politics.* New York, Random House, 1996.

Curtis, Richard K. *They Called Him Mister Moody.* Garden City, NY: Doubleday, 1962.

————. *Evolution or Extinction: The Choice Before Us. A Systems Approach to the Study of the Future.* New York: Pergamon Press, 1982.

Dallek, Robert. *Lone Star Rising: Lyndon Johnson and His Times. 1908–1960.* New York: Oxford, 1991.

————. "My Search for Lyndon Johnson," *American Heritage*, September 1991, 84–88.

David, Lester. *Lonely Lady at San Clemente: The Story of Pat Nixon.* New York: Thomas Y. Crowell, 1978.

Deak, Istvan. "The Fuhrer Furor." *The New Republic*, December 15, 1997.

Dean, John. *Blind Ambition.* New York: Simon and Schuster, 1976.

de Toledano, Ralph. *One Man Alone: Richard Nixon.* New York: Funk and Wagnalls, 1969.

DeWaal, Frans. *Chimpanzee Politics: Power and Sex Among Apes.* New York: Harper & Row, 1982.

Dobzhansky, Theodosius. *Genetics and the Origin of the Species.* 3rd ed. New York: Columbia University Press, 1951.

————. *The Biological Basis of Human Freedom.* New York: Columbia University Press, 1956.

————. *The Biology of Ultimate Concern.* New York: New American Library, 1967.

Domhoff, G. William. *Who Rules America Now?* New York: Simon and Schuster, 1983.

Donovan, Hedley. "Job Specs for the Oval Office." *Time*, December 13, 1982, 21–29.

Dugger, Ronnie. *The Politician: The Drive for Power from the Frontier to Master of the Senate.* New York: W.W. Norton, 1982.

Edwards, George C. III, and Stephen Wayne. *Presidential Leadership.* New York: St. Martin's, 1985.

Ehrlichman, John. *Witness to Power.* New York: Simon and Schuster, 1982.

———. "Where's the Man I Knew?" *Parade Magazine,* February 5, 1995.

Eisenhower, Dwight D. *The White House Years: Mandate for Change, 1953–1956.* Garden City, NY: Doubleday, 1963.

Emery, Fred. *Watergate. The Corruption of American Politics and the Fall of Ric hard Nixon.* New York: Simon and Shuster, 1994.

Evans, Rowland, and Robert Novak. *Lyndon B. Johnson: The Exercise of Power.* New York: New American Library, 1966.

———. *Nixon in the White House: The Frustration of Power.* New York: Random House, 1971.

Farrell, John C., and Asa P. Smith, eds. *Image and Reality in World Politics.* New York: Columbia University Press, 1967.

Ferm, Vergilius, ed. *An Encyclopedia of Religion.* New York: Philosophical Library, 1945.

Finder, Joseph. "Good Riddance." *The New Republic,* December 30, 1996.

Ford, Gerald R. *A Time to Heal: The Autobiography of Gerald R. Ford.* New York: Harper & Row, 1979.

Frick, Don M., and Larry C. Spears, eds. *On Becoming a Servant Leader: The Private Writings of Robert K. Greenleaf.* San Francisco: Jossey-Bass, 1996.

Fromm, Eric. *Escape from Freedom.* New York: Reinhart and Company, 1941.

Frost, David. *I Gave Them a Sword: Behind the Scenes of the Nixon Interviews.* New York: William Morrow, 1978.

Frost, Elizabeth, ed. *The Bully Pulpit.* New York: Facts on File, 1988.

Fulbright, Senator J. William. *The Arrogance of Power.* New York: Vintage Books, 1966.

Gelb, Leslie. "Today's Lessons from the Pentagon Papers." *Life,* October, 1971, 34–36.

Gelb, Leslie and Richard K. Batts. *Washington, D.C.: Brookings Institution, 1979. The Irony of Vietnam: The System Worked.* New York: G.P. Putnam's Sons, 1994.

Gold, Gerald, ed. *The White House Transcripts*. New York: Bantam Books, 1974.

Goldman, Eric F. *The Crucial Decade and After: America 1945–1960*. New York: Vintage Books, 1960.

———. *The Tragedy of Lyndon Johnson*. New York: Alfred A. Knopf, 1969.

Goldwater, Barry M. *With No Apologies: Personal and Political Memoirs*. New York: William Morrow, 1979.

Gulley, Bill. *Breaking Cover*. New York: Warner Books, 1980.

Halberstam, David. *The Best and the Brightest*. New York: Random House, 1972.

———. *The Powers That Be*. New York: Alfred A. Knopf, 1979.

Haldeman, H.R., with Joseph DiMona. *The Ends of Power*. New York: Dell, 1978.

———. *The Haldeman Diaries. Inside the Nixon White House*. New York: G.P. Putnam's Sons, 1994.

Henry, Lewis C., ed. *Best Quotations for All Occasions*. New York: Premier Book, 1955.

Herring, George. *America's Longest War*. 2nd ed. New York: John Wiley and Sons, 1986.

Hersh, Seymour M. *The Price of Power: Kissinger in the Nixon White House*. New York: Summit Books, 1983.

Hilsman, Roger. *To Move a Nation: The Politics of Foreign Policy in the Administration of John F. Kennedy*. New York: Dell, 1967.

Hinckie, Warren and William Turner, *Deadly Secrets: The CIA–Mafia War Against Castro and the Assassination of J.F.K.* New York: Thunder's Mouth Press, 1992.

Hobbes, Thomas. *The Leviathon*. Great Books of the Western World Library, Vol. 23. Chicago: Encyclopedia Britannica, 1952.

Hodgson, Godfrey. *America in Our Time*. New York: Vintage, 1985.

Hoffman, Paul. *The New Nixon*. New York: Tower, 1970.

Hook, Sidney. *The Hero in History*. Boston: Beacon, 1943.

Hughes, Emmet John. *The Ordeal of Power: A Political Memoir of the Eisenhower Years*. New York: Atheneum, 1963.

Humphrey, Hubert. *The Education of a Public Man*. Garden City, NY: Doubleday, 1976.

Hunt, Michael H. *Lyndon Johnson's War. America's Cold War Crusade in Vietnam*, 1945-1968. New York: Hill and Wang, 1996.

Hutschnecker, Arnold A. *The Drive for Power*. New York: M. Evans, 1974.

Impeachment Report, The. New York: New American Library, 1974.

Issacson, Walter. *Kissinger. A Biography*. New York: Simon and Shuster, 1992

Janis, Irving. *Victims of Groupthink*. Boston: Houghton Mifflin, 1972.

———. *Groupthink*. 2nd ed. Boston: Houghton Mifflin, 1982.

Jaworski, Leon. *The Right and the Power: The Prosecution of Watergate*. New York: Reader's Digest Press/Houston, TX: Gulf, 1976.

Jefferson, Thomas. *The Declaration of Independence*. Great Books of the Western World Library, Vol. 43.. Chicago: Encyclopedia Britannica, 1952.

Johnson, Gerald W. "The Use and Abuse of Leadership." *The Saturday Review*, July 5, 1958.

Johnson, Lady Bird. *A White House Diary*. New York: Holt, Rinehart and Winston, 1970.

Johnson, Lyndon Baines. *The Vantage Point: Perspectives on the Presidency, 1963–1969*. New York: Popular Library, 1971.

Johnson, Sam Houston. *My Brother Lyndon*. New York: Cowles, 1970.

Judis, John B. "Chinatown." *The New Republic*, March 10, 1997, 17–20.

Kagan, Donald. *On the Origins of War and the Preservation of Peace*. Garden City, NY: Doubleday, 1995.

Kahn, Herman. *Thinking the Unthinkable*. New York: Horizon Press, 1962.

Kalb, Marvin, and Bernard Kalb. *Kissinger*. New York: Dell, 1975.

———. *The Nixon Memo*. Chicago: University of Chicago Press, 1994.

Karnow, Stanley. *Vietnam: A History*. New York: Viking, 1983.

Kearns, Doris. *Lyndon Johnson and the American Dream*. New York: Harper & Row, 1976.

Kennedy, Paul. *The Rise and Fall of the Great Powers*. New York: Random House, 1987.

Kessler, Ronald. *Inside the White House*. New York: Pocket Books, 1995.

———. *The Sins of the Father. Joseph P. Kennedy and the Dynasty He Founded*. New York: Warner Books, 1996.

Kissinger, Henry. *White House Years*. Boston: Little, Brown, 1979.

———. *Years of Upheaval*. Boston: Little, Brown, 1982.

Kluckhohn, Frank L. *Lyndon's Legacy*. Derby, CT: Monarch, 1964.

Kornitzer, Bela. *The Real Nixon: An Intimate Biography*. Chicago: Rand McNally, 1960.

Kraft, Joseph. "The Nixon Presidency." *Indianapolis Star*, August 12, 1974.

Kramer, Peter D. "Why Someone Would Risk It All." *U.S. News & World Report*, February 9, 1998, 40.

Krock, Arthur. "New Leader's Setback Needless." *New York Times*, January 20, 1965.

Kutler, Stanley I. *The Wars of Watergate. The Last Crisis of Richard Nixon.* New York: Alfred A. Knopf, 1990.

————. ed. *Abuse of Power: The New Nixon Tapes.* New York: Free Press, 1997.

L.B.J. PBS Home Video.

Lasky, Victor. *It Didn't Start with Watergate.* New York: Dell, 1977.

Leinster, Colin. "Nixon's Friend Bebe." *Life*, July 31, 1970.

Lewis, Michael. "Silver Medallists." *The New Republic*, October 21, 1996.

Lind, Michael. "The Out-of-Control Presidency." *The New Republic*, August 14, 1995, 18–23.

Lukas, J. Anthony. *Nightmare: The Underside of the Nixon Years.* New York: Viking, 1976.

Lurie, Leonard. *The Impeachment of Richard Nixon: A Call to Action Now!* New York: Berkley Medallion Books, 1973.

Lyon, Gene M. *America: Purpose and Power.* Chicago: Quadrangle Books, 1965.

Machiavelli, Nicolo. *The Prince.* Great Books of the Western World Library, Vol. 23. Chicago: Encyclopedia Britannica, 1952.

Maggs, John. "The Myth of the Corner Market." *The New Republic*, March 10, 1997, 15–17.

Magruder, Jeb Stuart. *An American Life: One Man's Road to Watergate.* New York: Atheneum, 1974.

Mankiewicz, Frank. *Perfectly Clear: Nixon from Whittier to Watergate.* New York: Quadrangle, 1973.

————. *U.S. v. Richard M. Nixon: The Final Crisis.* New York: Quadrangle, 1975.

Marcus, Joyce, and Kent T. Flannery. *Zapotec Civilization.* Reviewed in *Science*, August 30, 1996, 1178–1179.

Marks, John. "Sex, Drugs and the CIA." *Saturday Review*, February 3, 1979, 12–16.

Matthews, Christopher. *Kennedy and Nixon: The Rivalry That Shaped Post-War America.* New York: Simon and Schuster, 1996.

Mazo, Earl. *Richard Nixon: A Political and Personal Portrait*. New York: Harper & Brothers, 1959.

McCarry, Charles. "The Unasked Question." *U.S. News & World Report*, October 28, 1996, 7.

McConnell, Grant. *The Modern Presidency*. New York: St. Martin's Press, 1967.

McDougall, Walter A. *Promised Land, Crusader State: The American Encounter with the World Since 1776*. Boston: Houghton Mifflin, 1997.

McGinniss, Joe. *The Selling of the President*. New York: Penguin Books, 1988.

McMaster, H.R. *Dereliction of Duty*. New York: Harper Collins, 1997.

McNamara, Robert S., with Brian VanDeMark. *In Retrospect: The Tragedy and Lessons of Vietnam*. New York: Times Books, 1995.

McNeill, William H. *The Pursuit of Power*. Chicago: University of Chicago Press, 1982.

Mill, John Stuart. *On Liberty*. Great Books of the Western World Library Vol. 43. Chicago: Encyclopedia Britannica, 1952.

Miller, Merle. *Lyndon: An Oral Biography*. New York: G.P. Putnam's Sons, 1980.

Mintz, Morton, and Jerry Cohen. *America, Inc.: Who Owns and Operates the United States*. New York: Dial Press, 1971.

Mitchell, Jack. *Executive Privilege: Two Centuries of White House Scandals*. New York: Hippocrene Books, 1992.

Mitroff, Ian, and Warren Bennis. *The Unreality Industry*. New York: Oxford, 1989.

Monks, Robert A.G., and Nell Minnow. *Power and Accountability*. New York: Harper Business, 1991.

Mooney, Booth. *LBJ: An Irreverent Chronicle*. New York: Thomas Y. Crowell, 1976.

Morris, Roger. *Richard Milhouse Nixon. The Rise of an American Politician*. New York: Henry Holt, 1990.

Mumford, Lewis. *The Myth of the Machine: The Pentagon of Power*. New York: Harcourt Brace Jovanovich, 1970.

Murray, John C. "The Case for Consensus." *Center*, September, 1969.

Nixon, Richard M. *The Real War*. New York: Warner Books, 1981.

———. *No More Vietnams*. New York: Avon Books, 1985.

———. *The Memoirs of Richard Nixon.* New York: Simon and Schuster, 1990.

———.*Six Crises.* New York: Simon and Schuster, 1990.

Nye, Joseph S., Jr. *Bound to Lead: The Changing Nature of American Power.* New York: Basic Books, 1990.

O'Neill, Thomas, with William Novak. *Man of the House: The Life and Political Memoirs of Speaker Tip O'Neill.* New York: St. Martin's Press, 1987.

Ortega y Gasset, José. "The Barbarism of Specialization." *The Revolt of the Masses.* New York: W.W. Norton, 1932, 119–126.

Osborne, John. *The Last Nixon Watch.* New York: The New Republic Press, 1975.

Otto, Friedrich. "The Devilish Doctrine of Deniability." *Time*, December 15, 1986.

Oudes, Bruce, ed. *From: The President. Richard Nixon's Secret Files.* New York: Harper & Row, 1989.

Page, Benjamin I., and Mark P. Petracca. *The American Presidency.* New York: McGraw-Hill, 1983.

Parmet, Herbert S. *Richard Nixon and His America.* Boston: Little, Brown, 1990.

Pool, William C., et al. *Lyndon Baines Johnson: The Formative Years.* San Marcos, TX: Southwest Texas State Teachers College, 1965.

Powell, Colin. *My American Journey.* Reviewed by Charles Lane in *The New Republic*, October 16, 1995, 20–21.

Powers, William. "Scandal Shy." *The New Republic*, December 16, 1996.

Provence, Harry. *Lyndon B. Johnson: A Biography.* New York: Fleet, 1964.

Rapoport, Anatol. *Operational Philosophy.* New York: Harper & Brothers, 1953.

Rather, Dan, and Garry Paul Gates. *The Palace Guard.* New York: Harper & Row, 1974.

Rauch, Jonathan. "What Nixon Wrought." *The New Republic*, May 16, 1994.

Reedy, George. *Lyndon B. Johnson: A Memoir.* New York: Andrews McMeel, 1982.

Reston, James. *Deadline.* New York: Times Books, 1991.

Rosin, Hannah. "The Madness of Speaker Newt." *The New Republic*, March 17, 1997, 23.

Rovere, Richard H. *Senator Joe McCarthy*. New York: Harcourt Brace, 1959.

Rusk, Dean, as told to Richard Rusk. *As I Saw It*. New York: W.W. Norton, 1990.

Russell, Dick. *The Man Who Knew Too Much*. New York: Carroll and Grof, 1992.

Safire, William. *Before the Fall*. Garden City, NY: Doubleday, 1975.

Scheer, Robert. "Lord Russell." *Ramparts*, 1966, 15–23.

Schell, Jonathan. *The Time of Illusion*. New York: Vintage Books, 1976.

Schlesinger, Arthur M., Jr. *A Thousand Days: John F. Kennedy in the White House*. Boston: Houghton Mifflin, 1965.

———. *The Imperial Presidency*. Boston: Houghton Mifflin, 1973.

———. *Robert Kennedy and His Times*. Boston: Houghton Mifflin, 1978.

Schurmann, Franz, et al. *The Politics of Escalation in Vietnam*. Greenwich, CT: Fawcett Premier, 1966.

Sevareid, Eric, ed. *Candidates, 1960*. New York: Basic Books, 1959.

Sheehan, Neil. *A Bright and Shining Lie: John Paul Vann and America in Vietnam*. New York: Random House, 1988.

Shelton, Robert. "The Geography of Disgrace: A World Survey of Political Prisoners." *Saturday Review / World*, June 15, 1974.

Sherrill, Robert. *The Accidental President*. New York: Grossman, 1967.

Shenk, Joshua Wolf. "What Do We Know and Why Do We Know It?" *U.S. News & World Report*, June 23, 1997.

Shogan, Robert. *The Riddle of Power: Presidential Leadership from Truman to Bush*. New York: Penguin Books, 1992.

Sidey, Hugh. "The Presidency." *Life*, January 1968.

———. "Deep Grow the Roots of the Alamo." *Life*, May 1968.

———. *A Very Personal Presidency: Lyndon Johnson in the White House*. New York: Atheneum, 1968.

———. "The Mandate to Live Well." *Time*, April 15, 1974.

———. "Locking Eyes at the Top." *Time*, November 22, 1982.

———. "Above All, The Man Had Character." *Time*, February 21, 1983.

Sirica, John J. *To Set the Record Straight: The Break-in, The Tapes, The Conspirators, The Pardon*. New York: W.W. Norton, 1979.

Small, Melvin. *Johnson, Nixon and the Doves*. New Brunswick, NJ: Rutgers University Press, 1989.

Smith, Gerard. *Doubletalk: The Untold Story of SALT*. Garden City, NY: Doubleday, 1981.

Smith, Helen McCain, as told to Elizabeth Frank. "Ordeal! Pat Nixon's Final Days in the White House." *Good Housekeeping*, July 1976, 127–133.

Solberg, Carl. *Hubert Humphrey: A Political Biography*. New York: W.W. Norton, 1984.

Sorensen, Theodore C. *Kennedy*. New York: Harper & Row, 1965.

Spalding, Henry. *The Nixon Nobody Knows*. Middle Village, NY: Jonathan David, 1972.

Steinberg, Alfred. *Sam Johnson's Boy*. New York: Macmillan, 1968.

Stevenson, Adlai E. *The Papers of Adlai E. Steenson*. Boston: Little, Brown, 1977.

Stoessinger, John G. *Henry Kissinger: The Anguish of Power*. New York: W.W. Norton, 1976.

Strober, Gerald and Deborah. *Nixon. An Oral History of His Presidency*. New York: Harper, 1994.

Sullivan, George W.N. *The Limitations of Science*. New York: Mentor Books, 1950.

Sullivan, Michael John. *Presidential Passions*. New York: SPI Books, 1991.

Tabori, Paul. *The Natural Science of Stupidity*. Philadelphia: Chilton, 1959.

Taft, John. *American Power: The Rise and Decline of U.S. Globalism*. New York: Harper & Row, 1989.

Thomas, Helen. *Dateline: White House. A Warm and Revealing Account of America's Presidents and Their Families from the Kennedys to the Fords*. New York: Macmillan, 1975.

Thompson, Fred D. *At That Point in Time*. New York: Guadrangle/N.Y. Times Books, 1975.

Thompson, Hunter S. *Fear and Loathing on the Campaign Trail '72*. New York: Warner Books, 1973.

Tobin, Richard. "Who Makes Our Foreign Policy?" *Saturday Review*, February 14, 1970, 28.

Tuchman, Barbara W. *The March of Folly: From Troy to Vietnam*. New York: Alfred A. Knopf, 1984.

Turner, Stansfield. *Secrecy and Democracy: The CIA in Transition*. New York: Harper & Row, 1985.

Valenti, Jack. *A Very Human President*. New York: W.W. Norton, 1975.

Van Atta, Dale. "The Death of the State Secret." *The New Republic*, February 18, 1985.

Viorst, Milton. "Nixon of the O.P.A." *New York Times Magazine*, October 3, 1971.

Walker, Daniel. *Rights in Conflict: "The Chicago Police Riot."* New York: Signet Books, 1968.

Ward, Geoffrey. "The Full Johnson." *American Heritage*, September 1991, 14–16.

Welles, Sam, ed. *The World's Great Religions.* New York: Time, 1957.

Weinberg, Steven. "Out of the Public Eye." *Common Cause*, July/August 1983.

Weinstein, Allan. *Perjury. The Hiss Chambers Case.* New York: Random House, 1997.

White, Theodore H. *The Making of the President 1960.* New York: New American Library, 1961.

———. *The Making of the President 1964.* New York: Atheneum, 1965.

———. *The Making of the President 1972.* New York: Atheneum, 1973.

———. *Breach of Faith. The Fall of Richard Nixon.* New York: Dell, 1975.

White, William S. *The Professional: Lyndon B. Johnson.* Boston: Houghton Mifflin, 1964.

Whitehead, Alfred North. *Adventures in Ideas.* New York: Mentor Books, 1933.

Wicker, Tom. *One of Us: Richard Nixon and the American Dream.* New York: Random House, 1991.

Wilentz, Sean. "The Mandarin and the Rebel." *The New Republic*, December 22, 1997, 25–34.

Wills, Garry. *Nixon Agonistes: The Crisis of the Self-Made Man.* Boston: Houghton Mifflin, 1970.

Witcover, Jules. *The Resurrection of Richard Nixon.* New York: Putnam, 1970.

Woodward, Bob, and Carl Bernstein. *The Final Days.* New York: Simon and Schuster, 1976.

Yoder, Edwin M. "When Presidents Seek Immortality," *U.S. News and World Report*, November 24, 1986, 13.

Zimmerman, Paul D. "The Psychology of LBJ." *Newsweek*, October 24, 1966.

Zumwalt, Admiral Elmo, Jr. *On Watch.* New York: Quadrangle, 1976.

INDEX

Bowie, Jim, 103-4, 358
Bradlee, Ben, 114
Bradley, Bill, 645
Bradley, Omar, 27
Brandeis, Louis (Justice), 600
Brandenburg Gate, xv
Breslin, Jimmy, 147-8
Bretton Woods, 196
Brezhnev, Leonid, 39, 138, 178, 182-3, 580-1, 592, 599
Bridges, Styles, 316, 343
Bright, John, 628
Brinkley, David, 546
British Broadcasting Co. (BBC), 520
Brodie, Fawn, 134, 230, 242, 611
Brookings Institute, 283, 417
Browder, Earl, 373
Brown and Root, Inc., 21, 160, 163, 174-5, 202, 358, 403
Brown, George (General), 151
Brown, George, 21, 160ff, 174-5, 201, 250, 253, 273, 315, 343, 358, 403, 536
Brown, H. Rap, 409
Brown, Herman, 21, 160ff, 201, 250, 253, 273, 315, 343, 403, 536
Brown University, 220
Brown v. Board of Education, 28, 182
Brownell, Herbert, 240
Buchanan, James (Pres.), 637
Buchanan, James "Buck," 9, 100, 160, 315
Buchanan, Patrick, 328, 594, 606
Buckley, James, 595
Buckley, William 337, 595
Buffalo Evening News, 292
Bull, Steve, 334
Bullitt, William, 533
Bullock, Paul, 230
Bundy, McGeorge, 21, 56-7, 64, 98, 105-6, 209, 400-1, 404, 461ff, 502, 539-40
Bundy, William, 64, 106, 459, 461
Bunker, Ellsworth, 305, 413, 427, 482
Burch, Dean, 180, 525-6
Bureau of Reclamation, 160
bureaucracy, 66ff, 148, 639, 646ff
Burns, Arthur, 77, 121, 288

Busby, Horace, 48, 164, 314, 506, 540
Bush, George (Pres.), 81, 293-4, 508ff, 526
Bush, Prescott, 294
Butterfield, Alexander, 388, 443, 592
Butler, Paul, 317, 343-4
Buzhardt, Fred, 193, 223, 387, 529, 593, 604-5, 631
Byrd, Harry, 18-19

Cabinet, 574, 578, 646; FDR's,
46; Ike's, 283, 369, 386; LBJ's, 52, 578; RMM's, 33, 40, 67, 196, 283, 289, 386, 423, 512, 519, 552, 563; Agriculture, 46; Commerce, 55, 150; Defense, xii, xvi, 43, 45, 52, 57, 64, 69, 77, 175, 261, 290-1, 336, 362, 379ff, 391, 394, 398, 403, 408, 414, 563, 589, 650; Health, Education, and Welfare (HEW), vii, 56, 77, 94, 148, 650; Housing and Urban Development (HUD), 67, 574; Interior, 67, 148, 160; Justice, 32, 46, 68, 125, 189-90, 378-9, 649-50; Labor, 150; State, xii, 25, 34, 36, 39, 69-70, 85, 105-6, 283-4, 290-1, 336, 367, 370, 376, 562-3; Transportation, 553; Treasury, 26, 31, 77, 132, 329
Calhoun, John C., 511, 519
Califano, Joseph, 19, 51, 55-6, 106, 115, 206, 310, 365, 570, 579
Calley, William, 391
Cambodia, 71, 136, 150, 182, 283, 290-1, 443ff, 479, 512-3, 583, 613, 632, 650, 654
Camp David, xiii, 31, 175, 208, 297, 550, 584, 599
Cannon, Frank, 120
Capital Page School, vii
Capp, Al, iv, 635
Captive Nations Resolution, 386
Carmichael, Stokely, 409
Carnegie Endowment for International Peace, 382
Caro, Robert, 100, 199, 202, 263
Carroll, Lewis, 321
Carter, Clifford, 19
Carter, Jimmy (Pres.), 508, 615

Castro, Fidel, 26, 179, 521
Catton, Bruce, 107
Cavers, David, 67
Center for the Study of Democratic Institutes, 420, 582
Central Intelligence Agency (CIA), xii, 63, 189, 223, 391, 398, 404, 415, 419, 445-6, 499, 502, 571-2, 604, 650
Chamberlain, Neville, 355, 360, 399, 464
Chambers, Whittaker, 377ff
Chancellor, John, 83, 585
Chandler, Norman, 227
Chapin, Dwight, 77-8, 224, 298, 525
Chase, Stuart, 157, 474
Chennault, Anna, 481ff
Chennault, Claire, 481
Chicago Daily News, 377
Chicago Tribune, 308
China, iii, 38, 103-4, 132, 149, 178, 189, 250, 300, 336, 399ff, 407-8, 412-3, 420-1, 440, 488, 516, 593, 617, 621, 631-2, 645
Chotiner, Murray, 24, 134-5, 141, 225ff, 229-30, 237-8, 476
Chou En-Lai, 22, 35ff, 326, 399
Christian, George, 506
Christian Science Monitor, 589-90
Church, Frank, 391
Churchill, Winston, 54, 112, 117, 130, 314, 325, 376, 452, 539, 634
Civil Rights Act, 16, 63, 113ff, 181, 341
Civil Service Commission, 218
Civil War, 107, 136-7, 346, 365, 408, 418, 474, 504, 511, 615
Clark, Ed, 101
Clark, Ramsey, 271
Clay, Henry, 519
Clemenceau, Georges, 534, 550
Cleveland, Grover (Pres.), 45
Clifford, Clark, 64, 172, 319, 321, 412-3, 415ff, 479, 483, 488, 506, 539, 572-4, 577-9
Cohen, Wilbur, 94, 320
Cohn, Roy, 180, 512
Cold War, 104, 250, 419, 511, 637
Coles, Robert, 503
Colson, Charles, 133, 298-300, 328, 427, 433, 436, 521, 525, 560, 564, 591

Columbia Broadcasting
System (CBS), 166-70, 210,
311, 322, 360, 525
Columbia University, 46, 63-4,
325, 618-9
Commager, Henry Steele, 611
Commission on Organizing
the Executive Branch, 647
Committee to Reelect the
President (CREEP), 39, 184,
193, 298ff, 522
Communism, 418; v. Judeo-
Christian tradition, 251, 420-
1; v. capitalism, 104;
European, 373ff, 382, 399; v.
Nixon, 25, 38, 76, 134, 140,
183, 189, 229-230, 284ff; v.
McCarthy, 372-3; and State
Department, 382; v. LBJ, 106,
321ff, 538, 582
Conant, James B., 84, 107, 133
Congress
(see House and Senate)
Congressional Directory, 68
Congress of Industrial
Organizations, (CIO) 228
Connally, John, and.LBJ, 31, 50,
53, 95ff, 168ff, 174, 183,
254-5, 266, 272, 348, 499; and
RMN, 31ff, 38-9, 66ff, 72, 77,
95ff, 422, 527ff, 640
Connally, Nellie, 97
Connally, Tom, 160-1
Conrad, Joseph, ii-iii
Constitution, drafting vii, 5, 63,
89ff, 228, 589; provisions, vi-
vii, 89ff, 131, 337, 418-9, 469,
481, 511, 516ff, 596, 600, 611ff,
636, 641ff, 651; a model, 333,
624, 638, 641; amenable, 651;
subvertible, 126, 137, 552-4
Constitutional Convention,
589, 634
Consumer Product Safety Act,
622
Cook, Donald C., 360
Cooke, Alistair, 379
Coolidge, Calvin (Pres.), viii-
ix, 45-6, 201, 318, 354, 495,
522, 537, 606, 637
Corcoran, Tommy, 9, 11, 46,
167, 204, 215, 314, 339, 352
Corsican Network, 745-6
Corwin, Edward S., 92
Costello, William, 181, 510-1
Council on Foreign Relations,
230

Cousins, Norman, 406, 430
Cox, Archibald, 324, 510
Crider, Ben, 7
Crockett, Davy, 103, 358, 399
Cromwell, Oliver, 123
Cronkite, Walter, 119, 410-1,
572
Cross, Jim, 57
Cuba, 26, 417, 430, 445-6, 521;
Bay of Pigs, 417, 446, 521, 637;
Missile Crisis, 417, 430, 592;
drugs, 445
Curtis, Carl, 597
Curtis, Richard K., iii

Daedalus, ii, 570
Daley, Richard, 127, 368
dairy producers, 602
Dallas Morning News, 214
Dallek, Robert, 49, 216, 266
Dangerfield, Rodney, 290
Daniel, Price, 348
Daniels, Jonathan, 257, 262
Dante, ii
Davidson, David 479-80
Davidson, Whitfield, 277-8
Davies, John Paton, Jr., 408
Davis, A. L., 159
Davis, Carol, 158
Day, Roy, 134, 226
Dean, John, recruited 78, 296;
RMN enemies list, 519;
Fielding burglary, 558, 562;
Watergate burglary, 520-1,
557-8; cover-up, 66, 82, 192,
294, 330, 522ff, 554ff, 560ff;
RMN commends, 472, 522,
525, 557-8, 562; RNN
castigates, 148, 222, 330ff,
526, 561ff, 565ff; testimony,
559ff, 601; plausible
deniability, 330, 557-8, 564ff;
contradicts RMN, 193, 520,
554, 561ff; unreality of White
House, 509; Haldeman, 83-4,
561; Ehrlichman, 73, 561;
Mitchell, 561; Gray, 564;
McCord, 561; Petersen,
369-70; Magruder, 563;
firing, 561ff; imprisonment,
566
Deason, Willard, 168, 202-3
Declaration of Independence,
iv, 123, 641, 650
DeGaulle, Charles, v, 22, 30-1,
37, 121, 314, 327-8, 335, 632-3

Democratic National
Committee, 40, 97, 132,578
Democratic National
Convention (1968), 577-80
Demosthenes, ii
Descartes, Rene, 306
deTocqueville, Alexis, 1, 307
deToledano, Ralph, 185
Dewey, Thomas, 24, 234, 378,
382-4, 475
Diem, Bui, 445, 482-3
Diem, Ngo Dinh, 133, 400,
426-7, 431, 468, 563, 602
Dies, Martin, 167, 377
Dietrich, Noah, 191
Dirksen, Everett, xvi, 98,
111, 318-20
D'Israeli, Benjamin, 84, 454,
628
divine right of kings, iii, 650
Dixon, Tom, 235, 238, 245
Dobrynin, Anatoly, 580-1, 592
Dobzhansky, Theodosius, 155
Dodd, Thomas, 348, 458
Dole, Bob, 81, 293, 553, 603
domino theory
(see Vietnam War)
Donovan, Hedley, 615
Douglas, Helen Gahagen, 124,
135, 139, 179, 217, 230, 236,
282-4, 293, 296, 378, 475, 645
Douglas, Paul, 12, 63, 207-8,
271
Douglas, William O. (Justice),
167-8, 202
Drown, Helene, 244
Drummond, Roscoe, 637-8
Dugger, Ronald, 264
Duke University, 23, 67, 126,
129, 146, 236, 546
Dulles, John Foster, 36, 105,
283, 304-5, 375, 382, 391
Durbin, Deanna, 254
Durenberger, David, 652
Durr, Virginia, 174, 502-3

Eagleberger, Lawrence, 149
Eagleton, Tom, 298
Eastland, James, 596
Eastman Kodak Co., 380
Edwards, Augustine, 189
Ehrlichman, John,
background, 150;
enlistment, 70, 75, 78, 193;
RMN advisor, 68, 71ff, 295-7,
588; RMN decision-making,
85, 334; Miami convention,

Richardson, Elliott, 80, 125, 133, 324, 331-2
Richardson, Sid, 165-8, 273
Ridgeway, Matthew, 396-7, 403
Riegle, Donald, 567
Roberts, Chalmer, 512
Roberts, Joe, 214
Roche, John, 56
Rockefeller, Nelson (VP), 26, 69, 180, 232, 288, 368, 476-7, 488, 515-6, 549-50
Rockwell, Norman, 293
Rodino, Peter, 596-7, 599-600, 603-5, 610
Rogers, William, i, 37, 69ff, 85, 290-1, 299, 370, 376-7, 429
Rome (ancient), iv, 420-1, 440-1
Rommel, Erwin "Desert Fox," 326
Romney, George, 67, 288, 368
Roosevelt, Eleanor, 9-10
Roosevelt, Elliott, 168
Roosevelt, Franklin (Pres.), ix, 101, 140, 250, 329, 511, 534, 539; Navy, 10; paraplegic, 616ff; staff, 46-7, 49, 52, 68, 70; abuse of power, 90-1, 210, 341, 624, 655; criticism, 11, 504; v. Supreme Court, 10, 624; office, 360, 534, 646-7; press, 10, 518, 644; use of radio, 112-3; LBJ's sycophancy, 9-10, 12, 15, 165, 250, 253, 314f1 360ff, 504ff; LBJ favored, 9, 11-12, 96, 156-7, 169, 173;, WW II, 30-1, 416, 453ff, 458, 539, 599, 616; LBJ in WW II, 256ff, 262, 315; 1940 reelection, 210ff; LBJ's 1941 campaign, 209-10, 268; 1944 reelection, 210ff; death, 165-6; legacy, 637
Roosevelt, Theodore "T.R.," (Pres.), 16, 91, 112, 133, 162, 281, 409, 422, 495, 522, 534, 537, 637, 642, 644
Rosin, Hannah, 585
Ross, E. P., 159
Ross, Kitty Clyde, 158
Rossiter, Clinton, 556, 620
Rostow, Walt, 63, 321, 412, 538ff, 572-3
Rousseau, Jean-Jacques, 641
Rovere, Richard, 45
Rowe, Jim, 3, 49, 321, 355, 462
Ruckelshaus, William, 80, 528

Rusk, Dean, 15, 20, 53, 63-4, 106, 412-3, 453, 460ff, 483, 522-3, 581, 647, 653-4
Russell, Richard, 12ff, 18, 63, 96, 116-7, 171, 173, 207, 314, 316, 361, 391, 401, 414, 498
Ryan, Kate, 233
Ryan, Will, 233ff

Sadat, Anwar, 598
Safe Drinking Water Act, 621-2
Safire, William, i, 121, 124, 150, 326
St, Clair, James, 332, 596, 601, 604-6
St. John, Adela Rogers, 238, 243
St. Louis Post Dispatch, 210
Salas, Luis, 279
Salinger, Pierre, 115, 309, 497
San Clemente (W. White House), 187ff, 194-5, 289, 300, 544-5, 549ff, 603-4
San Francisco Examiner, 521
Santa Anna, 104
Santayana, George, 394, 457, 615
Sarnoff, David, 360
Saturday Evening Post, 571
Saturday Review, 430
Saxbe, William, 439
Sayre, Francis B., 205, 309
Scharnhorst Ranch, 171
Schell, Jonathan, 289, 649-50
Schlesinger, Arthur, Jr., 16, 48, 67, 91-2, 141, 152, 180, 283, 294-5, 329, 509, 517-8, 534-5, 589, 611, 620
Schultze, Charles, 574
Scott, George C., 290-1, 326-8
Scott, Hugh, 317-8, 558, 596, 601-2, 607
Scott, Sir Walter, 454
Scowcroft, Brent, 144-5
Scranton, William W., 368
Secret Service, viii, x-xiv, 59ff, 218, 354-5, 501, 504, 541, 578, 580, 598, 606-7, 609
Segretti, Donald, 78, 224, 298, 521-2, 525
Semple, Robert, 549
Senate (U.S.), vii, 11, 47, 98, 123, 135, 137, 202-3, 353, 383, 550, 638; League of Nations, 534, 550-1, 617; Federalist Papers, 457-8; LBJ's dominance, 13, 63, 305, 315,

317, 341, 637; RMN presides, 548, 637; McCarthy, 180, 512; Tonkin Gulf Res., 468ff; committees: Armed Services, 12-3, 29 401, 469, 498; Commerce, 175; Finance, 106; Foreign Relations, 20-1, 351, 465, 572, 637; Gov't. Operations, 638; Interstate and Foreign Commerce, 13; Judiciary, 530, 639ff; Watergate, 299, 530, 558, 590, 595, 600, 602, 620, 638
"Sequoia" (Pres. yacht), xiii, 175, 290
Service, John S., 408
Severeid, Eric, 141
Seward, William, 360
Shakespeare, William, ii, xv, 4, 41, 205, 245, 247, 290, 319, 393, 449, 457, 474, 491, 511, 570
Sharp, Ulysses S., 461ff
Shaw, George, Bernard, ii
Sheehan, Neil, 456
Shelton, Emmett, 161
Sheppard, Morris, 201
Sheridan, Richard, ii
Sherman, Tecumseh, 121, 618
Sherrill, Robert, 155, 409, 494
Sherwood, Jack, 513
Shoup, David, 411
Shriver, Sargent, 359
Sicilian Mafia (see also Mafia), 445
Sidey, Hugh, 19, 55, 89, 103-4, 209, 312-3, 349, 453, 456, 472, 513, 626
Simon, William, 132, 329, 332
Sirica, John, 85, 137, 149, 299-300, 368, 558, 562, 594-5, 596-7, 605
Skelton "Red," 337
Skinner, B.F., 130
slavery, 417, 421
Smathers, George, 47, 98, 152, 186, 194, 316, 596
Smith, Al, 234, 619
Smith, Asa P., 400
Smith, Gerard, 39
Smith, Helen McCain, 245
Smith, Paul, 24, 129, 236, 242-3
Smith, Stephen, 358
Smith, Walter Bedell "Beetle," 325

Van Dyke, Ted, 484
Vann, Jesse, 144
Vann, John Paul, 144-5
Vann, Peter, 145
Vaughan, Harry, 46
Vazzona, Nicholas, 380
Vietcong, 132, 319, 400, 404, 482-5
Vietminh, 25, 38, 375, 398
Vietnam, 55, 58, 104ff; LBJ visit 1961, 391, 394-5; contrast with U.S., 407-8; Saigon: corruption, 398, 400, 404, 426, 468, 477, 487, 497; suppression, 400ff
Vietnam War (see also Tonkin Gulf Res.), 92, 131, 394ff, 946-7; background, 26, 409ff; JFK, 4, 389, 399-400; rationale: 132; independence, 145; testing ground, 394, 452-453; domino theory, 104, 398, 454, 507; pledge to SEATO, 323, 572, 575, 577, 637; first Pres. to lose war?, 103-4, 136-7, 342, 459, 465ff, 470, 494, 506, 517, 551; Brown and Root payback, 21, 174; peace with honor, 80, 122, 131-2, 136, 143, 149, 293-4, 396-7, 437-8; noble purpose, 476-7; LBJ confronts, 16-7, 103, 317-8, 413-4; LBJ's ignorance, 63, 103-4, 107, 111, 132, 347-8, 575; LBJ's decision-making, 54-5, 60, 63ff, 104, 110, 458-9, 575-6, 632-3; LBJ's policies, 458-9, 577; LBJ's deceptions, 145, 162, 473, 476-7; (see also Geneva Accords); v. Great Society (see Great Society); LBJ's escalations, 104, 177, 208-9, 310ff; protests, 34, 74, 78, 182, 291, 320, 336, 415, 490, 499-500ff, 517, 530, 537ff, 556, 572-4, 610, 635; press, 209-10, 302, 323, 581; demilitarized zone (DMZ), 104; demonizing enemy, 385, 420ff; war crimes, 391, 505; Negroes, 104, 452-3; Tet offensive, 321, 409ff, 431, 476-7, 505, 552, 579; negotiations, 326, 399-400, 576; JCS, 414; "Wise Men,"

414; (see also Clifford) toll on LBJ, 200, 498-9; toll on U.S., 136, 398, 409; toll on Vietnam, 169, 406-7, 416, 444ff, 550, 571, 583, 590, 608; (see also MaNamara); RMN inherits war, 103; promises to end, 30, 125, 181-2, 240, 476-7; timed to reelection, 80, 130, 424ff, 432, 552; RMN's ignorance, 132; RMN broadens war, 289, 420, 423, 437-8, 523, 556, (see also Cambodia, Laos); RMN withdraws (Vietnamization), 125, 136, 406, 424ff, 480, 503, 516-7, 551ff; draft-evaders, 74, 440; veterans, 144; ARVN, 136, 145, 398, 406, 413, 422-4, 442-3, 459; negotiations, 420, 427ff, 436, 440ff; (see also RMN summits 1972); reparations, 80, 427, 443ff, 522, 613-4, 622-3; cease-fire, 80, 145, 425ff, 442ff, 516-7, 550, 613-4, 622-3; toll on RMN, 424; toll on U.S., 137, 176, 291ff, 391, 424, 445-7, 473, 512-3, 567, 571, 622; leads to Watergate, 136, 617-8, 622-3; leads to Cambodia genocide, 446-7, 613; legacy, 631
Vinson, Carl, 11
Vinson, Fred, 10
Vincent, John Carter, 408
Vista, 588
Vocational Rehabilitation Act, 621
Volpe, John, 553
Voorhis Act, 229
Voorhis, Jerry, 23-4, 29, 127, 133ff, 225ff, 285 302, 376-7, 475, 644

Waggoner, Joseph, 603
Wall St. Journal, 171, 173-4, 496, 571-2
Wallace, George, 34, 481, 494, 521-2, 603
Wallace, Gerald, 521-2
Wallace, Henry, 134, 264
Wallace, Mike, 80, 143-4
Walters, Vernon, 650
war, iii, 393 (see also each American war)

War Powers Act, 639
Ward, Barbara, 107, 504-5
Warnecke, Jack, 3, 4
Warner Books, Inc., 444
Warner-Lambert Co., 188
Warnke, Paul, 3, 4, 48
War of 1812, 91, 319, 539, 629-30
Warren Commission, 18, 362
Warren, Earl, Sr. (Justice), 325, 475, 647
Warren, Earl, Jr. 476
Washington, George, (Pres.), v-vi, ix, 2, 4-5, 46, 90ff, 109, 116, 133, 210, 293, 303, 308, 358, 409, 454, 539, 615, 617-8, 626ff, 642
Washington, Martha, xi
Washington Post, 114, 137, 151, 207, 212, 240-1, 467, 520; Watergate, 297, 332, 435, 439, 512, 525, 558, 582, 592-3, 601, 645
Washington Star-News, 483, 595
Watergate, 122, 125, 128, 130, 132, 139, 145, 193, 244, 385; burglary, 39, 40, 78, 82, 132, 295ff, 330-1, 424ff; cover-up, 40, 66, 78, 84, 125, 130, 132, 137, 283, 329-30, 387, 509-10, 521ff, 554; inevitability, 132, 136; RMN's innocence, 82-3; RMN's cynicism, 180; RMN's exploitation, 223ff; transcripts, 40, 132-3, 137, 148; press, 132; closing in, 139, 148-9, 151, 295ff, 435-6, 516, 555; Pat's resignation, 236; RMN's resignation, 41, 71, 74, 83ff, 243, 289ff, 301ff, 329ff, 590-1, 603; toll on RMN, 551; fallout, 654
Watergate Committee (see also Sam Ervin), 73, 82, 194-5, 299-300, 331, 387-8, 521, 526, 530, 554-5, 558-9, 561, 592
Watson, Marvin, 57, 499, 580
Weaver, Robert, 574
Webber, Palmer, 170
Weber, Elizabeth, 391
Weber, O. J., 256
Weber, William, 391
Webster, Daniel, 519
Weinberqer, Caspar, 77